ESG Frameworks for Sustainable Business Practices

Biju Ajithakumari Vijayappan Nair
University of Kerala, India

Glenn Muschert
Khalifa University of Science and Technology, UAE

Ambili Jayachandran
University of Kerala, India

A volume in the Advances in
Logistics, Operations, and
Management Science (ALOMS)
Book Series

Published in the United States of America by
    IGI Global
    Business Science Reference (an imprint of IGI Global)
    701 E. Chocolate Avenue
    Hershey PA, USA 17033
    Tel: 717-533-8845
    Fax: 717-533-8661
    E-mail: cust@igi-global.com
    Web site: http://www.igi-global.com

Library of Congress Cataloging-in-Publication Data

CIP DATA PROCESSING

2024 Business Science Reference
 ISBN: 9798369338803
 ISBN: 9798369349441
 eISBN: 9798369338810

British Cataloguing in Publication Data
A Cataloguing in Publication record for this book is available from the British Library.

All work contributed to this book is new, previously-unpublished material.
The views expressed in this book are those of the authors, but not necessarily of the publisher.

For electronic access to this publication, please contact: eresources@igi-global.com.

Advances in Logistics, Operations, and Management Science (ALOMS) Book Series

John Wang
Montclair State University, USA

ISSN:2327-350X
EISSN:2327-3518

MISSION

Operations research and management science continue to influence business processes, administration, and management information systems, particularly in covering the application methods for decision-making processes. New case studies and applications on management science, operations management, social sciences, and other behavioral sciences have been incorporated into business and organizations real-world objectives.

The **Advances in Logistics, Operations, and Management Science** (ALOMS) Book Series provides a collection of reference publications on the current trends, applications, theories, and practices in the management science field. Providing relevant and current research, this series and its individual publications would be useful for academics, researchers, scholars, and practitioners interested in improving decision making models and business functions.

IGI Global is currently accepting manuscripts for publication within this series. To submit a proposal for a volume in this series, please contact our Acquisition Editors at Acquisitions@igi-global.com or visit: http://www.igi-global.com/publish/.

Coverage

- Marketing engineering
- Operations Management

Titles in this Series

For a list of additional titles in this series, please visit: www.igi-global.com/book-series

Ensuring Security and End-to-End Visibility Through Blockchain and Digital Twins
Pankaj Dashore (Sandip University, India) and Rachana Dashore (Sandip Institute of Technology and Research Centre, India)
Business Science Reference • copyright 2024 • 459pp • H/C (ISBN: 9798369334942) • US $345.00 (our price)

Unleashing the Power of Basic Science in Business
Sonal Trivedi (VIT Business School, VIT Bhopal University, India) Veena Grover (Noida Institute of Engineering and Technology, India) Balamurugan Balusamy (Shiv Nadar University, India) and Abhijit Ganguly (Westford University College, UAE)
Business Science Reference • copyright 2024 • 459pp • H/C (ISBN: 9798369355039) • US $345.00 (our price)

Management Model for Building Trust and Upskilling the Workforce
B. D. Sharma (HROB Place, India) Rajni Sharma (HROB Place, India) Rashmi Michael (R&B Management Consulting Services, USA) and Boniface Michael (California State University, Sacramento, USA)
Business Science Reference • copyright 2024 • 323pp • H/C (ISBN: 9798369314432) • US $245.00 (our price)

Quantum Computing and Supply Chain Management A New Era of Optimization
Ahdi Hassan (Global Institute for Research Education and Scholarship, The Netherlands) Pronaya Bhattacharya (Amity University, Kolkata, India) Pushan Kumar Dutta (Indian Institute of Technology, Delhi, India) Jai Prakash Verma (Institute of Technology Nirma University, Ahmedabad, India) and Neel Kanth Kundu (Indian Institute of Technology, Delhi, India)
Business Science Reference • copyright 2024 • 519pp • H/C (ISBN: 9798369341070) • US $425.00 (our price)

701 East Chocolate Avenue, Hershey, PA 17033, USA
Tel: 717-533-8845 x100 • Fax: 717-533-8661
E-Mail: cust@igi-global.com • www.igi-global.com

Table of Contents

Detailed Table of Contents

Chapter 1

    Ambili Jayachandran, University of Kerala, India
    Jose John, Cochin University of Science and Technology, India
    Ann Susan Thomas, University of Kerala, India
    I. S. Smiju, Cochin University of Science and Technology, India

Corporate Social Responsibility (CSR) and Environmental, Social, and Governance (ESG) concepts have undergone significant evolution over the decades. A closer look at the evolution of these concepts on a country basis would achieve a better comprehension of nations' standpoints and the direction in which CSR and ESG are advancing. This study looks at the thematic evolution and trajectory of corporate social responsibility (CSR) and environmental, social, and governance (ESG) concepts in five different regions: the United States, the United Kingdom, Italy, China, and India. Using data analysis techniques facilitated by R software, the study examines patterns from 2001 to 2024 to identify shifts in CSR and ESG discourse. We find that developed countries focus on sustainability reporting, with the US preferring CSR and the UK and Italy progressing toward ESG disclosure practices. The emerging markets are heavily inclined towards ESG ratings, although sustainability disclosure remains to be in the nascent stage.

Corporate Social Responsibility (CSR) and pillars of Environmental, Social and Governance (ESG) are closely associated. The chapter aimed to review the scope of CSR in contributing to pillars of ESG in developing nations. The authors used the Joanna Briggs Institute Methods Manual guidelines and Preferred Reporting Items for Systematic Reviews and Meta-analysis for Scoping Review (PRISMA-ScR) as guidelines for this scoping review. Two databases (EBSCOhost and SCOPUS) and a reference list of the relevant systematic reviews were searched. After screening 320 titles and abstracts, followed by sixty-four full texts, thirteen unique documents that fulfilled the eligibility criteria were selected. The result highlighted CSR's role in promoting organizational sustainability through corporate governance, social sustainability. and environmental sustainability. The study gathered evidence to identify the contribution of CSR toward environmental social and governance sustainability and would contribute to the existing literature and further research on sustainable development.

This chapter explores the symbiotic relationship between ESG practices and SDGs, emphasizing the increasing trend of companies aligning their ESG performance with UN SDGs. This integration ensures that corporate practices positively impact ESG factors, addressing global challenges outlined by the United Nations. The study investigates the interrelation between SDGs and ESG factors to classify SDGs based on ESG considerations. By shedding light on the underlying dynamics shaping sustainable development initiatives, the study aims to offer valuable insights for practical ESG-based approaches to specific SDGs. The study engages a mixed-methods approach with knowledgeable participants, utilizing narrative, thematic analysis, and quantitative ranking through a structured questionnaire. At a practical level, the chapter extends its impact by offering applications for organizational strategy, ESG integration, policy implications, and stakeholder engagement.

Chapter 4

Hanaa Taji, Ibn Zohr University, Morocco
El Houssain Attak, Cadi Ayyad University, Morocco

This chapter explores the complex landscape of ESG (Environmental, Social, and Governance) ratings, focusing on their conceptual foundations, the methodologies employed by major rating agencies, the criteria used to evaluate corporate sustainability, and the significant divergences in ratings. It examines how different agencies interpret and apply ESG criteria, leading to varied ratings that complicate consistent comparisons for investors. Through a detailed analysis of sector-wise correlation and descriptive statistics, the chapter highlights the influence of sectoral characteristics on rating discrepancies and proposes recommendations for standardizing ESG reporting, enhancing transparency, integrating advanced technologies, and developing sector-specific guidelines to improve the reliability and comparability of ESG ratings.

Chapter 5

P. Fahad, RUA College, India & Farook College, India
Mubarak Rahman P., LEAD College of Management, India
Showkat Ahmad Busru, NMIMS, Hyderabad, India
Mohammed Shafeeque K., Farook College, India & University of
*   Calicut, India*

The study investigates the relationship between ESG disclosure, information asymmetry, cost of capital and earnings management in an emerging economy, India. The study uses PLS-SEM for a sample of 183 companies listed in BSE 500 index for a period of ten years from 2014 to 2023. The study finds that higher ESG disclosure leads to decrease in information asymmetry. While ESG disclosure increases the firm's cost of capital. The result also shows that firms with higher ESG disclosure have more social commitment and less chance for doing earnings management. An increase in information asymmetry increases the chance for managers to manipulate earnings. Similarly, higher information asymmetry leads to increase investor risk which results in increased cost of capital. Finally, earnings management practice reduces the firm cost of capital.

Chapter 6

Ramsha Noori, Indian Institute of Management, Udaipur, India
Vidya S. Athota, The University of Notre Dame, Australia

This book chapter discusses greenwashing within the domain of Environmental, Social, and Governance (ESG), reflecting upon the emergent dichotomy between espoused corporate sustainability and actual environmental stewardship. By systematically reviewing the pertinent literature, the chapter highlights the pivotal role of greenwashing as a deceptive tactic within ESG framework. It discusses the Volkswagen's and Coca-Cola's greenwashing practices and offer empirical insights into the inconsistencies in their marketing claims of producing sustainable and eco-friendly products. This chapter explores the variances in ESG reporting due to differing regulatory frameworks and emphasize on the importance of regulatory frameworks in enhancing or impeding transparency in corporate disclosures. The chapter outlines the pressing research questions and practical challenges in containing greenwashing strategies and advocate for future scholarly exploration into the uncharted areas of ESG and corporate sustainability.

Chapter 7

Aghila Sasidharan, Indian Institute of Forest Management, Bhopal, India
Sreelekshmi Geetha, University of Kerala, India
Biju Ajithakumari Vijayappan Nair, University of Kerala, India
Ambili Jayachandran, University of Kerala, India
Nisha Sheen, St. Lawrence College, Ontario, Canada

This study examines the effect of audit committees on corporate social performance. Using a sample of Indian firms for the 2008–2021 period, we find that the firm's corporate social performance is significantly higher in the presence of an audit committee. This relationship is stronger when the audit committee consists of more directors. Our results support the resource dependence theory, which indicates that the members of each committee on the board provide various resources to the firms in the form of their skills and expertise. Our study has an implication for the regulators that more transparency should be required in the audit committee to ensure better corporate governance.

Chapter 8

Aghila Sasidharan, Indian Institute of Forest Management, Bhopal,
*   India*
M. Thenmozhi, Indian Institute of Technology, Madras, India
Biju Ajithakumari Vijayappan Nair, University of Kerala, India
Sonam Chawla, O.P. Jindal Global University, Sonipat, India
Jane S. C. Liu, Chaoyang University of Technology, Taichung, Taiwan

The importance of gender diversity on corporate boards has increased in recent years because of its potential impact on Environmental, Social, and Governance (ESG) activities. This study investigates the link between gender diversity on corporate boards and the disclosure of ESG policies in Indian firms. Our study indicates a positive relationship between gender diversity and ESG performance. We used panel regression analysis on a sample of 250 companies that are publicly traded on India's National Stock Exchange (NSE). Companies that have a greater representation of women on their boards of directors are more likely to provide more extensive disclosures about ESG activities. There is a positive correlation between the involvement of female directors and the degree of transparency and comprehensiveness in ESG reporting. The presence of a diverse range of genders on boards can enhance the quality of disclosures by fostering a heightened emphasis on sustainability and ethical issues, as well as including a broader range of opinions.

    Vineetha Mathew, Cochin University of Science and Technology, India
    Haseena Akbar, Cochin University of Science and Technology, India
    Santhosh Kumar P. K., Cochin University of Science and Technology,
        India
    Vitaliy Serzhanov, Uzhhorod National University, Ukraine

This chapter delves into a novel exploration of the non-linear interdependence between the conventional market index and selected sustainability indices in India. While socially responsible investing has gained traction globally, its impact on emerging markets like India is less explored. This study assesses the relationship between the market index- Sensex and sustainability indices - ESG, Carbonex, and Greenex through copula models. By scrutinizing the relationship between them, this study breaks new ground in understanding investor preferences and market dynamics. Results indicate a strong positive association between Sensex and sustainable indices, underscoring investors' growing inclination towards sustainable investments. Moreover, the copula models reveal various degrees of dependency, with Carbonex demonstrating the highest dependency on Sensex. The findings of the study show the popularity of sustainable indices in the Indian landscape and provide insights for investors, companies and policymakers.

A. S. Aparna, University of Kerala, India
M. Moni, University of Kerala, India
V. Sreeraj, University of Kerala, India
M. P. Silpakrishnan, SN College, Kollam, India
Biju Ajithakumari Vijayappan Nair, University of Kerala, India

This study investigates the performance of Environmental, Social, and Governance
(ESG) mutual funds compared to conventional funds in the Indian financial market.
The objective is to determine if ESG funds can match or surpass the financial
performance of traditional funds. The methodology includes evaluating performance
using the Carhart Four-Factor Model, Jensen's Alpha, Treynor Ratio, and Sharpe
Ratio. Additionally, entropy measures—Shannon Entropy, Rényi Entropy, and
Approximate Entropy—are employed to assess the volatility and complexity of
fund returns. Findings indicate that while conventional funds often deliver higher
raw returns, ESG funds excel in risk-adjusted performance, evidenced by higher
Alpha and more favourable Treynor and Sharpe Ratios. Entropy analysis reveals that
ESG funds exhibit higher volatility and complexity, as elevated Shannon, Rényi,
and Approximate Entropy values indicate greater potential for significant returns
and increased risk.

Dany Thomas, School of Business Management and Legal Studies,
    Kollam, India
Ria Mammen, St. Thomas College, Kozhencherry, India
Vimal George Kurian, CMS College, Kottayam, India
S. P. Asha, SN College, Kollam, India

The study examine the influence of financial risk on the nature of the relationship between ESG and the financial performance of Indian banks. In India, loans are key financial products of banks that are exposed to carbon-intensive sectors, which hinder their efforts to mitigate against transition risks and global ESG standards, amid the growing pressure from international investors. The study uses ROA to measure financial performance. The independent variable ESG was measured using the ESG scores Indian banks indexed in the NIFTY 100 ESG Index. Altman's Z-score model which predicts the financial risk of Indian banks was considered as the mediating variable to assess its influence on the nature of the relationship between ESG and financial performance. The evidence from the study would be useful to identify the changes in the financial performance of Indian banks resulting from their sustainable performance.

Shreyanshu Singh, Babu Banarasi Das University, Lucknow, India
Rinki Verma, Babu Banarsi Das University, Lucknow, India
Afeefa Fatima, Babu Banarsi Das University, Lucknow, India
Manoj Kumar, Shri Ramswaroop Memorial University, Barabanki, India

This study investigates the intricate relationship between Environmental, Social, and Governance (ESG) practices and their influence on brand reputation and customer loyalty, within the goal of achieving competitive advantage. Employing a quantitative research methodology, this study utilizes a survey to gather insights from consumers regarding their perceptions of ESG initiatives and loyalty to sustainable brands. Through statistical analyses, including regression analysis, this paper furnishes empirical evidence of the strategic importance of ESG practices in bolstering brand reputation and nurturing customer loyalty. Additionally, this research explores challenges and opportunities in the adoption and implementation of ESG practices, shedding light on complexities faced by organizations. By elucidating the nexus between ESG initiatives and brand loyalty, this study contributes to the literature on sustainable business strategies and provides insights for businesses in a competitive and socially conscious marketplace.

Chapter 13

Faryal Razzaq, Karachi School of Business and Leadership, Pakistan
Sana Ashfaq, IMDC, Pakistan
Glenn Muschert, Khalifa University of Science and Technology, UAE
Muhammad Bin Ashfaq, RIHS, Pakistan

Startups success is detrimental to foster economic growth of any country. what are the criteria that the winning pitches/startups have? Do the evaluators give sufficient weightage to the business process's environmental sustainability practices and social aspects? We interviewed 13 most influential players in the Pakistani startup ecosystem engaged in the selection process. This is a qualitative study with constructivist grounded theory approach using thematic analysis. We found only 10% startup in Pakistani Eco-system are working on social and environment, and the judging criteria is also 0-10% only social and environment incubators use 20-40%. Developing countries could benefit from the findings and themes identified. The research will be significant for the policy makers, training for the startup evaluators and setting more robust criteria incorporating ESG frameworks for selection and funding. Study reveal the mindset that prevails among the decision makers selecting startups, as they have a trickledown effect for focusing on sustainability.

Chapter 14

P. K. Santhosh Kumar, Cochin University of Science and Technology,
    India
Haseena Akbar, Cochin University of Science and Technology, India
Barbara Pisker, University of Osijek, Croatia
Hareesh N. Ramanathan, Cochin University of Science and Technology,
    India

The textile industries, while important to employment and economic growth, also contribute to environmental damage. However, adopting a 'closed loop' production and supply chain model minimises environmental risks. Moreover, a circular framework in the textile sector will pace the path towards sustainability. So, the study explored sustainable production practices in the textile manufacturing units in Kerala based on the priority selections made by the manufacturers. The Fuzzy analytical hierarchy procedure application on the data gathered from 300 sample units from five cities of Kerala revealed that though the industries have consistent circular economic potentials, the majority exhibit inconsistency in their decisions to follow the sustainable production models.

Aparna Sajeev, Department of Commerce and Management Studies,
University of Calicut, India
Harpreet Kaur, Sri Guru Gobind Singh College of Commerce,
University of Delhi, India

Understanding the interrelationships between economic growth, environmental quality, and sustainable development is pertinent for India. This connection is marked by reciprocal causation and feedback mechanisms-energy consumption stimulates economic growth by providing the necessary fuel for production and consumption. However, economic expansion influences energy consumption patterns by altering the industrial structure, adopting new technologies, and changing income levels. This study investigates the relationship between economic growth, energy transition, and sustainable development in India from 1990 to 2020. It also estimates the impact of industrialisation and trade openness on economic growth using an Auto Regressive Distributed Lag (ARDL) approach. The results show a positive and significant relationship between environmental degradation (CO_2) and economic growth. Policymakers and stakeholders must develop efficient energy policies and effective, sustainable development strategies. The policies should facilitate economic expansion and safeguard energy stability, ecological endurance, and social well-being.

Chapter 16
The Costs and Concerns of Energy Transition: Energy Transition Should Be
Sanobar Imam, TISS, Mumbai, India
Adwait Madkaikar, TISS, Guwahati, India

The global transition from fossil fuels to clean energy is driven by the need to reduce carbon emissions and combat climate change. However, this transition has its own set of costs, benefits, and concerns. The top-down approach to the transition often fails to consider the social, economic, and environmental costs associated with it, leading to conflicts among stakeholders and social groups. The transition to net-zero emissions will increase job opportunities, but it also poses a risk of job loss and displacement, particularly in industries reliant on coal. The chapter explores the challenges and opportunities of the energy transition, in the Indian context, and the unequal distribution of resources among different regions and social groups. It adopts a three-pronged approach: an extensive literature review, a detailed case study, and stakeholder consultations. The chapter aims to offer actionable insights for policymakers, industry stakeholders, and communities to navigate the challenges, concerns, and opportunities of the ongoing energy transition towards a cleaner future.

Preface

The sustainability realm has been undergoing profound transformations, especially in the past few years, proving that sustainability has become one of the mainstream global initiatives. Even though the idea existed way back in the late 19th century, until recent times, it was treated as a niche concern confined to environmental conventions and natural resource preservation movements. The basic ideology of sustainability was focused on imparting conscious and responsible human activities, ensuring the sustenance of natural resources for future generations. As global warming, climate change, and environmental degradation started impacting the global community, sustainability emerged from the discussion forums to be considered more practically. An urgent need to impart sustainable practices was recognised, bringing nations together to join the global sustainability campaign.

Despite the growing recognition of sustainability as the need of the hour, the journey is far from complete, with the recent onslaught of climate disasters serving as a reminder of the dire need for decisive action. With the warnings from the scientific community for immediate action hanging as a sword above their heads, global leaders have resorted to bringing sustainable business operations to advance the sustainability agenda. Understanding the unique position of businesses in driving change, measures in the form of regulations have been implemented that intrinsically associate sustainability with business operations. While initially, sustainability was perceived as a niche concern among businesses and was pursued almost as an afterthought, the concept now stands at the forefront of corporate strategy, driven by an increasing understanding of the interconnectedness between social justice, environmental protection, and economic prosperity. Backed by the resources, large appetite for innovation, and ability to pioneer sustainable solutions, firms have the potential to take charge of leading the sustainability movement.

We have observed that the work has already started as businesses shift towards adopting sustainability frameworks by imbibing circular economy principles, using sustainable technologies, resorting to renewable resources, and imbibing more cost-effective operations. Furthermore, businesses have upgraded their Corporate Social

Responsibility (CSR) activities to Environmental, Social and Governance(ESG) principles to align their framework with cleaner and greener sustainable business practices. Regulations have further bolstered the adoption of ESG into business frameworks, bringing about the potential for a green economy and sustainable development. Integrating ESG into corporate strategies has opened up new opportunities as well as challenges in achieving a sustainable front. Ranging from identifying and mitigating environmental and social risks, adhering to consumer, investor, regulator and stakeholder demand for sustainable operations to achieving a competitive edge, ESG has offered many possibilities which remain to be fully explored.

The necessity to document ideas regarding the change in the corporate world as firms weave sustainable practices into their framework brought us to the title of "ESG Frameworks for Sustainable Business Practices". The rising popularity of ESG has taken the concept across borders and touched disciplines such as applied economics, sustainable development and sustainable development goals, supply chain management, investor and investment management, security and stock market studies, consumer and brand impact, human resource management and many more. This book explores the various ways businesses can and should use ESG integration to meet the issue of sustainability. The initiative aims to seek fresh outlook from varied disciplines on how aligning to sustainable practices under the ESG framework has affected businesses. It examines cutting-edge tactics, inspirational case studies, best practices and challenges of the system from around the world. We aim to collate systematic, clear, and concise research on the effectiveness of ESG as a modem for sustainable practices and to discern the future direction of sustainable business practices in light of the rapid technological advancements and changes in corporate board dynamics and regulatory frameworks.

Let's acknowledge that pursuing sustainability is not just a choice but a need of the hour as we step into the era of sustainable living. Together, we can build a future in which economic growth is balanced with the health of the earth and the welfare of all its people. This book acts as a spur to action, motivating, empowering and enlightening companies, regulatory bodies and the research fraternity on the metamorphosis of businesses into sustainable institutions.

Biju Ajithakumari Vijayappan Nair

Department of Commerce, School of Business Management and Legal Studies, University of Kerala, India

Glenn Muschert

Department of Public Health and Epidemiology, Khalifa University of Science and Technology, UAE

Ambili Jayachandran

Preface

*Department of Commerce, School of Business Management and Legal Studies,
University of Kerala, India*

Chapter 1
Evolution of CSR and ESG Concepts in the Frame of Sustainability:
Insights From Thematic Evolution Across Nations

Ambili Jayachandran
https://orcid.org/0000-0002-0062-6260
University of Kerala, India

Jose John
https://orcid.org/0000-0003-2024-2130
Cochin University of Science and Technology, India

Ann Susan Thomas
University of Kerala, India

I. S. Smiju
Cochin University of Science and Technology, India

ABSTRACT

Corporate Social Responsibility (CSR) and Environmental, Social, and Governance (ESG) concepts have undergone significant evolution over the decades. A closer look at the evolution of these concepts on a country basis would achieve a better comprehension of nations' standpoints and the direction in which CSR and ESG are advancing. This study looks at the thematic evolution and trajectory of corporate social responsibility (CSR) and environmental, social, and governance (ESG) concepts in five different regions: the United States, the United Kingdom, Italy, China, and

DOI: 10.4018/979-8-3693-3880-3.ch001

India. Using data analysis techniques facilitated by R software, the study examines patterns from 2001 to 2024 to identify shifts in CSR and ESG discourse. We find that developed countries focus on sustainability reporting, with the US preferring CSR and the UK and Italy progressing toward ESG disclosure practices. The emerging markets are heavily inclined towards ESG ratings, although sustainability disclosure remains to be in the nascent stage.

INTRODUCTION

The pressing need to address environmental, social, and economic concerns has led to the wide recognition of sustainable development notions. The new-found vigour in sustainability campaigns is visible in the United Nations (UN) Sustainable Development Goals (SDGs), formed with the intention of guiding nations in their sustainability pursuit (Leal Filho et al., 2018). Acknowledging businesses as the patrons of a nation's economic growth coupled with the rising call for responsible reporting has urged firms to integrate principles of sustainability into their corporate framework and align corporate strategies with social and environmental wellbeing (Crisóstomo et al., 2017). It is in this context that Corporate Social Responsibility (CSR) and Environmental Social Governance (ESG) come into play. CSR and ESG adorn a vital role in the corporate world since they are the sole indicators that address sustainability at the firm level, with the former being an existing concept and the latter a newer version (Halme et al., 2020). Despite the difference in the scope offered by CSR and ESG, diverse standpoints are noticed across nations on the adoption and execution of CSR and ESG (Bhatia & Makkar, 2020; Singhania & Saini, 2021).

CSR refers to the efforts taken up by firms to address their bearings on society and the environment while pursuing profit, with initial indications of philanthropic intention which later flourished into a stakeholder contentment strategy (Cheruvalath, 2017; Manchiraju & Rajgopal, 2017). CSR literature can be traced back to 1985, implying the long-standing practice of CSR in global markets (Pisani et al., 2017). The prime purpose behind integrating CSR initiatives into firm operations was to tamp down risks to augment their reputation and thereby creating longevity and value for stakeholders (Deng et al., 2013). Hence, CSR became a moral and strategic imperative for businesses to secure their license to operate in an increasingly interconnected world. Despite its benefits, CSR also faces criticisms mainly revolving around its focus on governance and ethical issues rather than environmental responsibility (Egri & Ralston, 2008). The initiative has been at the receiving end of controversies claiming CSR is more of a strategy for greenwashing than sustainability practice (Marquis et al., 2016).

CSR practice was synonymous with sustainability until the concept of sustainable business practices evolved to include environmental and social sustainability, making authors use ESG and CSR as substitutes for one another (Gillan et al., 2021). ESG's global acclamation has led many nations to encourage firms to adopt ESG activities (Jemel-Fornetty et al., 2011). ESG, defined by its foundational pillars, Environmental (which accounts for water use, carbon emissions, pollution among other variables), Social (accounts for workplace safety, gender discrimination, community development, etc.) and Governance (board independence, board diversity, transparency etc.), embodies a holistic and integrated approach to sustainability, bringing substantial attention to investing and reporting arenas, especially in the past few years (Clément et al., 2023). Unlike CSR, which often operates as a standalone initiative in corporate governance, ESG integrates sustainability principles into core business policies and decision-making courses (Saini et al., 2023). This shift echoes a wider recognition that ecological and social issues are integral factors that influence business performance and resilience. Moreover, ESG factors are increasingly seen as material to financial outcomes, with a majority of the ESG literature indicating a positive connection between financial performance and ESG (Aydoğmuş et al., 2022; Naeem et al., 2022). As such, ESG provides an all-inclusive framework for assessing and managing sustainability risks and opportunities, bringing business interests in line with the bigger picture of a sustainable future.

Developed and emerging nations all around the world have been joining the cause of sustainability by aggressively implementing regulations on corporate practices. Due to their economic, social, industrial, political and cultural differences, nations have adopted sustainability practices that often contrast with one another (Maletič et al., 2016). While the newer ESG initiatives have been gaining popularity, many still adhere to the time-tested and proven CSR practices. Moreover, Gillan et al. (2021) indicated that the ESG/CSR practices of firms are highly variable based on the regulatory frameworks and political inclinations of the region in which the firm is based.

Despite their increasing prominence as distinct domains within the sustainability framework, ESG and CSR practices have not been individually examined. Recent literature reviews (Bhatia & Makkar, 2020; Singhania & Saini, 2021) have tended to focus on either ESG or CSR independently, neglecting to examine them in tandem. Additionally, there has been insufficient study on the evolution of these practices and the shifts that have occurred over time. To address these gaps a comparative analysis from a country-wise perspective, is undertaken here. By exploring the diverse national perspectives on the adoption and implementation of CSR and ESG practices, we seek to advance existing knowledge in this field. Thus, our research sparks curiosity and offers a novel avenue for understanding how nations have accepted and adapted to these sustainability changes. The study undertakes the thematic evolution of five nations of prime importance which have embraced sustainability norms, to answer the following research questions:

RQ1: What is the pattern of evolution and the direction in which CSR and ESG concepts are advancing in the case of the U.S.?

RQ2: What is the pattern of evolution and the direction in which CSR and ESG concepts are advancing in the case of the U.K.?

RQ3: What is the pattern of evolution and the direction in which CSR and ESG concepts are advancing in the case of Italy?

RQ4: What is the pattern of evolution and the direction in which CSR and ESG concepts are advancing in the case of China?

RQ5: What is the pattern of evolution and the direction in which CSR and ESG concepts are advancing in the case of India?

The remaining chapter is sectioned to include Methodology, Discussion of Results, Summary of Insights and Conclusion.

METHODOLOGY

The chapter utilized a systematic methodological approach in order to answer the research questions. To filter out the sample for the study, appropriate search strategy, sources and eligibility criteria for selecting the research publications were fixed.

Information and Sources

A search was initiated in the SCOPUS database to find potentially significant documents. Scopus is thought to be the largest citation and abstract database encompassing a wide range of domains when compared to the Web of Science database (Hashem E et al., 2023). The detailed strategy is depicted in Figure 1.

Figure 1. Detailed search strategy generated using PRISMA

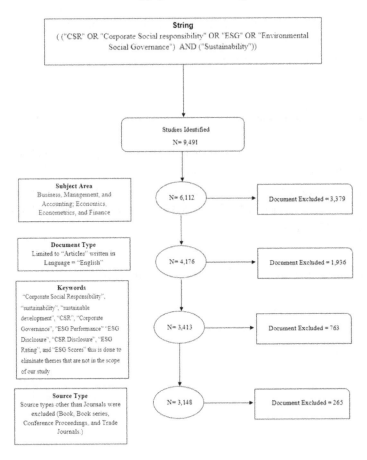

Selection of Studies

There were 3148 articles identified from the database (SCOPUS). The selection was based on the highest annual scientific production among the developed and emerging markets. On this basis, the US, UK and Italy, with 497, 365 and 281 studies respectively, were selected from the developed nations. China and India, with 205 and 197 studies respectively, were selected to represent the emerging nations. The studies from the selected nations were imported into the R software and analyzed using the "Bibliometrix" package. This comprehensive R package facilitates the extraction of pertinent bibliographic data from large datasets and offers robust statistical analyses to unveil patterns and trends within the literature (Aria & Cuccurullo, 2017). We utilized thematic evolution to explain the conceptual structure. A thematic map is a visual representation of the co-occurrence of terms extracted from a corpus of documents. It helps to identify clusters of related terms and visualize their relationships within the literature (Alkhammash, 2023).

The thematic maps captured the conceptual evolution of CSR and ESG criteria. Below are the explanations of the six cases as themes.

DISCUSSION OF RESULTS

RQ1: What is the pattern of evolution and the direction in which CSR and ESG concepts are advancing in the case of the U.S.?

The thematic evolution generated in the case of the U.S. has the evolution divided into 4-time slices: 2001-2014, 2015-2018, 2019-2022 and 2023-2024. The evolution is represented in Figure 1.

Figure 2. Thematic evolution of CSR and ESG in the U.S

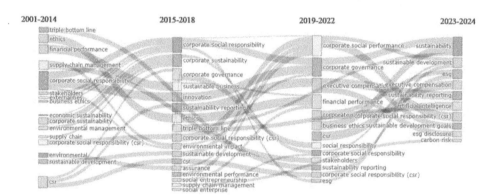

Examining the literature in the first time slice (2001-2014), we observe that CSR has already been thoroughly discussed at various levels. Persistent attempts to derive improved *CSR* frameworks and strategies to enhance *financial performance* and *stakeholder* engagement were evident (Cheng et al., 2014). With the growing awareness of *sustainable development* practices, stakeholders started to attach sustainability to the reputation of businesses (Peloza et al., 2012). Therefore, *ethical business* practices also received due importance (Balmer et al., 2011). CSR, as a mascot of sustainability practices, witnessed studies inquiring into the reasons, pressures, and effects of imbibing CSR practices in various fields of businesses (Holcomb et al., 2007; Levy & Park, 2011; Trendafilova et al., 2013). *Supply chain management* is another area where CSR in connection with the *triple bottom line* was pursued (Govindan et al., 2013; Hutchins & Sutherland, 2008). Another thematic association which was keenly followed was the CSR-sustainability reporting aspect. CSR communications or disclosures were found to be highly varying across industries and were generally found to be more of a signaling rather than a sustainability strategy (Mahoney et al., 2013).

Looking at the second time slice ranging from 2015-2018, we find that *CSR* commands a substantial share, implying the continuing importance of the topic in the U.S. academic audience. Articles looking into CSR practices cover a wide range of topics such as financial performance, rating divergence, assurances (verification of disclosures by external auditors) and customer response (Casey & Grenier, 2015; Chatterji et al., 2016; Jo et al., 2015). Along with CSR, *corporate governance*, especially in the context of employee engagement, has also gained significant traction during this period (Kim et al., 2014; Lamm et al., 2015). General confusion regarding how to define sustainability in the corporate world has led to the *corporate sustainability* conundrum (Landrum & Ohsowski, 2018). Landrum and Ohsowski sort through various corporate perspectives of sustainability conveyed through their reports. This confirms the notion that *sustainability reporting* of firms is the major measure of corporate accountability for their *sustainable business* practices (Medrado & Jackson, 2015). This inevitably gives leeway to firms to disclose or not sustainability reports according to their liking (Marquis et al., 2016).

Coming to the third time slice, we find that *Corporate Social Performance (CSP)* and *Corporate Governance* dominate the topic of discussion. CSP is seen to have arisen from the fusion of *CSR, assurance, sustainable development* and *environmental performance* themes. As a widely accepted means for weaving sustainability into the fabric of corporate operations, CSR also offers a pathway towards accomplishing improved environmental performance (Halme et al., 2020). CSR assurances seem to be a sought-after phenomenon for verifying a firm's sustainability disclosure to boost the credibility of the reports and directly affect the CSP and reputation of firms (Krasodomska et al., 2021). Since CSR has the ability to put a firm's reputation on the line, *corporate governance*, especially the board, has turned up efforts to ensure CSP (Uyar et al., 2020). During this period, ESG finally shows up on the chart, indicating an increase in research interest in ESG, and its influence on various facets of firm performance was also noticed during this time period. ESG, being the new means to realizing sustainability goals is also linked to the *financial performance* of firms (Minutolo et al., 2019). Studies have gone on to examine the divergence issue among ratings, calling for a standardization of the ratings and enabling comparability (Berg et al., 2022). Another topic of relevance that stands out during this phase is the *executive compensation practice*, where managers receive incentives based on the CSP of firms (Greiner & Sun, 2021).

Results generated in the final slice show that the research focus has come back to *Sustainability* and *Sustainable development*, with *CSR* and *ESG* representing sustainability at the corporate level. (Delgado-Ceballos et al., 2023) talk about scaling up sustainable practices through ESG to meet SDGs, implying the important role played by businesses in a nation's sustainability schema. The newfound importance of ESG as a sustainability indicator has generated studies on the topic, although some studies dwell on reputation risk and enhancing ESG disclosure practices (Asante-Appiah & Lambert, 2023). The final time slice also shows the emergence of *executive compensation* in discussion forums due to its potential to inspire sustainability reporting practices and ESG performance (Lee et al., 2024). A new data-driven methodology using artificial intelligence has also been explored for developing better and more reliable sustainability ratings (Asif et al., 2023).

RQ2: What is the pattern of evolution and the direction in which CSR and ESG concepts are advancing in the case of the UK?

The analysis of CSR and ESG literature in the case of the UK generated the thematic evolution map, as depicted in Figure 5. Research spanning across 2002-2024 was seen to be divided into four time slices: 2002-2015, 2016-2020, 2021-2023 and 2024.

Figure 3. Thematic evolution of CSR and ESG in the UK

Between 2002 and 2015, the landscape of CSR in the UK underwent a significant transformation. Initially, the focus was on regional and person-centered philanthropy, reminiscent of age-old tensions between business and social goals (Hopkins &

Crowe, 2003). However, the emergence of *CSR* as a sustainable business strategy began to reshape corporate practices. This shift was buoyed by the UK's stature as a CSR vanguard, attributed to factors such as the presence of major accountancy firms and early experiences with privatization, contributing to the evolution of CSR perspectives (Ward & Smith, 2006). Mainstreaming CSR within *corporate governance* structures signaled a paradigm shift towards stakeholder-centric approaches, balancing short-term financial imperatives with long-term sustainability goals (Money & Schepers, 2007). Various sectors grappled with the integration of CSR principles and despite notable efforts to report on CSR activities, discrepancies in implementation and measurement persisted (Jones et al., 2006). On the contrary, in the business front, superior CSR strategies correlated with improved access to finance and stakeholder engagement (Cheng et al., 2013). This parallels the temporal evolution of sustainability reporting, which transitioned from standalone reports to integrated policy statements aligned with global reporting initiatives (Jenkins, 2006). While the emphasis on CSR expanded to encompass sustainable business strategies, challenges persisted in translating CSR rhetoric into tangible outcomes (Bonilla-Priego et al., 2004; Font & Harris, 2004). Companies began recognizing the impacts of their operations on society and the environment, leading to the development of responsible policies on sustainability and corporate reporting (Bonilla-Priego et al., 2004). However, reports often echoed corporate voices rather than stakeholder demands, suggesting a nascent stage in understanding and adopting CSR's broader implications. Nevertheless, the proliferation of CSR processes underscored a wider societal shift towards corporate accountability (Wheeler et al., 2002).

During the period 2016 – 2020, this discourse expanded to include *ESG* factors, reflecting a broader consideration of sustainability beyond traditional CSR frameworks. *Sustainability reporting* emerged as a key practice, with research showing its influence on firm *performance* (Buallay, 2020; Koroleva et al., 2020). This relationship became more nuanced, with *ESG disclosure* demonstrating a positive impact on market performance but potentially negative effects on financial and operational performance (Albitar et al., 2020). While sustainability reporting positively influenced market performance, it also raised questions about the rationality of capital market participants in interpreting CSR information (Arnold et al., 2018). Adopting the SDGs provided a framework for addressing environmental and social impacts, guiding investments, and highlighting ESG-aligned practices (Consolandi et al., 2020). SMEs began recognizing the economic benefits of sustainability initiatives, with CSR becoming integral to long-term financial success (Bartolacci et al., 2019). The multidisciplinary nature of CSR committees underscored diverse stakeholder expectations, influencing overall firm performance (Baraibar-Diaz & Odriozola, 2019). These developments emphasized the growing integration of sustainability principles into corporate strategies and governance mechanisms, signaling a more nuanced understanding of business responsibilities.

From 2021 to 2023, further refinements emerged in the relationship between CSR, ESG, and corporate sustainability. Board characteristics and country governance quality were identified as significant determinants of environmental performance, highlighting the importance of governance structures in driving sustainability initiatives (Orazalin & Mahmood, 2021). The impact of corporate governance and shareholding structure on *CSR* performance deepened the role of institutional and managerial factors in shaping corporate behavior (Sarhan & Al-Najjar, 2022). Higher levels of *ESG* disclosure were linked to increasing female participation on boards, reflecting the impact of diversity on corporate transparency and account-ability (Buallay et al., 2022). Startups with strong *ESG performance* attracted higher valuations, indicating growing investor interest in sustainable entrepreneurship (Mansouri & Momtaz, 2022). Mandatory CSR regulation in the UK improved CSR reporting quality, enhancing stakeholder perceptions and market valuations (Hamed et al., 2022).

In the most recent years, the dialogue surrounding *ESG* considerations has contin-ued to evolve, with a focus on investment choices and financial stability (Kraussl et al., 2024; Orazalin et al., 2024). Studies highlighted the role of corporate governance mechanisms in curbing earnings management practices and improving *sustainability reporting* (Adeneye et al., 2024). Sustainability committees were identified as vital for driving corporate sustainability and *environmental performance*, emphasizing the importance of organizational factors and governance structures (Abdullah et al., 2024). Additionally, there is growing attention to the role of social media in *CSR* disclosure, with studies exploring the credibility of CSR narratives on platforms like Twitter (Amin et al., 2024).

RQ3: What is the pattern of evolution and the direction in which CSR and ESG concepts are advancing in the case of Italy?

The analysis of CSR and ESG literature in the case of Itay generated the thematic evolution map, as depicted in Figure 2. Research spanning across 2008-2024 was seen to be divided into four time slices: 2008-2018, 2019-2021, 2022-2023 and 2024.

Figure 4. Thematic evolution of CSR and ESG in Italy

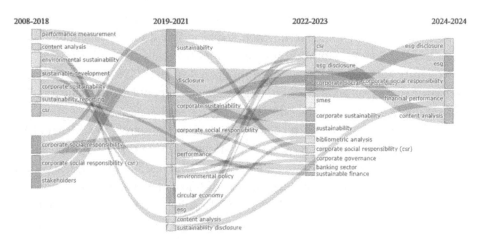

The first time slice 2008-2018 gleans the importance given by Italian researchers to sustainability and *sustainable development* initiatives and the rising environmental consciousness among firms (Bran et al., 2011). The studies during this period have explored *CSR* as a means to an end for non-financial disclosure in attaining *Corporate Sustainability* (Lai et al., 2016). As a *sustainability reporting* method, the direct implications of improved CSR disclosures on the firm *performance* were acknowledged (Lawal et al., 2017) along with the inconsistencies in the quality of CSR disclosures (Michelon et al., 2015). This emphasized the rising discontent regarding the lack of a comprehensive sustainability reporting framework (Sodano & Hingley, 2018) and the need for a strong integrated reporting process (Montecchia et al., 2016).

Italian literature on CSR and ESG shows a significant growth in the second phase, reinforcing their focus on *Sustainability* taking cues from the global sustainability agenda. *Corporate sustainability* through *CSR* has again attained prime significance where strategies to attain the same were explored in the avenues of *corporate governance* and *circular economy* (Aureli et al., 2020; Khan et al., 2020). The period also earmarks the advent of studies on ESG linking it to business profitability and reporting fronts with special attention to its non-financial *disclosure* prospects (Clementino & Perkins, 2021). Apart from the regulatory push mandating companies to disclose non-financial information among the European countries, COVID 19 was also a disruptive force which stimulated stakeholders towards favoring *ESG* rated avenues (Ferriani & Natoli, 2021).

In the third phase CSR and ESG disclosure dominates the thematic discourse. Here we notice a convergence of CSR, corporate sustainability, and environmental policy in the *ESG disclosure* indicating the acceptance of ESG disclosure as the new all-inclusive measure (environmental, social and governance sustainability) for non-financial and sustainable business operations (Cerciello et al., 2023). *CSR* still retains significant research interest since on a practical level CSR through corporate governance initiatives and CSR committees remains a popular modus operandi of firms for implementing sustainability practices (Ginesti et al., 2023).

The final time slice shows the course in which the research on CSR and ESG is traversing. Insights obtained from the evolution indicate that *ESG disclosure* is more often being used as a sustainability measure (Baldi & Lambertides, 2024). At this point in time, CSR and ESG are being used almost interchangeably to represent sustainability at the corporate level, with CSR looking into more of the managerial side of sustainable business conduct (Ahsan, 2024). *Content analysis* has found a place along with ESG and CSR in the final slice, indicating the popular use of the methodology in analyzing the disclosure practices of Italian firms (Crapa et al., 2024).

RQ4: What is the pattern of evolution and the direction in which CSR and ESG concepts are advancing in the case of China?

Figure 3 depicts the thematic evolution of the sustainability reporting field, with an emphasis on China, throughout the period 2010-2024, divided into three time slices or subperiods.

Figure 5. Thematic evolution of CSR and ESG in China

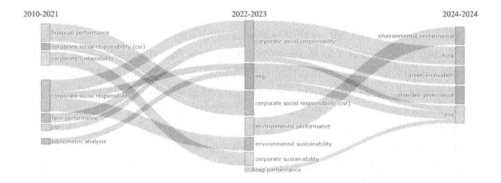

The main themes from 2010 to 2021 are *financial performance, Corporate Social Responsibility*, and *corporate sustainability*. There is a strong emphasis on understanding the relationship between CSR programs and corporate performance, showing a growing appreciation for the importance of social and environmental factors in business practices. This period saw an increase in studies exploring the impact of CSR on areas of company performance, indicating a broader social trend towards more responsible and sustainable business practices. The growing relevance of integrating technical improvements with sustainability goals was witnessed in the study of Khadke et al. (2021), where it was found that Block Chain Technology enables improvements in circular economy practices such as circular procurement and recycling, thereby improving firms' environmental performance and outcomes. The era faces emerging research in financial performance, CSR, business sustainability and its relationships and influence on organizational performance. The relationship between firm performance and CSR initiatives gained increased emphasis in the literature (Govind et al., 2021). An increasing importance was given in this period to social and environmental factors in business operations, resulting in a spike in the studies on these themes and thereby contributing to responsible and sustainable corporate practices.

CSR and Sustainability were the areas of interest in the second phase (2022-2023). A shift to *environmental performance and sustainability*, with a focus on integrating ESG principles into organizational culture is transparent in this phase. Green Human Resource Management, business strategy, and environmental responsibility were a few of the specific areas researched and the results project its relationships in navigating environmental challenges (Zhang et al., 2023). The study by Ye et al. (2022) explored the influence of CSR and environmental responsibility on investment efficiency and financial performance in Chinese institutions. The implication of the study lies in highlighting the strategies for ESG promotion in organizations on the backdrop of international markets. Certain studies also dealt with different aspects of organizational performance, ranging from green stock to liquidity (Long et al., 2023). These studies initiated broader discussions on sustainability and responsible corporate practices looking into the association between ESG and firm performance. The end of the phase looked into how ESG principles can be accommodated into the decision-making framework of the organization.

The key theme of the last slice is *environmental performance and green innovation*. The research in this period gains wider recognition of environmental responsibility and sustainable development and asks corporates to prioritize these principles in their operations. Corporates started to invest in eco-friendly technologies, products, and processes to reduce wastage and boost long-term competitiveness. The studies in this period investigated green financial policies, boardroom diversity, artificial intelligence, and green transformational leadership, and its impact on corporate behavior and performance in the context of sustainability and innovation (Chen et al., 2024). Furthermore, using "China" as a keyword implies a regional focus or specific context for understanding sustainability and innovation practices, emphasizing the importance of these studies in the current phase.

RQ 5: What is the pattern of evolution and the direction in which CSR and ESG concepts are advancing in the case of India?

Thematic evolution of CSR and ESG literature in the context of India can be seen in Figure 4. The period has been divided into three time slices: 2008-2019, 2020-2022 and 2023-2024.

Figure 6. Thematic evolution of CSR and ESG in India

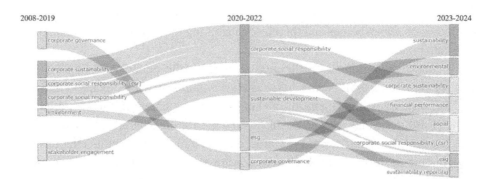

During the first period (2008-2019), significant emphasis was placed on *corporate governance*, *corporate sustainability*, *CSR*, the *environment*, and *stakeholder engagement* indicating a growing awareness of the impact of business activities on society and the environment. Studies during this time period, investigated the relationship between CSR initiatives, green practices, and organizational performance, emphasizing the importance of incorporating sustainability principles into business strategies (Raj et al., 2018). Environmental sustainability was an issue which received increasing research interest. For instance, Modak et al. (2019) investigated sustainable and closed-loop supply chains and highlighted the importance of coordination and collaboration among supply chain agents in addressing environmental and social responsibility issues. Furthermore, Raut et al. (2019) examined the green management practices in industries such as agriculture and highlighted the importance of implementing sustainable practices to reduce environmental impact while improving operational efficiency. The period also saw the active involvement of stakeholders, such as employees, customers, communities, and investors, in corporate decision-making processes which is referred to as stakeholder engagement. Gardas et al. (2019)

evaluated the social sustainability performance and barriers to sustainable human resource management which emphasized the importance of taking into account social factors and stakeholder interests when making business decisions. Overall, research conducted during this period demonstrated a concerted effort to address corporate governance, sustainability, CSR, and stakeholder engagement, indicating a shift towards more responsible and sustainable business practices.

During the second phase, 2020-2022, the emphasis shifted slightly to include *CSR, sustainable development, ESG* considerations, and *corporate governance.* CSR remained important, highlighting the ongoing concerns about business ethics and social impact. Sustainable development emerged as a key theme, focusing the importance of environmentally responsible and socially inclusive economic growth. Furthermore, ESG factors have received increased attention from investors and businesses, emphasizing the importance of including environmental, social, and governance issues in investment and decision-making processes. Sardana et al. (2020) investigated the impact of environmental sustainability on firm performance and the importance of taking sustainability into account in the institutional and business environments. The study also talks about the importance of environmentally sustainable economic growth. Rajesh and Rajendran (2020) reinforced the period's heightened focus on ESG factors by investigating the relationship between ESG scores and global firm sustainability performance. This is consistent with the broader trend of incorporating ESG criteria into investment and decision-making processes, emphasizing the importance of ESG factors in corporate governance and sustainability. The findings of these studies add to our understanding of how ESG considerations have become an integral part of assessing firm sustainability and performance, reflecting the changing landscape of corporate governance and responsible investment practices.

The popular themes in the final time slice (2023-2024) were *Sustainability, environmental issues, corporate sustainability, financial performance, social impact, CSR, ESG*, and *sustainability reporting*. Sustainability remains a top priority, highlighting the ongoing importance of balancing economic, social, and environmental considerations in business practices. Many studies during this phase revealed a comprehensive understanding of the current landscape of sustainability, CSR, and environmental factors (Fatimah et al., 2023). From the implementation of circular economy principles in food supply chains to the creation of innovative e-business models for sustainability, these studies highlight the importance of incorporating sustainable practices into business strategies and operations. Furthermore, the emphasis on consumer perceptions of sustainable marketing strategies, as well as top management support for CSR initiatives, reflects the growing recognition of sustainability as a critical factor in business success. ESG adoption has been increasingly stressed on with due emphasis on the interplay between technology, sustainability, and stakeholder perceptions (Efthymiou et al., 2023). The significance of considering stakeholders' needs and expectations in enterprising sustainable practices has been gaining recognition in the Indian academia. Looking into corporate sustainability, Yadav and Prashar (2022) finds the importance of gender diversity in improving ESG performances. The research contributes to understanding the implications of board composition and gender diversity in promoting sustainability. Prashar (2021) study on the linkage between sustainability reporting and firm performance, reveals that level and quality of sustainability reporting influence a variety of performance metrics. On the whole, corporate governance, sustainability reporting, CSR and ESG remain important themes of research with a focus on incorporating sustainable principles into business strategies and operations. ESG factors continue to gain popularity, with a particular emphasis on their impact on financial performance and risk management.

FINDINGS AND IMPLICATIONS

The insights gathered through the thematic evolution of the five country cases are summarized in Table 1. From the thematic evolution of the five cases, the main implications, the respective regulatory frameworks, the overall preferred strategy (CSR vs ESG) and future research themes are listed.

Table 1. Summary of insights

Countries	Time period	Preferred Strategy	Disclosure Norms	Implications	Future Research Themes
U. S.	2001-2024	CSR is more preferred than ESG	**Voluntary disclosure:** supported by a few guidelines such as Global Reporting Initiatives (GRI), Securities Exchange Commission Guidance and New York Stock Exchange Listing Standards.	• CSR has expanded beyond a focus on business sustainability • Focus on broader topics of sustainability and sustainable development • A growing discontent with the reliability of ESG measures observed • Rise in assurance practices due to non-reliability of disclosures • Voluntary disclosure norms resulting in lack of uniformity in sustainability disclosure practices	• CSR committees and sustainability disclosure practices • Meeting SDGs through sustainable practices • ESG disclosure as a sustainability indicator • ESG divergence and reliability • Executive compensation and sustainability agenda • AI methodology in developing reliable ESG rating standards
United Kingdom	2002-2024	CSR and ESG coexist within companies' strategic frameworks.	**Mandatory Disclosure:** Companies (Strategic Report) (Climate-related Financial Disclosure) Regulations 2022[1] The Limited Liability Partnerships (Climate-related Financial Disclosure) Regulations 2022[2] **Voluntary Disclosure:** Task Force on Climate-Related Disclosures (TCFD)	• A clear preference for ESG as a sustainability metric. • More importance to environmental sustainability • Despite having voluntary disclosure norms, sustainability disclosure is widely practised	• Double materiality assessment in CSR and ESG disclosure • Impact investing and ESG • Effect of Climate Risk Disclosure and Net Zero Commitments in attaining sustainability • AI-based sustainability tracing
Italy	2008-2024	CSR broader scope and ESG disclosure as a directive of CSR strategy.	**Mandatory Disclosure:** Non-Financial Reporting Directive (2014/95/EU) requires all public interest companies with employees above 500 to disclose their sustainability information mandatorily. This has brought a major improvement in sustainability reporting among European firms (Aureli et al., 2020).	• Italy has a pronounced shift from CSR to ESG • More importance is given to sustainability disclosures • The increased disclosure practices attributed to the mandatory disclosure norms	• Association of CSR committees and assurances with Corporate Governance • Effectiveness of ESG disclosure as a Sustainability reporting practice • Influence of CSR/ ESG on Financial performance

continued on following page

Table 1. Continued

Countries	Time period	Preferred Strategy	Disclosure Norms	Implications	Future Research Themes
China	2010-2024	Focus on both CSR and ESG disclosures but by limited corporations.	**Mandatory Disclosure** Measures on Open Environmental Information 2007[3] Environmental Protection Law 2014[4] By 2026 All firms listed on the Shanghai Stock Exchange 180 Index and the Kechuang 50 Index, as well as components from the Shenzhen Stock Exchange 100 Index and the ChiNext Index.	• A shift from CSR to a broader sustainability framework was observed • China is heavily reliant on ESG ratings in corporate decision-making processes • Existing environment protection laws have a huge effect on ESG adoption • New regulations in the pipeline which has fueled adoption of ESG.	• Green Innovations and Eco-Friendly Technologies • Board room cultures and association with ESG • Green Human Resource Management (GHRM) roles for CSR and ESG promotions • Association between sustainable investment and green finance
India	2008-2024	ESG more popular than CSR. Mandatory ESG disclosure by corporates may include CSR information.	**Mandatory Disclosure** Section 135 of the Companies Act, 2013 mandates disclosure of CSR activities which increased CSR activity in Indian firms (Dharmapala & Khanna, 2018) Business Responsibility and Sustainability Report (BRSR)[5] National Guidelines for Responsible Business Conduct 2019[6]	• CSR system ingrained into the corporate framework as a beacon of sustainability practices • Yet, increasing change towards a holistic approach to sustainability, in the form of ESG, was observed. • Recent studies give more weightage to ESG ratings • Mandatory disclosure norms have encouraged firms to level up CSR activities into ESG disclosure frameworks	• Full disclosure of individual pillars of ESG • Integration of advanced technologies in CSR and ESG reporting. • Sector-specific differences in ESG adoption and financial performance • Sustainability reporting and stakeholder trust

Apart from the country-wise implications listed in Table 1, we also come upon a few distinctions on the basis of developed and developing categorization. Research interest in developed countries revolved around qualitative sustainability disclosure practices, while emerging nations are seen to rely on the quantitative ESG ratings of external agencies. This indicates a divergence in the perspective of sustainability practices among the nations. Additionally, mandatory disclosure norms are seen to be more effective in nudging firms to disclose their sustainable business practices. Despite the differences, ESG disclosure is acknowledged as the new wave in the sustainability realm with a dire need for standardization.

CONCLUSION

CSR and ESG concepts have taken over the sustainability research field in a significant way. In the context of growing literature on CSR and ESG, this study tries to understand the evolution and trajectory of CSR and ESG concepts in developed and developing countries, focusing on the US, the UK, Italy, China, and India. These choices were made based on their importance and representation in the global landscape of CSR and ESG initiatives. Thematic evolution was analyzed utilizing R software to discern patterns and trends in advancing CSR and ESG concepts across different periods and regions. The analysis revealed that while the US, UK, and Italy defer in terms of their disclosure norms, they unanimously focus on qualitative sustainability disclosure practices. The US still prefers CSR and is skeptical of ESG reliability, with the UK and Italy enthusiastically accepting ESG as a better sustainability principle. The emerging countries China and India both display similar patterns of evolution where they initially took up CSR activities, but with stringent norms, they shifted to ESG reporting with more emphasis on ratings. The findings add to the ongoing discussion about environmental sustainability and innovation, providing useful insights for policymakers, managers, and practitioners working to incorporate ESG principles into corporate strategies and practices.

REFERENCES

Abdullah, A., Yamak, S., Korzhenitskaya, A., Rahimi, R., & McClellan, J. (2024). Sustainable development: The role of sustainability committees in achieving ESG targets. *Business Strategy and the Environment*, 33(3), 2250–2268. 10.1002/bse.3596

Adeneye, Y. B., Fasihi, S., Kammoun, I., & Albitar, K. (2024). Does earnings management constrain ESG performance? The role of corporate governance. *International Journal of Disclosure and Governance*, 21(1), 69–92. 10.1057/s41310-023-00181-9

Ahsan, M. J. (2024). Unlocking sustainable success: Exploring the impact of transformational leadership, organizational culture, and CSR performance on financial performance in the Italian manufacturing sector. *Social Responsibility Journal*, 20(4), 783–803. 10.1108/SRJ-06-2023-0332

Albitar, K., Hussainey, K., Kolade, N., & Gerged, A. M. (2020). ESG disclosure and firm performance before and after IR: The moderating role of governance mechanisms. *International Journal of Accounting and Information Management*, 28(3), 429–444. 10.1108/IJAIM-09-2019-0108

Alkhammash, R. (2023). Bibliometric, network, and thematic mapping analyses of metaphor and discourse in COVID-19 publications from 2020 to 2022. *Frontiers in Psychology*, 13, 1062943. 10.3389/fpsyg.2022.106294336726506

Amin, M. H., Ali, H., & Mohamed, E. K. (2024). Corporate social responsibility disclosure on Twitter: Signalling or greenwashing? Evidence from the UK. *International Journal of Finance & Economics*, 29(2), 1745–1761. 10.1002/ijfe.2762

Aria, M., & Cuccurullo, C. (2017). bibliometrix: An R-tool for comprehensive science mapping analysis. *Journal of Informetrics*, 11(4), 959–975. 10.1016/j.joi.2017.08.007

Arnold, M., Bassen, A., & Frank, R. (2018). Timing effects of corporate social responsibility disclosure: An experimental study with investment professionals. *Journal of Sustainable Finance & Investment*, 8(1), 45–71. 10.1080/20430795.2017.1368229

Asante-Appiah, B., & Lambert, T. A. (2023). The role of the external auditor in managing environmental, social, and governance (ESG) reputation risk. *Review of Accounting Studies*, 28(4), 2589–2641. 10.1007/s11142-022-09706-z

Asif, M., Searcy, C., & Castka, P. (2023). ESG and Industry 5.0: The role of technologies in enhancing ESG disclosure. *Technological Forecasting and Social Change*, 195, 122806. 10.1016/j.techfore.2023.122806

Aureli, S., Del Baldo, M., Lombardi, R., & Nappo, F. (2020). Nonfinancial reporting regulation and challenges in sustainability disclosure and corporate governance practices. *Business Strategy and the Environment*, 29(6), 2392–2403. 10.1002/bse.2509

Aydoğmuş, M., Gülay, G., & Ergun, K. (2022). Impact of ESG performance on firm value and profitability. *Borsa Istanbul Review*, 22, S119–S127. 10.1016/j.bir.2022.11.006

Baldi, F., & Lambertides, N. (2024). Exploring the role of ESG for the performance and risks of infrastructure investing: Evidence from the international funds' market. *Managerial Finance*, 50(1), 92–117. 10.1108/MF-01-2023-0024

Balmer, J. M. T., Powell, S. M., & Greyser, S. A. (2011). Explicating Ethical Corporate Marketing. Insights from the BP Deepwater Horizon Catastrophe: The Ethical Brand that Exploded and then Imploded. *Journal of Business Ethics*, 102(1), 1–14. 10.1007/s10551-011-0902-1

Baraibar-Diez, E., & Odriozola, D., M. (2019). CSR committees and their effect on ESG performance in UK, France, Germany, and Spain. *Sustainability*, 11(18), 5077. 10.3390/su11185077

Bartolacci, F., Caputo, A., & Soverchia, M. (2020). Sustainability and financial performance of small and medium sized enterprises: A bibliometric and systematic literature review. *Business Strategy and the Environment*, 29(3), 1297–1309. 10.1002/bse.2434

Berg, F., Kölbel, J. F., & Rigobon, R. (2022). Aggregate Confusion: The Divergence of ESG Ratings. *Review of Finance*, 26(6), 1315–1344. 10.1093/rof/rfac033

Bonilla-Priego, M. J., Font, X., & del Rosario Pacheco-Olivares, M. (2014). Corporate sustainability reporting index and baseline data for the cruise industry. *Tourism Management*, 44, 149–160. 10.1016/j.tourman.2014.03.004

Bhatia, A., & Makkar, B. (2020). CSR disclosure in developing and developed countries: A comparative study. *Journal of Global Responsibility*, 11(1), 1–26. 10.1108/JGR-04-2019-0043

Bran, F., Ioan, I., Radulescu, C. V., & Ardeleanu, M. P. (2011). Sustainable development at corporate level. *Rivista di Studi sulla Sostenibilità*, 1(1), 101–131. 10.3280/RISS2011-001012

Buallay, A. (2020). Sustainability reporting and firm's performance: Comparative study between manufacturing and banking sectors. *International Journal of Productivity and Performance Management*, 69(3), 431–445. 10.1108/IJPPM-10-2018-0371

Buallay, A., Hamdan, R., Barone, E., & Hamdan, A. (2022). Increasing female participation on boards: Effects on sustainability reporting. *International Journal of Finance & Economics*, 27(1), 111–124. 10.1002/ijfe.2141

Casey, R. J., & Grenier, J. H. (2015). Understanding and Contributing to the Enigma of Corporate Social Responsibility (CSR) Assurance in the United States. *Auditing*, 34(1), 97–130. 10.2308/ajpt-50736

Cerciello, M., Busato, F., & Taddeo, S. (2023). The effect of sustainable business practices on profitability. Accounting for strategic disclosure. *Corporate Social Responsibility and Environmental Management*, 30(2), 802–819. 10.1002/csr.2389

Chatterji, A. K., Durand, R., Levine, D. I., & Touboul, S. (2016). Do ratings of firms converge? Implications for managers, investors and strategy researchers. *Strategic Management Journal*, 37(8), 1597–1614. 10.1002/smj.2407

Chen, P., Chu, Z., & Zhao, M. (2024). The Road to corporate sustainability: The importance of artificial intelligence. *Technology in Society*, 76, 102440. 10.1016/j.techsoc.2023.102440

Cheng, B., Ioannou, I., & Serafeim, G. (2014). Corporate social responsibility and access to finance. *Strategic Management Journal*, 35(1), 1–23. 10.1002/smj.2131

Cheruvalath, R. (2017). NEED FOR A SHIFT FROM A PHILANTHROPIC TO A HUMANISTIC APPROACH TO CORPORATE SOCIAL RESPONSIBILITY. *Annals of Public and Cooperative Economics*, 88(1), 121–136. 10.1111/apce.12146

Clément, A., Robinot, É., & Trespeuch, L. (2023). The use of ESG scores in academic literature: a systematic literature review. *Journal of Enterprising Communities*. https://doi.org/10.1108/JEC-10-2022-0147/FULL/XML

Clementino, E., & Perkins, R. (2021). How Do Companies Respond to Environmental, Social and Governance (ESG) ratings? Evidence from Italy. *Journal of Business Ethics*, 171(2), 379–397. 10.1007/s10551-020-04441-4

Consolandi, C., Phadke, H., Hawley, J., & Eccles, R. G. (2020). Material ESG outcomes and SDG externalities: Evaluating the health care sector's contribution to the SDGs. *Organization & Environment*, 33(4), 511–533. 10.1177/1086026619899795

Crapa, G., Latino, M. E., & Roma, P. (2024). The performance of green communication across social media: Evidence from large-scale retail industry in Italy. *Corporate Social Responsibility and Environmental Management*, 31(1), 493–513. 10.1002/csr.2581

Crisóstomo, V. L., De Azevedo Prudêncio, P., & Forte, H. C. (2017). An analysis of the adherence to GRI for disclosing information on social action and sustainability concerns. *Advances in Environmental Accounting and Management*, 6, 69–103. 10.1108/S1479-359820160000006002

Delgado-Ceballos, J., Ortiz-De-Mandojana, N., Antolín-López, R., & Montiel, I. (2023). Connecting the Sustainable Development Goals to firm-level sustainability and ESG factors: The need for double materiality. *Business Research Quarterly*, 26(1), 2–10. 10.1177/23409444221140919

Deng, X., Kang, J., & Low, B. S. (2013). Corporate social responsibility and stakeholder value maximization: Evidence from mergers. *Journal of Financial Economics*, 110(1), 87–109. 10.1016/j.jfineco.2013.04.014

Dharmapala, D., & Khanna, V. (2018). The impact of mandated corporate social responsibility: Evidence from India's Companies Act of 2013. *International Review of Law and Economics*, 56, 92–104. 10.1016/j.irle.2018.09.001

Efthymiou, L., Kulshrestha, A., & Kulshrestha, S. (2023). A Study on Sustainability and ESG in the Service Sector in India: Benefits, Challenges, and Future Implications. *Administrative Sciences*, 13(7), 7. 10.3390/admsci13070165

Egri, C. P., & Ralston, D. A. (2008). Corporate responsibility: A review of international management research from 1998 to 2007. *Journal of International Management*, 14(4), 319–339. 10.1016/j.intman.2007.09.003

Fatimah, Y. A., Kannan, D., Govindan, K., & Hasibuan, Z. A. (2023). Circular economy e-business model portfolio development for e-business applications: Impacts on ESG and sustainability performance. *Journal of Cleaner Production*, 415, 137528. 10.1016/j.jclepro.2023.137528

Ferriani, F., & Natoli, F. (2021). ESG risks in times of Covid-19. *Applied Economics Letters*, 28(18), 1537–1541. 10.1080/13504851.2020.1830932

Font, X., & Harris, C. (2004). Rethinking standards from green to sustainable. *Annals of Tourism Research*, 31(4), 986–1007. 10.1016/j.annals.2004.04.001

Gardas, B. B., Mangla, S. K., Raut, R. D., Narkhede, B., & Luthra, S. (2019). Green talent management to unlock sustainability in the oil and gas sector. *Journal of Cleaner Production*, 229, 850–862. 10.1016/j.jclepro.2019.05.018

Gillan, S. L., Koch, A., & Starks, L. T. (2021). Firms and social responsibility: A review of ESG and CSR research in corporate finance. *Journal of Corporate Finance*, 66, 101889. 10.1016/j.jcorpfin.2021.101889

Ginesti, G., Campa, D., Spano', R., Allini, A., & Maffei, M. (2023). The role of CSR committee characteristics on R&D investments. *International Business Review*, 32(5), 102147. 10.1016/j.ibusrev.2023.102147

Govindan, K., Khodaverdi, R., & Jafarian, A. (2013). A fuzzy multi criteria approach for measuring sustainability performance of a supplier based on triple bottom line approach. *Journal of Cleaner Production*, 47, 345–354. 10.1016/j.jclepro.2012.04.014

Govindan, K., Kilic, M., Uyar, A., & Karaman, A. S. (2021). Drivers and value-relevance of CSR performance in the logistics sector: A cross-country firm-level investigation. *International Journal of Production Economics*, 231, 107835. 10.1016/j.ijpe.2020.107835

Greiner, M., & Sun, J. (2021). How corporate social responsibility can incentivize top managers: A commitment to sustainability as an agency intervention. *Corporate Social Responsibility and Environmental Management*, 28(4), 1360–1375. 10.1002/csr.2148

Halme, M., Rintamäki, J., Knudsen, J. S., Lankoski, L., & Kuisma, M. (2020). When Is There a Sustainability Case for CSR? Pathways to Environmental and Social Performance Improvements. *Business & Society*, 59(6), 1181–1227. 10.1177/0007650318755648

Hamed, R. S., Al-Shattarat, B. K., Al-Shattarat, W. K., & Hussainey, K. (2022). The impact of introducing new regulations on the quality of CSR reporting: Evidence from the UK. *Journal of International Accounting, Auditing & Taxation*, 46, 100444. 10.1016/j.intaccaudtax.2021.100444

Holcomb, J. L., Upchurch, R. S., & Okumus, F. (2007). Corporate social responsibility: What are top hotel companies reporting? *International Journal of Contemporary Hospitality Management*, 19(6), 461–475. 10.1108/09596110710775129

Hopkins, M., & Cowe, R. (2003). *Corporate social responsibility: is there a business case*. ACCA UK.

Hutchins, M. J., & Sutherland, J. W. (2008). An exploration of measures of social sustainability and their application to supply chain decisions. *Journal of Cleaner Production*, 16(15), 1688–1698. 10.1016/j.jclepro.2008.06.001

Jemel-Fornetty, H., Louche, C., & Bourghelle, D. (2011). Changing the dominant convention: The role of emerging initiatives in mainstreaming ESG. *Critical Studies on Corporate Responsibility. Governance and Sustainability*, 2, 85–117. 10.1108/S2043-9059(2011)0000002011/FULL/XML

Jenkins, H., & Yakovleva, N. (2006). Corporate social responsibility in the mining industry: Exploring trends in social and environmental disclosure. *Journal of Cleaner Production*, 14(3-4), 271–284. 10.1016/j.jclepro.2004.10.004

Jo, H., Kim, H., & Park, K. (2015). Corporate Environmental Responsibility and Firm Performance in the Financial Services Sector. *Journal of Business Ethics*, 131(2), 257–284. 10.1007/s10551-014-2276-7

Jones, P., Comfort, D., & Hillier, D. (2006). Reporting and reflecting on corporate social responsibility in the hospitality industry: A case study of pub operators in the UK. *International Journal of Contemporary Hospitality Management*, 18(4), 329–340. 10.1108/09596110610665339

Katmon, N., Mohamad, Z. Z., Norwani, N. M., & Farooque, O. A. (2019). Comprehensive Board Diversity and Quality of Corporate Social Responsibility Disclosure: Evidence from an Emerging Market. *Journal of Business Ethics*, 157(2), 447–481. 10.1007/s10551-017-3672-6

Khan, A., Muttakin, M. B., & Siddiqui, J. (2013). Corporate Governance and Corporate Social Responsibility Disclosures: Evidence from an Emerging Economy. *Journal of Business Ethics*, 114(2), 207–223. 10.1007/s10551-012-1336-0

Khan, O., Daddi, T., & Iraldo, F. (2020). Microfoundations of dynamic capabilities: Insights from circular economy business cases. *Business Strategy and the Environment*, 29(3), 1479–1493. 10.1002/bse.2447

Khadke, S., Gupta, P., Rachakunta, S., Mahata, C., Dawn, S., Sharma, M., Verma, D., Pradhan, A., Krishna, A. M. S., Ramakrishna, S., Chakrabortty, S., Saianand, G., Sonar, P., Biring, S., Dash, J. K., & Dalapati, G. K. (2021). Efficient Plastic Recycling and Remolding Circular Economy Using the Technology of Trust–Blockchain. *Sustainability (Basel)*, 13(16), 16. 10.3390/su13169142

Koroleva, E., Baggieri, M., & Nalwanga, S. (2020). Company performance: Are environmental, social, and governance factors important. *International Journal of Technology*, 11(8), 1468–1477. 10.14716/ijtech.v11i8.4527

Krasodomska, J., Simnett, R., & Street, D. L. (2021). Extended external reporting assurance: Current practices and challenges. *Journal of International Financial Management & Accounting*, 32(1), 104–142. 10.1111/jifm.12127

Kräussl, R., Oladiran, T., & Stefanova, D. (2024). A review on ESG investing: Investors' expectations, beliefs and perceptions. *Journal of Economic Surveys*, 38(2), 476–502. 10.1111/joes.12599

Lai, A., Melloni, G., & Stacchezzini, R. (2016). Corporate Sustainable Development: Is 'Integrated Reporting' a Legitimation Strategy? *Business Strategy and the Environment*, 25(3), 165–177. 10.1002/bse.1863

Lamm, E., Tosti-Kharas, J., & King, C. E. (2015). Empowering Employee Sustainability: Perceived Organizational Support Toward the Environment. *Journal of Business Ethics*, 128(1), 207–220. 10.1007/s10551-014-2093-z

Landrum, N. E., & Ohsowski, B. (2018). Identifying Worldviews on Corporate Sustainability: A Content Analysis of Corporate Sustainability Reports. *Business Strategy and the Environment*, 27(1), 128–151. 10.1002/bse.1989

Lawal, E., May, G., & Stahl, B. (2017). The Significance of Corporate Social Disclosure for High-Tech Manufacturing Companies: Focus on Employee and Community Aspects of Sustainable Development. *Corporate Social Responsibility and Environmental Management*, 24(4), 295–311. 10.1002/csr.1397

Leal Filho, W., Azeiteiro, U., Alves, F., Pace, P., Mifsud, M., Brandli, L., Caeiro, S. S., & Disterheft, A. (2018). Reinvigorating the sustainable development research agenda: The role of the sustainable development goals (SDG). *International Journal of Sustainable Development and World Ecology*, 25(2), 131–142. 10.1080/13504509.2017.1342103

Lee, J., Koh, K., & Shim, E. D. (2024). Managerial incentives for ESG in the financial services industry: Direct and indirect association between ESG and executive compensation. *Managerial Finance*, 50(1), 10–27. 10.1108/MF-03-2023-0149

Levy, S. E., & Park, S. Y. (2011). An Analysis of CSR Activities in the Lodging Industry. *Journal of Hospitality and Tourism Management*, 18(1), 147–154. 10.1375/jhtm.18.1.147

Long, H., Feng, G.-F., Gong, Q., & Chang, C.-P. (2023). ESG performance and green innovation: An investigation based on quantile regression. *Business Strategy and the Environment*, 32(7), 5102–5118. 10.1002/bse.3410

Mahoney, L. S., Thorne, L., Cecil, L., & LaGore, W. (2013). A research note on standalone corporate social responsibility reports: Signaling or greenwashing? *Critical Perspectives on Accounting*, 24(4–5), 350–359. 10.1016/j.cpa.2012.09.008

Maletič, M., Maletič, D., & Gomišček, B. (2016). The impact of sustainability exploration and sustainability exploitation practices on the organisational performance: A cross-country comparison. *Journal of Cleaner Production*, 138, 158–169. 10.1016/j.jclepro.2016.02.132

Manchiraju, H., & Rajgopal, S. (2017). Does Corporate Social Responsibility (CSR) Create Shareholder Value? Evidence from the Indian Companies Act 2013. *Journal of Accounting Research*, 55(5), 1257–1300. 10.1111/1475-679X.12174

Mansouri, S., & Momtaz, P. P. (2022). Financing sustainable entrepreneurship: ESG measurement, valuation, and performance. *Journal of Business Venturing*, 37(6), 106258. 10.1016/j.jbusvent.2022.106258

Michelon, G., Pilonato, S., & Ricceri, F. (2015). CSR reporting practices and the quality of disclosure: An empirical analysis. *Critical Perspectives on Accounting*, 33, 59–78. 10.1016/j.cpa.2014.10.003

Minutolo, M. C., Kristjanpoller, W. D., & Stakeley, J. (2019). Exploring environmental, social, and governance disclosure effects on the S&P 500 financial performance. *Business Strategy and the Environment*, 28(6), 1083–1095. 10.1002/bse.2303

Money, K., & Schepers, H. (2007). Are CSR and corporate governance converging?: A view from boardroom directors and company secretaries in FTSE100 companies in the UK. *Journal of General Management*, 33(2), 1–11. 10.1177/030630700703300201

Montecchia, A., Giordano, F., & Grieco, C. (2016). Communicating CSR: Integrated approach or Selfie? Evidence from the Milan Stock Exchange. *Journal of Cleaner Production*, 136, 42–52. 10.1016/j.jclepro.2016.01.099

Modak, N. M., Kazemi, N., & Cárdenas-Barrón, L. E. (2019). Investigating structure of a two-echelon closed-loop supply chain using social work donation as a Corporate Social Responsibility practice. *International Journal of Production Economics*, 207, 19–33. 10.1016/j.ijpe.2018.10.009

Naeem, N., Cankaya, S., & Bildik, R. (2022). Does ESG performance affect the financial performance of environmentally sensitive industries? A comparison between emerging and developed markets. *Borsa Istanbul Review*, 22, S128–S140. 10.1016/j.bir.2022.11.014

Nayal, K., Raut, R. D., Yadav, V. S., Priyadarshinee, P., & Narkhede, B. E. (2022). The impact of sustainable development strategy on sustainable supply chain firm performance in the digital transformation era. *Business Strategy and the Environment*, 31(3), 845–859. 10.1002/bse.2921

Orazalin, N., & Mahmood, M. (2021). Toward sustainable development: Board characteristics, country governance quality, and environmental performance. *Business Strategy and the Environment*, 30(8), 3569–3588. 10.1002/bse.2820

Orazalin, N., Kuzey, C., Uyar, A., & Karaman, A. S. (2024). Does CSR contribute to the financial sector's financial stability? The moderating role of a sustainability committee. *Journal of Applied Accounting Research*, 25(1), 105–125. 10.1108/JAAR-12-2022-0329

Pisani, N., Kourula, A., Kolk, A., & Meijer, R. (2017). How global is international CSR research? Insights and recommendations from a systematic review. *Journal of World Business*, 52(5), 591–614. 10.1016/j.jwb.2017.05.003

Prashar, A. (2021). Moderating effects on sustainability reporting and firm performance relationships: A meta-analytical review. *International Journal of Productivity and Performance Management*, 72(4), 1154–1181. 10.1108/IJPPM-04-2021-0183

Qian, W., Parker, L., & Zhu, J. (2024). Corporate environmental reporting in the China context: The interplay of stakeholder salience, socialist ideology and state power. *The British Accounting Review*, 56(1), 101198. 10.1016/j.bar.2023.101198

Raj, A., Biswas, I., & Srivastava, S. K. (2018). Designing supply contracts for the sustainable supply chain using game theory. *Journal of Cleaner Production*, 185, 275–284. 10.1016/j.jclepro.2018.03.046

Rajesh, R. (2020). Exploring the sustainability performances of firms using environmental, social, and governance scores. *Journal of Cleaner Production*, 247, 119600. 10.1016/j.jclepro.2019.119600

Rajesh, R., & Rajendran, C. (2020). Relating Environmental, Social, and Governance scores and sustainability performances of firms: An empirical analysis. *Business Strategy and the Environment*, 29(3), 1247–1267. 10.1002/bse.2429

Raut, R. D., Luthra, S., Narkhede, B. E., Mangla, S. K., Gardas, B. B., & Priyadarshinee, P. (2019). Examining the performance oriented indicators for implementing green management practices in the Indian agro sector. *Journal of Cleaner Production*, 215, 926–943. 10.1016/j.jclepro.2019.01.139

Sachin, N., & Rajesh, R. (2022). An empirical study of supply chain sustainability with financial performances of Indian firms. *Environment, Development and Sustainability*, 24(5), 6577–6601. 10.1007/s10668-021-01717-134393619

Saini, M., Aggarwal, V., Dhingra, B., Kumar, P., & Yadav, M. (2023). ESG and financial variables: A systematic review. *International Journal of Law and Management*, 65(6), 663–682. 10.1108/IJLMA-02-2023-0033

Sardana, D., Gupta, N., Kumar, V., & Terziovski, M. (2020). CSR 'sustainability' practices and firm performance in an emerging economy. *Journal of Cleaner Production*, 258, 120766. 10.1016/j.jclepro.2020.120766

Sarhan, A. A., & Al-Najjar, B. (2023). The influence of corporate governance and shareholding structure on corporate social responsibility: The key role of executive compensation. *International Journal of Finance & Economics*, 28(4), 4532–4556. 10.1002/ijfe.2663

Singhania, M., & Saini, N. (2023). Institutional framework of ESG disclosures: Comparative analysis of developed and developing countries. *Journal of Sustainable Finance & Investment*, 13(1), 516–559. 10.1080/20430795.2021.1964810

Sodano, V., & Hingley, M. (2018). Corporate social responsibility reporting: The case of the agri-food sector. *Economia Agro-Alimentare*, 20(1), 93–120. 10.3280/ECAG2018-001006

Trendafilova, S., Babiak, K., & Heinze, K. (2013). Corporate social responsibility and environmental sustainability: Why professional sport is greening the playing field. *Sport Management Review*, 16(3), 298–313. 10.1016/j.smr.2012.12.006

Uyar, A., Kilic, M., Koseoglu, M. A., Kuzey, C., & Karaman, A. S. (2020). The link among board characteristics, corporate social responsibility performance, and financial performance: Evidence from the hospitality and tourism industry. *Tourism Management Perspectives*, 35, 100714. 10.1016/j.tmp.2020.100714

Wang, K., Li, T., San, Z., & Gao, H. (2023). How does corporate ESG performance affect stock liquidity? Evidence from China. *Pacific-Basin Finance Journal*, 80, 102087. 10.1016/j.pacfin.2023.102087

Ward, H. (2006). *Corporate Social Responsibility at a Crossroads: Futures for CSR in the UK to 2015*. IIED.

Wheeler, D., Fabig, H., & Boele, R. (2002). Paradoxes and dilemmas for stakeholder responsive firms in the extractive sector: *Lessons from the case of Shell and the Ogoni.Journal of Business Ethics*, 39(3), 297–318. 10.1023/A:1016542207069

Wong, W. C., Batten, J. A., Ahmad, A. H., Mohamed-Arshad, S. B., Nordin, S., & Adzis, A. A. (2021). Does ESG certification add firm value? *Finance Research Letters*, 39, 101593. 10.1016/j.frl.2020.101593

Yadav, P., & Prashar, A. (2022). Board gender diversity: Implications for environment, social, and governance (ESG) performance of Indian firms. *International Journal of Productivity and Performance Management*, 72(9), 2654–2673. 10.1108/IJPPM-12-2021-0689

Zhang, Y., Mirza, S. S., Safdar, R., Huang, C., & Zhang, C. (2023). Business strategy and sustainability of Chinese SMEs: Determining the moderating role of environmental uncertainty. *Ekonomska Istrazivanja*, 36(3), 2218468. 10.1080/1331677X.2023.2218468

Zhou, D., Saeed, U. F., & Agyemang, A. O. (2024). Assessing the Role of Sustainability Disclosure on Firms' Financial Performance: Evidence from the Energy Sector of Belt and Road Initiative Countries. *Sustainability (Basel)*, 16(2), 2. Advance online publication. 10.3390/su16020930

ENDNOTES

[1] Mandatory climate-related financial disclosure requirements under the Companies (Strategic Report) (Climate-related Financial Disclosure) Regulations introduced in 2022 https://www.legislation.gov.uk/uksi/2022/31/memorandum/contents

[2] Limited Liability Partnerships (Climate-related Financial Disclosure) Regulations introduced in 2022 https://www.legislation.gov.uk/uksi/2022/46/contents/made

[3] The Measures on Open Environmental Information was introduced by Congressional-Executive Commission on China to promote and standardize the disclosure of environmental information among Chinese firms https://www.cecc.gov/resources/legal-provisions/measures-on-open-environmental-information-trial-cecc-full-translation

[4] The Environmental Protection Law of China revised in 2014 mandates firms to disclose environmental information https://leap.unep.org/en/countries/cn/national-legislation/environmental-protection-law-peoples-republic-china

[5] SEBI mandated disclosure of BRSR for the top 1000 listed companies (as per market capitalization) https://www.sebi.gov.in/legal/circulars/jul-2023/brsr-core-framework-for-assurance-and-esg-disclosures-for-value-chain_73854.html

[6] National Guidelines for responsible Business Conduct was revised in 2019 to encourage disclosure of responsible business activities https://www.mca.gov.in/Ministry/pdf/NationalGuildeline_15032019.pdf

Chapter 2
Environmental, Social, and Governance (ESG) Sustainability Through Corporate Social Responsibility:
A Scoping Review

Jose John

https://orcid.org/0000-0003-2024-2130

Cochin University of Science and Technology, India

I. S. Smiju

Cochin University of Science and Technology, India

Kiran Thampi

https://orcid.org/0000-0002-7976-1317

Rajagiri College of Social Sciences (Autonomous), India

M. K. Joseph

https://orcid.org/0009-0001-0458-6227

Rajagiri College of Social Sciences (Autonomous), India

ABSTRACT

Corporate Social Responsibility (CSR) and pillars of Environmental, Social and Governance (ESG) are closely associated. The chapter aimed to review the scope of CSR in contributing to pillars of ESG in developing nations. The authors used the Joanna Briggs Institute Methods Manual guidelines and Preferred Reporting Items

DOI: 10.4018/979-8-3693-3880-3.ch002

for Systematic Reviews and Meta-analysis for Scoping Review (PRISMA-ScR) as guidelines for this scoping review. Two databases (EBSCOhost and SCOPUS) and a reference list of the relevant systematic reviews were searched. After screening 320 titles and abstracts, followed by sixty-four full texts, thirteen unique documents that fulfilled the eligibility criteria were selected. The result highlighted CSR's role in promoting organizational sustainability through corporate governance, social sustainability. and environmental sustainability. The study gathered evidence to identify the contribution of CSR toward environmental social and governance sustainability and would contribute to the existing literature and further research on sustainable development.

1. INTRODUCTION

Corporate Social Responsibility (CSR) is a social science concept in which organisations amalgamate societal and environmental interests in their business operations. CSR highlights the role of organisations in the development of the community in which it functions. It can also turn out to be a good avenue for attaining higher performance and a basis for competitive advantage (Porter & Kramer, 2007).

ESG, containing environmental, social, and governance, are the three focus pillars in ESG frameworks and are the key thematic areas on which companies must report. The goal of ESG is to cover all non-monetary risks and opportunities integral to a company's daily processes (Goodell et al., 2024; Wang & Chang, 2024).

Economic, social, and environmental sustainability are all included in the concept of sustainability. To secure both economic and social progress, it is necessary to respect the environment in which activities are carried out (Purvis et al., 2019). With the introduction of the Sustainable Development Goals (SDGs) of the United Nations, the discussion of global sustainability has advanced to the point where it cannot be separated from the function of the organisation (Marcus et al., 2010).

CSR uses the Triple Bottom Line Approach and ensures that a company attains a balance of economic, environmental, and social imperatives (Gu et al., 2022). According to Branco and Lima Rodrigues, (2006), CSR goes "beyond compliance" and moves toward a social goal; it does not entail "sacrificing profits for the common good" (Stavins et al., 2008). According to CSR, company decision-makers should consider "ethical and socially supporting" factors in addition to "economically lucrative, law-abiding" considerations (Carroll, 1999).

CSR and ESG is more prevalent and widespread in developed nations compared to underdeveloped countries, due to greater resource availability and higher public awareness. National CSR agendas in medium and low-income nations have garnered less international attention, particularly in the realm of sustainable development

(Sharma, 2019),. Research on CSR in developing economies is still in its early stages (Jamali & Karam, 2018). While there are studies on CSR and ESG with respect to sustainable development, research specific to the context of developing nations is still limited. In this backdrop, a scoping review was conducted to identify knowledge gaps and implications for decision-making in corporate social responsibility and sustainable development in developing nations.

The study area's underlying concepts, primary sources, and kinds of accessible data evidence are mapped through scoping reviews (Tricco et al., 2016). It was decided to answer the following research question: *How does Corporate Social Responsibility (CSR) contribute to the pillars of ESG in Developing Nations?* It was found that CSR could promote sustainable development through, Environment Sustainability, Social Sustainability, and Corporate Governance.

The paper is arranged in to 5 sections. Section 2 deals with the methodology for undertaking the scoping review. Section 3 presents the important results through thematic analysis. Section 4 represents the discussion. Finaly section 5 concludes the article with implications and potential future directions.

2. METHOD

2.1 Protocol

We utilized Joanna Briggs Institute Methods Manual guidelines for scoping reviews to construct the scoping review protocol (Peters et al., 2020). We then documented our findings using the components from the Preferred Reporting Items for Systematic Reviews and Meta-analysis for Scoping Review (PRISMA-ScR) (Tricco et al., 2018).

2.2 Eligibility Criteria

Inclusion criteria:

1. The papers need to have dimensions or focus on CSR and ESG in developing nations.
2. The Study examined journal papers that were written in English.
3. Given the scarcity of review papers, the study utilized quantitative, qualitative, and mixed studies from the context of developing nation.

Exclusion criteria:

1. It does not have the aspects of CSR or ESG or Sustainable Development;
2. Those studies, which were not original but were a review, commentary, letter to the editor, or case report;
3. Those articles were not in the context of a developing country.

2.3 Information and Sources

A search was initiated in both the *EBSCOhost* and SCOPUS databases to find potentially significant documents. The search strategies were drafted after the discussion among the authors. The search results were exported into Zotero, and duplicates were removed.

2.4 Search Strategy

The reviewers developed search strategy jointly and used the PCC framework put forward by Joanna Briggs Institute Methods Manual guidelines for scoping reviews for developing the string (Pollock et al., 2023) (Table 1). The developed string was peer-reviewed by the college librarian through the Peer Review of Electronic Search Strategies (PRESS) checklist.

Table 1. Development of string from PCC framework (JBIM)

PCC Framework	TERM	Keyword	String
Participant	NA	NA	TITLE-ABS-KEY ("corporate social responsibility" OR "csr" AND "ESG" OR "social responsibility" OR "environment sustainability" OR "corporate governance" AND "developing countries" OR "developing nations" OR "third world" OR "low-income countries")
Concept	Corporate Social Responsibility and Environmental, Social and Governance	CSR, Corporate Social Responsibility, Environment Responsibility, Social Responsibility, Corporate Governance	
Context	Developing Countries	emerging economy, developing countries, emerging nation	

2.5 Selection of Sources

There were 708 articles identified from the database (EBSCO*host and* SCOPUS) and through reference. 92 duplicates were eliminated. In the initial stage, the authors screened the titles and abstracts of the articles. 232 papers were eliminated, and

64 full papers were assessed for eligibility (Figure 1). During the full-text review process, the authors got together to settle disagreements and ensure uniformity among the authors and the proposed study question. 12 articles that came under the inclusion criteria were selected for the Study. Each author reviewed the whole text of the publications and excerpted the data that satisfied the requirements for inclusion. The author and year of publication, Study's goals, methodology, geography, number of participants, study's theme, and findings were all extracted from each study in a table (Table 3).

2.6 Synthesis of Result

Once the table was reviewed, the studies were prioritized according to the focus of review related to CSR and Sustainable Development grounded on the objective, geography, and result from the Study. The authors discussed and reviewed the codes developed from the selected articles. The codes were then grouped into three main themes.

Figure 1. PRISMA flow dia

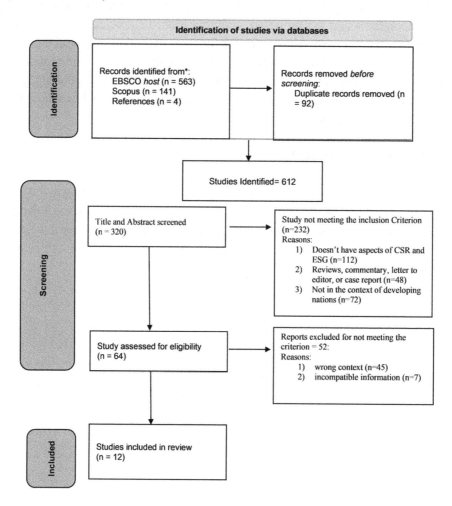

3. RESULTS

3.1 Characteristics of Source of Evidence

Out of 88 studies published, 12 met the inclusion criterion. The studies include 4 studies from the Asian continent (India, Bangladesh, China, Vietnam); 4 from the African continent (Nigeria, Egypt, Uganda); and 1 from South America (Brazil) (Table 2). The participants in the Study range from *n=2* in qualitative (case studies) to *n=1200* in quantitative Study.

Table 2. Source of articles

Continent	Countries	No of Studies
Africa	Nigeria	2
	Egypt	1
	Uganda	1
Asian	India	1
	Bangladesh	2
	China	1
	Vietnam	1
	Pakistan	2
Latin America	Brazil	1

According to the focus of the research, the reviewed studies are classified into three themes: 1) CSR for promoting corporate governance, 2) CSR for promoting Social Sustainability, and 3) CSR for promoting environmental sustainability

Table 3. Data charting form including author and year of publication, objectives, method used, country of the study, SDG theme, samples and result

	Objective			SDG	N	Results
	looked into the factors that influence how corporate social responsibility (CSR) practices are implemented in Brazil.			CSR and	Managers and	revealed the role of factors like Exogenous constituency, organizational leadership, organizational knowledge, and exogenous revolutionary changes in institutions for CSR practices.
	identified CSR barriers and investigated sustainable CSR possibilities while taking those barriers into consideration in the Bangladeshi RMG industry..			CSR and	Case Study on RMG	The Study analyzed the internal positive and negative significance of RMG industries. The positive significance involves Organisations CSR practices for secure working, environmental management, and provision of wholesome work environments. The negative significance involves a lack of proper care taken for hazards, political barriers, corruption, and poor reporting.
	Created and analyzed a CSR evaluation model that takes into account the context of developing nations and emphasizes sustainable development indicators as the most recent global framework for development.			CSR and	2 Case study with $n=$ 14	CSR organizations should be evaluated on their contribution to the SDGs and their alignment with the global sustainable development agenda.
	examined the sustainability of CSR activities related to the health care system and to understand the CSR activities of the dominant PFPC.			CSR and	Case study on 5 major business sectors. Interview n=38 managers	sustainability is ensured by organizational CSR practice through (1) funding, (2) institutionalization and top-management engagement, and (3) external stakeholder engagement.

continued on following page

Table 3. Continued

		Objective			SDG	*N*	Results
		Examined the relationship between stakeholder influence, CSR types and corporate reputation.			CSR and	*n* = 869	Revealed the positive effect of stakeholder influence (STAHIN) on CSR practices and corporate reputation (COREPU). A substantial effect was identified between environmental CSR and corporate reputation, Ethical Corporate Social Responsibility and corporate reputation, Legal Corporate Social Responsibility and corporate reputation and Philanthropic Corporate Social Responsibility and corporate reputation.
		Examined the extent of CSR contributions made by global oil firms in discussions and promotion for the reach of women to agricultural land in Nigeria's Niger Delta.			CSR and	n=700 Females	Any CSR initiative aimed at enhancing the reach of women to land and resources will result in significant inclusive growth in such communities. The study also point out that deliberate CSR efforts directed towards women farmers(rural), particularly in advocating for their right to access land and farm, will significantly increase the productivity of rural women.
		Investigated the effect of MOCs' CSR investments on youth employment in rural Nigeria's Niger Delta.			CSR and	n=1200	A general understanding of CSR involvement is common with communities with greater possession allowing for enhanced sustainability, initiatives, and improved trust.; yet, they have little effect on entrepreneurial growth and job creation.
Kao et al.,		Investigated how businesses might use their managerial and corporate resources to address poverty problems			CSR and	Case Study on XRC Industry	The case study demonstrates how a company successfully implements a proactive CSR strategy by using the poverty reduction model. First, from a personal perspective, by improving the working capacities of the underprivileged through the sharing of technologies and resources, the provision of skill development, and education; second, from a social and structural perspective, by establishing businesses to give the underprivileged access to employment opportunities or by introducing social network resources to help them launch a business.
		To map the CSR activities put forward by Indian businesses that have sustainable development goal as its objectives To explore the pattern of CSR spending of selected companies in India			CSR and	*n*=40	The research identified that the objectives of CSR and SDG overlap in terms of activities and focal areas, and aim to create a sustainable future. Total capital used for CSR, Total strength of companies, and total number of CSR projects have increased from 2014 to 2017.
		Investigated the impact of several CSR factors on green innovation and sustainable environmental growth.			CSR and	n=282	CSR to Environment and CSR to Community positively impacted Environment Sustainable Development (ESD) and positively affected Green Innovation (GI).
		concentrated on the interaction between perceptions of CSR and Pro-Environmental Behaviour (PEB).			CSR and	*Multiple case studies on 3 business schools.*	This research proposed additional CSR motivations for pro-environmental behavior: eco-civic sensibility and religious viewpoint. Stakeholder salience improves CSR research in this study.
		evaluated Lever Brothers Bangladesh Limited's (LBBL) environmental and social performance and pinpointed development opportunities.			CSR and	*Case Study of LBBL*	For environmental sustainability, the corporation must adapt its stakeholder response. Finally, this research suggests practical tools and ways to overcome restrictions.

3.2 CSR Promoting Corporate Governance

Five studies examined the role of CSR in promoting Corporate Governance. Among the studies, there were 4 qualitative studies and 1 quantitative study. All the qualitative studies used the case study design, with samples falling within the limit of n=5 to n=16.

Organizational leadership plays an essential role in corporate social responsibility. The Study by Pureza and Lee, (2020) described the "leadership style" as short-term thinking (leading to low-level CSR practices) and long-term thinking (advanced CSR practices), linked to the returns on the investment of the organization. The organizations with long-term-focused leadership claimed that potentially negative financial performance had no impact on their CSR initiatives. In addition, the long-term thinking leadership style was linked to strong corporate governance and to what long-term investment shareholders wanted. P. K. Saha et al. (2021) explains the internal CSR factors by examining the internal (positive and negative) significance of studying the RMG industry of Bangladesh. The positive components of the organization account for effective CSR propagation, which involves a healthy working climate, a safe working process, and environmental management. At the same time, the negative aspects of lack of care on workplace hazards, long working hours, and poor reporting of stakeholders' concerns, along with political barriers and corruption, create a direct or indirect impact on CSR implementation. The Study by Abdelhalim and Eldin, (2019) conducted a case study on two corporates (a family-owned business and a multinational company) in Egypt. From the semi-structured interview (n=14) conducted, it was found that there is a lack of strategy as the foundations' target areas (education, health, and capacity) lack coherence. The foundation's CSR initiatives exhibit a certain amount of informality and improvisation. The foundation does lack a clearly defined CSR practice approach. The second case study depicted the CSR initiatives of a multinational company and identified that the group has a solution-focused sustainable business approach, which was derived from the business model itself.

Katamba, (2017) emphasizes that the sustainability in CSR implementation could be ensured through top management engagement and institutionalization, funding, and external stakeholder engagement. The Study also revealed that the private for-profit companies (PFPCs) under Study had excellent CSR initiatives. They have independence, continuity, and CSR governance procedures in the organization. This reveals that when these firms execute CSR ideas, they must be converted or taken on as an organizational issue (that is, "institutionalized") and senior management must be involved in them to see their effectiveness.

P. K. Saha et al. (2021) propose the "ABCD" model for sustainable organizational practices, focusing on awareness, identifying sustainability gaps, brainstorming creative solutions, and prioritizing areas of action based on social, ecological, and economic returns on investment. This model helps organizations build an academic foundation for future sustainability efforts.

Another quantitative research by Khuong et al. (2021) identifies a positive relationship between stakeholder influence and CSR. Also, a positive association between stakeholder influence and Economical CSR, stakeholder influence and Environmental CSR Practices, stakeholder influence and Ethical CSR Practices, stakeholder influence and Legal CSR Practices and stakeholder influence and Philanthropic CSR Practices. The Study by P. K. Saha et al. (2021) also talks about the local community pressure for organizational change, thus leading to CSR practice changes.

3.3 CSR Promoting Social Sustainability

Among the 12 selected studies, 4 articles emphasize the theme of CSR for Social Responsibility. Out of 4 studies, three were quantitative studies with sample size ranging from n=40 to n=1200. The other Study is qualitative (case study design) in nature. The studies represent countries from African and Asian demography.

2 quantitative studies examined the essential significance of the Global Memorandum of Understanding (GMOU) of Multinational Oil Companies (MOC) for empowerment in Nigeria. Among the 2 studies by Uduji et al. (2021) focuses on youth empowerment, and the other on women's empowerment. The first Study (n=1200) found that GMOU involvement has substantially affected youth empowerment in Nigeria. In addition, the predictor-perception of GMOU points out that youth empowerment and job creation could be enhanced if MOCs raised their GMOU. Another study Uduji et al. (2019) concluded that the CSRs of the Multi Oil Companies under the Global Memorandum of Understanding (GMOU) had not had an influence on the rural womenfolk farmers empowerment (access to farm input) based on the established 5% significant level. However, the odds ratio is 7.0 times larger if MOCs increase their CSR program, which is intended to provide farm-related guidance to women farmers, by one unit, which is equal to $1 (as the EXP(B) value of the Predictor—GMOU is 5.614). As a result, women farmers in rural areas have seven times more possibilities to enhance their productivity by spending more on farming. According to the findings, any CSR initiative to enhance women's access to resources and land will result in significant inclusive growth in such communities.

Kao et al. (2016) examined an organization named XRC in China through a case study and found that when it comes to empowering individuals, XRC utilises skill development to improve the human capital of underprivileged individuals and give them the ability to seize appropriate career possibilities. XRC has coached over 300,000 people across China. Workers, students and farmers are among these folks. Twelve years old was the youngest trainee, while seventy-five was the oldest. 90% of these trainees overcame poverty, and 65% found success; the business has produced thousands of millionaires. Also Mishra, (2021) examines the Corporate Social Responsibility practices of n=40 companies in India and, in the preliminary analysis, found a significant increase in the CSR spending of companies with a contribution of more than 10000 crores. The study also gathered data from the National CSR Portal, which the Corporate Affairs Ministry runs. The first year that CSR was implemented saw a massive investment of \$ 1263691.68 (2014-2016) by 16,785 companies to, contributing \$180351625.96 (2016-2017) in the year 2016–201 by 21,498 companies. Ten CSR activity areas under Schedule VII, Section 135 of the 2013 Companies Act have been identified and is connected with 17 Sustainable Development Goals. When ranked by the percentage of funds spent, the top areas of CSR intervention by Indian companies were found to be 34.84% of funds spent on education, employment creation, and skill enhancement, 27.64% on projects to end hunger, poverty, and improve health, sanitation, and cleanliness, 12.63% on environmental issues, and 10.83% on projects to develop rural and slum areas.

3.4 CSR for Promoting Environment Sustainability

Three of twelve studies deal with environment sustainability. Among them three studies were qualitative (case studies) in nature and one study is quantitative (n=282). The study represented Pakistan and Bangladesh.

Shahzad et al. (2020) empirically explored the impact of four Corporate Social Responsibility aspects (environment, workers, community, and customers) on the environmental component of organisational sustainability leaning toward green innovation. It was found that CSR dimensions were positively significant with "Environment Sustainable Development (ESD)". The study unveiled that Corporate Social Responsibility for the Environment has a more substantial effect on ESD, but CSR on consumers has a weaker effect on ESD. Businesses in Pakistan are involved in CSR activities as part of their philanthropic and humanitarian duties to promote social issues, including environmental preservation, employee and community well-being, and education in society leading to the cause of customers giving CSR high thoughts in terms of enhancing environmentally sustainable growth. The study also presented a positive and noteworthy relationship between ESD and Green Innovation (GI). ESD and GI stimulated firms to engage in innovative manufacturing technologies and processes that enable them to develop more environmentally friendly while also reaping financial rewards by lowering material costs, using less energy, and producing less waste. Organisations that were more aware of the harm that their products due to the environment were more likely to innovate and implement green technologies.

In another study, Tariq et al. (2022) disseminated perspectives of faculty and management on CSR towards "pro-environmental behavior" in the framework of business academies in Pakistan. According to research, business academies' environmental domains include ecological aspects such as waste reduction, energy saving, and cleanliness. The CSR-shaping parameters that influence the emergence of ecological-conscious attitudes in people include environmental awareness, eco-consciousness, faith-based perspective, and perceived organisational encouragement for the environment. In summary, empirical data showed that the management of all the chosen business academies consider environmental challenges to be a component of their Corporate Social Responsibility initiatives and were generally engaged in green and clean initiatives. The study also indicated that the perceived endorsement of environmental sustainability within the organisation played a role in the environmentally responsible actions of managers and faculty. Employees were motivated to exhibit their environmental commitment in response to the perceived backing and encouragement from the organisation. Kabir and Rabbi, (2017) put forward an integrated management framework for CSR reporting on environmental issues. The framework had a sustainability vision and various actions to achieve policy objectives as its major component. The Sustainability vision included the prevention of pollution, product stewardship, and green technology to advance the business leading to sustainable development. Tools like Code of Business Principled, Environmental Management System (EMS) and Tripe Bottom Line Reporting are used to understand environmental performance.

4. DISCUSSION

This scoping review identified 12 studies focusing on corporate social responsibility and Environment, Social, and Governance concepts in developing nations. Our findings indicate that CSR can contribute to environmental sustainability, social sustainability, and Corporate Governance.

CSR plays a noteworthy role in promoting corporate governance through leadership, internal stakeholder engagement, and external stakeholder engagement. Long-term thinking is necessary for corporate leaders while practicing CSR as it showcases advanced knowledge (Pureza & Lee, 2020). A knowledge-driven CSR accommodates sustainable development and attracts long-term investment returns for the organization's shareholders. The engagement of CSR towards internal stakeholders plays a lead role in organizational sustainability. The internal negative factors, political barriers, corruption, and environmental mismanagement must be rectified

(P. Saha et al., 2021). These include proper human resource practices, a fulfilling and motivational work environment alongside employee development, an environmental management system, and codes of conduct. The study also put forward the ABCD model, which CSR practitioners and corporate leaders could adopt to promote organizational sustainability. Like internal stakeholders, external stakeholders are also crucial for CSR practices. Also, Khuong et al. (2021) shows that CSR has a positive association with stakeholder engagement. Organizations engaged in CSR practices should also note that continuous practice is always better than one-time practice to maintain a positive relationship between the organization and external stakeholders. The Study by Katamba, (2017) ensures organizational sustainability through external stakeholder engagement. The company's relationship with the target community is vital for delivering effective CSR practices. Also, Khuong et al. (2021) shows that CSR has a positive association with stakeholder engagement. Organizations engaged in CSR practices should also note that continuous practice is always better than one-time practice to maintain a positive relationship between the organization and external stakeholders.

Social sustainability is the second theme discussed in the Study. The studies under the theme emphasize the role of CSR in promoting human empowerment. Uduji et al. (2021) highlighted how the CSR of multinational oil companies contributed to youth and women's empowerment. This implies that the services delivered by the organization through CSR will impact the community and lead to social sustainability. As far as developing countries are concerned, empowerment is necessary, and CSR practices of organizations in partnership with the government could help them empower people. The study of Kao et al. (2016) that XRC in China had given skill training to more than 3 lakh people, leading to employment generation and livelihood empowerment. The Study also put forward a CSR strategy for power reduction through empowerment, which could be utilized by policymakers and practitioners related to CSR for livelihood empowerment in developing nations. Enterprise in a developing country could initiate personal empowerment through vocational education and training and by implementing a social business model through CSR, creating empowerment within the organization and poverty reduction in society, leading to social sustainability.

The triple bottom line idea serves as the cornerstone of CSR and focuses on profit, people, and the environment. In the 21st century, "planet" is an essential component of this group. (Brammer et al., 2007) identified organisational ethics, such as environmental preservation and environmental management, as a crucial part of external CSR. The literature is supported by the research findings that experimentally explored the beneficial correlations between CSR and Environmental Sustainability in Pakistan (Shahzad et al., 2020). This article demonstrated the significance of CSR in supporting Green Innovations and using green technologies to minimise environmental damage in developing countries, where Green Innovations is a crucial aspect. This supported the claims by Das Gupta, (2022) which asserted that the natural environment is everyone's duty and that organisations have a more significant role in removing the adverse effects of the environment since they are the largest emitters of dangerous chemicals. Green innovations and proactive environmental management practices promote sustainability and mitigate ecological damage. Organizations reduce their environmental footprint and contribute to natural resource preservation. This proactive approach supports environmental sustainability efforts, advancing and protecting the planet for present and future generations.

Based on the findings, stakeholder engagement is a critical component of CSR and ESG initiatives. Table 4 summarises the key stakeholders, their roles, and the impact they have through CSR and ESG initiatives.

Table 4. Key stakeholders, their roles and impact

Stakeholders	Role	Impact
Government	• Regulation and Legislation • Providing incentives to companied adhereing to CSR and ESG • Monitoring and Enforcement for effective implementation of CSR and ESG	• In countries like India, the mandatory 2% CSR spending requirement has significantly increased corporate contributions to social and environmental causes. • The voluntary King Codes on business Governance have been widely embraced in South Africa, improving business sustainability and responsibility.
Corporates	• Accommodating philosophy of CSR and ESG in their vision and mission • Implementing CSR and ESG initiatives • Disclosing their environmental impact, social initiatives, and governance practices in annual reports and sustainability reports.	• Multinational corporations frequently establish higher standards for CSR and ESG practices, which can trickle down to local enterprises via supply chain regulations and collaborations. • Businesses that understand the socioeconomic backdrop can modify CSR programmes to meet unique community needs, resulting in more effective interventions.
Non-Governmental Organizations (NGOs)	• Advocacy and Awareness • Collaboration with corporates • NGOs can act as independent monitors, assessing the impact of corporate CSR and ESG activities.	• NGOs in countries like Brazil have been instrumental in highlighting environmental issues, such as deforestation in the Amazon, pressuring companies to adopt more sustainable practices. • NGOs and corporations work together in many African countries to provide underprivileged people with healthcare, education, and other social services.

continued on following page

Table 4. Continued

Stakeholders	Role	Impact
Investors	• Increasingly prioritize ESG factors in their investment decisions. • Investors can influence corporate behavior through shareholder activism. • Investors view strong ESG performance as a proxy for sound risk management.	• In developing countries, impact investors and social venture funds are providing critical capital to businesses that prioritise social and environmental goals, fostering a culture of responsible business practices. • Shareholder activism is growing, with investors demanding greater transparency and accountability from companies' ESG initiatives.
Consumers	Stronger demand for ethical products Consumers provide feedback on corporate behaviour through reviews, ratings, and social media.	• Companies are increasingly adopting eco-friendly practices and launching green products to meet the growing consumer awareness of sustainability in markets such as China and India. • Consumer boycotts and campaigns targeting companies with poor CSR and ESG records have resulted in significant changes in corporate behaviour, demonstrating the power of consumer influence.

5. THEORETICAL AND PRACTICAL IMPLICATIONS

5.1 Theoretical Implications

The study on CSR for organisational sustainability provides theoretical insights that are consistent with Stakeholder Theory and the Triple Bottom Line (TBL) approach to sustainable development. Pureza and Lee (2020) define leadership styles, which influence CSR practices, with long-term-oriented leadership correlating with sophisticated CSR activities that cater to varied stakeholder interests, mirroring Stakeholder Theory's focus on stakeholder alignment. Saha et al.'s (2021) investigation of internal CSR factors emphasises the importance of addressing positive workplace conditions while overcoming barriers such as political influence, which aligns with Stakeholder Theory's call for holistic stakeholder consideration and the TBL approach's emphasis on systemic challenges. Katamba's (2017) emphasis on top management engagement emphasises the role of leadership in institutionalising CSR, reflecting Stakeholder Theory's advocacy for stakeholder engagement and the TBL approach's incorporation of social and environmental concerns into core business strategies. These implications highlight the importance of organisations incorporating Stakeholder Theory and the TBL approach into their CSR practices in order to achieve sustainable development outcomes that balance stakeholder interests and maximise value creation across economic, social, and environmental dimensions.

5.2 Practical Implications

The practical implications drawn from these studies offer actionable strategies for organizations aiming to enhance their CSR efforts and contribute to sustainability. By investing in leadership development programs that cultivate long-term thinking, organizations can foster a culture conducive to sustainable CSR practices, aligning leadership behaviors with organizational sustainability goals. Additionally, implementing systematic assessments of internal factors and stakeholder engagement processes can help organizations identify areas for improvement and tailor CSR initiatives to address specific needs, thereby enhancing the effectiveness and impact of their sustainability efforts. By translating theoretical insights into practical actions, organizations can navigate the complex landscape of CSR and contribute meaningfully to both organizational success and societal well-being. CSR and sustainability are based on the triple bottom line (economic, social, and environmental). A detailed recommendation for leveraging CSR and ESG practices to achieve sustainable development goals are described in Table 5.

Table 5. Recommendations for leveraging CSR and ESG practices to achieve sustainable development goals

Recommendations	Description	Implementations
Stakeholder Engagement	Stakeholders, including employees, customers, suppliers, investors, and the community, should actively engage with companies to shape CSR and ESG strategies, ensuring alignment with community needs and global sustainability goals.	• Establish stakeholder advisory boards. • Conduct regular stakeholder surveys and town hall meetings. • Create feedback loops for continuous improvement of CSR initiatives.
Leadership Commitment	Organisational leaders should consider long-term and show a strong commitment to CSR and ESG values. This requires incorporating sustainability into the basic corporate strategy and decision-making processes.	• Provide training for leaders on the importance of sustainable practices. • Have an Agile Mindset • Develop and communicate a long-term sustainability vision and roadmap
Sustainable Technologies and Practices	Invest in sustainable technologies like Blockchain, AI, Internet of Things and innovative practices that enhance resource efficiency.	• Research and development of green technologies. • Implementation of energy-efficient processes and renewable energy. • Encouragement of circular economy practices.

continued on following page

Table 5. Continued

Recommendations	Description	Implementations
Transparent Reporting and Communication	Regular reporting and communication of CSR and ESG efforts and outcomes fosters transparency, trust, and accountability among stakeholders.	• Publish annual sustainability reports to international standards. • Use digital platforms for real-time CSR updates. • Engage in third-party audits and certifications.
Collaborative Partnerships	Collaborate with other organizations, governments, and NGOs to enhance the impact of CSR and ESG initiatives.	• Participate in multi-stakeholder initiatives and forums on sustainability. • Collaborate on community projects. • Share best practices and resources.
Social Equity and Inclusion	The goal is to ensure that Corporate Social Responsibility and Environmental and Social Governance practices promote social equity and inclusion, particularly for marginalized and vulnerable populations.	• Improve education, health, livelihoods. • Implement diversity and inclusion. • Support fair trade and ethical sourcing.
Monitoring and Evaluation	Continuously monitor and evaluate the effectiveness of CSR and ESG initiatives to ensure they contribute to the Sustainable Development Goals (SDGs).	• Set clear, measurable goals and KPIs for sustainability initiatives. • Utilizing data analytics for progress tracking. • Regularly reviewing and adjusting strategies based on evaluation findings.

6. CONCLUSION AND FUTURE DIRECTIONS

Our Study adds to this by understanding the contribution of corporate social responsibility to the pillars of ESG in the context of developing nations from the available literature. It was found that CSR could promote organizational sustainability through corporate governance, social sustainability, and environmental sustainability to bring about sustainable development. Organizational leadership and ensuring internal and external stakeholder engagement could be accommodated in CSR practices to bring sustainability to organizations. Policymakers could also draft public-private partnership designs for effectively utilizing CSR to empower people, thus bringing social sustainability. CSR will also contribute effectively to the sustainable development goals of the United Nations for global sustainability.

The study encompasses certain limitations that offer avenues for prospective investigation in the future. Even though the string was developed after checking all the possibilities for getting accurate results, there can be chances of unidentifying studies related to the subject. To avoid this, the researchers have scoped more journals and utilized references to accommodate valid research. The review revealed that CSR and ESG research is still in its early stages, with significant methodological challenges ahead. The majority of studies are cross-sectional, which limits the ability to observe long-term effects and causality. Researchers should consider designing longitudinal studies, which can provide more clarity and depth into the domain's existing problems.

REFERENCES

Abdelhalim, K., & Eldin, A. (2019). Can CSR help achieve sustainable development? Applying a new assessment model to CSR cases from Egypt. *The International Journal of Sociology and Social Policy*, 39(9–10), 773–795. 10.1108/IJSSP-06-2019-0120

Branco, M., & Lima Rodrigues, L. (2006). Corporate Social Responsibility and Resource-Based Perspectives. *Journal of Business Ethics*, 69(2), 111–132. 10.1007/s10551-006-9071-z

Camilleri, M. A. (2017). Corporate sustainability and responsibility: Creating value for business, society and the environment. *Asian Journal of Sustainability and Social Responsibility*, 2(1), 59–74. 10.1186/s41180-017-0016-5

Carroll, A. B. (1999). Corporate Social Responsibility: Evolution of a Definitional Construct. *Business & Society*, 38(3), 268–295. 10.1177/000765039903800303

Goodell, J. W., Li, M., Liu, D., & Wang, Y. (2024). Aligning empirical evidence on ESG with ancient conservative traditions. *International Review of Financial Analysis*, 94, 103284. 10.1016/j.irfa.2024.103284

Gu, W., Pan, H., Hu, Z., & Liu, Z. (2022). The Triple Bottom Line of Sustainable Entrepreneurship and Economic Policy Uncertainty: An Empirical Evidence from 22 Countries. *International Journal of Environmental Research and Public Health*, 19(13), 7758. 10.3390/ijerph1913775835805416

Jamali, D., & Karam, C. (2018). Corporate Social Responsibility in Developing Countries as an Emerging Field of Study. *International Journal of Management Reviews*, 20(1), 32–61. 10.1111/ijmr.12112

Kabir, S. M., & Rabbi, F. (2017). Corporate sustainability reporting on environmental issue: An assessment of CSR framework for Lever Brothers Bangladesh. *Malaysian Construction Research Journal, Special Issue 1*(1). https://researchonline.nd.edu.au/bus_article/90

Kao, T.-Y., Chen, J. C. H., Wu, J.-T. B., & Yang, M.-H. (2016). Poverty Reduction through Empowerment for Sustainable Development: A Proactive Strategy of Corporate Social Responsibility. *Corporate Social Responsibility and Environmental Management*, 23(3), 140–149. 10.1002/csr.1365

Katamba, D. (n.d.). *STRENGTHENING HEALTH CARE SYSTEMS: PRIVATE FOR-PROFIT COMPANIES' CORPORATE SOCIAL RESPONSIBILITY ENGAGEMENTS - Document - Gale Academic OneFile*. Retrieved June 22, 2024, from https://go .gale.com/ps/i.do?id=GALE%7CA513854428&sid=googleScholar&v=2.1&it= r&linkaccess=abs&issn=23304103&p=AONE&sw=w&userGroupName=anon %7E29efc51f&aty=open-web-entry

Khuong, M. N., Truong an, N. K., & Thanh Hang, T. T. (2021). Stakeholders and Corporate Social Responsibility (CSR) programme as key sustainable development strategies to promote corporate reputation—Evidence from vietnam. *Cogent Business & Management*, 8(1), 1917333. 10.1080/23311975.2021.1917333

Marcus, J., Kurucz, E. C., & Colbert, B. A. (2010). Conceptions of the Business-Society-Nature Interface: Implications for Management Scholarship. *Business & Society*, 49(3), 402–438. 10.1177/0007650310368827

Mishra, L. (2021). Corporate social responsibility and sustainable development goals: A study of Indian companies. *Journal of Public Affairs*, 21(1), e2147. 10.1002/pa.2147

Peters, M., Godfrey, C., Mcinerney, P., Munn, Z., Trico, A., & Khalil, H. (2020). *Scoping Reviews.*, 10.46658/JBIMES-20-12

Pollock, D., Peters, M. D. J., Khalil, H., McInerney, P., Alexander, L., Tricco, A. C., Evans, C., de Moraes, É. B., Godfrey, C. M., Pieper, D., Saran, A., Stern, C., & Munn, Z. (2023). Recommendations for the extraction, analysis, and presentation of results in scoping reviews. *JBI Evidence Synthesis*, 21(3), 520–532. 10.11124/ JBIES-22-0012336081365

Porter, M. E., & Kramer, M. R. (2006, December 1). Strategy and Society: The Link Between Competitive Advantage and Corporate Social Responsibility. *Harvard Business Review*. https://hbr.org/2006/12/strategy-and-society-the-link-between -competitive-advantage-and-corporate-social-responsibility

Pureza, A. P., & Lee, K.-H. (2020). Corporate social responsibility leadership for sustainable development: An institutional logics perspective in Brazil. *Corporate Social Responsibility and Environmental Management*, 27(3), 1410–1424. 10.1002/csr.1894

Purvis, B., Mao, Y., & Robinson, D. (2019). Three pillars of sustainability: In search of conceptual origins. *Sustainability Science*, 14(3), 681–695. 10.1007/ s11625-018-0627-5

Saha, P., Akhter, S., & Hassan, A. (2021). Framing Corporate Social Responsibility to Achieve Sustainability in Urban Industrialization: Case of Bangladesh Ready-Made Garments (RMG). *Sustainability (Basel)*, 13(13), 6988. Advance online publication. 10.3390/su13136988

Saha, P. K., Akhter, S., & Hassan, A. (2021). Framing Corporate Social Responsibility to Achieve Sustainability in Urban Industrialization: Case of Bangladesh Ready-Made Garments (RMG). In *SUSTAINABILITY* (Vol. 13, Issue 13). MDPI. 10.3390/su13136988

Shahzad, M., Qu, Y., Javed, S. A., Zafar, A. U., & Rehman, S. U. (2020). Relation of environment sustainability to CSR and green innovation: A case of Pakistani manufacturing industry. *Journal of Cleaner Production*, 253, 119938. 10.1016/j.jclepro.2019.119938

Sharma, E. (2019). A review of corporate social responsibility in developed and developing nations. *Corporate Social Responsibility and Environmental Management*, 26(4), 712–720. 10.1002/csr.1739

Stavins, R., Reinhardt, F., & Vietor, R. (2008). Corporate Social Responsibility Through an Economic Lens. *Review of Environmental Economics and Policy*, 2(2), 219–239. 10.1093/reep/ren008

Tariq, S., Yunis, M. S., Shoaib, S., Abdullah, F., & Khan, S. W. (2022). Perceived corporate social responsibility and pro-environmental behaviour: Insights from business schools of Peshawar, Pakistan. In *Frontiers in Psychology* (Vol. 13). Frontiers Media S.A., 10.3389/fpsyg.2022.948059

Tricco, A. C., Lillie, E., Zarin, W., O'Brien, K., Colquhoun, H., Kastner, M., Levac, D., Ng, C., Sharpe, J. P., Wilson, K., Kenny, M., Warren, R., Wilson, C., Stelfox, H. T., & Straus, S. E. (2016). A scoping review on the conduct and reporting of scoping reviews. *BMC Medical Research Methodology*, 16(1), 15. 10.1186/s12874-016-0116-426857112

Tricco, A. C., Lillie, E., Zarin, W., O'Brien, K. K., Colquhoun, H., Levac, D., Moher, D., Peters, M. D. J., Horsley, T., Weeks, L., Hempel, S., Akl, E. A., Chang, C., McGowan, J., Stewart, L., Hartling, L., Aldcroft, A., Wilson, M. G., Garritty, C., & Straus, S. E. (2018). PRISMA Extension for Scoping Reviews (PRISMA-ScR): Checklist and Explanation. *Annals of Internal Medicine*, 169(7), 467–473. 10.7326/M18-085030178033

Uduji, J. I., Okolo-Obasi, E. N., & Asongu, S. A. (2019). Corporate social responsibility and the role of rural women in sustainable agricultural development in sub-Saharan Africa: Evidence from the Niger Delta in Nigeria. *Sustainable Development (Bradford)*, 27(4), 692–703. 10.1002/sd.1933

Uduji, J. I., Okolo-Obasi, E. N., & Asongu, S. A. (2021). Sustainable peacebuilding and development in Nigeria's post-amnesty programme: The role of corporate social responsibility in oil host communities. *Journal of Public Affairs*, 21(2), e2200. 10.1002/pa.2200

Wang, S., & Chang, Y. (2024). A study on the impact of ESG rating on green technology innovation in enterprises: An empirical study based on informal environmental governance. Journal of Environmental Management, 358. *Journal of Environmental Management*, 358, 120878. Advance online publication. 10.1016/j.jenvman.2024.120878

Chapter 3
Navigating Sustainability:
Assessing the Imperative of ESG Considerations in Achieving SDGs

A. Ayyoob
https://orcid.org/0009-0003-2839-3598
Department of Commerce and Management Studies, University of Calicut, India

Aparna Sajeev
Department of Commerce and Management Studies, University of Calicut, India

ABSTRACT

This chapter explores the symbiotic relationship between ESG practices and SDGs, emphasizing the increasing trend of companies aligning their ESG performance with UN SDGs. This integration ensures that corporate practices positively impact ESG factors, addressing global challenges outlined by the United Nations. The study investigates the interrelation between SDGs and ESG factors to classify SDGs based on ESG considerations. By shedding light on the underlying dynamics shaping sustainable development initiatives, the study aims to offer valuable insights for practical ESG-based approaches to specific SDGs. The study engages a mixed-methods approach with knowledgeable participants, utilizing narrative, thematic analysis, and quantitative ranking through a structured questionnaire. At a practical level, the chapter extends its impact by offering applications for organizational strategy, ESG integration, policy implications, and stakeholder engagement.

DOI: 10.4018/979-8-3693-3880-3.ch003

1. INTRODUCTION

The integration of Environmental, Social, and Governance (ESG) criteria and Sustainable Development Goals (SDGs) has become a focal point in corporate practices, reflecting a strategic commitment to global sustainability challenges (Radu et al., 2023). This alignment has gained traction, with companies increasingly mapping their ESG performance to the United Nations SDGs, indicating a broader commitment to sustainable growth at both microeconomic and macroeconomic levels. Research studies emphasize a positive correlation between firm-level ESG disclosures and country-level SDG scores, particularly in emerging markets, underscoring the intricate relationship between corporate sustainability practices and national sustainability goals (Soni, 2023). By aligning with SDGs, companies can enhance their corporate sustainability profiles without compromising economic growth, offering substantial advantages, particularly in emerging markets (Markopoulos & Maria, 2022). The linkage between ESG and SDGs is crucial for assessing the progress of ESG and SDG implementation and serves as a framework for evaluating the effectiveness of corporate sustainability practices (Radu et al., 2023; Soni, 2023; Markopoulos & Maria, 2022). This integration aligns with the global agenda for sustainable development set by the United Nations and holds strategic importance in the corporate landscape. The symbiotic relationship between ESG criteria and SDGs allows organizations to contribute meaningfully to global sustainability objectives while fostering corporate sustainability.

In parallel, integrating ESG factors in investing faces challenges, partly due to perceived conflicts with fiduciary duties and concerns about the quality of ESG data (Antoncic et al., 2020). Research explores the correlation between alpha generation and ESG metrics, emphasizing the impact on achieving the United Nations' SDGs (Antoncic et al., 2020). Addressing bidirectional causality between ESG disclosures and firm value, research studies contribute to a nuanced understanding of this intricate relationship in various sectors, such as the Indian energy sector (Behl et al., 2021). Simultaneously, studies delve into the nuanced connections between ESG activity and bank value, revealing positive relationships with cash flows and efficiency (Azmi et al., 2020). Pioneering investigations in East Asian listed firms explore the ESG-Corporate Financial Performance (CFP) relationship, revealing associations with stock return and price-to-book ratio (Naimy et al., 2021).

Additionally, research investigates the impact of rapid urbanization on the ESG-SDG relationship, employing structural equation models to identify key factors influencing this dynamic interaction (Xu et al., 2022). Investigations into the relationship between a company's ESG performance and financial performance offer empirical evidence to resolve contradictions in the existing literature (Ademi & Klungseth, 2022). These studies contribute valuable insights into the interconnected nature of

ESG considerations in shaping financial performance and contributing to broader sustainability objectives.

1.1 Research Questions

R1: How do ESG considerations contribute to the achievement of SDGs, and what is their significance in fostering sustainable development?

R2: What are the essential procedures in classifying each Sustainable Development Goal (SDG) based on relevant ESG factors, and how do these procedures aid in promoting a holistic approach to sustainable development?

R3: In what ways do advancements in ESG factors intersect with progress in SDGs, and how do these interconnections impact outcomes across different domains of sustainability?

1.2 Objectives

1. To examine the importance of addressing SDGs through ESG considerations and clarify the holistic approach essential for sustainable development.
2. To elucidate the procedures for classifying each Sustainable Development Goal (SDG) based on pertinent ESG factors.
3. To examine the interconnectedness between SDGs and ESG factors, revealing how advancements in one domain often influence outcomes in another.

2. LITERATURE REVIEWS

2.1 Environmental, Social, and Governance (ESG)

ESG (Environmental, Social, and Governance) encapsulates critical factors for evaluating enterprises' dedication to sustainable development, social accountability, and corporate governance (Kihn et al., 2004). The significance of ESG has surged owing to the imperative to tackle environmental impacts, foster social progress, and enhance governance standards in business activities. ESG principles underline the amalgamation of environmental considerations, social endeavours, and governance methodologies into organizational frameworks (Lapsley & Eggertsson, 2022). This inclusive approach fosters sustainable behaviours, social accountability, and principled governance within organizational structures (Harnos, 2022). Notably, ESG frameworks are experiencing heightened regulation, particularly within the financial realm, to ensure adherence to sustainability preferences and disclosure mandates. ESG is a comprehensive framework guiding organizations toward conscientious and sustainable behaviours in today's interconnected world. It evaluates how organizations handle sustainability issues across environmental impact, social responsibility, and corporate governance. Initially focused on investments, ESG now extends to various stakeholders, offering a structured approach to tackle sustainability challenges. Its evolution reflects a holistic view of sustainability, influencing investment strategies and prompting a rise in specialized expertise. ESG drives transformative change across sectors, promoting sustainability and resilience.

A company's environmental impact, particularly its carbon footprint and resource utilization, is the emphasis of the environmental component (Glushakova & Chernikova, 2023). To foster diversity, equity, and inclusion, the social dimension evaluates how an organization handles connections with its customers, suppliers, employees, and the communities in which it operates (Serra & Teresa, 2023). According to Luk et al. (2023), governance concerns a company's leadership, internal controls, and shareholder rights. It places a strong emphasis on accountability, transparency, and moral behaviour. Incorporating Environmental, Social, and Governance (ESG) considerations into corporate strategy not only advances the Sustainable Development Goals (SDGs) but also fosters stakeholder trust and long-term value generation (Sarkar et al., 2023).

ESG has gained significant attention amid growing concerns about environmental sustainability, social responsibility, and corporate accountability. Businesses face increasing pressure to address these issues, meet stakeholder expectations, and positively impact society and the environment. Investors are integrating ESG criteria into their decisions, aligning financial goals with ethical values. ESG investing blends environmental, social, and governance factors with financial metrics, offering a comprehensive perspective on investment analysis. A growing trend in ESG reporting involves organizations disclosing ESG metrics in annual reports, providing valuable insights into their sustainability performance. Transparent reporting allows organizations to demonstrate progress, compare against industry standards, and identify areas for improvement. Frameworks like the Task Force on Climate-related Financial Disclosure (TCFD) and the Sustainability Accounting Standards Board (SASB) support best practices in ESG disclosure. Regulators also encourage ESG integration through directives like the Corporate Sustainability Reporting Directive (CSRD) and the Sustainable Finance Disclosure Regulation (SFDR), which standardise reporting and promote transparency. Initiatives from the Carbon Disclosure Project (CDP) and the Global Reporting Initiative (GRI) further enhance ESG disclosure, reinforcing accountability and driving progress toward sustainability goals.

2.2 Sustainable Development Goals (SDGs)

The SDGs represent a comprehensive framework comprising 17 global development objectives, succeeding the Millennium Development Goals (MDGs), with the overarching aim of addressing economic, social, and environmental concerns while ensuring inclusivity through the principle of 'leaving no one behind' (Yi & Yi, 2023). Research findings suggest a predominant concentration of SDG-related research activities in developed nations such as the USA, China, and the UK, with a noticeable scarcity of focus in developing and underdeveloped regions (Mishra et al., 2023). These goals catalyse shedding light on crucial sustainable development facets, including the issue of fossil fuel subsidies, thereby indirectly bolstering endeavours to instigate reforms at the national level (Harro, 2023). However, despite the widespread global acceptance of the SDGs, their practical implementation encounters hurdles stemming from political influences and vested interests, thereby impeding the transformative potential envisaged within the agenda (Weiss & Wilkinson, 2023). The SDGs, adopted unanimously by all UN Member States in 2015, comprise 17 global objectives targeting poverty eradication, environmental preservation, and global well-being. They form a comprehensive agenda for collective action over 15 years. Interconnected and requiring collaboration among governments, the private sector, civil society, and the UN, the SDGs face challenges like climate disasters, conflicts, economic downturns, and the COVID-19 pandemic. The upcoming SDG Summit in September 2023 is crucial for refocusing efforts to achieve these goals. The SDGs are

1. No Poverty
2. Zero Hunger
3. Good Health and Well-being
4. Quality Education
5. Gender Equality
6. Clean Water and Sanitation
7. Affordable and Clean Energy
8. Decent Work and Economic Growth
9. Industry, Innovation, and Infrastructure
10. Reduced Inequality
11. Sustainable Cities and Communities
12. Responsible Consumption and Production
13. Climate Action
14. Life Below Water
15. Life on Land
16. Peace, Justice, and Strong Institutions

17. Partnerships for the Goals

2.3 Historical perspectives on ESG evolution and SDG implementation

The progression of ESG practices and the enforcement of Sustainable Development Goals have seen notable advancements in recent years. Introduced in 2015, the SDGs have directed various sectors towards sustainable development (Díaz-López et al., 2021). ESG reporting became more prominent with the Global Reporting Initiatives and received further momentum following the United Nations' adoption of the SDGs in 2015 (Soni, 2023). Studies have demonstrated a positive correlation between firm-level ESG disclosures and country-level SDG scores, underscoring the critical role of aligning ESG practices with SDGs to achieve sustainable development in emerging markets (Pokrovskaia et al., 2023). The ESG framework has expanded to incorporate new core elements, particularly within the energy sector, underscoring the significance of regulation, public involvement, and corporate governance in addressing new challenges (Gwalani & Mazumdar, 2022). Detailed reviews of SDG-related research have offered valuable insights into future research trajectories, supporting the formulation of strategies for SDG implementation (Markopoulos & Maria, 2022).

The historical development of ESG practices and the implementation of SDGs mark a significant shift towards integrating sustainability into business and governance. SDGs provide a structured approach to sustainable development, while ESG reporting enhances transparency and accountability. The positive correlation between ESG disclosures and SDG performance highlights their synergistic potential in driving sustainability. Expanding the ESG ecosystem to include new components, especially in critical sectors like energy, shows its adaptive nature to evolving challenges. This chapter explores the intricate relationship between SDGs and ESG factors, categorizing each SDG within an ESG framework to understand their connections. It aims to provide insights into the dynamics influencing socio-environmental outcomes and offer recommendations for organizations and policymakers to leverage ESG considerations in pursuing SDGs and fostering sustainable development.

3. RESEARCH METHODOLOGY

This study employs a comprehensive mixed methods approach to connect SDGs with ESG factors based on data collected from business experts using a purposive sampling technique. The selection criteria ensured the inclusion of participants knowledgeable about ESG and SDGs. This mixed-methods design, blending qualitative narrative thematic analysis and quantitative analysis of multiple response questions, was strategically crafted to provide a holistic understanding of the intricate dimensions within participants' perspectives with specific knowledge about ESG and SDGs. Through this intentional and selective approach, the study sought to gather insights from individuals with an understanding of the subject matter, enriching the qualitative and quantitative data collection process. The structured questionnaire, featuring multiple response questions related to connecting SDGs with ESG factors and analysing the literature based on the problems, is aimed to elicit detailed narratives and prioritize critical areas through quantitative ranking based on the data collected from 200 experts in the field of ESG and SDGs. The ethical approach, emphasizing participant autonomy and confidentiality, was communicated transparently, fostering trust and ensuring the voluntary nature of participation.

4. RESULTS AND DISCUSSION

This section presents a comprehensive analysis of the results obtained from the study and discusses their implications for the research questions posed. The findings are structured around four key areas, each addressing specific research questions and themes central to the study. Section 4.1 addresses Research Question 1 by exploring the importance of addressing Sustainable Development Goals (SDGs) via Environmental, Social, and Governance (ESG) considerations, emphasizing the necessity of a holistic approach to sustainable development. Section 4.2 focuses on Research Question 2, detailing the procedures for integrating ESG factors into the SDGs, outlining a systematic method for understanding, classifying, and mapping these factors while engaging stakeholders and implementing a comprehensive framework. Section 4.3 addresses Research Question 3 by examining the interconnected nature of SDGs and ESG factors, demonstrating how advancements in ESG can influence progress across various sustainability domains. Finally, Section 4.4 provides background on integrating ESG practices with SDGs, discusses the challenges and limitations, and presents relevant case studies to offer practical insights.

4.1 Importance of Addressing SDGs via ESG: A Holistic Approach to Sustainable Development

In addressing Research Question 1, which examines the importance of addressing Sustainable Development Goals (SDGs) through Environmental, Social, and Governance (ESG) considerations, it is essential to discuss how a holistic approach is crucial for achieving sustainable development. This involves aligning ESG practices with SDGs to tackle global sustainability challenges, manage risks, foster innovation, and create long-term value for stakeholders.

Integrating Sustainable Development Goals (SDGs) with Environmental, Social, and Governance (ESG) practices is crucial for achieving a sustainable future (Faria et al., 2024; Cem et al., 2024; Khutorova et al., 2023; Sekar & Krishnan, 2022). By considering ESG factors in business strategies, companies contribute to global sustainability while ensuring economic growth that benefits everyone (Faria et al., 2024). This approach helps businesses align their operations with environmental protection and social responsibility, enhancing the quality of life for communities worldwide. Tailored strategies based on ESG principles, like those seen in India's Business Responsibility and Sustainability Report framework, demonstrate how a multidisciplinary approach can effectively advance SDGs (Sekar & Krishnan, 2022). Fostering sustainability through quality education and holistic development of professionals is essential for achieving SDGs and raising awareness about sustainable development goals (Goswami & Krishnan, 2022).

Aligning ESG practices with SDGs is not just about corporate responsibility; it also makes good business sense. Companies that prioritize ESG factors manage risks better, foster innovation, and create long-term value for stakeholders (Cem et al., 2024). This alignment helps businesses develop competitive and reputable strategies, attracting customers and investors who care about sustainability. Understanding how ESG influences consumer behavior, especially regarding eco-friendly and ethical products, is crucial for meeting social responsibilities and building stronger relationships with stakeholders. By focusing on ESG, businesses drive progress toward sustainable development, benefiting both their operations and society as a whole.

4.1.1. Alignment with Global Agendas: Incorporating ESG considerations into business strategies and operations ensures alignment with the SDGs, addressing critical sustainability challenges comprehensively (Cem Işık et al., 2024; Sekar & Krishnan, 2022). Embracing ESG principles signals a commitment to advancing shared goals like poverty alleviation, environmental protection, social equity, and economic growth. Integrating ESG allows proactive addressing of interconnected environmental, social, and governance issues outlined in the SDGs, contributing to specific goals such as reducing carbon emissions (SDGs 13 and 7), promoting diversity and fair labor practices (SDGs 5 and 8), and fostering transparency and ethical practices (SDG 16). This integration demonstrates alignment with global agendas and enables meaningful contributions to sustainable development goals (Ruhana et al., 2024).

4.1.2. Risk Management and Resilience: ESG factors are crucial for managing risks and building resilience. By engaging with ESG issues, organizations can mitigate environmental, social, and governance risks, ensuring business continuity and sustainability. This includes managing environmental risks through sustainable practices, social risks by prioritizing responsibility and stakeholder engagement, and governance risks with robust oversight and transparency (Ademi & Klungseth, 2022; Khutorova et al., 2023). Integrating ESG into business strategies enhances resilience and positions organizations for long-term success (Cem Işık et al., 2024).

4.1.3. Value Creation and Innovation: Embracing ESG principles drives value creation and innovation. Environmental initiatives reduce costs and attract eco-conscious consumers, while social responsibility boosts employee engagement and brand reputation. Community engagement and partnerships contribute to sustainable development and spur innovation, creating long-term value for stakeholders (Sekar & Krishnan, 2022).

4.1.4. Access to Capital and Markets: In today's business environment, integrating ESG factors is critical for companies aiming to access capital and markets. This integration attracts socially responsible investors, fosters innovation, and expands customer bases. Transparent ESG disclosure builds stakeholder trust, enables benchmarking, and showcases progress toward sustainability goals. Prioritizing ESG considerations enhances investment attractiveness, market access, and stakeholder trust, helping companies thrive in a sustainable economy (Ademi & Klungseth, 2022; Khutorova et al., 2023).

4.1.5. Regulatory Compliance and Legal Obligations: In today's regulatory landscape, integrating ESG considerations is essential for organizations to ensure compliance, meet legal obligations, and mitigate risks. By embedding ESG into operations, companies align with regulations, anticipate future requirements, and enhance their reputation and competitiveness as sustainability leaders, reducing potential fines and penalties (Ruhana et al., 2024).

4.1.6. Stakeholder Expectations and Social License to Operate: Maintaining a social license requires addressing ESG issues in today's business environment. Prioritizing diversity, employee well-being, and community engagement builds stakeholder trust and loyalty. Addressing ESG also boosts investor confidence and enhances access to capital. Proactively integrating ESG considerations ensures long-term legitimacy and value creation (Goswami & Krishnan, 2022; Cem Işık et al., 2024).

4.1.7. Long-Term Value Creation and Reputation Management: Sustainable businesses integrate SDGs into their ESG frameworks, linking success with societal and environmental well-being. This alignment enhances risk management, drives innovation, and fosters growth, positioning companies as sustainability leaders. Addressing SDGs through ESG is crucial for reputation management, building stakeholder trust, and attracting talent. It enables businesses to create value, drive positive outcomes, and demonstrate commitment to meaningful change (Ruhana et al., 2024; Cem Işık et al., 2024).

Integrating SDGs into ESG considerations is crucial for achieving sustainable development objectives, managing risks, fostering innovation, accessing capital, ensuring compliance, meeting stakeholder expectations, and creating long-term value. Embracing ESG principles enables organizations to drive global sustainability efforts and contribute to a prosperous future for all stakeholders (Sekar & Krishnan, 2022; Khutorova et al., 2023).

4.2 Procedures for Integrating ESG Factors into SDGs

In addressing Research Question 2, which seeks to elucidate the procedures for classifying each Sustainable Development Goal (SDG) based on pertinent Environmental, Social, and Governance (ESG) factors, it is crucial to outline a systematic approach for integrating ESG considerations into the framework of the SDGs. This involves understanding the SDGs, identifying relevant ESG factors, creating an ESG framework, mapping these factors to the SDGs, engaging stakeholders, implementing and monitoring the framework, and reporting and communicating the results. Understanding the SDGs is foundational for classifying each Sustainable Development Goal (SDG) based on relevant ESG factors and formulating an ESG framework. The procedures for developing a framework are as follows:

4.2.1. Understand the SDGs: Begin by thoroughly understanding the 17 SDGs established by the United Nations in 2015. Each goal represents a distinct aspect of sustainable development, addressing critical global challenges ranging from poverty eradication to climate action. Take the time to delve into the specific targets and indicators associated with each SDG, as they provide valuable insights into the areas of focus and the desired outcomes. By understanding the SDGs comprehensively, you can grasp the interconnected nature of various sustainability issues and appreciate the holistic approach required to achieve meaningful progress. Moreover, familiarizing with the SDGs enables one to identify the overarching themes and priorities that underpin the global sustainability agenda, serving as a foundation for developing a practical ESG framework tailored to the organization's objectives and context.

4.2.2. Identify Relevant ESG Factors: After understanding the SDGs, delve into each goal to pinpoint the ESG factors that are most pertinent to its objectives. This involves analyzing the specific themes and targets within each SDG to determine the key areas where ESG considerations play a significant role. For instance:

- Environmental factors[1]: Certain SDGs primarily focus on environmental sustainability, such as SDG 13 (Climate Action), which addresses efforts to combat climate change and its impacts. Other SDGs, such as SDG 6 (Clean Water and Sanitation) and SDG 12[2] (Responsible Consumption and Production), highlight environmental concerns related to water management, waste reduction, and sustainable resource use.

- Social factors: Many SDGs emphasize social issues related to human well-being, equality, and community development. For instance, SDGs 1 (No Poverty) and 5 (Gender Equality) address poverty alleviation and gender empowerment, respectively and SDG 8 (Decent Work and Economic Growth)[3] promotes inclusive employment opportunities and social protection.
- Governance factors[4]: Governance plays a crucial role in several SDGs, particularly those related to justice, accountability, and effective institutions. SDG 16 (Peace, Justice, and Strong Institutions) highlights the importance of promoting peaceful societies, access to justice, and transparent governance structures. SDG 17 (Partnerships for the Goals) also underscores the need for collaboration between governments, businesses, and civil society to achieve sustainable development objectives

Identifying these relevant ESG factors within each SDG provides a framework for assessing how organizations can contribute to sustainable development across environmental, social, and governance dimensions. This process lays the groundwork for developing an integrated ESG strategy aligned with the broader objectives of the SDGs.

4.2.3. Create an ESG Framework: Building upon the identified ESG factors for each SDG, the next step is to develop a comprehensive framework that aligns these factors with the specific objectives of the Sustainable Development Goals. This framework should encompass several key components:

- Key ESG Metrics and Indicators: Define the ESG metrics and indicators most relevant to measuring progress toward each SDG. These metrics should be specific, measurable, and aligned with the targets and indicators outlined within each goal. For example, for SDG 13 (Climate Action), relevant metrics may include greenhouse gas emissions reduction, renewable energy adoption, and climate resilience measures.
- Data Sources and Methodologies: Identify the data sources and methodologies required to collect, analyse, and report ESG performance related to each SDG. This may involve leveraging internal data, external databases, stakeholder surveys, and third-party assessments. Establishing precise data collection and calculation methodologies is essential to ensuring consistency and accuracy in reporting.
- Reporting Mechanisms: Determine how ESG efforts and outcomes will be communicated to stakeholders through reporting mechanisms. This may involve the development of sustainability reports, ESG disclosures, integrated

annual reports, and other forms of communication. The reporting should be transparent, accessible, and aligned with relevant reporting frameworks such as the Global Reporting Initiative (GRI) or the Sustainability Accounting Standards Board (SASB) standards.

- Integration into Decision-Making: Embed ESG considerations into organizational decision-making processes and strategic planning. This involves incorporating ESG metrics and insights into risk assessments, investment decisions, product development strategies, and stakeholder engagement initiatives. By integrating ESG into decision-making, organizations can ensure that sustainability considerations are prioritized across all aspects of operations.

Developing a robust ESG framework that aligns with each SDG enables organizations to systematically measure, monitor, and manage their sustainability performance in alignment with global development objectives. This framework serves as a roadmap for driving continuous improvement in ESG practices and contributing to achieving the Sustainable Development Goals.

4.2.4. Map ESG Factors to SDGs: In this step, the identified ESG factors are classified and aligned with each of the 17 SDGs. This mapping exercise illustrates the interconnectedness between sustainability objectives and ESG considerations, facilitating a deeper understanding of how addressing ESG issues can contribute to achieving the SDGs. Here is how one can proceed:

- Environmental Factors: Identify the ESG factors related to environmental sustainability and map them to the corresponding SDGs. For instance, factors such as climate action, clean energy, sustainable consumption, and biodiversity conservation can be aligned with SDG 7 (Affordable and Clean Energy), SDG 12 (Responsible Consumption and Production), and SDG 15 (Life on Land), among others.
- Social Factors: Determine the ESG factors associated with social aspects such as human rights, gender equality, community development, and labour practices. These factors can then be mapped to the relevant SDGs, such as SDG 1 (No Poverty), SDG 5 (Gender Equality), SDG 8 (Decent Work and Economic Growth), and SDG 10 (Reduced Inequalities).
- Governance Factors: Identify governance-related ESG factors encompassing corporate governance, ethics, transparency, and anti-corruption measures. These factors can be mapped to SDGs such as SDG 16 and SDG 17 (Partnerships for the Goals), highlighting the importance of effective governance in achieving sustainable development.

By mapping ESG factors to the SDGs, organizations gain insights into the areas where their sustainability efforts can have the most significant impact. This mapping exercise facilitates strategic alignment, enabling businesses to prioritize initiatives that address the most pressing sustainability challenges while contributing to the broader agenda of sustainable development outlined by the United Nations.

4.2.5. Engage Stakeholders: To enrich the ESG framework and ensure its effectiveness, it is essential to engage internal and external stakeholders. Here is how to proceed:

- Internal Stakeholders: Engage with various departments and teams within the organization, including senior management, sustainability teams, human resources, finance, operations, and compliance. Seek their perspectives on how ESG factors align with their respective areas of responsibility and how they can contribute to achieving the SDGs. Encourage cross-functional collaboration to foster a comprehensive understanding of ESG issues and their implications across the organizations.
- External Stakeholders: Reach out to external stakeholders such as investors, customers, suppliers, NGOs, industry associations, and community representatives. Conduct stakeholder consultations, surveys, or focus groups to gather feedback on the relevance and effectiveness of the proposed ESG framework. Understand their expectations regarding sustainability performance, reporting, and transparency. Incorporate stakeholder feedback into the framework to ensure that it reflects the interests and concerns of all relevant parties.
- Partnerships and Collaborations: Explore opportunities for partnerships and collaborations with external stakeholders to enhance the organization's ESG efforts. Collaborate with industry peers, academic institutions, government agencies, and civil society organizations to share best practices, leverage resources, and address shared sustainability challenges. Engaging in multi-stakeholder initiatives can amplify the impact of ESG initiatives and foster collective action toward achieving the SDGs.

By engaging stakeholders throughout the development and implementation of the ESG framework, organizations can build trust, foster buy-in, and cultivate a sense of shared ownership and responsibility for sustainability goals. This collaborative approach ensures that the ESG framework reflects diverse perspectives, incorporates valuable insights, and is aligned with stakeholder expectations, ultimately enhancing its effectiveness and impact.

4.2.6. Implement and Monitor: Executing the ESG framework involves translating plans into action and consistently tracking performance to ensure alignment with sustainable development objectives. Here is a systematic approach to implementation and monitoring:

- Roll-out Across Business Functions: Introduce ESG framework to all departments, train employees, and embed sustainability into daily operations.
- Establish Key Performance Indicators (KPIs): To monitor progress effectively, define measurable KPIs aligned with ESG factors and SDG targets.
- Data Collection and Reporting: Implement robust data collection methods, leverage technology for data analysis, and ensure transparent reporting to stakeholders.
- Continuous Improvement and Adaptation: Foster a culture of continuous improvement, review performance regularly, engage in benchmarking, and encourage innovation to address emerging challenges.

By systematically implementing the ESG framework and rigorously monitoring performance, organizations can make meaningful progress toward achieving sustainable development goals, mitigating risks, enhancing stakeholder value, and creating long-term positive impacts for society and the environment.

4.2.7. Report and Communicate: Transparency and accountability are integral to effective ESG management. A robust reporting and communication strategy informs stakeholders about the organization's ESG performance, progress, and impact. By adopting a proactive approach to reporting and communication, organizations can enhance transparency, build credibility, and strengthen stakeholder relationships, ultimately driving more significant support for ESG initiatives and advancing sustainable development goals. Here is how to effectively report and communicate ESG initiatives:

- Develop Comprehensive ESG Reports: Compile detailed reports covering environmental, social, and governance performance aligned with SDGs, using frameworks like GRI or SASB for consistency.
- Tailor Communication Channels: Share ESG information using digital platforms, social media, and stakeholder sessions, adjusting messaging for different stakeholder groups.
- Highlight Achievements and Challenges: Transparently showcase successes and areas for improvement, providing context for variances and demonstrating a commitment to continuous enhancement.

- Set Clear Objectives and Targets: Communicate ESG objectives, targets, and progress clearly to stakeholders, using visual aids for clarity and comprehension.
- Engage in Dialogue and Feedback: Foster open dialogue with stakeholders through surveys, forums, and feedback channels, incorporating their input into decision-making processes.
- Demonstrate Long-Term Vision and Impact: Articulate the organization's commitment to sustainable development, emphasizing long-term societal and environmental impacts beyond financial returns.

By following these steps, organizations can effectively classify each Sustainable Development Goal (SDG) based on relevant ESG factors and develop a robust ESG framework aligned with sustainable development objectives. This approach enables organizations to integrate ESG considerations into their decision-making processes, measure and monitor performance, engage stakeholders, and drive meaningful progress toward achieving the SDGs. By aligning ESG practices with the broader goals of sustainable development, organizations can enhance their resilience, mitigate risks, seize opportunities, and contribute to positive social and environmental outcomes on a global scale.

4.3 The Interconnected Nature of SDGs and ESG Factors

This section addresses Research Question 3 (R3) by exploring how advancements in ESG factors intersect with progress in SDGs and impact outcomes across different domains of sustainability, highlighting the interconnected nature of environmental, social, and governance aspects within the framework of sustainable development goals. The classification of SDGs through the ESG framework involves a comprehensive assessment of their impacts on society, the environment, and the local economy. This approach, as outlined by Hoyas (2022) and Davino & D'Alesio (2023), categorizes SDGs into these three main blocks to evaluate the effects generated by projects. Maileen et al. (2022) noted that such a framework facilitates the identification of synergies and trade-offs concerning global development goals, allowing for a thorough analysis of how projects align with the SDGs.

Table 1. Classification of SDGs based on ESG

SDGs		ESG Considerations						
SDGs Number	SDGs	E only	S only	G only	Both E & S	Both E & G	Both S & G	All E, S, & G
SDG 1	No Poverty	8	**165**	12	2	3	5	5
SDG 2	Zero Hunger	4	**125**	6	46	4	10	5
SDG 3	Good Health and Well-being	5	**113**	2	67	3	8	2
SDG 4	Quality Education	12	**171**	5	1	2	6	3
SDG 5	Gender Equality	3	**124**	6	1	5	56	5
SDG 6	Clean Water and Sanitation	39	8	2	**141**	5	2	3
SDG 7	Affordable and Clean Energy	41	6	3	**139**	1	7	3
SDG 8	Decent Work and Economic Growth	4	21	20	25	5	**120**	5
SDG 9	Industry, Innovation, and Infrastructure	10	15	15	22	36	11	**91**
SDG 10	Reduced Inequality	1	40	9	5	5	**88**	52
SDG 11	Sustainable Cities and Communities	72	2	8	2	14	6	**96**
SDG 12	Responsible Consumption and Production	8	6	6	4	4	2	**170**
SDG 13	Climate Action	**115**	4	3	3	36	5	34
SDG 14	Life Below Water	**181**	1	5	2	2	5	4
SDG 15	Life on Land	**176**	2	4	4	5	5	4
SDG 16	Peace, Justice, and Strong Institutions	1	19	18	4	6	**150**	2
SDG 17	Partnerships for the Goals	1	2	2	4	6	32	**153**

E (Environmental), S (Social), G (Governance)
Source: Field data 2024

Moreover, by employing the ESG framework, projects can conduct meticulous technical analyses to identify internal shortcomings and failures, enabling informed decision-making for future improvements and adjustments in alignment with the SDGs (Kilanioti & Papadopoulos, 2023). Exploring the interconnectedness between SDGs and ESG factors reveals how progress in one area often influences outcomes in another. Table 1 provides a valuable framework for understanding how different SDGs align with various ESG considerations, emphasizing the interconnectedness and complexity of sustainable development challenges. Table 2 and Figure 1 categorize the SDGs based on different ESG aspects. Tables 1 and 2 show a breakdown of this interconnectedness:

Table 2. SDGs under different ESG aspects

ESG	SDGs
Environment only	SDG 13, SDG 14, and SDG 15
Social only	SDG 1, SDG 2, SDG 3, SDG 4, and SDG 5
Governance only	-
Both environmental and social	SDG 6 and SDG 7
Both environmental and governance	-
Both social and governance	SDG 8, SDG 10, and SDG 16
All ESG	SDG 9, SDG 11, SDG 12, and SDG 17

Source: Authors own based on Table 1

Pursuing progress in one Sustainable Development Goal (SDG) often generates synergistic effects that contribute to simultaneously advancing multiple SDGs. For instance, initiatives to achieve SDG 7 (Affordable and Clean Energy) by investing in renewable energy sources can yield numerous co-benefits across various SDGs. By reducing reliance on fossil fuels and promoting sustainable energy practices, such efforts can mitigate greenhouse gas emissions (SDG 13), foster economic growth and job creation (SDG 8), enhance access to clean and affordable energy (SDG 7) and bolster energy security (SDG 7). Conversely, adequately addressing ESG factors may result in trade-offs or negative consequences that affect progress toward multiple SDGs. Recognizing the interconnectedness of SDGs and integrating ESG considerations is essential for fostering synergies and maximizing positive impacts across diverse, sustainable development objectives. For instance, environmental degradation can exacerbate challenges related to poverty, inequality, and health disparities, hindering advancements in SDGs promoting well-being, equality, and sustainability. By acknowledging these interdependencies, entities can formulate comprehensive approaches to expedite progress toward sustainable development objectives, aligning business practices, policies, and investments with broader agendas. Table 1 represents the breakdown of categories in the "ESG Considerations" column, aiding in understanding how each SDG relates to environmental, social, and governance aspects. This facilitates a targeted approach to prioritizing initiatives and effectively addressing complex economic, social, and environmental challenges.

Based on table 1 and 2, the interconnectedness and synergies are explained and reported under the head 4.3.1 to 4.3.7

4.3.1. Environmental Factors and SDGs:

The environmental dimensions of ESG principles are intricately linked with the SDGs established by the United Nations. While ESG principles lack legal binding, they significantly influence the development of legal frameworks concerning sustainable development (Sokolova & Teymurov, 2022). Asset managers integrating ESG factors into investment decisions can enhance alpha generation while adhering to the SDGs (Maria, 2022). The SDGs serve as a vital framework connecting environmental intelligence systems with public policies, research endeavours, and technology transfers to address global environmental challenges such as climate change, biodiversity loss, and water access (Bekaert et al., 2023). Nevertheless, research spanning European countries highlights a funding gap in achieving environmentally focused SDGs despite investments in environmental protection, underscoring the challenges in swiftly addressing environmental issues (Cruz, 2022). The Sustainable Development Goals (SDGs) provide a crucial framework for addressing environmental sustainability alongside social and economic challenges. Integrating environmental concerns into these objectives underscores the interconnectedness of environmental issues with societal well-being and economic prosperity. Environmental sustainability includes preserving natural resources, protecting ecosystems, mitigating climate change impacts, and promoting human health and economic development. Despite global agreements, environmental degradation persists, necessitating concerted efforts to preserve ecosystems and promote sustainable resource management. Addressing challenges like biodiversity loss and climate change is essential for the health of human and ecological communities. Aligning efforts with the SDGs allows stakeholders to collaborate effectively toward achieving environmental sustainability and fostering a resilient and prosperous future.

The SDGs encompass a range of environmental challenges, illustrating the interconnectedness between human well-being and the planet's health. For instance, SDG 13, "Climate Action," focuses on mitigating the impacts of climate change. SDGs 14 and 15, "Life Below Water" and "Life on Land," respectively, aim to protect marine and terrestrial ecosystems. Environmental considerations are integral to achieving these goals. Carbon emissions, water usage, waste management, and biodiversity conservation are crucial in advancing environmental sustainability. By addressing these ESG factors, organizations can contribute to attaining environmental SDGs. The linkages are briefly explained below:

- Goal 13—Climate Action: Goal 13 of the SDGs underscores the urgency of combating climate change by reducing emissions and enhancing resilience to climate-related disasters for long-term environmental sustainability.

- Goal 14—Life Below Water: Goal 14 of the SDGs emphasizes conserving and sustainably using oceans, seas, and marine resources to prevent pollution, protect ecosystems, and manage resources effectively. It aims for environmental sustainability and supports coastal communities' livelihoods. Therefore, Goal 14 is a critical component of integrated environmental, social, and governance frameworks, preserving marine ecosystems and promoting sustainable development.

- Goal 15—Life on Land: SDG 15 highlights the importance of protecting, restoring, and promoting the sustainable use of terrestrial ecosystems, forests, and biodiversity. Preserving biodiversity and ecosystems on land is essential for maintaining ecosystem services, combating desertification, and ensuring the sustainability of life on earth.

Despite the SDGs' comprehensive framework, challenges like climate change and biodiversity loss persist, requiring a multi-dimensional approach integrating environmental considerations into development planning and promoting sustainable practices. Strengthening policy frameworks, investing in renewable energy, and conserving biodiversity are vital strategies to accelerate progress towards environmental sustainability, emphasizing the imperative of investing in nature for a resilient and prosperous future.

4.3.2. Social Factors and SDGs:

The social dimensions of ESG factors are closely linked with the United Nations SDGs (Szetey et al., 2023; Sokolova & Teymurov, 2022), highlighting the importance of societal well-being, community engagement, and workforce considerations in achieving sustainable development goals. Corporate ESG performance contributes to the SDGs, particularly in the social sphere (Maria, 2022). Aligning ESG indicators with the 17 SDGs provides companies with insights into their impact on sustainable growth at micro and macroeconomic levels (Bekaert et al., 2023). Emphasizing social dimensions within the SDGs underscores the need for local engagement and understanding, as societal issues often have profound local impacts. Integrating social aspects into ESG practices is crucial for advancing SDGs and promoting sustainable development.

Social sustainability, integral to numerous SDGs, addresses societal challenges like poverty eradication (SDG 1), zero hunger (SDG 2), good health (SDG 3), quality education (SDG 4), and gender equality (SDG 5). ESG factors, encompassing fair labor practices, human rights protection, diversity, community relations, and ethical supply chains, are crucial for progress in these areas, driving social sustainability and SDG advancement. The linkages are briefly explained below:

- Goal 1 - No Poverty: This goal aims to eradicate poverty in all its forms, emphasizing social inclusion and economic empowerment. Poverty alleviation fosters social equality and human dignity, contributing to sustainable development.
- Goal 2 - Zero Hunger: This goal focuses on ending hunger, achieving food security, and promoting sustainable agriculture. Addressing food insecurity is essential for ensuring social well-being and reducing inequalities.
- Goal 3 - Good Health and Well-being: This goal advocates for ensuring healthy lives and promoting well-being for all ages, addressing disease prevention and healthcare access. Health and well-being are fundamental social factors that underpin sustainable development and human flourishing.
- Goal 4 - Quality Education: Goal 4 underscores the importance of inclusive and equitable quality education for all, promoting lifelong learning opportunities. Education is a crucial social determinant that empowers individuals, reduces inequalities, and fosters economic prosperity.
- Goal 5 - Gender Equality: This goal seeks to achieve gender equality and empower all women and girls, addressing gender-based discrimination and violence. Gender equality is essential for promoting social justice, enhancing economic productivity, and achieving sustainable development.

Efforts in poverty alleviation, healthcare, education, gender equality, and economic opportunities are crucial for social development and SDG progress. However, challenges like poverty, inequality, healthcare gaps, gender discrimination, and unemployment persist, demanding actions for social inclusion and empowerment. Strengthening safety nets, investing in education and healthcare, promoting gender equality, and fostering inclusive growth accelerate social development and SDG achievement for a fairer, more resilient, and sustainable world.

4.3.3. Governance Factors and SDGs

Governance aspects are pivotal in bridging the connection between ESG factors and SDGs. Studies reveal a notable emphasis on governance-related disclosures by companies in emerging markets, with a significant positive correlation observed between mean ESG scores and country-specific SDG scores (Radu et al., 2023). Additionally, aligning ESG indicators with SDG performance is crucial for national SDG achievement, as governance standards and sustainability reporting offer a competitive advantage for stakeholders and investors (Ainul, 2022). Moreover, the research underscores the contribution of corporate ESG performance, particularly in the governance pillar, to the pursuit of SDGs, underscoring the significance of governance practices in driving sustainable development goals at both micro and macroeconomic levels (Sarkar et al., 2023). Governance is pivotal in advancing SDGs, particularly in ensuring peace, justice, and strong institutions (SDG 16) and fostering partnerships for the goals (SDG 17). ESG factors, integral to governance, encompass transparency, accountability, ethics, anti-corruption measures, stakeholder engagement, and regulatory compliance, which are crucial for responsible conduct. Strong governance optimizes resource allocation and builds trust, stability, and collaboration, amplifying sustainable development efforts globally. Adherence to sound governance principles empowers stakeholders to unite effectively, confronting complex challenges and driving progress towards SDGs worldwide.

4.3.4 Integrated Social and Environmental Factors and SDGs

The alignment between social and environmental dimensions is exemplified in SDGs 6 and 7, highlighting the interconnected nature of human well-being and environmental sustainability. SDG 6, "Clean Water and Sanitation," emphasizes universal access to clean water and sanitation, addressing water scarcity and pollution issues vital for social welfare and ecosystem health. Similarly, SDG 7, "Affordable and Clean Energy," advocates universal access to affordable, reliable, and clean energy, promoting renewable energy sources and energy efficiency to mitigate climate change impacts and advance environmental sustainability. The linkages are briefly explained below:

- Goal 6 - Clean Water and Sanitation: This goal underscores the imperative of ensuring universal access to clean water and sanitation, addressing issues like water scarcity and pollution. Environmental sustainability hinges on the availability of clean water, which is vital for human health and ecosystem integrity.
- Goal 7—Affordable and Clean Energy: Goal 7 advocates universal access to affordable, reliable, and clean energy, emphasizing renewable energy sources and energy efficiency. Adoption of clean energy is pivotal for reducing greenhouse gas emissions and advancing environmental sustainability.

ESG factors are vital for advancing SDGs by promoting equitable and sustainable development. Initiatives fostering social inclusivity, clean water, energy access, environmental justice, and sustainable resource management contribute to social and environmental goals. Integrating these considerations into development strategies accelerates progress towards SDGs 6 and 7, addressing interconnected challenges and building resilient communities for a sustainable future.

4.3.5 Integrated Environmental and Governance Factors

The linkage between environmental and governance factors is crucial for advancing sustainable development objectives. Environmental considerations encompass pollution control, resource conservation, renewable energy adoption, and ecosystem preservation, all of which are vital for environmental sustainability. On the other hand, governance factors, including transparent regulatory frameworks, effective institutions, stakeholder engagement mechanisms, and anti-corruption measures, play a pivotal role in enforcing and implementing environmental policies and initiatives. Effective governance structures enhance accountability, promote transparency, and facilitate collaboration among diverse stakeholders, fostering trust and stability in institutions. By integrating environmental and governance factors, stakeholders can develop comprehensive strategies to address environmental challenges, promote sustainable resource management, and mitigate climate change impacts. This integrated approach enables organizations and policymakers to create synergies between environmental conservation efforts and governance practices, ultimately contributing to the broader goals of sustainable development.

4.3.6. Integrated Social and Governance Factors

The nexus between social and governance factors is instrumental in advancing SDGs 8, 10, and 16, which focus on decent work and economic growth, reduced inequalities, and peace, justice, and strong institutions, respectively. Social considerations encompass labor rights, equality, diversity and inclusion, community well-being, and access to justice, all essential for fostering social sustainability. Governance factors, including transparency, accountability, ethics, stakeholder engagement, and adherence to laws and regulations, are critical for ensuring effective governance structures and institutions. By integrating social and governance factors, stakeholders can promote inclusive economic growth, reduce inequalities, and strengthen institutions to uphold justice and peace. The linkages are briefly explained below:

- Goal 8 - Decent Work and Economic Growth: Goal 8 promotes sustained, inclusive, sustainable economic growth, full and productive employment, and decent work. Access to decent work and economic opportunities is crucial for social stability and poverty reduction.
- Goal 10 - Reduced Inequalities: Goal 10 aims to reduce inequality within and among countries, addressing income inequality, social exclusion, and discrimination. Promoting social, economic, and political inclusion is essential for fostering social cohesion and sustainable development.

- Goal 16 - Peace, Justice, and Strong Institutions: Goal 16 aims to foster peaceful, inclusive societies with access to justice and effective institutions. Promoting transparency, accountability, and participation advances social stability, addresses inequalities, and creates an environment conducive to sustainable development. This goal is integral to integrating social considerations into governance frameworks and promoting inclusive development alongside environmental sustainability.

This integrated approach enables organizations, governments, and civil society to address social disparities, promote social cohesion, and build resilient and equitable societies. By aligning efforts with SDGs 8, 10, and 16, stakeholders can contribute to sustainable development outcomes prioritizing social well-being and justice.

4.3.7. Integrated Environmental, Social, and Governance Factors

The amalgamation of ESG factors is pivotal for advancing SDGs 9, 11, 12, and 17, focusing on industry, innovation, and infrastructure; sustainable cities and communities; responsible consumption and production; and partnerships for the goals. Environmental considerations encompass resource management, pollution control, climate resilience, and sustainable practices, all crucial for fostering environmental sustainability. Social factors, including equality, inclusivity, community engagement, and labour rights, are essential for promoting social sustainability and fostering resilient communities. Governance factors, including transparency, accountability, ethical business practices, and collaboration, are vital for effective decision-making and implementation of sustainable policies and initiatives. The linkages are briefly explained below:

- Goal 9 focuses on building resilient infrastructure, fostering innovation, and promoting sustainable industrialization to support economic growth and societal well-being, which are crucial for advancing environmental sustainability and economic prosperity.
- Goal 11: Prioritize building inclusive, safe, and sustainable cities, addressing urbanization challenges such as air pollution and waste management, which are essential for environmental sustainability.
- Goal 12: advocates for responsible consumption and production patterns, emphasizing resource efficiency and waste reduction to minimize environmental impacts and promote sustainable development.
- Goal 17 highlights the significance of global partnerships in achieving all SDGs, including environmental sustainability. It stresses collaboration

among stakeholders to mobilize resources and implement effective environmental initiatives.

Integrating environmental, social, and governance factors enables stakeholders to drive innovation, build resilient infrastructure, promote sustainable consumption, and foster partnerships for sustainable development. This approach aligns with SDGs 9, 11, 12, and 17, facilitating progress towards a more sustainable and resilient future.

Figure 1. SDGs based on ESG

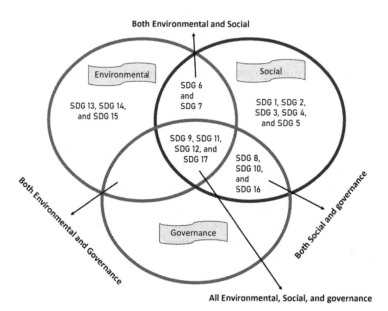

Source: Authors own based on Table 1

The analysis highlights several critical observations regarding the distribution and interconnectedness of ESG considerations across SDGs. Different SDGs align with various ESG factors, such as SDG 13 (Climate Action) focuses on environmental aspects, while SDG 16 emphasizes governance. Some SDGs, like SDG 11 (Sustainable Cities and Communities), intersect with multiple ESG factors, showcasing their interconnected nature. The distribution of ESG considerations across SDGs is uneven, reflecting differing priorities and challenges; for instance, SDG 14 (Life Below Water) primarily addresses environmental considerations, signalling the need to address neglected social and governance aspects. This underscores the importance of holistic approaches to sustainable development, as seen in SDG 9 (Industry, Innovation, and Infrastructure), which balances ESG considerations. Table

1 is a policy tool for identifying areas needing more attention, such as promoting clean energy in SDG 7 (Affordable and Clean Energy). The categorization in Table 2 further highlights the diverse dimensions of sustainable development, with SDGs grouped by their focus on environmental, social, governance, or a combination of these factors. This analysis emphasizes the need for integrated approaches to tackle complex challenges and achieve the SDGs, promoting a sustainable and resilient future.

4.4 Integrating ESG Practices with SDGs: Challenge, Limitations, and Case Studies

Companies grapple with challenges when integrating Environmental, Social, and Governance (ESG) practices with the Sustainable Development Goals (SDGs). These challenges encompass the struggle to align corporate reporting with the SDGs due to the lack of a universal conceptual framework, the necessity to prioritize specific SDGs based on ESG strategies and capabilities (Berrone et al., 2023), and the need to engage with either the entire set of SDGs or a specific subset to enhance financial performance (Markopoulos & Ramonda, 2022). For instance, a sustainability road-map devised for a Norwegian oil and gas company demonstrated how segregating programs into ESG pillars aligned with the SDGs can help address these challenges through targeted environmental, social, and governance initiatives (Gabriel et al., 2023). Successful integration of ESG with SDGs necessitates strategic alignment, well-defined reporting frameworks, and a comprehensive understanding of the interaction between sustainability goals and financial performance (Galeazzo et al., 2023).

Companies encounter significant obstacles when integrating ESG principles with the SDGs due to various factors. These include the necessity for robust ESG planning (Berrone et al., 2023), institutional pressures based on industry type and country of origin that affect SDG engagement (Gabriel et al., 2023), an unbalanced focus on societal issues over environmental concerns in emerging markets (Galeazzo et al., 2023), and discrepancies between assigned roles and actual practices in small- to medium-sized enterprises (SMEs) concerning the SDGs (Nygaard et al., 2022). For instance, companies may need help to align ESG strategies with SDGs. However, addressing these obstacles through comprehensive planning, stakeholder collaboration, and strategic initiatives can lead to more effective integration and positive impacts on financial performance and sustainability outcomes.

Research indicates that companies face challenges integrating ESG principles with SDGs due to factors such as a lack of commitment at the highest decision-making level, limited integration into reporting and management systems, a focus on societal issues over environmental concerns, and inconsistencies between reporting and practices (Idoya et al., 2023; Nygaard et al., 2022; Diaz-Sarachaga, 2021).

For instance, SMEs in Denmark often engage with SDGs less proactively, citing uncertainty, resource constraints, and low demand for SDG compliance. Lack of standardization, poor comparability, and omitting negative impacts in reporting further complicate integration efforts. Balancing strategies, managing institutional pressures, and addressing these challenges through comprehensive planning and stakeholder engagement are crucial for effective integration, improving financial performance, and achieving sustainable development goals globally.

5. THEORETICAL AND PRACTICAL IMPLICATIONS

This study draws from Stakeholder Theory, Institutional Theory, and CSR theories to provide a conceptual foundation for understanding the interplay between SDGs and ESG factors. It contributes to the discourse on sustainable development, corporate governance, and social responsibility by offering an interdisciplinary approach that integrates environmental science, social sciences, and management studies, thus providing a holistic understanding of these dynamics. Comparisons with previous studies highlight the evolving landscape of ESG and SDG integration. For instance, previous research has primarily focused on the isolated impact of ESG factors on corporate performance (Azmi et al., 2020; Behl et al., 2021) and also on financial performance (El et al., 2021; Galeazzo & Miandar, 2023). In contrast, this study emphasizes the interconnectedness of ESG and SDGs, demonstrating how comprehensive integration can drive more significant sustainable outcomes. The interdisciplinary methodology adopted in this research aligns with findings by Berrone et al. (2023) and Díaz-López et al. (2021), who also advocate for a multifaceted approach to sustainability challenges. By building on these studies, this research advances the theoretical understanding of how ESG practices can effectively contribute to achieving the SDGs. Practically, the findings can guide organizations in aligning ESG practices with SDGs, adopting responsible business strategies, and integrating sustainability into decision-making through tools like an ESG matrix. Policymakers can use these insights to craft regulations that promote ESG integration and sustainable development. Additionally, organizations can enhance stakeholder engagement by transparently communicating their ESG initiatives, improving their reputation, attracting responsible investors, and fostering positive stakeholder relationships. The study advances academic knowledge and actionable strategies for organizations and policymakers by combining theoretical and practical insights.

6. CONCLUSION

Global sustainability efforts can be advanced by integrating Environmental, Social, and Governance (ESG) criteria with the Sustainable Development Goals (SDGs). This connection substantially contributes to national and international sustainability agendas and fortifies business sustainability profiles (Radu et al., 2023). Research demonstrates that firm-level ESG disclosures and national SDG scores are positively correlated, with emerging economies significantly affected (Soni, 2023; Pokrovskaia et al., 2023). This emphasizes the crucial role that corporate practices play in advancing more general societal and environmental goals. However, there are obstacles to consider when incorporating ESG aspects into investment decisions, including fiduciary requirements and questions about the integrity of the data.

For this reason, solid frameworks and clear reporting procedures are required for successful implementation. Empirical studies highlight the complex connections between organizational resilience and value creation through ESG practices and financial success in many industries. Essential routes for sustainable development are illuminated by the investigation of ESG's influence on SDGs and the categorization of SDGs according to pertinent ESG elements. Comprehending these interdependencies enables entities to embrace comprehensive strategies that simultaneously tackle environmental, social, and governance aspects, guaranteeing enduring results in various industries and geographical settings. In addition to improving operational resilience and growth, the symbiotic relationship between ESG criteria and SDGs offers firms a strategic framework for making meaningful contributions to global sustainability objectives. By utilizing this integration, stakeholders may promote a sustainable future that balances economic growth with environmental stewardship and social justice. This holistic viewpoint highlights how business practices are linked to the earth's health and society's general well-being, opening the door to a more just and sustainable future.

REFERENCES

Ademi, B., & Klungseth, N. J. (2022). Does it pay to deliver superior ESG performance? Evidence from US S&P 500 companies. *Journal of Global Responsibility*, 13(4), 421–449. Advance online publication. 10.1108/JGR-01-2022-0006

Antoncic, M., Bekaert, G., Rothenberg, R. V., & Noguer, M. (2020, August 1). *Sustainable Investment - Exploring the Linkage between Alpha, ESG, and SDG's*. Papers.*ssrn*.com. https://ssrn.com/abstract=362345910.2139/ssrn.3623459

Azmi, W., Hassan, M. K., Houston, R., & Karim, M. S. (2020). ESG activities and banking performance: International evidence from emerging economies. *Journal of International Financial Markets, Institutions and Money*, 70, 101277. 10.1016/j.intfin.2020.101277

Bandeira, G. L., Duarte, Gardi, L. H., Sodario, M., & Simioni, C. G. (2023). *Developing an ESG Strategy and Roadmap: An Integrated Perspective in an O&G Company*. 10.4043/32600-MS

Behl, A., Kumari, P. S. R., Makhija, H., & Sharma, D. (2021). Exploring the relationship of ESG score and firm value using cross-lagged panel analyses: Case of the Indian energy sector. *Annals of Operations Research*, 313(1), 231–256. 10.1007/s10479-021-04189-8

Bekaert, G., Rothenberg, R., & Noguer, M. (2023). Sustainable investment – Exploring the linkage between alpha, ESG, and SDGs. *Sustainable Development (Bradford)*, 31(5), 3831–3842. 10.1002/sd.2628

Berrone, P., Rousseau, H. E., Ricart, J. E., Brito, E., & Giuliodori, A. (2023). How Can Research Contribute to the Implementation of Sustainable Development goals? an Interpretive Review of SDG Literature in Management. *International Journal of Management Reviews*, 25(2), 318–339. 10.1111/ijmr.12331

Cruz Villares, L. (2022). *Environmental Management and Data for the SDGs*. IoT Applications Computing., 10.5772/intechopen.97685

Davino, C., & D'Alesio, N. (2023). Sustainable development goals: classifying European countries through self-organizing maps. *Proceedings E Report (Online)*, 95–100. 10.36253/979-12-215-0106-3.17

Díaz-López, C., Martín-Blanco, C., De la Torre Bayo, J. J., Rubio-Rivera, B., & Zamorano, M. (2021). Analyzing the Scientific Evolution of the Sustainable Development Goals. *Applied Sciences (Basel, Switzerland)*, 11(18), 8286. 10.3390/app11188286

Diaz-Sarachaga, J. M. (2021). Shortcomings in reporting contributions towards the sustainable development goals. *Corporate Social Responsibility and Environmental Management*, 28(4), 1299–1312. Advance online publication. 10.1002/csr.2129

El Khoury, R., Nasrallah, N., & Alareeni, B. (2021). ESG and financial performance of banks in the MENAT region: Concavity–convexity patterns. *Journal of Sustainable Finance & Investment*, ●●●, 1–25. 10.1080/20430795.2021.1929807

Ferrero-Ferrero, I., Muñoz-Torres, M. J., Rivera-Lirio, J. M., Escrig-Olmedo, E., & Fernández-Izquierdo, M. Á. (2023). SDG reporting: An analysis of corporate sustainability leaders. *Marketing Intelligence & Planning*, 41(4), 457–472. 10.1108/MIP-07-2022-0332

Fuadah, L. L., Mukhtarudin, M., Andriana, I., & Arisman, A. Luk Luk Fuadah. (2023). Environmental, Social and Governance (ESG). *Integrated Journal of Business and Economics*, 7(2), 459–459. 10.33019/ijbe.v7i2.706

Galeazzo, A., Miandar, T., & Carraro, M. (2023). SDGs in corporate responsibility reporting: A longitudinal investigation of institutional determinants and financial performance. *The Journal of Management and Governance*. Advance online publication. 10.1007/s10997-023-09671-y

Glushakova, O. V., & Chernikova, O. P. (2023). Institutionalization of ESG-principles at the international level and in the Russian Federation, their impact on ferrous metallurgy enterprises. Part 1. *Izvestiâ Vysših Učebnyh Zavedenij. Černaâ Metallurgiâ*, 66(2), 253–264. 10.17073/0368-0797-2023-2-253-264

Goswami, M., & Krishnan, B. (2022). eHED2SDG: A Framework Towards Sustainable Professionalism and Attaining SDG Through Online Holistic Education in Indian Higher Education. *ECS Transactions*, 107(1), 15337–15347. 10.1149/10701.15337ecst

Gwalani, H., & Mazumdar, S. (2022). ESG Reporting – Genesis And Significance. *The Management Accountant Journal*, 57(3), 53. 10.33516/maj.v57i3.53-57p

Harnos, R. (2022). ESG (Environmental Social Governance) beim Vertrieb von Finanzprodukten. *Zeitschrift Für Das Gesamte Bank- Und Börsenwesen*, 70(12), 882. 10.47782/oeba202212088201

Hoyas, S. (2022). *ASDG — An AI-based framework for automatic classification of impact on the SDGs*. 10.1145/3560107.3560128

Ilieva, M. V. (2022). Chapter 7. The Interconnection Among Social, Environmental, and Economic Aspects of the 17 SDGs. *Nomos Verlagsgesellschaft mbH & Co. KG EBooks*, 127–150. 10.5771/9783748933090-127

Işık, C., & Ongan, S. Islam, H., Pinzon, S., & Jabeen, G. (2024). Navigating sustainability: Unveiling the interconnected dynamics of ESG factors and SDGs in BRICS-11. *Sustainable Development*. Advance online publication. 10.1002/sd.2977

Khutorova, N. A., Gazizova, A. V., & Gazizov, D. N. (2023). ESG approaches in strategic management of economic systems at the federal and regional levels. *Nacional nye Interesy: Prioritety I Bezopasnost*, *19*(5), 866–882. https://doi.org/10.24891/ni.19.5.866

Kihn, E. A., Zhizhin, M., Siquig, R., & Redmon, R. (2004). The Environmental Scenario Generator (ESG): A distributed environmental data archive analysis tool. *Data Science Journal*, 3, 10–28. 10.2481/dsj.3.10

Kilanioti, I., & Papadopoulos, G. A. (2023). A knowledge graph-based deep learning framework for efficient content similarity search of Sustainable Development Goals data. *Data Intelligence (Online)*, 1–19. 10.1162/dint_a_00206

Lapsley, J., & Eggertsson, M. (2022). Managing ESG in a Global Enterprise. *International Journal of Business Research*, 22(2), 14–24. 10.18374/IJBR-22-2.2

Maidin, A. J. (2022). Governance of SDGs. *Routledge EBooks*, 222–231. 10.4324/9781003230724-19

Markopoulos, E., & Maria Barbara Ramonda. (2022). An ESG-SDGs alignment and execution model based on the Ocean Strategies transition in emerging markets. *AHFE International*. 10.54941/ahfe1001511

Markopoulos, E., & Barbara Ramonda, M. (2022). An ESG-SDGs alignment and execution model based on the Ocean Strategies transition in emerging markets. *Creativity. Innovation and Entrepreneurship*, 31. Advance online publication. 10.54941/ahfe1001511

Markopoulos, E., Zhao, K., Samkova, M., & Vanharanta, H. (2023). *ESG and UN SDGs Driven Strategy Generation Process for Green and Pink Oceans*. Openaccess. cms-Conferences.org; AHFE Open Acces. 10.54941/ahfe1003878

Mishra, M., Sudarsan, D., Santos, Mishra, S. K., Abu, Goswami, S., Kalumba, A. M., Biswal, R., Silva, Antonio, C., & Baral, K. (2023). *A bibliometric analysis of SDGs: a review of progress, challenges, and opportunities*. 10.1007/s10668-023-03225-w

Naimy, V., El Khoury, R., & Iskandar, S. (2021). ESG Versus Corporate Financial Performance: Evidence from East Asian Firms in the Industrials Sector. *Estudios de Economía Aplicada*, 39(3). Advance online publication. 10.25115/eea.v39i3.4457

Nygaard, S., Kokholm, A. R., & Huulgaard, R. D. (2022). Incorporating the sustainable development goals in small- to medium-sized enterprises. *Journal of Urban Economics*, 8(1), juac022. Advance online publication. 10.1093/jue/juac022

Pokrovskaia, N. N., Mordovets, V. A., & Nataly Yu. Kuchieva. (2023). Regulation of ESG-Ecosystem: Context and Content Evolution: Energy Sector Study. *Springer Proceedings in Business and Economics*, 159–179. 10.1007/978-3-031-30498-9_15

Radu, O.-M., Dragomir, V. D., & Feleagă, L. (2023). The Link between Corporate ESG Performance and the UN Sustainable Development Goals. *Proceedings of the ...International Conference on Business Excellence, 17*(1), 776–790. 10.2478/picbe-2023-0072

Ruhana, F., Suwartiningsih, S., Mulyandari, E., Handoyo, S., & Afrilia, U. A. (2024). Innovative Strategies for Achieving Sustainable Development Goals Amidst Escalating Global Environmental and Social Challenges. *The International Journal of Science in Society*, 6(1), 662–677. 10.54783/ijsoc.v6i1.1054

Sarkar, S., Nair, S., & Datta, A. (2023). *Role of Environmental, Social, and Governance in achieving the UN Sustainable Development Goals: A special focus on India*. https://doi.org/10.1002/ep.14204

Sekar, A., & Krishnan, R. (2022). ESG - Marching Towards Sustainable Development Goals. *The Management Accountant Journal*, 57(3), 17. 10.33516/maj.v57i3.17-21p

Serra, D., & De Oliveira, T. (2023). Environmental, Social and Governance (ESG). *Revista Direito E Sexualidade*, 49–71. 10.9771/rds.v4i1.52207

Simao, M. S., Dagnese, L. L., Ribeiro, E., Aurelio, M., Green, V., & Tomaz, K. D. (2022). Multisectoral Sustainable Development Impacts Survey From the Application of the SDGs-IAE Framework: A Case Study. *2022 IEEE Sustainable Power and Energy Conference (ISPEC)*. 10.1109/iSPEC54162.2022.10032985

Sokolova, N. A., & Teymurov, E. S. (2022). Correlation of Sustainable Development Goals and ESG principles. [MSAL]. *Courier of Kutafin Moscow State Law University*, 12(12), 171–183. 10.17803/2311-5998.2021.88.12.171-183

Soni, T. K. (2023). Demystifying the relationship between ESG and SDG performance: Study of emerging economies. *Investment Management and Financial Innovations*, 20(3), 1–12. 10.21511/imfi.20(3).2023.01

Szetey, K., Moallemi, E. A., & Bryan, B. A. (2023). Knowledge Co-Production Reveals Nuanced Societal Dynamics and Sectoral Connections in Mapping Sustainable Human–Natural Systems. *Earth's Future*, 11(9), e2022EF003326. Advance online publication. 10.1029/2022EF003326 van Asselt, H. (2023). The SDGs and fossil fuel subsidy reform. *International Environmental Agreement: Politics, Law and Economics*, 23(2), 191–197. 10.1007/s10784-023-09601-1

Weiss, T. G., & Wilkinson, R. (2023). *International Organization and Global Governance*. Taylor & Francis. 10.4324/9781003266365

Xu, Z., Peng, J., Qiu, S., Liu, Y., Dong, J., & Zhang, H. (2022). Responses of spatial relationships between ecosystem services and the Sustainable Development Goals to urbanization. *The Science of the Total Environment*, 850, 157868. 10.1016/j.scitotenv.2022.15786835944627

Yi, I., & Yi, I. (2023). The Sustainable Development Goals. *Edward Elgar Publishing EBooks*, 310–320. 10.4337/9781803920924.00054

Zhang, D., Wang, C., & Dong, Y. (2022). How Does Firm ESG Performance Impact Financial Constraints? An Experimental Exploration of the COVID-19 Pandemic. *European Journal of Development Research*, 35(1), 219–239. Advance online publication. 10.1057/s41287-021-00499-635002102

ENDNOTES

[1.] United Nations. (2024). The 17 Sustainable Development Goals. United Nations. https://sdgs.un.org/goals

[2.] National Geographic Society. (2019, September 30). Sustainable Development Goals. National Geographic Society. https://www.nationalgeographic.org/article/sustainable-development-goals/

[3.] Unicef. (2024). SDG Goal 10: Reduced Inequalities. UNICEF DATA. https://data.unicef.org/sdgs/goal-10-reduced-inequalities/

[4.] United Nations. (2022). Goal 16: Peace, justice and strong institutions. The Global Goals. https://www.globalgoals.org/goals/16-peace-justice-and-strong-institutions/

Chapter 4
Exploring the Nexus of Objectives and Rating Disparities:
An In-Depth Examination of ESG Rating Agencies

Hanaa Taji
https://orcid.org/0009-0008-2213-7469
Ibn Zohr University, Morocco

El Houssain Attak
https://orcid.org/0009-0007-4228-1057
Cadi Ayyad University, Morocco

ABSTRACT

This chapter explores the complex landscape of ESG (Environmental, Social, and Governance) ratings, focusing on their conceptual foundations, the methodologies employed by major rating agencies, the criteria used to evaluate corporate sustainability, and the significant divergences in ratings. It examines how different agencies interpret and apply ESG criteria, leading to varied ratings that complicate consistent comparisons for investors. Through a detailed analysis of sector-wise correlation and descriptive statistics, the chapter highlights the influence of sectoral characteristics on rating discrepancies and proposes recommendations for standardizing ESG reporting, enhancing transparency, integrating advanced technologies, and developing sector-specific guidelines to improve the reliability and comparability of ESG ratings.

DOI: 10.4018/979-8-3693-3880-3.ch004

1. INTRODUCTION

ESG (Environmental, Social, and Governance) investment has become a fundamental aspect of modern finance, reflecting a growing awareness of global issues such as climate change, social justice, and corporate governance. Investors now incorporate ESG criteria into their decision-making processes to align their portfolios with ethical and sustainable values. In 2022, ESG assets under management reached approximately $41 trillion, representing about 36% of global assets under management, a notable increase from $22.8 trillion in 2016 (Bloomberg Intelligence, 2022). This substantial growth highlights the increasing significance of ESG criteria in guiding investment choices.

For many institutional and individual investors, integrating ESG criteria into investment strategies has become standard practice. These investors aim not only to achieve financial returns but also to foster responsible practices and mitigate risks associated with companies that neglect environmental, social, or governance issues. Research indicates that incorporating ESG criteria can enhance risk-adjusted returns and reduce portfolio volatility (Friede et al., 2015; Clark et al., 2015; Nofsinger & Varma, 2014).

The prominence of ESG criteria is also bolstered by regulatory and governmental support. For example, the European Union introduced the Taxonomy for Sustainable Investments in 2020 to establish a coherent framework for classifying sustainable economic activities (European Commission, 2020). This initiative seeks to improve transparency and provide a common basis for evaluating ESG impacts.

The ESG market is a dynamic ecosystem involving various stakeholders, including investors, companies, regulators, consumers and, all working towards integrating environmental, social, and governance criteria into business practices and investment decisions (PwC Global, 2022; EY Global Insights Team, 2022). ESG rating agencies, such as MSCI, Sustainalytics, LSEG (Refinitiv), and Moody's (Vigeo Eiris), evaluate companies' ESG performance and provide extra-financial scores to investors (Gibson et al., 2021; Escrig-Olmedo et al., 2019).

However, ESG rating agencies face significant challenges in producing reliable and comparable ratings. The methodologies used by different agencies vary considerably, leading to variations and sometimes contradictions in ESG scores assigned to the same companies. These discrepancies create uncertainty for investors seeking to align their portfolios with specific ethical criteria, as evidenced by score differences that can reach 30% for the same company (Berg et al., 2022). Additionally, sector-specific factors such as the unique ESG risks and opportunities presented by technology and financial services are not uniformly evaluated by all agencies, contributing to the inconsistency in ESG scores.

Despite the growing importance of ESG ratings, there is a lack of standardization and transparency in the methodologies used by rating agencies. Previous studies have highlighted the disparities in ESG ratings but have not comprehensively analyzed the impact of sector-specific factors on these divergences. This study aims to fill this gap by analyzing and comparing the rating methodologies adopted by leading ESG rating agencies and exploring how sector-specific factors affect the reliability and comparability of ESG scores for investors. The research addresses the critical question:

To what extent have ESG rating agencies developed reliable and easily comparable extra-financial ratings for investors, and how do sector-specific factors influence these divergences?

This study seeks to analyse the methodologies of leading ESG rating agencies, understand the impact of sector-specific factors on rating divergences, and provide recommendations for improving the reliability and comparability of ESG ratings.

Understanding the reasons behind the discrepancies in ESG ratings is crucial for investors, policymakers, and companies striving for transparency and reliability in ESG reporting. This study is expected to reveal significant methodological differences and sector-specific factors that contribute to rating inconsistencies. The findings will provide insights into improving ESG rating practices and developing more standardized and transparent rating frameworks, ultimately contributing to more informed investment decisions and better corporate governance practices.

This chapter is organized into distinct sections. It begins with a literature review that examines the concept of ESG ratings and the disparities observed among different rating agencies. The next section describes the methodology employed for the analysis. This is followed by the results section, which presents descriptive statistics and correlation analyses. The final section offers a summary of the main findings, explores the implications, and highlights the limitations of the research.

2. LITERATURE REVIEW

This review aims to elucidate the key aspects of ESG ratings, the roles and methodologies of major rating agencies, and the criteria they use to evaluate corporate sustainability. Additionally, it explores the divergence in ESG ratings, providing insights into the challenges and implications of using these ratings in investment decision-making.

2.1 Concept of ESG Rating

ESG ratings are metrics used to evaluate a company's adherence to sustainable practices across environmental, social, and governance dimensions. They provide insights into a company's management of non-financial risks and opportunities, reflecting its long-term sustainability and ethical practices.

Environmental criteria assess a company's impact on the natural environment through metrics such as carbon emissions, energy efficiency, and waste management (Hummel & Schlick, 2016). Social criteria evaluate the company's societal impact, including its relationships with employees, suppliers, customers, and communities, encompassing labor practices, human rights, and community engagement (Fatemi et al., 2018). Governance criteria focus on internal practices and policies, such as board structure, executive compensation, audit practices, and shareholder rights, ensuring ethical conduct and operational transparency (Bebchuk et al., 2009).

The primary purpose of ESG ratings is to offer a comprehensive assessment that extends beyond traditional financial metrics, aiding investors in making informed decisions. These ratings identify environmental and social risks that might affect a company's performance and reveal opportunities related to sustainability (Giese et al., 2019). They promote transparency by encouraging companies to disclose their ESG practices, leading to greater accountability (Gillan et al., 2021). ESG ratings also support investors in aligning their portfolios with their ethical values and long-term financial goals (Amel-Zadeh & Serafeim, 2018), while influencing corporate behaviour by linking ESG performance to investment attractiveness (Schoenmaker & Schramade, 2018).

The evolution of ESG ratings reflects the increasing emphasis on sustainability in investment. Originally, ESG ratings evolved from socially responsible investing (SRI) practices in the 1960s and 1970s when investors began excluding stocks of companies involved in activities deemed harmful, such as tobacco and alcohol (Hawley & Williams, 2000). By the 1990s and early 2000s, structured frameworks for evaluating ESG factors emerged, driven by growing corporate responsibility and sustainable development awareness. Organizations like the Global Reporting Initiative (GRI) and the Carbon Disclosure Project (CDP) established standards for ESG reporting (Matten & Moon, 2008).

In the 2010s, ESG ratings became integral to investment analysis, supported by technological advancements and regulatory frameworks. Standardized guidelines for ESG reporting, such as those provided by the Task Force on Climate-related Financial Disclosures (TCFD) and the Sustainability Accounting Standards Board (SASB), were developed to enhance the reliability and comparability of ESG data (Eccles & Klimenko, 2019). Technologies like artificial intelligence and machine learning are now utilized to process extensive ESG datasets, uncovering insights that traditional methods might miss (Macpherson et al., 2021; Hawn et al., 2018).

Ongoing efforts to harmonize ESG reporting standards aim to address challenges related to methodological discrepancies. Initiatives such as the International Financial Reporting Standards (IFRS) Foundation's move to create a global sustainability standards board illustrate attempts to standardise ESG metrics (Petersen et al., 2022). Governments and regulatory bodies are increasingly mandating ESG disclosures and integrating ESG considerations into financial reporting, enhancing the credibility and consistency of ESG ratings (Ammann et al., 2011).

2.2 ESG Rating Agencies and Criteria

ESG rating agencies play a pivotal role in evaluating how well companies adhere to Environmental, Social, and Governance standards. These agencies provide assessments and scores based on various ESG factors, offering valuable insights into non-financial risks and opportunities that significantly influence investment decisions. ESG ratings encompass three key dimensions: environmental, social, and governance criteria.

Environmental Criteria assess how companies manage their environmental impact through metrics such as carbon emissions, energy efficiency, waste management, and biodiversity conservation. These criteria evaluate strategies for climate change mitigation, resource management, and pollution control, as well as the transparency of environmental reporting (Clark et al., 2015; UNEP, 2011; Rand et al., 2010; GRI, 2020).

Social Criteria evaluate a company's impact on society and relationships with stakeholders, including labor practices, human rights, diversity and inclusion, community engagement, and product responsibility. These criteria cover the treatment of employees, adherence to human rights principles, promotion of diversity, community development contributions, and the safety and quality of products and services (ILO, 2021; UN, 2011; Grissom, 2018; Porter & Kramer, 2011; ISO, 2021).

Governance Criteria focus on a company's internal structures and ethical standards, including board composition, executive compensation, shareholder rights, ethical conduct policies, and risk management. These criteria assess the effectiveness of the board of directors, alignment of executive pay with company performance, protections afforded to shareholders, anti-corruption measures, and processes for identifying and managing risks (OECD, 2015; Bebchuk et al., 2009; Bebchuk, 2005; Transparency International, 2020).

ESG rating agencies such as MSCI, Sustainalytics, and Refinitiv use these criteria to evaluate companies' ESG performance, each with proprietary methodologies leading to variations in ratings. For instance:

- **MSCI**: Uses a rules-based methodology that includes over 1000 data points across 33 ESG key issues, assigning weights to these issues to derive overall ESG scores (MSCI, 2024).
- **Sustainalytics**: focuses on material ESG issues and assesses companies based on their management of these issues, deriving risk ratings that indicate the company's exposure to ESG risks. Supporting their core material ESG issues are over 250 ESG indicators, providing investors with insights into both the extent of companies' exposure to specific challenges and the effectiveness of their management strategies for these issues (Sustainalytics, 2024)
- **Refinitiv (LSEG)**: captures and calculates over 630 company-level ESG measures, of which a subset of 186 of the most comparable and material per industry powers the overall company assessment and scoring process. Refinitiv employs a data-driven approach, collecting data from publicly available information and assessing companies across ten ESG themes (LSEG, 2024).

2.3 ESG Rating Divergence

ESG ratings are essential tools for evaluating the sustainability and ethical practices of companies. Despite their growing importance, there is significant divergence in ESG ratings provided by different agencies. This divergence stems from variations in methodologies, data sources, weighting of ESG factors, and subjective judgment calls. Understanding these differences is crucial for stakeholders who rely on ESG ratings for making informed investment decisions and corporate strategies.

Several studies have explored the causes and implications of ESG rating divergence. Chatterji et al. (2016) provided foundational insights into the lack of convergence among ESG ratings from different agencies. Their comparative analysis highlighted significant discrepancies in ratings, underscoring the complexity of measuring corporate social responsibility, as different agencies prioritize various aspects of ESG performance. This initial exploration spurred extensive academic interest in understanding the implications of such divergences.

Building on these insights, Berg et al. (2022) examined how the absence of standardized metrics and frameworks among rating agencies contributes to divergent ratings, even when assessing the same companies. They suggest that these inconsistencies reflect inherent subjectivities in the interpretation of ESG data. The lack of a unified approach to evaluating ESG performance exacerbates the divergence in ratings, leading to varied assessments of the same company's practices.

Gibson et al. (2021) explored the influence of data availability and processing on ESG ratings, highlighting that discrepancies often arise from differences in data sources and the extent of data coverage. Their findings emphasize the varying levels of transparency and completeness in data collection across rating agencies. The disparity in data sources means that agencies might rely on different information to assess the same ESG criteria, resulting in divergent ratings.

Eccles and Stroehle (2018) discussed how divergent methodological approaches, such as the choice of indicators and the assignment of weights to various ESG factors, contribute to rating variations. They emphasize the need for a more harmonized approach to ESG evaluation to reduce discrepancies and improve the reliability of ESG ratings. Harmonization would involve developing standardized criteria and weighting systems that all rating agencies could adopt, thus minimizing subjective judgment calls.

Kotsantonis et al. (2016) explored the role of cultural and geographical factors, showing that regional differences and cultural biases significantly influence ESG rating variations. This perspective broadens the understanding of how global contexts affect ESG assessments. For example, environmental criteria might be weighted more heavily in regions where environmental issues are a critical concern, while social criteria might be emphasized in regions with significant social inequalities.

Dimson et al. (2023) examined the relationship between ESG ratings and financial performance, suggesting that rating divergence can lead to varied interpretations of a company's long-term value. This research underscores the financial implications of differing ESG assessments, as investors might make different decisions based on the rating agency they rely on. Divergent ratings can thus impact investment strategies and market perceptions of a company's sustainability and ethical practices.

Christensen et al. (2022) provided insights into how changes in regulatory frameworks influence ESG rating methodologies. They argue that evolving regulations are prompting agencies to adapt their assessment criteria, contributing to rating divergence. As regulatory requirements become more stringent or specific, rating agencies adjust their methodologies to comply, leading to temporary divergences until new standards are universally adopted.

In summary, the literature highlights the complexities and inconsistencies in ESG rating methodologies and the impact of these differences on ratings. The divergent approaches to data collection, indicator selection, weighting of ESG factors, cultural and regional biases, and evolving regulatory frameworks all contribute to the variation in ESG ratings. These discrepancies present challenges for investors and stakeholders who seek reliable and comparable ESG assessments.

3. STUDY METHODOLOGY AND SAMPLE

To analyse the divergence in ESG ratings across major rating agencies, this study adopts a systematic approach that integrates both quantitative and qualitative methods. This section outlines the research design, detailing the processes used for data collection, the criteria for selecting the sample, and the analytical techniques employed to examine the data.

3.1 Research Design

This study This study adopts a quantitative approach to analyse the divergence in ESG ratings across major rating agencies. The primary focus is on quantitatively comparing and contrasting the ratings assigned by MSCI, Sustainalytics, and Refinitiv to a selection of large multinational corporations. This analysis aims to identify patterns, discrepancies, and the underlying factors contributing to rating divergence.

3.2 Data Collection

This study employs a quantitative approach to analyse the reliability and comparability of ESG ratings among leading rating agencies. The core dataset includes ESG ratings for a selection of companies from MSCI, Sustainalytics, and Refinitiv. To facilitate comparison, these ratings are converted into a uniform numerical scale. MSCI ratings are converted from letter grades to numerical scores: AAA (100), AA (85), A (70), BBB (55), BB (40), B (25), CCC (10). Sustainalytics scores are collected on a scale from 0 (lowest risk) to 100 (highest risk), while Refinitiv ratings are provided on a scale from 0 (worst) to 100 (best). Additionally, companies are categorized into sectors according to the Global Industry Classification Standard (GICS) to enable sector-specific analysis of ESG ratings. Separate ratings for environmental (E), social (S), and governance (G) dimensions are analyzed to identify how each dimension is evaluated differently by the rating agencies. This quantitative data collection and analysis aim to provide insights into the methodologies of leading ESG rating agencies and the impact of sector-specific factors on rating divergences.

3.3 Sample

The sample includes the top 10 largest companies by market capitalization within each sector, resulting in a total of 100 companies across ten sectors: Consumer Discretionary (CD), Consumer Staples (CS), Energy (EN), Financials (FN), Health Care (HC), Industrials (IN), Information Technology(IT), Materials (MT), Real Estate (RE), and Utilities (UT). These companies were sampled from the global market, ensuring the inclusion of prominent firms with significant market influence and comprehensive ESG reporting.

Companies are selected based on their ranking as the largest by market capitalization within each sector as of 2023. The sample spans various sectors to provide a broad perspective on ESG rating divergence. Additionally, companies with ESG ratings available from MSCI, Sustainalytics, and Refinitiv are included to ensure comparability.

4. RESULTS AND ANALYSIS

This section presents the key findings from the analysis of ESG ratings provided by Sustainalytics, Refinitiv, and MSCI. The results are structured to first display the descriptive statistics by sector, followed by the correlation analysis of ESG ratings across different sectors. These results are then discussed in terms of their alignment and divergence, offering insights into the consistency and variability in ESG assessments across agencies.

Mean scores and standard deviations for ESG ratings within each sector summarize central tendencies and dispersion, highlighting agreement or disagreement between agencies. Pearson correlation coefficients assess relationships between ESG ratings from the three agencies, revealing convergence or divergence in ratings.

The study compares ratings across agencies to identify patterns and discrepancies, analyzing sector-wise differences and evaluating the consistency of ratings for individual ESG dimensions. This comparison identifies significant divergences and their potential causes.

4.1 Descriptive Statistics by Sector

The following table presents the descriptive statistics for ESG ratings provided by MSCI, Sustainalytics, and Refinitiv. The mean scores and standard deviations indicate the average rating and the dispersion of ratings within each sector. The analysis includes a total of 300 observations.

Table 1. Descriptive Statistics of ESG Ratings by Sector

	Sustainalytics	Refinitiv	MSCI	Numerical MSCI
Consumer Discretionary				
Average Score	21.69	73.69	A	70.00
Standard Deviation	7.45	6.19		10.61
Consumer Staples				
Average Score	23.15	81.38	AA	85.00
Standard Deviation	3.89	4.81		0.00
Energy				

continued on following page

Table 1. Continued

	Sustainalytics	Refinitiv	MSCI	Numerical MSCI
Average Score	32.83	78.27	A	67.14
Standard Deviation	8.25	11.79		21.96
Financials				
Average Score	26.59	73.71	A	67.14
Standard Deviation	4.98	17.10		16.23
Health Care				
Average Score	23.69	81.69	A	70.00
Standard Deviation	4.86	6.72		10.61
Industrials				
Average Score	23.62	78.12	AA	82.50
Standard Deviation	7.27	7.48		8.93
Information Technology				
Average Score	19.64	75.92	AA	85.00
Standard Deviation	7.50	10.65		7.94
Materials				
Average Score	29.06	73.75	A	68.57
Standard Deviation	7.89	8.90		19.61
Real Estate				
Average Score	12.78	68.00	AA	82.50
Standard Deviation	4.15	8.19		20.41
Utilities				
Average Score	29.28	78.25	AA	82.50
Standard Deviation	6.55	5.64		7.94

Source: The authors

Note: This table shows average ESG ratings and standard deviations by sector from Sustainalytics, Refinitiv, and MSCI

The comparison of ESG ratings across sectors reveals notable patterns in convergence and divergence among different rating agencies. Each sector demonstrates varying degrees of alignment in ESG ratings provided by Sustainalytics, Refinitiv, and MSCI, reflecting the distinct methodological approaches, criteria, and data sources used by these agencies. The following analysis provides a sector-wise breakdown of the average scores and standard deviations, highlighting the level of consistency or variability in ESG ratings.

Consumer Discretionary: The average Sustainalytics score is 21.69 with a standard deviation of 7.45, indicating moderate variability. Refinitiv's scores are higher and less variable, with an average of 73.69 and a standard deviation of 6.19.

MSCI ratings average at 'A' (70), reflecting moderate convergence but with some divergence shown by the standard deviation.

Consumer Staples: Sustainalytics and Refinitiv ratings converge closely with averages of 23.15 and 81.38, respectively. MSCI consistently rates this sector higher with an average of AA (85), showing strong alignment.

Energy: This sector has a higher average Sustainalytics score (32.83), with Refinitiv and MSCI also showing higher variability in ratings. MSCI's ratings show divergence with a lower average of A (67.14), highlighting significant differences in evaluation criteria.

Financials: Sustainalytics gives an average score of 26.59, with Refinitiv's average score at 73.71. MSCI ratings show divergence with an average of A (67.14) and a higher standard deviation, indicating variability in assessment methods.

Health Care: The ratings are relatively consistent across agencies, with averages of 23.69 for Sustainalytics and 81.69 for Refinitiv. MSCI's average of A (70) reflects a good convergence in ESG evaluations.

Industrials: ESG ratings are quite convergent in this sector, with Sustainalytics at 23.62, Refinitiv at 78.12, and MSCI at AA (82.50). Standard deviations are relatively low, indicating consistent rating approaches.

Information Technology: There is notable divergence in this sector. Sustainalytics scores lower on average (19.64), while Refinitiv and MSCI give higher ratings, suggesting different prioritizations in ESG criteria.

Materials: Sustainalytics scores this sector higher (29.06), while Refinitiv and MSCI have similar but lower average scores, indicating some divergence in ESG assessments.

Real Estate: ESG ratings diverge significantly with Sustainalytics scoring much lower on average (12.78) compared to Refinitiv and MSCI. This indicates differing methodologies and priorities in ESG evaluations.

Utilities: This sector shows high convergence with similar averages from Sustainalytics (29.28), Refinitiv (78.25), and MSCI (AA, 82.50), reflecting consistent ESG criteria and assessment approaches across rating agencies.

This comparison highlights the degree of convergence and divergence in ESG ratings across different sectors, emphasizing the varying methodologies and criteria used by different rating agencies. Understanding the alignment and divergence in ESG ratings across different sectors provides valuable insights into the methodologies and criteria used by various rating agencies. This sector-specific analysis highlights how differences in approach can lead to varying assessments of the same companies.

4.2 Sector-Wise Correlation Analysis of ESG Ratings

The following table presents the correlation analysis of ESG ratings between Sustainalytics, Refinitiv, and MSCI.

Table 2. Sector-Wise Correlation Analysis of ESG Ratings (Pearson correlation)

	CD	CS	EN	FN	HC	IN	IT	MT	RE	UT
	S	R	M	S	R	S	R	M	S	R
S	1.00	0.40	0.34	1.00	0.61	1.00	0.62	0.45	1.00	0.37
R	0.40	1.00	0.75	0.61	1.00	0.62	1.00	0.54	0.37	1.00
M	0.34	0.75	1.00	0.74	0.76	0.45	0.54	1.00	0.51	0.42

Source: The authors

Note: This table shows Pearson correlation coefficients for ESG ratings from Sustainalytics (S), Refinitiv (R), and MSCI (M) across sectors, illustrating alignment or divergence in ratings.

The correlation table reveals varying degrees of alignment in ESG ratings across different sectors, with high correlation observed in Utilities, Consumer Staples, and Energy; moderate correlation in Financials, Health Care, and Industrials; and low correlation in Information Technology, Materials, and Real Estate.

High Correlation:

- **Utilities**: Sectors such as utilities exhibit high correlations in ESG ratings across different agencies, suggesting a robust consensus on ESG evaluation criteria within these sectors. Utilities operate within highly regulated environments where ESG factors like carbon emissions, energy efficiency, and water usage are rigorously monitored and reported. The regulatory frameworks provide a standardized set of criteria that agencies use to evaluate companies, resulting in consistent ESG assessments.

- **Consumer Staples**: In the consumer staples sector, uniform supply chain issues and well-established reporting standards contribute to high correlation. Companies in this sector, including those producing food, beverages, and household products, face similar ESG challenges related to supply chain management, sourcing practices, and product safety. This homogeneity in operational concerns leads to consistent evaluation metrics across rating agencies.

- **Energy**: The energy sector shows high correlation due to focused environmental risks and enhanced transparency. The primary concerns involve managing carbon emissions, pollution control, and resource extraction, which are well-defined and universally acknowledged risks. These consistent operational impacts allow agencies to apply standardized metrics in their assessments.

Moderate Correlation:

- **Financials**: In the financials sector, varied ESG factors and different business models contribute to moderate correlation. ESG assessments cover diverse factors such as investment policies, governance practices, and customer relations, leading to differences in focus and weight across agencies. The financial sector includes banks, insurance companies, and investment firms, each with distinct ESG risks and opportunities, necessitating different evaluation approaches.
- **Health Care**: The health care sector shows moderate correlation due to diverse operational risks and evolving standards. Health care companies face a range of ESG issues, from clinical trials and product safety to patient privacy and employee welfare. The diversity of these issues can lead to variability in how agencies assess and weigh different factors.
- **Industrials**: The industrials sector's complex supply chains and varied ESG impact lead to moderate correlation. This sector encompasses a wide array of manufacturing and production processes, each with distinct ESG challenges related to environmental impact, resource use, and safety practices. Companies in the industrials sector can range from heavy manufacturing to aerospace, each with unique ESG risks.

Low Correlation:

- **Information Technology**: The information technology sector exhibits low correlation due to rapid innovation and diverse business models. The sector is characterized by rapid technological advancements and innovation, leading to varying interpretations of ESG risks and opportunities. Agencies might weigh factors like data privacy, cybersecurity, and innovation differently.
- **Materials**: The materials sector shows low correlation due to complex environmental impacts and varied reporting practices. This sector involves industries such as mining, chemicals, and construction materials, each with complex environmental impacts. Agencies may have differing approaches to evaluating issues like resource extraction, waste management, and pollution control.
- **Real Estate**: The real estate sector's unique ESG challenges and inconsistent criteria result in low correlation. Real estate companies face unique ESG challenges related to property management, energy efficiency of buildings, and urban development. The specific nature of these challenges can lead to diverse evaluations by rating agencies.

The influence of sector on ESG rating correlation is evident. Sectors with more standardized and well-defined ESG criteria, such as utilities, consumer staples, and energy, exhibit higher correlations in ratings. In contrast, sectors with diverse business models and unique ESG challenges, such as information technology, materials, and real estate, show lower correlations, reflecting significant variability in ESG assessments. Understanding these sectoral influences is crucial for investors and stakeholders as they navigate the complexities of ESG ratings and make informed decisions based on these assessments.

4.3 Sector-Wise Correlation Analysis of ESG Dimension Ratings

The sector-wise correlation analysis of ESG dimension ratings is important for understanding the consistency of ESG assessments across different sectors. This analysis helps identify how closely aligned the ratings from Sustainalytics, Refinitiv, and MSCI are, providing insights into their reliability for investors and stakeholders. The Pearson correlation coefficient is used because it measures the linear relationship between two variables, offering a clear indication of rating alignment.

The following table presents the correlation analysis of ESG dimension ratings between Sustainalytics, Refinitiv, and MSCI. The analysis includes a total of 900 observations.

Table 3. Sector-Wise Correlation Analysis of ESG Dimension Ratings (Pearson correlation)

Sector	E	S	G
Consumer Discretionary	0.53	0.16	-0.05
Consumer Staples	0.50	0.27	0.32
Energy	0.61	0.49	0.21
Financials	0.89	0.81	0.63
Health Care	0.14	0.58	0.71
Industrials	0.13	0.47	0.57
Information Technology	0.28	0.51	0.62
Materials	0.21	0.53	0.67
Real Estate	0.34	0.39	0.52
Utilities	0.28	0.19	0.33

Source: The authors

Note: This table shows Pearson correlation coefficients for Environmental (E), Social (S), and Governance (G) ratings across sectors, highlighting alignment between rating agencies.

The analysis of ESG dimension correlations highlights how each specific dimension contributes to the overall ESG rating consistency across different sectors. This understanding is crucial because ESG ratings aggregate these dimensions, and discrepancies in individual dimensions can lead to variability in the composite ESG scores.

Environmental (E) Dimension Correlation: The environmental dimension shows moderate to high correlation in sectors such as Energy (0.61), Financials (0.89), and Consumer Staples (0.50). This suggests that environmental factors are evaluated relatively consistently across agencies within these sectors. In sectors like Energy, where environmental impact is a critical concern, the high correlation of environmental scores (0.61) aligns with the strong overall rating correlation, indicating that consistent environmental evaluation drives ESG rating agreement.

In contrast, lower environmental correlations in sectors such as Industrials (0.13) and Information Technology (0.28) reflect more significant divergence in how environmental impacts are assessed, contributing to lower overall ESG rating correlations. This divergence in the environmental dimension likely causes the lower alignment seen in the ESG ratings for these sectors, as varying methodologies and focus areas among agencies lead to discrepancies in environmental assessments.

Social (S) Dimension Correlation: The social dimension exhibits moderate correlation across sectors, with notable alignment in Financials (0.81), Health Care (0.58), and Materials (0.53). The moderate to high social correlation suggests that social factors such as labor practices, community engagement, and customer relations are assessed with some consistency in these sectors. For instance, in the Financials sector, high correlations in social scores (0.81) align with the moderate overall rating alignment, reflecting consistent evaluation of social criteria.

Lower social correlations in sectors like Consumer Discretionary (0.16) and Utilities (0.19) reflect greater divergence in how social issues are evaluated, which may contribute to the moderate or lower overall ESG rating correlations observed. The variability in social dimension assessments could be due to different approaches in evaluating social impacts, such as community relations or labor practices, leading to discrepancies in the composite ESG ratings.

Governance (G) Dimension Correlation: The governance dimension generally shows moderate to high correlation, particularly in Health Care (0.71), Information Technology (0.62), and Materials (0.67). This high correlation in governance suggests that factors such as board effectiveness, executive compensation, and ethical practices are evaluated with greater consistency across agencies. For example, high governance correlations in Health Care (0.71) indicate that agencies agree more on governance criteria, contributing to overall rating consistency.

Lower governance correlations in sectors such as Consumer Discretionary (-0.05) indicate significant divergence in governance evaluations, contributing to lower overall ESG rating consistency. This divergence can be attributed to differences in how governance practices are prioritized and assessed by different agencies, leading to variability in the composite ESG scores for these sectors.

The correlation analysis of individual ESG dimensions helps explain the overall alignment or divergence in ESG ratings across sectors. High correlations in the environmental, social, and governance dimensions generally align with high overall ESG rating correlations, indicating that consistent evaluations of these dimensions contribute to greater agreement in ESG ratings. Conversely, lower correlations in individual dimensions reflect greater divergence in ESG assessments, leading to variability in the composite ESG ratings across agencies.

Sectors with well-defined and consistently evaluated ESG criteria, such as Energy and Financials, exhibit higher overall ESG rating correlations, driven by strong alignment in environmental and social assessments. In contrast, sectors with more complex or diverse ESG challenges, such as Consumer Discretionary and Industrials, show lower correlations in specific dimensions, contributing to greater divergence in overall ESG ratings. Understanding these correlations provides valuable insights for investors and stakeholders, highlighting the importance of considering sector-specific ESG dimensions and methodologies when evaluating and comparing ESG ratings.

5. INSIGHTS AND IMPLICATIONS

The results of the analysis reveal notable patterns and variations in ESG ratings across different sectors and rating agencies. Understanding these outcomes requires a closer examination of the underlying factors that contribute to these divergences. This section delves into the causes of the observed differences in ESG ratings, focusing on three key areas: methodological differences, variations in scoring models, and the influence of subjective judgments and data quality.

5.1 Methodological Differences

Methodological differences are a primary driver of ESG rating divergence. Agencies employ diverse frameworks and prioritize different indicators based on their proprietary methodologies. For instance, some agencies may emphasize environmental metrics like carbon emissions and energy efficiency, while others may focus more on social metrics such as labor practices and community engagement (Kotsantonis et al, 2019; Berg et al., 2020). This variation in focus leads to discrepancies in overall ESG scores, as each agency uses unique criteria to evaluate company performance.

The weighting systems used by rating agencies also contribute to divergent ESG scores. Different agencies assign varying weights to ESG factors, reflecting their perspectives on the relative importance of each aspect (Escrig-Olmedo et al., 2021). For example, Sustainalytics may place a higher weight on environmental factors, whereas MSCI might emphasize governance aspects more strongly (Busch et al., 2016). These weighting differences can significantly affect the final ratings assigned to companies.

5.2 Differences in Scoring Models

Scoring models employed by ESG rating agencies differ in several key aspects, including normalization techniques and aggregation methods. Agencies use various normalization techniques to standardise raw data, which can affect the comparability of ESG scores (Chatterji et al., 2016). Additionally, the methods for aggregating individual indicators into a composite score vary, leading to different overall ratings (Christensen et al., 2022). These methodological variations highlight the subjective nature of ESG rating assessments and the potential for divergence in final scores.

5.3 Subjective Judgments and Data Quality

Human judgment plays a significant role in ESG rating processes, particularly in assessing qualitative aspects of company performance. Differences in analyst opinions, biases, and interpretations contribute to rating divergence (Hartzmark & Sussman, 2019). The subjective nature of evaluating ESG factors means that ratings can vary based on the perspectives of the individuals conducting the assessments.

The quality and extent of company disclosures also impact ESG ratings. Inconsistent reporting standards and voluntary disclosures lead to gaps and variances in the data used for ratings (Marquis, et al., 2016). Incomplete or unaudited data can result in poor-quality inputs, which ultimately affect the accuracy of ESG ratings. As Pucker (2021) aptly describes, "Garbage in, garbage out," underscoring the importance of high-quality, comparable data for reliable ESG assessments.

5.4 Implications

The findings of this study have several important implications for the field of ESG rating and investment practices. The observed divergence in ESG ratings underscores the complexities and challenges associated with evaluating corporate sustainability and ethical performance. The lack of standardization and transparency in ESG rating methodologies can lead to confusion and misalignment in investment decisions, highlighting the need for more uniform and transparent rating practices.

One significant implication is that investors must exercise caution when relying on ESG ratings for making investment decisions. The variability in ratings across different agencies means that a comprehensive due diligence process is essential to ensure that investments align with ethical and sustainability goals. Investors should consider cross-referencing ratings from multiple agencies and seek additional qualitative insights to make informed decisions.

For companies, the findings suggest that greater consistency in ESG disclosures and reporting is crucial for improving their ESG ratings across different agencies. Companies should strive to align their reporting practices with recognized frameworks such as GRI and SASB to provide more consistent and comparable ESG data. Additionally, engaging with rating agencies to understand their evaluation criteria can help companies improve their ESG performance and ratings.

Regulators and policymakers also have a role to play in addressing the divergence in ESG ratings. By establishing clear guidelines and standards for ESG reporting, regulators can enhance the quality and comparability of ESG data. This can facilitate more effective oversight and enforcement of sustainability practices, contributing to more reliable and consistent ESG assessments.

6. CONCLUSION

This study provides an analysis of the divergence in ESG ratings from MSCI, Sustainalytics, and Refinitiv, revealing how variations in methodologies, data sources, and criteria contribute to significant inconsistencies across these ratings. Particularly notable were the discrepancies in ratings for sectors like Information Technology and Real Estate, which highlight the substantial methodological differences among these agencies. The findings underscore a critical need for harmonization and greater transparency in ESG rating practices to enhance their reliability and utility for investors and other stakeholders.

The analysis of ESG ratings demonstrates considerable variability, with significant implications for stakeholders who rely on these ratings for investment decisions. While Environmental (E) ratings tend to show higher alignment across agencies compared to Social (S) and Governance (G) ratings, the divergence in ESG scores points to a lack of standardization in assessing social and governance factors. This variability can undermine the credibility and comparability of ESG ratings, complicating efforts to integrate ESG considerations into investment strategies and corporate governance practices (Berg et al., 2022).

6.1 Recommendations

To address the inconsistencies in ESG ratings, there is a pressing need for the standardization of ESG reporting frameworks. The adoption of established frameworks such as the Global Reporting Initiative (GRI) and the Sustainability Accounting Standards Board (SASB) should be promoted to provide uniform guidelines for ESG disclosures. Standardized reporting can reduce data variability and enhance the comparability of ESG ratings across different agencies (Eccles et al., 2014).

Regulatory bodies should consider mandating standardized ESG reporting to ensure consistency in the data provided by companies. Such regulations could include specific requirements for the scope, format, and frequency of ESG disclosures, thereby improving the quality and reliability of the information used for ESG assessments (Christensen et al., 2022). Effective regulation can enhance the credibility of ESG data, making it more comparable and useful for investors and other stakeholders.

Greater transparency from ESG rating agencies regarding their methodologies, criteria, and data sources is crucial for improving the comparability and credibility of ESG ratings. Agencies should disclose the specific criteria used in their evaluations, the weighting of different ESG factors, and the sources of their data. Greater clarity on the assumptions and subjective judgments influencing ratings would enable users to better understand the basis of the ratings and make more informed decisions (Gibson et al., 2021).

Integrating advanced technologies such as artificial intelligence (AI) and big data analytics can significantly enhance the accuracy and consistency of ESG assessments. These technologies can process large datasets more efficiently, identify patterns in ESG performance, and improve the objectivity of evaluations. AI-driven analysis can help mitigate human biases and provide more robust and dynamic ESG ratings. Advanced technologies can also facilitate the continuous monitoring and updating of ESG data, ensuring that ratings reflect current and accurate information (Visalli et al., 2023; Tse et al., 2024).

Collaboration among rating agencies, companies, investors, and regulators is vital for developing shared standards and best practices in ESG rating. Stakeholders should engage in dialogue and cooperation to harmonize ESG assessment approaches, reduce rating discrepancies, and promote greater consistency in ESG evaluations. Joint initiatives, such as the creation of industry working groups or regulatory task forces, can facilitate the development of aligned and reliable ESG assessment frameworks (Dimson et al., 2015). Such collaborative efforts can also support the dissemination of best practices and innovative approaches to ESG evaluation.

ESG rating agencies should commit to regular updates and reviews of their methodologies to reflect evolving best practices and emerging risks. This will ensure that ESG ratings remain relevant and aligned with current standards and expectations. Continuous improvement and adaptation of rating methodologies will help address the dynamic nature of ESG issues and maintain the credibility of ESG ratings (Orlitzky et al., 2003). Agencies should also be responsive to stakeholder feedback and emerging trends in sustainability to ensure that their ratings remain comprehensive and accurate.

Given the observed sectoral differences in ESG ratings, developing sector-specific guidelines for ESG assessments can help address the unique challenges and opportunities within each industry. These guidelines should be tailored to the specific ESG risks and performance metrics relevant to different sectors, thereby improving the accuracy and relevance of ESG ratings for sector-specific analyses (Kotsantonis et al., 2016). Sector-specific guidelines can also provide a more nuanced understanding of ESG performance, accounting for industry-specific factors and challenges.

Investors and companies should be provided with education and capacity-building resources to better understand ESG ratings and integrate them into decision-making processes. Training programs, workshops, and educational materials can help stakeholders navigate the complexities of ESG assessments and make more informed choices based on ESG performance (Eccles & Stroehle, 2018). Such initiatives can also promote greater engagement with ESG issues and support the development of more effective sustainability strategies.

6.2 Limitations

The limitations of this study include the reliance on publicly available data and the focus on a specific set of companies. The findings may not be generalizable to all sectors or regions, and further research is needed to explore the divergence in ESG ratings in different contexts. Additionally, the study's analysis is based on the methodologies of three major rating agencies, and incorporating insights from additional agencies could provide a more comprehensive understanding of ESG rating divergence.

Future research should explore the impact of regulatory changes on ESG rating practices and investigate the potential benefits of integrating advanced technologies such as AI and machine learning in ESG assessments. By addressing these areas, researchers can contribute to the development of more accurate, consistent, and reliable ESG rating systems, ultimately supporting better-informed investment decisions and more effective corporate sustainability practices.

REFERENCES

Amel-Zadeh, A., & Serafeim, G. (2018). Why and how investors use ESG information: Evidence from a global survey. *Financial Analysts Journal*, 74(3), 87–103. 10.2469/faj.v74.n3.2

Ammann, M., Oesch, D., & Schmid, M. M. (2011). Corporate governance and firm value: International evidence. *Journal of Empirical Finance*, 18(1), 36–55. 10.1016/j.jempfin.2010.10.003

Bebchuk, L. A. (2005). The case for increasing shareholder power. *Harvard Law Review*, 118(3), 833–914. https://ssrn.com/abstract=387940

Bebchuk, L. A., Cohen, A., & Ferrell, A. (2009). What matters in corporate governance? *Review of Financial Studies*, 22(2), 783–827. 10.1093/rfs/hhn099

Berg, F., Kölbel, J., & Rigobon, R. (2022). Aggregate confusion: The divergence of ESG ratings. *Review of Finance*, 26(6), 1315–1344. 10.1093/rof/rfac033

Bloomberg Intelligence. (2022). ESG assets may hit $53 trillion by 2025, a third of global AUM. Retrieved from https://www.bloomberg.com/professional/blog/esg-assets-may-hit-53-trillion-by-2025-a-third-of-global-aum/

Busch, T., Bauer, R., & Orlitzky, M. (2016). Sustainable development and financial markets: Old paths and new avenues. *Business & Society*, 55(3), 303–329. 10.1177/0007650315570701

Chatterji, A. K., Durand, R., Levine, D. I., & Touboul, S. (2016). Do ratings of firms converge? Implications for managers, investors, and strategy researchers. *Strategic Management Journal*, 37(8), 1597–1614. 10.1002/smj.2407

Christensen, D. M., Hail, L., & Leuz, C. (2019). Economic analysis of widespread adoption of CSR and sustainability reporting standards. *SSRN*, 57(4), 931–972. 10.2139/ssrn.3315673

Christensen, H. B., Serafeim, G., & Sikochi, A. (2022). Why is corporate virtue in the eye of the beholder? The case of ESG ratings. *The Accounting Review*, 97(1), 147–175. 10.2308/TAR-2019-0506

Clark, G. L., Feiner, A., & Viehs, M. (2015). From the stockholder to the stakeholder: How sustainability can drive financial outperformance. *University of Oxford and Arabesque Partners*. 10.2139/ssrn.2508281

Dimson, E., Karakaş, O., & Li, X. (2015). Active ownership. *Review of Financial Studies*, 28(12), 3225–3268. 10.1093/rfs/hhv044

Dimson, E., Karakaş, O., & Li, X. (2023). Coordinated engagements. *European Corporate Governance Institute–Finance Working Paper, 721*. 10.2139/ssrn.3209072

Eccles, R. G., Ioannou, I., & Serafeim, G. (2014). The impact of corporate sustainability on organizational processes and performance. *Management Science*, 60(11), 2835–2857. 10.1287/mnsc.2014.1984

Eccles, R. G., & Klimenko, S. (2019). The investor revolution. *Harvard Business Review*, 97(3), 106–116. https://hbr.org/2019/05/the-investor-revolution

Eccles, R. G., & Stroehle, J. C. (2018). Exploring social origins in the construction of ESG measures. *Available at SSRN* 3212685. 10.2139/ssrn.3212685

Escrig-Olmedo, E., Fernández-Izquierdo, M. Á., Ferrero-Ferrero, I., Rivera-Lirio, J. M., & Muñoz-Torres, M. J. (2019). Rating the raters: Evaluating how ESG rating agencies integrate sustainability principles. *Sustainability (Basel)*, 11(3), 915. 10.3390/su11030915

European Commission. (2020). *Taxonomy: Final report of the technical expert group on sustainable finance*. Retrieved from https://ec.europa.eu/info/sites/info/files/business_economy_euro/banking_and_finance/documents/200309-sustainable-finance-teg-final-report-taxonomy_en.pdf

EY Global Insights Team. (2022, July 14). Five priorities to build trust in ESG. EY. https://www.ey.com/en_gl/insights/public-policy/five-priorities-to-build-trust-in-esg

Fatemi, A., Glaum, M., & Kaiser, S. (2018). ESG performance and firm value: The moderating role of disclosure. *Global Finance Journal*, 38, 45–64. 10.1016/j.gfj.2017.03.001

Friede, G., Busch, T., & Bassen, A. (2015). ESG and financial performance: Aggregated evidence from more than 2000 empirical studies. *Journal of Sustainable Finance & Investment*, 5(4), 210–233. 10.1080/20430795.2015.1118917

Gibson, R., Krueger, P., & Schmidt, P. S. (2021). ESG rating disagreement and stock returns. *Financial Analysts Journal*, 77(4), 104–127. 10.1080/0015198X.2021.1963186

Giese, G., Lee, L. E., Melas, D., Nagy, Z., & Nishikawa, L. (2019). Foundations of ESG investing: How ESG affects equity valuation, risk, and performance. *Journal of Portfolio Management*, 45(5), 69–83. 10.3905/jpm.2019.45.5.069

Gillan, S. L., Koch, A., & Starks, L. T. (2021). Firms and social responsibility: A review of ESG and CSR research in corporate finance. *Journal of Corporate Finance*, 66, 101889. 10.1016/j.jcorpfin.2021.101889

Global Reporting Initiative (GRI). (2020). *GRI standards: Consolidated set of GRI standards 2020*. Retrieved from https://www.globalreporting.org/standards/gri-standards-download-center/consolidated-set-of-gri-standards-2020/

Grissom, A. R. (2018). Workplace diversity and inclusion. *Reference and User Services Quarterly*, 57(4), 242–247. https://www.jstor.org/stable/90022643. 10.5860/rusq.57.4.6700

Hartzmark, S. M., & Sussman, A. B. (2019). Do investors value sustainability? A natural experiment examining ranking and fund flows. *The Journal of Finance*, 74(6), 2789–2837. 10.1111/jofi.12841

Hawley, J. P., & Williams, A. T. (2000). *The rise of fiduciary capitalism: How institutional investors can make corporate America more democratic*. University of Pennsylvania Press.

Hawn, O., Chatterji, A. K., & Mitchell, L. (2018). Do investors actually value sustainability? New evidence from investor reactions to the Dow Jones sustainability index (DJSI). *Strategic Management Journal*, 39(4), 949–976. 10.1002/smj.2752

Hummel, K., & Schlick, C. (2016). The relationship between sustainability performance and sustainability disclosure–Reconciling voluntary disclosure theory and legitimacy theory. *Journal of Accounting and Public Policy*, 35(5), 455–476. 10.1016/j.jaccpubpol.2016.06.001

ILO. (2021). *ILO global estimates on international migrant workers: Results and methodology*. International Labour Organization. Retrieved from https://www.ilo.org/international-labour-standards

ISO. (2021). *ISO 26000: Guidance on social responsibility*. Retrieved from https://www.iso.org/standard/42546.html

Kotsantonis, S., Pinney, C., & Serafeim, G. (2016). ESG integration in investment management: Myths and realities. *The Bank of America Journal of Applied Corporate Finance*, 28(2), 10–16. http://highmeadowsinstitute.org/wp-content/uploads/2014/05/JACF-ESG-Integration-Myths-and-Realities.pdf. 10.1111/jacf.12169

LSEG (2024). https://www.lseg.com/content/dam/marketing/en_us/documents/methodology/refinitiv-esg-scores-methodology.pdf

Macpherson, M., Gasperini, A., & Bosco, M. (2021). Implications for artificial intelligence and ESG data. 10.2139/ssrn.3863599

Marquis, C., Toffel, M. W., & Zhou, Y. (2016). Scrutiny, norms, and selective disclosure: A global study of greenwashing. *Organization Science*, 27(2), 483–504. 10.1287/orsc.2015.1039

Matten, D., & Moon, J. (2008). "Implicit" and "explicit" CSR: A conceptual framework for a comparative understanding of corporate social responsibility. *Academy of Management Review*, 33(2), 404–424. 10.5465/amr.2008.31193458

MSCI (2024) https://www.msci.com/documents/1296102/34424357/MSCI+ESG+Ratings+Methodology+-+Process.pdf/820e4152-4804-fe33-0a67-8ee4c6a8fd7d?t=1666300410683

Nofsinger, J., & Varma, A. (2014). Socially responsible funds and market crises. *Journal of Banking & Finance*, 48, 180–193. 10.1016/j.jbankfin.2013.12.016

OECD. (2015). *G20/OECD principles of corporate governance*. OECD Publishing., 10.1787/9789264236882-

Orlitzky, M., Schmidt, F. L., & Rynes, S. L. (2003). Corporate social and financial performance: A meta-analysis. *Organization Studies*, 24(3), 403–441. 10.1177/0170840603024003910

Petersen, A., Herbert, S., & Daniels, N. (2022). The likely adoption of the IFRS Foundation's proposed sustainability reporting standards. *The Business and Management Review*, 13(2). Advance online publication. 10.24052/BMR/V13NU02/ART-03

Porter, M. E., & Kramer, M. R. (2011). Creating shared value. *Harvard Business Review*, 89(1/2), 62–77. https://hbr.org/2011/01/the-big-idea-creating-shared-value

Pucker, K. P. (2021). Overselling sustainability reporting. *Harvard Business Review*, 99(3), 90–99. https://hbr.org/2021/05/overselling-sustainability-reporting

PwC Global. (2022, December 6). The CEO's ESG dilemma. PwC. https://www.pwc.com/gx/en/issues/esg/ceo-esg-dilemma.html

Rands, M. R., Adams, W. M., Bennun, L., Butchart, S. H., Clements, A., Coomes, D., Entwistle, A., Hodge, I., Kapos, V., Scharlemann, J. P. W., Sutherland, W. J., & Vira, B. (2010). Biodiversity conservation: Challenges beyond 2010. *Science*, 329(5997), 1298–1303. 10.1126/science.118913820829476

Schoenmaker, D., & Schramade, W. (2018). *Principles of sustainable finance*. Oxford University Press., https://www.researchgate.net/profile/Dirk-Schoenmaker/publication/330359025_Principles_of_Sustainable_Finance/links/5c3c3d1992851c22a3736593/Principles-of-Sustainable-Finance.pdf

Sustainalytics (2024). https://www.sustainalytics.com/material-esg-issues-resource -center

Transparency International. (2020). *Corruption perceptions index 2020*. Retrieved from https://www.transparency.org/en/cpi/2020/index/nzl

Tse, , TEsposito, , MGoh, , D. (2024). The impact of artificial intelligence on environmental, social and governance investing: the case of Nexus FrontierTech. *International Journal of Teaching and Case Studies*, *14*(3), 256-275. https://doi.org/ 10.1504/IJTCS.2024.137516

UN. (2011). *Guiding principles on business and human rights: Implementing the United Nations "Protect, Respect and Remedy" framework*. United Nations Human Rights Office of the High Commissioner. Retrieved from https://www.ohchr.org/ documents/publications/guidingprinciplesbusinesshr_en.pdf

United Nations Environment Programme. International Resource Panel, United Nations Environment Programme. Sustainable Consumption, & Production Branch. (2011). *Decoupling natural resource use and environmental impacts from economic growth*. UNEP/Earthprint. Retrieved from https://www.unep.org/resources/report/ decoupling-natural-resource-use-and-environmental-impacts-economic-growth

Visalli, F., Patrizio, A., Lanza, A., Papaleo, P., Nautiyal, A., Pupo, M., Scilinguo, U., Oro, E., & Ruffolo, M. (2023). ESG data collection with adaptive AI. In *Proceedings of the 25th International Conference on Enterprise Information Systems - Volume 1: ICEIS* (pp. 468-475). SciTePress. https://doi.org/10.5220/0011844500003467

KEY TERMS AND DEFINITIONS

Correlation Analysis: A statistical method to measure the relationship between two variables, used to assess agreement or divergence in ESG ratings from different agencies.

Data Normalization: Adjusting values to a common scale for comparing ESG data across different rating systems.

Environmental, Social, and Governance (ESG): Factors evaluating the sustainability and ethical impact of investments, including environmental stewardship, social responsibility, and corporate governance.

ESG Ratings: Assessments of a company's ESG performance, provided by agencies, varying in format from letter grades to numerical scores.

Methodological Differences: Variations in frameworks, criteria, and evaluation processes used by ESG rating agencies.

Scoring Models: Techniques and algorithms used by ESG rating agencies to convert raw data into final ratings, including normalization, aggregation, and weighting of ESG factors.

Sectoral Analysis: Examining ESG rating data by industry sectors to identify trends and patterns.

Chapter 5
The Relationship Between ESG Disclosure, Information Asymmetry, Cost of Capital, and Earnings Management

P. Fahad

RUA College, India & Farook College, India

Mubarak Rahman P.

LEAD College of Management, India

Showkat Ahmad Busru

NMIMS, Hyderabad, India

Mohammed Shafeeque K.

https://orcid.org/0009-0009-6151-3698

Farook College, India & University of Calicut, India

ABSTRACT

The study investigates the relationship between ESG disclosure, information asymmetry, cost of capital and earnings management in an emerging economy, India. The study uses PLS-SEM for a sample of 183 companies listed in BSE 500 index for a period of ten years from 2014 to 2023. The study finds that higher ESG disclosure leads to decrease in information asymmetry. While ESG disclosure increases the firm's cost of capital. The result also shows that firms with higher ESG disclosure have more social commitment and less chance for doing earnings management. An

DOI: 10.4018/979-8-3693-3880-3.ch005

increase in information asymmetry increases the chance for managers to manipulate earnings. Similarly, higher information asymmetry leads to increase investor risk which results in increased cost of capital. Finally, earnings management practice reduces the firm cost of capital.

1 INTRODUCTION

Environmental, Social and Governance (ESG) disclosure has garnered significant attention, fueled by increasing interest from investors, academicians, and researchers alike. The terms ESG disclosure is frequently interchanged with sustainability and CSR disclosures, this study exclusively employs the term ESG disclosure throughout its content. ESG disclosure furnishes the public with detailed insight into a company's performance in areas related with environmental impact, social responsibility, and corporate governance practices, thereby mitigating information asymmetry among certain stockholders. The consequential reduction in information asymmetry plays a pivotal role in shaping the cost of capital and deterring earning manipulation. From the earlier studies, the researcher has found that ESG disclosure, information asymmetry, cost of capital and earnings management are associated with each other. Information asymmetry causes adverse selection problems, lack of investor confidence, reduces market liquidity and increases firms required rate of return (Easely and O'Hara, 2004). Information asymmetry problem arises when some investor has information advantage about firms' operation than other investors. This can be solved by providing information voluntarily, so that information asymmetry could be reduced (Hung et al. 2015). Thus, the level of information asymmetry reduced as a result of ESG disclosure is important in determining its effect on cost of capital and earnings management (Hung et al. 2015). In short information asymmetry acts as a mediator in this interrelationship (Cuadrado et al., 2016). ESG disclosure reduces both information asymmetry and cost of capital (Michaels and Gruning, 2010; Mazumdar and Sengupta, 2005; Khanchel & Lassoued, 2022)

Companies with ESG disclosure are expected to act responsibly by providing quality and consistent financial data and show its obligation towards responsible business practices (Jones, 1995; Kim et al., 2012; Chouaibi & Affes, 2021). ESG disclosure is often used as a mask by managers to cover their unfair business practices through earning management (Choi et al., 2013). Existing studies also show mixed results regarding the ESG disclosure and earnings management relationship (Prior et al., 2008; Choi et al., 2013; Muttakin et al., 2015; Alsaadi et al., 2017; Gaio et al., 2022). One line of research indicates that firm with higher ESG disclosure provides better financial disclosures and reduces the chance for any sort of accounting manipulation (Alsaadi et al., 2007; Choi et al., 2013; Rezaee & Tuo, 2019).

Whereas another line of research noticed that some manager's uses ESG disclosure for their personal benefit, promoting ESG activities may help managers to secure their job by avoiding any stakeholder pressure (Prior et al., 2008; Muttakin et al., 2015; Raghunandan & Rajgopal, 2022). Similarly, earnings management is high in socially responsible firms (Chih et al., 2008; Hoang et al., 2022). Trueman and Titman (1998) stated that earnings management increases along with increase in information asymmetry. Because information asymmetry creates uncertainty among investors regarding firms' future operation and increases the chance for earnings management (Bhattacharrya et al. 2012). Whereas Strobl et al. (2008) opined that earnings management reduces the risk premium investor demands and influences firms' cost of capital. It has been argued that earnings management improves the cost of capital because earnings management creates a bad image among investors and reduces the investor's expectation about future cash flow level (Kim et al., 2013).

Previous studies investigated the association between ESG disclosure, information asymmetry, cost of capital and earnings management, separately, by employing different methodologies, samples, and proxy variables. These studies are mostly based on developed economies and the results are contradictory. While the present study aims to examine the relationship between ESG disclosure, information asymmetry, cost of capital and earnings management in an emerging economy, India.

2 REVIEW OF LITERATURE AND HYPOTHESIS DEVELOPMENT

2.1 ESG Disclosure and Information Asymmetry

Agency theory states that information asymmetry arises when one investor has an information advantage over other investors regarding firms operations (Jensen and Meckling, 1976). According to Akerlof (1970), higher information asymmetry creates difficulty for investors to exchange the assets and securities at the best price with lower transaction cost by creating an inefficient market condition, which reduces market liquidity (Leuz and Verrecchia, 1999) and increases the cost of capital (Brennan and Subrahmanyam, 1996). Transactions with more informed participants make the investor demand higher returns and end up in discounting future expected payoffs at a increased rate (Easley and O'hara, 2004). In this scenario, it is essential to identify various elements that can reduce information asymmetry. Diamond and Verracchia (1991) considers less disclosure as an important factor which increases information asymmetry by motivating investors to gain information privately. Transparency reduces such asymmetry between participants, with more amount of disclosure firm can overcome the asymmetric situation and ensure an ideal market situation for investors (Healy and Palepu, 2001). Information disclosure provides equality between stakeholders and reduces the risk arising out of speculative positions (Diamond, 1985). This is supported by Akerlof (1970), who opined that transparent disclosure of information reduces information asymmetry among investors because disclosure offers information about firm valuation, and it affects market price during Efficient Market Hypothesis (EMH).

Financial disclosure concentrates about the financial and economic position of firm but there are more an investor wanted to know in the light of recent trend on socially responsible investment including environmental, social and governance activities (Jensen and Berg, 2012), which motivate companies to make further disclosure of information to gain competitive advantage. In short, from the literature it is evident that firms provide information to reduce information asymmetry, whether it is financial or nonfinancial and mandatory or voluntary (Grossman and Hart, 1980; Veracchia, 1983).

The present study is focusing on ESG disclosure which is in limelight at present scenario because of underlying importance for socially responsible investment and CSR guideline as per Companies Act 2013. As a result, investors are also considering ESG activities while making investment decisions (Cohen et al., 2011; Park & Jang, 2021). ESG reports cover a wide variety of social, environmental, governance activities and also companies' relationship with suppliers, customers, workforce, social contribution, public safety and so on (Camilleri, 2015; Lofort and Gonzalez, 2008). Even though ESG activities are not directly associated to balance sheet, it helps the investor to make investment decision, capital raising and increases value of firm (Cho et al., 2013; Cheng et al., 2014). Recent studies find that ESG disclosure and information asymmetry are negatively related, which means that more ESG disclosure decreases information asymmetry and enhance the availability of information environment (Cho et al., 2013; Hung et al., 2015; Lu and Chueh, 2015; Siew et al., 2016; Michaels and Gruning, 2017; Hamrouni et al., 2021). Whereas Martinez-Ferroro et al. (2016) find voluntary disclosure and information asymmetry have two-way (bidirectional) associations between them. Cui et al., (2018) identified reduction in the information asymmetry issue of less informed investors to justify the negative association. (Siew et al., 2016; Martinez-Ferroro et al., 2016) found that insider trading by institutional investors, informed investors and family owners may reduce the benefit of ESG disclosure attained through reduction of information asymmetry. Cormier and Ledoux (2011) find environmental disclosure replace social disclosure and vice versa in reducing the information asymmetry among market players and managers. Elbadry et al. (2015) identified that information asymmetry weakens governance mechanism. Siew et al. (2016) finds out information asymmetry negatively influences ESG disclosures. The following hypothesis is developed after considering above studies:

H1: ESG disclosure negatively related with information asymmetry.

2.2 ESG Disclosure and Cost of Capital

The association between ESG disclosure and cost of capital has become a major theme in ESG research over the past. According to Agency Cost Theory and Positive Accounting Theories of the firm, the firm consists of contracts and contacts with a number of stakeholders. ESG disclosure would reduce conflicts among stakeholders, lowers business risk and reduce cost of capital (Core, 2001). ESG disclosure decreases non-diversifiable risk, and it leads to reduce the cost of capital in different ways. First, ESG disclosure weakens information asymmetry among stakeholders. It motivates investors to trade more, and it results in increased volume (Verrecchia, 2001; Amihud and Mendelson, 1986). Efficient market hypothesis assumptions are not always matching with real world situation, difference exists among investors regarding time and accuracy of the information and it increases risk as well as the cost of capital (Noe and Rebello, 1996). It has been argued that firms disclose more ESG activities to build a positive image in the minds of stakeholders as a responsible corporate citizen, which helps to reduce information asymmetry (Dhaliwal et al., 2011; Cho et al., 2012; Lee et al., 2022) and it increases transparency, liquidity and reduces risk, which leads to reduce the cost of capital (Coles et al., 1995; Chen et al., 2011; Khanchel and Lassoued, 2022). Second, ESG disclosure weakens the possible risk and uncertainty for investors. Cost of capital is the required rate of return an investor demands for taking a firm's riskiness. When the risk increases, the expected rate of return by shareholder also increases. Whereas companies with good ESG activities are less risky, which offer investors better investment condition with socially responsible companies (Lambert et al., 2007). Third, more ESG disclosure leads to enhanced risk sharing by increasing investor recognition (Merton, 1987; Lomberdo and Pagano, 2002). An investor with long term vision considers firms with better ESG performance in his investment portfolio. Because such firms exhibit a positive signal regarding their long term survival and achieving expected rate of return more easily (Cox and Wicks, 2011). Finally, high transparent disclosure lowers the agency cost and reduces the cost of capital (Lombardo and Pagano, 2002). The portfolio of institutional investors consists of fewer 'sin' stocks, that is firm operating in liquor, tobacco and gaming industries and they mostly prefer firms with high ESG practices (Hong and Kacperczy, 2009; Peternsen and Vredenburg, 2009).

One of the early research projects in this area was conducted by Richardson and Welker (2001) and the study finds that the cost of capital is reduced by financial disclosure, but social disclosure increases the cost of capital. It has been observed that voluntary disclosure quality reduces the cost of capital in environment-oriented firms (Plumlee et al., 2008). El Ghoul et al. (2010) found ESG ranked firms in US benefits with cheaper equity financing. The study also found that investment in the tobacco and nuclear power industries (the study considers it as sin industries) increases firms' cost of capital. The study identified that cost of capital is reduced by factors such as environmental policies, product strategies and investments in improving responsible employee relations. Reverte (2012) and Xu et al. (2015) identified a similar inverse connection, which is more predominant in environmentally sensitive industries. Later, El Ghoul et al. (2016) established their findings taking a sample from 30 countries, found lower cost of capital for higher environmentally responsible firms. Companies with a higher cost of capital during last year promote ESG activities and it helps to lessen the cost of capital in the coming years (Dhaliwal et al., 2011). Later, Dhaliwal et al. (2014) expanded their study and added that this inverse association is more evident in investor friendly countries. Ng and Rezaee (2015) advanced the literature by examining how the cost of capital is influencing the different sustainable approaches and the study confirms that financial and non-financial sustainable performance is always associated to cost of capital. The study of Ferris et al. (2017) identified that social capital reduces the cost of capital. Based on the above studies the researcher framed the following hypothesis.

H2: ESG disclosure is negatively affecting the cost of capital.

2.3 ESG Disclosure and Earnings Management

Accounting scandals such as Satyam computers, Enron and WorldCom confirm that insiders are exploiting their advantage in computing earnings of the company to mislead outsiders for their personal benefit (Laux and Leuz, 2009; Bhasin, 2016). Earnings management misleads investors and influences the results by an insider through manipulation of accounting records (Healy and Wahlen, 1999). Investor's expectation is one of the major reasons for earning manipulation (Teoh et al., 1998; DeGeorge et al., 1999) and to avoid Losses (Burgstahler and Dicher, 1997). Heal (2008) suggests that transparent reporting of accounting records is important for ESG as it provides confidence and trust to stakeholders regarding firms operations. Especially, when ESG disclosure is beyond what is required by rules and regulations, hence these disclosures help companies to decrease the problem of information asymmetry among managers and shareholders (Eng and Mak, 2003). Stakeholder Theory explains why companies involve themselves in socially responsible activities. According to the Stakeholder Theory, it is vital for companies to disclose more information relevant to stakeholders (Buhr, 2001). Stakeholder Theory states that ESG activities help to make more benefit than cost by maintaining good rapport with stakeholders including employees, customers, and community (Freeman, 1999). Transparent disclosure of information and earnings quality is important for companies because it is essential to satisfy the stakeholders, so companies keen to keep long term relationship with stakeholders rather than maximizing short term profit (Choi et al., 2013).

Previous studies observed that higher ESG activities reduces earning manipulation (Chih et al., 2008; Kim et al., 2012; Choi et al., 2013; Scholtens and Kang, 2013; Martinez-Ferroro et al., 2015; Cho and Chun, 2016; Gil et al., 2016; Alsaadi et al., 2016; Gavana et al., 2017; Almahrog et al., 2018). Chih et al., (2008) find that the type of earning manipulation determines the connection among ESG disclosure and earnings manipulation. Kim et al., 2012 analyzed financial reporting practices of the socially responsible firms using a sample of US firms and results find a weak probability for earnings management in socially responsible firm. Choi et al. (2013) carried out a study on Korean firms during 2002-2008 to study the association between ESG rating and quality of earnings for firms with different ownership structure. The study confirms the inverse relationship, which is weaker for firms with ownership concentration. The study by Scholtens and Kang (2013) indicates that firm with higher ESG activities are less engaged in earning manipulation in Asia. Martinez-Ferrero et al. (2015) find an inverse bidirectional effect of ESG on earnings management. Cho and Chun (2016) observe that ESG oriented firms are not interested in real activities earnings manipulation and corporate governance moderates this association. Similarly, Gil et al. (2016) found negative relationships and argue that socially responsible activities increase goodwill and stakeholder satisfaction. Alsaadi et al. (2016) studied the influence of ESG and Shariah index membership on financial reporting quality using a sample from 10 European countries. The result shows that ESG reduces earnings manipulation. In contrast, Shariah index membership has an opposite effect on earnings quality. The study concluded that institutional factors have a significant role in determining the link between these three factors. Gavana et al. (2017) carried out a similar study on family and nonfamily owned firms and the study indicates that family-oriented firms engage in earnings manipulation more often than nonfamily owned firms. Almahrog et al. (2018) found that ESG sub-themes such as community, employees, environment and product and services are negatively associated to the extent of earnings management.

In contrast, from the opportunistic behavior perspective, there are few studies which find a positive link between ESG disclosure and information asymmetry (Chih et al., 2008; Mcwilliams et al., 2006). Executives use ESG disclosure to mask their earnings manipulation (Chih et al., 2008) and to protect their personal interest (Mcwilliams et al., 2006). Prior et al. (2008), Gargouri et al. (2010) and Muttakin and Khan (2015) empirically supported this argument. The studies show earnings manipulation leads towards more ESG activities. Prior et al. (2008) argue that to deal with the stakeholder pressure managers use ESG initiatives as a tool to manipulate earnings. Gargouri et al. (2010) opined that the benefits of earnings management may be shared among managers and employees. Muttakin and Khan (2015) find that ESG disclosure increases earnings management. On the basis of the above studies, it can be said that majority of studies observe that ESG disclosure could reduce the information advantage of insiders over outsiders. So firms with strong social commitment neither undertake earnings management nor hide unfavorable earnings realization (Chih et al., 2008). Earnings manipulations happen very often in socially responsible firms (Schafer, 2004). Despite India's poor legal and institutional setting, poor investor protection and lack of shareholder awareness regarding ESG and financial disclosures which is mainly driven by Companies Act and SEBI regulations. Managers under the influence of foreign shareholders and public pressure towards good corporate citizenship are forced to provide more disclosure of ESG activities.

Consistent with past research (Chih et al., 2008; Martinez-Ferroro et al., 2015; Cho and Chin, 2015; Gil et al., 2016; Alsaadi et al., 2016; Gavana et al., 2017; Almahrog et al., 2018), the present study anticipate that earnings management is less in firms with strong social commitment, while firms with weak ESG performance have more incentive towards earnings manipulation. The present study therefore proposes the hypothesis that;

H3: ESG disclosure is negatively affecting earnings management.

2.4 Information Asymmetry and Cost of Capital

Existing literature indicates that availability of information is important in determining the cost of capital (Leuz and Verrecchia, 2000). Information disclosure weakens information asymmetry and reduces firms cost of capital as a result of large investment because of higher liquidity of the shares (Diamond and Verrecchia, 1991; Leland, 1992; Wang, 1993). Easley and O'Hara (2004) argue that investors will not take any risk by holding security with information disadvantage instead they move to securities with less information asymmetry, hence this will increase the cost of capital of companies with higher information asymmetry. Hughes et al. (2007) identified that higher information asymmetry increases the risk premium and cost of capital.

Armstrong et al. (2011) observed the role of market competition in this relationship and the study find positive association during imperfect competition, while finding no association during perfect competition. Lambert et al. (2011) find an inverse association, while Kazemi and Rahmani (2013) find information asymmetry increases cost of capital, such relationship is rare in the competitive world. He et al. (2013) identified that information asymmetry influences cost of capital and the study explain that the information disadvantage of less informed investors make the difference as they don't hold security with information disadvantage, hence increases the price and cost of capital. Rymar (2016) investigated the effect of information asymmetry on cost of capital and find that it is affected by the type of information disclosed.

To conclude, most of the prior studies indicated a positive relationship between information asymmetry and cost of capital, because holding the securities of companies with higher information asymmetry is risky for investors. Since they know that they are at an information disadvantage and it is not wise to hold such securities for long. At the same time, there are studies which find no significant relationship under different market conditions, which indicate that degree of market condition plays a role in determining the relationship (Armstrong et al., 2011; Kazemi and Rahmani, 2013). Considering these arguments researcher hypothesis that:

H4: Information asymmetry is positively affecting the cost of capital.

2.5 Information Asymmetry and Earnings Management

The study of Easley and O'Hara (2004) find that market participants try to make profit using of their information advantage when they have more information than others. The level of earnings management can be higher for firms with higher information asymmetry (Trueman and Titman, 1988; Dye, 1988). In turn, earnings management creates uncertainty among investors regarding firm's operation and future cash flow, which may cause information asymmetry (Bhattacharya et al., 2012). Chaney and Lewis (1995) empirically proved that the information gap among managers and owners leads to earnings management, and it affects firm's valuation. Richardson (2000) tested how information asymmetry motivates managers to participate in earnings management and find positive association. Francis et al. (2005) proved that information asymmetry improves the possibility for earnings management, which leads to an increase in the cost of capital. Ascioglu et al. (2012) argued that the extent of earnings management reduces disclosure quality and increases information asymmetry. Cormier et al. (2013) opined that higher information asymmetry improves the chance for earning management.

Dai et al. (2013) investigated how information asymmetry affects earnings management and find that decrease in information asymmetry increases firms' earnings quality. This encourages effective monitoring and motivates managers of the company to furnish needed data to improve transparency. Bhattacharya et al. (2013) documented that information asymmetry is connected with poor earnings quality. The relationship is affected by the information environment of the firm and more evidence are found from poor disclosure environment. Sougne and Ajina (2014) identified that firms that manage earnings have higher information asymmetry measured with the help bid ask spread. Wiyadi et al. (2015) showed that information asymmetry and corporate governance affect earnings management. The study also found that corporate governance acts as a mediator in this relationship. Abad et al. (2018) observed high real earnings management in firms with higher information asymmetry.

To conclude, transparent, frequent, and quality information disclosure reduces the information asymmetry problem faced by investors leading to low earnings management and better performance (Xia and Lu, 2005; Hunton et al., 2006; Fang and Hong, 2007; Jo and Kim, 2007). Higher information asymmetry motivates managers to do manipulation in the accounting records for their personal benefits and overstate the revenue to avoid stakeholder pressure and attract new investors. Hence the researcher hypothesis that:

H5: Information asymmetry is positively affecting earnings management.

2.6 Earnings Management and Cost of Capital

Previous studies found a conflicting result regarding the earnings management and cost of capital relationship. Many studies indicated that both have a positive correlation (Aboody et al., 2005; Bharath et al., 2008; Kim and Sohn, 2013), while few other studies found negative relationship (Francis et al., 2004; Gray et al., 2009; Strobl, 2013) or no relationship (McInnis, 2010; Putra et al., 2016). Earnings management measured as unsigned abnormal accruals increase the cost of equity capital (Aboody et al., 2005). Earnings management leads to an increase in the cost of debt capital (Bharath et al., 2008). Lambert et al. (2007) demonstrate that the cost of capital has direct and indirect effect on the quality of accounting information. The study argues that earnings management intends to cover actual earnings performance. The study also found that cost of capital will increase through manipulations in the accounting records. Kim and Sohn (2013) identified that there is a positive association between the two concepts and it is caused by managerial opportunism rather than measurement error and such earnings management weakens the quality of information, hence investors demand a high risk premium and improves the cost of capital.

Francis et al. (2004) found a negative association between seven earnings management variables and cost of capital. Gray et al. (2009) identified that earnings management and cost of capital are negatively related. Strobl (2013) demonstrates that earning manipulation influences firms cost of capital, earnings manipulation reduces the correlation between firms cash flow and reduces the risk premium demanded by investors. Further, earnings manipulation varies upon business cycle and earnings manipulation is more during economic expansion. Patro and Kanagaraj (2016) indicate that firm with poor performance has more inducement to involve earnings management, the managers of these companies overstate their earnings to avoid the undervaluation of stock and hence reduces the cost of capital represented by WACC (weighted average cost of capital). Eliwa et al. (2016) identified negative link among each earnings quality proxies and cost of capital and this relationship is more prominent during the crisis period than the pre-crisis period. In contrast, McInnis (2010) and Putra et al. (2016) didn't find any association between earnings management and the cost of capital.

To conclude, the association between earnings management and cost of capital has undergone rigorous studies and their findings are conflicting. One line of research indicates that earning manipulation or earnings management questions the credibility of the accounting record of the company and lose investors' confidence in companies' performance which creates a bad image among the investors and public, hence investor think it is risky and demands higher risk premium, thus earnings management increases firms cost of capital (Bharath et al., 2008; Kim and Sohn, 2013). Another line of research indicate that earnings management is carried by firms with poor financial performance and managers of such firms wanted to attract investors by overstating their accounting records and reduces the risk premium of investors and reduces cost of capital (Francis et al., 2004; Gray et al., 2009; Strobl 2013). There are studies which failed to establish any connection between earnings management and the cost of capital (McInnis, 2010; Putra et al., 2016). Considering all this argument the researcher hypothesis that:

H6: Earnings management is positively affecting the cost of capital.

3 METHODOLOGY

3.1 Sample

The present study collected data for a sample of 183 companies listed in BSE 500 index, India. The study covers all major players in the capital market, for a period of 10 years from 2014 to 2023.

3.2 Method

The present study investigates the relationship between ESG disclosure, information asymmetry, cost of capital and earnings management using a series of interdependent constructs. The study used Partial Least Square Structural Equation modeling (PLS-SEM) to construct the model, which allows analyzing the association between variables. PLS-SEM modeling is useful when there are many factors which are highly collinear, and this technique is mainly used for prediction in social sciences. PLS-SEM is a variance-based method considered as an alternate to covariance based SEM for testing models and it verifies the interrelated dependent relationship among different constructs (Rigdon, 1998). PLS-SEM is better suited for studies with small samples and when the aim is to predict and develop theory (Hair et al., 2014). SEM consists of two sub models, outer model (to verify the relationship between latent variable and indicators) and inner model (to verify the connection among explanatory and explained latent variables) (Wong, 2013). Based on the direction of arrows in the path diagram variables can be exogenous (inward) and endogenous (outward). PLS-SEM analysis consists of the series of steps that are: First, arrangement of the SEM. Second, specify the model measurement. Third, collection and examination of data. Fourth, model estimation. Fifth, assessment of measurement model and finally, structural model assessment.

3.3 Measurement of Variables

This study is based on four latent constructs namely ESG disclosure, information asymmetry, earnings management and cost of capital. Data were collected from Prowess and Bloomberg online database.

3.4 ESG Disclosure

The present study used ESG disclosure score, a third-party rating scale calculated by Bloomberg database to assure a subjective assessment. Bloomberg analysis wide sources related with the environment (e.g., Greenhouse gas emissions, climate change), social (e.g., health and security, fair trade principles) and governance (e.g., reporting and disclosure, shareholder protection)

3.5 Information Asymmetry

Different techniques are employed to calculate information asymmetry. Bid-ask spread and share price volatility are the proxy for information asymmetry mostly used in previous studies (Leuz and Verracchia, 2001; Francis et al., 2005; Siew et al., 2016). Consistent with previous studies, the present study uses bid ask spread and share price volatility to represent information asymmetry.

3.6 Cost of Capital

Cost of capital is measured in many ways, such as cost of equity capital (Reverte, 2012; Botosan et al., 2011) or cost of debt capital (Anis and Utama, 2016; Goss and Roberts, 2011; Menz, 2010) or both (Suto and Takehara, 2017). In line with this, the present study use cost of equity capital and debt capital to represent cost of capital.

3.7 Earnings Management

Different studies use different techniques to measure earnings management (Mouseli et al., 2012; Beattie, 2005; Wang, 2006). The present study uses the absolute value of discretionary accruals as a proxy for earnings management. The researcher used both Modified Jones model (Dechow et al., 1995) and Kothari model (Kothari et al., 2005). Modified Jones model is the most used model to measure discretionary accruals because of its higher specification and limited data requirements. As per this model, the level of discretionary accruals (DA) is the difference between total accruals (TA) and non-discretionary accruals (NDAC). The below given equation may use to measure discretionary accruals:

$$\frac{TACC_t}{A_{t-1}} = \alpha_1 \frac{1}{A_{t-1}} + \alpha_2 \frac{\left(\Delta REV_t - \Delta REC_t\right)}{A_{t-1}} + \alpha_3 \frac{PPE_t}{A_{t-1}} + \varepsilon_t$$

However, Kothari et al. (2005) questioned the accuracy of Jones model as the model didn't adjust firm performance, and the omission of firm performance will cause misspecification in the earnings management model and proposed a model that include an intercept and control over firm performance using ROA. Many previous studies used Kothari Model (Chang et al., 2010; Cornett et al., 2009). So present study used performance adjusted Kothari model as well, estimated using the given formula:

$$\frac{TACC_t}{A_{t-1}} = \alpha_1 \frac{1}{A_{t-1}} + \alpha_2 \frac{\left(\Delta REV_t - \Delta REC_t\right)}{A_{t-1}} + \alpha_3 \frac{PPE_t}{A_{t-1}} + \alpha_3 \frac{ROA_t}{A_{t-1}} + \varepsilon_t$$

Where, "TACC$_t$ is the Total accruals in year t, ΔREV$_t$ is the Revenue in the year t less revenue in the year t-1, ΔREC$_t$ is Delta revenue in year t less delta net receivables in year t-1, PPE$_t$ is the Gross property plant and equipment in year t, A$_{t-1}$ is the

Total asset in year t-1, ROA_t is the Return on asset of firm in year t, α_1, α_2, and α_3 are the parameters to be estimated, namely alphas, ε_t is the Residuals in year t".

Total accruals (TACC) are measured by the difference between net income (NI) and net cash flow from operating activities (CFO) as follows:

$$TACC_t = \Delta CA_t - \Delta Cash - \Delta CL_t + \Delta DCL_t - DEP_t$$

Where, "$TACC_t$ is the Total accruals in year t, ΔCA_t is the Change in current assets in year t, $\Delta Cash$ is the Change in cash and cash equivalents in year t, ΔCL_t is the Change in current liabilities in year t, ΔDCL_t is the change in short term debt included in current liabilities in year t, DEP_t is the depreciation and amortization in year t".

3.8 Control Variables

The present study used different control variables for different constructs, because the variables which influence the constructs are not the same as indicated in existing studies (Prior et al., 2008; Chil et al., 2008; Muttakin and Khan, 2015). After considering the previous studies the present study used control variables namely firm size, leverage, profitability, growth, firm age and promoter's ownership. Log of total assets is used to measure firm size, debt to equity ratio is used to measure firms leverage, return on asset is used to measure profitability, percentage of increase in EPS is used to measure the growth of the firm, years since establishment used to determine firm age and percentage of promoter's ownership is used to calculate promoter's ownership.

Figure 1. Path model

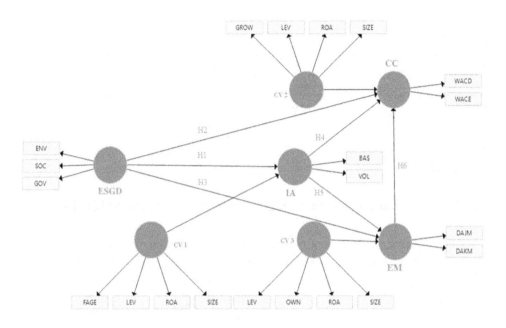

Table 1. Constructs and indicator description

Construct and indicator	Description
ESGD (Latent construct)	Environmental, Social, Governance disclosure score
ENV	Environmental disclosure score
SOC	Social disclosure score
GOV	Governance disclosure score
IA (Latent construct)	Information asymmetry
BAS	Average annual Bid/Ask spread computed daily basis
VOL	Standard Deviation of % changes in daily stock prices
CC (Latent construct)	Cost of capital
WACE	Weighted average cost of equity capital
WACD	Weighted average cost of debt capital
EM (Latent construct)	Earnings management
DAJM	Discretionary accruals (Modified Jones model)
DAK M	Discretionary accruals (Kothari model)
CV (Latent construct)	Control variable

continued on following page

Table 1. Continued

Construct and indicator	Description
SIZE	Firm size - log of total assets
GROW	Percentage increase in EPS
LEV	Financial leverage / debt-equity ratio
ROA	Return on asset
OWN	Percentage of promoter's ownership

4 RESULTS

4.1 Validity Assessment of Reflective Measurement Models

The reflective measurement model validates the addition of a construct measure in the path model by ensuring its reliability and validity (Hair et al., 2017). The measurement models for constructs with reflective measures are accessed through indicator reliability, internal consistency reliability (Composite reliability), convergent validity (AVE), and discriminant validity.

According to Hair et al. (2014) indicator reliability measures the level of variation of an item explained in a single variable. Outer loadings are used to assess the indicator reliability and higher outer loading shows that the related measure has much in common that is measured by the variable. Generally the acceptable limit of outer loading should be greater than 0.70 and the outer loading between 0.70 and 0.40 can be removed if the removal helps to improve the composite reliability (CR) and AVE. Similarly, items with outer loading of less than 0.40 must be deleted if the value of AVE and CR reach above the threshold value after such deletion; otherwise, it should be taken. The result of indicator reliability is displayed in the following table (Table 2). After running the PLS algorithm the researcher removed an indicator (representing information asymmetry) with low loading, even though the researcher retained few indicators with low loading, which is used as a control variable to get the true effect on explaining variables. All other variables in the path model show higher loading (Table 2).

Convergent validity measures the degree to which the construct is correlated with each other. The value of Average Variance Explained (AVE) is used to measure convergent validity. If the AVE value for all the variables is higher than 0.5 (cut off limit) the conditions for convergent validity will be satisfied (Hair et al., 2014). The result of convergent validity of the latent variables used in this study is given in Table 2. Since the value of AVE for all the study variables (except control variables) is greater than other than the cut of limit 0.50 (Hair et al., 2014), it can be interpreted that, the study establish convergent validity.

Reliability or internal consistency is a measure of how well our instrument measures what the researcher wants to measure. It determines the similarity in their score while measuring a variable (Hair at al., 2014). Cronbach's alpha is the common statistical tool used to identify the internal consistency of multiple scale items. It is the mean of all possible split-half correlations for a set of items. The coefficient value lies between zeros to one. Value zero means no consistency and one means the complete consistency. The Cronbach's alpha value above 0.70 is satisfactory and indicates good reliability (Reynold & Santos, 1999). Table 2 shows the CR and Cronbach's Alpha values of variables used in this study, variables other than the cost of capital (weak Cronbach's Alpha but high CR) found to have the required value, which establishes internal consistency.

Discriminant validity measures the amount to which a construct is well defined by another construct. It is the degree to which a variable is different from other variables, in terms of its correlation with other variables, and how much indicator represents only a single variable (Hair et al., 2014). The higher the discriminant value means the construct is more distinctive. The cross loadings and Fornell Lacrker criterion are commonly used to measure discriminant validity. As per Fornell Larcker criterion, the square root of the AVE of all construct must be greater than highest correlation with any other construct in the model (Forenell and Larcker, 1981). Table 3 explains the results of discriminant validity of the construct used in the study. The AVE (in bold) is higher than its own highest construct correlation with any other construct, so the researcher concludes that the criteria for discriminant validity has been satisfied. Further, Table 4 shows the cross-loading criterion results. Since the individual loading of all variables is greater than their cross loadings (Hair et al., 2014), which provides further proof for discriminant validity.

Table 2. Construct reliability and validity

Construct	Items	Loadings	AVE	Composite Reliability	Cronbach's Alpha
ESGD	ENV	0.818	0.712	0.88	0.837
	SOC	0.952			
	GOV	0.749			
IA	BAS	0.901	0.838	0.912	0.808
	VOL	0.93			
CC	WACD	0.674	0.563	0.719	0.229
	WACE	0.82			

continued on following page

Table 2. Continued

Construct	Items	Loadings	AVE	Composite Reliability	Cronbach's Alpha
EM	DAJM	0.938	0.867	0.929	0.846
	DAKM	0.923			
CV 1	FAGE	0.111	0.34	0.626	0.396
	LEV	0.798			
	ROA	0.581			
	SIZE	0.612			
CV 2	GROW	0.809	0.477	0.21	0.139
	LEV	-0.299			
	ROA	0.872			
	SIZE	-0.635			
CV 3	LEV	-0.78	0.262	0.044	0.139
	OWN	0.372			
	ROA	0.372			
	SIZE	0.404			

Table 3. Discriminent validity: Fornell-Larcker criterion

Construct	ESGD	IA	CC	EM	CV 1	CV 2	CV 3
ESGD	**0.844**						
IA	-0.012	**0.916**					
CC	0.100	0.01	**0.75**				
EM	-0.062	-0.026	-0.16	**0.931**			
CV 1	0.036	0.52	-0.141	0.042	**0.585**		
CV 2	0.193	-0.128	0.344	-0.168	-0.443	**0.581**	
CV 3	-0.082	0.306	0.374	-0.157	0.033	0.129	**0.512**

Table 4. Discriminant validity: Cross loadings criterion

Construct	ESGD	IA	CC	EM	CV 1	CV 2	CV 3
ENV	**0.818**	0	0.035	-0.008	0.029	0.103	-0.133
SOC	**0.952**	-0.013	0.116	-0.08	0.023	0.226	-0.033
GOV	**0.749**	-0.009	0.05	-0.018	0.057	0.065	-0.138
BAS	-0.014	**0.901**	0.02	-0.039	0.434	-0.152	0.372
VOL	-0.009	**0.93**	-0.001	-0.011	0.512	-0.088	0.202

continued on following page

Table 4. Continued

Construct	ESGD	IA	CC	EM	CV 1	CV 2	CV 3
WACD	0.132	0.06	**0.675**	-0.16	-0.005	0.193	0.187
WACE	0.032	-0.034	**0.818**	-0.09	-0.185	0.313	0.357
DAJM	-0.063	-0.019	-0.139	**0.938**	0.043	-0.172	-0.168
DAKM	-0.052	-0.03	-0.16	**0.923**	0.035	-0.139	-0.122
GROW	0.011	0.487	0.01	0.005	**0.796**	-0.044	0.096
LEV	0.023	-0.027	0.096	-0.03	**0.113**	0.352	0.03
ROA	0.051	0.157	-0.274	0.127	**0.588**	-0.783	-0.17
SIZE	0.039	0.278	-0.184	0.015	**0.613**	-0.485	0.009
GROW	0.011	0.487	0.01	0.005	0.796	**-0.044**	0.096
LEV	0.023	-0.027	0.096	-0.03	-0.113	**0.352**	0.03
ROA	0.051	0.157	-0.274	0.127	0.588	**-0.783**	-0.17
SIZE	0.369	-0.067	0.272	-0.146	-0.147	**0.782**	0.032
LEV	0.099	-0.033	-0.086	0.127	0.103	-0.225	**-0.78**
OWN	-0.087	0.119	0.013	-0.051	-0.036	-0.06	**0.372**
ROA	-0.014	0.901	0.02	-0.039	0.434	-0.152	**0.372**
SIZE	0.062	0.05	0.676	-0.071	0.043	0.018	**0.404**

4.2 Assessment of the Structural Model

Structural model assessment includes five phases. In the initial phase, the collinearity issue is measured. Collinearity is a tool used to find out whether two or more independent variables interrelate with one another or not. The collinearity effects reduce the ability to predict the dependent measures as well to ascertain the relative role of each independent variable. Variance Inflation Factor (VIF) is adopted to measure the collinearity and the result is shown in Table 5. Since the value of VIF for all construct is less than 5 (i.e., threshold value), the problem of collinearity does not exist in the measurement model.

Table 5. Collinearity assessment for inner model: VIF values

Variable	VIF
ENV	2.549
SOC	1.845
GOV	1.95
BAS	1.853

continued on following page

Table 5. Continued

Variable	VIF
VOL	1.853
WACD	1.017
WACE	1.017
DAJ	2.166
DAMJ	2.166
FAGE	1.009
LEV	1.017
ROA	1.586
SIZE	1.571
GROW	2.821
LEV	1.024
ROA	2.976
SIZE	1.104
LEV	1.005
OWN	1.055
ROA	1.058
SIZE	1.005

Table 6. Significance testing results of the structural model path coefficients

Path Direction	Original Sample	Sample Mean	Standard Deviation	t Statistics	P Values	Significance
ESGD -> IA	-0.036	-0.037	0.021	1.708	0.088	*
ESGD ->CC	0.045	0.047	0.019	2.381	0.017	**
ESGD ->EM	-0.075	-0.08	0.023	3.293	0.001	**
IA -> CC	0.052	0.051	0.017	3.023	0.003	**
IA -> EM	0.025	0.027	0.009	2.671	0.008	**
EM -> CC	-0.106	-0.108	0.029	3.685	0.000	***
CV 1 -> IA	0.522	0.544	0.115	4.523	0.000	***
CV 2 -> CC	-0.323	-0.325	0.024	13.207	0.000	***
CV 3 -> EM	-0.17	-0.182	0.027	6.393	0.000	***

Note: * $p < 0.10$, ** $p < 0.05$, *** $p < 0.01$; (based on t(55), one tail test).
Bootstrap confidence intervals for 5% probability of error ($\alpha = 0,05$).

The next stage consists of the measurement of significance and relevance of model. Path coefficient analysis shows the relevance of path coefficient, higher and absolute values indicate higher predictive association among constructs (Hair et al., 2013). Path coefficient value lies between -1 to +1. Table 6 explains the path coefficients of variables used in the study. A weak positive relationship is found between ESGD and CC, IA and CC and IA with EM. A negative relationship is found between ESGD and IA, ESGD and EM and EM with CC. The third step consists of measuring the significance of structural models. In smart PLS, Bootstrapping procedure is employed to test the significance of the structural model. It is a nonparametric method to measure whether coefficients are significant or not, by estimating standard error for the estimates. Bootstrapping procedure explains the importance of path coefficient values and it gives t statistics and p values. The t statistics is calculated by dividing path coefficient value with standard error. Then the t value is compared with critical value, to check whether t value is greater than the critical value which is desired. The critical values are 2.57, 1.96 and 1.65 for significance level of 1%, 5% and 10% respectively. After the analysis an indicator is deleted when the outer loading is less than 0.5 and insignificant, removal of an indicator is considered when outer loading is less than 0.5 and insignificant, while an insignificant indicator is retained if the outer loading is greater than 0.5. Based on all these selection criteria the researcher developed the model and results of bootstrapping are given in Table 6, which shows all our constructs and variables are significant.

Table 7. Variance explained

Construct	R^2	Adj. R^2
IA	0.272	0.271
CC	0.131	0.129
EM	0.031	0.029

The third stage includes the identification of coefficient of determination (R^2). R^2 is the assessment of predictive accuracy of the model (Hair et al., 2014). Table 7 shows the adjusted R^2 value of our study. IA and CC show a higher adjusted R^2 of 0.271 and 0.129 respectively, whereas EM with show a weak adjusted R^2 of 0.029.

Table 8. Effect size (F^2)

Construct	ESGD	IA	CC	EM
ESGD		0.002	0.002	0.006
IA			0.003	0.001
CC				
EM			0.013	
CV 1		0.374		

continued on following page

Table 8. Continued

Construct	ESGD	IA	CC	EM
CV 2			0.112	
CV 3				0.027

The fourth stage consists of the assessment effect size with the help of F square. F^2 or effect size evaluates the difference in R^2 when exogenous variable is included or excluded from the model (Hair et al., 2015). F^2 value effect size indication: 0.02 (small), 0.15 (medium) and 0.35 (high) (Cohen, 1998). Table 8 shows the effect size results and the effect size fall between small to medium effect, which is understandable considering the model and data we have taken.

Table 9. Predictive relevance (Q^2)

Construct	SSO	SSE	Q^2 (=1- SSE/SSO)
CC	3,294.00	3,067.76	0.069
ESGD	4,941.00	4,941.00	
EM	3,294.00	3,217.67	0.023
IA	3,294.00	2,647.17	0.196
CV 1	6,588.00	6,588.00	
CV 2	6,588.00	6,588.00	
CV 3	6,588.00	6,588.00	

The final stage includes the estimation of Q square to identify the predictive relevance through blindfolding. Blindfolding is used to cross-validate the model's predictive relevance for each of the individual endogenous variables, the stone-Geisser Q^2 value (Stone, 1974; Geisser, 1974). According to Chin (1998), the Q^2 explains how well observed values are reconstructed by its model and its parameter estimates. A model with Q^2 higher than zero is measured to have predictive relevance. Increase in Q^2 value also increases the predictive relevance. Table 9 provides the Q^2 value of endogenous construct which is above zero (0.069, 0.023 and 0.196), thus providing support for the relevance of model regarding endogenous latent variable.

Figure 2. Final path model

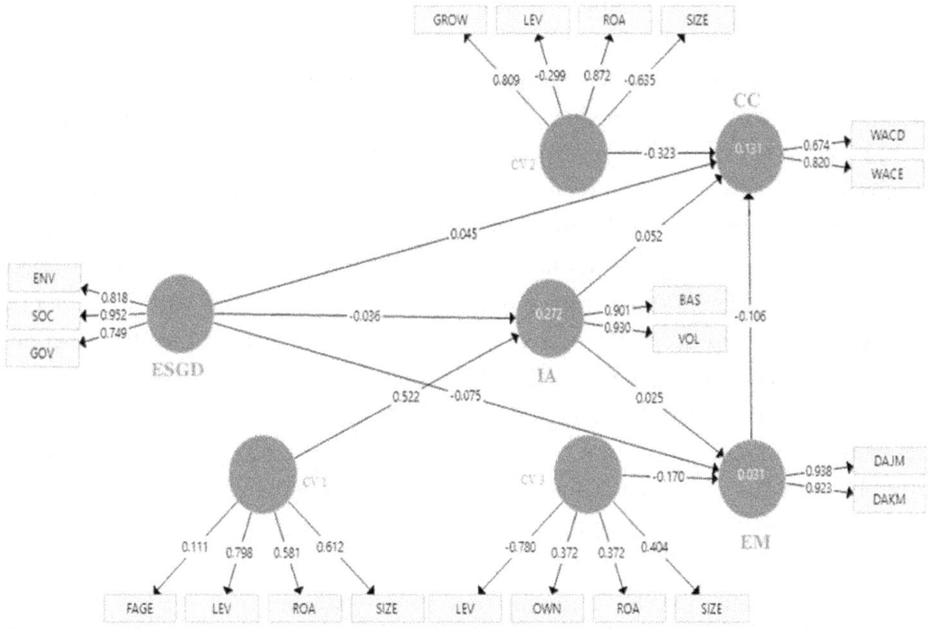

5 DISCUSSIONS

5.1 ESG Disclosure and Information Asymmetry

The empirical studies showing the effect of ESG disclosure on information asymmetry is limited in spite of its importance. The present study finds that ESG disclosure reduces information asymmetry. This inverse relationship is rightly explained by Cui et al. (2016), Hamrouni et al. (2021), voluntary disclosure ensures the equal availability of information to a certain extent which reduces the agency problem. Additional information through ESG disclosure reduces the information gap between informed and uninformed investors and reduces information asymmetry. The result extends the empirical findings of Welker (1995), Leuz and Verrecchia (2000), Healy et al. (1999) and Cormier et al. (2013) who also observed a similar inverse association, hence H1 accepted.

5.2 ESG Disclosure and Cost of Capital

Investors require a minimum return for their investment to the firm and they are very much concerned about how ESG activities of the firm affect their investment. The present study empirically examines how ESG disclosure affects the cost of capital. In contrast and inconsistent with H2, the study finds that ESG disclosure increases cost of capital. The results are against the findings of Plumlee et al. (2008), Dhaliwal et al. (2011) and El Ghoul et al. (2010), Khanchel and Lassoued (2022). But the result supports the findings of Richardson and Welker (2001), the study gives several possible explanations for this positive relationship. Firstly, investors are looking for firms with a higher profit margin and not ones with more social activities. The present values of socially responsible investment by the firm are lower, which increases firm risk. While SRI concept aims towards the potential cost saving, long term advantage and social welfare (Scaltegger and Figge, 2000) but the investors mostly didn't care much about anything other than the profit margin, in such a situation the result could hold. Especially in a country like India, where investors are not that sensitive towards ESG activities. Secondly, the firm may use ESG disclosure as a measure to hide their activities with negative social impacts and for self-promotion. Several literatures on social disclosure have opined that there happened to be errors in disclosures (Gutherin and Parker, 1990; Wiseman, 1982).

5.3 ESG Disclosure and Earnings Management

The empirical result explains that ESG disclosure is negatively affecting the earnings management, i.e., higher ESG disclosure results in lower earnings management and more earnings quality, Thus H3 accepted. The findings corroborates with most of the existing studies, which found a negative impact of ESG disclosure on earnings management (Chih et al., 2008; Kim et al., 2012; Alsaadi et al., 2013; Martinez-Ferroro et al.,2016; Choi et al., 2016; Cho and Chun, 2016; Gaio et al., 2022). Companies integrating ESG initiatives are not supposed to do manipulation of earnings since they will not hide unfavorable earnings realization (Chih et al., 2008). Similarly, earnings management stands against the ESG principles, companies which plan and execute ESG activities act responsibly and have less chance to do earnings management (Kim et al., 2012). The findings contradict with previous studies (Prior et al., 2008; Gargouri et al., 2010; Jo Hoje and Harjoto, 2011; Scholtens and Kang, 2013; Muttakin et al., 2015; Almubarak et al., 2023), who find a positive influence of ESG disclosure and earnings management and explained that organizations adopt ESG initiatives as a mask to cover their earnings manipulations and to divert stakeholder activism and vigilance.

5.4 Information Asymmetry and Cost of Capital

The findings explain that information asymmetry is positively affecting the cost of capital, thus H4 is accepted. The study argues that lack of availability of information leads to a reduction in the price of the assets of the investors, which increases the cost of capital. Investors always prefer companies with a good reputation and track history, and they try to access maximum information regarding the company from whatever sources available before taking investment decisions. Investors avoid taking unwanted risk by investing in stocks with high information differences (asymmetry), which leads to an increase in the cost of capital. The findings provide an additional proof to the conceptual model proposed by He et al. (2013), Cuadrado et al. (2016) and Amstrong et al. (2010), Abu Afifa and Saadeh (2023).

5.5 Information Asymmetry and Earnings Management

The influence of information asymmetry on earnings management is analyzed and the empirical result identified that information asymmetry positively influencing the earnings management. The results corroborate with the results of earlier studies (Bhattacharya et al., 2013; Cormier et al., 2013; Masud et al., 2017), thus H5 accepted. The study argued that if the information asymmetry is higher, stakeholders may not be able to access the significant information to observe the actions manager; it motivates managers to take advantage of the situation and increases the chance for earnings management (Schipper, 1989; Warfield et al., 1995). Information asymmetries motivate managers to manipulate the earnings for their personal benefits like promotion, bonus and pay hike and the information gap and lack knowledge about firm operation will make it difficult for the owners to find out any sort of earnings management.

5.6 Earnings Management and Cost of Capital

The study found that earnings management and cost of capital are negatively related. The findings are in line with Francis et al. (2004), Gray et al. (2009) and Strobl (2013), Gao et al. (2020), Le and Moore (2021), thus rejects H6. Companies with poor performance have higher inducement for earnings management; it leads to conceal their poor financial performance and helps to reduce stakeholder pressure. Managers of these firms try to overstate the earnings to avoid undervaluation of their stock and it reduces the cost of capital (Patro and Kanagraj, 2016). This is similar to what happened with Satyam computers in 2009; they overstated the financial records and reduced their cost of capital to attract more investors. In contrast, few studies have identified the positive influence of earnings management on cost of capital (Bharath et al., 2008; Kim and Sohn, 2013; Chouaibi and Zouari, 2022).

6 CONCLUSION

The study aims to shed lights into the literature by examining the relationship between ESG disclosure, information asymmetry, cost of capital and earnings management in India. The study finds that higher ESG disclosure leads to decrease information asymmetry, because the additional information disclosed helps to mitigate the information asymmetry and agency conflicts between owners and managers. While ESG disclosure increases firms cost of capital, because Indian investors are more concerned about short term profit than long term advantage through ESG activities. The result also shows that firm with higher ESG disclosure have more social commitment and less chance for doing earnings management and increase in information asymmetry increases the chance for managers to manipulate earnings. Similarly, higher information asymmetry led to increase the investors risk which results in increased cost of capital. Finally, earnings management practice reduces firm costs of capital by easily attracting investors through manipulated accounting records.

To conclude, from the results it is evident that in Indian capital market ESG disclosure has significant role to play, as the additional ESG information disclosure reduces the information asymmetry by means of reducing the agency conflict and the gap between informed and uninformed investors. This improves transparency, earnings quality and reduces the chance for earnings management. But at the expense of a higher cost of capital as Indian investors are more concerned about the short-term profit than the future value addition. It is also evident that higher information asymmetry increases the firm's risk which increases firms cost of capital and high information asymmetry creates agency problem among owners and managers which motivates the Indian managers to do accounting fraud. So firm with higher earnings management window dresses its accounting records to attract investors and it helps to reduce cost of capital.

The findings are important for investors, managers, and policymakers. Investors should understand that higher ESG disclosure reduces information asymmetry, reduces the chance for earnings management and increases the cost of capital. Investors must be vigilant while investing in companies with less information availability, because higher information asymmetry increase chance for earnings management and increases cost of capital. Managers need to analyze how ESG disclosure gain investor confidence by reducing information asymmetry and the chance for earnings management and increases the cost of capital, to come up with an optimal level of

ESG disclosure and also need to make sure that various ESG initiatives reaches to people to reduce the cost of capital. Policy makers need to formulate more policies and guidelines to promote ESG disclosure and reduce information asymmetry and earnings management. More investor awareness programs have to be conducted to make investors sensitive towards ESG activities. This study is subject to certain limitations. Firstly, it considered only listed companies, thereby neglecting the behavior of unlisted companies. Secondly, the Bloomberg database does not provide the methodology used to measure the ESG disclosure score, which limits the transparency of the data used. Thirdly, the study employed a variety of variables and methodologies for modeling, which may raise questions regarding the accuracy and consistency of the findings.

REFERENCES

Abad, D., Cutillas-Gomariz, M. F., Sánchez-Ballesta, J. P., & Yagüe, J. (2018). Real earnings management and information asymmetry in the equity market. *European Accounting Review*, 27(2), 209–235. 10.1080/09638180.2016.1261720

Aboody, D., Hughes, J., & Liu, J. (2005). Earnings quality, insider trading, and cost of capital. *Journal of Accounting Research*, 43(5), 651–673. 10.1111/j.1475-679X.2005.00185.x

Abu Afifa, M. M., & Saadeh, M. (2023). Does information asymmetry mediate the relationship between voluntary disclosure and cost of capital? Evidence from a developing economy. *Journal of Financial Reporting and Accounting, ahead-of-print*(ahead-of-print).

Akerlof, G. A. (1970). The Market for" Lemons": Quality Uncertainty and the Market Mechanism, 84Q. *Journal of Economics*, 488, 489–490.

Almubarak, W. I., Chebbi, K., & Ammer, M. A. (2023). Unveiling the Connection among ESG, Earnings Management, and Financial Distress: Insights from an Emerging Market. *Sustainability (Basel)*, 15(16), 16. 10.3390/su151612348

Alsaadi, A., Ebrahim, M. S., & Jaafar, A. (2017). Corporate social responsibility, Shariah-compliance, and earnings quality. *Journal of Financial Services Research*, 51(2), 169–194. 10.1007/s10693-016-0263-0

Amihud, Y., & Mendelson, H. (1986). Asset pricing and the bid-ask spread. *Journal of Financial Economics*, 17(2), 223–249. 10.1016/0304-405X(86)90065-6

Armstrong, C. S., Core, J. E., Taylor, D. J., & Verrecchia, R. E. (2011). When does information asymmetry affect the cost of capital? *Journal of Accounting Research*, 49(1), 1–40. 10.1111/j.1475-679X.2010.00391.x

Ascioglu, A., Hegde, S. P., Krishnan, G. V., & McDermott, J. B. (2012). Earnings management and market liquidity. *Review of Quantitative Finance and Accounting*, 38(2), 257–274. 10.1007/s11156-010-0225-9

Beattie, V. (2005). Moving the financial accounting research front forward: The UK contribution. *The British Accounting Review*, 37(1), 85–114. 10.1016/j.bar.2004.09.004

Bharath, S. T., Sunder, J., & Sunder, S. V. (2008). Accounting quality and debt contracting. *The Accounting Review*, 83(1), 1–28. 10.2308/accr.2008.83.1.1

Bhasin, M. L. (2016). Unethical accounting practices in connivance with top management: A case study of satyam. *International Journal of Management Sciences and Business Research*, 5(9), 5–19.

Bhattacharya, N., Desai, H., & Venkataraman, K. (2013). Does earnings quality affect information asymmetry? Evidence from trading costs. *Contemporary Accounting Research*, 30(2), 482–516. 10.1111/j.1911-3846.2012.01161.x

Botosan, C. A. (1997). Disclosure level and the cost of equity capital. *The Accounting Review*, ●●●, 323–349.

Brennan, M. J., & Subrahmanyam, A. (1996). Market microstructure and asset pricing: On the compensation for illiquidity in stock returns. *Journal of Financial Economics*, 41(3), 441–464. 10.1016/0304-405X(95)00870-K

Buhr, N. (2001). Corporate silence: Environmental disclosure and the North American free trade agreement. *Critical Perspectives on Accounting*, 12(4), 405–421. 10.1006/cpac.2000.0434

Burgstahler, D. C., & Dichev, I. D. (1997). Earnings, adaptation and equity value. *The Accounting Review*, ●●●, 187–215.

Camilleri, M. A. (2015). Environmental, social and governance disclosures in Europe. *Sustainability Accounting. Management and Policy Journal*, 6(2), 224–242.

Chaney, P. K., & Lewis, C. M. (1995). Earnings management and firm valuation under asymmetric information. *Journal of Corporate Finance*, 1(3-4), 319–345. 10.1016/0929-1199(94)00008-I

Chang, S. C., Chung, T. Y., & Lin, W. C. (2010). Underwriter reputation, earnings management and the long-run performance of initial public offerings. *Accounting and Finance*, 50(1), 53–78. 10.1111/j.1467-629X.2009.00329.x

Chen, H., Chen, J. Z., Lobo, G. J., & Wang, Y. (2011). Effects of audit quality on earnings management and cost of equity capital: Evidence from China. *Contemporary Accounting Research*, 28(3), 892–925. 10.1111/j.1911-3846.2011.01088.x

Cheng, B., Ioannou, I., & Serafeim, G. (2014). Corporate social responsibility and access to finance. *Strategic Management Journal*, 35(1), 1–23. 10.1002/smj.2131

Chih, H. L., Shen, C. H., & Kang, F. C. (2008). Corporate social responsibility, investor protection, and earnings management: Some international evidence. *Journal of Business Ethics*, 79(1-2), 179–198. 10.1007/s10551-007-9383-7

Chih, H. L., Shen, C. H., & Kang, F. C. (2008). Corporate social responsibility, investor protection, and earnings management: Some international evidence. *Journal of Business Ethics*, 79(1-2), 179–198. 10.1007/s10551-007-9383-7

Chin, W. W. (1998). The partial least squares approach to structural equation modeling. *Modern methods for business research, 295*(2), 295-336.

Cho, C. H., Freedman, M., & Patten, D. M. (2012). Corporate disclosure of environmental capital expenditures: A test of alternative theories. *Accounting, Auditing & Accountability Journal*, 25(3), 486–507. 10.1108/09513571211209617

Cho, E., & Chun, S. (2016). Corporate social responsibility, real activities earnings management, and corporate governance: Evidence from Korea. *Asia-Pacific Journal of Accounting & Economics*, 23(4), 400–431. 10.1080/16081625.2015.1047005

Cho, S. Y., Lee, C., & Pfeiffer, R. J.Jr. (2013). Corporate social responsibility performance and information asymmetry. *Journal of Accounting and Public Policy*, 32(1), 71–83. 10.1016/j.jaccpubpol.2012.10.005

Choi, B. B., Lee, D., & Park, Y. (2013). Corporate Social Responsibility, Corporate Governance and Earnings Quality: Evidence from K orea. *Corporate Governance*, 21(5), 447–467. 10.1111/corg.12033

Chouaibi, S., & Affes, H. (2021). The effect of social and ethical practices on environmental disclosure: Evidence from an international ESG data. *Corporate Governance (Bradford)*, 21(7), 1293–1317. 10.1108/CG-03-2020-0087

Chouaibi, Y., & Zouari, G. (2022). The mediating role of real earnings management in the relationship between CSR practices and cost of equity: Evidence from European ESG data. *EuroMed Journal of Business, ahead-of-print*(ahead-of-print).

Cohen, J. (1998). *Statistical power analysis for the behavioural sciences, xxi*. L Erlbaum Associates.

Cohen, J., Holder-Webb, L., Nath, L., & Wood, D. (2011). Retail investors' perceptions of the decision-usefulness of economic performance, governance, and corporate social responsibility disclosures. *Behavioral Research in Accounting*, 23(1), 109–129. 10.2308/bria.2011.23.1.109

Coles, J. L., Loewenstein, U., & Suay, J. (1995). On equilibrium pricing under parameter uncertainty. *Journal of Financial and Quantitative Analysis*, 30(3), 347–364. 10.2307/2331345

Core, J. E. (2001). A review of the empirical disclosure literature [discussion]. *Journal of Accounting and Economics*, 31(1-3), 441–456. 10.1016/S0165-4101(01)00036-2

Cormier, D., Houle, S., & Ledoux, M. J. (2013). The incidence of earnings management on information asymmetry in an uncertain environment: Some Canadian evidence. *Journal of International Accounting, Auditing & Taxation*, 22(1), 26–38. 10.1016/j.intaccaudtax.2013.02.002

Cornett, M. M., McNutt, J. J., & Tehranian, H. (2009). Corporate governance and earnings management at large US bank holding companies. *Journal of Corporate Finance*, 15(4), 412–430. 10.1016/j.jcorpfin.2009.04.003

Cox, P., & Wicks, P. G. (2011). Institutional interest in corporate responsibility: Portfolio evidence and ethical explanation. *Journal of Business Ethics*, 103(1), 143–165. 10.1007/s10551-011-0859-0

Cuadrado-Ballesteros, B., Garcia-Sanchez, I. M., & Martinez Ferrero, J. (2016). How are corporate disclosures related to the cost of capital? The fundamental role of information asymmetry. *Management Decision*, 54(7), 1669–1701. 10.1108/MD-10-2015-0454

Cuadrado-Ballesteros, B., Garcia-Sanchez, I. M., & Martinez Ferrero, J. (2016). How are corporate disclosures related to the cost of capital? The fundamental role of information asymmetry. *Management Decision*, 54(7), 1669–1701. 10.1108/MD-10-2015-0454

Cuadrado-Ballesteros, B., Garcia-Sanchez, I. M., & Martinez Ferrero, J. (2016). How are corporate disclosures related to the cost of capital? The fundamental role of information asymmetry. *Management Decision*, 54(7), 1669–1701. 10.1108/MD-10-2015-0454

Cui, J., Jo, H., & Na, H. (2018). Does corporate social responsibility affect information asymmetry? *Journal of Business Ethics*, 148(3), 549–572. 10.1007/s10551-015-3003-8

Dai, Y., Kong, D., & Wang, L. (2013). Information asymmetry, mutual funds and earnings management: Evidence from China. *China Journal of Accounting Research*, 6(3), 187–209. 10.1016/j.cjar.2013.03.001

Dechow, P. M., Sloan, R. G., & Sweeney, A. P. (1995). Detecting earnings management. *The Accounting Review*, •••, 193–225.

Degeorge, F., Patel, J., & Zeckhauser, R. (1999). Earnings management to exceed thresholds. *The Journal of Business*, 72(1), 1–33. 10.1086/209601

Dhaliwal, D. S., Li, O. Z., Tsang, A., & Yang, Y. G. (2011). Voluntary nonfinancial disclosure and the cost of equity capital: The initiation of corporate social responsibility reporting. *The Accounting Review*, 86(1), 59–100. 10.2308/accr.00000005

Dhaliwal, D. S., Radhakrishnan, S., Tsang, A., & Yang, Y. G. (2012). Nonfinancial disclosure and analyst forecast accuracy: International evidence on corporate social responsibility disclosure. *The Accounting Review*, 87(3), 723–759. 10.2308/accr-10218

Diamond, D. W. (1985). Optimal release of information by firms. *The Journal of Finance*, 40(4), 1071–1094. 10.1111/j.1540-6261.1985.tb02364.x

Diamond, D. W., & Verrecchia, R. E. (1991). Disclosure, liquidity, and the cost of capital. *The Journal of Finance*, 46(4), 1325–1359. 10.1111/j.1540-6261.1991.tb04620.x

Dye, R. A. (1988). Earnings management in an overlapping generations model. *Journal of Accounting Research*, 26(2), 195–235. 10.2307/2491102

Easley, D., & O'hara, M. (2004). Information and the cost of capital. *The Journal of Finance*, 59(4), 1553–1583. 10.1111/j.1540-6261.2004.00672.x

El Ghoul, S., Guedhami, O., Kwok, C. C., & Mishra, D. R. (2011). Does corporate social responsibility affect the cost of capital? *Journal of Banking & Finance*, 35(9), 2388–2406. 10.1016/j.jbankfin.2011.02.007

El Ghoul, S., Guedhami, O., & Pittman, J. (2016). Cross-country evidence on the importance of Big Four auditors to equity pricing: The mediating role of legal institutions. *Accounting, Organizations and Society*, 54, 60–81. 10.1016/j.aos.2016.03.002

Elbadry, A., Gounopoulos, D., & Skinner, F. (2015). Governance quality and information asymmetry. *Financial Markets, Institutions and Instruments*, 24(2-3), 127–157. 10.1111/fmii.12026

Eliwa, Y., Haslam, J., & Abraham, S. (2016). The association between earnings quality and the cost of equity capital: Evidence from the UK. *International Review of Financial Analysis*, 48, 125–139. 10.1016/j.irfa.2016.09.012

Eng, L. L., & Mak, Y. T. (2003). Corporate governance and voluntary disclosure. *Journal of Accounting and Public Policy*, 22(4), 325–345. 10.1016/S0278-4254(03)00037-1

Fang, J. X., & Hong, J. Q. (2007). Listed firms' information disclosure quality and securities analysts' earnings forecasts. *Securities Market Herald*, 3, 25–30.

Ferris, S. P., Javakhadze, D., & Rajkovic, T. (2017). The international effect of managerial social capital on the cost of equity. *Journal of Banking & Finance*, 74, 69–84. 10.1016/j.jbankfin.2016.10.001

Fornell, C., & Larcker, D. F. (1981). Evaluating structural equation models with unobservable variables and measurement error. *JMR, Journal of Marketing Research*, 18(1), 39–50. 10.1177/002224378101800104

Francis, J., LaFond, R., Olsson, P. M., & Schipper, K. (2004). Costs of equity and earnings attributes. *The Accounting Review*, 79(4), 967–1010. 10.2308/accr.2004.79.4.967

Freeman, R. E. (1999). Divergent stakeholder theory. *Academy of Management Review*, 24(2), 233–236.

Gaio, C., Gonçalves, T., & Sousa, M. V. (2022). Does corporate social responsibility mitigate earnings management? *Management Decision*, 60(11), 2972–2989. 10.1108/MD-05-2021-0719

Gao, H., Shen, Z., Li, Y., Mao, X., & Shi, Y. (2020). Institutional Investors, Real Earnings Management and Cost of Equity: Evidence from Listed High-tech Firms in China. *Emerging Markets Finance & Trade*, 56(14), 3490–3506. 10.1080/1540496X.2019.1650348

Gargouri, R. M., Shabou, R., & Francoeur, C. (2010). The relationship between corporate social performance and earnings management. *Canadian Journal of Administrative Sciences/Revue Canadienne Des Sciences De l'Administration, 27*(4), 320-334.

Gavana, G., Gottardo, P., & Moisello, A. (2017). Earnings management and CSR disclosure. Family vs. non-family firms. *Sustainability (Basel)*, 9(12), 2327. 10.3390/su9122327

Geisser, S. (1974). A predictive approach to the random effect model. *Biometrika*, 61(1), 101–107. 10.1093/biomet/61.1.101

Gras-Gil, E., Manzano, M. P., & Fernández, J. H. (2016). Investigating the relationship between corporate social responsibility and earnings management: Evidence from Spain. *Business Research Quarterly*, 19(4), 289–299. 10.1016/j.brq.2016.02.002

Gray, P., Koh, P. S., & Tong, Y. H. (2009). Accruals quality, information risk and cost of capital: Evidence from Australia. *Journal of Business Finance & Accounting*, 36(1-2), 51–72. 10.1111/j.1468-5957.2008.02118.x

Grossman, S. J., & Hart, O. D. (1980). Disclosure laws and takeover bids. *The Journal of Finance*, 35(2), 323–334. 10.1111/j.1540-6261.1980.tb02161.x

Guthrie, J., & Parker, L. D. (1990). Corporate social disclosure practice: a comparative international analysis. *Advances in public interest accounting, 3*, 159-175.

Hair, F.Jr, J., Sarstedt, M., Hopkins, L., & G. Kuppelwieser, V. (. (2014). Partial least squares structural equation modeling (PLS-SEM) An emerging tool in business research. *European Business Review*, 26(2), 106–121. 10.1108/EBR-10-2013-0128

Hair, J.Jr, Sarstedt, M., Hopkins, L., & Kuppelwieser, G., V. (. (2014). Partial least squares structural equation modeling (PLS-SEM) An emerging tool in business research. *European Business Review*, 26(2), 106–121. 10.1108/EBR-10-2013-0128

Hair, J. F.Jr, Matthews, L. M., Matthews, R. L., & Sarstedt, M. (2017). PLS-SEM or CB-SEM: Updated guidelines on which method to use. *International Journal of Multivariate Data Analysis*, 1(2), 107–123. 10.1504/IJMDA.2017.087624

Hamrouni, A., Bouattour, M., Ben Farhat Toumi, N., & Boussaada, R. (2021). Corporate social responsibility disclosure and information asymmetry: Does board-room attributes matter? *Journal of Applied Accounting Research*, 23(5), 897–920. 10.1108/JAAR-03-2021-0056

He, W. P., Lepone, A., & Leung, H. (2013). Information asymmetry and the cost of equity capital. *International Review of Economics & Finance*, 27, 611–620. 10.1016/j.iref.2013.03.001

Heal, G. M. (2008). *When principles pay: corporate social responsibility and the bottom line*. Columbia University Press. 10.7312/heal14400

Healy, P. M., & Palepu, K. G. (2001). Information asymmetry, corporate disclosure, and the capital markets: A review of the empirical disclosure literature. *Journal of Accounting and Economics*, 31(1-3), 405–440. 10.1016/S0165-4101(01)00018-0

Healy, P. M., & Wahlen, J. M. (1999). A review of the earnings management literature and its implications for standard setting. *Accounting Horizons*, 13(4), 365–383. 10.2308/acch.1999.13.4.365

Hoang, H. V., Ha, S. T., Tran, M. L., & Nguyen, T. T. T. (2022). Is auditor tolerant of earnings management in socially responsible firms? Evidence from China. *Asian Review of Accounting*, 30(5), 669–690. 10.1108/ARA-01-2022-0001

Hong, H., & Kacperczyk, M. (2009). The price of sin: The effects of social norms on markets. *Journal of Financial Economics*, 93(1), 15–36. 10.1016/j.jfineco.2008.09.001

Hughes, J. S., Liu, J., & Liu, J. (2007). Information asymmetry, diversification, and cost of capital. *The Accounting Review*, 82(3), 705–729. 10.2308/accr.2007.82.3.705

Hung, M., Shi, J., & Wang, Y. (2015). Mandatory CSR disclosure and information asymmetry: Evidence from a quasi-natural experiment in China. In *The Asian Finance Conference 2013*.

Hunton, J. E., Libby, R., & Mazza, C. L. (2006). Financial reporting transparency and earnings management (retracted). *The Accounting Review*, 81(1), 135–157. 10.2308/accr.2006.81.1.135

Jensen, J. C., & Berg, N. (2012). Determinants of traditional sustainability reporting versus integrated reporting. An institutionalist approach. *Business Strategy and the Environment*, 21(5), 299–316. 10.1002/bse.740

Jensen, M. C., & Meckling, W. H. (1976). Theory of the firm: Managerial behavior, agency costs and ownership structure. *Journal of Financial Economics*, 3(4), 305–360. 10.1016/0304-405X(76)90026-X

Jo, H., & Harjoto, M. A. (2011). Corporate governance and firm value: The impact of corporate social responsibility. *Journal of Business Ethics*, 103(3), 351–383. 10.1007/s10551-011-0869-y

Jo, H., & Kim, Y. (2007). Disclosure frequency and earnings management. *Journal of Financial Economics*, 84(2), 561–590. 10.1016/j.jfineco.2006.03.007

Jones, T. M. (1995). Instrumental stakeholder theory: A synthesis of ethics and economics. *Academy of Management Review*, 20(2), 404–437. 10.2307/258852

Kazemi, H., & Rahmani, F. (2013). Relationship between information asymmetry and cost of capital. *Management Science Letters*, 3(1), 321–328. 10.5267/j.msl.2012.10.026

Khanchel, I., & Lassoued, N. (2022). ESG Disclosure and the Cost of Capital: Is There a Ratcheting Effect over Time? *Sustainability (Basel)*, 14(15), 9237. 10.3390/su14159237

Kim, J. B., & Sohn, B. C. (2013). Real earnings management and cost of capital. *Journal of Accounting and Public Policy*, 32(6), 518–543. 10.1016/j.jaccpubpol.2013.08.002

Kim, Y., Park, M. S., & Wier, B. (2012). Is earnings quality associated with corporate social responsibility? *The Accounting Review*, 87(3), 761–796. 10.2308/accr-10209

Kothari, S. P., Leone, A. J., & Wasley, C. E. (2005). Performance matched discretionary accrual measures. *Journal of Accounting and Economics*, 39(1), 163–197. 10.1016/j.jacceco.2004.11.002

Lambert, R., Leuz, C., & Verrecchia, R. E. (2007). Accounting information, disclosure, and the cost of capital. *Journal of Accounting Research*, 45(2), 385–420. 10.1111/j.1475-679X.2007.00238.x

Lambert, R. A., Leuz, C., & Verrecchia, R. E. (2011). Information asymmetry, information precision, and the cost of capital. *Review of Finance*, 16(1), 1–29. 10.1093/rof/rfr014

Laux, C., & Leuz, C. (2009). The crisis of fair-value accounting: Making sense of the recent debate. *Accounting, Organizations and Society*, 34(6-7), 826–834. 10.1016/j.aos.2009.04.003

Le, B., & Moore, P. H. (2021). The impact of audit quality on earnings management and cost of equity capital: Evidence from a developing market. *Journal of Financial Reporting and Accounting*, 21(3), 695–728. 10.1108/JFRA-09-2021-0284

Lee, M. T., Raschke, R. L., & Krishen, A. S. (2022). Signaling green! Firm ESG signals in an interconnected environment that promote brand valuation. *Journal of Business Research*, 138, 1–11. 10.1016/j.jbusres.2021.08.061

Lefort, F., & González, R. (2008). Hacia un mejor gobierno corporativo en Chile. *Revista Abante*, 11(1), 17–37.

Leland, H. E. (1992). Insider trading: Should it be prohibited? *Journal of Political Economy*, 100(4), 859–887. 10.1086/261843

Leuz, C., & Verrecchia, R. (2000). The economic consequences of increased disclosure. *Journal of Accounting Research*, 38, 91–124. 10.2307/2672910

Leuz, C., & Verrecchia, R. E. (1999). The economic consequences of increased disclosure. *Available atSSRN* 171975.

Lombardo, D., & Pagano, M. (2002). Law and equity markets: A simple model. *Corporate governance regimes: Convergence and diversity*, 343-362.

Lu, C. W., & Chueh, T. S. (2015). Corporate social responsibility and information asymmetry. *Journal of Applied Finance & Banking*, 5(3), 105–122.

Martínez-Ferrero, J., Banerjee, S., & García-Sánchez, I. M. (2016). Corporate social responsibility as a strategic shield against costs of earnings management practices. *Journal of Business Ethics*, 133(2), 305–324. 10.1007/s10551-014-2399-x

Martínez-Ferrero, J., Gallego-Álvarez, I., & García-Sánchez, I. M. (2015). A bidirectional analysis of earnings management and corporate social responsibility: The moderating effect of stakeholder and investor protection. *Australian Accounting Review*, 25(4), 359–371. 10.1111/auar.12075

Masud, M. H., Anees, F., & Ahmed, H. (2017). Impact of corporate diversification on earnings management. *Journal of Indian Business Research*, 9(2), 82–106. 10.1108/JIBR-06-2015-0070

Mazumdar, S. C., & Sengupta, P. (2005). Disclosure and the loan spread on private debt. *Financial Analysts Journal*, 61(3), 83–95. 10.2469/faj.v61.n3.2731

McInnis, J. (2010). Earnings smoothness, average returns, and implied cost of equity capital. *The Accounting Review*, 85(1), 315–341. 10.2308/accr.2010.85.1.315

McWilliams, A., Siegel, D. S., & Wright, P. M. (2006). Corporate social responsibility: Strategic implications. *Journal of Management Studies*, 43(1), 1–18. 10.1111/j.1467-6486.2006.00580.x

Menz, K. M. (2010). Corporate social responsibility: Is it rewarded by the corporate bond market? A critical note. *Journal of Business Ethics*, 96(1), 117–134. 10.1007/s10551-010-0452-y

Merton, R. C. (1987). A simple model of capital market equilibrium with incomplete information. *The Journal of Finance*, 42(3), 483–510. 10.1111/j.1540-6261.1987.tb04565.x

Michaels, A., & Grüning, M. (2017). Relationship of corporate social responsibility disclosure on information asymmetry and the cost of capital. *Journal of Management Control*, 28(3), 251–274. 10.1007/s00187-017-0251-z

Muttakin, M. B., Khan, A., & Subramaniam, N. (2015). Firm characteristics, board diversity and corporate social responsibility: Evidence from Bangladesh. *Pacific Accounting Review*, 27(3), 353–372. 10.1108/PAR-01-2013-0007

Ng, A. C., & Rezaee, Z. (2015). Business sustainability performance and cost of equity capital. *Journal of Corporate Finance*, 34, 128–149. 10.1016/j.jcorpfin.2015.08.003

Noe, T. H., & Rebello, M. J. (1996). Asymmetric information, managerial opportunism, financing, and payout policies. *The Journal of Finance*, 51(2), 637–660. 10.1111/j.1540-6261.1996.tb02697.x

Park, S. R., & Jang, J. Y. (2021). The Impact of ESG Management on Investment Decision: Institutional Investors' Perceptions of Country-Specific ESG Criteria. *International Journal of Financial Studies*, 9(3), 3. 10.3390/ijfs9030048

Patro, A., & Kanagaraj, A. (2016). Is Earnings Management a Technique to Reduce Cost of Capital? Exploratory Study on Indian Companies. *Journal of Modern Accounting and Auditing*, 12(5), 243–249.

Petersen, H., & Vredenburg, H. (2009). Corporate governance, social responsibility and capital markets: exploring the institutional investor mental model. *Corporate Governance: The international journal of business in society, 9*(5), 610-622.

Plumlee, M., Brown, D., & Marshall, S. (2008). The impact of voluntary environmental disclosure quality on firm value. *Available atSSRN* 1140221.

Prior, D., Surroca, J., & Tribó, J. A. (2008). Are socially responsible managers really ethical? Exploring the relationship between earnings management and corporate social responsibility. *Corporate Governance*, 16(3), 160–177. 10.1111/j.1467-8683.2008.00678.x

Putra, H. B. D., Trisnawati, R., & Sasongko, N. (2016). Cost of Equity Capital and Real Earnings Management on Listed Companies in LQ-45 and Jakarta Islamic Index.

Raghunandan, A., & Rajgopal, S. (2022). Do ESG funds make stakeholder-friendly investments? *Review of Accounting Studies*, 27(3), 822–863. 10.1007/s11142-022-09693-1

Reverte, C. (2012). The impact of better corporate social responsibility disclosure on the cost of equity capital. *Corporate Social Responsibility and Environmental Management*, 19(5), 253–272. 10.1002/csr.273

Reynold, J., & Santos, A. (1999). Cronbach's alpha: A tool for assessing the reliability of scales. *Journal of Extension*, 37(7), 36–35.

Rezaee, Z., & Tuo, L. (2019). Are the Quantity and Quality of Sustainability Disclosures Associated with the Innate and Discretionary Earnings Quality? *Journal of Business Ethics*, 155(3), 763–786. 10.1007/s10551-017-3546-y

Richardson, A. J., & Welker, M. (2001). Social disclosure, financial disclosure and the cost of equity capital. *Accounting, Organizations and Society*, 26(7-8), 597–616. 10.1016/S0361-3682(01)00025-3

Richardson, V. J. (2000). Information asymmetry and earnings management: Some evidence. *Review of Quantitative Finance and Accounting*, 15(4), 325–347. 10.1023/A:1012098407706

Rigdon, E. E. (1998). The equal correlation baseline model for comparative fit assessment in structural equation modeling. *Structural Equation Modeling*, 5(1), 63–77. 10.1080/10705519809540089

Rymar, I. E. (2016). Information asymmetry and its impact on cost of equity capital: Volkswagen case.

Schäfer, H. (2004). Ethical Investment of German Non-Profit Organzations-Conceptual Outline and Empirical Results. *Business Ethics (Oxford, England)*, 13(4), 269–287. 10.1111/j.1467-8608.2004.00370.x

Schaltegger, S., & Figge, F. (2000). Environmental shareholder value: Economic success with corporate environmental management. *Eco-Management and Auditing*, 7(1), 29–42. 10.1002/(SICI)1099-0925(200003)7:1<29::AID-EMA119>3.0.CO;2-1

Schipper, K. (1989). Earnings management. *Accounting Horizons*, 3(4), 91.

Scholtens, B., & Kang, F. C. (2013). Corporate social responsibility and earnings management: Evidence from Asian economies. *Corporate Social Responsibility and Environmental Management*, 20(2), 95–112. 10.1002/csr.1286

Siew, R. Y., Balatbat, M. C., & Carmichael, D. G. (2016). The impact of ESG disclosures and institutional ownership on market information asymmetry. *Asia-Pacific Journal of Accounting & Economics*, 23(4), 432–448. 10.1080/16081625.2016.1170100

Sougné, D., & Ajina, A. (2014). Examining the Effect of Earnings Management on Bid-Ask Spread and Market Liquidity. *European Journal of Business and Management*, 9(28).

Stone, M. (1974). Cross-validation and multinomial prediction. *Biometrika*, 61(3), 509–515. 10.1093/biomet/61.3.509

Strobl, G. (2013). Earnings manipulation and the cost of capital. *Journal of Accounting Research*, 51(2), 449–473. 10.1111/1475-679X.12008

Suto, M., & Takehara, H. (2017). CSR and cost of capital: Evidence from Japan. *Social Responsibility Journal*, 13(4), 798–816. 10.1108/SRJ-10-2016-0170

Teoh, S. H., Welch, I., & Wong, T. J. (1998). Earnings management and the long-run market performance of initial public offerings. *The Journal of Finance*, 53(6), 1935–1974. 10.1111/0022-1082.00079

Trueman, B., & Titman, S. (1988). An explanation for accounting income smoothing. *Journal of Accounting Research*, 26, 127–139. 10.2307/2491184

Verrecchia, R. E. (1983). Discretionary disclosure. *Journal of Accounting and Economics*, 5, 179–194. 10.1016/0165-4101(83)90011-3

Verrecchia, R. E. (2001). Essays on disclosure. *Journal of Accounting and Economics*, 32(1-3), 97–180. 10.1016/S0165-4101(01)00025-8

Wang, J. (1993). A model of intertemporal asset prices under asymmetric information. *The Review of Economic Studies*, 60(2), 249–282. 10.2307/2298057

Wang, S., & D'Souza, J. (2006). Earnings management: The effect of accounting flexibility on R&D investment choices. *Johnson School Research Paper Series*, (33-06).

Warfield, T. D., Wild, J. J., & Wild, K. L. (1995). Managerial ownership, accounting choices, and informativeness of earnings. *Journal of Accounting and Economics*, 20(1), 61–91. 10.1016/0165-4101(94)00393-J

Welker, M. (1995). Disclosure policy, information asymmetry, and liquidity in equity markets. *Contemporary Accounting Research*, 11(2), 801–827. 10.1111/j.1911-3846.1995.tb00467.x

Wiseman, J. (1982). An evaluation of environmental disclosures made in corporate annual reports. *Accounting, Organizations and Society*, 7(1), 53–63. 10.1016/0361-3682(82)90025-3

Wiyadi, A Veno, N & Sasongko. (2015). Information Asymmetry And Earnings Management: Good Corporate Governance As Moderating Variable. South East Asia Journal of Contemporary Business. *Economics and Law*, 7, 54–61.

Wong, K. K. K. (2013). Partial least squares structural equation modeling (PLS-SEM) techniques using SmartPLS. *Marketing Bulletin*, 24(1), 1–32.

Xia, L. J., & LU, X. N. (2005). On the Relationship between Earnings Management and Information Disclosure Quality of Listed Firms [J]. *Geological Technoeconomic Management, 5*.

Xu, S., Liu, D., & Huang, J. (2015). Corporate social responsibility, the cost of equity capital and ownership structure: An analysis of Chinese listed firms. *Australian Journal of Management*, 40(2), 245–276. 10.1177/0312896213517894

Chapter 6
Greenwashing in ESG and Its Implications

Ramsha Noori

Indian Institute of Management, Udaipur, India

Vidya S. Athota

The University of Notre Dame, Australia

ABSTRACT

This book chapter discusses greenwashing within the domain of Environmental, Social, and Governance (ESG), reflecting upon the emergent dichotomy between espoused corporate sustainability and actual environmental stewardship. By systematically reviewing the pertinent literature, the chapter highlights the pivotal role of greenwashing as a deceptive tactic within ESG framework. It discusses the Volkswagen's and Coca-Cola's greenwashing practices and offer empirical insights into the inconsistencies in their marketing claims of producing sustainable and eco-friendly products. This chapter explores the variances in ESG reporting due to differing regulatory frameworks and emphasize on the importance of regulatory frameworks in enhancing or impeding transparency in corporate disclosures. The chapter outlines the pressing research questions and practical challenges in containing greenwashing strategies and advocate for future scholarly exploration into the uncharted areas of ESG and corporate sustainability.

Introduction

The contemporary corporate accountability has witnessed Environmental, Social, and Governance (ESG) considerations emerging as pivotal yardsticks in assessing organizational conduct and its long-term implications on sustainability and ethics

DOI: 10.4018/979-8-3693-3880-3.ch006

(Chouaibi & Affes, 2021). Today's discerning investors and stakeholders leverage ESG standards to gauge not just the immediate fiscal health of companies, but their broader commitment to ethical practices and environmental custodianship (Eccles & Klimenko, 2019; Friede et al., 2015). These standards delve into a corporation's ecological footprint, scrutinize its societal interactions, and evaluate governance structures overseeing fair and transparent business operations. A sound ESG protocol reflects a corporation's adept navigation through the complexities of ethical stewardship and strategic foresight, often translating into lower financial risks and augmented investor confidence (Khan et al., 2016). This trust, however, is premised on the authenticity and reliability of reported ESG conduct, underscoring the importance of the quality of non-financial disclosure practices. With ESG disclosures largely remaining voluntary, companies enjoy a substantial berth in defining the narrative of their sustainability and eco-friendly practices. While this autonomy is instrumental in fostering tailored sustainability strategies, it also paves the way for greenwashing—a practice where firms embellish their sustainability credentials, offering an illusion of environmental virtue that may not hold up under scrutiny.

While ESG has emerged as a vital framework in modern corporate analysis, there is a growing concern about 'greenwashing,' a form of deceptive marketing where a company presents itself as more environmentally friendly or socially responsible than it is (Nguyen et al., 2019). This practice misleads stakeholders into believing that the products, values, and policies of a company are eco-friendly. The dissonance between the publicly espoused Corporate Social Responsibility (CSR) narratives and the underlying corporate actions is at the heart of this issue, leading to criticism and scepticism about the authenticity of these proclaimed commitments towards environment (Gatti et al., 2019). When companies fudge or exaggerate their ESG compliance, it undermines the very objectives ESG standards aim to achieve: sustainable development, social equity, and transparent corporate governance. Governments worldwide are recognizing the importance of genuine ESG practices, often offering subsidies and support to companies that display genuine commitment to these principles. However, many companies have been found to engage in greenwashing strategy when it comes to their reported ESG performance, either through omission, embellishment, or outright deception.

While the extant studies have identified individual cases pertaining to greenwashing, less is known about the congruence between what companies report in their ESG disclosures and their actual practices. This chapter provide a critical analysis of reported ESG practices, thereby aiding in enhanced understanding of the credibility gap in corporate sustainability reporting. Another gap in extant research is understanding how different countries' regulatory frameworks affect the sincerity and thoroughness of ESG disclosures with an objective to contain greenwashing. This review article has twofold objectives – first is to critically assess the corporate

ESG disclosures, with an emphasis on how it could potentially be used to engage in 'greenwashing.' Within the ambit of the first objective, the chapter will delve into a case study of greenwashing practices within a leading beverage company (Coca-Cola) and unravel how 'corporate greenwashing' unfolds in the business context. This case will not only underscore the misalignment between reported and actual green practices, but also scrutinize the subtleties and tactics used in the crafting of (public) environmental narratives that may mask unsustainable practices. The second objective is to evaluate the role of regulatory environments in influencing the transparency and accuracy of ESG reporting across different geopolitical contexts. Within the scope of second objective, this chapter seek to examine how regulatory stringency, corruption, and political freedom can influence corporate transparency and potentially reduce greenwashing behaviours. Overall, this chapter delves into the intricacies of greenwashing within the ESG framework, illuminating the contrast between the facade of compliance and the actual practices of corporations. This chapter will explore how the act of greenwashing can erode trust and hinder the efforts toward a sustainable and equitable future.

Literature Review

The literature on greenwashing extends across multiple disciplines, exploring the phenomenon from environmental, ethical, marketing, and regulatory perspectives. The body of literature reveals an array of strategies employed by firms to appear more sustainable than they are, and the impacts of these practices on consumer behaviour and trust. This section first provides a brief summary of types of greenwashing, followed by how different academic disciplines approach greenwashing.

Tateishi (2017, p. 3) defines greenwashing as a form of messaging that deceives individuals regarding the environmental claims or benefits of a company, service, product by selectively withholding adverse details and overemphasizing favourable information. The extant literature has identified three primary types of greenwashing. The first involves tweaking of disclosure to inflate company valuation, misleading stakeholders by overstating environmental performance (Lyon & Maxwell, 2011; Lyon & Montgomery, 2013; Marquis et al., 2016). Another approach is the manipulation of investment funds labeled as "green" or "sustainable", where some corporations may rebrand existing funds as ESG funds without making substantial changes to the investment criteria, a practice known as "ESG integration." This can give the illusion that a company is prioritizing sustainable investments, when in reality, the underlying assets might not align with true ESG principles (Berg et al., 2022). The second type, selective disclosure, is characterized by firms reporting positive environmental information while concealing the negative, thus creating false impressions of their environmental performance (Kirk & Vincent, 2014; Lyon & Maxwell, 2011; Lyon & Montgomery, 2013; Marquis et al., 2016). Selective disclosure also involves the withholding of information pertaining to environmental damage created through its products or services. Moreover, marketing efforts often disproportionately highlight a minor green aspect of a product or service while ignoring its detrimental impact on environment, which broadly falls under the practice of "selective disclosure" (Delmas & Burbano, 2011). The third type pertains to product-level greenwashing, wherein firms may exaggerate the eco-friendly nature of their products to boost sales, impacting consumer decisions and the perceived value of green brands (Delmas & Burbano, 2011; Majid & Russell, 2015; Cho & Baskin, 2018). One common approach to product greenwashing is through ambiguous or broad claims that lack clarity or specificity. For instance, a company might tout its products as "green" or "eco-friendly" without providing concrete evidence or details to support such claims. This can also include the use of misleading labels or certifications that are either self-created or obtained through lenient standards, offering an unwarranted sheen of sustainability (Lyon & Maxwell, 2011).

Terrachoice Environmental Marketing Inc. (2007) conducted one of the earliest and most cited studies on greenwashing, producing the "Six Sins of Greenwashing" report, which categorizes common greenwashing tactics and discusses their prevalence in consumer markets (Terrachoice, 2007). The study identified six common misleading tactics deployed by companies to portray their products or services as eco-friendly. These include the "Sin of the Hidden Trade-Off," which emphasizes one eco-friendly attribute over others that may be more harmful; the "Sin of No Proof," where the claims made by the firms are not backed by scientific evidence or through endorsement by a third-party verifying agency; the "Sin of Vagueness," where claims are deliberately defined in abstract terms which either could not be easily interpreted or has the potential of deceiving the customers; the "Sin of Irrelevance," involving claims that could be correct, however has less bearing for customers soliciting eco-friendly products and services; the "Sin of Lesser of Two Evils," which creates a false sense of green by comparing a product to the worst options available; and the "Sin of Fibbing," where such claims made by the firms are outright false or grossly fudged. This study was crucial in shedding light on the deceptive practices of greenwashing, highlighting the urgent need for more rigorous standards and consumer education to combat such misleading tactics (Terrachoice, 2007).

The extant literature has explored the broader consequences of greenwashing. For instance, Zhang (2022) and Teichmann et al. (2023) investigate the adverse effects of greenwashing on the financial performance of companies and the regulatory environment. These studies reveal that stringent environmental regulations and negative media exposure can undermine the financial benefits that companies might initially gain from greenwashing. Teichmann et al. (2023) further discuss how consumer interactivity on corporate websites can provide insights into public perceptions of corporate sustainability, showing that perceived greenwashing correlates negatively with consumer trust and positively with consumer scepticism regarding corporate sustainability claims. The economic implications of greenwashing are profound, influencing not only corporate performance but also consumer behaviour and market dynamics.

Investigations by Friede et al. (2015) and Orlitzky et al. (2003) examine the correlation between ESG factors and financial results, whereas Zhang (2022) study addresses the detrimental effects of environmental regulations on firms with high pollution levels. Likewise, Walker and Wan (2012) discuss the financial implications of symbolic environmental actions, noting how these can serve as a form of greenwashing that may temporarily benefit firms at the expense of genuine sustainability. This body of work suggests that while greenwashing can temporarily enhance a company's image and financial standing, the long-term consequences—driven by consumer disillusionment and regulatory pressures—can be detrimental.

The literature on corporate governance suggests that vertical interlocking—where executives or directors are simultaneously holding positions across different firms, whether within a corporate group or among unrelated entities—can significantly influence a firm's adherence to Environmental, Social, and Governance (ESG) reporting standards. Haw et al. (2004) propose that governance structures, including ownership and control dynamics, are decisive in shaping management's disclosure behaviours, a premise applicable to ESG disclosures within vertical interlocks. Allen et al. (2005) discuss the broader consequences of such corporate governance arrangements, postulating their potential effects on economic growth and the efficacy of regulatory frameworks in China. Moreover, Marquis et al. (2016) delve into organizational norms and scrutiny as pivotal elements in forming corporate social responsibility behaviours, which implies that these could similarly affect the integrity of ESG reporting in scenarios where vertical interlocking is present. Exploring the context of emerging markets, Khanna and Palepu (2000) examine vertical interlocks' contributions to strategic coherence and the performance of corporate groups. Bizjak et al. (2009) provide insights into how board interlocks, which can be analogous to vertical interlocks, might significantly sway managerial decisions and affect the transparency of corporate practices. This body of literature collectively underscores the potential of vertical interlocking to shape corporate governance outcomes, including the quality and transparency of ESG reporting.

Greenwashing across academic disciplines

Within the broader realm of economics, studies have revealed the effect of capital market liberalization on the greenwashing of ESG reporting (Liu et al., 2024). While the influx of foreign investors under liberalization is expected to establish de facto regulation, compelling corporations to curtail information manipulation, it has been observed that private firms often resort to deceptive greenwashing practices to attract foreign investors (Bae et al., 2006; Chen & Wang, 2023). This opportunistic behaviour remains unchecked by foreign investors and analysts, and thus they fail to act as regulators that could restrain ESG report greenwashing. However, the propensity for greenwashing was found to be significantly lower in the case of state-owned enterprises with a mandatory ESG disclosure imperative. This underscores how the ownership structure can have an impact on the authenticity of ESG disclosures. For private sector firms under liberalized market conditions, financial pressures may exacerbate the divergence between reported and actual ESG practices. From a theoretical viewpoint, these nuanced insights highlight the strong prevalence of a catering effect, wherein local firms may tailor their ESG disclosures to attract (and cater to) the preferences of foreign investors. Such tailored disclosures could potentially include embellishments or omissions, leading to practices such as greenwashing (Hou et al., 2019; Jiao et al., 2021).

Both green loans and green bonds (GBs) issued by public and private sector entities aim to provide sustainable financing models that accelerate the transition to sustainable development practices (Baldi & Pandimiglio, 2022). Green loans represent a significant component of green finance, wherein banks and financial institutions provide funds specifically earmarked for projects that yield environmental benefits. These loans are integral in promoting sustainability across various sectors by offering financial incentives for adopting environmentally friendly practices (Mirovic et al., 2023). The theoretical underpinning of green loans lies in their potential to facilitate the transition to a low-carbon economy by mitigating the financial barriers associated with sustainable projects. For instance, the European Investment Bank (EIB) has played a crucial role in this domain by extending green loans to support renewable energy projects, energy efficiency upgrades, and sustainable urban infrastructure. The alignment of green loans with broader environmental, social, and governance (ESG) criteria underscores their importance in contemporary financial markets, promoting both economic and environmental objectives. Green bonds, on the other hand, represent a burgeoning class of fixed-income securities designated to generate funds for climate and environmentally friendly business ventures. Green bonds have emerged as a crucial vehicle for financing projects with environmental benefits, often with favourable yield dynamics for investors. These dynamics are not solely driven by traditional financial metrics but are increasingly influenced by the project's

ESG credentials and the associated risk of greenwashing. As Baldi & Pandimiglio (2022) assert, green bonds with substantial underlying projects, reflected in high ESG scores, tend to attract investors even at lower yields, underlining the financial market's growing valuation of sustainability. However, the yields on green bonds are not immune to the pervasive issue of greenwashing. The risk associated with issuers' potential overstatement of their environmental commitment is a significant concern for investors, often resulting in a greenwashing premium on the yield of green bonds. This necessitates a higher yield to mitigate the risk of investments not delivering the environmental impact as promised (Baldi & Pandimiglio, 2022). The integrity of green bonds is therefore a critical factor in determining their attractiveness and efficacy as instruments for sustainable development.

From economic gains viewpoint, the profit motive of firms can create a dichotomy, where the immediacy of financial returns (profit-seeking imperative) is seen as fundamentally at odds with the resource allocation necessary for sustainable practices (Ashforth & Reingen, 2014; Hahn et al., 2015). When companies prioritize short-term gains, the authenticity of their ESG claims can come into question, leading to accusations of greenwashing. Hengst et al. (2020) argue for a dynamic and iterative process of making sustainability strategies legitimate in action. In this case, a firm might choose to invest in sustainable technology that, while initially more costly, could lead to operational efficiencies and long-term cost savings, aligning with both sustainability and profit seeking objectives (Hengst et al., 2020).

In the realm of finance and corporate governance, the literature on financial implications (such as firms valuation) of greenwashing has become increasingly nuanced, reflecting growing concerns over the authenticity of corporate sustainability efforts. Central to this debate is the strategic disclosure of ESG information by corporates, which is intricately linked to their valuation and environmental risk management (Lyon et al., 2013; Marquis et al. 2016; Yu et al. 2020). These scholars contend that ESG factors significantly influence a firm's valuation, implying that investors integrate such non-financial information into their decision-making processes. Another essential element in the financial discourse of greenwashing is the voluntary disclosure of CSR information. Study by Laufer (2003) suggest that the lack of standardization and verification in CSR reporting can lead to information asymmetry, allowing companies to overstate their environmental efforts without substantial evidence to back their claims. Likewise, Lu et al. (2024) suggest that CSR reports could improve monitoring of firm managers and result in more efficient cash management. Complementing this, Dhaliwal et al. (2011) demonstrate the financial benefits of initiating voluntary CSR disclosure, as evidenced by companies with superior CSR performance gaining cheaper access to equity capital. Meanwhile, Ghoul et al. (2018) find that adherence to sustainability and environmental standards can lower the business risk and thereby reduce the cost associated with accessing equity capital.

A critical aspect of greenwashing research is the sociological and psychological underpinnings that explain why companies engage in such practices and how consumers interpret and react to them. Nyilasy et al. (2014) investigated the cognitive processes that lead consumers to be sceptical of corporate environmental claims. They found that consumer scepticism is influenced by the perceived motives behind the company's environmental actions, affecting the social acceptance and overall trust in the brand (Nyilasy et al., 2014). For instance, Pascual et al. (2017) note that extreme scrutiny and negative reporting from NGOs and other civil society organizations could be detrimental to a firm's social acceptance, especially if the firm do not perform well on parameters pertaining to mitigating environmental impact and sustainability. In contrast, Marquis et al. (2016) suggest that firms with superior adherence with environmental standards might have high social acceptance and thus engage less in greenwashing because they have fewer negative aspects to conceal.

From a marketing standpoint, scholars have investigated the persuasive techniques used in green marketing and their effects on consumers. Parguel et al. (2011) delved into the deceptive use of eco-labels and environmental product attributes. They highlighted the issue of 'hidden trade-offs', where companies may exaggerate the significance of one environmentally friendly attribute to distract from other, more harmful environmental impacts. Such tactics exploit consumer confusion and result in misplaced trust in the brands (Parguel et al., 2011).

Within the strategic management studies, incorporating ESG considerations offers a pathway to sustainability that is both genuine and aligned with business objectives. Strategic management as a discipline is increasingly recognizing the necessity of integrating ESG criteria into the core of business strategy, moving away from the peripheral, check-box approach that often leads to greenwashing. Hengst et al. (2020) provide a framework for understanding this integration, emphasizing the need for iterative action cycles that align sustainability strategies (SUST) with mainstream strategies (MAST), thus enabling firms to negotiate between profitability and sustainability objectives. This transformation involves establishing a symbiotic relationship between SUST and MAST, wherein each strategy is continuously redefined to support the other's objectives, thereby ensuring that ESG considerations are not peripheral but integral to the firm's core operational logic (Hengst et al., 2020).

Strategic management studies advocate for a holistic approach where sustainability is not an afterthought but a cornerstone of competitive advantage and value creation. According to Hengst et al. (2020), this integration demands a reinterpretation of business models and operational processes that can adaptively align sustainability goals with strategic business outcomes. It requires organizations to engage in legitimate action that reinforces their commitment to sustainability while ensuring economic viability. This adaptive alignment is a strategic endeavour where firms continuously reassess and realign their ESG initiatives with business goals, resulting in strategies that are sustainable in both environmental and economic terms (Hengst et al., 2020).

Theoretical Perspectives

Political economy theories, stakeholder theory, and legitimacy theory provide lenses through which we can understand corporate ESG disclosures and ensuing corporate greenwashing practices (Deegan, 2000). Political economy theory posits that corporate disclosures are not merely neutral or technical practices but are embedded within the broader socio-political and economic context. From this perspective, ESG disclosures are seen as strategic instruments used by firms to navigate and influence the societal structures and economic conditions within which they operate (Gray et al., 1995). This theory suggests that firms will disclose ESG information to align with the prevailing economic and political climate, ensuring their survival and profitability. When ESG disclosures are manipulated to create a misleadingly positive perception of the firm's sustainability practices, this can be understood as a form of greenwashing that seeks to exploit and influence societal and political structures for economic benefit. Gesso and Lodhi (2024) present a review of theories in the domain of accounting, focused on ESG disclosure, revealing the prominence of stakeholder theory and legitimacy theory. These theoretical frameworks offer fresh perspectives on how ESG disclosures are not just compliance exercises but strategic communications shaped by multiple stakeholder demands and societal norms.

Stakeholder theory focusses on the nexus between the firm and various stakeholders, ranging from shareholders and employees to communities and governments (Mitchell et al., 1997). Within the ambit of this theory, stakeholders are considered to have distinct interests and power over the firm, and their needs and concerns can drive the quantity and quality of ESG disclosures. Firms use ESG reporting as a way to demonstrate that they are attentive to their stakeholders demands for transparency and accountability, thus securing necessary support to manage its stakeholder relationships (Donaldson & Preston, 1995). However, this too can be co-opted into greenwashing when firms selectively disclose information to appease certain stakeholders or to defuse potential criticisms pertaining to environmental impact of their operations, without making substantive changes to their practices (Donaldson & Preston, 1995).

Legitimacy theory complements stakeholder theory by emphasizing the societal expectations and norms that firms must conform to maintain their 'license to operate.' According to this theory, firms engage in ESG disclosures to legitimize their activities and to demonstrate that their operations are aligned with the values and norms of society (Suchman, 1995). This involves managing perceptions and constructing a narrative that reflects the firm as a responsible corporate citizen. Since legitimacy is not static but evolves with societal values and expectations, the ESG disclosures may change over time to reflect these shifts and to continuously seek societal approval for corporate strategies and actions (Deegan, 2002). Yet, when such disclosures are more about crafting a socially responsible image than about reporting actual sustainable practices, they can contribute to a firm's greenwashing strategy, wherein they seek legitimacy through an illusion of conformity to societal expectations (Deegan, 2002). Legitimacy theory, dovetailing with stakeholder theory, underlines the need for companies to adapt to the prevailing societal expectations and norms to secure their operational legitimacy. For instance, Rahman and Alsayegh (2021) add empirical weight to this discourse, noting that a firm's size and economic performance can influence the depth of its ESG disclosures, which can either bolster or undermine their legitimacy efforts. This interplay suggests that firms must go beyond mere reporting enhancement; they need to embed actual sustainable practices into their ESG efforts, meeting the rising stakeholder demand for genuine transparency and corporate sustainability.

It is pertinent to underscore that these theoretical perspectives are not mutually exclusive but rather interlinked, offering a combined view that corporations use ESG reporting as a means to manage stakeholder relations and maintain societal legitimacy (Amran et al., 2015; Soobaroyen & Mahadeo, 2016). The combined view offered by these theories illustrates that ESG reporting serves multiple purposes: it is a means for navigating socio-political contexts, managing stakeholder relations, and maintaining societal legitimacy. However, there is a risk that ESG reporting, by the corporations, can be used to greenwash, thereby distorting these purposes.

Case 1: The Greenwashing Strategy of Volkswagen (VVW)

In 2015, Volkswagen (VW) Group, a prominent automaker known globally for its engineering prowess and environmental claims, became embroiled in a scandal that rocked the automotive industry. The company had marketed its diesel-powered vehicles, particularly in the United States, as environmentally friendly with low emissions of nitrogen oxides (NOx), branding them as "clean diesel" cars (Ewing & Boudette, 2015). However, investigations by the Environmental Protection Agency (EPA) and the California Air Resources Board (CARB) revealed that VW had equipped its diesel engines with software designed to detect when the vehicles were undergoing emissions testing. During these tests, the software activated emissions control systems, leading the cars to emit significantly lower levels of pollutants compared to real-world driving conditions (Hakim, 2015). Upon detection of real-world driving conditions, the software deactivated these controls, allowing the vehicles to emit pollutants, including NOx, at levels up to 40 times higher than permitted under US environmental regulations (Ewing & Boudette, 2015). This deliberate manipulation of emissions data affected approximately 11 million vehicles worldwide, spanning several VW brands including Volkswagen, Audi, and Porsche (Hakim, 2015). The implications were profound and multifaceted. Beyond the immediate environmental impact of increased NOx emissions, VW faced severe legal consequences, including fines and settlements amounting to billions of dollars. The scandal tarnished VW's reputation as a leader in environmental sustainability and raised questions about the effectiveness of regulatory oversight in the automotive sector (Ewing & Boudette, 2015; Hakim, 2015).

Case 2: The Greenwashing Strategy of Coca-Cola Marketing of Bottled Water

Greenwashing in the beverage industry is a significant concern, with corporations like Coca-Cola often at the centre of this debate due to their extensive marketing campaigns. The marketing strategies of Coca-Cola, especially for its bottled water products (such as *Dasani)*, have been criticized for overstating environmental stewardship and sustainability while downplaying the ecological impacts of bottled water production and disposal. This practice essentially is an instance of greenwashing, where the corporations uses marketing tactics to create a 'green' brand image that may not align with the actual environmental impact of their products (Bruce & Laroiya, 2007). Critics argue that the company's promotion of bottled water as a "pure" and "natural" alternative to tap water, alongside investments in water efficiency and recycling programs, are efforts to deflect attention from the environmental costs of producing and distributing bottled water (Hawkins, 2011). Through a semiotic analysis of advertising campaigns, Lanthorn (2013) contends that Coca-Cola's greenwashing efforts—while sophisticated in their integration of ecological imagery and discourse—are fundamentally driven by capitalistic motives rather than genuine environmental concern.

Research by Lanthorn (2013) further indicates that Coca-Cola's use of plant-based plastics and commitments to water replenishment can be seen as strategic greenwashing. It has been argued that *Dasani* "PlantBottle" (which claims to mix thirty percent plant based plastic material with the conventional petroleum based plastic material), despite being marketed as an ecologically responsible product, are not as environmentally beneficial (Jones, 2019; Lanthorn, 2013). While the advertisements created an association of the PlantBottles with nature and cleanness through the use of colours, symbols, and metaphors that suggest environmental responsibility, the reality is that the *Dasani* brand PlantBottles are still PET plastic bottles that are not biodegradable (Blanding, 2011; Lanthorn, 2013). The environmental benefits, such as reduced carbon emissions and recyclability, are therefore overshadowed by the broader ecological impacts of the bottled water industry (Haws, 2022). Despite Coca-Cola's products often bearing recycling symbols and certifications, some argue that these eco-labels can be misleading and serve as a form of greenwashing by implying a level of environmental friendliness that does not fully align with the product's life cycle impact (Halttunen & Inkilä, 2014).

Coca-Cola's global water management strategies have been scrutinized, where water scarcity is exacerbated by the company's extraction of local water resources for bottling (Holzendorff, 2013). Further examination by Holzendorff (2013) points to the discrepancy between Coca-Cola's marketing of bottled water as environmentally friendly and the reality of its water source depletion for communities in India. Furthermore, corporate social responsibility (CSR) reports from Coca-Cola emphasize water efficiency and recycling, but independent analyses suggest that these reports might selectively disclose information to improve the company's image (Lyon & Maxwell, 2011). The greenwashing tactics adopted by corporations like Coca-Cola exploits the public's growing environmental consciousness and manipulates consumers into making purchases based on a false perception of environmental benefit. This misrepresentation leads to consumer confusion and contributes to the commodification of the environment, where eco-friendliness becomes another marketing tool rather than a practice of actual sustainability. These greenwashing practices not only perpetuate a superficial consumer identity aligned with environmentalism but also mask the environmental costs of the various products, such as bottled water.

Despite these concerns, Coca-Cola has been recognized for some genuine environmental efforts. For instance, third-party organizations have acknowledged the company for improving water efficiency in its operations and for its global partnerships aimed at water conservation.

ESG Reporting and Greenwashing - Role of Institutional and Regulatory Environments

The regulatory framework within which firm's operate tend to have an impact on accuracy and transparency of ESG reporting. Studies have found that the corporates based in countries with robust regulatory environments usually have more comprehensive and transparent ESG disclosures (Ioannou & Serafeim, 2012). This is often attributed to the stringent reporting requirements and oversight mechanisms that compel corporations to adhere to higher standards of transparency while making ESG disclosures. For instance, the European Union's Non-Financial Reporting Directive (EU-NFRD) mandates big corporate entities to declare their operations and management of social and environmental challenges in a prescribed manner. This has enhanced the quality of information disclosed by companies on ESG matters, aligning with the findings of Eccles and Krzus (2010), who assert that mandatory reporting can significantly improve the trustworthiness of corporate ESG disclosures.

In contrast, the regulatory environment in some jurisdictions may not provide the same level of oversight or demand for ESG transparency, leading to greater variability in reporting practices. Companies in these regions may engage in ESG disclosures more as a response to market pressures than regulatory compulsion, which can result in inconsistent and less reliable reporting (Chen & Bouvain, 2009). For instance, research by Dhaliwal et al. (2011) indicates that voluntary ESG reporting without regulatory enforcement often leads to selective disclosure, allowing companies to highlight favourable activities while minimizing or omitting less flattering information. The need for harmonized global reporting standards is underscored by the work of KPMG (2020), which calls for international alignment in ESG reporting frameworks to enhance comparability and reliability across different geopolitical contexts.

The literature on greenwashing, when examined through the lens of public policy and regulatory practices, suggests a strong connection between corporate transparency and the socio-political context of a company's headquarters. It is posited that increased public scrutiny and pressure are conducive to more trustworthy corporate disclosure concerning ESG issues, a stance supported by multiple studies that scrutinize the influence of the regulatory framework on corporate behaviour (Vormedal & Ruud, 2009; Marquis et al., 2016). The regulatory landscape and public policy of a country play pivotal roles in shaping corporate disclosures. Marquis and Qian (2014) and Marquis et al. (2016) observed that firms are more forthcoming with their environmental and sustainability reports when located in nations where environmental NGOs are active and regulatory oversight is stringent. Delmas and Toffel (2004) further illustrate that firms may adopt various environmental strategies in response to different institutional pressures. Cooper and Uzun (2022) and Cuervo-Cazurra (2006) highlight that societies with diminished political and civil rights are often constrained in freely voicing apprehension through social media outlets or non-governmental organizations, potentially reducing corporate incentives to maintain transparency. Additionally, the prevalence of corruption in a given geography can directly affect the disclosures and transparency, as bribery and other corrupt practices can obscure the true nature of ESG implementation. In a comparative study, Ioannou and Serafeim (2012) reveal that firms in Japan experience relatively less pressure to bolster their sustainability and corporate social responsibility compared to their German counterparts, attributing this difference to the lower prevalence of corruption in Germany. These findings reveals that firms may be deterred from indulging in greenwashing strategies in countries with lower corruption levels and greater freedom for media and civil society organizations. Therefore with increased public scrutiny and pressure, fostered by a robust political and anti-corruption framework, could compel firms to provide more reliable ESG disclosures. Prakash and Potoski (2006) advocate for governmental and non-governmental organizations to develop clearer guidelines and certification processes to prevent greenwashing. They propose that third-party certifications could be instrumental in legitimizing environmental claims and restoring consumer confidence (Prakash & Potoski, 2006).

While the role of the regulatory environment is crucial, it is essential to emphasize that firms must substantively implement sustainability policies and move beyond merely symbolic green strategies. Yuan et al. (2011) support a close intertwining of the sustainability strategy with the prevailing competitive strategy of business organizations. This implies that firms, whose ultimate goal is to merely seek external legitimacy, may inadvertently end up decoupling sustainability from their core organizational activities and processes (Crilly et al., 2012; 2016; MacLean & Behnam, 2010).Top of Form

Recent research by Todaro and Torelli (2024) emphasizes the evolution of greenwashing into a broader context of 'ESG-washing,' wherein companies manipulate disclosures not just environmentally, but also in social and governance dimensions. Todaro and Torelli's (2024) investigation also sheds light on the complex relationship between circular economy (CE) adoption and ESG-washing practices. The circular economy (CE) concept is characterized by a closed-loop circulation of materials, coupled with the utilization of raw materials and energy across various phases (Geissdoerfer et al., 2017). The key objective of the circular economy is to extend the life cycle of materials by promoting their recycling and reusing waste as a resource. In this economic model, the intention is to minimize or eliminate waste so that materials and products are reused, recycled, and recovered, rather than discarded. Todaro and Torelli (2024) found that companies actively engaged in circular economy practices are less likely to engage in ESG-washing, suggesting a negative correlation between genuine circular economy adoption and the prevalence of misleading ESG communication (Todaro & Torelli, 2024). This supports the notion that substantive circular economy initiatives can serve as a mitigating factor against the risks of greenwashing, fostering more transparent and action-oriented sustainability strategies within firms.

Theoretical Implications

The exploration of greenwashing through the lenses of political economy, stakeholder, and legitimacy theories presents a detailed examination of corporate disclosure strategies and their societal reception. The intersection of these theories highlights the multifaceted motivations behind corporate disclosures and the complex demands placed on firms by various stakeholders.

Incorporating political economy theory, the chapter acknowledges that firms operate within a complex interplay of market demands, regulatory landscapes, and socio-political conditions. These factors collectively shape the strategic deployment of ESG disclosures as firms navigate through pressures to maintain market legitimacy and competitive advantage. This view aligns with the suggestion that firms use ESG reporting as a strategic instrument, one that is not only about compliance but also about influencing and responding to the socio-political and economic environment (Gray et al., 1995). This chapter underscores the necessity of considering the broader political and economic incentives that drive corporate behaviour, particularly in the context of greenwashing within ESG disclosures. It highlights the potential for firms to manipulate disclosures to present a socially responsible image in line with the prevailing economic and political climate, thus ensuring their survival and profitability.

Stakeholder theory demands that attention be paid to the power dynamics inherent in corporate relationships with diverse stakeholder groups. This theory posits that stakeholder influences, interests, and the power dynamics between them and the firm are central to understanding the motivations behind ESG reporting (Mitchell et al., 1997). This chapter contends that selective disclosure may occur when firms seek to appease specific stakeholder groups, thereby risking greenwashing if these disclosures are not aligned with actual sustainable practices. This chapter advocates for a more critical examination of ESG reports and the motivations behind them, recognizing that disclosures may be selectively presented to appease stakeholders rather than to reflect genuine sustainable practices.

Finally, legitimacy theory highlights the need for firms to conform to societal norms and values to maintain their license to operate. Legitimacy theory provides a framework for understanding corporate behaviour in seeking social approval and aligning operations with societal values. The chapter suggests that corporate narratives of responsibility constructed through ESG disclosures are aimed at securing operational legitimacy (Suchman, 1995). However, this pursuit is challenged by the need for disclosures to reflect not just current societal norms but also evolving expectations. This dynamic nature of legitimacy underscores the need for continuous alignment between corporate actions and societal values. This chapter contributes to the legitimacy theory by exploring how firms employ ESG disclosures to construct a narrative of responsibility and to align themselves with societal expectations. The cases of Coca-Cola and Volkswagen group reveal the potential for firms to craft such narratives as a form of greenwashing, seeking legitimacy through an illusion of conformity to societal expectations. It prompts a re-evaluation of how societal norms shape corporate disclosures and the importance of scrutinizing these disclosures to ensure they genuinely reflect responsible corporate behaviour.

In essence, this chapter call for a reassessment of corporate motivations and strategies in ESG disclosures, the influence of socio-political contexts on corporate behaviour, and the effectiveness of existing frameworks in detecting and discouraging greenwashing. The insights provided by this chapter serve to inform and refine these theories, suggesting a need for stronger governance, greater accountability, and more transparent reporting mechanisms to combat the adverse effects of greenwashing on sustainability initiatives. Therefore, this chapter enriches the theoretical dialogue by positioning greenwashing not only as a deceptive practice but also as a potential stimulus for corporate and societal change, calling for empirical research to delve deeper into how corporate disclosures can contribute to both perpetuating and mitigating greenwashing within the ESG framework.

Practical Implications

The practical implications of the critical analysis presented in this chapter are threefold. Firstly, there is a need for heightened consumer awareness and education that can augment the ethical dimension of sustainable consumption and counteract the allure of using greenwashed products. Consumers must be equipped with the cognitive tools to discern between authentic environmental stewardship and corporate greenwashing. Secondly, regulatory bodies need to impose more stringent standards for eco-labelling and advertising, ensuring that claims of environmental responsibility are substantiated by tangible, positive environmental impacts. Such measures would mitigate the risk of greenwashing, compelling corporations to commit to genuine sustainability if they wish to benefit from the market advantages associated with producing environment friendly products. Lastly, the discourse around greenwashing should foster a more critically engaged consumers, regulators and civil society organizations, who are able to interrogate and challenge the corporate manipulations pertaining to offering of eco-friendly products and services. The practical implications for firms extend to a re-evaluation of internal governance structures to ensure that ESG reporting goes beyond surface-level disclosures and reflects genuine sustainable practices. Top of FormBottom of Form

The critical insights from Liu et al. (2024) underscore the pressing need for corporate governance reforms that address vertical interlocking, a factor contributing to the pervasive issue of ESG report greenwashing. This practice, prevalent among financially well-off firms (example, Chinese A-share listed companies), not only undermines the integrity of ESG reporting but also distorts the true sustainable trajectory of an enterprise. Therefore, strengthening internal governance mechanisms is essential to counteract this trend. Instituting rigorous supervisory frameworks and cultivating executives with authentic green expertise are necessary steps toward ensuring transparent and honest ESG disclosures. As such, companies need to prioritize building a governance culture that values ethical reporting and aligns executive motivations with long-term sustainability goals, thereby enabling stakeholders to make more informed decisions.

Future Research Scope

In light of the pervasive phenomenon of greenwashing, future scholarly inquiries could further reveal the nuances of greenwashing tactics and its implications. For instance, a comparative analysis across diverse business organizations could elucidate the variance in greenwashing tactics and consumer perception, thereby establishing a typology of greenwashing practices. Future research could also investigate the efficacy of regulatory measures on green marketing claims and evaluate the robustness of legal frameworks to contain greenwashing malpractices. It could also delve into the consumer psyche, to understand how the purchasing behaviours of consumers are manipulated by deceptive marketing and suggest strategies to inoculate consumers against misleading claims. The veracity and influence of third-party environmental certifications on corporate and consumer behaviours present yet another area for future research.

From the viewpoint of business corporations, probing into the financial ramifications of greenwashing could unravel its impact on corporate profitability and sustainability. From the organization behaviour viewpoint, future research could focus on revealing organizational culture factors that motivate the corporates to indulge in greenwashing practices. The role of social media in amplifying or mitigating greenwashing, coupled with the potency of digital activism could be further studied. Additionally, research pertaining to technological advancements that facilitate the real-time identification of greenwashing claims thus enabling consumers to make informed decisions, can be undertaken. From the consumer's viewpoint, empirical research focusing on the development of sustainable consumption patterns amidst widespread greenwashing could provide actionable insights. The long-term ecological implications of greenwashing could be another area of potential study. Lastly, from the viewpoint of public policy, analysis pertaining to determining the state's role in either perpetuating or inhibiting corporate greenwashing could be undertaken. These research themes holds the potential to advance the dialogue on greenwashing and drive the momentum towards promoting ethical and environmentally responsible consumption.

Limitations

This chapter provides an overview of greenwashing within the context of ESG practices, enriched by discussion of case studies. However, the scope and approach of this work entail certain limitations. The focus on specific case studies, such as Volkswagen's and Coca-Cola's greenwashing practices, may not fully represent the diversity of greenwashing strategies employed across different industries and companies. This narrow scope limits the generalizability of the conclusions drawn from these case studies. Additionally, while the chapter emphasizes the role of regulatory frameworks in mitigating greenwashing, it may not sufficiently account for the varying effectiveness of these regulations in different geopolitical contexts. Differences in enforcement and cultural attitudes toward regulation can significantly impact the efficacy of these frameworks, which the chapter may not fully address. Furthermore, the chapter primarily discusses greenwashing from a corporate and regulatory perspective, potentially overlooking the crucial consumer perspective. Understanding how consumers perceive and react to greenwashing is essential for developing effective counter-strategies. Lastly, ESG practices and greenwashing tactics are continuously evolving, and the chapter may not capture the most recent developments or innovations in these areas, potentially rendering some of its findings outdated. These limitations suggest a need for broader case studies, a comprehensive analysis of consumer perceptions, and an updated examination of regulatory effectiveness to enhance the chapter's insights.

Conclusion

In conclusion, the critical examination of greenwashing within the ESG framework sheds light on the intricate ways corporations may present themselves as environmentally responsible. Through the review of existing literature and the case studies on Coca-Cola and Volkswagen group, this chapter has underscored the significant gap between ESG narratives and actual practices, revealing the nuanced strategies that constitute greenwashing. By juxtaposing Coca-Cola's public sustainability narratives with its tangible actions, this chapter provided clarity on the dissonance often present in corporate reporting, thus offering a critical lens through which greenwashing can be recognized and assessed. The case of Coca-Cola highlights the complexities of corporate sustainability claims and the potential for such claims to be used to mislead consumers and investors.

This chapter's analysis has also revealed that in regions with stringent ESG reporting regulations, such as the European Union, corporations exhibit a higher level of disclosure accuracy and transparency. Contrastingly, in jurisdictions with more lenient oversight, the variance in reporting quality is significant, often leading to superficial or deceptive portrayals of corporate sustainability. Moreover, without stringent disclosure mandates, corporations may selectively report on favourable sustainability initiatives while obscuring less commendable practices. This review has raised critical questions about the authenticity of corporate sustainability efforts and their alignment with broader societal values and expectations. It emphasizes the role of public policy and regulatory practices in shaping corporate behaviour and calls for more stringent and enforceable standards to combat greenwashing. It has also highlighted the need for consumer education and the importance of transparent and reliable ESG disclosures. The implications of this chapter stretch beyond academic inquiry, touching on practical aspects of business ethics, regulatory policy, and consumer activism. As corporations continue to navigate the growing demands for sustainability, the insights gleaned from this review can inform the development of more ethical business practices.

The theoretical framing of sustainability objectives within corporations often paints a picture of inherent 'duality', 'conflict', and 'paradoxes', portraying firms as being torn between the 'moral high ground' of sustainability and the 'profit-seeking' imperatives of business organizations. Yet, navigating these competing priorities is not a zero-sum game; they can coexist, enabling organizations to pursue dual strategies effectively through dynamic people's action cycles. This integrative approach positions sustainability as a driver of innovation and competitive advantage, rather than as a mere compliance or ethical consideration. Future empirical research could further explore greenwashing's impact on corporate valuation, stakeholder trust, and consumer behaviour. This would improve understanding of greenwashing strategies and help develop more effective strategies to deter such practices.

References

Abdul Rahman, R., & Alsayegh, M. F. (2021). Determinants of corporate environment, social and governance (ESG) reporting among Asian firms. *Journal of Risk and Financial Management*, 14(4), 167. 10.3390/jrfm14040167

Allen, F., Qian, J., & Qian, M. (2005). Law, finance, and economic growth in China. *Journal of Financial Economics*, 77(1), 57–116. 10.1016/j.jfineco.2004.06.010

Amran, A., Lee, S. P., & Devi, S. S. (2015). The influence of governance structure and strategic corporate social responsibility toward sustainability reporting quality. *Business Strategy and the Environment*, 23(4), 249–264. 10.1002/bse.1767

Ashforth, B. E., & Reingen, P. H. (2014). Functions of dysfunction: Managing the dynamics of an organizational duality in a natural food cooperative. *Administrative Science Quarterly*, 59(3), 474–516. 10.1177/0001839214537811

Bae, K. H., Bailey, W., & Mao, C. X. (2006). Stock market liberalization and the information environment. *Journal of International Money and Finance*, 25(3), 404–428. 10.1016/j.jimonfin.2006.01.004

Baldi, F., & Pandimiglio, A. (2022). The role of ESG scoring and greenwashing risk in explaining the yields of green bonds: A conceptual framework and an econometric analysis. *Global Finance Journal*, 52, 100711. 10.1016/j.gfj.2022.100711

Berg, F., Koelbel, J. F., & Rigobon, R. (2022). Aggregate confusion: The divergence of ESG ratings. *Review of Finance*, 26(6), 1315–1344. 10.1093/rof/rfac033

Bizjak, J., Lemmon, M., & Whitby, R. (2009). Option backdating and board interlocks. *Review of Financial Studies*, 22(11), 4821–4847. 10.1093/rfs/hhn120

Blanding, M. (2011). *The coke machine: The dirty truth behind the world's favorite soft drink*. Penguin.

Bruce, C., & Laroiya, A. (2007). The production of eco-labels. *Environmental and Resource Economics*, 36(3), 275–293. 10.1007/s10640-006-9028-9

Chen, G., & Wang, M. (2023). Stock market liberalization and earnings management: Evidence from the China–Hong Kong stock connects. *Finance Research Letters*, 58, 104417. 10.1016/j.frl.2023.104417

Chen, L., & Bouvain, P. (2009). Is corporate responsibility converging? A comparison of corporate responsibility reporting in the USA, UK, Australia, and Germany. *Journal of Business Ethics*, 87(1), 299–317. 10.1007/s10551-008-9794-0

Cho, Y. N., & Baskin, E. (2018). It's a match when green meets healthy in sustainability labeling. *Journal of Business Research*, 86, 119–129. 10.1016/j.jbusres.2018.01.050

Chouaibi, S., & Affes, H. (2021). The effect of social and ethical practices on environmental disclosure: Evidence from an international ESG data. *Corporate Governance (Bradford)*, 21(7), 1293–1317. 10.1108/CG-03-2020-0087

Cooper, E. W., & Uzun, H. (2022). Busy outside directors and ESG performance. *Journal of Sustainable Finance & Investment*, 1–20. Advance online publication. 10.1080/20430795.2022.2122687

Crilly, D., Hansen, M., & Zollo, M. (2016). The grammar of decoupling: Stakeholder heterogeneity and firm decoupling of sustainability practices. *Academy of Management Journal*, 59, 705–729. 10.5465/amj.2015.0171

Crilly, D., Zollo, M., & Hansen, M. T. (2012). Faking it or muddling through? Understanding decoupling in response to stakeholder pressures. *Academy of Management Journal*, 55(6), 1429–1448. 10.5465/amj.2010.0697

Cuervo-Cazurra, A. (2006). Who cares about corruption? *Journal of International Business Studies*, 37(6), 807–822. 10.1057/palgrave.jibs.8400223

de Freitas Netto, S. V., Sobral, M. F. F., Ribeiro, A. R. B., & Soares, G. R. D. L. (2020). Concepts and forms of greenwashing: A systematic review. *Environmental Sciences Europe*, 32(1), 1. Advance online publication. 10.1186/s12302-020-0300-3

Deegan, C. (2000). *Financial Accounting Theory*. McGraw-Hill Education Australia.

Deegan, C. (2002). Introduction: The legitimising effect of social and environmental disclosures–a theoretical foundation. *Accounting, Auditing & Accountability Journal*, 15(3), 282–311. 10.1108/09513570210435852

Del Gesso, C., & Lodhi, R. N. (2024). Theories underlying environmental, social and governance (ESG) disclosure: A systematic review of accounting studies. *Journal of Accounting Literature*. Advance online publication. 10.1108/JAL-08-2023-0143

Delmas, M., & Toffel, M. W. (2004). Stakeholders and environmental management practices: An institutional framework. *Business Strategy and the Environment*, 13(4), 209–222. 10.1002/bse.409

Delmas, M. A., & Burbano, V. C. (2011). The drivers of greenwashing. *California Management Review*, 54(1), 64–87. 10.1525/cmr.2011.54.1.64

Dhaliwal, D. S., Radhakrishnan, S., Tsang, A., & Yang, Y. G. (2011). Nonfinancial disclosure and analyst forecast accuracy: International evidence on corporate social responsibility disclosure. *The Accounting Review*, 87(3), 723–759. 10.2308/accr-10218

Donaldson, T., & Preston, L. E. (1995). The stakeholder theory of the corporation: Concepts, evidence, and implications. *Academy of Management Review*, 20(1), 65–91. 10.2307/258887

Eccles, R. G., & Klimenko, S. (2019). The Investor Revolution. *Harvard Business Review*, 97(3), 106–116.

Eccles, R. G., & Krzus, M. P. (2010). Integrated Reporting for a Sustainable Strategy. *Financial Executive*, 26(2), 28–32.

El Ghoul, S., Guedhami, O., Kim, H., & Park, K. (2018). Corporate environmental responsibility and the cost of capital: International evidence. *Journal of Business Ethics*, 149(2), 335–361. 10.1007/s10551-015-3005-6

Friede, G., Busch, T., & Bassen, A. (2015). ESG and financial performance: Aggregated evidence from more than 2000 empirical studies. *Journal of Sustainable Finance & Investment*, 5(4), 210–233. 10.1080/20430795.2015.1118917

Gatti, L., Pizzetti, M., & Seele, P. (2021). Green lies and their effect on intention to invest. *Journal of Business Research*, 127, 228–240. 10.1016/j.jbusres.2021.01.028

Gatti, L., Seele, P., & Rademacher, L. (2019). Grey zone in–greenwash out. A review of greenwashing research and implications for the voluntary-mandatory transition of CSR. *International Journal of Corporate Social Responsibility*, 4(1), 1. Advance online publication. 10.1186/s40991-019-0044-9

Geissdoerfer, M., Savaget, P., Bocken, N. M., & Hultink, E. J. (2017). The Circular Economy – A new sustainability paradigm? *Journal of Cleaner Production*, 143, 757–768. 10.1016/j.jclepro.2016.12.048

Gray, R., Kouhy, R., & Lavers, S. (1995). Corporate social and environmental reporting: A review of the literature and a longitudinal study of UK disclosure. *Accounting, Auditing & Accountability Journal*, 8(2), 47–77. 10.1108/09513579510146996

Hahn, T., Pinkse, J., Preuss, L., & Figge, F. (2015). Tensions in corporate sustainability: Towards an integrative framework. *Journal of Business Ethics*, 127(2), 297–316. 10.1007/s10551-014-2047-5

Halttunen, L., & Inkilä, J. (2014). Corporate responsibility reporting on the consumer perspective: Case: Coca-Cola Company.

Haw, I., Hu, B., Hwang, L. S., & Wu, W. (2004). Ultimate ownership, income management, and legal and extra-legal institutions. *Journal of Accounting Research*, 42(2), 423–462. 10.1111/j.1475-679X.2004.00144.x

Hawkins, G. (2011). Packaging water: Plastic bottles as market and public devices. *Economy and Society*, 40(4), 534–552. 10.1080/03085147.2011.602295

Haws, J. W. (2022). Cherry red greenwashing: The rhetoric behind corporate recycling narratives (Doctoral dissertation, Brigham Young University). ProQuest Dissertations Publishing.

Hengst, I. A., Jarzabkowski, P., Hoegl, M., & Muethel, M. (2020). Toward a process theory of making sustainability strategies legitimate in action. *Academy of Management Journal*, 63(1), 246–271. 10.5465/amj.2016.0960

Holzendorff, G. D. (2013). Living on the Coke side of thirst: The Coca-Cola Company and responsibility for water shortage in India. *Journal of European Management & Public Affairs Studies*, 1(1), 1–4. 10.15771/2199-1618_2013_1_1_6

Hou, F., Ng, J., Rusticus, T., & Xu, X. (2019). Foreign capital and earnings management: International evidence from equity market openings. University of Hawai'i. http://hdl.handle.net/10125/59269

Huang, Q., Li, Y., Lin, M., & McBrayer, G. A. (2022). Natural disasters, risk salience, and corporate ESG disclosure. *Journal of Corporate Finance*, 72, 102152. 10.1016/j.jcorpfin.2021.102152

Ioannou, I., & Serafeim, G. (2012). What drives corporate social performance? The role of nation-level institutions. *Journal of International Business Studies*, 43(9), 834–864. 10.1057/jibs.2012.26

Janjuha-Jivraj, S., & Pasha, N. (2021). *Futureproof Your Career: How to Lead and Succeed in a Changing World*. Bloomsbury Publishing.

Jiao, J., Tong, L., & Yan, A. (2021). Catering incentive and corporate social responsibility. [Preprint]. *SSRN*. http://dx.doi.org/10.2139/ssrn.3536960

Jones, E. (2019). Rethinking greenwashing: Corporate discourse, unethical practice, and the unmet potential of ethical consumerism. *Sociological Perspectives*, 62(5), 728–754. 10.1177/0731121419849095

Khan, M., Serafeim, G., & Yoon, A. (2016). Corporate sustainability: First evidence on materiality. *The Accounting Review*, 91(6), 1697–1724. 10.2308/accr-51383

Khanna, T., & Palepu, K. (2000). Is group affiliation profitable in emerging markets? *The Journal of Finance*, 55(2), 867–891. 10.1111/0022-1082.00229

Kirk, M. P., & Vincent, J. D. (2014). Professional investor relations within the firm. *The Accounting Review*, 89(4), 1421–1452. 10.2308/accr-50724

KPMG. (2020). *KPMG International Survey of Sustainability Reporting 2020.* KPMG International Cooperative.

Lanthorn, K. R. (2013). It's all about the green: The economically driven greenwashing practices of Coca-Cola. *Augsburg Honors Review, 6*(1), 13. https://idun.augsburg.edu/honors_review/vol6/iss1/13

Laufer, W. S. (2003). Social accountability and corporate greenwashing. *Journal of Business Ethics*, 43(3), 253–261. 10.1023/A:1022962719299

Liu, G., Qian, H., Shi, Y., Yuan, D., & Zhou, M. (2024). How do firms react to capital market liberalization? Evidence from ESG reporting greenwashing. *Corporate Social Responsibility and Environmental Management*, csr.2808. Advance online publication. 10.1002/csr.2808

Lu, Z., Liang, Y., Hu, Y., & Liu, Y. (2024). Is managerial myopia detrimental to corporate ESG performance? *International Review of Economics & Finance*, 92, 998–1015. Advance online publication. 10.1016/j.iref.2024.02.061

Lyon, T. P., & Maxwell, J. W. (2011). Greenwash: Corporate environmental disclosure under threat of audit. *Journal of Economics & Management Strategy*, 20(1), 3–41. 10.1111/j.1530-9134.2010.00282.x

Lyon, T. P., & Montgomery, A. W. (2013). Tweetjacked: The impact of social media on corporate greenwash. *Journal of Business Ethics*, 118(4), 747–757. 10.1007/s10551-013-1958-x

MacLean, T. L., & Behnam, M. (2010). The dangers of decoupling: The relationship between compliance programs, legitimacy perceptions, and institutionalized misconduct. *Academy of Management Journal*, 53(6), 1499–1520. 10.5465/amj.2010.57319198

Majid, K. A., & Russell, C. A. (2015). Giving green a second thought: Modeling the value retention of green products in the secondary market. *Journal of Business Research*, 68(5), 994–1002. 10.1016/j.jbusres.2014.10.001

Marquis, C., & Qian, C. (2014). Corporate social responsibility reporting in China: Symbol or substance? *Organization Science*, 25(1), 127–148. 10.1287/orsc.2013.0837

Marquis, C., Toffel, M. W., & Zhou, Y. (2016). Scrutiny, norms, and selective disclosure: A global study of greenwashing. *Organization Science*, 27(2), 483–504. 10.1287/orsc.2015.1039

Mirovic, V., Kalas, B., Djokic, I., Milicevic, N., Djokic, N., & Djakovic, M. (2023). Green loans in bank portfolio: Financial and marketing implications. *Sustainability (Basel)*, 15(7), 5914. 10.3390/su15075914

Mitchell, R. K., Agle, B. R., & Wood, D. J. (1997). Toward a theory of stakeholder identification and salience: Defining the principle of who and what really counts. *Academy of Management Review*, 22(4), 853–886. 10.2307/259247

Nguyen, T. T. H., Yang, Z., Nguyen, N., Johnson, L. W., & Cao, T. K. (2019). Greenwash and green purchase intention: The mediating role of green skepticism. *Sustainability (Basel)*, 11(9), 2653. 10.3390/su11092653

Nyilasy, G., Gangadharbatla, H., & Paladino, A. (2014). Perceived greenwashing: The interactive effects of green advertising and corporate environmental performance on consumer reactions. *Journal of Business Ethics*, 125(4), 693–707. 10.1007/s10551-013-1944-3

Orlitzky, M., Schmidt, F. L., & Rynes, S. L. (2003). Corporate social and financial performance: A meta-analysis. *Organization Studies*, 24(3), 403–441. 10.1177/0170840603024003910

Parguel, B., Benoit-Moreau, F., & Larceneux, F. (2011). How sustainability ratings might deter 'greenwashing': A closer look at ethical corporate communication. *Journal of Business Ethics*, 102(1), 15–28. 10.1007/s10551-011-0901-2

Pascual, U., Balvanera, P., Díaz, S., Pataki, G., Roth, E., Stenseke, M., Watson, R. T., Başak Dessane, E., Islar, M., Kelemen, E., Maris, V., Quaas, M., Subramanian, S. M., Wittmer, H., Adlan, A., Ahn, S. E., Al-Hafedh, Y. S., Amankwah, E., Asah, S. T., & Yagi, N. (2017). Valuing nature's contributions to people: The IPBES approach. *Current Opinion in Environmental Sustainability*, 26, 7–16. 10.1016/j.cosust.2016.12.006

Prakash, A., & Potoski, M. (2006). *The voluntary environmentalists: Green clubs, ISO 14001, and voluntary environmental regulations*. Cambridge University Press. 10.1017/CBO9780511617683

Seele, P., & Gatti, L. (2017). Greenwashing revisited: In search of a typology and accusation-based definition incorporating legitimacy strategies. *Business Strategy and the Environment*, 26(2), 239–252. 10.1002/bse.1912

Soobaroyen, T., & Mahadeo, J. D. (2016). Community disclosures in a developing country: Insights from a neo-pluralist perspective. *Accounting, Auditing & Accountability Journal*, 29(3), 452–482. Advance online publication. 10.1108/AAAJ-08-2014-1810

Suchman, M. C. (1995). Managing legitimacy: Strategic and institutional approaches. *Academy of Management Review*, 20(3), 571–610. 10.2307/258788

Szabo, S., & Webster, J. (2021). Perceived greenwashing: The effects of green marketing on environmental and product perceptions. *Journal of Business Ethics*, 171(4), 719–739. 10.1007/s10551-020-04461-0

Tateishi, E. (2017). Craving gains and claiming "green" by cutting greens? An exploratory analysis of greenfield housing developments in Iskandar Malaysia. *Journal of Urban Affairs*, 40(3), 370–393. 10.1080/07352166.2017.1355667

Teichmann, F. M. J., Wittmann, C., & Sergi, B. S. S. (2023). What are the consequences of corporate greenwashing? A look into the consequences of greenwashing in consumer and financial markets. *Journal of Information. Communication and Ethics in Society*, 21(3), 290–301. 10.1108/JICES-10-2022-0090

Terrachoice Environmental Marketing Inc. (2007). *The 'Six Sins of Greenwashing': A study of environmental claims in North American consumer markets*. Global Ecolabelling Network.

Todaro, D. L., & Torelli, R. (2024). From greenwashing to ESG-washing: A focus on the circular economy field. *Corporate Social Responsibility and Environmental Management*, csr.2786. Advance online publication. 10.1002/csr.2786

Torelli, R., Balluchi, F., & Lazzini, A. (2020). Greenwashing and environmental communication: Effects on stakeholders' perceptions. *Business Strategy and the Environment*, 29(2), 407–421. 10.1002/bse.2373

Vormedal, I., & Ruud, A. (2009). Sustainability reporting in Norway: An assessment of performance in the context of legal demands and socio-political drivers. *Business Strategy and the Environment*, 18(4), 207–222. 10.1002/bse.560

Walker, K., & Wan, F. (2012). The harm of symbolic actions and green-washing: Corporate actions and communications on environmental performance and their financial implications. *Journal of Business Ethics*, 109(2), 227–242. 10.1007/s10551-011-1122-4

Walsh, H., & Dowding, T. J. (2012). Sustainability and The Coca-Cola Company: The global water crisis and Coca-Cola's business case for water stewardship. *International Journal of Business Insights & Transformation, 4*.

Wu, Y., Zhang, K., & Xie, J. (2020). Bad greenwashing, good greenwashing: Corporate social responsibility and information transparency. *Management Science*, 66(7), 3095–3112. 10.1287/mnsc.2019.3340

Yang, Z., Nguyen, T. T. H., Nguyen, H. N., Nguyen, T. T. N., & Cao, T. T. (2020). Greenwashing behaviours: Causes, taxonomy and consequences based on a systematic literature review. *Journal of Business Economics and Management*, 21(5), 1486–1507. 10.3846/jbem.2020.13225

Yu, E. P. Y., Van Luu, B., & Chen, C. H. (2020). Greenwashing in environmental, social and governance disclosures. *Research in International Business and Finance*, 52, 101192. 10.1016/j.ribaf.2020.101192

Zhang, D. (2022). Environmental regulation and firm product quality improvement: How does the greenwashing response. *International Review of Financial Analysis*, 80, 1–8. 10.1016/j.irfa.2022.102058

Chapter 7
Does Audit Committee Matter for Corporate Social Performance?
Evidence From India

Aghila Sasidharan
http://orcid.org/0000-0002-9254-6291
Indian Institute of Forest Management, Bhopal, India

Sreelekshmi Geetha
https://orcid.org/0000-0002-0114-1951
University of Kerala, India

Biju Ajithakumari Vijayappan Nair
https://orcid.org/0000-0001-5583-6495
University of Kerala, India

Ambili Jayachandran
https://orcid.org/0000-0002-0062-6260
University of Kerala, India

Nisha Sheen
https://orcid.org/0000-0003-2174-5215
St. Lawrence College, Ontario, Canada

ABSTRACT

This study examines the effect of audit committees on corporate social performance. Using a sample of Indian firms for the 2008–2021 period, we find that the firm's corporate social performance is significantly higher in the presence of an audit

DOI: 10.4018/979-8-3693-3880-3.ch007

committee. This relationship is stronger when the audit committee consists of more directors. Our results support the resource dependence theory, which indicates that the members of each committee on the board provide various resources to the firms in the form of their skills and expertise. Our study has an implication for the regulators that more transparency should be required in the audit committee to ensure better corporate governance.

1. INTRODUCTION

Corporate social responsibility (CSR) has gained wide market interest globally, in emerging as well as advanced economies, as globalization came and the international trade volume attained mass scale (Jamali & Mirshak, 2006; Thomas et al., 2024). This has motivated academicians, businesses, and policymakers to give substantial attention to CSR. Firms are under pressure not merely to achieve financial objectives but also to meet and balance numerous bottom lines and address the demands of multiple stakeholders (Jamali, 2008; Pfajfar et al., 2022). CSR disclosure contributes to the company's overall competency and financial performance and enhances stakeholder value by minimizing the management-stakeholder information asymmetry (Cho et al., 2013; Coelho et al., 2023; Cui et al., 2018; Kaur & Singh, 2021; Maqbool & Zameer, 2018; Naqvi et al., 2021). Customers aware of CSR initiatives can raise the corporate image and brand value, increasing demand for the company's products (Ali et al., 2019; Brown & Dacin, 1997).

Firms and the public in general pretty much unaware of their rights and responsibilities, with firms considering CSR as a liability rather than a source of long-term interest (Ying et al., 2021). Against this backdrop, regulations have been implemented in some countries which mandate CSR spending to ensure social performance. These mandatory requirements, especially in India, China, and South Africa, made the companies increasingly spend a certain sum of money on CSR activities. In India, the Companies Amendment Act of 2013 made it compulsory for companies to divulge their average profit for the preceding three years spent on CSR activities in their annual reports. In an investigation of the consequence of the amendment on stock returns, Manchiraju and Rajgopal (2017) show that mandatory CSR regulations had an unfavorable effect on the shareholder wealth goal, inhibiting firms from spending on CSR. Thus, earlier, firms hesitated to invest in CSR activities due to the conservative thinking that the return to shareholders may decrease if companies start spending on CSR. The mandatory requirements brought a radical change to the Indian CSR initiatives that were undertaken.

Generally, almost all companies report the amount spent on social activities such as education and community development, which is available in their yearly reports. Nonetheless, concerns exist towards the quality and extent of CSR disclosure. Choi et al. (2013) point out that executives might use CSR disclosure to hide their opportunistic behavior. Management utilizes CSR disclosure to develop its reputation rather than to reduce information disconnect between stakeholders and managers. Although the laws are implemented across countries, there must be some mechanisms to monitor whether the firms comply with the laws enacted by the various regulators (Proimos, 2005). In this regard, corporate governance plays a significant part in channeling CSR funds towards real sustainability outcomes. It involves striking an equilibrium between social and economic objectives and individual and communal interests. As the Cadbury Report of 1992 rightly points out the sole aim behind a corporate governance framework is to urge the efficient use of resources and to require accountability for managing those resources. The objective is to align the individuals, corporations and society's interests to the utmost extent possible.[1]

Corporate governance has become an important aspect of CSR as it deals with a firm's association with its stakeholders, which is why CSR may be tackled from a corporate governance perspective (Parmar et al., 2010). Both share a closely knit linkage, leading to higher transparency. As a result, companies have incorporated corporate governance as an integral part of their CSR reporting, and it highly enhanced the quality of the CSR disclosure agenda (Ali et al., 2017; Eng & Mak, 2003; Kolk & Pinkse, 2010). The concept of an audit committee (hereafter AC) has been among the most crucial corporate governance mechanisms. The traditional AC position is largely concerned with compulsory financial disclosure. Still, after the financial scandals such as Enron and WorldCom in the United States and the Satyam scandal in India, the significance of the AC has extended to oversee non-financial disclosure, such as CSR (Kolk & Pinkse, 2010). The Satyam company crisis in India exposed the governance systems that supervise the financial reporting process in developing nations (Lal Bhasin, 2013). There exists a critical question of whether corporate governance workings, such as that of ACs have any impact on CSR spending to ensure corporate social performance (CSP) in countries like India, where concentrated ownership is high.

Against this backdrop, this study adds to the current literature by probing into the role of AC characteristics, such as AC size and independence, on CSR to ensure social performance and to inspect how the Companies Act 2013 regulation impacts the ACs' CSR. This study is theoretically founded on the stakeholder theory, making a unique contribution to the CSR literature. Moreover, this study also discusses the AC-CSR association. To the best of our understanding, our attempt can be deemed as the first to explore the impact of ACs on various kinds of CSR activities including environmental and community CSR activities. The study's findings inform the regulatory authorities about the corporate governance effects on ACs and in turn on CSR.

2. THEORETICAL LINKAGES AND HYPOTHESIS DEVELOPMENT

The social and environmental repercussions of Firms' operations have become a global concern. Numerous consequences result from a company's antisocial behavior, including the rising costs of related higher energy prices and the impact of climate change policy, threatening the corporate reputation and value. Climate risk has become a boardroom issue (KPMG, 2021). Companies are now under stakeholder pressure to broaden their goals and actions to include CSR dimensions in their activities. However, concerns about the quality and materiality of CSR exist, making it critical that corporate governance measures such as the AC act as a supervisory mechanism to alleviate these concerns while simultaneously monitoring and improving CSR. The core function and prime responsibility of the AC is to review the company's risk management strategies and internal control systems. With the unveiling of financial scandals and mismanagement cases, ACs gain huge importance in ensuring the quality and timeliness of corporate financial reporting (Lin et al., 2006). With the emergence of the CSR agenda, a global trend for boards to increasingly emphasize their role in ensuring social and environmental reporting quality is rising. Implementation of the International Financial Reporting Standards (IFRS) is one element that has improved the quality and openness of financial reporting, and it has also enhanced the wider AC's role in monitoring mandatory disclosures such as CSR.

From the standpoint of risk management and reporting oversight, the AC might be crucial in ensuring these issues receive the necessary attention. Annually, the AC evaluates CSR-related risks and monitors performance via the annual control self-assessment process conducted by the internal audit function and through regular meetings with the board and CSR committee. Based on the agency theory, firms having considerable information asymmetry and agency costs will be inclined to reduce these costs by providing substantive supervision of financial reporting via ACs (Collier & Gregory, 1999). According to Porter and Kramer (2006), the resource-based view (RBV) signaling method expands upon the agency approach and emphasizes the relationship between competitive advantage and CSR. When a firm is endowed with resources, such as a larger size that results in effects of scale and scope and a higher profit, it can offer its management the resource base necessary to invest in firm-specific resources that provide competitive advantages.

The resource base is evaluated based on historical profitability, which stands in as a proxy for cash flow, and size, which is evaluated based on the natural log of total assets, which stands in as a proxy for the scale and scope of the resource base. This evaluation is done using the RBV signaling method. Environmental disclosure, precisely the quality of environmental disclosure, is controlled by CG mechanisms and defined by the resource base.

The existence of ACs and their characteristics improves board oversight and auditor efficiency and reduces the information disconnect between managers and various stakeholders, thereby improving the credibility of CSR disclosure (Al-Shaer & Zaman, 2018; Dwekat et al., 2022; Hosseinniakani et al., 2024; Mangena & Pike, 2005). ACs help in overseeing risk management, and the AC's knowledgeable independent directors are well-positioned to determine the management actions to adequately identify, manage, monitor, and control risks (Keinath & Walo, 2004). Beasley et al. (2009) opines that an effective board of directors comprises an AC that supervises financial statements, maintains their accuracy, boosts audit quality, and improves financial reporting. When inspecting financial reports, an AC can also assist in evaluating non-financial matters, such as the value of assets that may be affected by environmental concerns, social issues, and the costs of product redesign (Dixon et al., 2004). It can provide accurate information to all relevant stakeholders, enhance the credibility of financial reporting (Ghafran & O'Sullivan, 2013), and develop the firm's reputation.

AC size is an important attribute driving the significance of an AC as a corporate governance mechanism. The larger the AC, the more legitimacy and power it receives. A minimum of three people is required to serve on the AC. Large ACs are an important monitoring tool as they contribute diverse talents, experiences, and energy, consequently increasing the possibility of resolving problems in the reporting process (Appuhami & Tashakor, 2017; Smith, 2003). They have the potential to achieve greater power and monitoring practices over top management executives because they will strengthen the internal audit mechanism (Abbott et al., 2004; Al-Hadrami et al., 2020; Alqudah et al., 2023). AC independence also has similar results. Raimo et al. (2020) provide evidence that both AC size and independence positively influenced integrating reporting quality. Based on Australian companies, Appuhami and Tashakor (2017) found that AC size and independence influence the quantity and quality of CSR information disclosure. Dwekat et al. (2022) also found similar results based on Europe. Although these research domains have been explored, research has yet to investigate the influence of the AC or the prospective influence it could have on enhancing the overall quality of environmental disclosures in the emerging economy of India.

Numerous policies pertaining to AC composition have been implemented in India with the aim of safeguarding investor interests. On April 1, 1997, India's first set of best practices was drafted by a group of twelve people led by Rahul Bajaj and was published by the Confederation of Indian Industry (CII). This report is the first to offer suggestions about, the creation of the AC, the required minimum number of non-executive directors on the board, and management transparency regarding the disclosure of financial as well as non-financial matters. This report was acknowledged by the Securities Exchange Board of India (SEBI), which took a step further and appointed the Kumara Mangalam Birla committee to raise the bar for corporate governance in India.

Among the recommendations made by this committee, a notable recommendation was that the AC should meet at least three times annually, once every six months, and once prior to the finalization of the accounts. The AC should also consist of at least three non-executive directors, the majority of whom should be independent. Many of the committee's recommendations were accepted by SEBI, which also imposed mandatory governance transparency laws. By virtue of Listing Agreement Clause 49, this advice was implemented. A thorough report on the AC's operations and the company-auditor relationship was provided by the Naresh Chandra Committee in 2000, among which certain suggestions were consequently made part of the 2009 Companies Bill. According to Section 292A of the Companies Act of 1956, a public company with paid-up capital of at least Rs. 5 crore is mandated to establish an AC. The Act gave the board the authority to determine the committee's functions and authority. Furthermore, the Companies (Amendment) Act of 2002 introduced the requirement for AC powers. Apart from this, the Companies Amendment Act, 2013's Rules 6 and 7 of Section 177 acknowledged the significance of an AC and provided it extra duties and responsibilities. The Indian Companies Act of 2013 requires that the board form an AC with a minimum of three members where independent directors are its members with at least one person having recent and pertinent financial experience. The Act also specifies that the committee should be led by an independent director. To improve the AC's oversight, SEBI introduced the LODR (Listing Obligations and Disclosure Regulation), 2015, which concentrates on the AC composition and membership qualifications in particular. All members shall be financially educated and at least one among them a finance expert. Additionally, it stipulates that disclosure of specific transactions in annual reports would need the prior approval of the AC.

Based on the facts gathered from the prevailing literature, this study adopts the following hypothesis:

H1: The audit committee characteristics enhance the corporate social performance of emerging economy firms

3. DATA & METHODOLOGY

3.1 Data

All firms listed in the National Stock Exchange (NSE) in the period between 2008 and 2021 that disclose their financial data as of 31st March every year were taken for the study. The data related to financial statement variables and CSR variables are collected from the Prowess IQ database maintained by the Center for Monitoring Indian Economy (CMIE). The preliminary study involved interviews with ACs of a few companies to understand the implications and validation of the approach.

3.2 Methodology

The fixed effect panel regression model and difference in difference analysis have been used to estimate the effect of audit committees on CSR. Appropriate measures to validate and test the robustness of the results and case studies to substantiate the results are used.

$$CSP = \alpha_0 + \beta_1 Size_{it} + \beta_2 LEVE + \beta_3 Profit_{it} + \beta_4 BS_{it} + \beta_5 INST_{it} + \beta_5 ACSIZE + \beta_5 ACIND_{it} \ U_i + V_t + \epsilon_{it} \tag{1}$$

CSP is the dependent variable measured by using the proportion of the amount spent on CSR activities to total assets. ACIND and ACSIZE are the independent variables measured by using the AC's number of directors and the ratio number of independent directors on the AC to board size respectively. Size, leverage, profit, institutional ownership, and board size were taken as the control variables.

Table 1. Variable definition

Variables	Definition
Corporate Social Performance (CSP)	Ratio of the amount spent on activities carried under CSR to total assets
Audit committee size (ACSIZE)	Total number of directors in the AC
Audit Committee Independence (ACIND)	Ratio number of independent directors on the AC to board size
Board Size (BS)	Number of directors on the board
Institutional investors (INSTI)	Percentage of shares held by institutional investors
Size	Natural log of total assets
Leverage	Ratio of borrowings to total assets
Growth	Current sales-previous sales/Previous sales

4. EMPIRICAL RESULTS

4.1 Descriptive Statistics

Table 2 details the descriptive statistics of the main variables of the study. The mean value of the dependent variable CSR is 3.22 implying that firms are spending more on CSR, indicating the growing significance firms attribute to the global sustainability developments. The average value of the AC size is 0.553 and the AC independence is 3.11. The mean value of board size is 8.8852.

Table 2. Descriptive statistics

Variable	Obs	Mean	Std.Dev	Min	Max
CSP	20392	0.0322	0.0017	-0.0006	0.1792
Size	20392	8.3717	1.9126	4.7908	12.1049
Leverage	20392	0.2840	0.2260	0.0000	0.7531
Growth	20392	0.3876	1.6772	-1.0000	5.8374
INSTI	20392	0.3350	0.2522	0.0000	1.0000
BS	20392	8.8582	3.4738	0.0000	25.0000
ACSIZE	20392	0.5530	0.2359	0.0000	1.0000
ACIND	20392	0.3115	0.3180	0.0000	0.9000

Note. This table reports the descriptive statistics. For each variable, we report the sample average and number of observations. Detailed definitions of the variables are listed in Table 1.

4.2 Correlation Matrix

The correlation matrix reported in Table 3 implies that the number of directors in the AC has a negative and significant relationship with CSP. Institutional investors have a positive and significant impact on CSP. The board of directors has a positive and significant relationship with CSP. Among the control variables, size has a positive and significant impact on CSP whereas leverage is inversely related to CSP.

Table 3. Correlation matrix

Variable	CSP	Size	Leverage	Growth	Insti	noofdirect~d	ACSIZE	ACIND
CSP	1							
Size	0.0578*	1.0000						
Leverage	-0.0735*	0.0210*	1.0000					

continued on following page

Table 3. Continued

Variable	CSP	Size	Leverage	Growth	Insti	noofdirect~d	ACSIZE	ACIND
Growth	0.0008	0.0439*	0.0046	1.0000				
INSTI	0.0145*	0.2648*	0.0037	0.0472*	1.0000			
BS	-0.0227*	0.0052	-0.0094	0.0026	-0.0011	1.0000		
ACSIZE	0.0141*	0.0211*	-0.0241*	-0.0024	0.0151*	0.4320*	1.0000	
ACIND	0.0010	-0.0045	0.0008	-0.0044	-0.0020	0.0011	0.1703*	1

Note. This table reports the correlation of variables used in this study.

4.3 Impact of Audit Committee on CSP

Table 4 reports the results of the impact of the AC on CSP. We find that the number of directors in the AC has a positive and significant impact on CSP, implying that an AC comprising a more significant number of directors possesses an enhanced capacity to supervise and analyze corporate activities, including their social and environmental practices. Enhanced oversight of the organization's activities by more directors results in heightened responsibility for achieving social responsibility objectives and maintaining ethical practices (Khan et al., 2013). This enhanced supervision may lead to improved monitoring of critical performance indicators associated with CSP, including initiatives for community engagement, labor practices, and environmental impact assessments. This confirms the results of Appuhami and Tashakor (2017) and Dwekat et al. (2022), who found similar results in different countries.

Firms can strengthen their oversight systems, encourage inclusive decision-making, and make substantial progress in achieving their social and environmental goals by increasing the size of the committee and guaranteeing variety and expertise among its members. Institutional investors, such as pension funds, mutual funds, and insurance firms, favorably correlate with CSP progress in achieving social and environmental objectives. Following the ESG (environmental, social, and governance factors) agenda in investment decision-making, engaging with companies on CSR issues, and leveraging their shareholder influence, institutional investors help promote sustainable business practices and create long-term value for both investors and society. As Al-Shaer and Zaman (2018) rightly assert, ACs improve the credibility of sustainability reporting with their auditing expertise, although it may be burdensome for some firms. This is critical, especially against the backdrop of greenwashing practices being adopted by firms to champion the demand for sustainability existing in the market.

Table 4. Baseline results

Variables	CSP	CSP
Size	0.0003***	0.0003***
	(11.62)	(11.58)
Leverage	-0.0008***	-0.0008***
	(-5.74)	(-5.71)
Growth	-0.0000	-0.0000
	(-0.44)	(-0.45)
INSTI	0.0321**	0.0465**
	(2.02)	(2.03)
BS	-0.0000***	-0.0000***
	(-2.89)	(-2.91)
ACSIZE	0.0002**	0.0002**
	(2.52)	(2.49)
ACIND		0.0000
		(0.07)
Constant	-0.0017***	-0.0017***
	(-7.67)	(-7.57)
R-Squared	0.30	0.32
No: of observations	20392	20392

Note: Table 4 presents the results showing the impact of the audit committee on CSP. All regressions control for industry and year-fixed effects. t-statistics are in brackets. ***, **, * denote significance at the 1%, 5%, and 10% significance level, respectively.

4.4 Robustness Check

Table 5 portrays the results of the robustness analysis. We have used three-stage least squares (3SLS) instrumental regression to examine the AC's impact on CSP. We have used the following procedure for robustness analysis. In the first stage, we ran the first-stage regression by regressing the endogenous variable (AC qualities) against the instrumental factors and any exogenous variables. We also obtained the predicted values for the endogenous variable. In the second stage, we regressed the CSP proxy (lagged value) on the endogenous variable's anticipated values from the first stage and additional control variables. This step evaluates the AC's effect on CSP while accounting for endogeneity. We have used the Wu-Hausman test for endogeneity to evaluate the instruments' validity.

Table 5. Robustness check

Variables	CSP
Size	0.9450**
	(2.28)
Leverage	-1.5388***
	(-4.25)
Growth	0.8155
	(1.46)
INSTI	0.1590 **
	(2.37)
BS	-1.0518***
	(-2.70)
ACSIZE	0.0400***
	(2.94)
ACIND	0.0093
	(0.13)
Constant	-0.1074
	(-0.74)
R-Squared	0.33
No: of observations	19632

Notes: This table reports the impact of the audit committee on CSP. All regressions control for industry and year fixed effects. t-statistics are in brackets. ***, **, * denote significance at the 1%, 5%, and 10% significance level, respectively.

5. CONCLUSION

This study examines the impact of ACs on CSP in India. Our results show that AC size positively impacts CSP, indicating that the greater the size of the AC greater the prospects of incorporating a wider variety of viewpoints, experiences, and areas of expertise, which can result in more comprehensive decision-making processes. A diverse AC can be crucial in ensuring that a wider variety of social issues and stakeholder interests are addressed when developing CSR plans. Different perspectives can assist in identifying blind spots or risks that could have gone unidentified by a smaller, less diverse group, resulting in more comprehensive and effective CSR programs. Our results also indicates that institutional investors wield a positive impact on CSP which proposes that institutional investors can advocate for improvements in CSP practices by engaging in shareholder activism, voting by proxy, and engaging in communication with company leaders. These improvements may include enhanced transparency, improved diversity and inclusion policies, and stronger environmental stewardship. This shows the significance of governance mechanisms in promoting environmentally responsible business conduct.

Our study makes a valuable contribution to corporate governance and social responsibility literature by analysing the influence of audit committees on CSP. Our findings could potentially provide policymakers and regulators with significant insights regarding the efficacy of ACs in advancing CSP. The results have direct implications on regulatory frameworks that are devised to improve practices related to CSR. However, as businesses shift from CSR to ESG and the sustainability agenda keeps on gaining emergency considerations, studying the effect of ACs on ESG performance is timely. Further research can attempt to unveil the role of AC existence and committee characteristics on corporate environmental, social, and governance practices in emerging countries. A deeper understanding of the corporate governance mechanisms' effect on ESG can yield far-reaching results in achieving the UN Sustainable Development Goals.

REFERENCES

Abbott, L. J., Parker, S., & Peters, G. F. (2004). Audit Committee Characteristics and Restatements. *Auditing*, 23(1), 69–87. 10.2308/aud.2004.23.1.69

Al-Hadrami, A., Rafiki, A., & Sarea, A. (2020). The impact of an audit committee's independence and competence on investment decision: A study in Bahrain. *Asian Journal of Accounting Research*, 5(2), 299–313. 10.1108/AJAR-02-2020-0008

Al-Shaer, H., & Zaman, M. (2018). Credibility of sustainability reports: The contribution of audit committees. *Business Strategy and the Environment*, 27(7), 973–986. 10.1002/bse.2046

Ali, H. Y., Danish, R. Q., & Asrar-ul-Haq, M. (2019). How corporate social responsibility boosts firm financial performance: The mediating role of corporate image and customer satisfaction. *Corporate Social Responsibility and Environmental Management*, 27(1), 166–177. 10.1002/csr.1781

Ali, W., Frynas, J. G., & Mahmood, Z. (2017). Determinants of Corporate Social Responsibility (CSR) Disclosure in Developed and Developing Countries: A Literature Review. *Corporate Social Responsibility and Environmental Management*, 24(4), 273–294. 10.1002/csr.1410

Alqudah, H., Amran, N. A., Hassan, H., Lutfi, A., Alessa, N., alrawad, M., & Almaiah, M. A. (2023). Examining the critical factors of internal audit effectiveness from internal auditors' perspective: Moderating role of extrinsic rewards. *Heliyon*, 9(10), e20497. 10.1016/j.heliyon.2023.e2049737842607

Appuhami, R., & Tashakor, S. (2017). The Impact of Audit Committee Characteristics on CSR Disclosure: An Analysis of Australian Firms. *Australian Accounting Review*, 27(4), 400–420. 10.1111/auar.12170

Beasley, M. S., Carcello, J. V., Hermanson, D. R., & Neal, T. L. (2009). The Audit Committee Oversight Process*. *Contemporary Accounting Research*, 26(1), 65–122. 10.1506/car.26.1.3

Brown, T. J., & Dacin, P. A. (1997). The Company and the Product: Corporate Associations and Consumer Product Responses. *Journal of Marketing*, 61(1), 68–84. 10.1177/002224299706100106

Cho, S. Y., Lee, C., & Pfeiffer, R. J.Jr. (2013). Corporate social responsibility performance and information asymmetry. *Journal of Accounting and Public Policy*, 32(1), 71–83. 10.1016/j.jaccpubpol.2012.10.005

Choi, B. B., Lee, D., & Park, Y. (2013). Corporate Social Responsibility, Corporate Governance and Earnings Quality: Evidence from <scp>K</scp> orea. *Corporate Governance*, 21(5), 447–467. 10.1111/corg.12033

Coelho, R., Jayantilal, S., & Ferreira, J. J. (2023). The impact of social responsibility on corporate financial performance: A systematic literature review. *Corporate Social Responsibility and Environmental Management*, 30(4), 1535–1560. 10.1002/csr.2446

Collier, P., & Gregory, A. (1999). Audit committee activity and agency costs. *Journal of Accounting and Public Policy*, 18(4–5), 311–332. 10.1016/S0278-4254(99)00015-0

Cui, J., Jo, H., & Na, H. (2018). Does Corporate Social Responsibility Affect Information Asymmetry? *Journal of Business Ethics*, 148(3), 549–572. 10.1007/s10551-015-3003-8

Dixon, R., Mousa, G. A., & Woodhead, A. D. (2004). The necessary characteristics of environmental auditors: A review of the contribution of the financial auditing profession. *Accounting Forum*, 28(2), 119–138. 10.1016/j.accfor.2004.01.001

Dwekat, A., Meqbel, R., Seguí-Mas, E., & Tormo-Carbó, G. (2022). The role of the audit committee in enhancing the credibility of CSR disclosure: Evidence from STOXX Europe 600 members. *Business Ethics, the Environment & Responsibility*, 31(3), 718–740. 10.1111/beer.12439

Eng, L. L., & Mak, Y. T. (2003). Corporate governance and voluntary disclosure. *Journal of Accounting and Public Policy*, 22(4), 325–345. 10.1016/S0278-4254(03)00037-1

Ghafran, C., & O'Sullivan, N. (2013). The Governance Role of Audit Committees: Reviewing a Decade of Evidence. *International Journal of Management Reviews*, 15(4), 381–407. 10.1111/j.1468-2370.2012.00347.x

Hosseinniakani, M., Overland, C., & Samani, N. (2024). Do key audit matters matter? Correspondence between auditor and management disclosures and the role of audit committees. *Journal of International Accounting, Auditing & Taxation*, 55, 100617. 10.1016/j.intaccaudtax.2024.100617

Jamali, D. (2008). A Stakeholder Approach to Corporate Social Responsibility: A Fresh Perspective into Theory and Practice. *Journal of Business Ethics*, 82(1), 213–231. 10.1007/s10551-007-9572-4

Jamali, D., & Mirshak, R. (2006). Corporate Social Responsibility (CSR): Theory and Practice in a Developing Country Context. *Journal of Business Ethics*, 72(3), 243–262. 10.1007/s10551-006-9168-4

Kaur, N., & Singh, V. (2021). Empirically examining the impact of corporate social responsibility on financial performance: Evidence from Indian steel industry. *Asian Journal of Accounting Research*, 6(2), 134–151. 10.1108/AJAR-07-2020-0061

Keinath, A. K., & Walo, J. C. (2004). Audit Committee Responsibilities: Focusing on Oversight, Open Communication, and Best Practices. *The CPA Journal*, ●●●, 22–28.

Khan, A., Muttakin, M. B., & Siddiqui, J. (2013). Corporate Governance and Corporate Social Responsibility Disclosures: Evidence from an Emerging Economy. *Journal of Business Ethics*, 114(2), 207–223. 10.1007/s10551-012-1336-0

Kolk, A., & Pinkse, J. (2010). The integration of corporate governance in corporate social responsibility disclosures. *Corporate Social Responsibility and Environmental Management*, 17(1), 15–26. 10.1002/csr.196

KPMG. (2021). *Climate change and corporate value.* https://assets.kpmg.com/content/dam/kpmg/xx/pdf/2021/03/climate-change-and-corporate-value.pdf

Lal Bhasin, M. (2013). Corporate Accounting Fraud: A Case Study of Satyam Computers Limited. *Open Journal of Accounting*, 02(02), 26–38. 10.4236/ojacct.2013.22006

Lin, J. W., Li, J. F., & Yang, J. S. (2006). The effect of audit committee performance on earnings quality. *Managerial Auditing Journal*, 21(9), 921–933. 10.1108/02686900610705019

Manchiraju, H., & Rajgopal, S.MANCHIRAJU. (2017). Does Corporate Social Responsibility (CSR) Create Shareholder Value? Evidence from the Indian Companies Act 2013. *Journal of Accounting Research*, 55(5), 1257–1300. 10.1111/1475-679X.12174

Mangena, M., & Pike, R. (2005). The effect of audit committee shareholding, financial expertise and size on interim financial disclosures. *Accounting and Business Research*, 35(4), 327–349. 10.1080/00014788.2005.9729998

Maqbool, S., & Zameer, M. N. (2018). Corporate social responsibility and financial performance: An empirical analysis of Indian banks. *Future Business Journal*, 4(1), 84–93. 10.1016/j.fbj.2017.12.002

Naqvi, S. K., Shahzad, F., Rehman, I. U., Qureshi, F., & Laique, U. (2021). Corporate social responsibility performance and information asymmetry: The moderating role of analyst coverage. *Corporate Social Responsibility and Environmental Management*, 28(6), 1549–1563. 10.1002/csr.2114

Parmar, B. L., Freeman, R. E., Harrison, J. S., Wicks, A. C., Purnell, L., & de Colle, S. (2010). Stakeholder Theory: The State of the Art. *The Academy of Management Annals*, 4(1), 403–445. 10.5465/19416520.2010.495581

Pfajfar, G., Shoham, A., Małecka, A., & Zalaznik, M. (2022). Value of corporate social responsibility for multiple stakeholders and social impact – Relationship marketing perspective. *Journal of Business Research*, 143, 46–61. 10.1016/j.jbusres.2022.01.051

Porter, M. E., & Kramer, M. R. (2006). Strategy and society: The link between competitive advantage and corporate social responsibility. *Harvard Business Review*, 84(12).17183795

Proimos, A. (2005). Strengthening corporate governance regulations. *Journal of Investment Compliance*, 6(4), 75–84. 10.1108/15285810510681900

Raimo, N., Vitolla, F., Marrone, A., & Rubino, M. (2020). Do audit committee attributes influence integrated reporting quality? An agency theory viewpoint. *Business Strategy and the Environment*, 30(1), 522–534. 10.1002/bse.2635

Smith, R. (2003). *Audit Committtees Combined Code Guidance*. https://www.ecgi.global/sites/default/files/codes/documents/ac_report.pdf

Thomas, A. S., Jayachandran, A., & Biju, A. V. N. (2024). Strategic mapping of the environmental social governance landscape in finance – A bibliometric exploration through concepts and themes. *Corporate Social Responsibility and Environmental Management*, 1–26. 10.1002/csr.2805

Ying, M., Tikuye, G. A., & Shan, H. (2021). Impacts of Firm Performance on Corporate Social Responsibility Practices: The Mediation Role of Corporate Governance in Ethiopia Corporate Business. *Sustainability (Basel)*, 13(17), 9717. 10.3390/su13179717

[1] The report titled 'Financial Aspects of Corporate Governance Committee' or 'Cadbury Report' was framed by the committee on corporate governance chaired by Sir Adrian Cadbury in 1992.

Chapter 8
Does Gender Diversity on the Board Matter for ESG Performance?
Evidence From India

Aghila Sasidharan
http://orcid.org/0000-0002-9254-6291
Indian Institute of Forest Management, Bhopal, India

M. Thenmozhi
https://orcid.org/0000-0002-8292-8042
Indian Institute of Technology, Madras, India

Biju Ajithakumari Vijayappan Nair
https://orcid.org/0000-0001-5583-6495
University of Kerala, India

Sonam Chawla
O.P. Jindal Global University, Sonipat, India

Jane S. C. Liu
Chaoyang University of Technology, Taichung, Taiwan

ABSTRACT

The importance of gender diversity on corporate boards has increased in recent years because of its potential impact on Environmental, Social, and Governance (ESG) activities. This study investigates the link between gender diversity on corporate boards and the disclosure of ESG policies in Indian firms. Our study indicates a positive relationship between gender diversity and ESG performance. We used panel

DOI: 10.4018/979-8-3693-3880-3.ch008

regression analysis on a sample of 250 companies that are publicly traded on India's National Stock Exchange (NSE). Companies that have a greater representation of women on their boards of directors are more likely to provide more extensive disclosures about ESG activities. There is a positive correlation between the involvement of female directors and the degree of transparency and comprehensiveness in ESG reporting. The presence of a diverse range of genders on boards can enhance the quality of disclosures by fostering a heightened emphasis on sustainability and ethical issues, as well as including a broader range of opinions.

1. INTRODUCTION

Gender diversity encompasses the presence of several genders within an institution, such as the board of directors. This involves enhancing the presence of women in top-level positions and significant decision-making roles within firms. In India, the implementation of Business Responsibility and Sustainability Reporting (BRSR) has resulted in the replacement of Corporate Social Responsibility (CSR) with ESG practices(Biju et al., 2023; Thomas et al., 2024). Thereupon, socially conscious investors employ ESG criteria, a collection of standards pertaining to a company's operations, to assess prospective investments(Kodiyatt et al., 2024). The manner in which a firm manages its interactions with customers, suppliers, employees, and the communities in which it works is among the evaluated social factors. The manner in which a firm behaves as a steward of the environment is evaluated using environmental standards. Shareholder rights, executive compensation, internal controls, and audits are all aspects of governance considered. Resource dependence theory contends that firms must frequently acquire resources from their environment to guarantee survival (Thomas et al., 2024). A diverse board may offer access to myriad resources and networks. Numerous studies have been conducted to examine the impact of female directors on firm performance, yielding inconclusive findings. This study shows that increasing the presence of women on a firm's board improves its financial performance and decision-making processes.

In the US, prior studies have shown a positive relationship between board diversity and firm value (Carter et al., 2023). Since investors realise how important ESG performance is as a metric, firms that effectively use ESG practices are viewed as less risky and more resilient(Geetha et al., 2023). Previous research has demonstrated that boards with a diverse gender composition are more likely to prioritise ESG concerns. As stated by Konrad et al. (2008), female directors tend to prioritise ecological and ethical corporate policies while simultaneously displaying a cautious approach towards taking risks. Most of the studies being done now focus on developed markets like the US and Europe. No research hasn't been done on how gender diversity affects ESG performance in developing nations like India. Our study provides a distinct path for examining the effect of female directors on the performance of Indian boardrooms, which significantly advances both academic debate and actual corporate governance.

In recent years, scholars and policymakers have shown significant interest in the influence of ESG dimensions on the value of firms. ESG is a novel idea gaining traction in emerging and developed economies. The prevalence of legislation mandating ESG practices is increasing due to a widespread lack of understanding among the general public and corporations regarding their legal rights and responsibilities. Businesses also see ESG as a liability rather than a source of long-term benefit. Previously, firms were hesitant to disclose their ESG activities because shareholders were concerned that if companies began to disclose ESG scores, the return to shareholders would decrease. Firms were compelled to invest in social activities by the mandated regulations in China, South Africa, and India. Most businesses disclose the amount they allocate to social activities, including education and community development, in their annual reports. Although laws are being implemented across many countries, certain mechanisms are necessary to ensure that firms adhere to the laws enacted by the various regulators. Hence, examining the effect of female directors on ESG activities is crucial.

The primary objective of the firm is to balance various bottom lines and meet the requirements of diverse stakeholders, in addition to meeting its financial goals(-Jamali et al., 2024). ESG disclosure may impact a company's financial performance and stakeholders by minimizing information asymmetry between management and stakeholders. Customers who are aware of ESG activities, according to Brown and Dacin (1997), can raise the brand value and increase demand for a company's products. Nevertheless, there are some individuals who are apprehensive about the quality of the disclosure of ESG activities. Management uses ESG disclosure scores to enhance its reputation rather than to mitigate information asymmetry between stakeholders and managers. Choi et al. (2019) suggest managers could use ESG disclosure to hide their opportunistic actions. Thus, it is imperative to create strong corporate governance systems that include gender diversity on boards in order to keep an eye on the operations of companies in nations like India, where concentrated ownership is highly prevalent.

Corporate governance is a critical component of ESG, as it pertains to the relationships between firms and all stakeholders. Consequently, ESG can be viewed from a corporate governance perspective. The majority of research contends that corporate governance and social activities are interrelated and that effective governance results in increased transparency. Corporate governance impacts the quality of ESG disclosure; effective regulation can lead to greater transparency (Cormier et al., 2011). Having a women director on the board and its presence and characteristics would enhance board oversight and efficiency, as well as reduce information asymmetry between managers and stakeholder groups. Consequently, the level of company disclosure, including ESG, would increase. India has enacted a range of policies to control the number of boards of directors. According to the Indian businesses Act of 2013, listed firms are required to have a minimum of one female director serving on their board. It has also expanded the scope of gender diversity's role in the oversight of mandatory disclosures, including ESG. The social and environmental impact of firms has become a global concern, and companies are now being compelled by stakeholders to expand their objectives and actions in these areas. Prior studies on ESG focus on the firm's obligations to its diverse stakeholders. Nevertheless, there are apprehensions regarding the quality and quantity of ESG disclosures. Women directors are crucial as a supervisory mechanism to mitigate these concerns, while simultaneously monitoring and enhancing ESG. The effectiveness of the monitoring process can be enhanced when the board is predominantly composed of women directors. The United Nations' Sustainable Development Goals (SDG Goal 5, gender equality) aim to promote gender diversity and ensure equitable opportunities for women in leadership and decision-making roles. Owing to their different interpersonal interactions, men and women view sustainability concerns from different angles. People therefore believe that women make more moral decisions. Female directors, by virtue of their personality, may possess a greater understanding of social and environmental issues, while simultaneously addressing the concerns of all stakeholders.

There are numerous contributions to the existing literature on ESG and sustainability reporting that this study makes. The paper first offers empirical support for the theory that, in the setting of Indian firms, female directors are related with ESG activities. This contributes to the existing research conducted in developing countries, expanding the geographical scope of the current body of research. Furthermore, this research enhances the existing body of literature and enables a more comprehensive examination of the correlation between gender diversity and ESG factors. This is achieved by focusing on particular ESG elements, such as performance and transparency criteria. In order to establish a theoretical foundation for the study, the third phase of the research involves examining multiple theoretical frameworks. The list includes the frameworks of resource dependency theory, agency theory, stakeholder theory, and social identity theory. Furthermore, it emphasises the significance of performing further study in the future to explore the fundamental mechanisms that underlie the correlation between female directors and ESG actions. The study's findings provide regulatory authorities with valuable insights into the impact of corporate governance systems, including gender diversity and environmental,

RQ1. To analyse how gender diversity influences ESG disclosure practices

RQ2. To assess the influence of female directors on board decisions ESG performance in Indian firms

2. REVIEW OF LITERATURE

2.1 Institutional Background

India has implemented legislative measures that mandate female diversity on corporate boards, including the Companies Act 2013 and SEBI regulations. The research evaluates how compliant businesses are, and what results arise from having more women in leadership roles. Studies on female directors provide insight into the variables affecting women's experiences in corporate environments, leadership trajectories, and career advancement (Biswas, 2021). Our findings help with leadership development initiatives, talent management plans, and campaigns against discrimination and gender bias.

A company's dedication to gender diversity may be seen positively by the public, which could increase trust and loyalty and improve its ESG performance (Chatterjee &Nath, 2023; Satter et al.,2023). In India, the significance of gender diversity and ESG disclosure is being emphasized more and more by regulatory frameworks and stakeholder expectations. While firms that show a commitment to diversity and sustainability are more likely to achieve compliance requirements and satisfy stakeholder demands, companies that ignore gender diversity may come under regulatory scrutiny and run the risk of damaging their brand(Marano, 2022). Firms that are gender diverse tend to be more creative and innovative, which leads to business models that address social demands and environmental challenges. Companies may generate sustainable innovation and positively impact ESG results by developing an inclusive culture encouraging different ideas.

2.2 The Impact of Female Directors on ESG Factors

Prior studies show that female directors are better at identifying and managing risks, especially those pertaining to social responsibility and environmental sustainability. Diverse boards can better foresee new possibilities and hazards, resulting in more proactive ESG strategies (Cambrea et al.,2023). The perception of gender-diverse boards as more inclusive and socially conscious is common, and it can improve their connections with communities, workers, investors, and other stakeholders (Bhattacharya et al.,2022). Good stakeholder interactions can generate long-term benefits for shareholders and enhance a company's reputation overall. Incorporating gender diversity onto boards promotes a culture of transparency, accountability, and moral leadership, all of which benefit long-term value generation. Businesses that emphasized ESG issues are better able to adjust to shifting market conditions, reduce risks, and take advantage of chances for long-term growth (Fan et al.,2024).

Adams and Ferreira (2009) find that having a board with a diverse gender composition in the US is associated with higher levels of attendance and monitoring. However, it does not necessarily result in enhanced performance for the company. The research undertaken by Carter et al. (2003) illustrates that boards with a varied composition can provide a multitude of viewpoints, resulting in enhanced decision-making and overall effectiveness. In their study, Nielsen and Huse (2010) discovered that having women on boards enhances board performance through their active involvement in addressing and tackling CSR matters. The study conducted by Bear et al. (2010) demonstrates that organisations with a greater proportion of women on their boards demonstrate superior performance in CSR. This implies that the presence of a variety of genders has a beneficial effect on the fulfilment of social obligations. Post et al. (2015) discovered that boards with a mix of genders are keenly interested in investing in renewable energy and implementing sustainable policies. Bernardi and Threadgill (2010) found that firms with a greater representation of women on their boards are more inclined to engage in community-oriented and philanthropic endeavors. In their study, Erhardt et al. (2003) found that having boards with various genders leads to better governance practices, such as increased accountability and transparency. In their study, Chakrabarti et al. (2019) examined the effect of female directors on firm value and discovered some significant conclusions. They highlighted the need for additional research to comprehend the contextual elements that impact these findings thoroughly.

ESG indicators are proxies for the non-financial performance of firms (Thomas et al. 2024), and it is worthwhile to investigate whether a diversity board has good ESG performance. While examining the BGD on disclosure practices, prior studies find that women directors fail to perform their fiduciary duties in firms where females are in the minority (Usman et al., 2018). Furthermore, studies have shown that female directors often exhibit risk-averse behavior and are strongly dedicated to sustainable and ethical corporate practices (Konrad et al., 2008). The literature needs to offer insight into whether female board members function more effectively when other independent directors are present. The relationship between female directors and ESG performance in emerging nations, such as India, has not been extensively examined and requires further investigation (Nekhili & Gatfaoui, 2013). Although extensive research has been carried out in developed countries, there is a conspicuous dearth of understanding on the influence of gender diversity on ESG performance in rising economies, such as India. Prior studies have mostly focused on identifying associations rather than causal relationships between gender diversity and ESG performance. Further study is needed to evaluate the impact of gender diversity on ESG performance. Thus, we put forward the subsequent hypothesis:

H1: Gender diversity on the board has a positive impact on ESG reporting of Indian firms

3. DATA AND METHODOLOGY

3.1 Data

The sample consists of all the companies that are listed in the NSE. The data was obtained from Bloomberg and the Prowess database, which is managed by the Centre for Monitoring the Indian Economy (CMIE). These are the sources from which NSE collects its historical data on the ESG disclosure score and other significant metrics. The Bloomberg ESG Database encompasses ESG data furnished by nearly 1000 firms, encompassing environmental, social, and governance dimensions. The disclosure scores assigned to a firm by Bloomberg's own ESG disclosure database do not accurately show its ESG performance. A score of 0.1 denotes no disclosure based on the company's reporting, while a score of 100 denotes full transparency. CMIE has created a database for Indian-listed firms that includes detailed financial and non-financial information specific to each firm. We have obtained ESG scores data from Bloomberg and financial and corporate governance data from Prowess IQ. The years 2013–2020 were selected due to the introduction of the CSR requirement and the appointment of women directors in 2013. We conducted additional research on these particular firms using the Bloomberg database and reviewing their most recent annual reports. Our final sample comprised of 250 firms covering 1000 firm year observation and our data is unbalanced panel data this is because the panel initially missed some observations. We have to hand collect the data related to women directors based on their salutations since it's not available in Prowess.

3.2 Methodology

The Hausman test served as the basis for our decision to conduct our research using fixed effect panel regression. The equation that follows illustrates the relationship between women directors and ESG.

$$ESG\ scores = \alpha_{it} + \beta_1 Size_{it} + \beta_2 LEVE_{it} + \beta_3 Growth_{it} + \beta_4 BS_{it} + \beta_5 B-IND_{it} + \beta_6 B_{Tenure} + \beta_7 WD + U_i + V_t + \epsilon_{it}$$

The term U_{-i}, V_{-t} and ϵ_{it} stands for industry-fixed effects, time-fixed effects, and error term, respectively. Table 1 also includes definitions variables. The endogeneity problem was addressed by using the lagged value of the variable, and we found that our findings were robust as a result of this method.

3.2.1 Variables and Measurement

The study uses the ESG disclosure score as the primary dependent variable, supported by previous research (Filipiak & Kiestrzyn, M, 2021). The environmental disclosure score evaluates a company's involvement in controlling greenhouse gas (GHG) emissions, waste, water, energy, climate risk, air quality, and environmental impact. The social disclosure score evaluates companies' effectiveness in managing product quality, adhering to labor practices, promoting gender diversity in the Indian setting, upholding ethical standards, and protecting the general public's rights. Similarly, the governance disclosure score represents a company's achievement in diversity, board responsibilities, obligations, and motivations. The number of women serving as directors on the board has been used as an independent variable. We have included several control variables in our analysis that are consistent with previous research (Bravo & Reguera-Alvarado, 2019; Cucari et al., 2018). These variables include board size, independence, tenure, growth, company size, and leverage.

Table 1. Variable definition

Variables	Definitions
Dependent Variable	
ESG	Total of E, S and G score, Scale ranges from 0 to 100 downloaded from Bloomberg
Independent Variable	
Women director(W_D)	The proportion of female directors in the board-to-board size
Control Variables	
Size	Natural log of total assets
Leverage	Ratio of borrowings to total assets
Growth	Difference between current sales and previous sales by previous sales
Size of the board	The number of directors on board
Independent Directors (B_IND)	The proportion of independent directors to the total size of the board
Tenure of the Board(B_Tenure)	The period of time an individual member serves on the board

4. EMPIRICAL RESULTS

4.1 Summary Statistics

Table 2 shows the descriptive statistics and correlation matrices of the main variables used in the study. The average value of ESG is 0.438. If ESG scores are assigned a number between 0 and 1, then a mean score of 0.438 means that, on average, the evaluated companies have obtained half of the highest possible ESG score. This points to a generally mediocre performance in terms of governance and social and environmental practices. The average value of board size is 10.03, and the mean value of women directors is 0.192. The average tenure of a board member is 6.701. The correlation matrix indicates that ESG is significantly and positively correlated with women directors. ESG is substantially and negatively correlated with board size, independence, and tenure. Leverage is negatively correlated with ESG among the control variables.

Table 2. Descriptive statistics and correlation matrix

Variable	Obs	Mean	Std. dev.	ESG	Size	LEVE	Growth	Board Tenure	BS	IND	
ESG		0.4388	0.3621	1							
Size			1.8728	0.0126	1						
LEVE		0.1281	0.1631	-0.0873*	0.2376*	1					
Growth		5.0395	3.8984	0.0144	-0.0601	0.0707*	1				
Board Tenure		6.7091	3.8561	-0.0833*	-0.1877*	-0.1470*	-0.0162	1			
BS			3.5451	-0.1334*	0.3459*	-0.0559	-0.0531	0.2556*	1		
IND		0.3473	2.1923	-0.1391*	0.2111*	-0.0673*	0.0899*	0.4193*		1	
WD		0.1902	0.4921	0.1042*	0.1396*	-0.0710*	0.0168	0.0189			1

Note: This table displays the descriptive statistics and correlation matrices of the variables used in the study. The asterisk (*) indicates significance at the 5% level.

4.2 The Impact of Female Directors on ESG

Table 3 displays the impact of female directors on ESG performance. Our findings indicate that gender diversity has a positive effect on ESG factors, thereby confirming our initial hypothesis. This is consistent with the results of previous research. Gender diverse boards are more inclined to prioritise ESG concerns. According to Konrad et al. (2008), female directors often display risk aversion and a strong dedication to sustainable and ethical company practices. Furthermore, Adams & Ferreira (2009) discovered, for instance, that gender-diverse boards in the US are linked to increased attendance and monitoring, contributing to enhanced ESG practices.

The perception that women directors are more socially responsible and inclusive is common. This perception can help boards improve their interactions with consumers, employees, investors, and communities (Sattar et al., 2023). Strong relationships with stakeholders not only contribute to the overall reputation of a company but also have the potential to provide long-term value for shareholders. In India, regulatory frameworks progressively emphasise the significance of board diversity and ESG disclosure. Regulatory scrutiny and reputational risks may be imposed on businesses that fail to address gender diversity and ecological, social, and governance issues. On the other hand, those who exhibit leadership in these areas have the potential to earn a competitive advantage and the ability to fulfil the ever-changing expectations of the market. By cultivating a culture that values accountability, transparency, and ethical leadership, gender diversity on boards of directors produces long-term value. To effectively react to shifting market conditions, manage risks, and grab opportunities for sustainable growth, businesses that emphasize ESG issues are better positioned.

Our results underscore that board size, board independence and board tenure negatively related to ESG suggesting power dynamics, conflicts of interest, or inadequate accountability mechanisms within the board may hinder the advancement of ESG initiatives. The presence of long-tenured directors can potentially impede the introduction of fresh viewpoints, the infusion of diverse talent onto the board, and the adaptation of governance practices to emergent ESG trends. A potential consequence of independent directors placing immediate financial interests ahead of long-term sustainability concerns is a problem between board decisions and ESG outcomes.

Table 3. The impact of board diversity on ESG

Variables	(1) ESG	(2) ESG	(3) ESG	(4) ESG	(5) ESG
Size	0.6250	0.4364	1.3652**	1.3522**	1.1167*
	(1.12)	(0.74)	(2.16)	(2.14)	(1.76)
LEVE	-17.2361***	-17.1169***	-20.0595***	-19.9900***	-18.2097***
	(-2.71)	(-2.60)	(-3.05)	(-3.04)	(-2.77)
Growth	0.0072	0.0069	0.0059	0.0051	0.0041
	(0.70)	(0.66)	(0.57)	(0.49)	(0.40)

continued on following page

Table 3. Continued

Variables	(1) ESG	(2) ESG	(3) ESG	(4) ESG	(5) ESG
Board Tenure		-0.6601**	-0.3582	-0.2634	-0.2892
		(-2.42)	(-1.27)	(-0.87)	(-0.96)
BS			-1.3427***	-0.9860*	-1.0154*
			(-3.81)	(-1.85)	(-1.92)
IND				-0.7499	-0.7186
				(-0.90)	(-0.86)
WD					6.0089***
					(2.83)
Constant	6.0598***	2.4119***	2.7092***	4.5292***	4.8943***
	(5.13)	(5.28)	(5.36)	(5.33)	(5.28)
No. of Obs.	1000.00	1000.00	1000.00	1000.00	1000.00
R-Squared	0.20	0.21	0.33	0.34	0.36
Year Effect	YES	YES	YES	YES	YES
Industry Effect	YES	YES	YES	YES	YES

Notes: This table presents the influence of female directors on ESG factors. All regressions incorporate industry and year fixed effects as control variables. The t-statistics are enclosed within brackets. The symbols ***, **, and * represent statistical significance at the 1%, 5%, and 10% levels, respectively.

4.3 Endogeneity Check

The relationship between ESG and women directors is investigated using the statistical method known as two-stage least squares regression, or 2SLS regression. Lagged values are used for the analysis. We have identified the instrument that correlates with the women directors but not with ESG performance. We have used legal requirements for gender diversity as instrumental variables. We regressed the binary variable representing the number of women directors on the selected instrumental factors. Using this model, get the fitted or expected values for female directors. We regress ESG performance (dependent variable) and any control factors on the women directors' anticipated values derived from the first stage. We incorporated lagged values of women directors to account for any temporal effects or time lags in establishing the relationship between the female directors and ESG. The model implies that our findings are comparable to those of the base model.

Table 4. Robustness check

Variables	ESG_{t-1}
Size	1.2113*
	(1.79)
LEVE	-9.1122
	(-1.30)
Growth	0.0159
	(1.45)
Board Tenure	-0.3817
	(-1.20)
BS	-1.0056*
	(-1.79)
IND	-0.3686
	(-0.42)
WD	7.6464***
	(3.39)
Constant	33.1459***
	(3.93)
No. of Obs.	600
R-Squared	0.36

Notes: This table presents the influence of female directors on ESG factors. All regressions incorporate industry and year fixed effects as control variables. The t-statistics are enclosed in brackets. The symbols ***, **, and * represent statistical significance at the 1%, 5%, and 10% levels, respectively.

5. CONCLUSION

We examine the impact of female directors on ESG factors using a sample of Indian companies registered on the NSE. We find that ESG performance is improved by BGD, especially for women directors. Practitioners may find use for the empirical data from our study, especially when it comes to improving corporate governance in Indian listed firms. Our findings indicate that increasing the number of directors on the board can lead to an increase in ESG reporting and a decrease in the board's involvement in ESG decision-making. Gender-diverse boards are related to improved ESG performance indicators and more open and thorough ESG disclosure procedures. These findings emphasise the crucial significance of gender diversity in corporate governance for establishing sustainable and responsible business practices in India. This study is a valuable contribution to academic research and has important practical implications for policymakers, corporate executives, and investors who are interested in advancing diversity and sustainability in corporate governance procedures. By presenting empirical evidence from the context of an emerging economy, this study addresses a gap in the existing literature.

More women directors should be promoted to the board, and their participation should be encouraged and promoted to provide better protection for shareholders. Consequently, legislators and regulators may advocate for the representation of a significant number of female members on corporate boards. The importance of this study for regulators and policymakers of Indian firms is its recognition of the impact of board features, such as gender diversity and the number of directors, on the reporting of ESG indicators.

REFERENCES

Adams, R. B., & Ferreira, D. (2009). Women in the boardroom and their impact on governance and performance. *Journal of Financial Economics*, 94(2), 291–309. 10.1016/j.jfineco.2008.10.007

Bear, S., Rahman, N., & Post, C. (2010). The impact of board diversity and gender composition on corporate social responsibility and firm reputation. *Journal of Business Ethics*, 97(2), 207–221. 10.1007/s10551-010-0505-2

Bernardi, R. A., & Threadgill, V. H. (2010). Women Directors and Corporate Social Responsibility. EJBO, Vol. 15, No. 2, p. 15-21. https://urn.fi/URN:NBN:fi:jyu-201201301096

Bhattacharya, B., Khadka, I., & Mani, D. (2022). Shaking up (and keeping intact) the old boys' network: The impact of the mandatory gender quota on the board of directors in India. *Journal of Business Ethics*, 177(4), 763–778. 10.1007/s10551-022-05099-w

Biju, A. V. N., Kodiyatt, S. J., Krishna, P. P. N., & Sreelekshmi, G. (2023). ESG sentiments and divergent ESG scores: Suggesting a framework for ESG rating. *SN Business & Economics*, 3(12), 209. 10.1007/s43546-023-00592-4

Biswas, S. (2021). Female directors and risk-taking behavior of Indian firms. *Managerial Finance*, 47(7), 1016–1037. 10.1108/MF-05-2020-0274

Bravo, F., & Reguera-Alvarado, N. (2019). Sustainable development disclosure: Environmental, social, and governance reporting and gender diversity in the audit committee. *Business Strategy and the Environment*, 28(2), 418–429. 10.1002/bse.2258

Brown, T. J., & Dacin, P. A. (1997). The company and the product: Corporate associations and consumer product responses. *Journal of Marketing*, 61(1), 68–84. https://psycnet.apa.org/doi/10.2307/1252190. 10.1177/002224299706100106

Cambrea, D. R., Paolone, F., & Cucari, N. (2023). Advisory or monitoring role in ESG scenario: Which women directors are more influential in the Italian context? *Business Strategy and the Environment*, 32(7), 4299–4314. 10.1002/bse.3366

Carter, D. A., Simkins, B. J., & Simpson, W. G. (2003). Corporate governance, board diversity, and firm value. *Financial Review*, 38(1), 33–53. 10.1111/1540-6288.00034

Chatterjee, C., & Nag, T. (2023). Do women on boards enhance firm performance? Evidence from top Indian companies. *International Journal of Disclosure and Governance*, 20(2), 155–167. 10.1057/s41310-022-00153-5

Choi, Y. K., Han, S. H., & Kwon, Y. (2019). CSR activities and internal capital markets: Evidence from Korean business groups. *Pacific-Basin Finance Journal*, 55, 283–298. 10.1016/j.pacfin.2019.04.008

Cormier, D., Ledoux, M. J., & Magnan, M. (2011). The informational contribution of social and environmental disclosures for investors. *Management Decision*, 49(8), 1276–1304. 10.1108/00251741111163124

Cucari, N., Esposito De Falco, S., & Orlando, B. (2018). Diversity of board of directors and environmental social governance: Evidence from Italian listed companies. *Corporate Social Responsibility and Environmental Management*, 25(3), 250–266. 10.1002/csr.1452

Erhardt, N. L., Werbel, J. D., & Shrader, C. B. (2003). Board of director diversity and firm financial performance. *Corporate Governance*, 11(2), 102–111. 10.1111/1467-8683.00011

Fan, Y., Li, S., & Yang, W. (2024). Research on the impact of the percentage of female directors on corporate ESG score. *Finance Research Letters*, 105376, 105376. Advance online publication. 10.1016/j.frl.2024.105376

Filipiak, B. Z., & Kiestrzyn, M. (2021). Potential ESG Risks in Entities of the Healthcare System. In Adapting and Mitigating Environmental, Social, and Governance Risk in Business (pp. 74-102). IGI Global. 10.4018/978-1-7998-6788-3.ch005

Geetha, S., & Biju, A. V. N. (2024). Is green FinTech reshaping the finance sphere? Unravelling through a systematic literature review. *Environmental Science and Pollution Research International*, 31(2), 1790–1810. 10.1007/s11356-023-31382-y38057679

Jamali, D. R., Ahmad, I., Aboelmaged, M., & Usman, M. (2024). Corporate social responsibility in the United Arab Emirates and globally: A cross-national comparison. *Journal of Cleaner Production*, 434, 140105. 10.1016/j.jclepro.2023.140105

Hillman, A. J., Cannella, A. A., & Paetzold, R. L. (2000). The resource dependency role of corporate directors: Strategic adaptation of board composition in response to environmental change. *Journal of Management Studies*, 37(2), 235–256. 10.1111/1467-6486.00179

Jensen, M. C., & Meckling, W. H. (1976). Theory of the firm: Managerial behavior, agency costs, and ownership structure. *Journal of Financial Economics*, 3(4), 305–360. 10.1016/0304-405X(76)90026-X

Kodiyatt, S. J., Nair, B. A. V., Jacob, M. S., & Reddy, K. (2024). Does green bond issuance enhance market return of equity shares in the Indian stock market?*. *Asia-Pacific Journal of Financial Studies*, 02(3), 1–20. 10.1111/ajfs.12459

Konrad, A. M., Kramer, V., & Erkut, S. (2008). The impact of three or more women on corporate boards. *Organizational Dynamics*, 37(2), 145–164. 10.1016/j.orgdyn.2008.02.005

Marano, V., Sauerwald, S., & Van Essen, M. (2022). The influence of culture on the relationship between women directors and corporate social performance. *Journal of International Business Studies*, 53(7), 1315–1342. 10.1057/s41267-022-00503-z

Nekhili, M., & Gatfaoui, H. (2013). Are Demographic Attributes and Firm Characteristics Drivers of Gender Diversity? Investigating Women's Positions on French Boards of Directors. *Journal of Business Ethics*, 118(2), 227–249. 10.1007/s10551-012-1576-z

Nielsen, S., & Huse, M. (2010). The contribution of women on boards of directors: Going beyond the surface. *Corporate Governance*, 18(2), 136–148. 10.1111/j.1467-8683.2010.00784.x

Post, C., Rahman, N., & McQuillen, C. (2015). From Board Composition to Corporate Environmental Performance Through Sustainability-Themed Alliances. *Journal of Business Ethics*, 130(2), 423–435. 10.1007/s10551-014-2231-7

Sattar, M., Biswas, P. K., & Roberts, H. (2023). Private firm performance: Do women directors matter? *Meditari Accountancy Research*, 31(3), 602–634. 10.1108/MEDAR-03-2021-1233

Thomas, A. S., Jayachandran, A., & Biju, A. V. N. (2024). Strategic mapping of the environmental social governance landscape in finance – A bibliometric exploration through concepts and themes. *Corporate Social Responsibility and Environmental Management*, ●●●, 1–26. 10.1002/csr.2805

Usman, M., Zhang, J., Wang, F., Sun, J., & Makki, M. A. M. (2018). Gender diversity in compensation committees and CEO pay: Evidence from China. *Management Decision*, 56(5), 1065–1087. 10.1108/MD-09-2017-0815

Chapter 9
Assessing the Dependence of Sustainability and Market Indices in India:
A Copula Approach

Vineetha Mathew
https://orcid.org/0000-0003-0671-5018
Cochin University of Science and Technology, India

Haseena Akbar
Cochin University of Science and Technology, India

Santhosh Kumar P. K.
https://orcid.org/0000-0002-2832-4635
Cochin University of Science and Technology, India

Vitaliy Serzhanov
Uzhhorod National University, Ukraine

ABSTRACT

This chapter delves into a novel exploration of the non-linear interdependence between the conventional market index and selected sustainability indices in India. While socially responsible investing has gained traction globally, its impact on emerging markets like India is less explored. This study assesses the relationship between the market index- Sensex and sustainability indices - ESG, Carbonex, and Greenex through copula models. By scrutinizing the relationship between them, this study breaks new ground in understanding investor preferences and market

DOI: 10.4018/979-8-3693-3880-3.ch009

dynamics. Results indicate a strong positive association between Sensex and sustainable indices, underscoring investors' growing inclination towards sustainable investments. Moreover, the copula models reveal various degrees of dependency, with Carbonex demonstrating the highest dependency on Sensex. The findings of the study show the popularity of sustainable indices in the Indian landscape and provide insights for investors, companies and policymakers.

1. INTRODUCTION

Socially responsible investing (SRI) is a long-term oriented investment approach which integrates environmental, social, and governance (ESG) factors in the research, analysis and selection process of securities within an investment portfolio (European Sustainable Investment Forum, 2018). In addition to delivering long-term returns for investors, SRI pushes companies towards socially responsible behaviour thus generating a positive societal impact (The Forum for Sustainable and Responsible Investment, 2018). As of the end of 2021, the US SIF Foundation reported $8.4 trillion in total assets under management in the United States, employing sustainable investment strategies. This constitutes 13 percent, or 1 in every 8 dollars, of the overall assets under professional management in the US (US SIF Foundation, 2022). The emergence of sustainability indices reflects a growing awareness and emphasis on incorporating ESG factors into investment decisions (Atz et al., 2023; Fowler & Hope, 2007; HKEX, 2020). However, most of the existing research on SRIs has focused primarily on the performance of socially responsible mutual funds (Kim, 2019; Renneboog et al., 2008; Statman & Glushkov, 2016).

Sustainable indices have not received the same level of attention in academic research, indicating the need for more research specifically dedicated to evaluating the effectiveness and impact of sustainability indices in promoting sustainable investing practices and driving positive environmental, social, and governance outcomes (Fowler & Hope, 2007; Jain et al., 2019; Plastun et al., 2022). These indices aim to reflect the performance of companies that adhere to sustainable practices, providing a benchmark for ESG-oriented investments. While the impact of socially responsible investing is well-documented in developed markets, its influence in emerging economies, such as India, remains underexplored (Jain & Tripathi, 2023; Talan & Sharma, 2019; Widyawati, 2019). This chapter seeks to fill this gap by examining the non-linear interdependence between conventional market indices and sustainability indices in India using a copula approach. The primary objective of this chapter is to assess the dependence between the Sensex and the selected sustainability indices (ESG, Carbonex, and Greenex) using copula models. Copula models offer a flexible and robust framework for analyzing the joint distribution of multiple variables, capturing both linear and non-linear dependencies (Patton, 2012). Unlike traditional correlation measures, copulas can model complex dependency structures, including tail dependencies, which are crucial for understanding the joint behaviour of financial variables during extreme market conditions (Hung, 2021).

It is crucial to understand the interdependence between conventional and sustainability indices for several reasons. Firstly, it provides insights into investor behaviour and preferences, highlighting the extent to which sustainable investing influences market dynamics. As investors increasingly prioritize ESG factors, the relationship between conventional and sustainability indices can shed light on the evolving landscape of investment strategies. Secondly, assessing the dependence between these indices can inform risk management and portfolio diversification strategies. Non-linear dependencies, particularly tail dependencies, can have significant implications for risk assessment, especially during periods of market stress. Finally, this analysis can guide policymakers and regulatory bodies in promoting sustainable practices within financial markets, contributing to the broader agenda of sustainable development.

2. REVIEW OF LITERATURE

2.1 Theoretical Background

The theoretical foundation of this study is rooted in the theories underlying socially responsible investing (SRI), which extend from Corporate Social Responsibility (CSR) frameworks. These theories—Instrumental Theory, Ethical Theory, and Normative Stakeholder Theory—provide critical insights into the motivations and impacts of incorporating ESG factors into investment decisions. The Instrumental Theory (Friedman, 1953), posits that the primary responsibility of a business is to maximize profits for shareholders within the legal and ethical confines of society, viewing social responsibilities as secondary to profit maximization. In contrast, ethical theory (Freeman, 1984) argues that corporations have a duty to act ethically and contribute to societal well-being, emphasizing that business decisions should consider broader ethical implications and the impact on various stakeholders. Normative Stakeholder Theory (Phillips, 2003) expands corporate responsibility, asserting that managers are accountable to all stakeholders, not just shareholders, and should integrate moral and social values into their decision-making processes. This perspective asserts that businesses can achieve long-term profitability and sustainability by addressing societal demands and integrating ethical considerations into their strategies. The increasing popularity of sustainability indices like ESG, Carbonex, and Greenex highlights investors' recognition of the value of ethical considerations and stakeholder interests. Grounding our analysis in these theoretical perspectives, we aim to enrich the discourse on business's societal role and the evolving landscape of sustainable investing.

2.2 Sustainability Indices: An Overview

Sustainability indices play a crucial role in examining and promoting sustainable practices among businesses (Miralles-Quiros et al., 2017; Plastun et al., 2022). These indices serve as benchmarks they are specifically designed to evaluate and rate companies based on their performance in areas related to sustainability and responsible business practices. The world's first sustainability index, the Domini 400 social index, was launched in May 1990 by Kinder, Lydenberg, Domini and Co. Other prominent sustainability indices include FTSE4Good, MSCI ESG Ratings and Dow Jones Sustainability Index (DJSI). These sustainability indices contribute to the growth of responsible investing by providing investors with valuable information on companies' ESG practices (Guerard, 1997). They also motivate businesses to adopt sustainable strategies, leading to a positive impact on the environment, society, and corporate governance. Thus, these indices help investors make informed decisions by considering not only financial performance but also a company's impact on the planet and society. The growing trend of sustainability indices demonstrates a shift towards including environmental concerns into mainstream financial markets (Fowler & Hope, 2007; Rodrigo et al., 2024; Talan & Sharma, 2019).

Sustainability indices include companies that prioritize environmentally friendly practices, such as renewable energy, energy efficiency, and waste reduction. They also promote investments in companies with positive social and governance practices, fair labour conditions, and ethical business conduct (Górka & Kuziak, 2022). By investing in such indices, investors can support businesses with a commitment to sustainability. Investing in sustainability indices allows individuals and institutions to align their investments with their values. This approach, known as ethical or socially responsible investing, enables investors to support companies that share their commitment to sustainability and responsible business practices. Companies with strong environmental, social and governance practices are better positioned for long-term performance (Renneboog et al., 2011), as they can potentially mitigate certain risks associated with environmental regulations, social unrest, and changing consumer preferences (Ortas et al, 2015). Sustainable companies are often at the forefront of innovation in areas such as clean energy, resource efficiency, and technology. Also, as the demand for sustainable products and services continues to grow, companies adopting environmentally friendly practices may attract more customers, potentially leading to increased revenues and market share. Studies suggest that companies with strong ESG performance may outperform their counterparts over the long term (Atz et al., 2023; Verheyden et al., 2016; Wu et al. 2017). Thus, investing in sustainability indices may provide exposure to companies that are well-positioned for future growth and profitability.

2.3 Sustainability Indices in the Indian Context

Most of the studies on sustainability indices were carried out in the U.S. and other developed economies. Research in the emerging markets is limited due to lack of awareness and lack of accurate and relevant ESG-related information (Jain & Tripathi, 2023; Talan & Sharma, 2019; Tripathi & Bhandari, 2015). However, sustainability indices have gained traction in India, reflecting a growing awareness of ESG factors among investors and businesses. The global trend of increasing assets managed with SRI strategies has slowly started to percolate in India as well. Mutual fund markets in India witnessed a record increase of 76% in ESG-based mutual fund schemes in the time period 2019-20, with assets under management increasing from Rs 2,094 crore to Rs 3,686 crore. Further, anticipating stable and long-term risk-adjusted returns, pension funds too have started integrating ESG factors. This gives evidence to the fact that stakeholders now recognize the importance of responsible investing and the role of financial markets in fostering sustainable development. S&P BSE Carbonex, S&P BSE Greenex, BSE SENSEX 50 ESG Index, Nifty100 ESG Index, and NSE ESG Index are the major sustainability indices in India. In the Indian financial landscape, where awareness of sustainable practices is on the rise and research is limited, understanding the relationship between sustainability indices - and traditional market indices is crucial (Alshehhi et al., 2018; Jain et al., 2019; Talan & Sharma, 2019).

2.4 Interdependence between Sustainable and Conventional Indices

Majority of existing research has primarily examined the returns of sustainable indices in comparison to traditional market indices (Atz et al., 2023; De la Torre et al. 2016; Fooladi & Hebb, 2022; Managi et al., 2012; Mensi et al. 2017) or the financial performance of companies listed on sustainability indices in contrast to those listed on conventional market indices (Ademi & Klungseth, 2022; Alshehhi et al. 2018; Lassala et al. 2017; Santis et al. 2016). Existing literature lacks an understanding of the inter-dependence between sustainable indices and conventional market indices (Friede, 2019; Jain et al., 2019; Sadorsky, 2014). Understanding the inter-dependence between sustainable and conventional market indices is essential for refining portfolio management strategies in the realm of sustainable investing. As sustainable investing continues to gain traction in financial markets, it is imperative to comprehend how movements in sustainable indices influence, and are influenced by, broader market dynamics. This understanding is essential for investors seeking to diversify their portfolios with sustainable assets while maintaining exposure to traditional markets (Hung, 2021; Rajwani & Kumar, 2019). Identifying the interdependence between sustainable and conventional indices can also help assess the resilience of sustainable investments during market fluctuations and economic downturns (Górka & Kuziak, 2022; Gupta & Chaudhary, 2023). Moreover, insights into inter-dependency can inform risk management strategies, enabling investors to better navigate volatility and uncertainty (Gordeev et al., 2012; McNeil et al., 2015).

2.5 Copula Models for Assessment of Inter-dependence

Traditional approaches rely on linear correlation coefficients, assuming elliptic distributions of returns. However, these methods might overlook nuances in dependence patterns, particularly during extreme market conditions. Empirical studies have revealed that stock returns exhibit asymmetric dependency, with a potentially stronger correlation observed during bearish markets compared to bullish markets, and notably heightened during periods of turbulent price fluctuations (Ang & Bekaert, 2002; Jondeau, 2016). Recognizing the detected asymptotic dependence of random variables in tails (Patton, 2012), researchers employ copula functions to address this phenomenon (Gordeev et al., 2012; Hung, 2021). Copula functions have emerged as a more suitable tool for dependency modelling, particularly due to their ability to capture the increasing correlation in the tails of return distributions. By separating the marginal distributions of individual variables from their joint dependency structure, copula models offer greater flexibility and precision in analyzing interdependencies.

In this study, we employ several copula families, including Gaussian, Student's t, Clayton, Gumbel, and Frank copulas, to model the dependence structure between the Sensex and sustainability indices. Each copula family has distinct characteristics, making them suitable for different types of dependencies. By comparing the performance of different copulas, we aim to identify the most appropriate model that accurately reflects the interdependence between the indices. By incorporating these copula distributions together, we aim to comprehensively analyze the dependency structures between sustainability and market indices, capturing both linear and non-linear relationships as well as extreme value dependencies. This approach facilitates a better understanding of their interrelationships, contributing to a more robust analysis of the study.

2.6 Analysing the Dependence of Sustainability and Market Indices in India

This chapter aims to explore and assess the dependence between the sustainability indices - S&P BSE Carbonex, S&P BSE Greenex, BSE SENSEX 50 ESG Index and market index BSE Sensex in India, employing a copula approach. This approach studies the non-linear dependence of sustainability indices and the market indices based on their marginal distribution (Patton, 2012). By doing so, this chapter aims to contribute to the evolving field of sustainable finance by providing a detailed understanding of the co-movement between sustainability indices and market indices in India. Understanding the co-movement between sustainability and market indices helps investors and businesses in effective risk assessment and its management. This can also help investors evaluate the potential for sustained performance in companies that prioritize sustainability, providing insights into their long-term financial performance. Findings from the study provide valuable insights for investors, businesses, and policymakers, helping them make informed decisions that consider both financial performance and broader societal and environmental impacts.

3. DATA AND METHODOLOGY

We used three selected sustainability indices: S&P BSE 100 ESG, S&P BSE Carbonex and S&P BSE Greenex as the sustainability indices, and S&P BSE Sensex as the conventional market index. The S&P BSE Sensex measures the performance of the 30 largest, most liquid and financially sound companies across key sectors of the Indian economy that are listed at BSE Ltd. The S&P BSE 100 ESG Index measures securities that meet sustainability investing criteria while maintaining a risk and performance profile similar to the S&P BSE 100. The S&P BSE Carbonex tracks the performance of the companies within the S&P BSE 100 index based on their commitment to mitigating risks arising from climate change. The S&P BSE Greenex measures the performance of the top 25 "green" companies in terms of greenhouse gas emissions, market cap and liquidity. Closing price data was obtained from the Bombay Stock Exchange, covering the period from 26 October 2017 to 4 January 2022. Logarithmic returns were computed by subtracting the logarithms of consecutive closing prices and then multiplying by 100 to represent percentage changes.

We use Copula, one of the popular time series modelling techniques to specify the marginal distribution of random variables separately from temporal dependence (Patton, 2012) and characterise the dependence in a sequence of observation (Joe,

1997). This offers higher flexibility in defining and estimating the model, as distinct estimation methods can be applied to the various components of the model. Initially introduced by Sklar (1959), copula models were to describe non-linear correlation and trial dependence between series. Now it finds applications in various areas of finance like portfolio diversification (Christoffersen & Langlois, 2013; Garcia & Tsafack, 2011), risk management (McNeil et al., 2015; Rosenberg & Schuermann, 2006) and derivative pricing (Cherubini et al., 2011; Salmon & Schleicher, 2006).

3.1 Model Specification

The selected sustainability indices such as Greenex, ESG and Carbonex was paired with Sensex to analyse the dependence structure of sustainability indices with the conventional market index. The study identified the Copula approach as a suitable tool to obtain the joint distribution and dependence parameter of pairs of time series stock returns under consideration. The Copula model was executed with Copula package [https://cran.r-project.org/web/packages/copula/index.html] of R Software (Hofert et al., 2014; Hofert & Mächler, 2011; Kojadinovic & Yan, 2010; Yan, 2007).

3.2 Copula Based Dependency Analysis

Sklar's theorem is popularly used to model bivariate relationships between variables. Sklar (1959) states that, by taking marginal distributions (CDFs) as arguments any joint probability distribution (PDFs) can written in terms of a copula function, on the other hand, a copula function with a univariate probability distribution provides a joint distribution. More specifically, random variables x_1, x_2 with respective marginal CDFs (x_1), $G(x_2)$, will have joint cumulative distribution functions (JCDFs) $G_{x_1 x_2}(x_1, x_2)$ and a copula function C.

$$G_{x_1 x_2}\left(x_1, x_2\right) = C\left(G_{x_1}(x_1), G_{x_2}\left(x_2\right)\right)$$

The general requirements for $C(x_1, x_2)$ to represent a joint probability distribution are

i) If one event has a zero probability, then one of the arguments of the function C (x_1, x_2) is zero and the function must return zero.

ii) If one event will occur, then the joint probability of both events happening corresponds to the probability of observing the second event. In other words, if one argument of $C(x_1, x_2)$ is one, the function must yield the other argument.

iii) It expects that if the probabilities of both events increase, the joint probabilities should also increase and not decrease.

Copula function, in short, helps to express joint probability distribution as a function of marginal ones. Under the assumption, marginal CDF distribution is continuous with PDFs $g\left(x_1\right)$ and $g\left(x_2\right)$ has JPDF,

$$g_{x_1,x_2}\left(x_1,x_2\right) = C\left(G_{x_1}(x_1), G_{x_2}\left(x_2\right)\right) \cdot g_{x_1}\left(x_1\right) \cdot g_{x_2}\left(x_2\right)$$

If u and z are transformations of marginal distributions G_{x_1} and G_{x_2} respectively, the double partial derivation of C over u and z is written as:

$$c(u,z) = \frac{\partial^2 C(u,z)}{\partial u, \partial z}$$

The following bivariate copula model is presented to represent the sustainability indices (E) and Sensex (S):

$$F_{S,E}(s,e) = C\left(F_E(e), F_S(s)\right)$$

Where, $F_{S,E}(s, e)$ is the JCDF and $F_E(e), F_S(s)$ are CDFs of the variables Sustainability indices (Greenex, Carbonex and ESG) and Sensex respectively.

3.3 Bivariate Copula

The copula classes are listed as a copula family with a minimum product and maximum one, called a comprehensive (Devroye, 1986) and explain conditional distribution via copula. For the bivariate Copula density functions used in the study take, $u = F_S(s)$ and $z = F_E(e)$ are the CDF of Sensex and Sustainability, the Copula parameter θ represents the dependency structure between F_S and F_E, the standard normal CDF and PDF are ϕ and Φ, respectively.

The bivariate Copula density functions employed in the present study are given as follows:

i)   Bivariate Gaussian Copula

The Gaussian copula can be defined as

$$C(u,z;\theta) = \phi_\theta(\phi^{-1}(u), \phi^{-1}(z)), -1 \le \theta \le 1$$

$$c(u,z) = \frac{\phi_\theta(\phi^{-1}(u), \phi^{-1}(z))}{\Phi(\phi^{-1}(u))\Phi(\phi^{-1}(z))}$$

ii) Bivariate Student's t Copula

A bivariate student's copulaC_v with v degrees of freedom is defined as

$$C_v(u,z) = t_v\left(t_v^{-1}(u) - t_v^{-1}(z)\right)$$

$$= \int_{-\alpha}^{t_v^{-1}(u)} \int_{-\alpha}^{t_v^{-1}(z)} \left(\frac{1}{z\pi\sqrt{1-\rho^2}}\right)\left(1 + \frac{s^2 + t^2 - 2\rho st}{v\sqrt{1-\rho^2}}\right)^{\frac{-v+2}{2}} dsdt$$

iii) Bivariate Clayton Copula

The Clayton copula can be defined as

$$C(u,z;\theta) = (u^{-\theta} + z^{-\theta} - 1)^{-1/\theta}, \theta > 0$$

$$c(u,z) = (\theta + 1)(u^{-\theta} + z^{-\theta} - 1)^{\frac{-1}{\theta}-2}(uz)^{-\theta-1}, \theta > 0$$

iv) Gumbel Copula

The Gumbel copula can be defined as

$$C(u,z;\theta) = exp\{-[-(Lu)^\theta + -(Lz)^\theta]^{1/\theta}\}, \theta \geq 1$$

$$c(u,z) = C(u,z)\frac{[(-Lu)(-Lz)]^{\theta-1}}{uz}[(-Lu)^\theta + (-Lz)^\theta]^{\frac{2}{\theta}-2}.\{(\theta-1)[(-Lu)^\theta + (-Lz)^\theta]^{\frac{-1}{\theta}} + 1\}$$

v) Frank Copula

The Frank copula can be defined as

$$C(u,z;\theta) = \frac{1}{\theta}L\left[1 + \frac{(v^{-\theta u} - 1)(v^{-\theta z} - 1)}{(v^\theta - 1)}\right], \theta \neq 0$$

$$C(u,z) = \frac{\theta v^{-\theta(u+z)}(v^{-\theta} - 1)}{[v^{-\theta(u+z)} - v^{-\theta u} - v^{-\theta z} + v^{-\theta}]^2}$$

4. RESULTS

Table 1. Descriptive statistics

	n	mean	sd	median	min	max	skew	kurtosis
ESG_ln	1039	5.26	0.2	5.2	4.78	5.73	0.85	-0.31
Sensex_ln	1039	10.61	0.18	10.55	10.17	11.03	0.75	-0.41
Carbonex_ln	1039	7.6	0.18	7.54	7.11	8.02	0.76	-0.09
Greenex_ln	1039	8.01	0.19	7.94	7.51	8.47	0.9	-0.01

Source: Author(s)'s calculation

Table 1 presents the descriptive statistics calculated from the log values of daily closing prices. When comparing the conventional and sustainable indices, Sensex has the highest average price. Among the sustainable indices, the average price of Greenex was the highest, followed by Carbonex and ESG. However, the variation is highest for ESG, followed by Carbonex and Greenex.

Table 2. Correlation

Correlation	Sensex&ESG	Sensex&Carbonex	Sensex&Greenex
Pearson's linear correlation	0.98	0.98	0.87
Kendall's Tau	0.87	0.89	0.69
Spearman's rho	0.98	0.98	0.87

Source: Author(s)'s calculation

The correlation between the sustainable indices shows that each has a high positive correlation with Sensex (Table 2). The three different correlations, Pearson's linear correlation, Kendall's Tau (τ) and Spearman's roh (ρ), show similar correlations. Unlike Pearson's linear correlation, ρ and τ are calculated after extracting the marginals from the actual data. So, the correlation between the indices from Kendall's Tau (τ) and Spearman's roh (ρ) is closer to the copula marginal correlations. The correlation between Sensex-Carbonex is higher than between Sensex-ESG and Sensex-Greenex. The Kendall's Tau on Sensex and Greenex is only .69, the lowest correlation between the indices. It suggests a weak association indicating a limited synchronicity between the movements of Sensex and Greenex.

4.1 Dependency Under Copula Family: Case of Sensex and ESG

The copula results in Table 3 allow us to understand the structure of joint distribution and the degree of dependency between the selected sustainable index, ESG and Sensex. The S&P BSE SENSEX 50 ESG index includes companies that meet sustainability criteria, thus providing avenues for investors interested in sustainability criteria. The Sensex ESG pair has strong linear dependence (Gaussian parameter 1) with heavier tails (Student's t parameter 1). Similarly, there is positive dependence (Frank parameter 1) with more robust positive tails (Clayton & Gumbel parameter 1). The tail dependency structure for the Sensex-ESG pair expresses that both indices move together in highly positive and negative scenarios. Kendall's tau of all copulas indicates a strong positive association between the Sensex ESG 50 index and Sensex. Moreover, large Kendall's tau indicates Sensex's association with large ESG values. The student's t Copula model is the better-fit model for the data, followed by the Gumbel and Gaussian models. In total, all the models capture the data characteristics.

Table 3. Copula result for Sensex ESG 50 index with Sensex

Sensex&ESG	Gaussian	Student's t	Gumbel	Clayton	Frank
θ_1	0.98	0.98	7.41	9.04	27.37
θ_2	0.00	4.04	0.00	0.00	0.00
β	0.87	NA	0.87	0.85	0.90
τ	0.87***	0.87**	0.87**	0.82**	0.86**
Log-likelihood	1642.02	1672.22	1642.17	1448.39	1490.21
Lower tail	0.00	0.82	0.00	0.93	0.00
Upper tail	0.00	0.82	0.90	0.00	0.00
AIC	-3282.05	-3340.44	-3282.34	-2894.77	-2978.43
BIC	-3277.10	-3330.55	-3277.40	-2889.83	-2973.48

Source: Author(s)'s calculation

*** and ** indicate significance at 1% and 5% level, respectively

4.2 Dependency under Copula family: Case of Sensex and Carbonex

S&P BSE Carbonex, India's first effective carbon efficient index, includes companies actively reducing their carbon footprint and reducing climate-related risks. The dependency structure between the Carbonex and Sensex (Table 4) presented with the first parameter of Gaussian and Student's t copula indicates that both the copula exhibit similar dependency structure. The Gumbel, Clayton and Frank Copula also exhibit that the indices pair has stronger tail dependences. Moreover, the strength of association between the variables (beta) indicates a stronger positive dependence between Sensex and Carbonex. Kendall's tau indicates an almost perfect positive correlation between Carbonex and Sensex. Student's t was the best model to fit the data compared to other copula models. Though the pair of Sensex and Carbonex exhibit the same level of dependence, there is no possible convergence of Student's t copula with Gaussian Copula in a short period.

Table 4. Copula result for Carbonex index with Sensex

Sensex&Carbonex	Gaussian	Student's t	Gumbel	Clayton	Frank
θ_1	0.99	0.99	9.07	11.09	34.45
θ_2	0.00	4.08	0.00	0.00	0.00
β	0.90	NA	0.89	0.88	0.92
τ	0.9***	0.89**	0.89**	0.85**	0.89**
Log-likelihood	1870.96	1895.58	1847.08	1621.68	1697.31
Lower tail	0.00	0.86	0.00	0.94	0.00
Upper tail	0.00	0.86	0.92	0.00	0.00
AIC	-3739.91	-3787.16	-3692.17	-3241.35	-3392.61
BIC	-3734.97	-3777.27	-3687.22	-3236.41	-3387.67

Source: Author(s)'s calculation

\# *** and ** indicate significance at 1% and 5% level, respectively

4.3 Dependency under Copula family: Case of Sensex and ESG

The S&P BSE Greenex measures the performance of 25 companies in terms of market capitalisation, Greenhouse gas emission and liquidity. This index also allows investors to participate in responsible investment practices. Across the copula models (Table 5), there is a strong, significant, and positive dependency between Sensex and Greenex. The tail dependency captured by Student's t, Gumbel and Clayton indicates positive and heavier tails. As such, the Sensex-Greenex pair moves together in extreme event situations. However, the positive correlation between the dependency structure of the Sensex-Greenex duo for all copula models is similar except for the Clayton copula. The higher likelihood values across the model indicate a strong fit between the model's assumptions and the data's underlying characteristics.

Table 5. Copula result for Carbonex index with Sensex

Sensex&Greenex	Gaussian	Student's t	Gumbel	Clayton	Frank
θ_1	0.89	0.89	3.25	10.95	10.95
θ_2	0.00	4.16	0.00	0.00	0.00
β	0.70	NA	0.70	0.65	0.75
τ	0.7**	0.69**	0.69**	0.62**	0.69**
Log-likelihood	799.89	825.82	820.06	721.64	721.64
Lower tail	0.00	0.60	0.00	0.81	0.00
Upper tail	0.00	0.60	0.76	0.00	0.00
AIC	-1597.79	-1647.65	-1638.12	-1438.09	-1441.28
BIC	-1592.84	-1637.76	-1633.18	-1433.15	-1436.34

Source: Author(s)'s calculation
*** and ** indicate significance at 1% and 5% level, respectively

5. DISCUSSION

The market sentiments towards socially responsible indices as well as its risk are the same as the conventional indices (Kim, 2019; Gorka & Kuziak, 2022). The feeling of assured return and less volatility makes sustainable indices attractive (Gupta & Chaudhary, 2023; Renneboog et al., 2011; Statman & Glushkov, 2016). This study shows that the variance of Greenex matches with the susceptible Sensex characteristics. However, ESG moves slower than Greenex and Carbonex regarding price and volatility. The relationship between sustainable indices and Sensex was assessed using Pearson's linear correlation, Spearman's rho, and Kendall's Tau. Unlike Pearson's linear correlation, Kendall's tau and Spearman's rho are calculated with marginals extracted from the price returns of each index. A high positive correlation between Sensex and the three sustainable indices during the study period has been identified. However, the correlation between Sensex and Carbonex is relatively higher, and the relationship between Sensex and Greenex is low during this period, indicating greater market sensitivity related to environmental considerations.

Marginal distributions for the series were calculated using the method of moments estimated based on Spearman's rho and Kendall's Tau. The major Copula methods applied to assess the bivariate movements of Sensex and sustainable indices are Gaussian, Student's t, Gumbel, and Frank. The Gaussian parameter of the model is higher for Sensex-Carbonex movements and lowest for the Sensex-Greenex pair, indicating higher volatility for the former and lower volatility for the latter. The Student's t parameters exhibit similar results. On the contrary, the indices' parameters are not the same for all the Archimedean models. As such, the bivariate movement of Sensex and Greenex has the lowest parameter for Gumbel and Frank while in Clayton, the lowest parameter is for Sensex and ESG, suggesting a weaker association under the models. The tail dependency of the Gumbel copula model exhibits lower tails at the left and right positions of the sustainable indices and Sensex. Meanwhile, the symmetric tail dependency is lower for Greenex and Sensex, indicating weaker associations in extreme market movements.

Moreover, there is consistent evidence of a robust positive association between the Sensex index and sustainable indices, namely ESG Carbonex and Greenex. Across different Copula models, Parameter 1 consistently indicates robust dependency among these pairs, with higher values suggesting stronger associations. Kendall's tau coefficients confirm significant positive correlations, indicating concordance between large values of Sensex and corresponding large values of ESG, Carbonex, and Greenex indicating consistent alignment between Sensex and sustainable indices. Although the rate of the relationship varies among the pairs, all models exhibit high log-likelihood values, indicating a good fit of the Copula to the data. As such, the chosen Copula models effectively represent the joint distribution of variables regardless of the varying degrees of intensity among the pairs. Moreover, despite differences in tail dependence structures and shape parameters, such as those observed in Student's t and Gumbel Copula models, the findings underscore a strong and positive dependency between the Sensex index and sustainable indices, reinforcing the joint behaviour of these financial and environmental performance metrics.

In short, the analysis highlights degrees of differences among Copula models regarding the strength and structure of dependencies. For instance, the Gumbel Copula suggests a stronger tail dependence between extreme events in Sensex and Carbonex compared to other pairs, while the Clayton Copula emphasizes a notable tail dependency among indices pairs, with Sensex-Carbonex exhibiting a better fit. Additionally, the Frank Copula underscores a strong underlying dependency between Sensex and Carbonex pairs, with better model performance than other pairs. The consistent findings across different Copula models provide robust evidence of joint behaviour between the Sensex index and sustainable indices, contributing to a deeper understanding of their interrelationships in financial and environmental contexts. Thus, the comparative analysis shows that Greenex shows higher marginal volatility than ESG and Carbonex. Thus, in the Indian context, investors' acceptance of sustainable indices is at par with conventional indices.

6. CONCLUSION

The market has witnessed tremendous growth in SRI investments in the last few decades due to increased concern among investors on ESG issues. These investments offer favourable risk-return profiles, diversification benefits, and the non-financial utility they achieve by consuming the social responsibility attribute. Sustainable investments have been in the limelight, especially in developed countries, which have paved the way for extensive research in this area. However, studies on the relative financial performance of such investments show mixed and contradictory results. Also, limited studies exist on such investments in emerging markets like India. This chapter addresses this lacuna in research on sustainable investments in India. This chapter contributes to the growing body of literature on sustainable investing by applying copula models to assess the non-linear interdependence between conventional and sustainability indices in India. The application of copula models in this study represents a novel methodological contribution.

The study on the dependency behaviour of sustainable indices and Sensex helped to draw insights into their joint behaviour, which can help investors make valuable decisions about portfolio diversification and hedging strategies to mitigate risks. The results highlight the significant and positive association between these indices, reflecting investors' increasing preference for sustainable investments. The copula models' results indicate that Carbonex and Sensex's dependency behaviour is higher than that of ESG-Sensex and Greenex-Sensex pairs. In short, the findings of strong positive dependence between Sensex and sustainable indices explain that the adoption of ESG strategies by the companies did not reduce its popularity among investors; instead, it exhibited its risk-adjusted return capability like other indices. So, investors choose sustainable market indices like the general market indices.

The findings of this study have several important implications. For investors, understanding the dependency structure between conventional and sustainability indices can enhance portfolio diversification and risk management strategies. Companies can leverage these insights to align their practices with investor expectations, potentially improving their market performance and attractiveness. Policymakers can use the results to foster a supportive environment for sustainable investments, promoting long-term economic stability and environmental sustainability.

Despite the valuable insights provided by this study, it also has limitations that warrant further research. One limitation is the focus on daily data, which, while providing a comprehensive view of market dynamics, may not capture intra-day fluctuations and high-frequency trading effects. Future research could explore the impact of high-frequency data on the relationship between sustainability and market indices. Additionally, longitudinal studies examining the long-term performance and dynamics of sustainability indices could provide deeper insights into their role in promoting sustainable practices. Further investigation of the long-term value-creation capacity of sustainable indices is needed. Moreover, a deeper understanding of the dynamics of extreme events and their interdependencies between financial and sustainable indices is necessary to design new policies for promoting ESG.

REFERENCES

Ademi, B., & Klungseth, N. J. (2022). Does it pay to deliver superior ESG performance? Evidence from US S&P 500 companies. *Journal of Global Responsibility*, 13(4), 421–449. Advance online publication. 10.1108/JGR-01-2022-0006

Alshehhi, A., Nobanee, H., & Khare, N. (2018). The impact of sustainability practices on corporate financial performance: Literature trends and future research potential. *Sustainability (Basel)*, 10(2), 494. 10.3390/su10020494

Ang, A., & Bekaert, G. (2002). International asset allocation with regime shifts. *Review of Financial Studies*, 15(4), 1137–1187. 10.1093/rfs/15.4.1137

Atz, U., Van Holt, T., Liu, Z. Z., & Bruno, C. C. (2023). Does sustainability generate better financial performance? Review, meta-analysis, and propositions. *Journal of Sustainable Finance & Investment*, 13(1), 1–24. 10.1080/20430795.2022.2106934

Cherubini, U., Mulinacci, S., Gobbi, F., & Romagnoli, S. (2011). *Dynamic copula methods in finance*. John Wiley & Sons. 10.1002/9781118467404

Christoffersen, P., & Langlois, H. (2013). The joint dynamics of equity market factors. *Journal of Financial and Quantitative Analysis*, 48(5), 1371–1404. 10.1017/S0022109013000598

De la Torre, O., Galeana, E., & Aguilasocho, D. (2016). The use of the sustainable investment against the broad market one. A first test in the Mexican stock market. *European Research on Management and Business Economics*, 22(3), 117–123. 10.1016/j.iedee.2015.08.002

Devroye, L. (1986). *Non-Uniform Random Variate Generation*. Springer-Verlag, New York European Sustainable Investment Forum. (2018). *European SRI Study 2018*. Brussels. 10.1007/978-1-4613-8643-8

Fooladi, I. J., & Hebb, G. (2022). Drivers of differences in performance of ESG-focused funds relative to their underlying benchmarks. *Global Finance Journal*, 56, 100745. 10.1016/j.gfj.2022.100745

Fowler, S. J., & Hope, C. (2007). A critical review of sustainable business indices and their impact. *Journal of Business Ethics*, 76(3), 243–252. 10.1007/s10551-007-9590-2

Freeman, R. E. (1984). *Strategic Management: A Stakeholder Approach*. Pitman Publishing.

Friede, G. (2019). Why don't we see more action? A meta-synthesis of the investor impediments to integrate environmental, social, and governance factors. *Business Strategy and the Environment*, 28(6), 1260–1282. Advance online publication. 10.1002/bse.2346

Friedman, M. (1953). *Essays in Positive Economics*. University Of Chicago Press.

Garcia, R., & Tsafack, G. (2011). Dependence structure and extreme comovements in international equity and bond markets. *Journal of Banking & Finance*, 35(8), 1954–1970. 10.1016/j.jbankfin.2011.01.003

Gordeev, V. A., Knyazev, A. G., & Shemyakin, A. E. (2012). Selection of copula model for inter-market dependence. *Model Assisted Statistics and Applications : An International Journal*, 7(4), 315–325. 10.3233/MAS-2012-0243

Górka, J., & Kuziak, K. (2022). Volatility modeling and dependence structure of ESG and conventional investments. *Risks*, 10(1), 20. 10.3390/risks10010020

Guerard, J. B. (1997). Is there a cost to being socially responsible in investing? *Journal of Forecasting*, 16(7), 475–490. 10.1002/(SICI)1099-131X(199712)16:7<475::AID-FOR668>3.0.CO;2-X

Gupta, H., & Chaudhary, R. (2023). An Analysis of Volatility and Risk-Adjusted Returns of ESG Indices in Developed and Emerging Economies. *Risks*, 11(10), 182. 10.3390/risks11100182

HKEX. 2020. Performance of ESG Equity Indices Versus Traditional Equity Indices. Available online: https://www.hkex.com.hk/-/media/HKEX-Market/News/Research -Reports/HKEx-Research-Papers/2020/CCEO_ESGEqIdx_202011_e.pdf

Hofert, M., Kojadinovic, I., Maechler, M., & Yan, J. (2014). Copula: Multivariate dependence with copulas. R package version 0.999-9, URL http://CRAN. R-project. org/package= copula, C225.

Hofert, M., & Mächler, M. (2011). Nested Archimedean copulas meet R: The na-copula package. *Journal of Statistical Software*, 39(9), 1–20. 10.18637/jss.v039.i09

Hung, N. T. (2021). Green bonds and asset classes: New evidence from time-varying copula and transfer entropy models. *Global Business Review*, 097215092110340. Advance online publication. 10.1177/09721509211034095

Jain, K., & Tripathi, P. S. (2023). Mapping the environmental, social and governance literature: A bibliometric and content analysis. *Journal of Strategy and Management*. 10.1108/JSMA-05-2022-0092

Jain, M., Sharma, G. D., & Srivastava, M. (2019). Can sustainable investment yield better financial returns: A comparative study of ESG indices and MSCI indices. *Risks*, 7(1), 15. 10.3390/risks7010015

Joe, H. (1997). *Multivariate Models and Multivariate Dependence Concepts.* Chapman and Hall.

Jondeau, E. (2016). Asymmetry in tail dependence in equity portfolios. *Computational Statistics & Data Analysis*, 100, 351–368. 10.1016/j.csda.2015.02.014

Kim, C.-S. (2019). Can socially responsible investments be compatible with financial performance? A meta-analysis. *Asia-Pacific Journal of Financial Studies*, 48(1), 30–64. 10.1111/ajfs.12244

Kojadinovic, I., & Yan, J. (2010). Modeling Multivariate distributions with continuous margins using the copula RPackage. *Journal of Statistical Software*, 34(9). Advance online publication. 10.18637/jss.v034.i09

Lassala, C., Apetrei, A., & Sapena, J. (2017). Sustainability matter and financial performance of companies. *Sustainability (Basel)*, 9(9), 1498. 10.3390/su9091498

Managi, S., Okimoto, T., & Matsuda, A. (2012). Do socially responsible investment indexes outperform conventional indexes? *Applied Financial Economics*, 22(18), 1511–1527. 10.1080/09603107.2012.665593

Mcneil, A. J., Frey, R., & Embrechts, P. (2015). *Quantitative Risk Management: Concepts, Techniques and Tools.* Princeton University Press.

Mensi, W., Hammoudeh, S., Al-Jarrah, I. M. W., Sensoy, A., & Kang, S. H. (2017). Dynamic risk spillovers between gold, oil prices and conventional, sustainability and Islamic equity aggregates and sectors with portfolio implications. *Energy Economics*, 67, 454–475. 10.1016/j.eneco.2017.08.031

Miralles-Quiros, M. del M., Miralles-Quiros, J. L., & Arraiano, I. G. (2017). Sustainable development, sustainability leadership and firm valuation: Differences across Europe. *Business Strategy and the Environment*, 26(7), 1014–1028. 10.1002/bse.1964

Ortas, E., Gallego-Alvarez, I., & Álvarez Etxeberria, I. (2014). Financial factors influencing the quality of corporate social responsibility and environmental management disclosure: A quantile regression approach. *Corporate Social Responsibility and Environmental Management*, 22(6), 362–380. 10.1002/csr.1351

Patton, A. J. (2012). A review of copula models for economic time series. *Journal of Multivariate Analysis*, 110, 4–18. 10.1016/j.jmva.2012.02.021

Phillips, R. (2003). *Stakeholder Theory and Organizational Ethics*. Berrett-Koehler Publishers.

Plastun, A., Bouri, E., Gupta, R., & Ji, Q. (2022). Price effects after one-day abnormal returns in developed and emerging markets: ESG versus traditional indices. *The North American Journal of Economics and Finance*, 59, 101572. 10.1016/j.najef.2021.101572

Rajwani, S., & Kumar, D. (2019). Measuring dependence between the USA and the Asian economies: A time-varying copula approach. *Global Business Review*, 20(4), 962–980. 10.1177/0972150919845240

Renneboog, L., Ter Horst, J., & Zhang, C. (2008). The price of ethics and stakeholder governance: The performance of socially responsible mutual funds. *Journal of Corporate Finance*, 14(3), 302–322. 10.1016/j.jcorpfin.2008.03.009

Renneboog, L., Ter Horst, J., & Zhang, C. (2011). Is ethical money financially smart? Nonfinancial attributes and money flows of socially responsible investment funds. *Journal of Financial Intermediation*, 20(4), 562–588. 10.1016/j.jfi.2010.12.003

Rodrigo, F. (2024). Impact on the performance of ESG indices: A comparative study in Brazil and international markets. *Applied Economics*, ●●●, 1–12. 10.1080/00036846.2024.2342069

Rosenberg, J. V., & Schuermann, T. (2006). A general approach to integrated risk management with skewed, fat-tailed risks. *Journal of Financial Economics*, 79(3), 569–614. 10.1016/j.jfineco.2005.03.001

Sadorsky, P. (2014). Modeling volatility and conditional correlations between socially responsible investments, gold and oil. *Economic Modelling*, 38, 609–618. 10.1016/j.econmod.2014.02.013

Salmon, M., & Schleicher, C. (2006). Pricing multivariate currency options with copulas. In *Copulas: From Theory to Application in Finance*. Risk Books, London.

Santis, P., Albuquerque, A., & Lizarelli, F. (2016). Do sustainable companies have a better financial performance? A study on Brazilian public companies. *Journal of Cleaner Production*, 133, 735–745. 10.1016/j.jclepro.2016.05.180

Sklar, M. (1959). Fonctions de répartition à n dimensions et leurs marges. In Annales de l'ISUP (Vol. 8, No. 3, pp. 229-231).

Statman, M., & Glushkov, D. (2016). Classifying and measuring the performance of socially responsible mutual funds. *Journal of Portfolio Management*, 42(2), 140–151. 10.3905/jpm.2016.42.2.140

Talan, G., & Sharma, G. (2019). Doing well by doing good: A systematic review and research agenda for sustainable investment. *Sustainability (Basel)*, 11(2), 353. 10.3390/su11020353

The Forum for Sustainable and Responsible Investment. (2018). *Report on US Sustainable*. Responsible and Impact Investing Trends.

Tripathi, V., & Bhandari, V. (2015). Socially responsible stocks: A boon for investors in India. *Journal of Advances in Management Research*, 12(2), 209–225. 10.1108/JAMR-03-2014-0021

US SIF Foundation. (2022). Highlights: 2022 Report on US Sustainable Investing Trends from US SIF Foundation. US SIF Trends 2022 Highlights. https://trends2022highlights.com/

Verheyden, T., Eccles, R. G., & Feiner, A. (2016). ESG for all? The impact of ESG screening on return, risk, and diversification. *The Bank of America Journal of Applied Corporate Finance*, 28(2), 47–55. 10.1111/jacf.12174

Widyawati, L. (2019). A systematic literature review of socially responsible investment and environmental social governance metrics. *Business Strategy and the Environment*, 29(2), 619–637. 10.1002/bse.2393

Wu, J., Lodorfos, G., Dean, A., & Gioulmpaxiotis, G. (2015). The market performance of socially responsible investment during periods of the economic cycle - Illustrated using the case of FTSE. *MDE. Managerial and Decision Economics*, 38(2), 238–251. 10.1002/mde.2772

Yan, J. (2007). Enjoy the joy of copulas: With a package copula. *Journal of Statistical Software*, 21(4). Advance online publication. 10.18637/jss.v021.i04

Chapter 10
Assessing the Performance of ESG Mutual Funds and Traditional Funds in Emerging Economies

A. S. Aparna
University of Kerala, India

M. Moni
University of Kerala, India

V. Sreeraj
https://orcid.org/0009-0001-1225-6279
University of Kerala, India

M. P. Silpakrishnan
SN College, Kollam, India

Biju Ajithakumari Vijayappan Nair
https://orcid.org/0000-0001-5583-6495
University of Kerala, India

ABSTRACT

This study investigates the performance of Environmental, Social, and Governance (ESG) mutual funds compared to conventional funds in the Indian financial market. The objective is to determine if ESG funds can match or surpass the financial

DOI: 10.4018/979-8-3693-3880-3.ch010

*performance of traditional funds. The methodology includes evaluating perfor-
mance using the Carhart Four-Factor Model, Jensen's Alpha, Treynor Ratio, and
Sharpe Ratio. Additionally, entropy measures—Shannon Entropy, Rényi Entropy,
and Approximate Entropy—are employed to assess the volatility and complexity of
fund returns. Findings indicate that while conventional funds often deliver higher
raw returns, ESG funds excel in risk-adjusted performance, evidenced by higher
Alpha and more favourable Treynor and Sharpe Ratios. Entropy analysis reveals
that ESG funds exhibit higher volatility and complexity, as elevated Shannon, Rényi,
and Approximate Entropy values indicate greater potential for significant returns
and increased risk.*

1. INTRODUCTION

ESG fund investing has become a trendsetter in the 21st century, capturing the
attention and interest of savvy investors worldwide (Thomas et al., 2024). Institutional investors across the globe have already shown considerable interest in ESG
investing, leading to fund inflows of $1.921 trillion in 2021 (Lee et al., 2023). Also,
access to a growing number of ESG-profiled mutual funds allowed retail investors
to consider sustainability factors when making investment decisions (Quirici,
2023). Over the years, ESG funds have demonstrated solid performance despite
the substantial variations among them. ESG mutual funds are equity funds of those
companies that operate sustainably, thus aligning with UN sustainability initiatives.
Even though ESG factors are non–financial, these funds tend to impact the returns of
long-term investments (Thomas et al., 2024). When traditional funds focus only on
the return aspect, ESG funds propagate the idea of sustainability. Recently, certain
US ESG-equity mutual funds have showcased consistent outperformance compared
to their conventional counterparts (Raghunandan & Rajgopal, 2022). According to
the Sustainable Reality Report 2023, performance sustainable funds have surpassed
traditional funds, with a median return of 6.9% for sustainable funds and only 3.8%
for the latter (Morgan Stanley, 2023).

ESG investing emerged as a popular investment trend due to the increasing
interest of the public in the impact of corporate actions on its stakeholders and society (Curtis et al., 2021). Investing in sustainable mutual funds is often presented
as a means of making a socially and financially responsible contribution to society
or generating long-term profit (Sandberg & Sjöström, 2021). Capotă et al. (2022)
compared conventional and ESG funds; results suggest that investors are ready to
return to ESG or environmental funds that have previously had low returns, thus
enabling sustainable funds to offer a more reliable source of financing for the green
transition. To optimize the performance of ESG investing strategies, it is suggested

to maintain a low concentration of holdings, diversify into stocks with high ESG scores, and retain stocks with high ESG scores for an extended period (Xia et al., 2023). "ESG Integration" seeks to enhance the effectiveness of ESG investing by combining style investing with ESG considerations, including factors like company size (Xia et al., 2023). It is adaptable across all hedge fund strategies, providing meaningful advantages to both hedge funds and their clients (Pancholi, 2022). Additionally, ESG screening can also influence the factor-risk-adjusted performance of portfolios, emphasizing the need for investors to carefully weigh the costs and benefits of incorporating ESG criteria (Jin, 2022). Enhancing fund performance is achievable by sustaining a minimal concentration of holdings, broadening investments into stocks with elevated ESG scores, and retaining these high-scoring ESG stocks over an extended period.

The performance of ESG funds is shaped by their ESG strategy, ESG scores, and ESG ratings. Assessing these elements can offer valuable insights into the sustainability and effectiveness of ESG mutual funds. In China, ESG funds have performed at varying levels; over time, their total factor productivity has decreased (Xia et al., 2023). In Norway, however, improved ESG ratings and fund performance are positively correlated without any proof of the risk-adjusted abnormal returns or ESG rating effect (Steen et al., 2020).

Although there have been substantial advancements in ESG investing, there is still a significant lack of comparison between the performance of ESG and conventional mutual funds in terms of both risk and return, particularly in emerging economies such as India. There are 10 funds available in India under ESG thematic funds; the oldest one is SBI Magnum Equity ESG 1; none of them has a long track record. This study aims to assess the financial viability of ESG and conventional mutual funds in the Indian financial market by comparing their performance in terms of both return and risk. This study incorporates momentum, in addition to traditional risk factors, by applying the Carhart Four-Factor Model. In the first phase, ratios such as Jensen's Alpha, Sharpe Ratio, and Treynor Ratio are utilized. In the second phase, we use entropy analysis to assess fund returns' volatility, complexity, and unpredictability. The selection of entropy measures, namely Shannon Entropy, Rényi Entropy, and Approximate Entropy, offer a thorough understanding of the volatility and consistency of the return series. This combination enables a more sophisticated understanding of the performance dynamics between ESG and conventional funds. The importance and pertinence of this study are emphasized by its concentration on the Indian market, a burgeoning economy with unique financial dynamics that diverge from those of industrialized economies. This research offers useful insights for investors and policymakers interested in sustainable investment in emerging markets by examining the performance of ESG mutual funds in India.

2. REVIEW OF LITERATURE

2.1 Evaluating Mutual Fund Performance: Metrics and Trends

Mutual funds have become a vital channel for resource mobilization, attracting investors worldwide (Nicolescu & Tudorache, 2018). The performance of mutual funds is closely monitored, particularly during market fluctuations such as bull and bear markets (Yousaf et al., 2023). Studies have shown that mutual fund investors prioritize funds with strong past performances (Nicolescu & Tudorache, 2018). Studies have explored the influence of several variables on mutual funds, including the effects of variations in accounting standards among nations (Yu, 2010). Furthermore, researchers have examined the utilization of credit default swaps by corporate bond mutual funds in times of financial crises to evaluate their role in providing liquidity and managing counterparty risk (Aragon & Li, 2019).

The evolution of mutual funds in specific regions, like Pakistan and Central and Eastern Europe, has been analyzed to understand investor behavior and market dynamics (Aslam et al., 2023; Naqvi, 2019). Such studies shed light on the significance of mutual funds in emerging capital markets and their role in driving economic growth (Nicolescu & Tudorache, 2018). In more mature markets like India, mutual fund industry showcases several challenges and opportunities, emphasizing the need for continuous research and development in this area (Panda, 2016). Natter et al., (2017) investigated the impact of complicated financial instruments used by mutual funds on fund performance and investor outcomes. Gaining a comprehensive understanding of the mechanics of soft-dollar contracts and the benefits that mutual funds gain from their access to skilled analysts can offer valuable insights into investing strategies and decision-making procedures (Gokkaya et al., 2023).

Mutual funds are instrumental in mobilizing savings and investing in capital markets, providing small investors access to diversified portfolios managed by professionals (Kumar & Srivastava, 2016; Prajapati, 2008; Vanaja & Karrupasamy, 2016). These funds face the dual challenge of managing portfolio risks while trying to outperform market benchmarks, a task complicated by varying market conditions and fund attributes (Coleman & Coleman, 2016). Studies extensively use metrics like alpha, beta, standard deviation, Sharpe ratio, and Jensen's measure to evaluate mutual funds' performance. For instance, Mateus et al. (2019) emphasized the importance of using benchmark-adjusted and peer-group-adjusted alphas to identify top-performing mutual funds, suggesting that these metrics can predict future performance with significant accuracy. Similarly, Narang, (2018) assessed 41 equity large-cap mutual funds, using these parameters to aid investors in making informed decisions. Soussou and Omri, (2022) demonstrated how these attributes affect mutual funds in the Saudi market, particularly highlighting differences between

Islamic and conventional funds. Additionally, the relationship between mutual fund expenses and performance was explored by Vidal-García and Vidal (2024), who found a complex interaction where expenses negatively impacted performance in parametric analyses but showed positive effects in non-parametric settings. Chu et al. (2022) successfully applied LSTM and GRU models, combined with ensemble techniques, to outperform traditional statistical methods in predicting mutual funds' performance. This breakthrough indicates a shift towards more reliable and precise predictive models in the financial industry, potentially reducing investment risks and enhancing portfolio management strategies.

2.2 The Dynamics of Conventional Funds

Several studies utilize standard performance metrics such as the Sharpe, Treynor, and Jensen's indices to compare these funds. Suharti et al., (2022) employed these methods to assess the sustainability of conventional funds during the COVID-19 pandemic, noting their attractiveness to new investors due to maintained risk-return balance. Similarly, conventional mutual funds were found to generally outperform Islamic funds in Pakistan with better market timing and selection abilities (Afridi et al., 2020; Zeeshan et al., 2020). The performance of mutual funds is also significantly influenced by internal and external factors. For example, conventional mutual funds in Saudi Arabia are impacted by fund growth and objectives, but not by fund size and management fees (Ashraf, 2013; BinMahfouz & Hassan, 2012). During the European financial crisis, conventional funds showed mixed results against different benchmarks, with negative abnormal adjusted-returns highlighted in some instances (Gonçalves et al., 2021).

The comparative performance of Islamic and conventional mutual funds during financial crises reveals interesting trends. (Mansor et al., 2020) found that conventional funds outperformed the market during extreme events, though ethical funds showed more resilience. In contrast, during the 2007-2008 financial crisis, Islamic funds offered better hedging and performed consistently better in asset allocation (Ahmed & Siddiqui, 2020). Recent studies have also incorporated advanced analytical techniques to refine the performance evaluation of these funds. For instance, (Marzuki & Atta, 2020) examined the selectivity skills and market timing ability of conventional versus Islamic funds within the same family, revealing nuanced insights into the internal fund management efficiencies.

2.3 Specialized Investments: Analyzing the Performance of ESG and Sustainability Mutual Funds

Thematic mutual funds, particularly those aligned with sustainability goals, have emerged as a focal point in investment discourse due to their specialized investment strategies. Studies of LLelasi et al., (2018) and Lelasi & Rossolini, (2019) indicate that sustainability-themed funds, emphasizing small caps and global sectors, display lower underperformance compared to ethical funds, particularly excelling during turbulent financial periods. Additionally, Altan, (2022); Methling & von Nitzsch, (2019) introduce a tri-criterion thematic portfolio optimization model, enhancing portfolio yield by optimizing correlation effects, offering a strategic advantage over traditional approaches. Conversely, Massa & Yadav, (2010) caution that thematic funds, especially those loaded with high-sentiment stocks, may prioritize marketing strategies over performance, potentially leading to underperformance. Despite these challenges, Ruan, (2018) demonstrates that geographically focused funds, like those targeting emerging markets, can outperform benchmarks post-expenses. Moreover, Lapointe, (2015) underscores the critical role of transparency within socially responsible investment funds, emphasizing its impact on performance outcomes.

Fong et al. (2018) emphasize the influence of algorithmic trading on the performance of mutual funds, uncovering possible trade-offs between the level of involvement with algorithmically traded stocks and the resulting returns, especially in small-cap companies. Lai and Li, (2008) compare genetic algorithms with mean-variance models in fund-of-funds, illustrating the higher performance and consistency of genetic algorithms. The innovations discussed in the study by Juliana Nascimento and Powell, (2010) pertain to dynamic programming models for mutual fund cash balance concerns. These models demonstrate improved adaptability to market changes. In addition, Tsai et al., (2011) demonstrate the effectiveness of genetic algorithms in choosing mutual funds based on historical performance, while Wang et al., (2008) provide adaptive neural network classifiers for evaluating performance, providing improved accuracy compared to conventional approaches. Alibakhshi and Sadeghi Moghadam, (2016) propose a novel algorithm that utilizes several attribute decision-making strategies to assess and prioritize mutual funds. This algorithm is designed to serve the needs of both inexperienced and experienced investors. Chiew et al., (2021) propose the use of the Expected Utility-Entropy model, which is more effective than standard Morningstar ratings in choosing U.S. mutual funds.

Our review suggests a critical gap in the comprehensive comparison of ESG and conventional mutual funds, particularly in terms of risk and return within emerging markets like India. This gap is notable because existing studies have predominantly focused on developed markets, leaving a void in understanding how these sustainable investments perform in diverse financial environments.

3. Data and Methodology

3.1. Data

The Net Asset Value (NAV) of the mutual funds was obtained from the Association of Mutual Funds in India (AMFI) website. This dataset included daily NAVs for a selected group of five Environmental, Social, and Governance (ESG) funds and five conventional funds, spanning from April 1, 2021, to March 31, 2024. This period was chosen to provide recent insights into the performance trends of these funds.

Additional data for the Fama-French 4 Factor Model was obtained from the database of the Indian Institute of Management (IIM) Ahmedabad. This model includes the momentum factor (WML), SMB (Small Minus Big) factor, HML (High Minus Low) factor, and market risk premium—all of which are necessary for a detailed examination of the funds over a range of market situations.

3.2. Methodology

The initial steps included cleaning the data to clear the missing values through imputation and identifying and correcting outliers using the interquartile range method. NAV data were normalized to adjust for corporate actions such as splits and dividends, ensuring consistency in historical data comparison. Standardization of data formats and an assessment for seasonality or trends were also conducted to maintain the robustness of the analysis. Following data cleaning, descriptive statistics were calculated, including mean, median, standard deviation, skewness, and kurtosis, to preliminarily understand the funds' performance distributions and volatility, setting a solid foundation for subsequent detailed analysis.

3.3. Statistical Tools for Performance Evaluation of Mutual Funds

3.3.1 Jensen's Alpha

Jensen's Alpha (Jensen, 1968) is a performance measure that determines the excess return a mutual fund generates over its expected return, as predicted by an asset pricing model. Earlier Capital Asset Pricing Model (CAPM) were largely used for calculating the expected return. Studies by Sehgal & Babbar, (2017); Sehgal & Jhanwar, (2007). Also, Sehgal & Jain, (2012) identified that the Carhart four factor model is better for this purpose.

Jensen's Alpha Based on CAPM

$$\alpha = R_p - \left(R_f + \left(R_m - R_f \right) \times \beta \right)$$

Where:

- R_p is the actual return of the fund
- R_f is the risk-free return
- R_m is the expected market return,
- β is the fund's sensitivity to movements in the market (systematic risk).

Jensen's Alpha Based on Carhart Four Factor Model

$$\alpha = R_p - \left(R_f + \beta_m \times \left(R_m - R_f \right) + \beta_s \times SMB + \beta_v \times HML + \beta_w \times WML \right)$$

Where,

- *SMB* (Small Minus Big) is the size premium,
- *HML* (Hiah Minus Low) is the value premium
- WML (Winners Minus Losers) captures the momentum effect.

This model adds a momentum factor to the Fama-French three factor model, enhancing the analysis of mutual fund performance (Carhart, 1997).

Jensen's Alpha helps in understanding how much a fund's return deviates from its expected return based on its risk profile. A positive alpha indicates outperformance relative to the fund's systematic risk, while a negative alpha suggests underperformance (Jensen, 1968). This metric is crucial for assessing whether the fund manager has successfully generated additional value.

3.4 Risk-Adjusted Performance Metrics

Sharpe Ratio:

Developed by William Sharpe, (1964), this ratio measures the risk-adjusted return of an investment compared to its risk. The Sharpe ratio is calculated as:

$$\text{Sharpe Ratio} = \frac{R_p - R_f}{\sigma_p}$$

Where:

- R_p is the return of the portfolio,
- R_f is the risk-free rate,
- σ_p is the standard deviation of the portfolio's excess return.

Treynor Ratio:

Introduced by Jack L. Treynor, (1961)This ratio assesses the returns earned more than the risk-free rate per unit of market risk and is defined as:

$$\text{Treynor Ratio} = \frac{R_p - R_f}{\beta_p}$$

Where:

- β_p is the beta of the portfolio.

3.5 Comparative Analysis

The final phase involves comparing the outcomes from Jensen's Alpha, Sharpe and Treynor ratios. This comprehensive analysis allows us to determine the mutual funds' performance in terms of both total and risk-adjusted returns. Positive outcomes from these comparisons (e.g., positive alpha, higher than expected returns from the models, and higher Sharpe and Treynor ratios) indicate superior fund performance relative to its risk and market benchmarks.

3.6 Entropy Measures

In this study, we utilize entropy measures to evaluate the volatility and complexity of mutual fund returns. The selected measures-Shannon Entropy, Rényi Entropy, and Approximate Entropy-provide comprehensive insights into the unpredictability and regularity of the return series (Ausloos et al., 2018; Ghasemi Doudkanlou et al., 2023; J.-R. Yu et al., 2017). Each method is rationalized based on its unique ability to capture different aspects of return variability and risk.

3.6.2. Shannon Entropy

Shannon Entropy measures the average level of uncertainty or unpredictability in a dataset, making it a fundamental concept in information theory (Shannon, 1948). It provides a quantitative measure of the randomness in the distribution of mutual fund returns. For a discrete set of probabilities p_i representing the distribution of returns, Shannon Entropy H is defined as:

$$H = -\sum_{i=1}^{n} p_i \log(p_i)$$

where:

- p_i is the probability of occurrence of the i-th return.
- n is the total number of different returns.

Shannon Entropy is utilized in this study to comprehensively measure the uncertainty and complexity in the return series. Higher values of Shannon Entropy indicate greater unpredictability, implying higher volatility and complexity in the mutual fund returns. This measure helps in understanding the overall risk profile of the funds by quantifying the level of disorder in the returns.

3.6.3. Rényi Entropy

Rényi Entropy generalizes Shannon Entropy by introducing a parameter α that adjusts the sensitivity to different probabilities (Rényi, 1961). This flexibility allows for emphasizing either more probable or less probable events, depending on the choice of α. Rényi Entropy H_α is defined as:

$$H_\alpha = \frac{1}{1-\alpha} \log\left(\sum_{i=1}^{n} p_i^\alpha\right)$$

where:

- α is a parameter that determines the order of the entropy ($\alpha \geq 0$ and $\alpha \neq 1$).
- p_i is the probability of occurrence of the i-th return.
- n is the total number of different returns.

The parameter α allows tuning the sensitivity of the entropy measure. For $\alpha = 1$, Rényi Entropy converges to Shannon Entropy. Higher values of α increase the weight of more probable events, while lower values increase the weight of less probable events. This makes Rényi Entropy a powerful tool for analyzing the complexity and variability of return distributions, providing a deeper understanding of the distribution characteristics beyond what Shannon Entropy offers.

3.6.4. Approximate Entropy (ApEn)

Approximate Entropy quantifies the amount of regularity and unpredictability of fluctuations in a time series (Pincus & Huang, 1992). It measures the likelihood that similar patterns of observations will not be followed by additional similar observations, thus identifying the regularity and complexity of time series data. ApEn is calculated as:

$$\text{ApEn}(m, r, N) = \Phi^m(r) - \Phi^{m+1}(r)$$

where:

- m is the length of compared runs.
- r is a tolerance (filtering level).
- N is the number of data points.
- $\Phi^m(r)$ is a measure of the frequency of similar runs of length m.

$$\Phi^m(r) = \frac{1}{N-m+1} \sum_{i=1}^{N-m+1} \log\left(C_i^m(r)\right)$$

where:

- $C_i^m(r)$ is the number of vectors x within r of x_i divided by $N - m + 1$.

Approximate Entropy evaluates the complexity of a time series by examining the prevalence of repetitive patterns. Lower values of ApEn indicate more regularity (less complexity), while higher values suggest more irregularity and unpredictability. This measure is particularly useful for assessing the stability and predictability of mutual fund returns over time, making it a valuable tool for investors and portfolio managers in understanding the consistency and risk associated with the funds.

4. RESULTS AND DISCUSSION

Tables 1 and 2, showing ESG funds' descriptive statistics, illustrate varying returns, risks, and volatility across different funds. ICICI Prudential ESG Exclusionary Strategy Fund stands out with the highest average and median returns, suggesting it generally outperforms the other funds. Conversely, Franklin India Fund shows the greatest volatility, with the widest range between its maximum and minimum returns and the highest standard deviation, indicating increased risk. Quantum ESG Best in class Strategy Fund and SBI Magnum Equity ESG Fund, while not leading in average returns, display substantial potential for both high gains and significant losses. All funds exhibit negative skewness, indicating more frequent extreme negative returns than positive ones. High kurtosis across the fund's points to a leptokurtic distribution, suggesting a higher likelihood of outlier returns. This is corroborated by significant Jarque-Bera statistics, confirming the non-normal distribution of returns. These statistics reveal a complex risk-return profile for each fund, highlighting the importance of understanding potential gains and risks for investors.

The descriptive statistics of conventional mutual funds display an extensive range of performance parameters that signify different degrees of return, risk, and volatility. The Nippon India Mutual Fund exhibits significantly greater average and median returns in comparison to the other funds, indicating a possibly superior performance profile. All funds exhibit substantial volatility in risk, with each fund having wide ranges between their highest and lowest returns and quite high standard deviations. The skewness of the funds is negative, suggesting that the returns tend to be skewed towards more negative outcomes. This trend is particularly evident in Nippon India Mutual Fund and Unit Trust of India Mutual Fund. Furthermore, all funds display a high level of kurtosis, indicating a tendency for extreme returns that is backed by significantly high Jarque-Bera statistics, confirming the non-normal distribution of returns. Both high kurtosis and strong Jarque-Bera values highlight the possibility of experiencing extreme returns, whether positive or negative. This is particularly important for investing strategies that prioritize risk management.

When comparing the performance of ESG and conventional mutual funds, it becomes apparent that conventional funds generally provide greater prospective returns. This is supported by higher mean and median values. Nevertheless, this benefit is accompanied by elevated risk and volatility, characterized by greater variations between the highest and lowest returns and bigger standard deviations. ESG funds, in comparison, have somewhat lower returns but demonstrate reduced volatility and slightly less pronounced minimum losses, indicating a steadier performance profile. Both ESG and conventional funds display negative skewness, suggesting a preference for negative extremes in returns. However, this tendency is more prominent in conventional funds, demonstrating higher kurtosis and Jarque-Bera statistics. These findings highlight a greater likelihood of significant outliers and deviations from a normal distribution in conventional funds. Generally, conventional funds may be attractive to investors looking for greater returns, even when a larger level of risk is involved. On the other hand, ESG funds may appeal to individuals who prioritize stability and decreased risk exposure.

Figures 1 and 2 depict the return plots for ESG and conventional mutual funds, respectively, over a specified period. The return plots for ESG funds in Figure 1 show noticeable fluctuations, with some funds experiencing sharp spikes and drops, indicative of higher volatility and complexity in their return patterns. This volatility reflects the dynamic nature of ESG investments, which can be influenced by various socio-environmental factors. In contrast, Figure 2 shows the return plots for conventional funds, which appear to have less pronounced fluctuations and relatively more stable return patterns. This stability suggests that conventional funds might offer lower volatility compared to ESG funds.

Figure 1. Return plot of ESG funds

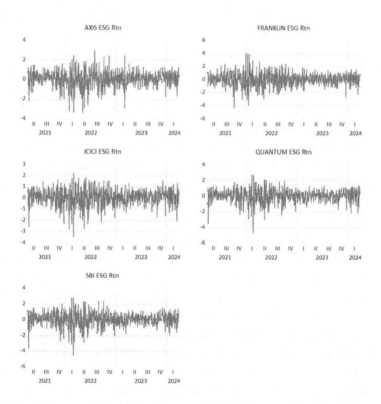

Note: Figure 1 illustrates the financial performance of ESG (Environmental, Social, and Governance) funds over a specified time period.

Figure 2. Return plot of conventional funds

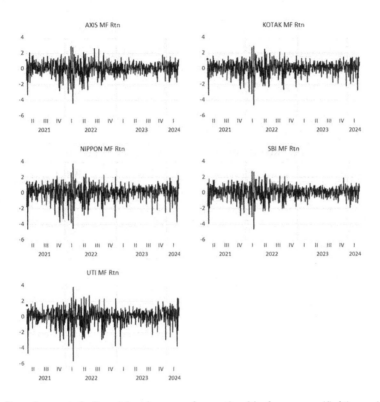

Note: Figure 2 presents the financial performance of conventional funds over a specified time period, offering insights into their comparative returns and market trends.

Table 1. Descriptive statistics – ESG funds

	AXIS_ESG_ RTN	FRANKLIN_ESG_ RTN	ICICI_ESG_ RTN	QUANTUM_ESG_ RTN	SBI_ESG_ RTN
Mean	0.0558	0.0445	0.0694	0.0588	0.0613
Median	0.0678	0.0759	0.1387	0.1361	0.1037
Maximum	2.9810	4.0860	2.2311	2.7590	2.8028
Minimum	-3.3865	-4.3268	-3.4615	-4.6695	-4.5410
Std. Dev.	0.8019	0.9919	0.7272	0.7990	0.8509
Skewness	-0.4850	-0.1348	-0.6481	-0.7741	-0.5823
Kurtosis	4.9212	4.6336	4.4970	5.7960	5.3408
Jarque-Bera	142.2370	84.1834	120.4123	313.6683	209.9006

continued on following page

Table 1. Continued

	AXIS_ESG_ RTN	FRANKLIN_ESG_ RTN	ICICI_ESG_ RTN	QUANTUM_ESG_ RTN	SBI_ESG_ RTN
Probability	0.0000	0.0000	0.0000	0.0000	0.0000
Observations	737	737	737	737	737

Note: Table 1 presents the descriptive statistics matrix of the data such as mean, median, standard deviation of ESG funds.

Table 2. Descriptive statistics- conventional funds

	AXIS_MF_RTN	KOTAK_MF_RTN	NIPPON_MF_RTN	SBI_MF_RTN	UTI_MF_RTN
Mean	0.0547	0.0798	0.1046	0.0653	0.0848
Median	0.0867	0.1643	0.2209	0.1014	0.2158
Maximum	2.8759	2.8704	3.7338	2.7298	3.7765
Minimum	-4.3813	-4.6271	-4.6275	-4.5930	-5.6031
Std. Dev.	0.8298	0.8374	0.9591	0.8206	1.0257
Skewness	-0.5691	-0.8113	-1.0421	-0.6806	-0.9703
Kurtosis	5.2984	5.5506	6.0447	5.7636	5.9040
Jarque-Bera	202.0051	280.6411	418.0667	291.4235	374.6242
Probability	0.0000	0.0000	0.0000	0.0000	0.0000
Observations	737	737	737	737	737

Note: Table 2 presents the descriptive statistics matrix of the data such as mean, median, standard deviation of conventional funds.

Table 3. Performance analysis of ESG funds

Funds	Mean Expected Return	Alpha	Mean Jensen's Alpha	Mean Treynor Ratio	Mean Sharpe Ratio	Mean Actual Return	SD
AXIS_ESG_RTN	-0.00538	0.029316	0.0612	0.044855	0.043424	0.0558	0.8019
FRANKLIN_ESG_RTN	0.012014	0.053507	0.0325	1.289644	0.023679	0.0445	0.9919
ICICI_ESG_RTN	0.058247	0.032146	0.0111	0.062837	0.066502	0.0694	0.7272
QUANTUM_ESG_RTN	0.029026	0.050744	0.0297	0.204242	0.04723	0.0588	0.7990
SBI_ESG_RTN	0.059885	0.022434	0.0014	0.042916	0.047347	0.0613	0.8509

Note: Table 3 summarizes the performance of selected ESG funds from April 1, 2021, to March 31, 2024, including metrics like NAV, Jensen's Alpha, and Sharpe and Treynor Ratios.

Table 4. Performance analysis of conventional funds

Funds	Mean Expected Return	Alpha	Mean Jensen's Alpha	Mean Treynor Ratio	Mean Sharpe Ratio	Mean Actual Return	SD
AXIS_MF_RTN	0.052492	0.023205	0.0022	0.037487	0.040567	0.0547	0.8298
KOTAK_MF_RTN	0.078229	0.022543	0.0015	0.065467	0.070146	0.0798	0.8374
NIPPON_MF_RTN	0.095788	0.02982	0.0088	0.087691	0.087138	0.1046	0.9591
SBI_MF_RTN	0.06359	0.022743	0.0017	0.049658	0.053986	0.0653	0.8206
UTI_MF_RTN	0.094342	0.011489	-0.0095	0.060264	0.062201	0.0848	1.0257

Note: Table 4 summarizes the performance of selected conventional funds from April 1, 2021, to March 31, 2024, including metrics like NAV, Jensen's Alpha, and Sharpe and Treynor Ratios.

When evaluating the performance of ESG and conventional mutual funds, it is essential to do a thorough analysis of several measures, including Mean Expected Return, Alpha, Mean Jensen's Alpha, Mean Treynor Ratio, Mean Sharpe Ratio, Mean Actual Return, and Standard Deviation (SD). ESG funds often have lower Mean Expected Returns than conventional funds, but they have much better Alpha values in certain situations. Franklin India Fund and Quantum ESG Best in class Strategy Fund exhibit significantly higher Alpha values than their conventional counterparts, indicating that these ESG funds were able to create a substantial return beyond what was expected based on their market exposure. Axis ESG Integration Strategy Fund and Franklin India Fund, which are ESG funds, provide superior risk-adjusted performance compared to conventional funds, as seen by their significant outperformance in terms of Mean Jensen's Alpha.

In addition, when evaluating performance using the Mean Treynor and Sharpe Ratios, which account for risk-adjusted returns, ESG funds such as Franklin India Fund and Quantum ESG Best in class Strategy Fund demonstrate higher statistics compared to the majority of traditional funds. These values indicate greater returns per unit of market risk and overall risk, respectively. These findings indicate that specific ESG funds not only have better risk management, but also take advantage of the risk to generate greater profits. Nevertheless, it is important to highlight that several ESG funds exhibit lower Mean Actual Returns compared to the top-performing conventional funds (such as Nippon India Mutual Fund and UTI Mutual Fund). However, their risk management and Alpha indicate a more efficient performance when considering risk-adjusted terms.

Table 1 and Table 2 of performance analysis shows that although conventional funds may have greater Mean Actual Returns in certain situations, ESG funds generally give superior risk-adjusted returns, as seen by their higher Mean Jensen's Alpha and favorable Treynor and Sharpe Ratios. Investors that prioritize consistency and efficiency in generating returns, rather than solely focusing on return indicators, may find this particularly attractive. Therefore, when considering both financial performance and risk factors, certain ESG mutual funds have shown the ability to outperform traditional funds. This aligns with the increasing preference among investors for sustainable investing options that provide satisfactory financial returns.

Table 5. Entropy analysis of mutual fund returns to assess volatility and complexity

Fund	Shannon Entropy	Rényi Entropy	Approximate Entropy
SBI ESG Rtn	4.9223	-0.4338	-0.4461
AXIS ESG Rtn	5.3299	-0.6523	-0.4487
FRANKLIN ESG Rtn	4.84	-0.1286	-0.44
ICICI ESG Rtn	5.5616	-0.8028	-0.4409
QUANTUM ESG Rtn	4.5768	-0.492	-0.4456
SBI MF Rtn	4.7491	-0.4794	-0.4486
NIPPON MF Rtn	4.5993	-0.2335	-0.4533
KOTAK MF Rtn	4.6322	-0.4611	-0.4461
AXIS MF Rtn	4.8685	-0.4619	-0.4449
UTI MF Rtn	4.3383	-0.0503	-0.4503

Note: This table presents the entropy analysis of mutual fund returns, assessing volatility and complexity through Shannon, Rényi, and Approximate Entropy metrics.

Entropy analysis provides insights into the volatility and complexity of the return distributions for both ESG and conventional mutual funds. Shannon Entropy values indicate that Axis ESG Integration Strategy Fund and ICICI Prudential ESG Exclusionary Strategy Fund have higher entropy, suggesting more unpredictable and complex return patterns, which can be associated with higher volatility. Conversely, conventional funds such as UTI Mutual Fund show lower Shannon Entropy, indicating less complexity and potentially lower volatility. The Rényi and Approximate Entropy values reinforce this observation, with more negative values typically representing more irregularity and potential risk. For instance, ICICI Prudential ESG Exclusionary Strategy Fund and Axis ESG Integration Strategy Fund display more negative Rényi Entropy values, aligning with higher risk levels. In contrast, conventional funds like UTI Mutual Fund have the least negative Rényi Entropy, suggesting lower risk. Overall, ESG funds exhibit higher entropy values, implying they experience greater volatility and risk compared to their conventional counterparts.

When considering the combined results for ESG and conventional mutual funds, the entropy metrics collectively indicate that ESG funds generally exhibit higher levels of volatility and risk compared to conventional funds. The higher Shannon Entropy values observed in ESG funds suggest that their returns are more unpredictable and complex, potentially reflecting the dynamic nature of ESG investments, which may be influenced by various socio-environmental factors. The Rényi and Approximate Entropy values further support this, with ESG funds showing more negative values, indicating greater irregularity and risk in their return distributions.

In contrast, conventional funds, with their relatively lower entropy values, exhibit more stable and predictable return patterns, implying lower volatility and risk. This overall assessment highlights that while ESG funds may offer potential for higher risk-adjusted returns, as previously discussed, they also come with increased volatility and complexity, requiring investors to carefully consider their risk tolerance and investment objectives when opting for ESG over conventional funds.

5. IMPLICATIONS

The findings that ESG funds generally exhibit higher entropy values, indicating greater volatility and complexity, suggest that these funds require more sophisticated risk management strategies to harness their potential for higher returns. Portfolio managers might need to develop advanced analytical tools and adopt dynamic investment approaches to navigate the unpredictability inherent in ESG investments. Additionally, the superior risk-adjusted performance of ESG funds, as evidenced by higher Alpha and favorable Treynor and Sharpe Ratios, underscores the viability of integrating ESG criteria into investment strategies not merely for ethical alignment but for financial performance enhancement. Investors should recognize the potential for higher returns alongside increased volatility, balancing their portfolios to optimize for both stability and growth. This nuanced understanding of ESG fund performance can guide more informed decision-making, encouraging a strategic shift towards sustainable investments that do not compromise on financial returns while managing the inherent risks more effectively.

6. CONCLUSION

The analysis comparing ESG mutual funds to conventional funds offered insightful results, particularly when viewed through risk-adjusted metrics and entropy measures. Conventional funds initially appeared to lead in terms of raw returns, but ESG funds distinguished themselves significantly by achieving higher Alpha and Mean Jensen's Alpha, underscoring their superior performance after adjusting for risk. This suggested that ESG funds managed risks effectively while capitalizing on opportunities aligned with sustainable investment principles, producing returns that often-exceeded market expectations. In terms of risk-adjusted performance, ESG funds demonstrated stronger Mean Treynor and Sharpe Ratios compared to their conventional counterparts, highlighting their efficiency in generating higher returns per unit of market risk and offering better returns relative to total risk. However, the entropy analysis provided deeper insights into the volatility and complexity of the returns. Shannon Entropy values for ESG funds were higher, indicating that their returns were more unpredictable and complex. This complexity might reflect the dynamic nature of ESG investments, influenced by various socio-environmental factors. Rényi Entropy values also showed that ESG funds had more negative readings, suggesting greater irregularity and risk in their return distributions. Approximate Entropy further supported these findings by revealing higher values for ESG funds, indicating less regularity and predictability in their returns. This increased volatility could imply a higher chance of achieving significant returns, although it also pointed to greater risk.

Conversely, conventional funds exhibited lower entropy values across Shannon, Rényi, and Approximate Entropy measures, indicating more stable and predictable return patterns. This implied lower volatility and risk compared to ESG funds. These findings reflected the advanced fund management strategies employed by ESG funds, which focused on long-term stability and risk mitigation—qualities highly valued in today's volatile market environment. The growing preference for sustainable investment options was evident as more investors aligned their portfolios with funds supporting responsible business practices, enhancing a fund's market strength and potential for accessing unique investment opportunities. This trend indicated the evolving dynamics in financial markets where ESG integration became synonymous with enhanced portfolio performance and resilience.

In summary, while conventional funds provided satisfactory immediate returns, ESG funds excelled in delivering commendable risk-adjusted returns, marking them as prudent choices for investors focused on long-term value and ethical investment practices. Since ESG funds exhibit higher volatility and complexity, indicating greater risk, they also provide a greater possibility for substantial returns. Our evidence aligned with the findings of Capotă et al., (2022) that ESG funds often outperformed conventional funds under broader risk factors, underscoring a transformative era in investing where sustainability considerations were integral to financial success and strategic fund management.

REFERENCES

Afridi, S. H. S., Rehman, A., Mubashir, M., & Zeeshan, M. (2020). Risk Adjusted Performance, Market Timing and Selectivity of Mutual Funds: A Comparative Analysis of Islamic and Conventional Mutual Funds of Pakistan. *Journal of Management Research*, 6(2), 1–22.

Ahmed, S., & Siddiqui, D. A. (2020). Factors affecting fund flows in islamic and conventional mutual funds of Pakistan. *Available atSSRN* 3681179. 10.2139/ssrn.3681179

Alibakhshi, R., & Sadeghi Moghadam, M. R. (2016). A new algorithm for mutual funds evaluation based on multiple attribute decision making techniques. *Kybernetes*, 45(8), 1194–1212. 10.1108/K-10-2015-0256

ALTAN, İ. M. (2022). Thematic investment strategies: Cointegration relationship between robotic investment index and Bist100. *International Journal of Mechanical Engineering*.

Aragon, G. O., Li, L., & Qian, J. Q. J. (2019). The use of credit default swaps by bond mutual funds: Liquidity provision and counterparty risk. *Journal of Financial Economics*, 131(1), 168–185. 10.1016/j.jfineco.2018.07.014

Ashraf, D. (2013). Performance evaluation of Islamic mutual funds relative to conventional funds: Empirical evidence from Saudi Arabia. *International Journal of Islamic and Middle Eastern Finance and Management*, 6(2), 105–121. 10.1108/17538391311329815

Aslam, F., Ferreira, P., & Mohti, W. (2023). Investigating efficiency of frontier stock markets using multifractal detrended fluctuation analysis. *International Journal of Emerging Markets*, 18(7), 1650–1676. 10.1108/IJOEM-11-2020-1348

Ausloos, M., Bartolacci, F., Castellano, N. G., & Cerqueti, R. (2018). Exploring how innovation strategies at time of crisis influence performance: A cluster analysis perspective. *Technology Analysis and Strategic Management*, 30(4), 484–497. 10.1080/09537325.2017.1337889

BinMahfouz, S., & Hassan, M. K.BinMahfouz. (2012). A comparative study between the investment characteristics of Islamic and conventional equity mutual funds in Saudi Arabia. *Journal of Investing*, 21(4), 128–143. 10.3905/joi.2012.21.4.128

Capotă, L.-D., Giuzio, M., Kapadia, S., & Salakhova, D. (2022). *Are ethical and green investment funds more resilient?* Carhart, M. M. (1997). On Persistence in Mutual Fund Performance. *The Journal of Finance*, 52(1), 57–82. https://doi.org/https://doi.org/10.1111/j.1540-6261.1997.tb03808.x

Chiew, D., Qiu, J., Treepongkaruna, S., Yang, J., & Shi, C. (2021). Performance of Portfolios Based on the Expected Utility-Entropy Fund Rating Approach. *Entropy (Basel, Switzerland)*, 23(4), 481. 10.3390/e2304048133919622

Chu, N., Dao, B., Pham, N., Nguyen, H., & Tran, H. (2022). Predicting Mutual Funds' Performance using Deep Learning and Ensemble Techniques. *ArXiv Preprint ArXiv:2209.09649.*

Coleman, L., & Coleman, L. (2016). The Mutual Fund Industry: Structure and Conduct. *Applied Investment Theory: How Markets and Investors Behave, and Why*, 121–129.

Curtis, Q., Fisch, J., & Robertson, A. Z. (2021). Do ESG mutual funds deliver on their promises? *Michigan Law Review*, 120(120.3), 393. 10.36644/mlr.120.3.ESG

Fong, K. Y. L., Parwada, J. T., & Yang, J. W. (2018). Algorithmic Trading and Mutual Fund Performance. *Available atSSRN* 3111598.

Ghasemi Doudkanlou, M., Chandro, P., & Banihashemi, S. (2023). The Effect of Exit Time and Entropy on Asset Performance Evaluation. *Entropy (Basel, Switzerland)*, 25(9), 1252. 10.3390/e2509125237761551

Gokkaya, S., Liu, X., Pool, V. K., Xie, F., & Zhang, J. (2023). Is there investment value in the soft-dollar arrangement? Evidence from mutual funds. *Review of Financial Studies*, 36(8), 3122–3162. 10.1093/rfs/hhad010

Gonçalves, T., Pimentel, D., & Gaio, C. (2021). Risk and performance of European green and conventional funds. *Sustainability (Basel)*, 13(8), 4226. 10.3390/su13084226

Hauff, J. C., & Nilsson, J. (2022). Is ESG mutual fund quality in the eye of the beholder? An experimental study of investor responses to ESG fund strategies. *Business Strategy and the Environment*. Advance online publication. 10.1002/bse.3181

Ielasi, F., & Rossolini, M. (2019a). A New Approach to Sustainable and Responsible Investment: The Sustainability-Themed Mutual Funds. *Socially Responsible Investments: The Crossroads Between Institutional and Retail Investors*, 125–148.

Ielasi, F., & Rossolini, M. (2019b). Responsible or thematic? The true nature of sustainability-themed mutual funds. *Sustainability (Basel)*, 11(12), 3304. 10.3390/su11123304

Ielasi, F., Rossolini, M., & Limberti, S. (2018). Sustainability-themed mutual funds: An empirical examination of risk and performance. *The Journal of Risk Finance*, 19(3), 247–261. 10.1108/JRF-12-2016-0159

Jack, L. Treynor. (1961). Market Value, Time, and Risk. SSRN.

Jensen, M. C. (1968). The performance of mutual funds in the period 1945-1964. *The Journal of Finance*, 23(2), 389–416.

Jin, I. (2022). ESG-screening and factor-risk-adjusted performance: The concentration level of screening does matter. *Journal of Sustainable Finance & Investment*, 12(4), 1125–1145. 10.1080/20430795.2020.1837501

Kumar, V., & Srivastava, A. (2016). Performance Evaluation of Private Sector Mutual Funds. *International Journal of Trend in Research of Development*, 3(1), 201–210.

Lai, S., & Li, H. (2008). The performance evaluation for fund of funds by comparing asset allocation of mean–variance model or genetic algorithms to that of fund managers. *Applied Financial Economics*, 18(6), 485–501. 10.1080/09603100600970099

Lapointe, V. (2015). Financial Performance of Socially Responsible Investment: Does the Visibility of Firms in the Portfolio Matter? *Available atSSRN* 2386015.

Lee, W. H., Han, M.-Y., & Kim, S. (2023). ESG, Style Investing, and Integration. *Asian Review of Financial Research*, 36(3), 105–145. 10.37197/ARFR.2023.36.3.4

Mansor, F., Bhatti, M. I., Rahman, S., & Do, H. Q. (2020). The investment performance of ethical equity funds in Malaysia. *Journal of Risk and Financial Management*, 13(9), 219. 10.3390/jrfm13090219

Marzuki, A., & Atta, A. A. B. (2020). *Mutual Fund Families in Saudi Arabia, Malaysia, Indonesia And Pakistan: How Persist Their Performance Are?*

Massa, M., & Yadav, V. (n.d.). *Do Mutual Funds Play a Sentiment-based Strategy?*

Mateus, , I. BMateus, , CTodorovic, , N. (2019). Review of new trends in the literature on factor models and mutual fund performance. *International Review of Financial Analysis, 63*, 344–354.

Methling, F., & von Nitzsch, R. (2019). Naïve diversification in thematic investing: Heuristics for the core satellite investor. *Journal of Asset Management*, 20(7), 568–580. 10.1057/s41260-019-00136-2

Morgan Stanley. (2023). *Sustainable Funds Show Continued Outperformance and Positive Flows in 2023 Despite a Slower Second Half.* Institute of Sustainable Investing.

Naqvi, N. (2019). Manias, panics and crashes in emerging markets: An empirical investigation of the post-2008 crisis period. *New Political Economy*, 24(6), 759–779. 10.1080/13563467.2018.1526263

Narang, M. (2018). Performance Evaluation of Selected Equity Mutual Funds. *Performance Evaluation.*

Nascimento, J., & Powell, W. (2010). Dynamic programming models and algorithms for the mutual fund cash balance problem. *Management Science*, 56(5), 801–815. 10.1287/mnsc.1100.1143

Natter, M., Rohleder, M., Schulte, D., & Wilkens, M. (2017). Bond mutual funds and complex investments. *Journal of Asset Management*, 18(6), 433–456. 10.1057/s41260-017-0046-7

Nicolescu, L., & Tudorache, F. G. (2018). Romania, Slovakia and Hungary: evolution of mutual funds in recent years. *Proceedings of the International Conference on Business Excellence, 12*(1), 695–710.

Pancholi, D. (2022). Hedge Funds: Resolving Myths about ESG Integration. *Journal of Alternative Investments*, 25(2), 8–13. 10.3905/jai.2022.1.172

Panda, P. K. (2016). A Review on Evolution of Mutual Funds Market in India: Current Status and Problems. *Indian Journal of Economics & Business*, 15(1), 153–172.

Pincus, S. M., & Huang, W.-M. (1992). Approximate entropy: Statistical properties and applications. *Communications in Statistics. Theory and Methods*, 21(11), 3061–3077. 10.1080/03610929208830963

Prajapati, K. N. S. H. M. F. (2008). *Performance Evaluation of Public & Private Mutual Fund Schemes in India.*

Quirici, M. C. (2023). The European Blue Economy Framework and Blue Bonds as New Instruments of Blue Finance. In *ESG Integration and SRI Strategies in the EU: Challenges and Opportunities for Sustainable Development* (pp. 175–194). Springer. 10.1007/978-3-031-36457-0_9

Raghunandan, A., & Rajgopal, S. (2022). Do ESG funds make stakeholder-friendly investments? *Review of Accounting Studies*, 27(3), 822–863. 10.1007/s11142-022-09693-1

Rényi, A. (1961). On measures of entropy and information. *Proceedings of the Fourth Berkeley Symposium on Mathematical Statistics and Probability,* Volume 1*: Contributions to the Theory of Statistics, 4*, 547–562.

Ruan, H. (2018). *Essays on Mutual Funds.*

Sandberg, J., & Sjöström, E. (2021). *Motivations for investment in sustainable consumption and production. Sustainable Consumption and Production* (Vol. I). Challenges and Development., 10.1007/978-3-030-56371-4_7/COVER

Sehgal, S., & Babbar, S. (2017). Evaluating alternative performance benchmarks for Indian mutual fund industry. *Journal of Advances in Management Research*, 14(2), 222–250. 10.1108/JAMR-04-2016-0028

Sehgal, S., & Jain, S. (2012). Short-term prior return patterns in stocks and sector returns: Evidence for BRICKS markets. *Investment Management and Financial Innovations*, 9(1), 93–114.

Sehgal, S., & Jhanwar, M. (2007). Short-term persistence in mutual funds performance: evidence from India. *10th Capital Markets Conference,* Indian Institute of Capital Markets. 10.2139/ssrn.962829

Shannon, C. E. (1948). A mathematical theory of communication. *The Bell System Technical Journal*, 27(3), 379–423. 10.1002/j.1538-7305.1948.tb01338.x

Sharpe, W. F. (1964). 1964 Sharpe - Capital Asset Prices. *The Journal of Finance*, 19(3).

Soussou, K., & Omri, A. (2022). Mutual Funds' Performance Sensitivity to Funds' Attributes. Case Study: Saudi Mutual Funds. *Financial Markets. Institutions and Risks*, 6(4), 32–50. 10.21272/fmir.6(4).32-50.2022

Steen, M., Moussawi, J. T., & Gjolberg, O. (2020). Is there a relationship between Morningstar's ESG ratings and mutual fund performance? *Journal of Sustainable Finance & Investment*, 10(4), 349–370. 10.1080/20430795.2019.1700065

Suharti, T., Aminda, R. S., Bimo, W. A., Nurhayati, I., & Dewi, S. M. (2022). Performance of Conventional and Sharia Mutual Funds Using Sharpe, Treynor and Jensens Methods. *Proceedings of The International Halal Science and Technology Conference, 15*(1), 48–58. 10.31098/ihsatec.v15i1.594

Thomas, A. S., Jayachandran, A., & Biju, A. V. N. (2024). Strategic mapping of the environmental social governance landscape in finance–A bibliometric exploration through concepts and themes. *Corporate Social Responsibility and Environmental Management*, csr.2805. 10.1002/csr.2805

Tsai, T.-J., Yang, C.-B., & Peng, Y.-H. (2011). Genetic algorithms for the investment of the mutual fund with global trend indicator. *Expert Systems with Applications*, 38(3), 1697–1701. 10.1016/j.eswa.2010.07.094

Vanaja, V., & Karrupasamy, R. (2016). Performance Evaluation of select Public Sector and Private Sector Mutual Funds in India. *Asian Journal of Research in Social Sciences and Humanities*, 6(7), 1532–1547. 10.5958/2249-7315.2016.00527.X

Vidal-García, J., & Vidal, M. (2024). The Relation between Mutual Fund Performance and Investment Style Changes. *Available atSSRN* 4021259.

Wang, K., Huang, S., & Chen, Y.-H. (2008). Mutual fund performance evaluation system using fast adaptive neural network classifier. *2008 Fourth International Conference on Natural Computation, 2*, 479–483. 10.1109/ICNC.2008.756

Xia, Q., Liu, Y., & Wei, F. (2023). How can ESG funds improve their performance? Based on the DEA-Malmquist productivity index and fsQCA method. *Journal of University of Science and Technology of China*, 53(8), 0803. Advance online publication. 10.52396/JUSTC-2023-0017

Yousaf, M., Ziaullah, M., & Tariq, M. G. (2023). The Performance of Pakistani Equity Mutual Funds During Bull and Bear Market. *Global Social Sciences Review*, VIII(II), 592–615. 10.31703/gssr.2023(VIII-II).53

Yu, G. (2010). Accounting standards and international portfolio holdings: Analysis of cross-border holdings following mandatory adoption of IFRS. *Unpublished Paper, Harvard University*.

Yu, J.-R., Chiou, W.-J. P., Lee, W.-Y., & Yu, K.-C. (2017). Does entropy model with return forecasting enhance portfolio performance? *Computers & Industrial Engineering*, 114, 175–182. 10.1016/j.cie.2017.10.007

Zeeshan, M., Han, J., Rehman, A., Saleem, K., Shah, R. U., Ishaque, A., Farooq, N., & Hussain, A. (2020). Conventional mutual funds out perform Islamic mutual funds in the context of Pakistan. A myth or reality. *International Journal of Economics and Financial Issues*, 10(4), 151–157. 10.32479/ijefi.10090

Chapter 11
Dynamics of Financial Risk on the Effect of Sustainable Practices on Financial Performance:
Evidence From the Indian Banking Companies

Dany Thomas
https://orcid.org/0000-0002-4938-7029
School of Business Management and Legal Studies, Kollam, India

Ria Mammen
https://orcid.org/0000-0003-1496-329X
St. Thomas College, Kozhencherry, India

Vimal George Kurian
https://orcid.org/0000-0002-6430-4383
CMS College, Kottayam, India

S. P. Asha
SN College, Kollam, India

ABSTRACT

The study examine the influence of financial risk on the nature of the relationship between ESG and the financial performance of Indian banks. In India, loans are key financial products of banks that are exposed to carbon-intensive sectors, which hinder their efforts to mitigate against transition risks and global ESG standards,

DOI: 10.4018/979-8-3693-3880-3.ch011

amid the growing pressure from international investors. The study uses ROA to measure financial performance. The independent variable ESG was measured using the ESG scores Indian banks indexed in the NIFTY 100 ESG Index. Altman's Z-score model which predicts the financial risk of Indian banks was considered as the mediating variable to assess its influence on the nature of the relationship between ESG and financial performance. The evidence from the study would be useful to identify the changes in the financial performance of Indian banks resulting from their sustainable performance.

INTRODUCTION

Sustainable and responsible investment techniques have gained importance due to the growing public interest in issues that relate to environmental security and social progress. The constant interaction of humans with the environment and their natural surroundings to enhance the quality of their lives intensifies issues such as global warming, industrial pollution, and environmental degradation. In the twenty-first century, information, progressive advancements, and the disruptions to environment provide humanity with its biggest challenge (Pater & Cristea, 2016), leading to the need for sustainability. Maintaining an ecological balance is the key to fostering sustainability (Yadav et al., 2021), the basic idea of which was rooted in the UN Conference in Stockholm during the early 1970s. Sustainability is guided by the principle of harmonising development and environment in a mutually beneficial manner (*History of SD · What Is Sustainable Development · Sustainable Development Commission*, n.d.). By fulfilling the Sustainable Development Goals (SDG) initiated by the UN, businesses can also take part in this process (*Sustainable Development | UN Global Compact*, n.d.) by making investments that take into consideration environmental, social and governance (ESG) factors to reduce risk and boost returns.

ESG is a key to obtain sustainability, which is also a self-driven contribution to Sustainable Development by focusing on the environment, society, stakeholders, ethical behaviour, and volunteering, which offers a balance between pursuing the present needs of corporations, while protecting the future of humans and natural resources.(Shayan et al., 2022). In this regard the Sustainable Development Goals contain a universally agreed-upon and delimited set of sustainable development issues, many of them broken down into targets that are directly relevant to business. In addition, it provides a framework against which companies may start to map their CSR activities in order to identify leverage points for enhancing positive impacts and mitigating negative ones (Schonherr et al., 2017) Through our research work we carry out an evaluation on how ESG pillars affect the performance of an organisation, which would help identify the obstacles in achieving SDGs. SDGs can serve as a reputable, comprehensive, and practical framework for ESG, which is also aligned with sustainability that benefit each entity. (Shayan et al., 2022).

The ESG concept imparts a strong governance framework for managing the social and environmental implications of businesses. It is a comprehensive strategy to foster the confidence of stakeholders by incorporating ESG in a company's operations and reporting. The mandatory implementation of ESG reporting has been the subject of an ongoing controversy in the United States. There has been a growing trend in ESG reporting and transparency, including among utility corporations, between 2011 and 2019 (Nicolo et al., 2023). ESG ratings and scores are of particular interest as they form a broadly homogeneous product group offered by companies aiming to provide investors with an objective data-driven third-party assessment of ESG-related aspects (Mazzacurati, 2021). Different rating agencies might give the same company different ESG scores based on subjective agency criteria and they must voluntarily disclose ESG practices to receive ESG ratings from an agency because there are no legal requirements for companies to provide standardized ESG information (Williams, 2022).

Since there is no official or common definition of ESG ratings, there have been a number of concerns and criticisms in the ESG investing space (Williams, 2022). In a recent letter to the European Commission, ESMA (2021) proposed the following broad definition: ESG rating means an opinion regarding an entity, issuer, or debt securities impact on or exposure to ESG factors, alignment with international climatic agreements or sustainability characteristics, issued using a defined ranking system of rating categories (Mazzacurati, 2021). ESG rating measures the long-term sustainability and the future societal and environmental impact of businesses. Though there is an increased number of firms adopting sustainability practices and disclosing environmental, social, and governance information (Xie et al., 2019), it is difficult to identify the nature of the relationship between sustainable performance and the financial performance (FP) of a company, as the sustainability reports stand divorced from financial reports (R. El Khoury, 2021).

Companies considering pursuing ESG goals are subjected to certain challenges while implementing them. The primary forces behind the implementation of ESG are positive indications from the government in the form of legislation, regulations, and appropriate business policy plans (Liou et al., 2023). In India, SEBI issued guidelines to all listed companies regarding business responsibility and sustainability reporting, which is also mandatory for top companies. As a result, all sectors including banking sector are scrutinized for their sustainable practices and are compelled to disclose their operations and adopt improved management practices because they understand the resulting financial advantages. (Ehrenhard & Fiorito, 2018). In addition to the regulatory pressure, the impact of top management, substantial capital expenditure, effect of external managers in establishing ESG goals, and internal governance structure act as challenges faced by enterprises while implementing ESG (Liou et al., 2023). Furthermore, challenges to the adoption of ESG include shareholder obstacles or staff resistance to ESG implementation, and the ESG issue assessment barrier, which demonstrates organizations' inability to assess and plan ESG efforts (Sheehan et al., 2023). Ensuring the holistic well-being of employees and maintaining appropriate communication about the objective of CSR are crucial aspects of CSR implementation (Dhanesh, 2020).

In banking sector, the values upheld by each bank serve as a reliable framework for promoting equality, fairness, and openness while formulating plans and approaches for engaging with various stakeholders (Ehrenhard & Fiorito, 2018). In India, loans are key financial products of banks that are exposed to carbon-intensive sectors, which hinder their efforts to mitigate against transition risks and global ESG standards, amid the growing pressure from international investors. Despite the mandatory disclosures, it is still difficult to make out the relationship between FP and sustainable performance (R. El Khoury, 2021). In this regard, the present study attempts to provide evidence on the relationship between sustainability and FP. In addition, the researchers venture into investigating whether financial risk has any effect on the nature of the relationship between FP and the sustainable performance of banking companies in India.

The present study contributes to the existing literature in many ways. It gives a panoramic view of how environmental, social, and governance (ESG) practices adopted by Banks in India affect their FP. In addition, we provide evidence on how financial risk influences the nature of the relationship between ESG and the FP of Indian banks. The evidence from the study would be useful to identify the changes in the FP of Indian banks resulting from their sustainable performance. Furthermore, the study provides evidence of the significance of financial risk in influencing the changes brought in by the sustainable performance of banking companies on their financial well-being in India.

The paper is divided into five sections. The second section which follows immediately after the introduction presents the review of extant literature and hypotheses formulation. The third section presents the methodology and model specifications. The results are presented and discussed in the fourth section which is followed by the conclusion in the fifth section.

LITERATURE REVIEW

Corporate Sustainability

One of the earliest and key conceptions in the academic study of business and society relations is Corporate Social Responsibility (CSR), which consider a wide range of stakeholders who have relationships with firms, as it goes beyond the general responsibility that firms must legally comply with and includes ethical and moral responsibilities (Lee & Yang, 2022). Whereas the term "corporate sustainability" describes a new corporate management model. It can also fall under the broader term "Environmental Social Governance" (ESG). Corporate sustainability emphasizes growth and profitability through intentional business practices that cater to environmental, social and governance pillars. The goal is to provide long-term value for stakeholders without compromising people, the planet, or the economy. Businesses always concentrate on developing a comprehensive long-term plan that will aim for financial success (Ukko et al., 2019). Though FP operates as a direct input to corporate control mechanisms (Bushman & Smith, 2001), their ability to wealth generation and value creation are dependent on social competence and ethical responsibility (Hardjono & Van Marrewijk, 2001).

Effect of ESG on Financial Performance

ESG is an aggregate measure that comprises various sustainable practices (Velte, 2017), the disclosure of which brings a competitive edge to firms in a rational market (Xie et al., 2019). The rationale behind the disclosure of ESG information, which according to Velte, (2017) is aimed at gaining legitimacy for environmental or social impacts caused by firms. It is a guide for companies' strategic management, risk management, and non-financial performance (H. Liu et al., 2022) and the transparency of ESG reporting and activities is expected to augment the FP of a company (Gao et al., 2023). Nevertheless, research on the relationship between corporate social performance and financial performance provide mixed results. While Rizqi and Munari, (2023) states that sustainability disclosure has no significant influence on FP, (Xiao, 2023) found a significant positive association between ESG and corporate financial performance. Similarly, Gonçalves et al., (2023) too had observed that ESG has a positive impact on corporate FP. Because of the impact of environmental disclosure, a small correlation can be seen in businesses outside of the finance sector (Bernardi & Stark, 2018). The conclusive question that has to be cracked is whether ESG serves and affects a company's FP (Docekalova & Kocmanova, 2015) and hence the following hypothesis has been formulated:

H1: The FP of banking companies in India is significantly influenced by ESG.

In addition to the relationship between FP and composite ESG, the literature provides evidence on the implications of individual pillars of ESG on a company's FP. Hence, the review of the ESG-FP relationship has been extended to the analysis of scientific evidence on how the individual pillars of the composite ESG influence FP, in the subsequent sections.

Environment and financial performance: Increased pollution and climate change had attracted public attention to the impact of enterprises on the environment (Xiao, 2023). With the increase in the degree of environmental uncertainty sustainable development of organisations is challenged (Zhang & Liu, 2022). The environment pillar of composite ESG provides a framework for companies to represent how well they integrate the climate variability and environment preservation into its decisions (Gao et al., 2023). While analysing the impact of environment pillar on financial performance, it was observed by Liu et al., (2022) that 'E' negatively influences the accounting-based financial performance, whereas there is no significant impact on the market-based financial performance of an organisation. Corporates must be careful while devoting the resources for investment on environment to improve corporate financial performance and enhance stakeholders' expectations (Teng et al., 2022). The positive effect of environment on financial performance observed by Ihsani et al., (2023) states that, environment is an important aspect that can generate a competitive advantage for organisations which will improve the corporate financial performance. Taking into account the evidences on the significant association between ESG and FP, this study proposes the following hypothesis:

H2: The FP of banking companies in India is significantly influenced by the environment pillar of the composite ESG.

Social responsibility and financial performance: Research indicates a significant positive relationship between a company's social performance, as part of the ESG framework, and its financial performance (Amaral et al., 2023). While examining the empirical literature, there were discussions on the relationship between Corporate Social Responsibility and FP (Velte, 2017). The concept of Corporate Social Responsibility (CSR) is growing due to a variety of factors, ethical, legal, and economic obligations (Carroll, 1991). Increased consciousness over Corporate Social Responsibility (CSR) and taking an active part in CSR activities gives a need to evaluate CSR activities and FP. Studies suggest that CSR governance contributes to superior FP by achieving good CSR outcomes in the IT (Information Technology) Sector (Lubbe et al., 1995), and tourism industries (Inoue & Lee, 2011, Alatawi et al., 2023). Similarly factors such as employees and product safety and quality have a direct impact on companies FP (Berman et al., 1999). Wang & Sarkis (2017) emphasise the importance of the strategies to implement CSR governance and explains previous heterogeneous findings on CSR- financial return relationships. When it pertains to the banking industry, taking part in CSR initiatives fosters not just social well-being but also banks' financial results and risk management (Gangi et al., 2019). It is seen that stakeholders' credibility and confidence have been enhanced (Miralles-Quirós et al., 2019) and have acquired competitive advantage (Forgione & Migliardo, 2020) in commercial banks' by the adoption of sustainable practices. Considering the significance of social responsibility on financial performance of an organisation, the study proposes the following hypothesis:

H3: The FP of banking companies in India is significantly influenced by the social pillar of the composite ESG.

Governance and financial performance: The number of firms that employ sustainable strategies and disclose ESG information continues to increase fundamental changes in business models and management theory. There is a conflict among managers regarding to what extent they should disclose corporate information. Even though it would make a little bit uncertain whether they are favourable or unfavourable to value the firm in a rational market, a positive consensus emerged among corporate social responsibility and FP. Companies give equal importance to sustainability and FP in order to improve wealth maximisation, and they keep track of corporate social responsibility in depth to demonstrate companies' accountability and performance (Hopkins, 2002). Corporate governance boils down to a set of policies and procedures that control businesses (Blair, 2001) that bring significant benefits to companies such as strengthening the rights of minority shareholders and their confidence (Johnson et al., 2000), boosting the stock prices, enhancing performance (Davis, 2002), and ensuring investor protection from expropriation of insiders (La Porta et al., 2000). In developing South Asian nations, the corporate governance mechanism of ownership, board independence, and returnee board members is positively correlated with post-entry success (Zahoor et al., 2023). Furthermore, corporate governance enabled multinational companies to develop long-term strategies of innovation, production of technology (Miozzo & Dewick, 2002), (Zhang & Zhang, 2023) and even to survive in the subprime crisis (Joh, 2003) or any other financial crisis (Mitton, 2002). Researchers demonstrate that, even amid Korea's economic crisis, corporate governance policies had a favourable impact on a firm's value (Joh, 2003). Considering the evidence from the literature, on the impact of governance on the FP of an organisation, the following hypothesis has been formulated:

H4: The FP of banking companies in India is significantly influenced by the governance pillar of the composite ESG.

ESG and Financial Risk

According to US companies' 2016–2020 outcomes, there is a relationship between ESG performance and the likelihood of bankruptcy, with FP serving as a mediating element (Habib, 2023). The relationship between credit risk and ESG characteristics was also found in a cross-sectional study of European listed corporations (Bonacorsi et al., 2024). ESG lowers the possibility of misclassifying troubled banks as healthy, according to research on the predictive capacity of ESG indicators to forecast bank financial crises in EU commercial banks (Citterio & King, 2023). Interestingly prior to the crisis, shareholder-oriented banks performed better, but due to differences in risk appetite, they later sustained significant losses (Wu et al., 2023).

ESG disclosures play a major role in corporate decision-making, bank branch expansion, (Tian et al., 2024) corporate characteristics, stakeholders' demand, external pressure (Wang et al., 2023), and are typically linked negatively to financial risk and a firm's FP (Brooks & Oikonomou, 2018). It was observed by (financial risk5) that improving the ESG score would help in improving the financial efficiency of a company. Implementing ESG has a favourable impact on efficiency (Cao et al., 2024), reduce financial regularities (D. Liu & Jin, 2023) and mitigate risks (Ihsani et al., 2023) of an organisation. Empirical studies show that companies with strong ESG ratings can withstand significant systemic bank risk spillovers (Ling et al., 2023). However, banks with higher ESG performance are exposed to climate risk (Erhemjamts et al., 2024). Based on the evidence on the association between ESG and risk appetite of an organisation the following hypotheses have been formulated:

H5: Financial risk significantly influences the nature of relationship between FP and ESG.
H6: Financial risk significantly influences the nature of relationship between FP and the environment pillar of the composite ESG.

Based on the observations of US listed companies, companies that implement stronger Corporate Social Responsibility (CSR) practices can reduce their risk exposure, which is determined by social performance metrics in the community (Boubaker et al., 2020). Comparable research, particularly during the global financial crisis, was conducted on the positive correlation between the default risk of foreign bank subsidiaries and their parent corporations in emerging nations (Anginer et al., 2017). Based on the bankruptcy code, there is empirical evidence that financial problems can be resolved by debt restructuring and unofficial reorganization in the US real and capital asset markets (Senbet & Seward, 1995). By allaying shareholder worries, the removal of the CEO successfully reduces the detrimental impact that high reputational risks associated with ESG issues have on the risk of financial difficulties for the company (Choi et al., 2024).

Improved systemic and stand-alone risk is linked to shareholder-friendly corporate governance, particularly for financial institutions (Anginer et al., 2018). Though the ability of banks to bear risk and their financial stability were challenged during the global financial crisis, the banking institutions with a governance model focused on stakeholders and shareholders survived better during the 2008 financial crisis (Wu et al., 2023). The United States created laws to control financial stress in the 1980s. In contrast, managers who held significant equity positions were able to assume less risk following legislative improvements that strengthened the financial stability of the banking sector (Anderson & Fraser, 2000). Transparency in governance has a positive connection with banks' risk appetite (Bellardini et al., 2024). Considering the association of banks' risk appetite with the social and governance pillars, the following hypotheses has been formulated:

H7: Financial risk significantly influences the nature of relationship between FP and the social pillar of the composite ESG.

H8: Financial risk significantly influences the nature of the relationship between FP and the governance pillar of the composite ESG.

DATA AND METHODOLOGY

Panel Data

The study considered 8 major banks that are indexed in the NIFTY 100 ESG index, which is a sustainability index developed by NSE, and the data on their FP was obtained from the annual reports for 10 years. Corresponding ESG data of each banking company for 10 years were obtained from Rifinitiv, which is a database hosted by Thomson Reuters.

Variables

Financial Performance: Financial performance forms the dependent variable in this study and return on asset values (ROA) of each bank were obtained from their respective annual reports for the period of 10 years. ROA is used as a measure of FP as it indicates the profitability and efficiency of a company.

ESG Score: ESG score is considered as the independent variable for this study. ESG scores indicate the sustainability of each company and it comprises three pillars namely:

1. Environment (E)
2. Social (S)
3. Governance (G)

The data on ESG was obtained from Rifinitiv for 10 years. Also, the scores on each pillar were obtained for each company corresponding to the sample period.

Financial risk: It was observed from the literature that most of the studies have ignored the role of financial risk in FP, while analyzing its association with ESG. Considering this, the current attempts to analyse how financial risk influences the nature of relationship between FP and ESG. To measure risk attributable to each banking company included in this study, Altman Z Score values were obtained, because it is the most commonly used measure of risk.

Model

For selecting the appropriate model, a panel diagnostics was performed by estimating a pooled OLS, Fixed Effects (FE) and Random Effects (RE) models, for comparison. While estimating the models the ESG scores and ESG pillar scores have been log-transformed for better comparability. The pooled OLS model estimated for panel diagnostics had the following specifications:

ESG-FP model

$$FP_{it} = \beta_0 + \beta_1 \log ESG_{it} + \varepsilon_{it}$$

ESG Pillars-FP model

$$FP_{it} = \beta_0 + \beta_1 \log E_{it} + \beta_2 \log S_{it} + \beta_3 \log G_{it} + \epsilon_{it}$$

where FP_{it} measures the financial performance of each banking company i, during time period t. β_0 represents the average financial performance of banking companies, during 10 years, when other factors remain constant. $\beta_1 logESG_{it}$ in the ESG-FP model measure the percentage change in FP of banking company i, as a result of a percentage change in the value of ESG during time t. Whereas, $\beta_1 logE_{it}$, $\beta_2 logS_{it}$ and $\beta_3 logG_{it}$ in the ESG Pillars-FP model measures the percentage change in FP of banking company i, as a result of a percentage change in ESG Pillars E, S, and G during time t. The difference between the predicted and actual value of FP is captured by ϵ_{it} in both models, i.e., it captures the disturbances caused by other determinants of FP that are not considered in this model.

Followed by the pooled OLS estimation, a fixed effects model with the following specifications was estimated:

ESG-FP Fixed Effects model

$$FP_{it} = \alpha_i + \beta_1 logESG_{it} + u_{it}$$

ESG Pillars-FP Fixed Effects model

$$FP_{it} = \alpha_i + \beta_1 logE_{it} + \beta_2 logS_{it} + \beta_3 logG_{it} + u_{it}$$

in which the intercept and error term are different from that of a pooled OLS. Here, α_i represents the average unobserved effects across each banking company i and represents the idiosyncratic error term.

Finally, a Random Effects model with the following specification was estimated for completing the panel diagnostics:

ESG-FP Random Effects model

$$FP_{it} = \beta_0 + \beta_1 logESG_{it} + v_{it}$$

ESG Pillars-FP Random Effects model

$$FP_{it} = \beta_0 = \beta_1 logE_{it} + \beta_2 logS_{it} + \beta_3 logG_{it} + v_{it}$$

Where there is a difference in the error term compared to Pooled OLS and FE models. Here, v_{it} represents a composite error term which is inclusive of the unobserved effects a_i and the error term u_{it}.

To begin with the panel diagnostics procedure, the estimated pooled OLS model was initially compared with FE by performing a 'Joint significance of group means' test, which indicated that the pooled OLS is inadequate against FE, with $p < .01$ for both ESG and ESG Pillars models. Furthermore, the pooled OLS was compared with the RE model by performing a 'Breusch-Pagan' test, which indicated that pooled OLS is inadequate against RE, with $p < .01$ for both ESG and ESG Pillars models. Now that both the tests had rejected pooled OLS in favour of FE and RE 'Hausman' test was performed to identify whether to estimate FE or RE model for analysis. The test results indicated that RE is not adequate against FE, with $p < .01$ for both ESG and ESG Pillars models. Thus, the ESG-FP Fixed effects model and ESG Pillar-FP Fixed effects model were selected for further analysis.

RESULTS

Summary Statistics

Table 1 presents the descriptive statistics for all the variables. The results indicate that for the banking companies E(M = 1.72) and S(M = 1.78) as the important pillars in ESG (M = 1.72) with a mean value greater than G(M = 1.58). It is also evident from the table that the variables a stationary at level with $p < .01$ for all the variables.

Table 1. Descriptive statistics of FP, financial risk, ESG, and ESG pillars

Variable	Mean	Median	S.D.	Min	Max	Stationarity
ROA	0.010	0.011	0.008	-0.008	0.025	.000***
Altmanzscore	0.801	0.691	0.804	0.346	7.74	.000***
logESG	1.72	1.71	0.127	1.39	1.94	.007***
loge	1.72	1.74	0.130	1.03	1.96	.001***
logS	1.78	1.79	0.0829	1.55	1.93	.000***
Log	1.58	1.72	0.332	0.553	1.98	.010***

The correlation matrix between the variable FP, Financial risk, ESG, and ESG pillars are presented in Table 2. FP is highly correlated with ESG and Governance pillar. Among the ESG pillars, Social and Governance scores are highly correlated with ESG scores, indicating the significance of S and G pillars in elevating the ESG scores.

Table 2. Correlation matrix

ROA	Altmanzscore	logESG	logE	logS	log	
1.0000	0.1422	0.6031	0.2817	0.3564	0.6529	**ROA**
	1.0000	-0.0210	-0.0017	-0.0032	0.0760	**Altmanzscore**

continued on following page

Table 2. Continued

ROA	Altmanzscore	logESG	logE	logS	log	
		1.0000	0.4039	0.8523	0.8780	**logESG**
			1.0000	0.4789	0.1606	**logE**
				1.0000	0.5489	**logS**
					1.0000	**logG**

Regression Results

ESG-FP Fixed Effects Model

Table 3 presents the ESG-FP FE model. The residual diagnostics results of the model indicate that the residuals are normally distributed with p > .05, and the Wooldridge test for autocorrelation indicates that there is no first order autocorrelation, with p > .05. However, the residuals fail to pass the heteroskedasticity test, and thus rosbuts standard errors were used while estimating the model. The H1 stated was that there exists a significant relationship between FP and ESG. However, it can be observed from the model that when ESG changes by 1% the change in FP is nominal (.003%) with p > .05. Thus, rejecting H1, which means that ESG does not significantly influence the FP.

Table 3. ESG-FP FE model

Variables	Coefficient	Std. Error	t-ratio	p-value
Const	0.00401505	0.0112476	0.3570	0.7316
logESG	0.00357187	0.00655792	0.5447	0.6029

Obs = 80
R squared = .69

However, it was stated in H5 that financial risk significantly influences the nature of relationship between ESG and FP. The results of the modified ESG-FP model with dummies for measuring the role of financial risk in ESG-FP relationship presented in Table 4 indicate that the average FP significantly decrease by -.04% when the banks are risky. Also, the .02% decrease in FP as a result of a 1% increase in ESG, is now significant at p < .01. The coefficient of ESGr which measures the change caused by risk in the ESG-FP relationship indicate that FP is .03% more sensitive to ESG when banks are at risk, with p < .01, thus accepting H5. This means that, financial risk has a mediating effect on the nature of relationship between FP and ESG.

Table 4. ESG-FP model with financial risk dummies

Variables	Coefficient	Std. Error	t-ratio	p-value
Const	0.0486910	0.00765057	6.364	0.0004
Risk	−0.0492393	0.00667997	−7.371	0.0002
logESG	−0.0230919	0.00462001	−4.998	0.0016
logESGr	0.0292859	0.00382940	7.648	0.0001

Obs = 80
R squared = .69

Table 5 presents the ESG Pillars-FP FE model. Normality test performed on the residuals indicate that the residuals are normally distributed with $p > .05$, and the Wooldridge test for autocorrelation indicates that there is no first order autocorrelation, with $p > .05$. However, the residuals fail to pass the heteroskedasticity test, and thus robust standard errors were used while estimating the model. It can be observed from the model that when there is a 1% increase in the Environment pillar of banking companies, there is a nominal increase in their FP which is significant, with $p < .05$. Thus, accepting the H2 that Environment score significantly influences the FP of banking companies. Whereas, the increase in FP as a result of 1% increase Social, and Governance pillars are not significant, with $p > .05$. Thus, rejecting H3 that Social score significantly influences the FP and H4 that the Governance score significantly influences the FP, of banking companies.

Table 5. ESG pillars-FP FE model

Variables	Coefficient	Std. Error	t-ratio	p-value
Const	0.00188722	0.009	0.2018	0.846
loge	0.00973803	0.003	2.800	0.0265
logS	0.000498253	0.006	0.085	0.935
log	−0.00594693	0.005	−1.231	0.258

Obs = 80
R squared = .71

However, the results of the modified ESG Pillar-FP FE model with dummies for measuring the role of financial risk in the nature of relationship between individual ESG Pillar and FP presented in Table 6 indicate that the average FP significantly decrease by -.07% when the banks are risky. Also, FP significantly increase by .02% with a 1% increase in Environmental score which is non-significant when the banks are at risk. On the other hand, FP significantly decreases by .04% when there is a 1% increase in social score while the banks are at risk. Since the p value for interactive dummy Er is greater than .05, H6 that financial risk significantly influences the nature of the relationship between pillar E and FP, is rejected. Whereas, H7 which states that financial risk significantly influences the nature of relationship between pillar S and FP is accepted with p < .01 for the interactive dummy Sr. Thus, it indicates that while financial risk significantly influence how FP reacts to social responsibility of banks, it does not influence how FP react to environmental investments by banks in India. For pillar G the model fails to obtain results for the interactive dummy due to exact multicollinearity.

Table 6. ESG pillar-FP FE model with financial risk dummies

Variables	Coefficient	Std. Error	t-ratio	p-value
const	0.0702784	0.0174534	4.027	0.0001
risk	−0.0727909	0.0199696	−3.645	0.0005
logE	0.0210778	0.0186269	1.132	0.2619
logS	−0.0494856	0.00507493	−9.751	<0.0001
logG	−0.00737634	0.00481302	−1.533	0.1302
logEr	−0.0115487	0.0191193	−0.6040	0.5479
logSr	0.0539207	0.00927884	5.811	<0.0001

Obs = 80
R squared = .72

DISCUSSION

The results presented in the previous section underscore the multifaceted nature of the ESG-FP relationship, highlighting the role played by financial risk and the impact of individual ESG pillars on FP within the banking sector. These insights contribute to the theoretical understanding of ESG integration and also possess practical implications for stakeholders seeking to navigate the evolving landscape of sustainable finance. The results emphasise the significance of Environmental and Social pillars within the ESG framework for banking companies. It is interesting to note the high correlation between FP and ESG, which is further accentuated by the strong association between FP and Governance (Lubbe et al., 1995; Inoue & Lee, 2011; Alatawi et al., 2023). Furthermore, within the ESG pillars, Social and Governance scores emerge as highly correlated with ESG scores, signifying their pronounced influence on the overall ESG scores among of the banking companies in India. Such insights underscore the interconnectedness between FP and ESG considerations, warranting deeper exploration.

The ESG-FP FE model provided valuable insights into the nuances in the nature of relationship between ESG and FP. Notably, the nominal change in FP in response to ESG variations failed to be significance, challenging the ESG-FP relationship. However, the subsequent introduction of financial risk in the modified model yields intriguing results, confirming the spillover effect of. The significant decrease in FP amidst heightened banking risk underscores the interplay between risk exposure and FP. Moreover, the heightened sensitivity of FP to ESG under risky conditions accentuates the nuanced nature of this relationship, providing empirical support for its significance.

Furthermore, the ESG Pillars-FP FE model delves into the differential influence of individual ESG pillars on FP. While the Environment pillar emerges as a significant influencer of FP, the Social and Governance pillars fail to exhibit significant effects. The negative values of social and governance pillars indicates that social and governance risk is negatively associated with FP of banks. This is in contrast to Wu et al., (2023), who had observed a positive association between the risk appetite and governance practices of banks. Nonetheless, the incorporation of financial risk in the modified model reveals further complexities, confirming the differential influence of risk exposure on FP across different pillars. While environmental considerations exhibit a modest yet significant influence on FP, the effects of social responsibility manifest more prominently under conditions of heightened risk. Notably, the nuanced dynamics highlighted by the interactive dummies underscore the multifaceted nature of the ESG-FP relationship, warranting a holistic approach to analysis.

CONCLUSION

The present study investigated the intricate relationship between environmental, social, and governance (ESG) factors and FP within the banking sector in India. It was found that the E and S pillars, surpass the G pillar, in shaping the overall ESG framework for banking companies. Evidence on stronger associations between FP, ESG, and its individual pillars were found, emphasizing the interconnectedness between the variables. While the direct ESG-FP relationship fails was not significant, the inclusion of financial risk unravels nuanced dynamics, highlighting its substantial impact on the nature of the ESG-FP relationship. Furthermore, the modified models elucidate the differential influence of financial risk across ESG pillars, with environmental considerations emerging as a significant influencer of FP. However, the effects of social and governance pillars were found to be more prominent during heightened risk, emphasising the multifaceted nature of the ESG-FP relationship. These findings contribute to both theoretical understanding and practical implications within sustainable finance, emphasizing the need for a holistic approach to analysis. By shedding light on the role of financial risk and the nuanced influence of individual ESG pillars, this study informs stakeholders navigating the evolving landscape of ESG integration in banking, facilitating informed decision-making and promoting sustainable practices. However, the study had considered only financial risk as a mediating factor, whereas the relationship between FP and ESG can influenced by other systematic and unsystematic risks. Future research can be directed towards identifying the quadratic relationship (R. El Khoury, 2021) between FP and ESG by comprehensively controlling the effects of both systematic and unsystematic risks.

REFERENCES

Alatawi, I. A., Ntim, C. G., Zras, A., & Elmagrhi, M. H. (2023). CSR, financial and non-financial performance in the tourism sector: A systematic literature review and future research agenda. *International Review of Financial Analysis*, 89, 102734. 10.1016/j.irfa.2023.102734

Amaral, M. R., Willerding, I. V. A., & Lapolli, É. M. (2023). ESG and sustainability: The impact of the pillar social. *Concilium*, 23(13), 186–199. 10.53660/CLM-1643-23J43

Anderson, R. C., & Fraser, D. R. (2000). Corporate control, bank risk taking, and the health of the banking industry. *Journal of Banking & Finance*, 24(8), 1383–1398. 10.1016/S0378-4266(99)00088-6

Anginer, D., Cerutti, E., & Martínez Pería, M. S. (2017). Foreign bank subsidiaries' default risk during the global crisis: What factors help insulate affiliates from their parents? *Journal of Financial Intermediation*, 29, 19–31. 10.1016/j.jfi.2016.05.004

Anginer, D., Demirguc-Kunt, A., Huizinga, H., & Ma, K. (2018). Corporate governance of banks and financial stability. *Journal of Financial Economics*, 130(2), 327–346. 10.1016/j.jfineco.2018.06.011

Bellardini, L., Murro, P., & Previtali, D. (2024). Measuring the risk appetite of bank-controlling shareholders: The Risk-Weighted Ownership index. *Global Finance Journal*, 60, 100935. 10.1016/j.gfj.2024.100935

Berman, S. L., Wicks, A. C., Kotha, S., & Jones, T. M. (1999). Does stakeholder orientation matter? The relationship between stakeholder management models and firm financial performance. *Academy of Management Journal*, 42(5), 488–506. 10.2307/256972

Bernardi, C., & Stark, A. W. (2018). Environmental, social and governance disclosure, integrated reporting, and the accuracy of analyst forecasts. *The Effects of Environmental. The British Accounting Review*, 50(1), 16–31. 10.1016/j.bar.2016.10.001

Bianchi, N., Carretta, A., Farina, V., & Fiordelisi, F. (2021). Does espoused risk culture pay? Evidence from European banks. *Journal of Banking & Finance*, 122, 105767. 10.1016/j.jbankfin.2020.105767

Blair, M. M. (2001). Corporate Governance. In Smelser, N. J., & Baltes, P. B. (Eds.), *International Encyclopedia of the Social & Behavioral Sciences* (pp. 2797–2803). Pergamon., 10.1016/B0-08-043076-7/04292-3

Bonacorsi, L., Cerasi, V., Galfrascoli, P., & Manera, M. (2024). ESG Factors and Firms' Credit Risk. *Journal of Climate Finance*, 6, 100032. 10.1016/j.jclimf.2024.100032

Boubaker, S., Cellier, A., Manita, R., & Saeed, A. (2020). Does corporate social responsibility reduce financial distress risk? *Economic Modelling*, 91, 835–851. 10.1016/j.econmod.2020.05.012

Broadstock, D. C., Matousek, R., Meyer, M., & Tzeremes, N. G. (2020). Does corporate social responsibility impact firms' innovation capacity? The indirect link between environmental & social governance implementation and innovation performance. *Journal of Business Research*, 119, 99–110. 10.1016/j.jbusres.2019.07.014

Brooks, C., & Oikonomou, I. (2018). The effects of environmental, social and governance disclosures and performance on firm value: A review of the literature in accounting and finance. *The Effects of Environmental. The British Accounting Review*, 50(1), 1–15. 10.1016/j.bar.2017.11.005

Bushman, R. M., & Smith, A. J. (2001). Financial accounting information and corporate governance. *Journal of Accounting and Economics*, 32(1), 237–333. 10.1016/S0165-4101(01)00027-1

Cao, Q., Zhu, T., & Yu, W. (2024). ESG investment and bank efficiency: Evidence from China. *Energy Economics*, 133, 107516. 10.1016/j.eneco.2024.107516

Carroll, A. B. (1991). The pyramid of corporate social responsibility: Toward the moral management of organizational stakeholders. *Business Horizons*, 34(4), 39–48. 10.1016/0007-6813(91)90005-G

Choi, D., Gam, Y. K., Kang, M. J., & Shin, H. (2024). The effect of ESG-motivated turnover on firm financial risk. *The British Accounting Review*, 101373, 101373. Advance online publication. 10.1016/j.bar.2024.101373

Citterio, A., & King, T. (2023). The role of Environmental, Social, and Governance (ESG) in predicting bank financial distress. *Finance Research Letters*, 51, 103411. 10.1016/j.frl.2022.103411

Curcio, D., Gianfrancesco, I., Onorato, G., & Vioto, D. (2024). Do ESG scores affect financial systemic risk? Evidence from European banks and insurers. *Research in International Business and Finance*, 69, 102251. 10.1016/j.ribaf.2024.102251

Danisman, G. O., & Tarazi, A. (2024). ESG activity and bank lending during financial crises. *Journal of Financial Stability*, 70, 101206. 10.1016/j.jfs.2023.101206

Davis, E. P. (2002). Institutional investors, corporate governance and the performance of the corporate sector. *Economic Systems*, 26(3), 203–229. 10.1016/S0939-3625(02)00044-4

Docekalova, M. P., & Kocmanova, A. (2015). Evaluation of the Effectiveness of Manufacturing Companies by Financial and Non-financial Indicators. *20th International Scientific Conference 'Economics and Management 2015 (ICEM-2015)', 213*, 491–496. 10.1016/j.sbspro.2015.11.439

Ehrenhard, M. L., & Fiorito, T. L. (2018). Corporate values of the 25 largest European banks: Exploring the ambiguous link with corporate scandals. *Journal of Public Affairs*, 18(1), e1700. Advance online publication. 10.1002/pa.1700

Erhemjamts, O., Huang, K., & Tehranian, H. (2024). Climate risk, ESG performance, and ESG sentiment in US commercial banks. *Global Finance Journal*, 59, 100924. 10.1016/j.gfj.2023.100924

Forgione, A. F., & Migliardo, C. (2020). CSR engagement and market structure: Evidence from listed banks. *Finance Research Letters*, 35, 101592. 10.1016/j.frl.2020.101592

Galletta, S., Goodell, J. W., Mazzù, S., & Paltrinieri, A. (2023). Bank reputation and operational risk: The impact of ESG. *Finance Research Letters*, 51, 103494. 10.1016/j.frl.2022.103494

Gangi, F., Meles, A., D'Angelo, E., & Daniele, L. M. (2019). Sustainable development and corporate governance in the financial system: Are environmentally friendly banks less risky? *Corporate Social Responsibility and Environmental Management*, 26(3), 529–547. 10.1002/csr.1699

Gao, W., Li, M., & Zou, C. (2023). Analysis of the Impact of ESG on Corporate Financial Performance under the Epidemic Based on Static and Dynamic Panel Data. *Wireless Communications and Mobile Computing*, 2023, 1–1. 10.1155/2023/9816809

Gonçalves, T. C., Barros, V., & Avelar, J. V. (2023). Environmental, social and governance scores in Europe: What drives financial performance for larger firms? *Economics and Business Letters*, 12(2), 121–131. 10.17811/ebl.12.2.2023.121-131

Habib, A. M. (2023). Do business strategies and environmental, social, and governance (ESG) performance mitigate the likelihood of financial distress? A multiple mediation model. *Heliyon*, 9(7), e17847. 10.1016/j.heliyon.2023.e1784737483754

Hardjono, T. W., & van Marrewijk, M. (2001). The Social Dimensions of Business Excellence. *Corporate Environmental Strategy*, 8(3), 223–233. 10.1016/S1066-7938(01)00125-7

Hopkins, M. J. D. (2002). Sustainability in the Internal Operations of Companies. *Corporate Environmental Strategy*, 9(4), 398–408. 10.1016/S1066-7938(02)00121-5

Ihsani, A. N., Nidar, S. R., & Kurniawan, M. (2023). Does ESG Performance Affect Financial Performance? Evidence from Indonesia. *Wiga : Jurnal Penelitian Ilmu Ekonomi*, 13(1), 46–61. 10.30741/wiga.v13i1.968

Inoue, Y., & Lee, S. (2011). Effects of different dimensions of corporate social responsibility on corporate financial performance in tourism-related industries. *Tourism Management*, 32(4), 790–804. 10.1016/j.tourman.2010.06.019

Joh, S. W. (2003). Corporate governance and firm profitability: Evidence from Korea before the economic crisis. *Journal of Financial Economics*, 68(2), 287–322. 10.1016/S0304-405X(03)00068-0

Johnson, S., Boone, P., Breach, A., & Friedman, E. (2000). Corporate governance in the Asian financial crisis. *Journal of Financial Economics*, 58(1), 141–186. 10.1016/S0304-405X(00)00069-6

Khurram, M. U., Abbassi, W., Chen, Y., & Chen, L. (2024). Outward foreign investment performance, digital transformation, and ESG performance: Evidence from China. *Global Finance Journal*, 60, 100963. 10.1016/j.gfj.2024.100963

La Porta, R., Lopez-de-Silanes, F., Shleifer, A., & Vishny, R. (2000). Investor protection and corporate governance. *Journal of Financial Economics*, 58(1), 3–27. 10.1016/S0304-405X(00)00065-9

Lee, C.-C., Lu, M., Wang, C.-W., & Cheng, C.-Y. (2024). ESG engagement, country-level political risk and bank liquidity creation. *Pacific-Basin Finance Journal*, 83, 102260. 10.1016/j.pacfin.2024.102260

Lee, J. E., & Yang, Y. S. (2022). The Impact of Corporate Social Responsibility Performance Feedback on Corporate Social Responsibility Performance. *Frontiers in Psychology*, 13, 893193. Advance online publication. 10.3389/fpsyg.2022.89319335664210

Ling, A., Li, J., & Zhang, Y. (2023). Can firms with higher ESG ratings bear higher bank systemic tail risk spillover?—Evidence from Chinese A-share market. *Pacific-Basin Finance Journal*, 80, 102097. 10.1016/j.pacfin.2023.102097

Liu, D., & Jin, S. (2023). How Does Corporate ESG Performance Affect Financial Irregularities? *Sustainability (Basel)*, 15(13), 9999. Advance online publication. 10.3390/su15139999

Liu, H., Wu, K., & Zhou, Q. (2022). Whether and How ESG Impacts on Corporate Financial Performance in the Yangtze River Delta of China. *Sustainability (Basel)*, 14(24), 16584. Advance online publication. 10.3390/su142416584

Liu, K., Wang, J., Liu, L., & Huang, Y. (2023). Mixed-ownership reform of SOEs and ESG performance: Evidence from China. *Economic Analysis and Policy*, 80, 1618–1641. 10.1016/j.eap.2023.10.016

Liu, Z., & Li, X. (2024). The impact of bank fintech on ESG greenwashing. *Finance Research Letters*, 62, 105199. 10.1016/j.frl.2024.105199

Lubbe, S., Parker, G., & Hoard, A. (1995). The profit impact of IT investment. *Journal of Information Technology*, 10(1), 44–51. 10.1177/026839629501000106

Maquieira, C. P., Arias, J. T., & Espinosa-Méndez, C. (2024). The impact of ESG on the default risk of family firms: International evidence. *Research in International Business and Finance*, 67, 102136. 10.1016/j.ribaf.2023.102136

Mazzacurati, J. (2021). *ESG ratings: Status and key issues ahead.*

Miozzo, M., & Dewick, P. (2002). Building competitive advantage: Innovation and corporate governance in European construction. *Research Policy*, 31(6), 989–1008. 10.1016/S0048-7333(01)00173-1

Miralles-Quirós, M. M., Miralles-Quirós, J. L., & Redondo-Hernández, J. (2019). The impact of environmental, social, and governance performance on stock prices: Evidence from the banking industry. *Corporate Social Responsibility and Environmental Management*, 26(6), 1446–1456. 10.1002/csr.1759

Mitton, T. (2002). A cross-firm analysis of the impact of corporate governance on the East Asian financial crisis. *Journal of Financial Economics*, 64(2), 215–241. 10.1016/S0304-405X(02)00076-4

Nicolo, G., Zampone, G., Sannino, G., & Tiron-Tudor, A. (2023). Worldwide evidence of corporate governance influence on ESG disclosure in the utilities sector. *Utilities Policy*, 82, 101549. 10.1016/j.jup.2023.101549

Pater, L. R., & Cristea, S. L. (2016). Systemic Definitions of Sustainability, Durability and Longevity. *13th International Symposium in Management: Management During and After the Economic Crisis, 221*, 362–371. 10.1016/j.sbspro.2016.05.126

Pham Vo Ninh, B., Do Thanh, T., & Vo Hong, D. (2018). Financial distress and bankruptcy prediction: An appropriate model for listed firms in Vietnam. *Economic Systems*, 42(4), 616–624. 10.1016/j.ecosys.2018.05.002

Rizqi, M. A., & Munari, M. (2023). Effect ESG on Financial Performance. *Owner*, 7(3), 2537–2546. 10.33395/owner.v7i3.1600

Sadaa, A. M., Ganesan, Y., Yet, C. E., Alkhazaleh, Q., Alnoor, A., & aldegis, A. M. (2023). Corporate governance as antecedents and financial distress as a consequence of credit risk. Evidence from Iraqi banks. *Journal of Open Innovation*, 9(2), 100051. 10.1016/j.joitmc.2023.100051

Schonherr, N., Findler, F., & Martinuzzi, A. (2017). Exploring the interface of CSR and the Sustainable Development Goals. *Transnational Corporations*, 24(3), 33–47. 10.18356/cfb5b8b6-en

Senbet, L. W., & Seward, J. K. (1995). Financial distress, bankruptcy and reorganization. In *Handbooks in Operations Research and Management Science* (Vol. 9, pp. 921–961). Elsevier., 10.1016/S0927-0507(05)80072-6

Shayan, N. F., Mohabbati-Kalejahi, N., Alavi, S., & Zahed, M. A. (2022). Sustainable Development Goals (SDGs) as a Framework for Corporate Social Responsibility (CSR). *Sustainability (Basel)*, 14(3), 1222. Advance online publication. 10.3390/su14031222

Teng, X., Ge, Y., Wu, K. S., Chang, B. G., Kuo, L., & Zhang, X. (2022). Too little or too much? Exploring the inverted U-shaped nexus between voluntary environmental, social and governance and corporate financial performance. *Frontiers in Environmental Science*, 10, 969721. Advance online publication. 10.3389/fenvs.2022.969721

Tian, Z., Shen, Y., & Chen, Z. (2024). How does bank branch expansion affect ESG: Evidence from Chinese commercial banks. *Economic Analysis and Policy*, 82, 502–514. 10.1016/j.eap.2024.03.025

Tykvová, T., & Borell, M. (2012). Do private equity owners increase risk of financial distress and bankruptcy? *Journal of Corporate Finance*, 18(1), 138–150. 10.1016/j.jcorpfin.2011.11.004

Ukko, J., Nasiri, M., Saunila, M., & Rantala, T. (2019). Sustainability strategy as a moderator in the relationship between digital business strategy and financial performance. *Journal of Cleaner Production*, 236, 117626. 10.1016/j.jclepro.2019.117626

Velte, P. (2017). Does ESG performance have an impact on financial performance? Evidence from Germany. *Journal of Global Responsibility*, 8(2), 169–178. 10.1108/JGR-11-2016-0029

Wang, K., Chen, X., & Wang, C. (2023). The impact of sustainable development planning in resource-based cities on corporate ESG–Evidence from China. *Energy Economics*, 127, 107087. 10.1016/j.eneco.2023.107087

Wang, Z., & Sarkis, J. (2017). Corporate social responsibility governance, outcomes, and financial performance. *Journal of Cleaner Production*, 162, 1607–1616. 10.1016/j.jclepro.2017.06.142

Williams, Z. (2022). The Materiality Challenge of ESG Ratings. *Economics and Culture*, 19(2), 97–108. 10.2478/jec-2022-0019

Wu, M.-W., Shen, C.-H., Hsu, H.-H., & Chiu, P.-H. (2023). Why did a bank with good governance perform worse during the financial crisis? The views of shareholder and stakeholder orientations. *Pacific-Basin Finance Journal*, 82, 102127. 10.1016/j.pacfin.2023.102127

Xiao, K. (2023). How does Environment, Social and Governance Affect the Financial Performance of Enterprises? *SHS Web of Conferences, 163*, 04015. 10.1051/shsconf/202316304015

Xie, J., Nozawa, W., Yagi, M., Fujii, H., & Managi, S. (2019). Do environmental, social, and governance activities improve corporate financial performance? *Business Strategy and the Environment*, 28(2), 286–300. 10.1002/bse.2224

Yadav, P., Singh, J., Srivastava, D. K., & Mishra, V. (2021). Environmental pollution and sustainability. In Singh, P., Verma, P., Perrotti, D., & Srivastava, K. K. (Eds.), *Environmental Sustainability and Economy* (pp. 111–120). Elsevier., 10.1016/B978-0-12-822188-4.00015-4

Yu, J. (2024). Stabilizing leverage, financial technology innovation, and commercial bank risks: Evidence from China. *Economic Modelling*, 131, 106599. 10.1016/j.econmod.2023.106599

Zahoor, N., Lew, Y. K., Arslan, A., Christofi, M., & Tarba, S. Y. (2023). International corporate social responsibility and post-entry performance of developing market INVs: The moderating role of corporate governance mechanisms. *Journal of International Management*, 29(4), 101036. 10.1016/j.intman.2023.101036

Zhang, C., & Zhang, D. (2023). Executive incentives, team stability and corporate innovation performance. *Finance Research Letters*, 58, 104690. 10.1016/j.frl.2023.104690

Zhang, D., & Liu, L. (2022). Does ESG Performance Enhance Financial Flexibility? Evidence from China. *Sustainability (Basel)*, 14(18), 11324. Advance online publication. 10.3390/su141811324

Chapter 12
Building Brand Reputation and Fostering Customer Loyalty Through ESG Practices:
A Strategic Imperative for Competitive Advantage

Shreyanshu Singh
https://orcid.org/0000-0001-8745-6227
Babu Banarasi Das University, Lucknow, India

Rinki Verma
Babu Banarsi Das University, Lucknow, India

Afeefa Fatima
Babu Banarsi Das University, Lucknow, India

Manoj Kumar
https://orcid.org/0000-0002-8325-6612
Shri Ramswaroop Memorial University, Barabanki, India

ABSTRACT

This study investigates the intricate relationship between Environmental, Social, and Governance (ESG) practices and their influence on brand reputation and customer loyalty, within the goal of achieving competitive advantage. Employing a quantitative research methodology, this study utilizes a survey to gather insights from consumers regarding their perceptions of ESG initiatives and loyalty to sus-

DOI: 10.4018/979-8-3693-3880-3.ch012

tainable brands. Through statistical analyses, including regression analysis, this paper furnishes empirical evidence of the strategic importance of ESG practices in bolstering brand reputation and nurturing customer loyalty. Additionally, this research explores challenges and opportunities in the adoption and implementation of ESG practices, shedding light on complexities faced by organizations. By elucidating the nexus between ESG initiatives and brand loyalty, this study contributes to the literature on sustainable business strategies and provides insights for businesses in a competitive and socially conscious marketplace.

1. Introduction

Environmental, Social, and Governance practices have become increasingly important to organizations as they acknowledge the significance of addressing sustainability and social responsibility concerns. ESG practices encompass a company's policies and actions pertaining to environmental impact, social issues, and corporate governance. These practices are designed to foster constructive transformation, advocate for moral conduct, and mitigate potential hazards in order to attain enduring value for the firm and its stakeholders. Companies that prioritize environmental, social, and governance (ESG) practices not only contribute to the well-being of the environment and society but also stand to benefit from improved brand reputation and heightened customer loyalty. The implementation of Environmental, Social, and Governance (ESG) principles can significantly influence a company's brand reputation and customer loyalty. Modern consumers prioritize not only the quality and cost of goods and services, but also seek to endorse companies that share their values and contribute positively to society and the environment. Evidence suggests that there is an increasing need for sustainable and socially conscious products and services, with customers being prepared to spend more money on them (Guerrero, 2020; Demitriades & Zilakaki, 2019). Companies are reassessing their sustainability strategies and giving priority to efforts that line with environmental, social, and governance (ESG) principles because to the increasing recognition of climate change, social inequity, and corporate accountability (Grewal et al., 2021). This change demonstrates a wider acknowledgment of the interdependence between corporate activities, the welfare of society, and the responsible management of the environment. Establishing and enhancing brand reputation and cultivating customer loyalty through Environmental, Social, and Governance (ESG) policies has become a crucial strategic priority for organizations in the current highly competitive business environment. Multiple studies have established a correlation between Environmental, Social, and Governance (ESG) practices and the reputation of a company as well as the loyalty of its customers. For instance, a study conducted by Atkinson and

Rosler in 2017 discovered that organizations that prioritize environmental, social, and governance (ESG) policies are more inclined to possess a favorable brand reputation. Consequently, this favorable reputation results in higher levels of customer loyalty and trust. Moreover, a study conducted by Kiel and colleagues emphasized the favorable influence of ESG practices on a company's financial performance, indicating that organizations that prioritize sustainability and social responsibility might attain a competitive edge in the market. Brands that adopt ESG principles not only improve their reputation but also cultivate closer connections with customers who hold similar values (Saeidi et al., 2015). Furthermore, implementing ESG principles can assist organizations in reducing risks and developing the ability to withstand environmental and social difficulties.

This study distinguishes itself from previous research by conducting a thorough investigation into the interaction between ESG practices, brand reputation, and customer loyalty. Additionally, it examines the mediating role of brand reputation and the moderating influence of demographic characteristics. This comprehensive method offers a detailed comprehension of how ESG activities impact consumer behavior and purchasing choices, providing significant information for organizations seeking to utilize ESG for a competitive edge.

1.1 Objectives of the Research

The main aims of this study are as follows:

1. To thoroughly analyze the influence of ESG practices on brand reputation by clarifying the several aspects that drive consumer perceptions and attitudes towards sustainability initiatives.
2. To examine the complex connection between ESG practices and customer loyalty, by identifying the fundamental factors that generates consumer loyalty in the context of corporate sustainability initiatives.
3. To examine how brand reputation acts as a mediator in the connection between ESG practices and customer loyalty. This involves understanding the ways in which ESG activities impact consumer behavior and purchasing choices.
4. To evaluate how demographic variables influence the connection between ESG practices, brand reputation, and customer loyalty. This analysis aims to discover potential differences across various consumer categories and demographic profiles.

2. The Strategic Imperative of ESG Practices

ESG considerations cover a variety of measures that corporations use to assess their influence on society and the environment, as well as their governance systems. ESG factors encompass environmental considerations such as mitigating climate change, improving resource efficiency, and preventing pollution; social factors such as labor practices, human rights, and community engagement; and governance factors such as transparent corporate practices, diverse board composition, and ethical leadership (PwC, 2023).

ESG has seen a significant transformation in recent years, transitioning from a specialized issue to a widely recognized and essential aspect of business. Businesses in all sectors are progressively acknowledging the significance of incorporating ESG factors into their fundamental business strategies. The transition has occurred due to various factors, such as evolving consumer preferences, increased regulatory scrutiny, and rising investor desire for sustainable investment options (Deloitte, 2022).

The rationale for incorporating ESG standards into corporate operations is persuasive and has multiple aspects. First and foremost, organizations that give priority to ESG efforts have the potential to gain financial advantages through increased operational efficiency, decreased expenses, and higher revenue prospects. Investments in energy efficiency and renewable energy technology have the potential to generate substantial long-term cost savings. Similarly, efforts to minimize waste and improve resource efficiency can strengthen the resilience and competitiveness of supply chains (Accenture, 2023).

Furthermore, the incorporation of ESG standards can assist organizations in reducing the potential negative impacts linked to environmental, social, and governance concerns. Companies can mitigate their vulnerability to regulatory fines, legal liabilities, and reputational harm by aggressively addressing environmental risks, such as the impacts of climate change, and social risks, such as labor disputes or community conflicts (EY, 2023).

Ultimately, adopting ESG principles is crucial for generating sustainable value over an extended period of time and establishing trust with stakeholders. Companies that exhibit a dedication to sustainability and conscientious business practices are more inclined to attract and retain consumers, employees, and investors that prioritize ethical and socially responsible conduct (McKinsey & Company, 2022). Furthermore, when organizations match their commercial aims with wider societal and environmental goals, they can make a positive impact on social and environmental issues while simultaneously improving their brand image and market competitiveness.

The importance and necessity of ESG practices are of utmost significance. Companies can uncover financial opportunities, manage risks, and create long-term value for stakeholders by incorporating ESG concerns into their business plans. This also helps contribute to a more sustainable and fair future.

3. Building Brand Reputation through ESG Practices

ESG practices have become influential means of improving brand reputation and perception in the current corporate environment. This section examines the influence of ESG activities on how a brand is perceived, showcases examples of organizations successfully utilizing ESG to improve their brand, and emphasizes the significance of openly and genuinely conveying ESG commitments to stakeholders.

ESG initiatives are crucial in influencing consumers' perception and engagement with brands. Research has demonstrated that organizations that prioritize and excel in ESG policies are perceived more positively by customers, resulting in improved brand reputation and customer loyalty (Ali et al., 2021; Flammer & Luo, 2017). By incorporating sustainability concepts into their operations, organizations can distinguish themselves from rivals, appeal to ecologically and socially aware consumers, and establish enduring partnerships founded on trust and credibility (Luo & Bhattacharya, 2006; Fatma & Khan, 2023).

Companies in several sectors have showcased the efficacy of ESG practices in enhancing brand reputation. Patagonia's dedication to environmental sustainability and ethical sourcing has not only appealed to consumers but has also bolstered the company's expansion and profitability (Accenture, 2023). Unilever's Sustainable Living Plan is a prime illustration of how a thorough ESG strategy may stimulate innovation, entice top-notch personnel, and enhance brand devotion (Deloitte, 2022).

Transparency and sincerity are fundamental principles of effective communication when it comes to ESG commitments. It is imperative for companies to not only adopt sustainable practices but also effectively and openly communicate them to stakeholders, such as consumers, investors, and workers (PwC, 2023). Establishing trust through transparent and sincere communication enhances connections with stakeholders and bolsters the legitimacy of a company's environmental, social, and governance (ESG) initiatives (Ernst & Young, 2023).

By strategically incorporating ESG practices, organizations can seize a distinct opportunity to improve their brand reputation, distinguish themselves in the market, and establish significant relationships with stakeholders. Organizations can use ESG as a powerful tool to strengthen their brand and achieve long-term success by placing importance on transparency, authenticity, and a sincere dedication to sustainability.

4. ESG as a Driver of Competitive Advantage

ESG aspects serve as catalysts for gaining a competitive edge. Companies can utilize their ESG performance to distinguish themselves in the market, gain entry into new markets and customer segments, and generate enduring value.

Companies that give priority to ESG factors can set themselves apart from their competitors by showcasing a firm dedication to sustainability, ethics, and social responsibility (Guerrero, 2020). Companies can improve their brand name, attract environmentally and socially conscious consumers, and charge higher prices for their products and services by adopting strong ESG principles in their operations (Kim & Lyon, 2011).

Companies that demonstrate ESG leadership can gain entry into emerging markets and attract customer segments that place a high value on sustainability and ethical business practices (Lee et al., 2021). Companies can obtain a competitive advantage in emerging markets by integrating their products, services, and marketing strategies with ESG principles, which will allow them to meet the increasing demand for sustainable alternatives (Kim et al., 2021).

ESG practices have been acknowledged as a means of achieving a lasting competitive advantage, fostering long-term value generation, and enhancing organizational resilience (Jones, 1995). Companies that incorporate ESG factors into their strategic decision-making processes are more capable of reducing risks, adjusting to evolving market conditions, and taking advantage of emerging prospects. This enhances their long-term sustainability and achievement (Barney, 1991).

ESG aspects act as influential catalysts for gaining a competitive edge, allowing organizations to distinguish themselves, penetrate untapped markets, and generate enduring value over time. Companies can strengthen their competitiveness and contribute to positive societal and environmental results by incorporating sustainability, ethics, and social responsibility into their business plans.

5. Literature Review

5.1 ESG Practices and Brand Reputation

The relationship between ESG practices and brand reputation has received significant attention in recent academic research. Companies are rapidly realizing that strong ESG strategies are not only crucial for ethical and sustainable company operations but also essential for improving brand reputation. This section examines recent research that emphasizes the significance of ESG practices in establishing and preserving a favorable brand image.

5.1.1 ESG and Brand Trust

Recent research highlights the crucial significance of ESG practices in promoting brand confidence. Tripopsakul & Puriwat (2022) contend that organizations possessing robust ESG credentials are regarded as more reliable and socially conscientious, resulting in an improved brand reputation. Khan & Fatma (2023) have shown evidence that consumers' trust in a business experiences a notable boost when they see the company as dedicated to ESG principles. Flammer and Luo (2017) provide evidence that transparent and authentic disclosures of ESG activities can greatly enhance a company's reputation among stakeholders, hence strengthening the connection between ESG practices and brand trust.

5.1.2 Perception of Consumers and Differentiation of Brands

ESG standards have emerged as a crucial factor that sets companies apart in highly competitive marketplaces. (Tran, 2022) It has been emphasized that customers are increasingly assessing brands based on their ESG performance, and brands that excel in ESG are viewed more positively. Having a positive perception is essential for distinguishing a brand in a competitive market. In addition, Tripopsakul and Puriwat (2022). It is important to highlight that effectively communicating sustainability activities can set a company apart and improve its reputation. Given that consumers nowadays are well-informed and conscientious, it is crucial to consider that they frequently select products that align with their personal beliefs and dedication to sustainability.

5.1.3 Impact on Financial Performance and Brand Value

Increasing research indicates that robust ESG performance has a favorable effect on financial success, ultimately leading to the enhancement of brand value. In their study, Eccles et al. (2014) discovered that organizations that implement strong environmental, social, and governance (ESG) practices generally have reduced capital costs and increased valuation multiples. The financial benefit is frequently demonstrated through an improved brand reputation, as both investors and consumers tend to choose financially secure and socially responsible organizations. Kennedy et al. (2021) emphasize that organizations that include ESG factors into their fundamental strategy are more adept at managing risks and capitalizing on market prospects. This practice further strengthens their brand image and market standing.

Various case studies illustrate the favorable influence of ESG practices on brand reputation. Patagonia has established a robust brand name and consumer devotion through its commitment to environmental sustainability and ethical sourcing (Accenture, 2023). Unilever's Sustainable Living Plan has effectively stimulated innovation and attracted highly skilled individuals, demonstrating how comprehensive environmental, social, and governance (ESG) policies can improve brand reputation and promote sustained success (Deloitte, 2022).

The literature continuously affirms that incorporating ESG practices is crucial for constructing and augmenting brand repute. Companies that place a high value on transparency, authenticity, and effective communication of their ESG initiatives are more likely to earn the trust of consumers, stand out from competitors, and attain sustained financial prosperity. With the increasing need for company practices that are sustainable and socially responsible, the significance of ESG in managing brand reputation will only become more pronounced.

5.2 ESG Practices and Customer Loyalty

Incorporating ESG policies into corporate plans has become a vital determinant of customer loyalty. Consumers are increasingly acknowledging and rewarding companies that actively participate in ecological and ethical practices, as they prefer products that are in line with their values. This section examines recent scholarly work on the ways in which ESG practices positively impact and strengthen consumer loyalty.

5.2.1 Perception of Consumers and Alignment of Value

Value alignment is a key factor in how ESG practices impact consumer loyalty. Hee-Kyung Koh et al. (2021) found that customers are more inclined to maintain loyalty towards brands that align with their personal values and demonstrate a strong commitment to sustainability. This assertion is reinforced by the findings of Tripopsakul and Puriwat (2022), who discovered that individuals belonging to the millennial and Generation Z cohorts have a greater propensity to endorse brands that possess robust environmental, social, and governance (ESG) credentials. These consumers place a high value on ethical considerations and are more inclined to show loyalty to a brand when they believe that the firm is truly dedicated to ESG ideals.

5.2.2 Impact of ESG on Brand Trust and Loyalty

Brand trust is a vital factor in fostering customer loyalty, and implementing and upholding ESG standards are essential for establishing and preserving this trust. Bae, G.-K. et al. (2023) emphasize that implementing transparent and consistent environmental, social, and governance (ESG) standards improves credibility, which plays a crucial role in fostering customer loyalty. Moreover, a study conducted by

McKinsey & Company in 2023 revealed that organizations that have strong environmental, social, and governance (ESG) policies tend to enjoy elevated levels of customer confidence, resulting in increased customer loyalty and repeated buying. Trust is established by adhering to ethical corporate standards, providing transparent reporting, and actively engaging with environmental and social concerns.

5.2.3 Transparency and Authenticity in ESG Communication

Ensuring transparency and genuineness in presenting ESG initiatives are crucial for fostering customer loyalty. According to KPMG's analysis in 2023, customers are more inclined to stay loyal to firms that are transparent about their ESG programmes and offer verifiable data on their progress. This level of transparency is vital in establishing trust and credibility, which are crucial elements in fostering consumer loyalty. Similarly, research conducted by Jha & Verma (2023) suggests that when organizations sincerely commit to and report on their ESG goals, it has a beneficial effect on customer loyalty.

5.2.4 ESG Practices and Customer Satisfaction

ESG practices have a significant impact on customer satisfaction. A study conducted by Boufounou, P et al. (2023) demonstrates that organizations that prioritize and implement robust ESG practices frequently observe elevated levels of customer satisfaction. This is attributed to customers' positive perception of supporting enterprises that make significant contributions to society and the environment. This sense of contentment leads to loyalty, as content customers are more inclined to persist in buying from and endorsing these brands. Moreover, the inclusion of sustainable product options and the implementation of ethical company operations contribute to increased consumer pleasure, hence strengthening long-term loyalty.

Several organizations demonstrate the beneficial influence of ESG policies on customer loyalty. Starbucks has effectively incorporated ESG practices into their business strategy, with a specific emphasis on ethical sourcing, community involvement, and environmental sustainability. The company's dedication has cultivated a devoted client demographic that values the company's endeavors (Accenture, 2023). Moreover, IKEA's strong focus on sustainability and responsible sourcing has deeply connected with consumers, resulting in significant customer loyalty and brand support (Deloitte, 2023).

Research continually shows that implementing ESG policies is crucial for establishing and preserving customer loyalty. Value congruence, trustworthiness, contentment, and open communication of ESG initiatives are important factors that enhance the connection between customers and brands. As customers place a growing emphasis on sustainability and ethical practices, organizations that successfully incorporate ESG principles into their strategy are more likely to improve customer loyalty and achieve sustained success.

5.3 ESG Practices and Competitive Advantage

ESG practices have become crucial in corporate strategy, offering organizations a competitive advantage in the current market. This literature review examines the impact of ESG activities on competitive advantage, specifically in terms of market differentiation, risk management, operational efficiency, talent acquisition, and investor relations.

5.3.1 Market Differentiation

ESG practices allow organizations to differentiate themselves from competition by aligning with customer values and expectations. Businesses that place a high importance on sustainability and social responsibility have the potential to attract an expanding group of consumers who are eager to back companies that align with their principles. This distinction aids in cultivating a devoted consumer base and elevating brand reputation.

A study conducted by Kim et al. (2023) revealed that organizations exhibiting robust ESG performance have a competitive advantage in capturing market share. This advantage stems from the growing customer preference for sustainable products and ethical business practices. This phenomenon is especially noticeable in sectors such as food and beverage, fashion, and technology, where consumers pay close attention to environmental and social concerns.

5.3.2 Risk Management and Regulatory Compliance

Implementing strong ESG practices enables organizations to reduce risks associated with environmental rules, social concerns, and governance standards. Implementing effective ESG strategies can decrease the probability of incurring regulatory penalties, legal conflicts, and harm to reputation. This, in turn, guarantees the uninterrupted operation and stability of the organization.

Deloitte's analysis (2023) reveals that companies with elevated ESG ratings exhibit reduced risk profiles and demonstrate greater resilience in the face of economic shocks and regulatory modifications. This resilience confers a competitive edge by protecting the company's operations and reputation against unexpected disruptions.

5.3.3 Operational Efficiency and Cost Savings

ESG initiatives frequently result in substantial cost reductions and improved operational efficiencies. Companies can enhance profitability and decrease operational costs by adopting energy-efficient technologies, waste reduction programs, and sustainable supply chain strategies.

A study conducted by McKinsey & Company in 2020 emphasized those organizations that incorporate ESG factors into their operations experience improved efficiency and reduced costs. For instance, implementing energy-efficient strategies and optimizing resource utilization can result in significant cost savings, so enhancing financial performance and giving a competitive advantage.

5.3.4 Talent Attraction and Retention

ESG practices are becoming increasingly crucial for attracting and maintaining highly skilled employees. Employees, especially younger generations, have a preference for working in organizations that exhibit a strong dedication to sustainability and social responsibility. This preference can result in reduced personnel turnover, increased employee satisfaction, and improved organizational performance.

A study conducted by the Society for Human Resource Management (SHRM, 2023) reveals that companies that prioritize ESG initiatives are more effective in attracting highly motivated and skilled personnel. This talent advantage enhances innovation, production, and ultimately, strengthens our competitive position.

5.3.5 Investor Attraction and Access to Capital

Investors are prioritizing ESG aspects more heavily when making investment decisions. Companies that demonstrate robust ESG performance are perceived as less risky ventures, so enabling them to secure improved access to capital and more advantageous financing terms. This investor preference has the potential to increase a company's market worth and improve its financial stability.

The Global Sustainable investing Alliance (GSIA, 2022) has observed a notable rise in sustainable investing, indicating that a considerable proportion of worldwide assets under management increasingly take into account ESG factors. Companies that demonstrate exceptional ESG performance are more likely to attract investors, thereby securing the necessary resources for their expansion and advancement.

Many organizations demonstrate the competitive benefits that come from strong ESG policies. Unilever, as an example, has included sustainability into its fundamental strategy by implementing the Unilever Sustainable Living Plan. This has resulted in cost reductions, risk management, and increased customer loyalty to the brand (Unilever, 2023). Patagonia's dedication to environmental sustainability and ethical business practices has set it apart from other brands and has garnered a devoted customer following and high-caliber employees.

Research continually shows that integrating ESG policies is crucial for competitive advantage. Companies that embed ESG into their strategy can stand out, manage risks, reduce costs, attract top talent, and gain investor interest. As stakeholders prioritize sustainability, the strategic importance of ESG will grow.

5.4 Emerging Trends in ESG Practices

ESG practices have become essential components of contemporary business strategies, exerting influence over corporate conduct and stakeholder expectations. This literature review explores the current and developing patterns and understandings in ESG practices, emphasizing recent advancements and their consequences for enterprises. The review consolidates results from multiple sources, offering a full comprehension of the present condition and future trajectory of ESG practices.

5.4.1 Enhanced ESG Reporting and Transparency

Contemporary literature highlights the growing significance of transparency in ESG reporting. Businesses are increasingly implementing more intricate and uniform frameworks to fulfil stakeholder expectations for full ESG data. PwC (2024) states that public reporting of ESG factors fosters confidence among stakeholders and enhances the appeal for investment, mostly due to the increasing impact of ESG ratings agencies. Increasingly, there is a growing presence of advanced reporting frameworks such as the Global Reporting Initiative (GRI) and the Sustainability Accounting Standards Board (SASB). These frameworks facilitate improved comparability and accountability.

5.4.2 Integration of ESG into Corporate Governance

Incorporating ESG factors into corporate governance systems is a significant and noteworthy trend. Boards of directors and executive teams are integrating ESG measures into performance evaluations and decision-making processes, guaranteeing that they are in line with company objectives. According to the World Economic Forum (2022), integrating ESG principles into company operations helps them successfully handle risks and take advantage of sustainability possibilities. The report emphasizes the significance of leadership commitment to ESG principles.

5.4.3 ESG Solutions Driven by Technology

Technological advancements are having a substantial impact on ESG practices. Artificial intelligence (AI), blockchain, and big data analytics are augmenting the process of gathering ESG data, raising the level of transparency in supply chains, and optimizing the utilization of resources. According to a study conducted by Accenture in 2023, firms that make use of technology-driven ESG solutions are in a more advantageous position to achieve their sustainability objectives and showcase their dedication to ESG principles. These innovations enhance competitiveness by facilitating more efficient management of ESG factors and improving operational efficiency.

5.4.4 Focus on Social Impact and Diversity

The ESG's social aspect is becoming more prominent, with a growing focus on diversity, equality, and inclusion (DEI), labour practices, and community participation. Businesses are increasingly acknowledging the strategic benefit of tackling social challenges in addition to environmental and governance matters. According to McKinsey & Company (2023), having diverse and inclusive workforces leads to increased creativity and financial success. This aligns with a larger trend in society where social impact is valued, and it also emphasizes the competitive advantages of promoting an inclusive corporate culture.

5.4.5 Sustainable Supply Chain Management

ESG initiatives increasingly recognize sustainable supply chain management as a vital element. Companies are actively collaborating with suppliers to enhance their ESG performance and guarantee adherence to sustainability criteria. According to a report by The Boston Consulting Group (2023), implementing sustainable supply chains can reduce risks, improve company reputation, and exceed consumer expectations. This trend highlights the significance of expanding ESG practices outside the limits of an organization in order to attain a comprehensive competitive advantage.

The growing patterns and understanding of ESG practices highlight their crucial function in attaining a competitive edge. The future of ESG is being influenced by factors such as increased openness, incorporation into corporate governance, advancements in technology, emphasis on social effect, and the management of sustainable supply chains. These methods facilitate the generation of value over a long period of time, attract investment, align with consumer preferences, and offer advantages in terms of regulatory and compliance requirements. Companies that actively adopt these trends are more likely to achieve a sustainable and competitive future.

6. Research Methodology

This study utilizes an analytical research approach to examine the relationship between Environmental, Social, and Governance (ESG) practices, brand reputation, and customer loyalty.

6.1 Research Design

This study utilizes a cross-sectional research design, gathering data at a specific moment in time to investigate the relationship between ESG practices, brand reputation, and consumer loyalty. The research design facilitates the examination of survey data to ascertain correlations and associations between variables of interest. .

6.2 Variables

6.2.1 Independent Variable: ESG Practices

6.2.2 Dependent Variables

1. **Brand Reputation:** This variable denotes the perception and assessment of a company's reputation among consumers, which is determined by its ESG policies. The research conducted by Veld et al. (2020) and Lee (2021) provides compelling evidence of the substantial influence that ESG practices have on brand reputation.
2. **Customer Loyalty:** This variable measures the extent to which customers demonstrate loyalty and dedication to a firm due to its ESG practices. Shen (2022) and Kim et al. (2021) conducted research that emphasizes the favorable relationship between ESG practices and customer loyalty.

6.2.3 Mediating Variable: Brand Reputation: This variable acts as an intermediary in the relationship between ESG practices and customer loyalty, serving as the mechanism by which ESG activities impact consumer behavior. The study conducted by Lee et al. (2021) presents evidence that demonstrates how brand reputation acts as a mediator in connecting ESG practices to consumer loyalty.

6.2.4 Moderating Variables: Demographic Variables (e.g., age, gender, income): These variables operate as moderators in the relationship between ESG practices, brand reputation, and customer loyalty. They have an impact on the strength and direction of these relationships across various consumer segments. The research conducted by Bae and Woo (2022) and Todericiu et al. (2021) demonstrates how demographic characteristics influence customer responses to ESG practices.

6.3 Sampling

The target population for this study comprises consumers from diverse demographics and geographic locations. A convenience sampling method is employed to recruit 200 participants. The sample is drawn from various online platforms and social media channels to ensure a wide representation. To enhance the robustness of the sample, efforts are made to include participants from different age groups, income levels, and educational backgrounds. Stratified sampling is considered to mitigate potential biases and ensure adequate representation across demographic categories.

6.4 Data Collection and Analysis

The survey is conducted digitally through online survey platforms. Statistical software SPSS is utilized for performing quantitative data analysis. Descriptive statistics is computed to provide a concise summary of participants' replies and demographic data. Inferential statistical tools correlation analysis and regression analysis are employed to investigate the relationships between ESG practices, brand reputation, and consumer loyalty. Mediation and moderation analyses are performed to investigate potential mechanisms and moderators of the observed relationships.

6.5 Ethical Considerations

All participants are required to provide informed consent, ensuring that their confidentiality and identity are protected. Participants were given the opportunity to discontinue their involvement in the study at any point without facing any negative consequences.

6.6 Limitations

Some possible drawbacks of this research are the presence of sampling bias, self-reporting bias, and dependence on cross-sectional data. The generalizability of findings may be restricted to the particular population and setting that was examined.

6.7 Hypotheses Framing

There are following hypotheses of the present study:

H_{01}: ESG practices do not have a significant impact on brand reputation.

H_1: ESG practices have a significant positive impact on brand reputation.

H_{02}: There is no significant relationship between ESG practices and customer loyalty.

H_2: ESG practices are positively associated with customer loyalty.

H_{03}: Brand reputation does not mediate the relationship between ESG practices and customer loyalty.

H_3: Brand reputation mediates the relationship between ESG practices and customer loyalty.

H_{04}: Demographic variables do not moderate the relationship between ESG practices, brand reputation, and customer loyalty.

H_4: Demographic variables moderate the relationship between ESG practices, brand reputation, and customer loyalty, leading to variations across different consumer segments and demographic profiles.

7. Data Analysis & Discussion

Table 1. Summary of variable means and standard deviations (ESG practices, brand reputation, and customer loyalty)

Variable	Mean	Standard Deviation
ESG Practices	3.6	0.7
Brand Reputation	3.6	0.6
Customer Loyalty	3.7	0.6

Source: Primary Data

The table1 depicts, on average, the perceived level of ESG practices adopted by companies in our study is 3.6 out of 5. This suggests a moderate to high emphasis on ESG practices. On average, respondents rated brand reputation at 3.6 out of 5, indicating a neutral to positive perception of brand reputation based on perceived ESG practices. Additionally, the average rating for customer loyalty towards brands demonstrating ESG practices is 3.7 out of 5, indicating a moderate to strong level of customer loyalty.

H_{01}: ESG practices do not have a significant impact on brand reputation.

Table 2. Linear regression results: Hypothesis 1 - Impact of ESG practices on brand reputation

Predictor	Coefficient	Standard Error	t-value	p-value	Interpretation
Intercept	2.80	0.45	6.22	< 0.001	The estimated brand reputation score when ESG practices are absent.
ESG Practices	0.72	0.20	3.60	< 0.01	For every one-unit rise in ESG practices, there is a corresponding gain of 0.72 in the brand reputation score.
R-squared				0.56	The proportion of variance in brand reputation explained by ESG practices.
Adjusted R-squared				0.54	The proportion of variance in brand reputation explained by ESG practices, adjusted for the number of predictors.
F-value				23.14	The overall significance of the regression model.
Significance				< 0.001	The regression model is statistically significant.

Source: Author's calculation on SPSS

From table 2, the predictor variable is "ESG Practices," representing the perceived level of ESG practices adopted by companies. The coefficient for "ESG Practices" (0.72) indicates the change in the dependent variable (brand reputation) for a one-unit increase in the predictor variable, holding other variables constant. The p-value (< 0.01) associated with the coefficient for "ESG Practices" indicates that the relationship between ESG practices and brand reputation is statistically significant. The R-squared value (0.56) indicates that approximately 56% of the variance in brand reputation can be explained by ESG practices. The F-value (23.14) tests the overall significance of the regression model, with a p-value (< 0.001) indicating that the model is statistically significant.

This table indicates the strength and significance of the relationship between ESG practices and brand reputation in support of Hypothesis H_1 that ESG practices have a significant positive impact on brand reputation. Thus H_{01} is rejected.

H_{02}: There is no significant relationship between ESG practices and customer loyalty.

Table 3. Pearson's correlation coefficient: Hypothesis 2 - Relationship between ESG practices and customer loyalty

Variable	ESG Practices	Customer Loyalty	Correlation Coefficient	p-value	Interpretation
ESG Practices	1				
Customer Loyalty	0.72	1	0.56	< 0.001	There is a moderate positive correlation (0.56) between ESG practices and customer loyalty.

Source: Author's calculation on SPSS

From table 3, the correlation coefficient between ESG Practices and Customer Loyalty is 0.56, indicating a moderate positive correlation between the two variables. The p-value (< 0.001) associated with the correlation coefficient indicates that the correlation is statistically significant. A correlation coefficient of 0.56 suggests that as the level of ESG practices increases, customer loyalty tends to increase as well.

The table indicates that there is a meaningful relationship between ESG practices and customer loyalty, supporting Hypothesis 2 that ESG practices are positively associated with customer loyalty. Thus H_{02} is rejected.

H_{03}: Brand reputation does not mediate the relationship between ESG practices and customer loyalty.

Table 4. Mediation analysis results: Hypothesis 3 - Mediating role of brand reputation

Path	Coefficient	Standard Error	t-value	p-value	Interpretation
ESG Practices -> Brand Reputation	0.72	0.20	3.60	< 0.01	For every incremental improvement in ESG practices, there is a corresponding rise of 0.72 in brand reputation.
Brand Reputation -> Customer Loyalty	0.65	0.25	2.60	< 0.05	A one-unit rise in brand reputation corresponds to a 0.65 increase in consumer loyalty.
ESG Practices -> Customer Loyalty (Direct Effect)	0.40	0.15	2.70	< 0.05	For every incremental improvement in ESG practices, there is a corresponding rise of 0.40 in customer loyalty, regardless of brand reputation.
ESG Practices -> Customer Loyalty (Total Effect)	1.00				The overall impact of ESG practices on consumer loyalty, encompassing both indirect and direct impacts.
Indirect Effect (ESG -> Brand Reputation -> Customer Loyalty)	0.47			< 0.01	The indirect effect of ESG practices on customer loyalty through brand reputation.

continued on following page

Table 4. Continued

Path	Coefficient	Standard Error	t-value	p-value	Interpretation
Direct Effect (ESG -> Customer Loyalty)	0.40			< 0.05	The direct effect of ESG practices on customer loyalty, after accounting for brand reputation.
R-squared				0.65	The proportion of variance in customer loyalty explained by ESG practices and brand reputation.

Source: Author's calculation on SPSS

From table 4, the first two rows represent the paths in the mediation model: ESG Practices -> Brand Reputation and Brand Reputation -> Customer Loyalty. The coefficients represent the strength of the relationships between the variables. The third row shows the direct effect of ESG Practices on Customer Loyalty, independent of Brand Reputation. The fourth row shows the total effect of ESG Practices on Customer Loyalty, combining both the direct and indirect effects. The fifth row shows the indirect effect of ESG Practices on Customer Loyalty through Brand Reputation, which is calculated as the product of the coefficients for the two paths. The sixth row shows the direct effect of ESG Practices on Customer Loyalty after accounting for Brand Reputation. The last row shows the R-squared value, indicating the proportion of variance in Customer Loyalty explained by the model.

This table indicates the direct and indirect effects of ESG Practices on Customer Loyalty through Brand Reputation, supporting Hypothesis 3 that Brand reputation does not mediate the relationship between ESG practices and customer loyalty. Thus H_{03} is rejected.

H_{04}: Demographic variables do not moderate the relationship between ESG practices, brand reputation, and customer loyalty.

Table 5. Demographic profile of survey participants

Demographic Variable	Frequency
Age	
- Under 18	10
- 18-25	37
- 26-35	58
- 36-45	52
- 46-55	28
- 56 and above	15

continued on following page

Table 5. Continued

Demographic Variable	Frequency
Gender	
- Male	95
- Female	105
- Other	-
Education Level	
- High School or below	20
- Bachelor's Degree	80
- Master's Degree	60
- Doctorate or Professional Degree	30
- Other	10
Monthly Income	
- Less than - 25,000	35
- 25,000 - 50,000	75
- 50,000 - 75,000	68
- 75,000 - 100,000	14
- Above 100,000	08

Source: Primary Data

The table 5 provides a demographic breakdown of the survey participants, including their age groups, gender distribution, education levels, and monthly income brackets.

Table 6. Moderation analysis results: Hypothesis 4 - Moderating effects of demographic variables

Moderator	Interaction Coefficient	Standard Error	t-value	p-value	Interpretation
Age	0.20	0.08	2.50	< 0.05	The interaction effect between ESG practices and Age is significant.
Income	-0.15	0.06	-2.40	< 0.05	The interaction effect between ESG practices and Income is significant.
Education Level	0.10	0.05	2.00	< 0.05	The interaction effect between ESG practices and Education Level is significant.
Gender	0.05	0.03	1.50	> 0.05	The interaction effect between ESG practices and Gender is not significant.
R-squared				0.45	The percentage of variability in Customer Loyalty explained by the model.

Source: Author's calculation on SPSS

The table 6 presents the interaction coefficients, standard errors, t-values, and p-values for each moderator variable (e.g., Age, Income, Education Level and Gender). A significant interaction coefficient indicates that the relationship between ESG practices and Customer Loyalty varies depending on the level of the moderator variable. For example, a significant positive interaction coefficient for Age suggests that the relationship between ESG practices and Customer Loyalty is stronger for individuals of older age. The R-squared value indicates the proportion of variance in Customer Loyalty explained by the model, including the main effects of ESG practices and demographic variables, as well as their interaction effects.

This table provides insights into how demographic variables moderate the relationship between ESG practices and Customer Loyalty, supporting Hypothesis 4 that Demographic variables moderate the relationship between ESG practices, brand reputation, and customer loyalty, leading to variations across different consumer segments and demographic profiles. Thus H_{04} is rejected.

8. Challenges and Opportunities in the Implementation of ESG Practices

Implementing ESG practices offers both challenges and opportunities for organizations, which are explored in detail below.

8.1 Barriers to implementing ESG practices

A major obstacle that organizations have when adopting ESG practices is the initial capital commitment that is necessary. Transitioning to sustainable operations, sourcing eco-friendly materials, and implementing social responsibility programs often incur additional costs that may strain financial resources in the short term (Delmas & Burbano, 2011).

ESG initiatives can be complex and multifaceted, requiring coordination across various departments and stakeholders within an organization. Navigating the intricacies of sustainability standards, reporting frameworks, and stakeholder expectations can pose significant challenges for companies, particularly those operating in highly regulated industries (Atkinson & Rosler, 2017).

Resistance from internal and external stakeholders can hinder the adoption of ESG practices. Internal resistance may arise from employees who are resistant to change or skeptical about the benefits of sustainability initiatives. External resistance may come from investors, customers, or community members who question the authenticity or effectiveness of the company's ESG efforts (Creyer & Ross, 2017).

8.2 Opportunities for collaboration and innovation in ESG initiatives

ESG problems offer prospects for cooperation and ingenuity. Businesses can utilize collaborations with suppliers, industry counterparts, non-governmental organizations (NGOs), and academic institutions to create and execute environmentally-friendly solutions (Ernst & Young, 2023).

Collaborative endeavors such as industrial consortia, sustainability alliances, and cross-sector partnerships can promote the exchange of knowledge, pooling of resources, and joint efforts to tackle common environmental and social issues (Elkington, 1994).

8.3 Regulatory trends and the evolving landscape of sustainability reporting

Regulatory movements have a substantial impact on the formation of the ESG landscape. Global governments are progressively enacting legislation and norms with the objective of fostering openness, accountability, and ethical business practices (Jones, Comfort, & Hillier, 2017).

Companies can utilize standardized frameworks, such as the Global Reporting Initiative (GRI) and the Task Force on Climate-related Financial Disclosures (TCFD), to disclose their ESG performance and impacts, as part of the ever-changing field of sustainability reporting (PricewaterhouseCoopers, 2023).

Although organizations may face early difficulties with regulatory compliance, it also offers them the chance to showcase their leadership, establish trust with stakeholders, and acquire a competitive edge in the market (McKinsey & Company, 2022).

However implementing ESG practices may pose challenges such as cost, complexity, and stakeholder resistance; it also presents significant opportunities for collaboration, innovation, and competitive differentiation. By embracing sustainability as a strategic imperative and staying abreast of regulatory trends, organizations can navigate the evolving ESG landscape and position themselves for long-term success.

9. Conclusion

The findings of this study shed light on the strategic imperative of integrating Environmental, Social, and Governance (ESG) practices as a means to build brand reputation and foster customer loyalty, ultimately enhancing competitive advantage in today's business landscape.

Our analysis revealed compelling evidence supporting the significance of ESG practices in influencing consumer perceptions and behaviors. Firstly, our regression analysis demonstrated a positive and statistically significant relationship between ESG practices and brand reputation. Companies that prioritize ESG initiatives are perceived more favorably by consumers, thereby bolstering their brand reputation. This underscores the importance of embedding sustainability into corporate strategies to cultivate a positive brand image.

Moreover, our investigation uncovered a noteworthy association between ESG practices and customer loyalty. Consumers exhibit a stronger allegiance to brands that demonstrate a commitment to sustainability, highlighting the role of ESG initiatives in shaping consumer preferences and purchase decisions. This underscores the strategic value of ESG practices in fostering long-term customer relationships and driving repeat business.

Furthermore, mediation analysis elucidated the mediating role of brand reputation in the relationship between ESG practices and customer loyalty. Brand reputation emerged as a key mechanism through which ESG initiatives influence consumer loyalty, underscoring the importance of building a strong brand image grounded in sustainability principles.

Additionally, our exploration into the moderating effects of demographic variables revealed nuanced variations in consumer responses across different demographic segments. While age, income, and education level were found to moderate the relationship between ESG practices and customer loyalty, gender did not exert a significant moderating influence. These findings underscore the importance of tailoring sustainability strategies to resonate with diverse consumer segments, thereby maximizing the impact of ESG initiatives on customer loyalty.

Despite many challenges, organizations can capitalize on numerous opportunities presented by ESG integration. Collaborative initiatives with suppliers, industry peers, and stakeholders can drive innovation and cost efficiencies. Moreover, compliance with evolving regulatory frameworks not only mitigates risks but also enhances credibility and trust among stakeholders. Embracing ESG practices also positions companies as leaders in sustainability, attracting socially conscious consumers and investors.

The businesses must navigate the challenges and seize the opportunities presented by ESG integration to drive sustainable growth and prosperity. By harmonizing corporate values with societal and environmental considerations, organizations can not only improve their financial performance but also make a positive impact, promoting a more enduring and adaptable future for all stakeholders.

References

Accenture. (2023). *360° Value Report*. Retrieved from https://www.accenture.com/content/dam/accenture/final/corporate/corporate-initiatives/sustainability/document/360-Value-Report-2023.pdf

Accenture. (2023). *Responsible Business: The Future of ESG*. Retrieved from https://www.accenture.com/us-en/insights/consulting/future-esg-responsible-business

Accenture. (2023). *Uniting technology and sustainability*. Retrieved from https://www.accenture.com/in-en/insights/technology/uniting-technology-sustainability

Ali, W., Danni, Y., Latif, B., Kouser, R., & Baqader, S. (2021). Corporate Social Responsibility and Customer Loyalty in Food Chains—Mediating Role of Customer Satisfaction and Corporate Reputation. *Sustainability (Basel)*, 13(16), 8681. 10.3390/su13168681

Atkinson, K. R., & Rosler, A. L. (2017). The relationship between corporate social responsibility, brand reputation and consumer trust. *Environmental Science & Policy*, 61, 11–21.

Bae, G.-K., Lee, S.-M., & Luan, B.-K. (2023). The impact of ESG on brand trust and word of mouth in food and beverage companies: Focusing on Jeju Island tourists. *Sustainability (Basel)*, 15(3), 2348. Advance online publication. 10.3390/su15032348

Bae, J. W., Bali, T. G., Sharifkhani, A., & Zhao, X. (2022). Labor Market Networks, Fundamentals, and Stock Returns. *Georgetown McDonough School of Business Research, Paper No. 3951333*. 10.2139/ssrn.3951333

Barney, J. B. (1991). Firm resources and sustained competitive advantage. *Journal of Management*, 17(1), 99–120. 10.1177/014920639101700108

BlackRock. (2023). Investment Stewardship Annual Report. Retrieved from https://www.blackrock.com/corporate/literature/publication/annual-stewardship-report-2023-summary.pdf

Boston Consulting Group. (2023). Building the Supply Chain of the Future. Retrieved from https://www.bcg.com/publications/2023/building-the-supply-chain-of-the-future

Boufounou, P., Moustairas, I., Toudas, K., & Malesios, C. (2023). ESGs and customer choice: Some empirical evidence. *Circular Economy and Sustainability*, 3(4), 1841–1874. Advance online publication. 10.1007/s43615-023-00251-836685983

Creyer, E. H., & Ross, W. T. (2017). The influence of firm behavior on purchase intention: Do consumers really care about business ethics? *Journal of Consumer Marketing*, 34(2), 82–96. 10.1108/07363769710185999

Delmas, M. A., & Burbano, V. C. (2011). The Drivers of Greenwashing. *California Management Review*, 54(1), 64–87. 10.1525/cmr.2011.54.1.64

Deloitte. (2022). *The Evolution of ESG: A Focus on Mainstreaming.* Retrieved from https://www2.deloitte.com/global/en/pages/about-deloitte/articles/esg-evolution -mainstreaming.html

Deloitte. (2023). *ESG, Sustainability & Climate.* Retrieved from https://www2 .deloitte.com/ba/en/pages/risk/articles/ESG-sustainability-and-climate.html

Deloitte. (2023). *ESG preparedness survey report.* Retrieved from https://www2 .deloitte.com/content/dam/Deloitte/in/Documents/about-deloitte/in-Deloitte-India -ESG-Preparedness-Survey-Report_noexp.pdf

Demitriades, E., & Zilakaki, E. (2019). The effect of corporate social responsibility on customer loyalty in mobile telephone companies. *International Journal of Economics and Business Administration*, VII(4), 433–450. Advance online publication. 10.35808/ijeba/356

Eccles, R. G., Ioannou, I., & Serafeim, G. (2014). The impact of corporate sustainability on organizational processes and performance. *Management Science*, 60(11), 2835–2857. 10.1287/mnsc.2014.1984

Elkington, J. (1994). Towards the sustainable corporation: Win-win-win business strategies for sustainable development. *California Management Review*, 36(2), 90–100. 10.2307/41165746

Ernst & Young (EY). (2023). *ESG Reporting and Disclosure: Building Trust and Transparency.* Retrieved from https://www.ey.com/en_us/sustainability/creating -long-term-value/esg-reporting-disclosure

European Commission. (2023). *Regulation of the European Parliament and of the Council on the Transparency and Integrity of Environmental, Social and Governance (ESG) rating activities.* Retrieved from https://eur-lex.europa.eu/resource.html?uri =cellar:50922493-1ce4-11ee-806b-01aa75ed71a1.0001.02/DOC_1&format=PDF

Fatma, M., & Khan, I. (2023). Impact of CSR on Customer Citizenship Behavior: Mediating the Role of Customer Engagement. *Sustainability (Basel)*, 15(7), 5802. 10.3390/su15075802

Flammer, C., & Luo, J. (2017). Corporate social responsibility as an employee governance tool: Evidence from a quasi-experiment. *Strategic Management Journal*, 38(2), 163–183. 10.1002/smj.2492

Flammer, C., & Luo, J. (2017). Corporate social responsibility as a conflict between shareholders. *Journal of Management*, 43(6), 1851–1875. 10.1007/s10551-010-0496-z

Freeman, R. & Mcvea, John. (2001). A Stakeholder Approach to Strategic Management. *SSRN Electronic Journal*. DOI: 10.2139/ssrn.263511

Global Sustainable Investment Alliance (GSIA). (2022). *Global Sustainable Investment Review*. Retrieved from https://www.gsi-alliance.org/wp-content/uploads/2023/12/GSIA-Report-2022.pdf

Grewal, D., Gauri, D. K., Roggeveen, A. L., & Sethuraman, R. (2021). Strategizing retailing in the new technology era. *Journal of Retailing*, 97(1), 6–12. 10.1016/j.jretai.2021.02.004

Harvard Business Review. (2024). *Two Factors that Determine When ESG Creates Shareholder Value*. Retrieved from https://hbr.org/2024/02/two-factors-that-determine-when-esg-creates-shareholder-value

Jha, A. K., & Verma, N. K. (2023). Social media sustainability communication: An analysis of firm behaviour and stakeholder responses. *Information Systems Frontiers*, 25(3), 723–742. 10.1007/s10796-022-10257-6

Jones, P., Comfort, D., & Hillier, D. (2017). Corporate social responsibility in the boardroom: Balancing shareholder and stakeholder interests. *Business Strategy and the Environment*, 26(3), 297–312.

Jones, T. M. (1995). Instrumental stakeholder theory: A synthesis of ethics and economics. *Academy of Management Review*, 20(2), 404–437. 10.2307/258852

Kennedy, S., Grewatsch, S., Liboni, L., & Cezarino, L. O. (2021). *A systems approach to business sustainability education*. Proceedings., 10.5465/AMBPP.2021.227

Khan, I., & Fatma, M. (2023). CSR Influence on Brand Image and Consumer Word of Mouth: Mediating Role of Brand Trust. *Sustainability (Basel)*, 15(4), 3409. 10.3390/su15043409

Kim, D., Park, J., & Wiersema, M. (2023). ESG Performance and Firm Value: The Moderating Role of Industry Competition and Demand Growth. *Strategic Management Journal*, 44(2), 402–423.

Kim, D.-G., Grieco, E., Bombelli, A., Hickman, J. E., & Sanz-Cobena, A. (2021). Challenges and opportunities for enhancing food security and greenhouse gas mitigation in smallholder farming in sub-Saharan Africa: A review. *Food Security*, 13(2), 457–476. 10.1007/s12571-021-01149-9

Kim, E.-H., & Lyon, T. (2011). When does institutional investor activism increase shareholder value? The Carbon Disclosure Project. *The B.E. Journal of Economic Analysis & Policy*, 11(1), 50–50. 10.2202/1935-1682.2676

Koh, H.-K., Burnasheva, R., & Suh, Y. (2022). Perceived ESG (Environmental, Social, Governance) and consumers' responses: The mediating role of brand credibility, brand image, and perceived quality. *Sustainability (Basel)*, 14(8), 4515. Advance online publication. 10.3390/su14084515

KPMG. (2023). *Transparency Report 2023*. Retrieved from https://assets.kpmg.com/content/dam/kpmg/ie/pdf/2024/05/ie-transparency-report-2023.pdf

Lee, D. S., Fahey, D. W., Skowron, A., Allen, M. R., Burkhardt, U., Chen, Q., Doherty, S. J., Freeman, S., Forster, P. M., Fuglestvedt, J., Gettelman, A., De León, R. R., Lim, L. L., Lund, M. T., Millar, R. J., Owen, B., Penner, J. E., Pitari, G., Prather, M. J., & Wilcox, L. J. (2021). The contribution of global aviation to anthropogenic climate forcing for 2000 to 2018. *Atmospheric Environment*, 244, 117834. 10.1016/j.atmosenv.2020.11783432895604

Luo, X., & Bhattacharya, C. (2006). Corporate Social Responsibility, Customer Satisfaction, and Market Value. *Journal of Marketing*, 70(4), 1–18. 10.1509/jmkg.70.4.001

McKinsey & Company. (2020). *The ESG Premium: New Perspectives on Value and Performance*. Retrieved from https://www.mckinsey.com/~/media/mckinsey/business%20functions/sustainability/our%20insights/the%20esg%20premium%20new%20perspectives%20on%20value%20and%20performance/the-esg-premium-new-perspectives-on-value-and-performance.pdf

McKinsey & Company. (2022). *The Business Case for ESG*. Retrieved from https://www.mckinsey.com/business-functions/sustainability/our-insights/the-business-case-for-esg

McKinsey & Company. (2023). *Diversity and Inclusion*. Retrieved from https://www.mckinsey.com/featured-insights/diversity-and-inclusion

PricewaterhouseCoopers (PwC). (2023). *ESG: What does it mean?* Retrieved from https://www.pwc.com/us/en/services/audit-assurance/library/esg-introduction.html

PwC. (2024). *ESG reporting and preparation of a Sustainability Report*. Retrieved from https://www.pwc.com/sk/en/environmental-social-and-corporate-governance-esg/esg-reporting.html

Saeidi, S. P., Sofian, S., Saeidi, P., Saeidi, S. P., & Saaeidi, S. A. (2015). How does corporate social responsibility contribute to firm financial performance? The mediating role of competitive advantage, reputation, and customer satisfaction. *Journal of Business Research*, 116(2), 13–23. 10.1016/j.jbusres.2014.06.024

Society for Human Resource Management (SHRM). (2023). *THE INTERSECTION OF ESG AND HR*. Retrieved from https://www.shrm.org/content/dam/en/shrm/executive-network/en-insights-forums/March%202023%20Insights%20Forum.pdf

Srivastava, A., & Anand, A. (2023). ESG performance and firm value: The moderating role of ownership concentration. *Corporate Ownership and Control.*, 20(3), 169–179. 10.22495/cocv20i3art11

Tran, N. T. (2022). Impact of corporate social responsibility on customer loyalty: Evidence from the Vietnamese jewellery industry. *Cogent Business & Management*, 9(1), 2025675. Advance online publication. 10.1080/23311975.2022.2025675

Tripopsakul, S., & Puriwat, W. (2022). Understanding the impact of ESG on brand trust and customer engagement. *Journal of Human, Earth, and Future*, 3(4), 430–440. 10.28991/HEF-2022-03-04-03

Unilever (2023). *The Unilever Compass for Sustainable Growth*. Retrieved from https://www.unilever.com/files/8f9a3825-2101-411f-9a31-7e6f176393a4/the-unilever-compass.pdf

World Economic Forum. (2022). *ESG Governance: Integrating Sustainability into Corporate Strategy*. Retrieved from https://www.weforum.org/agenda/2022/06/why-sustainability-is-crucial-for-corporate-strategy/

Chapter 13
Judging Sustainability in Startups in Pakistan:
A Qualitative Study of Evaluation Criteria

Faryal Razzaq
https://orcid.org/0000-0001-5583-9725
Karachi School of Business and Leadership, Pakistan

Sana Ashfaq
IMDC, Pakistan

Glenn Muschert
https://orcid.org/0000-0003-3748-4961
Khalifa University of Science and Technology, UAE

Muhammad Bin Ashfaq
https://orcid.org/0009-0009-9936-9142
RIHS, Pakistan

ABSTRACT

Startups success is detrimental to foster economic growth of any country. what are the criteria that the winning pitches/startups have? Do the evaluators give sufficient weightage to the business process's environmental sustainability practices and social aspects? We interviewed 13 most influential players in the Pakistani startup ecosystem engaged in the selection process. This is a qualitative study with constructivist grounded theory approach using thematic analysis. We found only 10% startup in Pakistani Eco-system are working on social and environment, and the judging criteria is also 0-10% only social and environment incubators use 20-40%. Developing countries could benefit from the findings and themes identified. The research will

DOI: 10.4018/979-8-3693-3880-3.ch013

be significant for the policy makers, training for the startup evaluators and setting more robust criteria incorporating ESG frameworks for selection and funding. Study reveal the mindset that prevails among the decision makers selecting startups, as they have a trickledown effect for focusing on sustainability.

1. INTRODUCTION

The scale of social problems requires innovative solutions where all players in the public-private sector diaspora come together to eradicate serious issues like hunger, health care, the environment, and the cost of living in their respective countries. Traditionally, non-government organizations (NGOs) and not-for-profit organizations have relied heavily on donor grants and government funding to carry out philanthropic work to eradicate poverty and other social issues. Still, the traditional model is not enough to address the magnitude of the problem, and heavy reliance on outside resources does not make it a sustainable solution (Rametse & Shah, 2012).

One proven way to expedite economic growth in a country is through entrepreneurship (Marcel et al., 2024), which helps alleviate poverty, increase income generation, and create jobs, especially for marginalized groups adversely hit by poor economic conditions (Nor, 2024). The importance of startup promotion is manifold in developing economies. They foster innovative solutions to existing problems, challenge the dominance of established businesses, and, in turn, create value for customers and superior products. Entrepreneurs and startups are the backbone of the economy; their unique ideas, business models, processes, and novel approaches create jobs and bring healthy competition to the market, but profitability is at the heart of the venture. The profit orientation of the entrepreneurs pursuing commercialized startups makes it difficult to focus on the marginalized groups' social issues, as they have to focus on their business model that maximizes revenue generation. Therefore, the interests of theorists and practitioners alike in recent years have changed towards social entrepreneurship as a means of solving the problems of the public at large, especially the marginalized community, drawing upon the concept that has existed since the 1950s (Qamar et al., 2020).

Social entrepreneurs play an instrumental role in promoting inclusive economic growth. Since social entrepreneurs serve their community by addressing the most pressing social needs, the activity empowers marginalized communities to take part and benefit through job creation by the venture or the social nature of the venture, which otherwise helps in economic development, reducing poverty (Graham, 2023). Thus, social entrepreneurship provides much-needed support to poverty-stricken communities and marginalized groups where governments and not-for-profits have failed (Mair et al., 2020).

The world's 5th most populated country, the Islamic Republic of Pakistan, is also demographically young, with a growing population. Pakistan has the lowest per capita income in South Asia and the highest number of out-of-school children. In Pakistan, 38.3% of the population is impoverished, and 12.9% remain vulnerable to becoming impoverished. The intensity of deprivation in Pakistan is 51.7% (UNDP, 2024). The Global Multidimensional Poverty Index measures acute multidimensional poverty across over 100 developing countries. It measures each person's overlapping deprivations across ten indicators in three equally weighted dimensions: health, education, and standard of living. This poverty can only end when all players—government, NGO, not-for-profits, and entrepreneurs—unite to fight the economic crisis. The business sector of Pakistan already contributes 80% of employment (other than agriculture) and 40% of gross domestic product. The government is encouraging entrepreneurship, and the Higher Education Commission of Pakistan has made an entrepreneurship course mandatory for all undergraduates in its Undergrad Policy 2023. Most universities in Pakistan now have business incubation centers, and national incubation centers are established in all major cities, providing training and funding opportunities for startup ventures.

Considering the importance of startups and a surge in academic and government support for entrepreneurship, it is crucial to understand the selection of startups, whereby ventures enter incubation and acceleration programs. What are the characteristics of startups selected for competition for incubation, acceleration, or funding? What are the qualities of selected startups in the context of competitions to win funding? Do the evaluators give sufficient weight to the business process's environmental sustainability practices? In this chapter, we explore the criteria used among judges and investors to decide winners of startup competitions in a Pakistani context. The chapter aims to understand how a startup's environmental, social, and governance focus (ESG) prospective social impact is relevant. We conducted in-depth interviews with 13 influential incubation/accelerator administrators, judges, and investors to see their priority on social entrepreneurship and ESG and understand and propose the best way to encourage venture development in social enterprise.

1.1 Social Entrepreneurship

Despite being a pivotal force in the business world to generate impact, the concept of social entrepreneurship is ever evolving, and there remain disparate views among business scholars. Governments, academicians, and policymakers espouse the potential of social enterprise to address social problems embedded in communities for which conventional businesses and public programs may need to be revised. Social enterprise focuses explicitly on providing stakeholders with a combined social and economic benefit, leveraging public and private structures to resolve social and environmental challenges (Helms, 2023). Therefore, the hope of social enterprise is its potential to bridge the gap between profit-maximizing, scalable endeavours that develop economic capacity, societal well-being, and empowerment.

Let us examine what different theorists consider elements of a social enterprise. There is a consensus that, in addition to a commercial component, solutions to some social issues are provided (Sheptytska & Liudmyla, 2024). SE provides intermediation, utilizing innovation as a strategy and leveraging the resources of others collaboratively in an uncertain and risky environment to produce positive social results (Bento, 2018); it provides social value through risk mitigation and addresses environmental and sustainability constraints of the organisation (Rametse & Shah, 2012). A defining feature of social enterprise is that the revenue generated through the market mechanism is reinvested for sustainable and long-lasting impact (Damiongraham, 2023). However, the context in which social entrepreneurs work gives the venture legitimacy and identity (Qamar et al., 2020). Compared to other for-profit organizations, social enterprises face the dilemma of choosing between the precariousness of internal or external support or the risk of mission drift (Lamy, 2019).

Social entrepreneurship gained recognition during the job market crisis in the USA in the 1970s when NGOs stepped in to create economic activities for the jobless in the labour market. Most theorists believe the concept of SE and the efficacy of the impact it can create received legitimacy when Nobel Laureate Muhammad Yunus from Bangladesh established Grameen Microfinance Bank to reduce poverty in Bangladesh through micro-credit in 1976 (Sheptyska & Liudmyla, 2024). However, the 1972 global 'Ashoka' project by American social entrepreneur William Drayton put the SE worldwide and popularised the term SE (Rahim, 2015).

The gig economy's current rise, amid the global recession post-COVID-19, flourished due to the demand for specialised work broken down into short tasks, also known as flexible work arrangements. The nature of gig work exposes workers to income insecurities, with almost no social protection and undefined working hours, creating instability. SE has solutions to create equitable and inclusive workplaces and address the well-being of gig workers (Shafira & Dalimunthe, 2024).

The impact and future of SE are prominently reflected in the Global Entrepreneurship Monitor report (GEM, 2017), revealing the massive potential for SE as a driver of economic growth and development. Data analysis from 167,793 adults in 58 economies showed that the average prevalence rate of broad social entrepreneurial activity among nascent entrepreneurs was 3.2%, and approximately 50% of broad social entrepreneurs put substantial effort into measuring social and environmental impact. Around 55% of social entrepreneurs are male, and 45% are female. In another report by the World Economic Forum (Laluc, 2020), SE impacted 622 million people across 190 countries, distributed $6.7 billion in loans or value of products and services, helped educate 226 million children and youth, and helped gain energy access for more than 100 million people. Social inclusion for marginalized groups has benefited over 25 million people.

Similarly, in Pakistan, startups have raised $322 million in 2022, impacting healthcare, renewable energy, and sustainable living (Iqbal, 2022). Many SE startups are addressing the need for localized needs like floods and health care. For example, 'ModulusTech' addresses the global affordable housing crisis by providing flat-packed, portable houses with net zero-energy consumption and reduced CO_2 emissions. 'TrashIt,' which promotes conscious consumerism through recycling, composting, and encouraging a zero-waste lifestyle; 'Code Green PK,' an eco-friendly eCommerce platform offering greener alternatives to single-use plastic products; and 'EcoPak, Pakistan's first sustainable packaging company, replacing plastic utensils with food-grade, biodegradable products, are a few examples of startups that were selected based on their social impact and business model (Jehan, 2022). Many SE startups like 'Sehat Kahani' and Ghar Par' have secured many funding rounds. As can be seen, SE has a far-reaching effect on tackling social and environmental issues, especially in developing economies like Pakistan, so the question arises: Do the people distributing funding and selecting startups also emphasize SE?

1.2 ESG

Another closely related term, Environment & Social Governance (ESG), emerged two decades ago. Historically, ESG was used to measure an organization's environmental and social impact. Initially, ESG was mainly relevant in the context of investment, but now its scope has broadened and includes customers, suppliers, employees, and the general public (IBM, 2023). The overall ESG model has a significant relationship with economic performance (Cek & Eyupolgu, 2023). ESG metrics assess an organization's impact on sustainability and can be taken as a proxy for sustainable performance and facilitate socially responsible investment (SRI) decisions. Large-scale studies also show that irrespective of the economic development level and institutional environment, there is a correlation between ESG and the financial performance of companies (Garcia & Orsatto, 2020).

Notwithstanding the importance of SEs for economies and the emphasis to assess the ESG framework, let us find out how Pakistani startup ecosystem managers, judges, and investors incorporate these elements when selecting startups.

2. METHODOLOGY

This study adopts a constructivist grounded theory approach, integrating elements from the methodologies of Strauss and Corbin (1990) and Charmaz (2014). This approach allows for an in-depth exploration of the experiences and perceptions of start-up selectors, mentors, judges, and investors.

The sample for this study includes 13 participants, including four women and nine men, in positions of authority to select startups from across Pakistani incubators, accelerators, chambers of commerce, and venture capitalists. Purposeful sampling was employed, selecting participants who met established criteria (influential selectors for winning startups) to ensure their insights aligned with the research focus. The lead researcher's personal experiences as a social entrepreneur and seminal startup mentor provided a basis for empathy and understanding, aiding in building rapport with the participants as a "human instrument."

The data for the study are from semi-structured, in-depth interviews. The interview guide included broad questions about the criteria for selecting startups, the weight of ES and ESG factors in evaluating startups, how to encourage SE, and what barriers exist. The interviews were audio recorded using participants' consent, and participants were allowed to opt out of recording (except for one participant who requested confidentiality). As outlined in the Helsinki Protocol, ethical considerations included ensuring voluntary participation and participant anonymity. Please refer to Table 1 for the participant's profile with pseudonyms. An effort was made to remove the company name, country of affiliation, or foreign funding agency they are associated with to maintain anonymity.

For data analysis, initially, the interviews were transcribed verbatim, ensuring the preservation of participants' narratives. Open coding was performed on all the transcripts using a line-by-line approach. The open codes were grouped into conceptual categories, capturing the common themes and patterns present in the data. The researcher engaged in reflective discussions to better understand the emergent themes and concepts. Axial coding facilitated the examination of relationships between the conceptual categories. The researcher re-examined the categories, identified their interconnections, and established linkages. To enhance the validity and credibility of the findings, researchers shared the emergent themes with the participants and peers. Multiple data sources were used for triangulation, including field notes from the researcher's observations and organizational charts from the institutions' websites, where the participants worked and public information regarding selection criteria by the incubator/accelerator/or VC shown on their website or brochures was consulted. This approach ensured that the interpretations and conclusions drawn from the data were well-founded and trustworthy.

Table 1. Participants demographics

Pseudo Name	Gender	Experience with startup mentoring & selection	Category
Muhammad	Male	34 years	Incubator Administrator, judge, investor
Rayyan	Male	6 years	Incubator Mentor, Angel Investor
Majeed	Male	10 years	Incubator Administration, Angel
Hafsa	Female	7 years	Incubator Administration, judge
Sajid	Male	7 years	Incubator Administration, Judge
Munawar	Male	16 years	Investor, Ecosystem enabler & Judge
Shehla	Female	8 years	Mentor, Investor, Consultant
Khayam	Male	11 years	Incubator Administration, Angel Investor
Zainab	Female	13 years	Incubator Administration, VC
Ayesha	Female	9 years	Angel Investor
Khalid	Male	7 years	Incubator Administration
Shahid	Male	11 years	Incubator Administration, Angel Investor
Altaf	Male	7-10 years	Mentor

2.1 Detailed Profiles of the Participants

Muhammad is one of the pioneers in creating the startup culture and developing this ecosystem in Pakistan. After completing his MBA in 1989, successful entrepreneur for 34 years. There was no mentorship, so, out of his experience, he started advising people and visiting universities as a guest lecturer in the 1990s. to start local city chapters to solve local problems in 2008. In 2011, another international startup event organizer came to Pakistan and created ripples in the startup culture through its hackathons. The Startup Cup was launched in 2013 and has trained more than 65,000 entrepreneurs to build winning pitches across seven cities in Pakistan. In 2015, he got involved in one of the world's largest accelerators. He now serves as country head for Pakistan's chapter, helping establish the National Incubation Center (NIC) and becoming their curriculum partner. He works with the most prestigious aid providers and regularly trains entrepreneurs for their different grants and schemes. Now, they are working on communities and, with the help of donors, imparting training for skills, helping students appear for international certifications in technology, and helping them with placement. They have just started another NIC in another industrial city in Pakistan, which is doing well.

Rayyan has had a software house for six years and two other startups, one overseas and the other in health technology. They provide solutions to startups and SMEs to build products, secure appropriate technology, enter markets, and raise capital. For their health startup, they are developing a contactless remote vital monitoring solution to help patients with early risk assessment. As an investor, mentor, and judge, he has been involved for more than 2.5 years in the tech ecosystem of startups through NICs.

Majeed has led one of very few SE ventures for a prestigious international social enterprise's Pakistan chapter for the last ten years. Their sole aim is to create a social impact in civil society and foster the culture of social entrepreneurship. They incubate startups with accountability or good governance-related ideas, build their capacity through training workshops, connect them with potential funders inside and outside of Pakistan, provide seed funding up to $10,000, arrange events, and provide all-inclusive support. Their international office is now responsible for looking after their incubator globally. They also host youth peace incubators to support youth with the technical, financial, and moral support required by eight major universities in Pakistan, impacting about 30,000 youth. The third initiative is a climate justice incubator focused on climate-related issues. The Pakistan chapter was established after winning a global event and getting the seed funding to establish this social enterprise in Pakistan.

Hafsa is a Pakistani living abroad and established a social enterprise in 2017, an international development organization that helps women in emerging markets launch and scale their businesses and careers. It is an online accelerator program offering courses, mentorship, and coaching to teach women about entrepreneurship online. She started 2016 with a copyrighting consultancy, realizing that women remain underrepresented in the startup ecosystem. She set out on a mission to crack the code of running a social enterprise while converting it into a business, making money, and training women to do the same. She believes that more organizations should step up and help women marginalized in Pakistan enter the entrepreneurial journey and join tech careers, giving them financial independence, tools, confidence, and everything else they need to succeed.

Sajid was an engineer who started a venture for hardware in 2006 for the defense industry and sold it for $100,000. He joined a government job related to research and development and stayed there till 2015, then went abroad to pursue an MBA from a very prestigious business school with various chapters worldwide for startup competitions. Sajid brought the competition from the foreign university for startups he studied at to Pakistan. He ventured into two more startups and started the consulting firm GHI, which got funding from a very influential aid agency in a foreign country. He initially established two incubation centers at two universities and seven more incubation centers across Pakistan at different universities. Lastly, they secured funding for a very high-tech incubation center, one of a kind in Pakistan, with a public-private partnership, and are its administrators.

Munawar is a hybrid corporate-type entrepreneur who lives abroad. He started his career with a corporate job and worked for Fortune 500 companies for many years. He entered the higher education sector and came to Pakistan to lead a prestigious university. He has a tech company that creates ecosystems for academia and corporations. He got involved in the Pakistani ecosystem when he was a pioneering member of a foreign entity that supported Pakistani startups in 2007 and then another enabler from abroad who fostered startup culture in Pakistan.

Shehla has been involved in the Pakistani ecosystem as a mentor and judge for six years and has evaluated many startups as a judge in many hackathons. Currently, she has also started consulting for startups; her focus is mainly on women-owned startups.

Khayam has been an entrepreneur since his teenage years in 1980, before he moved abroad. He launched many ventures, failed to do so, and accumulated knowledge and experience. In 2000, he decided to repay his native country, believing only entrepreneurship could salvage our economy. When incubation started popping up, he thought we did not have eggs to hatch, so he believed in a greenhouse model, replicated the popular reality shows of the West for entrepreneurs' funding, and launched significant events where investors, entrepreneurs, and all startup ecosystem players have come together for impact since 2013.

Zainab founded Pakistan's most prestigious acceleration program, which started in 2011 as an ecosystem builder and entrepreneurship acceleration program. She also manages a venture capital fund, which began in 2019. She has been involved in the ecosystem for 13 years and has been an investor for five years.

Ayesha was a credit risk analyst for a bank. Later, she gained syndicate financing experience for corporations. She started her venture in 2014. In 2017, she got involved in a very prestigious global start-up competition as a judge. She had been a very active member of the Chamber of Commerce and convener for the Commercial and Research Development Committee, which works on trade-academic linkage. She has worked as a judge for many NICs and other prestigious organizations in the Pakistani ecosystem and even for regional organizations for a consortium of countries.

Khalid was a telecom engineer who worked in the telecom sector in 1990 and, in 2001, set up his own IT company, a billion-dollar company working in four countries. He was the pioneer who convinced the government to set up the first national incubator center and kicked off the startup culture in Pakistan. From 2016 to now, hundreds of startups have been trained, and 1,000 startups have been interviewed.

Shahid owns an IT company that has offices in Pakistan and abroad. They complete projects in Pakistan and deliver them to foreign markets. He also runs a training institute in Pakistan where they teach IT and computer skills to university students and youth and even prepare them for international language testing tests. To give back to his native country, he started investing in startups and training youth instead of giving to charity. He began his incubation venture and provided opportunities to the brilliant founders for investment and mentoring. Along the way, he was involved as a judge for other prestigious funding and hackathon events for startups.

Last but not least, Altaf is a professional accountant. From early on, he was involved in market research and evidence-based decision-making for market-driven solutions. His involvement with startups came from his role in banks that financed startups 15 years ago, in a very nascent stage, even before the word startup was popularized in Pakistan. He then started consulting for FMCG, and as a researcher and financer, he got into the startup ecosystem and has served as a mentor and judge for seven years.

3. RESULTS AND ANALYSIS

The interviews occurred from the end of February 2024 to the middle of April 2024. When the respondents' responses showed no other emerging themes and the data saturation point was reached, we used only 13 interviews with the most influential figures in the Pakistani startup ecosystem.

3.1 Qualitative Themes from the Interviews

The interviews were typed up and examined for open codes. After the development of conceptual categories, data confirmation and axial coding of conceptual themes allowed the identification of trends and patterns in interview responses.

3.1.1. Start-Up Judging Criteria

The responses were fascinating for the current selection criteria practiced in incubators, accelerators, startup competitions and investors. Though the results may sound a little off topic but to understand the mind set prevailing we need to understand the current selection criteria in the ecosystem for the selection of startups. The results are and are summarised in Table 2

Table 2. Startup judging criteria

Theme	Description	Subthemes
Business Model	Will the startup earn enough revenues to sustain and stay profitable	● Market potential ● Product-Market fit
Idea	The problem that the idea will solve in the market	● Traction ● Growth strategy ● Understanding of business area/industry
Startup Founder's Personality	Does the Founder/CEO have the will to persevere for many years	● Execution plan
Potential and Capability of the Team	Has the team relevant experience and expertise to carry out the operations	● Stakes of the founder and their commitment ● The mindset of the Team
Scalability	Is the idea scalable and can see growth	● Go to Market Strategy ● Progress made.
Judges Priorities	How qualified were the judges, and which things they prioritize the most as per their interests	● Resources they have ● Value proposition
Presentation	How well they impress the judges with a vow effect	● Target audience ● Utilization of funding plan ● Benefit to society. ● Job Creations. ● Which SDG they target

It was shocking to learn that judges' focus on selecting startups in any capacity (administrator, investor, mentor) was hardly related to Social or environmental criteria. Only 0–10% weightage was given in general and 20–40% for SE ventures.

Muhammad elaborated, 'A good pitch should not be the reason to select someone. This is a very unfortunate aspect: in most competitions, when somebody pitches very well, even if the idea is not very good or the founder is not very good, it is likely to get selected.

About the selection Criteria Rayyan said, We need to understand here what sort of pitch that is and what sort of target audience it is. Because when you are pitching something to an investor, to be very honest, an investor only focuses on revenues regardless of what the technology is or what the idea is. But when we see a different target audience, like incubators and accelerators, where they focus on impact, then the CSR activities do matter.

Personally, Rayyan says, We see the market potential of the startup itself? What is the market size, what is the growth potential, what sort of audience that you're targeting, how much this startup can grow eventually, is the team capable enough to execute this product or not, product team fit, and then similarly, product-market fit? These are the main parameters that we judge'. For university incubators and NICs, he said, 'I've noticed that they don't have criteria while taking a startup, and if you do in-depth analysis, you'll see everybody wants numbers. They just want to fill their startup cohort.

Majid, since they run an ES base incubator, said, The personal commitment of the people who are pitching the idea is important, When you're working with young people, the moment they find the next cool thing, they would like to move on, so I look for people who are committed to their ideas. The second thing, after the commitment phase, is that I would like to assess in depth their understanding of the area around which they want to work.

Stressing upon the business model, Hafsa said, 'the most important thing to look for is a business model. I think the word entrepreneurship, the word startup, the word running your own company, being your own boss—all these statements have kind of democratized entrepreneurship a lot. So, everybody who thinks that they have an idea can convert it into a business pays very little attention to the business model. In our accelerators, we always see that this person has an idea, and I always see how this person is doing it differently. What is their business model? And what are their numbers'?

Regarding their evaluation criteria, Sajid said, We have a rubric for formal selection criteria and a scoring card. But primarily, we look for three things. Number one is the team, number two is the market size, and number three is the ability to execute. Mostly, it's the team that's the most critical part. I primarily look for a founder-incubator fit, which is very important. At least 10% of the criteria focus on sustainability.

Munawar said while judging, Is it affordable to a common person? What is the pricing scheme? Secondly, as a product or a service, how much of the product serves a social cause instead of just being a money maker? If it's a manufactured product, is it contributing negatively to the environment?

Shehla said, It's almost the same across all levels. We mostly look at the idea first, then the problem that somebody is solving, and the business model for the solution itself. How strong is their revenue model and value proposition, how well do they understand the target audience, and how good is their operational model? So, this is an overarching aspect of what we look at. Then we look at their marketing, like, what is their go-to marketing strategy. What is their plan for scaling?

Khayam believes, There is no way in 10 minutes you will hear the whole story or judge the person. So, we don't judge; we simply take it at face value. Okay, what is on offer? The criteria are simple in five aspects: One is the customer. The second is how you will identify that customer's problem and then fulfill it with your solution. Are you capable enough to achieve it? Which is the team itself? Then, fourth, is the progress: how much progress have you made, in what time, and what sort of resources you have available to yourself, you have put in, whether it is time or money?

Zainab said, 'Most of the companies in our investment portfolio (14) have an impact lens regarding job creation or industry disruption, so I would say 100% are SE companies, but they are not "social entrepreneurs" since they are commercial for-profit companies.'

Ayesha said, Evaluation criteria are mainly based on the attitude and the intra-preneurial skills that a person has, so the focus is more on individual evaluations than the business idea. When you talk about the Pakistani ecosystem, such as NIC, their evaluation criteria do not include individual evaluation; the main focus is on business and startup mode. whenever I attend university startup events or student entrepreneurs, my main aim is to teach them how their ideas can be commercialized.

Khalid believes, One of the major things is the mindset in terms of how people perceive ideas. How do they perceive the challenges around those ideas and the opportunities around those ideas? And also, how do they move on beyond the idea itself? Has it already been done anywhere else in the world? then, of course, we look at the founders themselves. So, for example, in our experience, if it's a one-solo founder, then that's not really considered to be something very positive.'

Shahid said, 'If they are not clear about their idea about their finance model, nobody is going to promote them at all.'

Altaf said that 'the judges on the panel are looking at the startups as their own sifting mechanism, where they filter their ideas, or how they assess the yardstick; all I'm saying is that it's not a collectively structured or agreed upon methodology, where they complement each other, and it funnels down in a structured way.'

Further adding to judges' mix in the selection penal and their background and priority to select startups, Muhammad said, problems with the selection criteria are that it should not be a democracy or democratic decision. However, most of the decisions happen more on a democratic basis, where everyone has an equal say. But sometimes one person can sway (the one pitching or any judge's opinion) the rest of the judges in the direction that they want. And that is something that happens quite regularly.

3.1.2 Weightage of Social Venture and Environmental Sustainability in the selection of Startups

The most interesting finding, due to the scope of the chapter, was the importance given to selecting SE or considering ESG factors. As can be seen from Table 3, the criteria of selection based on social or environmental factors are almost negligible for winning startups.

Table 3. Percentage of selection based on SE or ESG

Pseudo Name	% of selection based on SE or ESG	Comments
Muhammad	0%	'Based on our selection criteria, we believe every startup has a social impact. However, we are not specifically looking at the environment or its social impact.'
Rayyan	5%	It is very minute. Maybe around 5%. Not much, unfortunately
Majeed*	20% On average	We use a mix of methodology and criteria and try to headhunt people already creating an impact. However, 80% of our focus is on selecting social organizations.
Hafsa *	40%	'We only run social entrepreneurship accelerators. However, for us, it's extremely important to understand whether the organization applying is even a social enterprise. We give 40% weight to the business model.'
Sajid	10%	'Team, to me, is, like, 40%, or 50%. I want to select good teams so that these teams can, if required, change their ideas, change the market segment, change the business model, and everything else. But we have focused on sustainability
Munawar	N/A	'I think that's something I would take into account, which is the product. Is the output positively impacting the environment (but not as a major criterion)?
Shehla	For general startups, 0%	'In general, nowhere does this come into account, such as how your operations affect the environment and your governance. So, I think that is a big missing piece. We only ask these questions when a startup is sustainability-specific; they are being socially responsible. Then obviously, we ask those questions as a part of their business model conversation, but not as a separate sustainability angle question anyway.'
Khayam	0%	We don't have any criteria. Specifically, I would like to know if the woman-led startup is or if there's a startup that is fulfilling the SDG goal. This is counterproductive. This is a level playing field for everyone
Zainab	N/A	'I'm not a startup "judge," so this question doesn't pertain to me. (she is an investor and runs an accelerator.)
Ayesha	10-*25%	I don't like to see pitches that lack numbers. Because if there is a product or a service, I want to see numbers. I keep the green environment at 10% weightage, and CSR, I believe, gets 25% weightage
Khalid	Didn't specify	I do recall that social impact was considered a secondary thing. We are doing it for the money. And that was the primary objective
Shahid	10%	According to international standards, only five or 10% of startups are ready for international contestants.
Altaf	Didn't specify	'VC has moved away from the ESG passion, is less passionate about ESG, and is way more concerned about the viability of the business model

*Purely for Social Businesses Pitches

It was quite alarming to learn that most participants observed that not more than 10% of SE ventures are in the startup ecosystem.

Khalid said that a few years ago, the number of startups related to social impact was negligible—maybe one or two percent. The numbers have increased, but still, it's a minority. So, if you were to ask me today, I would say that perhaps five to 10 percent of them would be focused on environmental impact, SDGs, or social impact.

3.1.3 Themes Emerged Among Judges: Meagre Training, Nepotism, and Monopolies

The most astonishing thing that surfaced was that none of the judges received any formal training; only two were given a workshop before a globally prestigious pitching competition. To report the finding here is to draw attention that unless we have qualified professional with a focus and awareness on ESG as judges, how can we expect that the ESG and SE framework are the selection criteria? The idea is not to just understand but give some policy suggestions to the ecosystem enablers in selection of judges as well. Most were selected to judge based on their networking or reputation in the business community. After this discovery, we asked them about the status of nepotism and monopolies in the ecosystem. However, only the incubation administrator admitted to giving some training. Muhammad said, 'We're very careful. Who are we selecting, and then we brief them on what we are looking at, what sort of value we can add, and what sort of startup would be a good fit for us?'

Most people acknowledge favouritism, nepotism, and monopolies in the startup ecosystem but have a soft view of it, accepting it as a fact. Regarding monopolies, Rayyan said,' It is there. You see the same faces almost everywhere, and they have control of a lot of things, and that is why the ecosystem somehow stays stagnant in big incubators or accelerators. No startup has raised any significant amount as such'.

Majeed said, 'It's a very small circle, and people like to keep it that way. You know, they think that if they sort of open it up for everyone else, they might lose the discretionary power that they currently have.' Additionally, Sajid said, 'Pakistani startups ecosystem is in very early stage within the nascent stage. There are challenges. I would rather focus on other bigger challenges, which I believe are the most priority areas for us, than delving in nepotism, which I would not like to agree with.'

Zainab said, 'There is a general gender and class-based bias in the ecosystem. Founders who've had exposure to or studied abroad are seen more positively (as are people who can pitch/speak English well). '

Muhammad raised a fascinating point, saying, 'Can you be an entrepreneur if you're not connected? Most of the funding has gone to people who have some sort of foreign connection, who have either worked abroad in the biggest IT companies or who have connections with global VCs. Very few homegrown Pakistani entrepreneurs have managed to secure funding. Does this mean that there is nepotism or favoritism in the system? I don't think so. When you say there are very few players in the ecosystem or there's a monopoly No, these are the people taking the initial risks because they are not getting the return.'

Hafsa also had an exciting take: 'What I observed in Pakistan is that there is a huge gap between people who know their stuff and people who are loud about it. And a lot of people who are loud get to judge. It's not their fault that somebody who knows their stuff is not judging those competitions.'

3.1.4 Foster a Culture that Supports SE & ESG Framework

The following themes emerged regarding what is necessary to foster a culture of SE and encourage the ESG framework:

Table 4. What can foster SE and ESG

Theme	Description
Regulatory Penalties	Tax/fine the polluters, especially the big fish
SE & ESG training for all Entrepreneurs	So they know the impact and effect of their production and processes.
Government Monitoring for Eco-friendly Practices	In all stages of production and delivery, the government should monitor that regulations are followed
Viable and Cheaper Options to Adopt Green Practices	Make adopting green practices affordable on a large scale
Incentivize with Tax credits	Encouraging entrepreneurs to pursue SE and use green products and services through tax rebates and amnesties.
Educate and advocate for SE & ESG in universities.	university should be teaching the requisite knowledge and importance of SE and ESG
Educate the consumer	To purchase the products and services that are ESG and support SE for the greater good of society
Competitions, Hackathons, and for SE and ESG	Healthy competition with monetary rewards increases the interests of entrepreneurs
More funding opportunities and educating investors	It will ensure that new entrants will focus on SE and ESG to qualify for funding

Muhammad posited, 'When we talk about penalties for environmental violations, we have not to penalize the poorest first. We need to start taking action against those polluting on a large scale, and those are the industries. I would not force people to adopt green practices at all costs; I would rather change their perspective so that it makes sense for them to believe that being responsible also earns a good income. No anti-smoking campaign can work when I say, don't smoke. It's hazardous, right? It has 121 chemicals, and your lungs will turn black, and so on. No, I have to make it socially unacceptable. So now, I love it when I go to airports, especially internationally, and see these small blast cabins with people who look like they're in a zoo. Because that has had an impact, smoking has gone down. So, to have an impact, we have to find the right levers.'

Rayyan said, 'Pakistan is struggling economically, and the way forward is social entrepreneurship. Although we do not have much to do with environmental pollution, we are the worst-affected country in the world. The way forward to improve the economy is through industrialization. Moreover, if businesses are not taught from the start to be green, we are already in a disaster,' he added. Regarding the SDGs, 'I'll also tell you the other side: the consumer is unwilling to adopt these green products. I have observed that a lot of people are not even aware of what the SDGs are. What are the three sustainability rules?

About the government role, Hafsa said, 'I think it's going to be a struggle, until we hit those economies of scale, until the government steps in and says that we are promoting this XYZ thing until the government starts giving tax rebates, it will always be an issue for a country like Pakistan, where people would always choose lower priced products over protecting the environment.'

Munawar said about consumer awareness, 'We'll have to educate the customer about it. If I give a service where my car is environmentally sound, it means it's also costing a bit more. I'm passing the extra cost down to the consumer.' '

Shehla also believed that awareness and advocacy should be effective. 'So first, we need an understanding of what social enterprise is. Second, when it comes to sustainability and ESG-related things, there is a lot of education and awareness required at all levels.

Zainab believed that 'we can encourage SE via competitions and hackathons at the national level, and through incubation/acceleration programs, funding also increases interest.'

Munawwar also stressed investment opportunities. 'New ideas are very seldom supported. It's a shame, but I think part of that is because we have a very small investor footprint and therefore the very few that they have. They try to play safe.'

3.1.5 Antecedents that Impede SE

Table 5. Factors that hamper SE

Theme	Description
A culture of Rules and low Risk-Taking hampers SE	Pakistan is a collectivist society which is generally risk-averse
Parents aspiration for obedience and stable jobs	The familial system wants a secure and stable career and views entrepreneurship as risky

continued on following page

Table 5. Continued

Theme	Description
Untrained/unsuitable Faculty in universities are unable to encourage SE	Faculty values influence students; their myopic vision, lack of understanding and knowledge, and disconnect from corporate trends can create distorted and unrealistic views for students regarding SE
University Curriculum, Priority, and Lack of Industry-Related Understanding	The curriculum of universities is not being revised at the pace at which the industry is evolving. They are mostly creating managers, not leaders. Their disconnect with industry is a setback for students entering the practical world.
Lack of understanding of the Concept of SE	Most people don't even understand the concept and how it can improve the economy.
Celebrate Success stories of SE ventures	That way, people are motivated to be known for their success stories and work on SE and ESG.

The researcher noticed that most participants didn't have a clear view of social entrepreneurship, except for two incubator administrators who were predominantly working on SE and two others. Most believe entrepreneurship is inherently social in nature; therefore, all startups are social. This sociological insight calls for more concerted advocacy and information campaigns that stress what SE is and the benefits of adopting the SE and ESG frameworks on a mass scale.

Hafsa said, 'In an ecosystem like Pakistan, many people are not even aware of what social enterprises are; the term is very Western. When we launched our program with XYZ Social Entrepreneurship Center in North America, suddenly, everybody started talking about it. In any developed country, social enterprise is a legal kind of structure. So, in the US, a B-corp is not a nonprofit; B stands for benefits. It's an organization that stands for social benefit. And the law itself has given them a legal structure to register themselves as a B-corp. But in a country like Pakistan, the moment you utter the word social enterprise, a lot of people confuse it with nonprofits or NGOs.

Sajid said, 'People try to club social entrepreneurship with charity or CSR? It's not charity. It's not CSR. This is for good, but for profit.

Universities' role emerged as an issue in fostering a culture of green practices and encouraging them to use ESG frameworks and SE. Hafsa said, 'They're out of touch with reality. Universities in Pakistan have created their own bubble. They've created their universe and think this is where the world exists. Anything outside should come to them, not go out there and realize where the world has gone.'

Sajid said, 'We need improvement in HEC [Higher Education Commission] policies, where the current policy mandated publications only and teachers' promotion and perks were linked to publications only.' This is why faculty are not motivated to solve real-world problems but rather to focus on research.

Munawar said, 'We tend to be a culture emphasizing adherence to rules. We don't encourage our children to question or break the rules. By age 18 or 19, their thinking is already constrained. By the time they arrive at universities, business programs at our universities are meant to produce managers. Our education basically prepares them to know all the rules. and it is almost impossible to tell them all of a sudden and expect them to become great entrepreneurs. Faculty beliefs and values are important because students emulate them. There is no humility or collaborative mindset, and dictatorship is the concept being practiced by faculty, as opposed to, you know, learning together.

Shehla posited, 'I think there is a gap between academia, where research is happening, and industry, where action is happening. It is much easier to collaborate with an organization facing the issue and pilot the project for academics.

Ayesha also believes that, in general, 'we are saying our startup ecosystem isn't developed because we have people who are only good in theory.'

Khalid stated, "Unfortunately, professors who have never been entrepreneurs typically run business incubation centers within universities. So if I've never earned one rupee in my life through business, how can I teach somebody to make money?'

Altaf said, 'Embedding ESG in a better manner in startups requires education at all levels. You must educate the judges, financial institutions, and ministries. On a larger scale, it requires awareness and understanding of the sheer necessity of where we are now and how ESG will affect all our lives. I think more advocacy needs to be done, and more success stories must be told on a smaller scale. What will make a difference is how we highlight and showcase smaller startups with ESG as part of their business model, giving confidence to other startups and founders.'

4. DISCUSSION

This qualitative research was an eye-opener for the Pakistani Startup Ecosystem (PSE) in general and for all SE stakeholders. We came to understand that there are many multidimensional factors if we want to encourage SE and adopt ESG frameworks in the ecosystem, with many antecedents that serve as stumbling blocks. We also talked about solutions.

Since we targeted the most influential players in the PSE, mainly the top executives of the incubation centers at national levels, influential judges, angel investors, or venture capitalists, only 4/13 respondents could articulate a definition of SE. This finding is concerning, as two are leading incubators and accelerators established by international organizations with heavily foreign-funded ventures for SE. These are the ecosystem's movers, shakers, and influencers; their lack of awareness reflects a much deeper issue of understanding the real importance of SE for a country like

Pakistan. It calls for more tangible and concrete steps to create this awareness and train the judges for capacity-building and conceptual clarity.

When the youth reach universities, most universities focus again on subject and theoretical knowledge. A huge gap exists in academia-industry fit, and currently, our universities are lagging in developing a conducive learning environment that fosters SE. The faculty are mostly non-practicers, the syllabus needs to be aligned to industry trends, and there is much disconnect between research at universities and market realities or requirements. This industry-academia void needs to be bridged, and policymakers like HEC should encourage more faculty engagement with corporations. The capacity of faculty to be qualified to teach and encourage SE and ESG should also be considered, and practitioners should be engaged to teach these subjects about entrepreneurship. Similarly, corporations should see the benefit of reaching out to universities for their market research and analysis since universities have qualified faculty and resources to conduct such research. Governments need to step in to create policies that foster academic and industry partnerships and stress incorporating SE and ESG frameworks.

The themes emerging to encourage SE and ESG range from awareness to incentives at all levels. Social enterprises should also get incentives like tax exemptions or credits for practicing ESG elements. Making green/eco products affordable through subsidies encourages consumers to buy green products during this inflation. Similarly, such subsidies will encourage producers to opt for more environmentally friendly products or processes in their productions or services. Social entrepreneurs in almost every developing economy face financial difficulty due to a lack of funding for local solutions, and investors should be encouraged to patronize SE projects.

One of the interesting findings from the studies is what can we do to foster SE and ESG, kindly refer to **Table 4**, many interesting themes emerged, ranging from penalties from regulatory authorities. This in turn requires training and education of SE and ESG frameworks only then we can penalise the entrepreneurs breaching ESG frameworks. unless the policy makers are not taking active control for implementation of policies, and monitoring organisations on each stage of production to ensure safe environmental practices organizations and entrepreneurs will keep on cutting corners. Since organisations need to be profitable, the Governments must intervene to provide viable and cheap alternatives for green practices, must provide tax incentives for the proponents of ESG frameworks to foster ESG and SE. Over all universities should be hub for awareness, education and innovative solution provider, must encourage hackathons on campus and provide seed fundings for viable ideas, so the new entrants and entrepreneurs build their models on the themes of ESG.

The above finding corroborates with the fact as highlighted in **Table 5** that the factors that impede adopting ESG frameworks or pursue SE, that points towards the culture of low risk taking, since parents from the start encourages children to pursue careers in stable Government jobs, therefore, there is little support from home, to start and SE venture. Universities are also not playing their roles to create awareness that SE could be a profitable venture. The academia -industry void and dearth of research do not let the students and new entrants for entrepreneurial venture be able to know the huge potential that may exist in the market to start a venture for SE or based on ESG frameworks. One of the main issues highlighted was the fact that few people actually understand the concept of SE, therefore, success stories of SE and incorporation of ESG frameworks should be celebrated to motivate, create awareness and normalising practicing SE and ESG frameworks.

Although there is evidence of many efforts by Governments, funding agencies, and PSE to promote SE, the data reveal that the current ratio of social startups is (as per the participants' observations) between 5% and 10%. This low uptake of social capital within the entrepreneurship sector is alarming and severe. Immediate steps are required to address this gap and aid Pakistan's dwindling economy by promoting SE and ESG.

5. CONCLUSION

Our research indicates that a basic understanding of SE or ESG is required at all levels. Therefore, awareness and advocacy are required in the media and education sectors and mandatory for all incubators and accelerators, organized angel investor networks, venture capitalists, and policymakers at the government level, or, in short, for all stakeholders. We have seen that investing in and encouraging SE is essential for developing economies, as the poverty level persists in developing economies, meaning that governments and NGOs do not have the resources to tackle the problem (Marcel et al., 2024; Nor, 2024). Investing in awareness will have manifold effects, diluting the cultural impediment. As shown in Table 5, the mindset of parents to be risk-aversive and wanting their children to go for rule-based safe bets steers youth towards finding conventional jobs. With such a massive bulge of youth and the economy in shambles, the government and job market do not have enough jobs to offer. One solution lies in entrepreneurship for the livelihood of the youth.

From the qualitative discussions, it is evident that we can enforce green practices that are good for society by having legislation, regulatory checks, and penalties. Penalizing the big players, enforcing fines for breaching ESG principles, and regulatory authorities' role in ensuring that businesses adopt SE and ESG practices can ensure positive results for the startup ecosystem to adopt SE and ESG. For instance, Pakistan's corporate regulator has been building the governance architecture for corporate enterprises since 2002. The indigenous code of corporate governance, loosely based on OECD principles, emphasizes probity, transparency, and accountability. Good governance practices lead to share price stability, long-term sustainable growth, and attractiveness to institutional investors (SDPI, 2023). The Securities and Exchange Commission of Pakistan (SECP) has issued draft guidelines on voluntary ESG disclosures. These guidelines are part of the ESG Regulatory Roadmap issued in June 2022. The SECP aims to enhance transparency and encourage companies to report on their ESG performance (SECP, 2023). Such efforts have highlighted the importance of ESG and SE from regulatory authorities, and SE is embracing them gradually.

A chorus of stakeholders demanding progress can change the game, and more entrepreneurs will be interested in steering for SE and ESG and pivoting their business model to incorporate ESG aspects or make it altogether a social startup. Like sharing the success story of a newly launched NIC, Muhammad said, We asked the team lead (investors/sponsors) to commit to an X amount of investment every year. That has been the game changer. So, in the very first year, the sponsor has already invested a considerable amount of money, and they will continue doing this every year. Immediately after that, we also created a unique event where we invited Pakistan's leading venture capitalists to the city. And we also invited the top industrialists in the city. The VCs then educated the industrialists on the startup economy, VC math, and why they should invest in startups. As a result, we launched a local angel investment network of the city's industries, and they will be investing as well. Now, what happens when these things come into place? Our selection criteria start to change because now that we know we have an angel investment fund, we are looking at two tracks: one track is very small amounts of money—three, four lakh rupees—that somebody needs to test an idea, and the other track will be sort of a grant. So, industrialists know they should not expect results from it, but it's going to help the startup and only at scale-up level can investors make money.

Startup administrators and judges should also receive rigorous capacity-building training to promote and select high-impact social startups that promote ESG. Similarly, startup founders should receive training highlighting the importance of SE and ESG and the rewards of practicing such socially responsible practices to motivate them to practice SE and ESG.

The selection criteria of the startups in incubators, accelerators, or funding rounds must also be revised. Less than 10% is dedicated to SE and ESG; even incubators based on SE give 20–40% weight to social/environmental orientation. The maximum weighting of selection criteria is based on the business model and how it generates profits. While ideation, business/finance model, go-to-market strategy, customers, product-market fit, and a good pitch are all important factors to consider, training and clear rubrics that are carefully crafted could steer the focus on SE and ESG during the selection process.

This research is significant as many other developing countries could benefit from these findings with constraints and contexts similar to those in Pakistan. The research will be especially significant for policymakers, investors, and mentors to understand the importance of training startup evaluators and setting more robust criteria incorporating ESG frameworks for selection and funding. This study cannot be generalized due to its limited number of in-depth interviews. However, it could reveal the pulse of the mindset that prevails among the decision-makers selecting startups, as they have a trickledown effect on focusing on sustainability for the whole startup ecosystem.

The values of social entrepreneurship include the appropriate use of resources to promote a sustainable world where trust, honesty, respect, and hope are valued (Mathur 2011). We hope that this research will make ripples in the power corridors, create legislation, implement policies, and work on novel solutions to eliminate the areas we identified in Table 5 that impede SE and ESG adoption for a sustainable future for uplifting poverty and pressing issues in society using social entrepreneurship. We hope future research finds ways to address these challenges.

6. LIMITATIONS OF THE STUDY & FUTURE SCOPE

Due to the scope and timelines of the study, only influential incubators, accelerators, and VCs were considered for the interviews, based on the purposive sampling and availability. This limited data also restricts generalisability of the results, however economies with challenges similar to Pakistan can benefit from the findings. Since startup culture in Pakistan is just getting pace, and most of the respondents are somehow connected to each other as the influencers of the system, therefore, show similar tendencies and views to skew the results and influence the judging criteria.

For future we recommend a detailed study that include the major university incubators, and Government ministries involved in the propagation of startup culture should be included to understand their selection criteria and philosophy regarding the importance of SE and incorporating ESG frameworks. We also recommend quantitative analysis of the current startups and their orientation for the SE, understand barriers that impedes SE and adopting ESG.

REFERENCES

Abazi-Alili, H. R. Ç. (2016). Encouragement factors of social entrepreneurial activities in Europe. *International Journal of Foresight and Innovation Policy*, 11(4), 225. 10.1504/IJFIP.2016.084529

Asif, M. A. (2018). The Role of Social Entrepreneurship in Pakistan and its Impact on Economy. *International Journal of Business. Economics and Management*, 5(5), 117–127.

Bento, P. F. (2018). How Social Entrepreneurship Promotes Sustainable Development: With Some Examples from Developed and Developing Countries. *Studies on entrepreneurship, structural change and industrial dynamics*, 283–297.

Çek, K., & Eyupoglu, S. (2020). Does environmental, social and governance performance influence economic performance? *Journal of Business Economics and Management*, 21(4), 1165–1184. 10.3846/jbem.2020.12725

Coleman, J. S. (1988). Social Capital in the Creation of Human Capital. *American Journal of Sociology*, 94, S95–S120. 10.1086/228943

Damiongraham. (2023, August 29). *The Catalyst for Change: The Role of Social Entrepreneurship in Economic Development*. Retrieved from Economic Impact Catalyst: https://economicimpactcatalyst.com/social-entrepreneurship/

Elkington, J. (1997). *Cannibals with Forks: The Triple Bottom Line of 21st Century Business*. New Society Publishers.

Ferrero-Ferrero, I. I., Fernández-Izquierdo, M., & Muñoz-Torres, M. (2016). The effect of environmental, social and governance consistency on economic results. *Sustainability (Basel)*, 8(10), 1005. 10.3390/su8101005

Garcia, A. S., & Orsato, R. J. (2020). Testing the institutional difference hypothesis: A study about environmental, social, governance, and financial performance. *Business Strategy and the Environment*, 29(8), 3261–3272. 10.1002/bse.2570

GEM. (2017). *GEM 2016/2017 Global Report*. London: GEM. Retrieved from https://www.gemconsortium.org/report/gem-2016-2017-global-report

Hart, S. L., & Milstein, M. B. (2003). Creating Sustainable Value. *The Academy of Management Perspectives*, 17(2), 56–67. 10.5465/ame.2003.10025194

Helms, B. (2023). *5 Ways to Better support social entrepreneurs*. Forbes.

Iqbal, M. (2022). *Pakistan sees growing culture of innovation amid tech startup boom*. Atlantic Council.

Jehan. (2022). *10 sustainability startups in Pakistan.* Katalystlabs.

Kwok, K. (2022). *The 6 Ps of empowering youth social entrepreneurs.* World Economic Forum.

Laluc, C. (2020). *Social Entrepreneurs Have Improved 622 Million Lives: Schwab Foundation Report.* Davos: WEF. Retrieved from https://www.weforum.org/press/2020/01/social-entrepreneurs-have-improved-622-million-lives-schwab-foundation-report/

Lamy, E. (2019). How to Make Social Entrepreneurship Sustainable? A Diagnosis and a Few Elements of a Response. *Journal of Business Ethics*, 155(3), 645–662. 10.1007/s10551-017-3485-7

Le Blanc, D. (2015). Towards Integration at Last? The Sustainable Development Goals as a Network of Targets. *Sustainable Development (Bradford)*, 23(3), 176–187. 10.1002/sd.1582

Marcel, T., Zenglian, Z., Yanick, O. A., & Paulin, B. (2024). Entrepreneurship and High-Quality Development of Enterprises—Empirical Research Based on Chinese-Listed Companies. *Journal of the Knowledge Economy*, 1–27. 10.1007/s13132-024-01922-z

Neumann, T. (2021). The impact of entrepreneurship on economic, social and environmental welfare and its determinants: A systematic review. *Management Review*, 71, 553–584.

Niels Bosma, T. S. (2016). *Global Entrepreneurship Monitor 2015 to 2016: Special Report on Social Entrepreneurship.* Global Entrepreneurship Research Association.

Nor, A. I. (2024). Entrepreneurship Development as a Tool for Employment Creation, Income Generation, and Poverty Reduction for the Youth and Women. *Journal of the Knowledge Economy*, ●●●, 1–24. 10.1007/s13132-024-01747-w

Putnam, R. D. (1993). The Prosperous Community: Social Capital and Public Life. *The American Prospect*, 35–42.

Qamar, U. A. (2020). Social entrepreneurship in Pakistan: Challenges and prospects. *Journal of Management Research*, 7(2), 1–41.

Rahim, H. L.-1. (2015). Social Entrepreneurship: A Different Perspective. *International Academic Research Journal of Business and Technology*, 1(1), 9–15.

Rametse, N. a. (2012). Investigating Social Entrepreneurship in Developing Countries. *SSRN.* 10.2139/ssrn.2176557

Rogers, E. M. (2003). *Diffusion of Innovations*. Free Press.

Sachs, J. D.-T.-D. (2019). *SDG Index and Dashboards Report 2019*. Bertelsmann Stiftung and Sustainable Development Solutions Network (SDSN).

Schwab Foundation for Social Entrepreneurship. (2020). *Two Decades of Impact.* Geneva: World Economic Forum.

SECP. (2023). *Draft Guidelines on ESG Disclosures for Listed Companies*. Securities and Exchange Commission of Pakistan.

Sheptytska, L., & Liudmyla, K. O. (2024). Social entrepreneurship in scientific and social discourses of Ukraine (the beginning of the 21st century. *East European HistoricalBulletin*, (30), 191–199.

Sullivan, D. M. (2007). Stimulating social entrepreneurship: Can support from cities make a difference? *The Academy of Management Perspectives*, 21(1), 77–78. 10.5465/amp.2007.24286169

Syed Samar Hasnain, S. B. (2017). *Green Banking Guidelines*. State Bank of Pakistan.

The World Bank. (2024, April 20). *The World Bank*. Retrieved from Understanding Poverty: https://www.worldbank.org/en/topic/poverty/overview

UNDP. (2024, April 15). *Multi Dimensional Poverty Index2023*. Retrieved from UNDP. Paksitan: https://hdr.undp.org/sites/default/files/Country-Profiles/MPI/PAK .pdf#:~:text=The%20intensity%20of%20deprivations%20in%20Pakistan%2C%20 which,the%20intensity%20of%20the%20deprivations%2C%20is%200.198

Widyawati, L. (2019). A systematic literature review of socially responsible investment and environmental social governance metrics. *Business Strategy and the Environment*, 29(2), 619–637. 10.1002/bse.2393

Chapter 14
Sustainable Production Practices and Circular Economy:
Evidence From Textile Manufacturing Units in Kerala

P. K. Santhosh Kumar
https://orcid.org/0000-0002-2832-4635
Cochin University of Science and Technology, India

Haseena Akbar
Cochin University of Science and Technology, India

Barbara Pisker
https://orcid.org/0000-0001-9434-5541
University of Osijek, Croatia

Hareesh N. Ramanathan
Cochin University of Science and Technology, India

ABSTRACT

The textile industries, while important to employment and economic growth, also contribute to environmental damage. However, adopting a 'closed loop' production and supply chain model minimises environmental risks. Moreover, a circular framework in the textile sector will pace the path towards sustainability. So, the study explored sustainable production practices in the textile manufacturing units in Kerala based on the priority selections made by the manufacturers. The Fuzzy analytical hierarchy procedure application on the data gathered from 300 sample

DOI: 10.4018/979-8-3693-3880-3.ch014

units from five cities of Kerala revealed that though the industries have consistent circular economic potentials, the majority exhibit inconsistency in their decisions to follow the sustainable production models.

1. BACKGROUND

The Sustainable Development Goal (SDG-12.6) on sustainable production has gained momentum recently with the spread of the successful adoption of circular business practices by manufacturing industries. The circular business model brings production and consumption under the 'reduce, reuse and recycle' loop. With the increasing concerns and commitments towards mitigating environmental damage, manufacturing industries include circular business practices in their production and supply chain to achieve sustainable development goals. Moreover, circular economy practices increase resource efficiency by slowing, narrowing, and closing resource flows (Jørgensen & Remmen, 2018), easing manufacturers' journey to achieve SDG goals. Circular economy intersects with sustainability by offering practices optimising sustainability, enabling more sustainable operations within business organisations (Arantes et al., 2022). So, a circular business model aims to create, deliver and capture economic value while minimising adverse environmental effects either by closing or by slowing the loop (Bocken & Konietzko, 2022)

The textile industry is one of the oldest and most significant sectors in the global economy. It encompasses various activities, from preparing and spinning fibre to manufacturing finished textile products. The extensive value chain equips the textile industry to provide materials for clothing, home furnishing and various industrial appliances. So, the industry's market share is based on the end consumer price irrespective of the product's geographical origin. As such, leading textile exporters in the international market are China, India, Germany and Turkey, where China generated the largest revenue in 2021.

India's textile sector is a prominent part of the country's industrial landscape, contributing 2% of GDP and more than 12% of manufacturing GDP and employing 45 million people directly and 60 million indirectly. Similarly, India produces around one million tonnes of textile waste. However, a significant portion of it is produced from households. In 2019, the United Nations Environment Programme introduced a Textile Flagship initiative to reduce unsustainable consumption practices and bring systematic changes towards sustainability and circularity in the textile sector. However, the textile sector's complex business practices and supply chain pose challenges to effectively implementing upcycling and recycling practices in India. Though there are policy supports for promulgating and implementing sustainability in consumption practice and waste disposal, little attention has been given to incentivising producers. However, there are instances of successful application of sustainable production practices and transition towards a circular economy in the textile sector at the global level. The initiatives of luxury fashion brands like Kering, Gucci, and Stella McCartney showcase how these brands are implementing eco-friendly materials, recycling programs, and innovative production methods to create sustainable fashion (Moorhouse & Moorhouse, 2017)

Similarly, the majority of the medium-sized textile and apparel companies in Slovakia positively adopted circular economic practices (Daňo et al., 2020). Participatory research in Ghana demonstrates that upcycling can contribute to clothing sustainability by extending the life cycle of garments through design and creativity (James & Kent, 2019). Likewise, fashion designers in Lithuania are also optimistic about incorporating sustainability into their brands (Bartkutė et al., 2023). Though textile manufacturing creates an environmental impact in the raw material collection to disposal of the final product (Gbolarumi et al., 2021), there is the potential to wedge circular economic practices in all stages of production.

The textile industry operates predominantly in a linear take-make-disposal model. The sector contributes significantly to greenhouse gas emissions, water pollution, and textile waste. This is mainly due to unsustainable practices such as high chemical usage, resource waste, excessive energy and water consumption, and the generation of other effluents. It is imperative to mitigate negative externalities to make the industry more sustainable and resilient. Recently, there has been a growing recognition and adoption of sustainable production practices by textile manufacturing units. Implementing eco-friendly dyeing processes, promoting recycling and upcycling of textile wastes, using organic raw materials, implementing cleaner production techniques, environment-friendly packaging, and investing in sustainable manufacturing techniques are increasingly adopting sustainable production practices in textile industries. These practices reduce negative environmental impact and positively contribute to the competitiveness and market share of the economy (Gbolarumi et al., 2021). Moreover, the adoption of sustainable production practices and a shift towards a circular economy will reduce energy consumption, reduce production cost (Indrayani & Triwiswara, 2020), reduce carbon footprint, minimise waste generation (Islam et al., 2021) and reduce carbon emission through the supply chain (Gbolarumi et al., 2021).

The contrast between social development and the relative underdevelopment of industrial production adversely affects sustainability in Kerala's manufacturing vista (Norris, 2013). Because policy discourses only address the growth and employment potential of the manufacturing sector. On the contrary, the textile manufacturing units of the state have the least negative environmental externality. Kerala's textile industry encompasses the traditional handloom sector, silk manufacturing and other garment manufacturing units. It is the handloom sector that contributes a major share of textile manufacturing. The traditional Textile manufacturing industries of the state followed sustainable practices of disposing of and upcycling garment waste materials, using natural dyes, and using less water. Adopting new technology and large-scale production whittle away the textile industry's sustainable production and disposal techniques. In this context, the present research intends to trace the circular and sustainable manufacturing practices and the textile manufacturing units in Kerala.

Organisations' circular economic practices can only be assessed with inputs from experts within the business. However, the inherent uncertainties and ambiguities in human judgement (Keshavarz Ghorabaee et al., 2017) necessitate the use of fuzzy set theory. The fuzzy set allows the representation of vague or ambiguous information in the real world. It effectively deals with uncertainties in the circularity evaluation (Geissdoerfer et al., 2020; Caiado et al., 2021). Nevertheless, a fuzzy comprehensive evaluation is appropriate for analysing the ecoefficiency of manufacturing units (An et al., 2010). Moreover, to capture decision makers' amigos judgment, the Fuzzy Analytical Hierarchy Process (FAHP) is appropriately proposed by (Chang, 1996). The FAHP is recognised as the most significant MCDM method for aiding the decision making process (Wang et al., 2020) because it allows the decision-makers to express their judgement using linguist variables.

Though circular economy tools can be used as a framework for sustainable development challenges (Mamun et al., 2023), it is imperative to tailor circular strategies suitable for different regions. Kerala's geographic and industrial setting demands its own strategies and solutions to address the problems of sustainable production. Considering the status of textile manufacturing in the industrial space and the spread of micro, small and medium industries, it is necessary to analyse the existing production practices in the textile industry. So, the present study is modelled to trace circular and sustainable production practices from the decision-maker's perspectives. The detailed examination of the judgement of decision-makers of randomly selected textile manufacturers in Kerala exhibits that, though there is an inherent inconsistency in selecting circular production practices, elements of existing sustainable production practices provide the potential for transition to a circular economy.

2. LITERATURE REVIEW

The literature review on sustainable production practices and their link with sustainable development mainly focuses on transitioning from traditional linear production to circular production based on reducing, reusing and recycling ma-terials. The integration of circular economic practices in production practices in various industries is evolving as a paradigm to address environmental challenges.

The motivation to adapt and follow circular economic practices has several empirical evidences. For instance, a study on circular economic practices in Brazilian companies (Ostermann et al., 2021) found that internal drivers such as companies' core values and sustainable mission are more influential than laws and regulations in adopting circular economic practices. Similarly, a study among young Lithuanian designers (Bartkutė et al., 2023) found that the designers are positive about incorporating sustainability into their brands; however, their efforts are inconsistent and incomplete due to a lack of in-depth knowledge and necessary financial resources to adapt circular economy business model. However, the transition exists from fast fashion to sustainable practices in the industry.

Evidence from Slovakia's textile and apparel sector exhibits that the companies adopted circular economic practices due to economic motivations and to meet customer expectations. Rising entry costs, current market capacity, and technological and logistic challenges create concerns while implementing circular economic business models. Furthermore, lack of awareness and incomplete communication from the government also pose hurdles to implementing circular economic models (Daňo et al., 2020). While, (Machado et al., 2019) explored the motives of consumers for the reuse of fashion products. An in-depth interview among nine customers at thrift stores in the Brazilian Street fairs revealed that there is an increase in the popularity of thrift stores and the consumption of second-hand fashion products. The major motives are economic, critical, hedonic and recreational. Moreover, second-hand fashion consumes fewer resources and reduces waste.

The literature on sustainable and circular economic practices in textile industries mainly (Gbolarumi et al., 2021) discusses the environmental impact of all stages of production. High chemical usage, water and energy consumption, air pollution, and waste generation are the key pollutants generated by the industry. So, it is imperative to apply a triple bottom line approach for sustainability assessment. Moreover, company-level assessment will help achieve sustainability objectives. (Holtström et al., 2019) found the importance of incorporating strategies encompassing circular economic practices for long-term success. The close examination of apparel retailer Houdini Sportswear shows that their transition from a traditional business model to sustainability can be seen through product design, sale or rental services and end-of-life practices like repair, reuse and recycling. They have addressed the challenges of effective distribution networks for potential return and managing consumer consumption preferences and technological platforms. So, integration of sustainability into a business model is a feasible solution to long-term development. However, the circular economic transition in the Romanian textile and apparel industry (Staicu & Pop, 2018) reveals that the presence of a vicious cycle of resolution, the lack of collaboration, and the absence of awareness hinder stakeholder partnership. Moreover, evidence from the European and global textile, clothing, ether and footwear industries shows that the transition (Dziuba et al., 2022) incorporates digital technology. The EU and international organisations promote competitiveness by encouraging innovative and sustainable practices in these industries, which significantly contribute to the EU GDP. For countries like Ghana (James & Kent, 2019), upcycling (adding value to used clothing) can support economic development, create employment opportunities, and offer value-added products for sale. The major challenge in conventional textile manufacturing in adopting sustainable production practices is the heavy use of harmful chemicals and resources like water and energy. However, sustainable methods like plasma technology and efficient waste management can minimise ecological damage (Rahaman et al., 2024). Moreover, eco-friendly chemical processing methods such as ultrasound, microwave, enzymes, and digital printing reduce environment pollution by the industry (Nayak et al., 2019).

Textile manufacturing units across different geographical areas face unique sustainability challenges and opportunities. So, it is necessary to understand the regional cases to gain valuable insights and identify best practices. Moreover, it will help to update with emerging technologies in the circular production process in the textile industry (Hora et al., 2023). For instance, (Härri & Levänen, 2024) explored the multifaceted challenges associated with the transition to circular economy in the textile industry of Tamil Nadu in India. They found that there is complexity in integrating just transition and sustainable dimensions. They emphasised the importance of understanding the interplay between distributive, procedural justice, environment, and social and economic sustainability. Thus, the existing knowledge is directed towards developing more effective strategies to measure circular practices, thereby achieving sustainable development goals in textile manufacturing units.

3. DATA

The research is based on primary data collected from the textile manufacturing units registered with the Department of Industries in Kerala. The list of textile manufacturing units of Kollam, Alappuzha, Ernakulam, Thrissur, and Kannur was provided by the Department of Industries, Government of Kerala, on formal request. The list contains micro, small and medium manufacturing units in the districts' rural and urban centres. A separate list of manufacturing units in urban centers was made, and 300 firms were chosen using a simple random sample without replacement. Field visits were conducted in the identified sample units to administer the questionnaire. A part of the questionnaire was designed to explore the circular economic practices, benefits, and motivations to mitigate environmental damage and promote development. The respondents' preferences in decisions about production practices, potential benefits, and motivation, which lead to sustainability, were collected through a judgement scale. The respondents who participated in the survey were from managerial level staff or owners whose participation was voluntary.

4. METHOD

The fuzzy analytical hierarchy process was chosen for the present study due to its ability to handle uncertainty and subjectivity inherent in the decision-making process. Moreover, it captures the relative importance and interdependencies of various criteria in circular production practices, such as resource efficiency, waste reduction, and sustainable material usage. In brief, the methodology facilitates a comprehensive analysis and leads to more balanced decisions about implementing circular economy practices within the textile industry.

4.1 Fuzzy set

A fuzzy set deals with the ambiguous class with varying degrees of memberships. Suppose X represent a collection of objects, where a single object in X is denoted by z. Thus, $X = \{z\}$. A fuzzy set A with in the space X is defined by a membership function $f_A(z)$, where each point z in X is assigned a number between 0 and 1. This number reflects how much X belongs to A. The degree of membership of z in A increases as the value of, $f_A(z)$ approaches to unity. As such, $\nu_A(z) = 0$ implies z does not belong to A at all, $\nu_A(z) = 1$ implies z fully belongs to A, and $0 < \nu_A(z) < 1$ implies z partially belongs to A

The membership function $\nu_A(z)$ describe the shape of a fuzzy number. One common way to represent a fuzzy number is using a triangular membership function. Let a, b and c be real numbers with $a < b < a$, in which b represents the membership degree maximum part, and outside the range $[a, c]$, the membership degree is null, then the triangular membership function $\nu_A(z)$ is given as follows:

$$\nu_A(z) = \begin{cases} 0 \, if z \langle a \, or \, z \rangle c \\ \dfrac{z-a}{b-a} \, if a \leq z \leq b \\ \dfrac{c-z}{c-b} \, if b \leq z \leq c \end{cases} \tag{1}$$

Next, if the two triangular membership functions $\nu_A(z)$ anf $\nu_B(z)$ defined over the interval $[a, c]$, then the Euclidian distance ED between the function is defined as:

$$ED = \sqrt{\int_a^c (\nu_A(z) - \nu_B(z))^2 \, dz} \tag{2}$$

The fuzzy weighted average method is widely used to compute aggregated scores of judgements under a fuzzy environment. Let n alternatives being evaluated, and each alternative i is associated with a fuzzy rating z_i. There are m criterion dimensions associated with a fuzzy weight, $\widetilde{w}_j$ where $j = 1, 2, \ldots m$, then the fuzzy weighted average can be presented as:

$$FW_A = \frac{\sum_{i=1}^{n} (z_i * \widetilde{w}_i)}{\sum_{i=1}^{n} \widetilde{w}} \tag{3}$$

4.1.1 Fuzzy Analytical Hierarchy (FAHP) model

The fuzzy analytical hierarchy model is a decision-making tool used to determine the importance of different criteria and sub-criteria in a complex system (Chang, 1996). It integrates the traditional AHP with fuzzy logic to improve decision-making where there is imprecision uncertainty. The complex structure of the circular economy and the ambiguities in its decision and practice popularise the use of the FAHP model in measuring circular economic issues. In the present research, the FAHP method is used to evaluate the manufacturer's judgement towards circular economic practices and performance to explore its contribution to sustainable development goals. It facilitates to quantify the linguistic comparative judgment of decision makers (Lima Junior et al., 2014).

Let $Z = \{z_1, z_2, z_3, \ldots \ldots z_n\}$ be a set of objects and $H = \{h_1, h_2, h_3, \ldots \ldots h_n\}$ is set of goals. Each object must be analysed for each goal, leading to an extension of the analysis for each object (Chang, 1996), which is presented as:

$$Q_{hi}^1, \ Q_{hi}^j, \ldots \ldots \ldots Q_{hi}^p, \ i = 1, 2, 3, \ldots \ldots h \tag{4}$$

Where all the $Q_{hi}^j (j = 1, 2, 3, \ldots \ldots q)$ are Triangular Fuzzy Number (TFN). The FAHP calculation procedure is given as follows:

i)   The calculation of fuzzy synthetic extent value associated to the ith object is described as:

$$M_i = \sum_{j=1}^{p} Q_{hi}^1 \left[\sum_{i=1}^{n} \sum_{j=1}^{p} Q_{hi}^i \right] - 1 \tag{5}$$

Where, $\sum_{j=1}^{p} Q_{hi}^i$ is derived through the fuzzy addition operation of extent analysis values within the following matrix:

$$\sum_{j=1}^{p} Q_{hi}^{i} = \left(\sum_{j=1}^{p} r_{j}, \sum_{j=1}^{p} p_{j}, \sum_{j=1}^{p} d_{j} \right) \tag{6}$$

The $\left[\sum_{i=1}^{n} \sum_{j=1}^{p} Q_{hi}^{i} \right]^{-1}$ is calculated as:

$$\left[\sum_{i=1}^{n} \sum_{j=1}^{p} Q_{hi}^{i} \right]^{-1} = \left[\frac{1}{\sum_{i=1}^{n} \sum_{j=1}^{p} d_{i}}, \frac{1}{\sum_{i=1}^{n} \sum_{j=1}^{p} p_{i}}, \frac{1}{\sum_{i=1}^{n} \sum_{j=1}^{p} r_{i}} \right] \tag{7}$$

ii) The degree of possibilities of $M_2(r_2, p_2, d_2) \geq M_1(r_1, p_1, d_1)$ is defined as:

$$U(M_2 \geq M_1) = sup_{x \geq y} \left[\min \left(\nu_{M_2}(x), \nu_{M_2}(y) \right) \right] \tag{8}$$

The equivalent expression of equation (8) is given in (9) and (10):

$$U(M_2 \geq M_1) = hgt(M_1 \cap M_2) = \nu_{M_2}(a) \tag{9}$$

Where a shows the highest intersection point between ν_{M_1} and ν_{M_2}:

$$\nu_{M_2}(a) = \begin{cases} 1, if p_2 \geq p_1 \\ 0, if r_1 \geq d_2 \\ \dfrac{r_1 - d_2}{(p_2 - d_2) - (p_1 - 1)}, otherwise \end{cases} \tag{10}$$

iii) The procedure in equation (11) can compute the degree of possibility for a convex fuzzy number to be greater than s convex fuzzy number $M_i (i = 1,2,3\ldots\ldots s)$

$$U(M \geq M_1, M_2, M_3 \ldots M_s) = U[(M \geq M_1) and (M \geq M_2)$$
$$and(M \geq M_3) and \ldots\ldots and(M \geq M_s) = min U(M \geq M_i), i = 1,2,3\ldots s] \tag{11}$$

iv) The vector Y^* can be computed as:

$$Y^* = \left(a'(\tilde{f}_1), a'(\tilde{f}_2), \ldots\ldots a'(\tilde{f}_s) \right) \tag{12}$$

Assuming $a'(\tilde{f}_i) = U(M_i \geq M_j), for\, j = 1,2,3....,s, s \neq i$

Thus the normalised form of the vector can be presented as:

$$Y = \left(a(\tilde{f}_1), a(\tilde{f}_2), ...a(\tilde{f}_s)\right)^T \tag{13}$$

Where Y a non-fuzzy number, computed for each comparison matrix.

v) Followed by the pairwise comparison, the consistency of expert judgment should be assessed using the consistent ratio (T. L. Saaty, 2004), for which the matrix must be defuzzied using the graded mean integration, as described as:

$$P(\tilde{R}) = R = \tfrac{1}{6}(r_1, 4r_2, r_3) \tag{14}$$

For computing consistency ratio, the normalised weight $\tilde{w}_i$ of each alternative is determined using the defuzzied pairwise comparison alternatives x_{ij}.

$$\tilde{w}_i = \frac{\sum_{j=1}^{k} x_{ij}}{\Sigma_{j=1}^{k} \sum_{j=1}^{k} x_{ij}} \tag{15}$$

$$\theta_i = \frac{\sum_{j=1}^{k} \tilde{w}_i x_{ij}}{\tilde{w}_i} \tag{16}$$

Next, computing the principal eigen value, λ_{max} and consistency index (CI) is given as:

$$\lambda_{max} = \frac{\sum_{j=1}^{k} \theta_i}{k} \tag{17}$$

$$CI = \frac{(\lambda_{max} - k)}{(k-1)} \tag{18}$$

The CR obtained using the given formula

$$CR = \frac{CI}{R_n} \tag{19}$$

The consistency of the decision maker is decided with reference to the random index given (Table 1). If the CR is less than 0.1, the matrix will be considered as consistent, if it exceeds 0.1, then the matrix is inconsistent and necessitating revision of the judgement of decision makers.

Table 1. Random index of (R. W. Saaty, 1987)

n	3	4	5	6	7	8	9	10
R_n	0.58	0.9	1.12	1.24	1.32	1.41	1.45	1.49

5. RESULT

The Fuzzy analytical hierarchy model has been widely applied in circular economic studies to assess the environmental performance and sustainability of different alternatives. The model assists to identify the prioritisation of circular business models of different firms. Moreover, it will provide evidence regarding decision-makers prioritisation and weights for circular economic principles. Respondent's judgment between different sustainable production practices in the textile manufacturing units in Kerala was analysed using the FAHP method. The *'ahpsurvey'* package in R software(https://cran.r-project.org/web/packages/ahpsurvey/) was used to analyse the result.

5.1 Production Practice

The judgement of decision makers while choosing among the given circular production alternatives revealed that the highest average individual weight (Table 2) is attributed to 'natural raw materials' followed by 'clean energy for production 'and water-efficient production technology. As such, the decision makers consider natural raw materials to be the main factor in sustainable production. Similarly, the use of clean energy and water efficient production techniques are the other important sustainable production techniques. However, there is high inconsistency among these decisions, as the consistency ratio is less than 0.1 (Figure 1).

Table 2. Circular production practices

Code	Circular Production Practices	Individual Weight	Mean of Aggregated preference	SD of Aggregated preference
GPP1	Natural raw materials	0.333	0.056	0.011
GPP2	Clean energy for production	0.214	0.091	0.026
GPP3	Water efficient production technology	0.172	0.116	0.033
GPP4	Reusing raw material waste	0.141	0.153	0.050
GPP5	Prefer to sell raw material waste	0.066	0.318	0.039
GPP6	Recycling waste	0.073	0.266	0.088

Source: Authors' calculation

Figure 1. Individual priorities of circular production practices

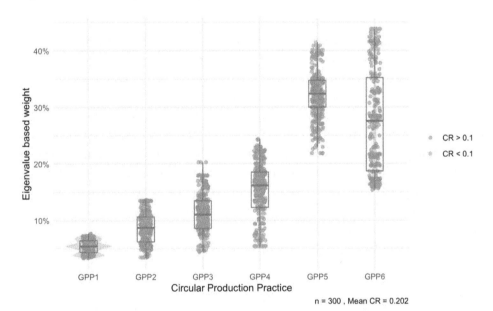

Source: author's calculation

The inconsistent pairs (Table 3) reveal conflicting rankings across different combinations of criteria in the decision-making process. The preference for natural raw material over recycling waste is exhibit high inconsistency, followed by water-efficient production over reusing and recycling waste materials. This inconsistency may arise due to the ambiguity in the actual practices of the provided criteria. As such, unlike energy-efficient and water-efficient technologies, the reuse and recycling of textile products are not highlighted in sustainable production practices. The inconsistencies highlight the uncertainties within the perspective of circular economic practices, which underscores the need for further examination and awareness creation.

Table 3. Top inconsistent pairs

Top 1	Top II	Top II
Natural raw materials vs Recycling waste	Prefer to sell raw material waste vs Recycling waste	Clean energy for production vs Prefer to sell raw material waste
Water efficient production technology vs Reusing raw material waste	Natural raw materials vs clean energy for production	Natural raw materials vs water efficient production technology
Water efficient production technology vs Recycling waste	Reusing raw material waste vs Recycling waste	Water efficient production technology vs Prefer to sell raw material waste

Source: Authors' calculation

5.2 Performance

Circular production performance indicates the creation of an effective and sustainable production loop while maximising profit. The manufacturers knowledge and consideration of the product's durability, recyclability and reproducibility will reflect in their choice of the performance benefits. The nature textile products have the potentials to choose circular production in the designing stage itself. However, the respondents' judgement (Table 4)revealed that 'reducing production cost' will have the highest weight, followed by increasing the customer base and increasing profitability while deciding to opt for circular production practices. However, 'decrease in environment damage' received the lowest individual weight. Thus, it indicates the manufacturers' choice of factors influencing the decision to adopt circular production. However, the individual consistency (Figure 2) exhibits that respondents exhibit strong consistency in profitability and decreased environmental damage.

Table 4. Circular performance benefits

Code	Circular Performance benefits	Individual Weight	Mean of Aggregated preference	SD of Aggregated preference
CEP1	Reduce the production cost	0.450	0.100	0.036
CEP2	Increase customer base	0.245	0.173	0.055
CEP3	Increase profitability	0.217	0.202	0.071
CEP4	Decrease environment damage	0.089	0.525	0.096

Source: Authors' calculation

Figure 2. Individual priorities of performance

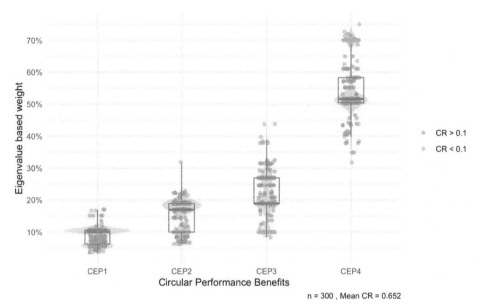

6. DISCUSSION

Transitioning to a Circular Economy is essential to mitigate resource extraction-related environmental impacts such as greenhouse gas emissions, biodiversity loss and water stress (Dziuba et al., 2022). Textile manufacturing units have the potential to minimise their negative environmental externalities by implementing sustainable production practices and embracing the principles of circular economy (Jia et al., 2020). However, policy intervention is necessary to promote sustainable farming practices, international energy policies, and societal consumption patterns significantly influencing textile production practices (Fletcher, 2009). For instance, despite the low cost of natural gas in Iran, the implementation of pollution tax policies could make SIPH (solar industrial process heat) identified as a cost-effective alternative for the textile industry (Hosseini Dehshiri et al., 2023). The present research investigation of sustainable production practices in textile manufacturing in Kerala found that the manufacturing units exhibit consistency in production practices and circular performance. As such, some manufacturing units successfully experimented with the efficient use of inputs and waste reduction. This indicates the presence of production practices with sustainable elements. However, more focus on popularising existing sustainable practices is necessary to achieve the sustainable development goals on production.

The textile manufacturing units can contribute to the circular economy through sustainable production practices such as reducing waste and using recycling materials (Atstaja et al., 2020). Using sustainable materials in production, such as organic cotton or recycled polyester, can ensure sustainable production. Exploring the existing circular production practices helps uncover their sustainability potential, minimizing transition costs and encouraging wider adoption across the textile sector. For instance, the handloom manufacturing units in Kerala still use natural raw materials which can be widely adopted. Moreover, all the manufacturing units surveyed fall under the micro, small, and medium categories, which allow them to adapt circular practices comparatively more easily than the large manufacturing units. Though the state's spinning, stitching and garment production units do not use high water, the respondents know the efficient use of water in production. Because lack of efficient technology force them to use chemicals in the dying process, and washing contaminates water. Similarly, waste recycling and selling is a practice among the manufacturing units; however, it is not followed as a part of their environmental commitment. So, the inconsistent decisions on the production practices revealed that there is a need to educate the manufacturers about circular business practices.

7. CONCLUSION

Textile manufacturing in Kerala encompasses spinning, weaving and garment making, which mainly operate at micro, small or medium scale levels. Though the sector has umpteen limitations, it stands as a reliable source of income for the state and its people. Moreover, the concerns towards environmental damage provide room for introducing circular economic practices in all stages of production and distribution. The use of FAHP revealed the nature of the textile companies while making circular and sustainable production decisions. Though some textile manufacturing, including handloom, follows some sustainable way of production, there is no uniformity and plan. The study also revealed the inherent inconsistency in the manufacturers' decisions to practice and adapt sustainable production. Because the manufacturers' decisions are only based on their profitability and consumer base, not on environmental commitments. So, it is necessitated to implement incentivised circular production policies for the textile manufacturing units. Moreover, unsustainable production practices, waste, obsolete technology, and a lack of awareness regarding the environmental impact of textile production need to be addressed. So, there is scope for further research to investigate the perception of the manufacturers to adapt to a complete transition to circular economic practices.

ACKNOWLEDGMENT

This research was supported by the Rashtriya Uchchatar Shiksha Abhiyan (RUSA) 2.0, Cochin University of Science and Technology (CUSAT). The authors thank RUSA 2.0, CUSAT for their financial assistance.

REFERENCES

An, X., Cui, Y., & Qi, E. (2010). *Study on eco-efficiency evaluation of manufacturing system based on Circular economy*. https://doi.org/https://doi.org/10.1109/icieem.2010.5646545

Arantes, R. F. M., Zanon, L. G., Calache, L. D. D. R., Bertassini, A. C., & Carpinetti, L. C. R. (2022). A fuzzy multicriteria group decision approach for circular business models prioritization. *Production, 32*. https://doi.org/10.1590/0103-6513.20220019

Atstaja, D., Uvarova, I., Kamilla Kambala, D., Alberte, V., Stokmane, K., Gegere-Zetterstroma, A., Kraze, S., & Zapletnuka, G. (2020). Investments to Develop Business Models and Projects in the Circular Economy. *IOP Conference Series. Earth and Environmental Science*, 578(1), 012029. Advance online publication. 10.1088/1755-1315/578/1/012029

Bartkutė, R., Streimikiene, D., & Kačerauskas, T. (2023). Between Fast and Sustainable Fashion: The Attitude of Young Lithuanian Designers to the Circular Economy. *Sustainability (Basel)*, 15(13), 9986. Advance online publication. 10.3390/su15139986

Bocken, N., & Konietzko, J. (2022). Experimentation capability for a circular economy: A practical guide. *The Journal of Business Strategy*, 44(6), 406–414. https://doi.org/https://doi.org/10.1108/jbs-02-2022-0039. 10.1108/JBS-02-2022-0039

Caiado, R. G. G., Scavarda, L. F., Gavião, L. O., Ivson, P., Nascimento, D. L. de M., & Garza-Reyes, J. A. (2021). A fuzzy rule-based industry 4.0 maturity model for operations and supply chain management. *International Journal of Production Economics*, 231, 107883. Advance online publication. 10.1016/j.ijpe.2020.107883

Chang, D.-Y. (1996). Applications of the extent analysis method on fuzzy AHP. In *European Journal of Operational Research* (Vol. 95). 10.1016/0377-2217(95)00300-2

Daňo, F., Drábik, P., & Hanuláková, E. (2020). Circular Business Models in Textiles and Apparel Sector in Slovakia. *Central European Business Review, 9*(1), 1–19. https://doi.org/https://doi.org/10.18267/j.cebr.226

Dziuba, R., Jabłońska, M., Ławińska, K., & Wysokińska, Z. (2022). Overview of EU and Global Conditions for the Transformation of the TCLF Industry on the Way to a Circular and Digital Economy (Case Studies from Poland). *Comparative Economic Research*, 25(1), 75–94. 10.18778/1508-2008.25.05

Gbolarumi, F. T., Wong, K. Y., & Olohunde, S. T. (2021). Sustainability Assessment in The Textile and Apparel Industry: A Review of Recent Studies. *IOP Conference Series. Materials Science and Engineering*, 1051(1), 012099. 10.1088/1757-899X/1051/1/012099

Geissdoerfer, M., Pieroni, M. P. P., Pigosso, D. C. A., & Soufani, K. (2020). Circular business models: A review. In *Journal of Cleaner Production* (Vol. 277). Elsevier Ltd., 10.1016/j.jclepro.2020.123741

Härri, A., & Levänen, J. (2024). "It should be much faster fashion"—Textile industry stakeholders' perceptions of a just circular transition in Tamil Nadu, India. *Discover Sustainability*, 5(1), 39. Advance online publication. 10.1007/s43621-024-00211-8

Holtström, J., Bjellerup, C., & Eriksson, J. (2019). Business model development for sustainable apparel consumption: The case of Houdini Sportswear. *Journal of Strategy and Management*, 12(4), 481–504. 10.1108/JSMA-01-2019-0015

Hora, S. T., Bungau, C., Negru, P. A., & Radu, A.-F. (2023). Implementing Circular Economy Elements in the Textile Industry: A Bibliometric Analysis. *Sustainability (Basel)*, 15(20), 15130. 10.3390/su152015130

Indrayani, L., & Triwiswara, M. (2020). Implementation green industry standard at textile industry and textile product. *IOP Conference Series. Earth and Environmental Science*, 456(1), 012049. Advance online publication. 10.1088/1755-1315/456/1/012049

Islam, M. M., Perry, P., & Gill, S. (2021). Mapping environmentally sustainable practices in textiles, apparel and fashion industries: A systematic literature review. *Journal of Fashion Marketing and Management*, 25(2), 331–353. 10.1108/JFMM-07-2020-0130

James, A. S. J., & Kent, A. (2019). Clothing Sustainability and Upcycling in Ghana. *Fashion Practice*, 11(3), 375–396. 10.1080/17569370.2019.1661601

Jia, F., Yin, S., Chen, L., & Chen, X. (2020). The circular economy in the textile and apparel industry: A systematic literature review. In *Journal of Cleaner Production* (Vol. 259). Elsevier Ltd., 10.1016/j.jclepro.2020.120728

Jørgensen, M. S., & Remmen, A. (2018). A Methodological Approach to Development of Circular Economy Options in Businesses. *Procedia CIRP*, 69, 816–821. 10.1016/j.procir.2017.12.002

Keshavarz Ghorabaee, M., Amiri, M., Zavadskas, E. K., Turskis, Z., & Antucheviciene, J. (2017). A new multi-criteria model based on interval type-2 fuzzy sets and EDAS method for supplier evaluation and order allocation with environmental considerations. *Computers & Industrial Engineering*, 112, 156–174. 10.1016/j.cie.2017.08.017

Lima, F. R.Junior, Osiro, L., & Carpinetti, L. C. R. (2014). A comparison between Fuzzy AHP and Fuzzy TOPSIS methods to supplier selection. *Applied Soft Computing*, 21, 194–209. 10.1016/j.asoc.2014.03.014

Machado, M. A. D., de Almeida, S. O., Bollick, L. C., & Bragagnolo, G. (2019). Second-hand fashion market: Consumer role in circular economy. *Journal of Fashion Marketing and Management*, 23(3), 382–395. 10.1108/JFMM-07-2018-0099

Mamun, A., Torst, N., & Sabantina, L. (2023). Advancing towards a Circular Economy in the Textile Industry. *Engineering Proceedings*, 56(1), 18. Advance online publication. 10.3390/ASEC2023-15244

Moorhouse, D., & Moorhouse, D. (2017). Sustainable Design: Circular Economy in Fashion and Textiles. *Design Journal, 20*(sup1), S1948–S1959. https://doi.org/10.1080/14606925.2017.1352713

Nayak, R., Panwar, T., & Van Thang Nguyen, L. (2019). Sustainability in fashion and textiles: A survey from developing country. In *Sustainable Technologies for Fashion and Textiles* (pp. 3–30). Elsevier., 10.1016/B978-0-08-102867-4.00001-3

Norris, L. (2013). Aesthetics and ethics: Upgrading textile production in northern Kerala. *Geoforum*, 50, 221–231. 10.1016/j.geoforum.2013.09.006

Ostermann, C. M., Nascimento, L. da S., Steinbruch, F. K., & Callegaro-de-Menezes, D. (2021). Drivers to implement the circular economy in born-sustainable business models: A case study in the fashion industry. *Revista de Gestao*, 28(3), 223–240. 10.1108/REGE-03-2020-0017

Rahaman, M. T., Pranta, A. D., Repon, M. R., Ahmed, M. S., & Islam, T. (2024). Green production and consumption of textiles and apparel: Importance, fabrication, challenges and future prospects. In *Journal of Open Innovation: Technology, Market, and Complexity* (Vol. 10, Issue 2). Elsevier B.V. https://doi.org/10.1016/j.joitmc.2024.100280

Saaty, R. W. (1987). *The Analytic Hierarchy Process-What it is And How it is Used* (Vol. 9, Issue 5).

Saaty, T. L. (2004). *Decision Making-The Analytic Hierarchy and Network Processes (AHP/ANP)* (Vol. 13, Issue 1).

Staicu, D., & Pop, O. (2018). Mapping the interactions between the stakeholders of the circular economy ecosystem applied to the textile and apparel sector in Romania. *Management and Marketing*, 13(4), 1190–1209. 10.2478/mmcks-2018-0031

Wang, Z., Ran, Y., Chen, Y., Yu, H., & Zhang, G. (2020). Failure mode and effects analysis using extended matter-element model and AHP. *Computers & Industrial Engineering*, 140, 106233. Advance online publication. 10.1016/j.cie.2019.106233

Chapter 15
Sustainable Synergy:
Exploring the Environmental Landscape of Energy Transition and Economic Growth for India

Aparna Sajeev
Department of Commerce and Management Studies, University of Calicut, India

Harpreet Kaur
https://orcid.org/0000-0003-3095-2443
Sri Guru Gobind Singh College of Commerce, University of Delhi, India

ABSTRACT

Understanding the interrelationships between economic growth, environmental quality, and sustainable development is pertinent for India. This connection is marked by reciprocal causation and feedback mechanisms-energy consumption stimulates economic growth by providing the necessary fuel for production and consumption. However, economic expansion influences energy consumption patterns by altering the industrial structure, adopting new technologies, and changing income levels. This study investigates the relationship between economic growth, energy transition, and sustainable development in India from 1990 to 2020. It also estimates the impact of industrialisation and trade openness on economic growth using an Auto Regressive Distributed Lag (ARDL) approach. The results show a positive and significant relationship between environmental degradation (CO2) and economic growth. Policymakers and stakeholders must develop efficient energy policies and effective, sustainable development strategies. The policies should facilitate economic expansion and safeguard energy stability, ecological endurance, and social well-being.

DOI: 10.4018/979-8-3693-3880-3.ch015

1. INTRODUCTION

20th and 21st centuries have experienced economic growth accompanied with industrialization, massive population expansion and advancements in healthcare underlining overall human development. Economic growth has been accompanied with greater affluence, prolonged life expectancy, elevated living standards, and enhanced accessibility to education, knowledge, and opportunities. On the downside, this progression has also been accompanied with the collective challenges of increasing inequalities, poverty, and deprivation along with escalating environmental degradation. Energy use and economic prosperity and development are convolutedly correlated and the connection is bidirectional. Not only does energy consumption play a critical role in the expansion of production processes and the development of infrastructure, but it also complements and enhances the quality of life. In fact, the extent of energy utilisation is often cited as an index of economic development. Energy is an indispensable component of production and economic growth, and economic expansion propels energy consumption by rising living standards. The correlation between energy and growth has been an essential subject in economic literature (Stern, 1993; Cheng & Lai, 1997; Cheng, 1999; Stern, 2000; Chang, 2010, Bartleet & Gounder, 2010; Bekun et al., 2019). Increased levels of economic growth are typically accompanied by a rise in availability, dependability, and usage of power (energy)[1]. Although the direction of the causal relationship between economic growth and energy is debatable (Kraft & Kraft, 1978; Zhixin & Xin, 2011; Bildirici & Bakirtas, 2014), however, it is undeniable that increased energy use is essential for development.

Energy use and availability has undeniably played a crucial role in driving economic growth, however, in turn it has also given rise to pertinent and persistent concerns in the form of environmental degradation and pollution. Given the swift progress of urbanisation and industrialisation, economic growth is becoming more reliant on energy consumption. Greater economic activity, encompassing both production and consumption, necessitates greater amounts of energy and material inputs. Manufacturing, transportation, and infrastructure development use energy derived from resources including fossil fuels, leading to pollution, emissions, climate change and other environmental impacts. Intensified extraction of resources accompanied with the generation and accumulation of higher volumes of waste along with the concentration of pollutants will inevitably surpass the ecosystem's carrying capacity. Further, depletion of resources at a fast pace will ultimately jeopardise economic activity itself. Hence, attaining indefinite economic growth without confronting resource constraints or harsh environmental damage seems overtly ambitious.

According to the United Nations Environment Programme (UNEP, 1991, p.9), sustainable development aims to enhance human well-being while remaining within the capability of supporting systems. Sustainable development aims to achieve a harmonious equilibrium between economic expansion, social advancement, and environmental preservation. It ensures that present requirements are fulfilled without jeopardising the capacity of future generations to fulfil their own demands. The primary objective is to disentangle economic advancement from ecological harm. In this regard adopting measures that promote resource efficiency, curb pollution and are in tandem with overall conservation is pertinent. Fostering responsible purchasing and manufacturing will help reduce the ecological footprint. This entails reducing waste production and safeguarding ecosystems to guarantee their sustained survival. Economic growth activities must consider environmental effects and social marginal costs to realise sustainable development and warrant long-term success.

The social, economic, and environmental facets of sustainable development pose extraordinary problems. Significant challenges that both prosperous and developing countries must deal with include managing urbanisation, food, water, and energy security, as well as climate change. In the framework of sustainable development, the necessity of switching to renewable energy sources has long been debated (Abbasi et al., 2011; Owusu & Asumadu-Sarkodie, 2016). Sustainable Development Goal (SDG) 7- "Access to Clean and Affordable Energy", focuses on renewable energy sources-solar, wind, biofuels and hydroelectric power, for ensuring universal access to cost-effective, clean, and sustainable energy. However, availability and access to green, and inexhaustible energy is inadequate to meet the energy demands globally, making a complete transition a concern for policymakers. In general, the rapid pace of economic expansion outpaces attempts to establish sustainable energy solutions and environmental legislation, thereby resulting in imbalances between economic growth and environmental protection. SDG 13- "Take Urgent Action to Combat Climate Change and Its Impacts", realises that climate change is real with impacts already apparent. Education, innovation, and adherence to climate commitments, play important roles in this regard in terms of according to future protection. Also important is the need to remodel production processes and infrastructure for creation of new jobs and overall global prosperity.

There have been many studies conducted on the topic of energy transition and economic development in emerging countries. With their substantial population, GDP, and energy consumption, the BRICS countries possess immense adeptness to shape global clean energy practices (Jana, 2022). Studies validate the EKC hypothesis for BRICS countries and have identified economic freedom, international trade, Foreign direct investment (FDI) and subsidies as essential factors (Wu et al., 2022; Sarwat et al., 2022; Akadiri et al., 2021; Leitão et al., 2021; Sajeev & Kaur, 2020). Further studies (Bryndin, 2023; Jana, 2022) comment on the need to prioritise the development of renewable energy sources and advocate for reforms to promote their use, though they do not predominantly discuss the interrelationship between energy transition and economic development. The relationship between energy use and economic development in the Indian economy has been the subject of numerous studies (Cheng, 1999; Paul & Bhattacharya, 2004; Yang & Zhao, 2014). Studies have been conducted to analyse the relationship between energy consumption, carbon emissions, and economic growth in India (Vidyarthi, 2013; Nain, et al., 2017). These studies have contributed to our understanding of the relationship between energy and economic growth in India. They are essential for creating effective policies that promote energy efficiency and the development of carbon-free energy sources such as nuclear, hydrogen, and renewables. However, there is a need for more research to fully understand the relationship between renewable energy consumption and economic growth, as well as the significance of renewable and non-renewable energy sources for economic development.

With this background, *the present Chapter studies the interrelationship between economic growth, environmental quality, and sustainable development for India*[2]. India's recognition of the intricate connection between energy consumption and economic progress is vital for sustainable development. It is in line with the UN's sustainable development goals and contributes to the achievement of Goals 7 and 13 pertaining to energy and climate change respectively.

India has experienced relatively faster economic growth in recent decades and now also has the world's largest population. Further, the current fifth-largest economy in the world, will become the third largest by 2032. This economic expansion will push the demand for swift urbanisation, entailing extensive development of new structures, industry, electricity and transportation systems driven by conventional energy sources. Therefore, it is necessary to enhance the availability of affordable power to achieve faster, sustainable, and more equal economic development.

Greater economic prosperity has led to an escalation in the country's carbon emissions. India is the world's third-largest emitter[3] and pledged to reach net zero by 2070 at the COP26 climate conference in Glasgow in 2021. Due to its vast geography, large population, and unrealized economic potential, the country is projected to have a greater increase in energy demand compared to any other country in the future decades. Being energy-dependent, the country must implement energy efficiency measures, super critical power plant technologies, and renewable energy investment to reduce fossil fuel use and carbon emissions for faster, more inclusive, and sustainable growth (Vidyarthi, 2013). Therefore, it is crucial to grasp the interplay and interdependence between economic growth, environmental quality, sustainable development as measured by HDI, and ecological footprint, industrialization, and trade openness in India. This is the specific area of focus for the current study. Energy usage drives the economy forward by supplying the essential energy needed for production and consumption. At the same time, economic expansion affects energy consumption patterns by modifying the industrial composition, adopting innovative technologies, and shifting income levels. Policymakers and stakeholders need to curate efficient state and global energy policies and effective sustainable development strategies. Importantly, these policies should facilitate economic expansion along with safeguarding energy stability, ecological endurance, and social well-being.

The study offers an extensive literature review in section 2, followed by a brief examination of the correlation between economic expansion and energy usage in India in section 3. Section 4 provides a description of the data and empirical methodology used to examine the interconnection between economic growth, environmental quality, sustainable development (measured by HDI), ecological footprint, industrialization, and trade openness in India. The data and analysis may be found in part 5, while the conclusion from a broad policy perspective is presented in section 6.

2. RELATIONSHIP BETWEEN ENERGY, ECONOMIC GROWTH, CARBON EMISSIONS AND ENERGY TRANSITION: EMPIRICAL EVIDENCE

Causal relationship between the energy consumption and economic growth: The existence of an association between economic growth and energy is axiomatic. In fact, it is the direction of this association that is often debated. Energy is the primary catalyst for economic growth. Access to affordable and reliable energy sources stimulates economic growth and boosts productivity, unleashes new economic opportunities and spurs investment. Hence availability, accessibility, and affordability of appropriate energy drives economic growth. Economic growth and expansion accompanied with industrialisation and improved standards of living drive up energy usage. Therefore, the relationship between economic growth and energy use is complex and dynamic, characterised by reciprocal influences and interconnections.

The literature between economic growth and energy use talks about four possible forms that the relationship takes - *growth hypothesis*, *conservation hypothesis*, *feedback hypothesis* and *neutrality hypothesis* depending on the direction of causality (Tiba & Omri, 2017). Under *growth* and *conservation* hypothesis there is unidirectional causality going from energy use to economic growth in the former and from economic growth to energy use in the latter. Under *feedback* hypothesis there is bidirectional causality between economic growth and energy consumption. Finally in *neutrality* hypothesis there is no apparent causal relationship between economic growth and energy use.

Cheng (1999) in his study for India based on data from 1952 to 1995 and using Cointegration, Error Correction Modelling and Granger causality tests find no causality running from energy intake to growth. Another important conclusion of the study is that economic progress leads to greater energy consumption in the short as well as long run. Paul and Bhattacharya (2004), using Granger causality test, Engle–Granger and Johansen multivariate cointegration on data for the period 1950-96, conclude that greater energy usage positively impacts economic growth and that higher growth also brings about higher energy consumption. Yang and Zhao (2014) study the relationship between growth, energy, and carbon emissions for India using data from 1970–2008. The study employs Granger tests and directed acyclic graphs (DAG) and finds evidence of causality running from energy use to growth and greenhouse gases (GHG) emissions. Their analysis also supports existence of a two-way linkage connecting emissions and growth. The study also considers the extent of trade as a variable and finds trade to be a significant factor impacting both emissions and growth. Dergiades et al. (2013) also find evidence supporting the "growth hypothesis" as greater energy consumption appears to promote greater growth for Greece. Their linear and non-linear analysis uses data for the country from 1960-2008. However, according to the researchers given the bivariate formulation used for the analysis the omitted variable bias is likely to exist. Paul and Bhattacharya (2004) use the Engle–Granger cointegration approach and Granger causality tests. The study uses Indian data from 1950 to 1996 and finds evidence of two-way association running from energy to economic growth and vice versa. Alam et al. (2011) using data for India from 1971-2006 on energy, emissions and income in India conclude that a two-way causality is apparent between energy usage and emissions, however they find that there is no linkage running from energy use to income in the long-run. These results are based on dynamic modelling approach employing the Toda and Yamamoto model and using labour force and fixed capital stock as additional variables in the analysis. In the sample of G-7 countries, capital, conventional energy consumption, government expenditure, and CO2 emissions have been found to increase GDP. At the same time, there are feedback relationships between GDP and capital, modern energy consumption, and government expenses (He, 2022, pp. 343–364).

Causal relationship between renewable energy and economic growth: The energy transition involves the transition from conventional fossil fuel-based energy sources to renewable and sustainable alternatives (Tuğcu et al., 2012). There are various factors that contribute to this transition, such as the growing concerns surrounding climate change, the limited availability of fossil fuel resources, and the aspiration for energy security and independence. The shift towards renewable energy is widely recognised as a crucial measure in attaining sustainable development and addressing the challenges posed by climate change (Gozgor et al., 2018). The relationship between growth and energy transition is complex and interconnected, as highlighted by Khan et al. (2021). The connection between energy transition and growth has been a subject of fascination in the field of energy economics. Increased energy usage can be driven by higher growth and income. The recognition of the significance of the role of renewable energy in the growth of an economy has been gaining traction and is driving global initiatives to conserve energy and decrease emissions (Tuğcu et al., 2012). Many nations are actively exploring methods to shift from non-renewable energy sources to renewable ones to foster sustainable development.

Numerous empirical studies have been conducted to explore this relationship using various methodologies and datasets. These studies have provided varying results, with some finding a positive liaison between renewable energy use and economic development, while others report bidirectional causality.

Growth of an economy and the energy used are strongly correlated as evidenced in the case of European transition countries. Pejovic & Kardzic (2023) find evidence of increased energy use (in the long run) following increases in gross domestic product. In a study conducted by Inglesi-Lotz (2016), the relationship between renewable energy and economic growth was examined for a panel of 34 OECD countries from 1990 to 2000. It has been observed that the utilisation of renewable energy has a favourable impact on economic growth. Further, the promotion of renewable energy sources also plays a crucial role in preserving the environment. A study by Gozgor et al. (2018), using a panel of 29 OECD countries, and data from 1990 to 2013 concludes that there is a significant and positive connection between economic complexity, renewable and non-renewable energy use, and higher growth. The study employs panel ARDL and panel quantile regression techniques.

Furthermore, researchers have analysed the relationship between the utilisation of renewable energy and development, uncovering a non-linear connection. Over time, the use of renewable energy hampers the growth of real GDP, but it has a beneficial effect in the short term. Furthermore, there are notable threshold effects related to the intensity and transformation of energy usage. Encouraging renewable energy consumption may hinder growth under specific circumstances, as highlighted by Feng and Zhao (2022). Wang et al. (2022) investigate the linkage between the renewable energy consumption and growth by applying a panel threshold model. They use balanced panel data from 1997-2015 for 34 OECD nations. The study, conducted from a risk-based standpoint, examines political, financial, and economic concerns. It concludes that the impact of use of renewable energy on development is nonlinear and varies depending on the specific risks associated with each country. According to Wang et al. (2018), a stable political environment is crucial for ensuring that greater renewable energy consumption has a significant impact on economic development. Baz et al. (2018) examine the association between fossil fuel consumption, renewable energy, and growth in Pakistan by using time series data from 1980 to 2017. The researchers employ non-linear autoregressive distributed lag and asymmetric causality methodologies and discover the presence of asymmetric and nonlinear co-integration among the variables. It has been discovered that favourable changes in economic growth have an uneven effect on the usage of renewable energy. Furthermore, both positive and negative impacts on fossil fuel and economic growth do not have a significant influence, whereas there seems to be a balanced reciprocal relationship between the use of fossil fuels and growth.

In addition, previous research has examined the reciprocating interaction among the utilisation of renewable and other energy sources and their impact on growth (Al-Mulali et al., 2013; Apergis & Danuletiu, 2014). Apergis and Payne (2010) explore the correlation between renewable energy and economic expansion. They analyse multivariate panel data and use cointegration and VECM techniques for twenty OECD countries from 1985 to 2005. According to their findings from Granger-causality tests, they have determined that there is a causal connection in both directions between use of renewable energy and growth, both in the short term and the long term. In their study, Apergis and Danuletiu (2014) analyse the correlation between renewable energy and economic growth across 80 countries from 1990 to 2012. They conclude that a two-way relationship exists between use of renewable energy and GDP in various regions, including the European Union, Western Europe, Asia, Latin America, and Africa. In their study, Saad and Taleb (2018) examine the association between use of renewable energy and growth in 12 European Union countries over a span of 25 years, from 1990 to 2014. They find that that there is a one-way association running from growth to use of renewable energy in the short term, and a two-way linkage exists between the variables in the long run.

Overall, energy transitions have implications for economic growth and environmental sustainability, and policies must consider the lasting and nonlinear effects of using renewable energy (Loewen, 2022).

Given that India relies heavily on energy, it is imperative for the country to adopt energy efficiency measures, employ extremely important energy-generation technological advances, and invest in renewable energy. These actions will help reduce the consumption of traditional sources of energy and decrease carbon emissions, ultimately leading to more rapid more inclusive, and sustainable economic growth (Vidyarthi, 2013). Although there have been studies investigating the influence of technological advancements on the utilisation of alternative and renewable sources of energy, there is need for further empirical research (Alam & Murad, 2020). This study adds to the existing body of literature on the evolving association between renewable sources of energy and growth.

3. ECONOMIC GROWTH AND ENERGY USE IN INDIA

India is presently the fifth largest economy in the world, behind only the United States of America, China, Germany and Japan. It is in fact projected to surpass Germany and Japan and become the third largest economy within the next three years and become a $7 trillion economy by 2030. India's present share in world GDP based on PPP is around 7.86 percent[4] even though it has now surpassed China to become the most populous country in the world.

The Indian economy has experienced fluctuating growth rates over the period 1983–2022 (Figure 1). The average growth rate for India has consistently stayed above 5 percent for all periods except for the period inclusive of the global pandemic. From the early 1980s, with an average growth rate of 5 percent over 1983–87, the economy grew at 5.5, 6.1, and 5.5 percent, respectively, in 1988–92, 1993–97, and 1998–02. The economy attained the highest average growth rate of 7.9 percent in 2003–07. The average growth rate during 2008–12 fell to 6 percent before rising to 7.4 percent. The COVID pandemic led to a lower average growth rate of 4.2 percent in the most recent five-year period. However, despite the global slowdown, the Indian economy grew and emerged as the third largest.

Figure 1. Average growth rate of Indian economy, 1983-2022

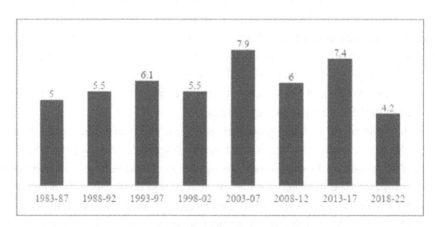

The growth in the Indian economy has been fuelled by greater energy use, as illustrated in Figure 2, where we plot GDP per capita measured in PPP along with Energy use per person in the country measured in kilowatt-hours per person[5][REMOVED HYPERLINK FIELD]. Both series show an increasing trend and appear to move together. At about 2002, primary energy consumption was pulling economic growth. From 2002 to 2006, it is the other way around, with economic growth pulling energy intake. The roles again reversed post-2006 till about 2015, when energy utilisation appeared to be leading economic growth. Post-2015 economic growth leads to an increase in primary energy consumption. The GDP per capita series attained a relatively high value of 6617.13 in 2018 before achieving its highest value of 6677.19 $ in 2020. India's primary energy consumption per capita was highest in 2019 at 6731.81 kWh/person and fell in 2020 to 6317.1 kWh/person despite the increase in GDP. Theoretically, the Environmental Kuznets curve approach expects that as growth increases, after threshold levels along with an increase in primary energy use, the levels of environmental pollution are anticipated to diminish.

Figure 2. GDP per capita and energy use per person in India (1990-2020)

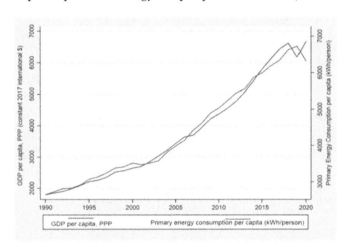

In understanding the relationship between growth and energy consumption, it is also essential to understand the energy intensity pattern in an economy, which is studied in Figure 3. Based on data from the Energy Statistics 2023[6] Report, it is evident that energy consumption has been increasing steadily from 2011-12 to 2018-19, after marginally declining in 2019-20 and 2020-21 on account of the slowdown in the economic experienced owing to the pandemic and again picks up to 33502 petajoules in 2021-22. Per capita energy consumption measured in megajoules also reflects a similar behaviour, rising from 19769 megajoules to 24699 megajoules in 2018-19 before falling marginally in 2019-20 and further declining to 22369 megajoules in 2020-21 and rising to a new high of 24453 megajoules in 2021-22. Interestingly, energy intensity is declining throughout and shows an increasing growth rate only between 2020-21 and 2021-22

Figure 3. Per capita energy consumption and energy intensity for India (2011- 2022)

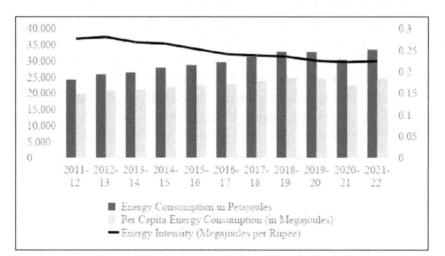

Energy consumption for the economy has been continuously rising. It stood at 514 Mtoe in 2010 and has risen by about 1.5 times to 754 Mtoe in 2022. The various primary energy sources for the Indian economy are examined in Figure 4.

Figure 4. Primary energy supply sources for India (2011- 2022)

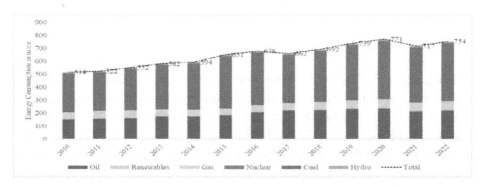

Energy consumption for the economy has been continuously rising. It stood at 514 Mtoe in 2010 and has risen by about 1.5 times to 754 Mtoe in 2022. The principal primary energy source continues to be coal in India contributing between 55 to 61 percent of the total primary energy supply throughout the 2010 to 2022 period. Oil is the second largest primary energy source contributing between 28 to 31 percent of total primary energy requirements. Interestingly the contribution of renewables as a primary energy source has also been continuously increasing throughout the period. It was 3.12 Mtoe in 2010 and increased to 15.43 in 2022 marking an increase of more nearly 400 percent. Hydro as a primary energy source is also continuously increasing its contribution. It was 9.19 Mtoé in 2010, increased to 11.13 Mtoe in 2015 and in 2022 has increased to 13.07 Mtoe. Nuclear energy is also being utilised as a primary energy source with its contribution increasing from 1.6 Mtoe in 2010 to 4.05 Mtoe in 2022.

India's greenhouse gas emissions have also been increasing continuously. There is a very close correlation between the country's energy consumption pattern and emissions, as shown in Figure 5. However, with its reaffirmed commitment to Nationally Determined Contributions to reduce carbon emissions (45 percent of GDP by 2030), India aims to diversify primary energy consumption sources (50 percent cumulative electric power from non-fossil fuel sources).

Figure 5. Primary energy consumption and greenhouse gas emissions for India (1990- 2020)

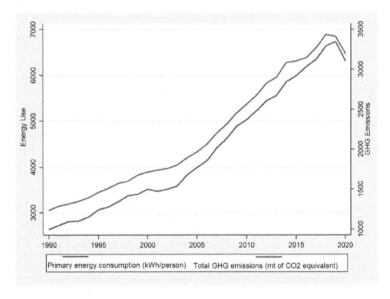

4. DATA AND METHODOLOGY

4.1 Data and Variables

This study aims to understand the interrelationship between economic growth, energy transition, and sustainable development in India. It measures economic growth using India's real gross domestic product per capita (GDPPC). It uses carbon emissions per capita and total ecological footprint as system performance imperative of energy transition indicators. Further, the Human Development Index is employed in the model to indicate sustainable development and energy transition readiness (H.V. Sing et al., 2019). Annual time series data for the given variables from 1990 to 2020 of India is used to study the relationship. Table 1 provides variable explanations used in the study and their sources.

Table 1. Variable description

Variables	Explanation	Source
Real GDP per capita (GDP_{PC})	"Total gross value added by all resident producers in the economy, less any product taxes and any subsidies not included in the depreciation of manufactured assets or the depletion of natural resources, divided by population at midyear."	WDI
Carbon emissions (CO_2) in a million metric tons per capita	Emissions from petroleum, natural gas, coal consumption, natural gas flaring, and cement manufacturing include carbon dioxide produced during the consumption of solid, liquid, and gas fuels and gas flaring.	WDI
Human Development Index (HDI)	It is a summary measure of average achievement in UNDP key dimensions of human development vis-à-vis a long and healthy life, knowledge, and decent living standards.	UNDP
Industrialisation (IND)	Industry comprises value added in mining, manufacturing (also reported as a separate subgroup), construction, electricity, water, and gas. Industry (including construction), value added (% of GDP).	WDI
Trade Openness (TO)	It is the aggregate of exports and imports of goods and services measured as a share of gross domestic product.	WDI
Renewable Energy Consumption (REC)	The share of renewable energy in total final energy consumption.	WDI
Total Ecological Footprint (EF)	Ecological Footprint is defined as the area used to support a defined population's consumption.	Global Footprint Network

4.2 Methodology

The following tests examined the interrelationship between economic growth, environmental quality, sustainable development measured by HDI, and ecological footprint, industrialisation, and trade openness in India.

a)   Structural Break Unit root test

In applied economics, multiple unit root tests are available to test the variables' stationarity features. Nevertheless, knowledge of the series' structural breakpoints is optional, leading to skewed and false conclusions. We carry out a unit root test with breakpoints similar to Perron's (1989). The null hypothesis states that the time series has a unit root.

b)   Autoregressive Distributed Lag Model (ARDL)

The study employs the robust ARDL cointegration analysis approach to investigate the single-level relationship between the dependent and independent variables. By incorporating the lagged and contemporaneous values of the independent variables and the lags of the dependent variable, this model not only allows for the indirect estimation of the long-run equilibrium connection but also enables the direct estimation of the short-run impacts, thereby ensuring the validity and reliability of our research findings.

The residuals are tested for serial correlation using the Breusch-Godfrey Serial Correlation LM test. The heteroskedasticity test is the Breusch-Pagan-Godfrey test. Our model, which has an autoregressive structure, undergoes a rigorous stability check to ensure it is "dynamically stable." A cumulative sum of recursive residuals (CUSUM) test evaluates the stability of long-run relationships over time. This stability check is particularly suitable in time series data, especially when we do not know when structural change might happen.

The section below explores the impact of energy transitions, sustainable development, industrialisation, and trade on economic growth.

5. EMPIRICAL RESULTS

5.1 Unit root test

Results statistics of ADF and breakpoint unit root tests are given in table 2. The test statistics indicate the presence of stationarity at the level and for some variables while first differencing. It shows that all variables are stationary at I (0) or I (1), except for renewable energy consumption in the breakpoint unit root method (stationary at I (2)).

Table 2. Unit root test

Variables	ADF		Break Point			
	Level	1ˢᵗ Difference	Level		1ˢᵗ Difference	
	t-statistic	t-statistic	t-statistic	Time Break	t-statistic	Time Break
GDP_{PC}	-2.3091	-1.3499	-2.8638	2000	- 5.6048***	2008
CO_2	- 4.0095**	-	- 8.1785***	2005	-	-
HDI	-0.8907	-2.7120*	-3.0323	2002	-4.2033*	2016
REC	-0.7955	-1.6319*	-3.5476	2006	-3.3436	2019
IND	-0.8328	-2.1451**	-2.2488	2014	- 5.3851***	1995
TO	-1.5872	- 4.5762***	-2.5892	2003	- 6.0387***	2013
EF	-0.7209	-2.6509*	- 5.8682***	2006	-	-

Results generated by EViews 12. Note: ***, **, and * denote significance at 1%, 5%, and 10%, respectively.

5.2 Autoregressive Distributed Lag Model (ARDL)

The present study aims to investigate the relationship between economic growth (measured by GDP per capita), carbon emissions (CO2), and sustainable development (measured by HDI and ecological footprint) using the ARDL bound testing approach.

The general empirical form of the model[7] is:

Model 1: $GDP_{PC} = f\left(CO_2, HDI \right)$

Model 2: $GDP_{PC} = f\left(CO_2, HDI, IND, TO \right)$

Model 3: $GDP_{PC} = f\left(CO_2, HDI, IND, TO, EF \right)$

The results of the ARDL bounds testing approach to cointegration in the presence of a structural break in the series is presented in Table 3. Using the multiple breakpoint tests for 'model 1', 2014[8] is identified as the breakpoint[9] and a lag length of 2 is determined using the lag length criteria[10]. Similarly, for models 2 and 3, the lag of 2[11] and structural break in 2016[12] is considered. The results indicated that the calculated F-statistics is greater than the upper bound at the 1 percent level. Thus, the null hypothesis of no cointegration is rejected for this model. This indicates that a cointegrating relationship exists among the variables in the long run.

Table 3. Bounds testing for cointegration

F-statistics		
$F_{Model\,1}\left(GDP_{PC}/CO_2, HDI\right)$	19.87***	
*F-critical at 1% level (k=3)	I (0)	I (1)
	4.29	5.61
$F_{Model\,2}\left(GDP_{PC}/CO_2, HDI, IND, TO\right)$	15.84***	
*F-critical at 1% level (k=5)	I (0)	I (1)
	3.41	4.68
$F_{Model\,3}\left(GDP_{PC}/CO_2, HDI, IND, TO, EF\right)$	12.15***	
*F-critical at 1% level (k=6)	I (0)	I (1)
	3.15	4.43

Note: ***, **, and * indicate significant levels at 1%, 5%, and 10%, respectively.

The long-run estimates of the cointegration models are reported in Table 4, and Table 5 reports the short-run estimates of the cointegration models. In models 1, 2, and 3, the coefficient of CO2 and HDI is positive and significant; this implies that higher levels of carbon emissions and human development are expected to be linked with higher levels of growth in the long run. The ecological print has a negligible negative but significant effect on economic growth in model 3. This result implies the delinking of economic growth and the ecological footprint of consumption. The coefficient of break term is positive and significant in models 1 and 2. (Annexure Figures 6, 7 and 8 give information of stability diagnostics.)

Table 4. Long-run estimates of ARDL

Variables	Model 1[13]	Model 2[14]	Model 3[15]
CO_2	324.7637*** (116.5147)	422.3255* (211.8628)	1007.252*** (182.8300)

continued on following page

Table 4. Continued

Variables	Model 1[13]	Model 2[14]	Model 3[15]
HDI	3546.217*** (580.8765)	3995.760*** (1276.568)	6155.437*** (1168.641)
IND	-	-16.8687 (13.7387)	7.7000 (7.6313)
TO	-	-3.7562 (3.9107)	-6.5004 (3.9057)
EF	-	-	-1.07E-06** (3.31E-07)
Break$_{2014}$	325.7329*** (51.3763)	-	-
Break$_{2016}$	-	250.4215*** (74.8072)	97.37524 (99.1340)
C	-633.1589*** (68.1607)	-427.7787 (261.8031)	-1994.072*** (266.5787)

Notes: *, **, *** indicate statistical significance at the 10%, 5%, and 1% levels, respectively. (.) Gives S.E values.

Firstly, the coefficient of the error correction terms is negative and significant across models (1 percent level.) In the short run, the coefficient of economic growth lag is positive and significant across models. Similar to the long run, the coefficient of carbon emissions across models is positive and significant, which is expected to imply a monotonic relationship between growth and carbon emissions. Even in the short run, the coefficient of human development is positively related to economic growth and is significant across models.

The coefficient of industrialisation lag is positive and significant at the 1 percent level. Similarly, the coefficient of trade openness in the short run is negative and significant at the 1 percent level in models 2 and 3. Also, in the short run, the coefficient of ecological footprint lag is negative and significant. Finally, the coefficient of the breaks in models 1 and 3 is positive and significant in the short run.

Table 5. Short-run estimates of ARDL

Variables	Model 1 (1,2,2,2)	Model 2 (1,2,1,2,1,0)	Model 3 (2,1,2,0,2,2)
Δ (GDP)	0.4908*** (0.1060)	0.5951*** (0.0970)	0.5268 (0.3226)
Δ (GDP$_{t-1}$)	-	-	0.4021*** (0.0885)
Δ (CO$_2$)	474.5016*** (73.2758)	463.0343*** (47.0671)	258.7233** (83.5597)

continued on following page

Table 5. Continued

Variables	Model 1 (1,2,2,2)	Model 2 (1,2,1,2,1,0)	Model 3 (2,1,2,0,2,2)
$\Delta(CO_{2(t-1)})$	363.6696*** (88.2033)	613.3158*** (74.5360)	-
Δ (HDI)	3203.988*** (892.9950)	4982.238*** (767.7859)	1924.927** (845.8315)
Δ (HDI$_{t-1}$)	-3159.645** (1160.742)	-	-4906.568*** (972.8355)
Δ (IND)	-	5.4578 (3.4687)	-
Δ (IND$_{t-1}$)	-	8.3898*** (2.8449)	-
Δ (TO)	-	-3.2053*** (0.7158)	-3.0395*** (0.4871)
$\Delta(To_{t-1})$		-	3.3226*** (0.6826)
Δ (EF)	-	-	6.52E-08 (1.21E-07)
Δ (Ef$_{t-1}$)		-	4.15E-07** (1.24E-07)
Δ (Break$_{2014}$)	16.3062 (15.6929)	-	-
Δ (Break$_{2014(t-1)}$)	-76.0721*** (23.8386)	-	-
Δ (Break$_{2016}$)	-	-	47.7302*** (12.7438)
Δ (Break$_{2016(t-1)}$)	-	-	-34.7955** (14.3548)
ect	-0.5092*** (0.0528)	-0.4048*** (0.0363)	-0.8752*** (0.0763)
R^2	0.9381	0.9514	0.9771
F-stat P(F-stat)	45.46942 (0.0000)	58.6783 (0.0000)	65.9507 (0.0000)

Notes: *, **, *** indicate statistical significance at the 10%, 5%, and 1% levels, respectively. (.) Gives S.E values.

To conclude, a monotonic relationship exists between economic growth and carbon emissions across models for India. There is also evidence to support sustainable development and economic growth.

6. CONCLUSION AND POLICY IMPLICATION

The current ambiguity in understanding the integration of global economic, environmental, and human sustainable development indicates the need for a study to explore the relationship described above at a disaggregated country level. The study explores the relationship between India's economic growth, energy transition, and sustainable development from 1990 to 2020. The study further estimates the long-term impact of industrialisation and trade openness on economic growth using an ARDL approach.

The essential results are as follows:

- The analysis results reveal a significant long-run cointegrating relationship. Our findings align with previous studies in India (Paul & Bhattacharya, 2004), which show a positive and significant relationship between environmental degradation (CO_2) and economic growth.
- The inverse relationship between energy transition and economic growth signifies a crucial shift for India. The disentangling of environmental degradation and economic growth can be achieved only by realising higher levels of energy efficiency and sustainable development for India. This delinking of growth and environmental degradation is a significant finding with practical implications. Moreover, the positive and significant relationship between HDI and economic growth underscores the role of sustainable development in driving economic growth. Similarly, the positive and significant relationship between economic growth and trade openness highlights the potential of trade policies to stimulate economic growth. The structural break, a critical methodological tool adopted in our study, aligns with the period of significant global shifts in adoption and mitigation commitments. This temporal alignment underscores the relevance and timeliness of our research in the current global context.

To drive sustainable economic growth, the urgency for policymakers and organizations to focus on enhancing energy transition and readiness parameters cannot be overstated. They must adopt interventionist policies to improve renewable energy consumption and increase energy efficiency. This is crucial to ensure that the monotonic relationship between carbon emissions and growth does not hinder emerging countries like India. For instance, the 'National Biofuel Policy 2018' of India, as indicated in previous studies (Sajeev et al., 2015), aim to reduce the import dependence of India on imported fossil fuels by fostering domestic biofuel production. The inverse relationship between economic growth and sustainable development also underscores the importance of policies for improving energy efficiency. Assertive initiatives in the direction of improving the energy intensity of households by 45 percent by 2030 and campaigns for behavioral changes in the consumption patterns of consumers are all efforts in the right direction. India has adopted a multi-pronged approach to make the country energy-independent and meet its climate change mitigation and adaptation obligations. Adopting measures like setting up the National Green Hydrogen Mission in January 2023 to facilitate demand creation, production, utilisation and export of Green Hydrogen are indicative of the country's allegiance to mitigate climate change (Economic Survey, 2023). The study's main limitation is that it needs more data on this country's renewable and fossil fuel energy consumption, limiting the model's predictability.

Further studies must use dynamic panel models for emerging countries as we move forward. This can provide significant results that are instrumental for policymakers. Additionally, including more variables of energy transition and readiness that may affect economic growth and carbon emissions can yield more comprehensive results, further emphasising the importance of ongoing research in this field.

REFERENCES

Abbasi, T., Premalatha, M., & Abbasi, S. A. (2011). The return to renewables: Will it help in global warming control? *Renewable & Sustainable Energy Reviews*, 15(1), 891–894. 10.1016/j.rser.2010.09.048

Akadırı, S. S., Alola, A. A., & Usman, O. (2021). Energy mix outlook and the EKC hypothesis in BRICS countries: A perspective of economic freedom vs. economic growth. *Environmental Science and Pollution Research International*, 28(7), 8922–8926. 10.1007/s11356-020-11964-w33410045

Alam, M. J., Begum, I. A., Buysse, J., Rahman, S., & Van Huylenbroeck, G. (2011). Dynamic modeling of causal relationship between energy consumption, CO2 emissions and economic growth in India. *Renewable & Sustainable Energy Reviews*, 15(6), 3243–3251. 10.1016/j.rser.2011.04.029

Alam, M. M., & Murad, M. W. (2020). The impacts of economic growth, trade openness and technological progress on renewable energy use in organization for economic co-operation and development countries. *Renewable Energy*, 145, 382–390. 10.1016/j.renene.2019.06.054

Apergis, N., & Danuletiu, D. C. (2014). Renewable energy and economic growth: Evidence from the sign of panel long-run causality. *International Journal of Energy Economics and Policy*, 4(4), 578–587.

Apergis, N., & Payne, J. E. (2010). Renewable energy consumption and economic growth: Evidence from a panel of OECD countries. *Energy Policy*, 38(1), 656–660. 10.1016/j.enpol.2009.09.002

Bartleet, M., & Gounder, R. (2010). Energy consumption and economic growth in New Zealand: Results of trivariate and multivariate models. *Energy Policy*, 38(7), 3508–3517. 10.1016/j.enpol.2010.02.025

Baz, K., Cheng, J., Xu, D., Abbas, K., Ali, I., Ali, H., & Fang, C. (2021). Asymmetric impact of fossil fuel and renewable energy consumption on economic growth: A nonlinear technique. *Energy*, 226, 120357. 10.1016/j.energy.2021.120357

Bekun, F. V., Emir, F., & Sarkodie, S. A. (2019). Another look at the relationship between energy consumption, carbon dioxide emissions, and economic growth in South Africa. *The Science of the Total Environment*, 655, 759–765. 10.1016/j. scitotenv.2018.11.27130476856

Bildirici, M. E., & Bakirtas, T. (2014). The relationship among oil, natural gas and coal consumption and economic growth in BRICTS (Brazil, Russian, India, China, Turkey and South Africa) countries. *Energy*, 65, 134–144. 10.1016/j.energy.2013.12.006

Breitung, J. 2000. The local power of some unit root tests for panel data. Advances in Econometrics, Volume 15: Nonstationary Panels, Panel Cointegration, and Dynamic Panels, ed. B. H. Baltagi, 161–178. Amsterdam: JAY Press. 10.1016/S0731-9053(00)15006-6

Bryndin, E. (2023). Transition of Countries to Currency and Trade Sustainable International Cooperation on the BRICS Platform. *Japan and the World Economy*, 2(1), 1–6. 10.56397/JWE.2023.03.01

Chang, C. C. (2010). A multivariate causality test of carbon dioxide emissions, energy consumption and economic growth in China. *Applied Energy*, 87(11), 3533–3537. 10.1016/j.apenergy.2010.05.004

Cheng, B. S. (1999). Causality between energy consumption and economic growth in India: An application of cointegration and error-correction modeling. *Indian Economic Review*, ●●●, 39–49.

Cheng, B. S., & Lai, T. W. (1997). An investigation of co-integration and causality between energy consumption and economic activity in Taiwan. *Energy Economics*, 19(4), 435–444. 10.1016/S0140-9883(97)01023-2

Dergiades, T., Martinopoulos, G., & Tsoulfidis, L. (2013). Energy consumption and economic growth: Parametric and non-parametric causality testing for the case of Greece. *Energy Economics*, 36, 686–697. 10.1016/j.eneco.2012.11.017

Feng, Y., & Zhao, T. (2022). Exploring the Nonlinear Relationship between Renewable Energy Consumption and Economic Growth in the Context of Global Climate Change. *International Journal of Environmental Research and Public Health*, 19(23), 15647. 10.3390/ijerph192315647 36497722

Gozgor, G., Lau, C. K. M., & Lu, Z. (2018). Energy consumption and economic growth: New evidence from the OECD countries. *Energy*, 153, 27–34. 10.1016/j.energy.2018.03.158

Harris, R. D. F., & Tzavalis, E. (1999). Inference for unit roots in dynamic panels where the time dimension is fixed. *Journal of Econometrics*, 91(2), 201–226. 10.1016/S0304-4076(98)00076-1

Im, K. S., Pesaran, M. H., & Shin, Y. (2003). Testing for unit roots in heterogeneous panels. *Journal of Econometrics*, 115(1), 53–74. 10.1016/S0304-4076(03)00092-7

Inglesi-Lotz, R. (2016). The impact of renewable energy consumption to economic growth: A panel data application. *Energy Economics*, 53, 58–63. 10.1016/j.eneco.2015.01.003

Jana, S. K. (2022). Sustainable energy development in emerging economies: A study on BRICS. In *Environmental Sustainability, Growth Trajectory and Gender: Contemporary Issues of Developing Economies* (pp. 23-35). Emerald Publishing Limited. 10.1108/978-1-80262-153-220221002

Kao C. Spurious regression and residual-based tests for cointegration in paneldata. J Econom 1999;90:1e44. .10.1016/S0304-4076(98)00023-2

Khan, I., Hou, F., Zakari, A., & Tawiah, V. K. (2021). The dynamic links among energy transitions, energy consumption, and sustainable economic growth: A novel framework for IEA countries. *Energy*, 222, 119935. 10.1016/j.energy.2021.119935

Kraft, J., & Kraft, A. (1978). On the relationship between energy and GNP. *The Journal of Energy and Development*, 401-403.

Leitão, N. C., Balsalobre-Lorente, D., & Cantos-Cantos, J. M. (2021). The impact of renewable energy and economic complexity on carbon emissions in BRICS countries under the EKC scheme. *Energies*, 14(16), 4908. 10.3390/en14164908

Loewen, B. (2022). Coal, green growth and crises: Exploring three European Union policy responses to regional energy transitions. *Energy Research & Social Science*, 93, 102849. 10.1016/j.erss.2022.102849

Ministry of Statistics and Programme Implementation. (2023). *Energy Statistics India*. Government of India.

Nain, M. Z., Ahmad, W., & Kamaiah, B. (2017). Economic growth, energy consumption and CO2 emissions in India: A disaggregated causal analysis. *International Journal of Sustainable Energy*, 36(8), 807–824. 10.1080/14786451.2015.1109512

Owusu, P. A., & Asumadu-Sarkodie, S. (2016). A review of renewable energy sources, sustainability issues and climate change mitigation. *Cogent Engineering*, 3(1), 1167990. 10.1080/23311916.2016.1167990

Paul, S., & Bhattacharya, R. N. (2004). Causality between energy consumption and economic growth in India: A note on conflicting results. *Energy Economics*, 26(6), 977–983. 10.1016/j.eneco.2004.07.002

Pejovic, B., Backovic, T., & Karadzic, V. (2023). Analysis of the Relationship Between Energy Consumption and Economic Growth in Transition Countries. *Eastern European Economics*, ●●●, 1–21. 10.1080/00128775.2023.2216690

Pesaran MH. General diagnostic tests for cross section dependence in panels. Iza 2004;1e42.

Pesaran MH. J Appl Econom 2007;21:1e21. https://doi.org/.10.1002/jae

Phillips PCB, Sul D. Dynamic panel estimation and homogeneity testing under cross section dependence. Econom J 2003;6:217e59. .10.1111/1368-423X.00108

Saad, W., & Taleb, A. (2018). The causal relationship between renewable energy consumption and economic growth: Evidence from Europe. *Clean Technologies and Environmental Policy*, 20(1), 127–136. 10.1007/s10098-017-1463-5

Sahin, G. (2022). Investigation into the Effects of Energy Transition in Terms. *Handbook of Energy Transitions*, 343.

Sajeev, A., Kaur, H., & Kaur, S. (2015). Cereal and fuel price interactions: Econometric evidence from India. *Journal of Business Thought*, ●●●, 14–43.

Sajeev, A., & Kaur, S. (2020). Environmental sustainability, trade and economic growth in India: Implications for public policy. *International Trade. Politics and Development*, 4(2), 141–160. 10.1108/ITPD-09-2020-0079

Sarwat, S., Godil, D. I., Ali, L., Ahmad, B., Dinca, G., & Khan, S. A. R. (2022). The role of natural resources, renewable energy, and globalization in testing EKC Theory in BRICS countries: Method of Moments Quantile. *Environmental Science and Pollution Research International*, 29(16), 1–13. 10.1007/s11356-021-17557-534811617

Singh, H. V., Bocca, R., Gomez, P., Dahlke, S., & Bazilian, M. (2019). The energy transitions index: An analytic framework for understanding the evolving global energy system. *Energy Strategy Reviews*, 26, 100382. 10.1016/j.esr.2019.100382

Stern, D. I. (1993). Energy and economic growth in the USA: A multivariate approach. *Energy Economics*, 15(2), 137–150. 10.1016/0140-9883(93)90033-N

Stern, D. I. (2000). A multivariate cointegration analysis of the role of energy in the US macroeconomy. *Energy Economics*, 22(2), 267–283. 10.1016/S0140-9883(99)00028-6

Stern, N. H. (2007). *The economics of climate change: the Stern review*. Cambridge University press. 10.1017/CBO9780511817434

Tiba, S., & Omri, A. (2017). Literature survey on the relationships between energy, environment and economic growth. *Renewable & Sustainable Energy Reviews*, 69, 1129–1146. 10.1016/j.rser.2016.09.113

Tugcu, C. T., Ozturk, I., & Aslan, A. (2012). Renewable and non-renewable energy consumption and economic growth relationship revisited: Evidence from G7 countries. *Energy Economics*, 34(6), 1942–1950. 10.1016/j.eneco.2012.08.021

United Nations Framework Convention on Climate Change. Secretariat. (1992). *United Nations framework convention on climate change.* UNFCCC.

Vidyarthi, H. (2013). Energy consumption, carbon emissions and economic growth in India. *World Journal of Science. Technology and Sustainable Development*, 10(4), 278–287. 10.1108/WJSTSD-07-2013-0024

Wang, Q., Dong, Z., Li, R., & Wang, L. (2022). Renewable energy and economic growth: New insight from country risks. *Energy*, 238, 122018. 10.1016/j.energy.2021.122018

Yang, Z., & Zhao, Y. (2014). Energy consumption, carbon emissions, and economic growth in India: Evidence from directed acyclic graphs. *Economic Modelling*, 38, 533–540. 10.1016/j.econmod.2014.01.030

Zhixin, Z., & Xin, R. (2011). Causal relationships between energy consumption and economic growth. *Energy Procedia*, 5, 2065–2071. 10.1016/j.egypro.2011.03.356

ENDNOTES

[1] https://blogs.worldbank.org/en/energy/how-much-do-we-know-about-development-impacts-energy-infrastructure

[2] India- ranks 67th in terms of System Performance and Transition Readiness globally on the Energy Transition Readiness Index (WEF, 2023). (https://www3.weforum.org/docs/WEF_Fostering_Effective_Energy_Transition_2023.pdf)

[3] https://www.newindianexpress.com/world/2023/Dec/08/global-emissions-of-fossil-carbon-dioxide-hit-record-high-in-2023-india-third-highest-emitter-2639836.html#~:text=India%20is%20now%20the%20world's,of%20the%20war%20in%20Ukraine.

[4] https://www.imf.org/external/datamapper/PPPSH@WEO/OEMDC/ADVEC/WEOWORLD

[5] The data is sourced from the U.S. Energy Information Administration (2023), Energy Institute - Statistical Review of World Energy (2023), Population-based on various sources (2023) – with major processing by Our World in Data. https://ourworldindata.org/grapher/per-capita-energy-use?region=Asia

6 https://www.mospi.gov.in/publication/energy-statistics-india-2023#

7   Models with renewable energy consumption was dropped for India, since variable is not stationary at $I(0)$ or $I(1)$.

8   Coincides with the great oil plunge, thereby affecting India's economic growth..

9   Result appendix Table A1.

10   The result of the lag length selection by different criteria is given in annexure Table A2.

11   Result appendix Table A3.

12   A primary reason for this structural break is the adoption of the Paris Agreement in 2015, which came into force in November 2016.

13   Relevant residual tests have been done on the estimated ARDL model (Table A4.1 and Figure A1)

14   Relevant residual tests have been done on the estimated ARDL model (Table A4.2 and Figure A2)

15   Relevant residual tests have been done on the estimated ARDL model (Table A4.3 and Figure A3)

APPENDIX

Table 6.

```
Multiple breakpoint tests
Bai-Perron tests of L+1 vs. L sequentially determined breaks
Date: 04/21/24   Time: 09:27
Sample: 1990 2020
Included observations: 31
Breaking variables: CO2 EMISSIONS HDI C
Break test options: Trimming 0.15, Max. breaks 5, Sig. level
   0.05
```

Sequential F-statistic determined breaks:			1

Break Test	F-statistic	Scaled F-statistic	Critical Value**
0 vs. 1 *	122.6356	367.9069	13.98
1 vs. 2	1.947381	5.842144	15.72

* Significant at the 0.05 level.
** Bai-Perron (Econometric Journal, 2003) critical values.

Break dates:

	Sequential	Repartition
1	2014	2014

Table 7.

```
VAR Lag Order Selection Criteria
Endogenous variables: GDP_PC_REAL CO2_EMISSIONS HDI
Exogenous variables: C
Date: 04/21/24   Time: 22:12
Sample: 1990 2020
Included observations: 29
```

Lag	LogL	LR	FPE	AIC	SC	HQ
0	-90.73133	NA	0.128823	6.464230	6.605674	6.508528
1	53.76533	249.1322	1.13e-05	-2.880368	-2.314590*	-2.703173
2	66.26593	18.96643*	9.11e-06*	-3.121789*	-2.131678	-2.811698*

* indicates lag order selected by the criterion
LR: sequential modified LR test statistic (each test at 5% level)
FPE: Final prediction error
AIC: Akaike information criterion
SC: Schwarz information criterion
HQ: Hannan-Quinn information criterion

Table 8.

```
VAR Lag Order Selection Criteria
Endogenous variables: GDP_PC_REAL CO2_EMISSIONS HDI INDUSTRY TR...
Exogenous variables: C
Date: 04/21/24   Time: 10:22
Sample: 1990 2020
Included observations: 29
```

Lag	LogL	LR	FPE	AIC	SC	HQ
0	-181.9580	NA	0.017172	12.96262	13.24551	13.05122
1	15.59078	299.7292	2.64e-07	1.821326	3.801547*	2.441506
2	74.13978	64.60579*	7.93e-08*	0.266222*	3.943777	1.417986*

```
* indicates lag order selected by the criterion
LR: sequential modified LR test statistic (each test at 5% level)
FPE: Final prediction error
AIC: Akaike information criterion
SC: Schwarz information criterion
HQ: Hannan-Quinn information criterion
```

Table 9. 1 LM test & BPG

Breusch-Godfrey Serial Correlation LM Test:
Null hypothesis: No serial correlation at up to 2 lags

F-statistic	0.166469	Prob. F(2,16)	0.8481
Obs*R-squared	0.591147	Prob. Chi-Square(2)	0.7441

Heteroskedasticity Test: Breusch-Pagan-Godfrey
Null hypothesis: Homoskedasticity

F-statistic	1.122963	Prob. F(10,18)	0.3979
Obs*R-squared	11.14141	Prob. Chi-Square(10)	0.3466
Scaled explained SS	9.820771	Prob. Chi-Square(10)	0.4564

Table 10. LM test &BPG

Breusch-Godfrey Serial Correlation LM Test: Null hypothesis: No serial correlation at up to 2 lags			
F-statistic	1.385959	Prob. F(2,14)	0.2824
Obs*R-squared	4.792870	Prob. Chi-Square(2)	0.0910
Heteroskedasticity Test: Breusch-Pagan-Godfrey Null hypothesis: Homoskedasticity			
F-statistic	0.731803	Prob. F(12,16)	0.7042
Obs*R-squared	10.27646	Prob. Chi-Square(12)	0.5917
Scaled explained SS	4.678506	Prob. Chi-Square(12)	0.9679

Table 11. LM test &BPG

Breusch-Godfrey Serial Correlation LM Test: Null hypothesis: No serial correlation at up to 2 lags			
F-statistic	1.926054	Prob. F(2,9)	0.2012
Obs*R-squared	8.692047	Prob. Chi-Square(2)	0.0130
Heteroskedasticity Test: Breusch-Pagan-Godfrey Null hypothesis: Homoskedasticity			
F-statistic	0.804322	Prob. F(17,11)	0.6675
Obs*R-squared	16.07114	Prob. Chi-Square(17)	0.5188
Scaled explained SS	1.111866	Prob. Chi-Square(17)	1.0000

Figure 6. CUSUM

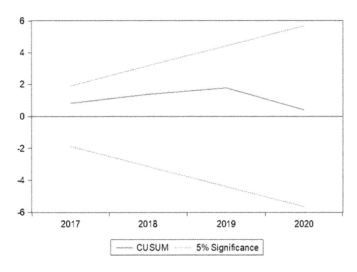

Figure 7. CUSUM

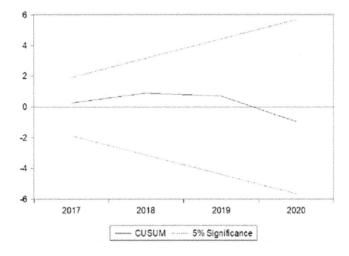

Figure 8. CUSUM

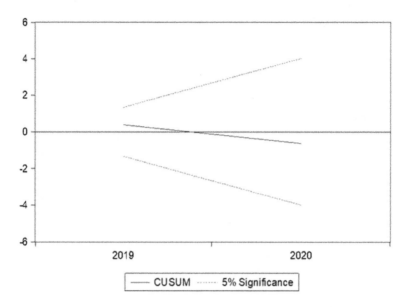

Chapter 16
The Costs and Concerns of Energy Transition:
Energy Transition Should Be Just and Inclusive

Sanobar Imam
TISS, Mumbai, India

Adwait Madkaikar
TISS, Guwahati, India

ABSTRACT

The global transition from fossil fuels to clean energy is driven by the need to reduce carbon emissions and combat climate change. However, this transition has its own set of costs, benefits, and concerns. The top-down approach to the transition often fails to consider the social, economic, and environmental costs associated with it, leading to conflicts among stakeholders and social groups. The transition to net-zero emissions will increase job opportunities, but it also poses a risk of job loss and displacement, particularly in industries reliant on coal. The chapter explores the challenges and opportunities of the energy transition, in the Indian context, and the unequal distribution of resources among different regions and social groups. It adopts a three-pronged approach: an extensive literature review, a detailed case study, and stakeholder consultations. The chapter aims to offer actionable insights for policymakers, industry stakeholders, and communities to navigate the challenges, concerns, and opportunities of the ongoing energy transition towards a cleaner future.

DOI: 10.4018/979-8-3693-3880-3.ch016

1. INTRODUCTION

The COVID-19 pandemic has intensified the disruption to the economic recovery. It has also led to widespread concerns about the affordability of energy primarily sourced from fossil fuels. It also pointed out the significant monetary burden of a centralized energy system. Intergovernmental Panel on Climate Change (IPCC) has stated that the effects of man-made climate changes are becoming increasingly evident. IPCC also points out that 3.3 billion to 3.6 people living in the region are vulnerable to Climate Change's impacts. The ongoing war in Ukraine further exacerbates the already soaring oil and gas prices. (Anisie et al, 2022)

To make the energy transition successful, India has set ambitious goals to achieve net-zero emissions by 2070 and to generate at least 50% of its electricity from non-fossil fuel sources by 2030. The country plans to harness its ample solar and wind resources. (Poudel, 2021).

Accelerating the transition to non-fossil fuel-based energy is essential. It will ensure long-term energy security, maintain price stability, and enhance national resilience. Currently, approximately 80% of the global population lives in countries that are net energy importers. By harnessing the abundant potential of renewable energy, this dependence on energy imports can be significantly reduced. An energy transition that includes phasing out coal and oil and switching to cleaner sources of energy would diminish countries' reliance on imported energy, provide a more diversified and stable energy supply, and shield economies from the volatility of fossil fuel prices. Moreover, transitioning to renewable energy sources would stimulate job creation, alleviate poverty, and support the development of an inclusive, climate-resilient global economy. (Anisie et al, 2022)

However, the transition to a low-carbon economy has various implications and concerns. Impact on labor markets is one of them. Workers in the fossil fuel sector may face job losses, while new opportunities may arise in the renewable energy sector. Geopolitical challenges, such as China's dominance in rare-earth materials critical to the manufacture of high-tech products like electric vehicles and solar panels, also pose barriers to the clean energy transition. (WEF, 2024) A study by the International Renewable Energy Agency predicts that the transition to renewable energies has the potential to create a substantial number of jobs in the renewable energy sector, with employment expected to rise to 42 million by 2050, representing a significant growth rate of 64%. However, the report also highlights the potential for job losses in the fossil fuel industries, which could offset some positive effects. Therefore, implementing a just policy framework for the energy transition is essential to ensuring a fair distribution of its benefits across society. (Carsals et al, 2020)

According to a review article published in the Institute of Global Environment Strategies, the energy transition can also exacerbate regional employment disparities. In regions heavily dependent on fossil fuels, job losses may outpace the growth of employment opportunities in low-carbon energy sectors, worsening regional employment inequalities. This geographic mismatch between the locations of displaced workers and new employment opportunities may hinder re-employment, even if workers possess the required skills for new roles. (Hanna et al, 2023) Workers and communities reliant on fossil fuels for jobs and economic prosperity need to be protected and prepared in this transition. (EDF,2020)

Without deliberate efforts to incorporate workforce goals, the economic changes triggered by climate policy could exacerbate existing trends in wage inequality and inequalities by race and gender. Thus, climate policy should be designed with explicit workforce goals to mitigate these adverse distributional effects. (Zabin,2020)

Furthermore, the transition to a low-carbon economy is expected to significantly impact financial systems and income distribution. Researchers state that inequality and energy prices can affect financial stability in a non-linear manner, as indicated by secondary literature. These findings highlight that changes in the energy sector extend beyond the sector itself, affecting broader economic and social stability. Therefore, policy frameworks must consider these complex interactions to ensure a just and equitable transition (Safarzynska, 2021).

This transition also risks creating new dividing lines in the global energy economy. Annual investment in clean energy is expected to increase by 24% between 2021 and 2023, driven by renewables and electric vehicles, compared to a 15% increase in fossil fuel investment over the same period. However, over 90% of this increase will come from advanced economies and China, posing a serious risk of new dividing lines in the global energy economy unless the clean energy transition gains momentum elsewhere. (IEA,2023)

The use of oil along with coal is being phased out. Oil-based internal combustion engine (ICE) vehicles are being replaced with electric vehicles. (Keith et al, 2023) Mining of cobalt and lithium has picked up pace because of this replacement. Mining of both lithium and cobalt poses environmental problems along with perpetuating social inequalities. It often produces pollution that leaches into neighboring rivers and water sources, contaminating them (Zheng, 2023).

2. RESEARCH OBJECTIVES

Keeping the above-mentioned points in mind, the objectives of this chapter are as follows:

- To identify the social, economic, and environmental impacts of transitioning from phasing out coal and moving to a renewable energy-based economy.
- To identify the effects of mining critical minerals to switch from oil-based Internal Combustion Engine Vehicles to Electric Vehicles.
- To investigate the shift in employment patterns due to changes in the shares of renewable and fossil energy in India.
- To evaluate the role of upskilling and reskilling in facilitating a smoother transition to clean energy.

3. RESEARCH PROBLEM

The chapter will try to explore whether the path toward sustainable development through phasing out fossil fuels has social, environmental, and economic implications. Keeping this in mind, the research problem is:

Question: Are there social, economic, and environmental implications associated with transitioning from a fossil fuel-based economy to a renewable energy-based economy?

4. METHODOLOGY

4.1. Literature Review

The literature review focuses on the transition from fossil fuels to renewable energy sources in India. The first part examines the five Indian states that are rich in renewable and fossil fuels to understand whether these resources are concentrated in different geographical areas, which could have an impact on migration and displacement of jobs in the energy sector. The second part discusses the social, economic, and environmental costs of phasing out coal and oil and switching to renewable energy sources such as solar and wind, as well as the consequences of mining critical minerals for electric vehicles. The economic costs of building new renewable energy infrastructure are also considered. Finally, the last part emphasizes the importance of upskilling and reskilling coal workers to enable a smooth transition to the clean energy sector and ensure a just transition for those affected by the transition.

The multi-stage literature review process encompassed:

- **Initial Search:** A comprehensive search of academic journals, papers (including sources such as Elsevier Science), reports (such as IRENA and IEA), and reputable websites (such as WEF, PIB The Wire, and Earth.Org) to identify relevant articles, reports, and papers. This initial search yielded 100 results.

- **Title Analysis:** Out of the initial 100 articles, 80 were retained after a title analysis, and 20 were excluded.
- **Policy Analysis:** Further analysis based on policy relevance reduced the number of articles to 60, with 10 excluded.
- **Full Paper Reading:** A thorough reading of the selected papers resulted in 50 articles being included for in-depth review, with an additional 26 excluded.

Table 1. Stages of a systematic review process for academic literature

Stage	Included	Excluded
Initial Search	100	-
Title Analysis	80	20
Policy analysis	60	10
Paper reading	50	26

The table begins with an initial search that yielded 100 articles, followed by a title analysis that retained 80 articles. Subsequent policy relevance analysis further reduced the number to 60 articles. Finally, a thorough reading of the papers resulted in 50 articles being included for an in-depth review. Each stage shows the number of articles included and excluded, demonstrating a methodical approach to narrowing down the most relevant literature.

4.2. Case Study

A case study of Cobalt Mining in Congo is used for this study. While the literature primarily focuses on the impacts of phasing out coal, this case study specifically examines the effects of transitioning away from oil. Electric vehicles, promoted as replacements for internal combustion engine-based vehicles running on petrol and diesel, pose several social implications for the communities involved in mining them and residing in their vicinity, alongside various environmental concerns. The case study thematically analyses these concerns.

4.3. Expert Consultations

Consultations with experts in the fields of energy and environment were conducted to gather professional insights and perspectives on the topic. These consultations helped to validate the findings and provide a comprehensive view of the issues involved.

5. LITERATURE REVIEW

The literature review of the chapter has focused on a few key aspects of energy transition that we have located in the following sub-headings. Coal is a major enabler of the Indian economy, and a phase-out of coal will have a large-scale impact on the economy as well as the social lives of the people dependent on its extraction. At the same time, an energy transition requires a strong focus on developing storage systems, which is again accompanied by the environmental costs of mining the critical minerals required for the same. The literature review also dwelled on the implications of phasing out oil through mining, which is critical for the rationalization of the transport sector. Along with this literature review, we also dealt with the impacts of constructing new renewable energy projects, examining their effects on both communities and the environment.

The focus of this review is not merely on understanding the multi-faceted impacts of the energy transition but also on the steps needed to upskill the workers to fit into the current workforce.

5.1. Renewable and Fossil Energy Share of States in India

The data gathered through the Press Information Bureau of India indicates the penetration of renewable energy (RE) and thermal energy across different regions. (PIB,2023) The purpose of identifying the concentration of RE and thermal energy in various geographies is to understand potential job-related migration patterns. Rajasthan leads in renewable energy sources, while Uttar Pradesh and Chhattisgarh predominantly rely on thermal energy sources like Coal, Lignite, Gas, and Diesel for their energy needs. The data points out that there is a possibility of energy-related displacement in India.

Table 2. Power generation in India for 2022-23 by source and state/UT

Serial Number	Power Generation Sources (2022-23)							
	Thermal (Coal/Lignite/Gas/Diesel)		Nuclear		Hydro (Large)		Other Renewable Energy Sources	
	State/UT	Production in Million Units (MUs)	State/UT	Production in MUs	State/UT	Production in MUs	State/UT	Production in MUs
1	Uttar Pradesh	152,063.22	Tamil Nadu	16,012.57	Himachal Pradesh	38,666.98	Rajasthan	40,990.05
2	Chhattisgarh	142,599.20	Maharashtra	8,985.48	Uttarakhand	15,435.77	Gujarat	29,575.44
3	Madhya Pradesh	135,838.47	Rajasthan	6,587.27	Karnataka	13,157.34	Karnataka	29,762.63
4	Maharashtra	126,907.03	Gujarat	3,639.91	Sikkim	11,696.79	Tamil Nadu	27,626.45
5	Gujarat	55,481.62	Uttar Pradesh	3,192.62	Kerala	7,989.00	Maharashtra	17,206.59

Source:Total power generated in the country grows by more than 8% year-on-year in 2021-22 and by 9% in 2022-23. (2023, August 10). Press Information Bureau. https://pib.gov.in/Pressreleaseshare.aspx?PRID=194738

Uttar Pradesh leads in thermal power with 152,063.22 MUs, while Tamil Nadu is highest in nuclear power with 16,012.57 MUs. Himachal Pradesh tops hydropower with 38,666.98 MUs, and Rajasthan leads in other renewable energy sources with 40,990.05 MUs.

Based on the provided table, four pie charts were illustrated, each focusing on the top 5 states or Union Territories (UTs) in India for different categories of power generation in the year 2022-2023. The categories and data sources are as follows:

● **Thermal Power Generation (Coal/Lignite/Gas/Diesel)**

This chart highlights the leading states/UTs in generating power through thermal sources such as coal, lignite, gas, and diesel based on data from the Press Information Bureau (PIB).

Figure 1. Top 5 states/UT in thermal (coal/lignite/gas/diesel) power generation year 2022-2023(PIB)

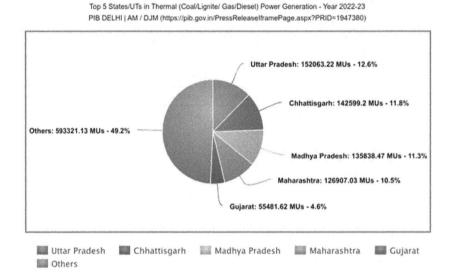

Top 5 States/UTs in Thermal (Coal/Lignite/ Gas/Diesel) Power Generation - Year 2022-23
PIB DELHI | AM / DJM (https://pib.gov.in/PressReleaseIframePage.aspx?PRID=1947380)

Uttar Pradesh: 152063.22 MUs - 12.6%

Chhattisgarh: 142599.2 MUs - 11.8%

Others: 593321.13 MUs - 49.2%

Madhya Pradesh: 135838.47 MUs - 11.3%

Maharashtra: 126907.03 MUs - 10.5%

Gujarat: 55481.62 MUs - 4.6%

Uttar Pradesh   Chhattisgarh   Madhya Pradesh   Maharashtra   Gujarat
Others

● **Nuclear Power Generation**

This chart showcases the top states/UTs contributing to nuclear power generation, based on data from the Press Information Bureau (PIB).

Figure 2. Top 5 states/UT in nuclear power generation year 2022-2023(PIB)

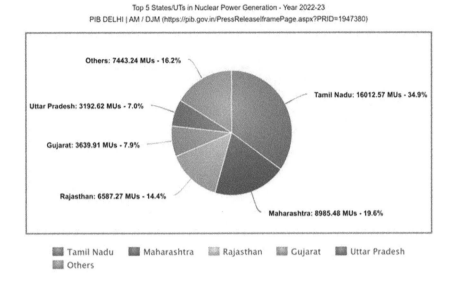

Top 5 States/UTs in Nuclear Power Generation - Year 2022-23
PIB DELHI | AM / DJM (https://pib.gov.in/PressReleaseIframePage.aspx?PRID=1947380)

- ● **Hydro (Large) Generation**

This chart displays the prominent states/UTs in large-scale hydroelectric power generation, with information sourced from PIB.

Figure 3. Top 5 states/UT in hydro (large) generation year 2022-2023 (PIB)

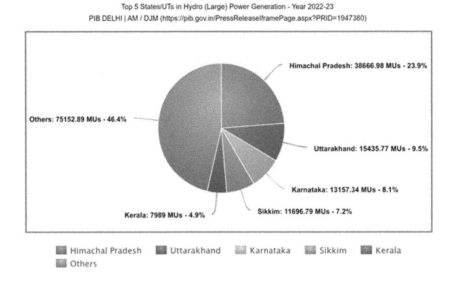

● **Other Renewable Energy Power Generation**

This chart illustrates the leading states/UTs in generating power from other renewable sources (such as solar, wind, biomass, etc.), using data from PIB.

Figure 4. Top 5 states/UT in other renewable energy power generation year 2022-2023(PIB)

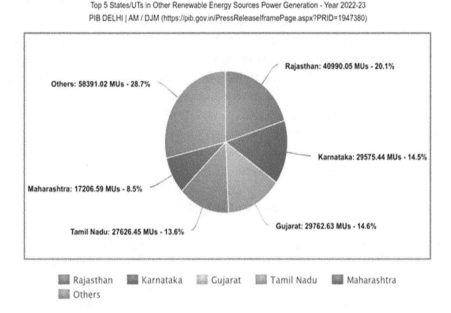

5.2. Economic Impact of Coal Phase-Out

Coal has historically been a key enabler for the Indian economy. Coal has been like the fuel that powered India's journey into modern industry. Since gaining independence, it has been the main source of energy for factories and industries and, most importantly, India's power sector. India has a total installed electricity capacity of over 441.19GW, but within that, 243.21 GW is coal-based (CEA, 2024). India has committed to achieving net zero by 2070, but the increasing dependence on thermal power and the commissioning of new coal-based plants tell us something else.

India is likely to add 19.6 GW of coal-based thermal power plants in the coming 18 months. (Varadhan,2024) The share of coal in India's power mix is also increasing faster than that of renewable energy. Such increasing dependence on coal contradicts India's commitment to developing low-carbon electricity systems at COP26. (PIB,2023) About three-quarters of the power generation capacity is coal-dependent, and India consumed about 777 MT of coal in the last fiscal year. (BS,2023) This is one narrative that is used by the Indian Government to increase coal mining, that is, for the expansion of the electricity system to meet the needs of the population (Roy & Schaffartzik, 2021). The Ministry of Coal has also released data showing that India's coal production has reached over 900 MT and that the coal industry employs some 3.69 lakh individuals, of which 1.28 lakh are contractual.

The coal phase-out in India represents a multifaceted challenge and opportunity. While coal has fueled the country's industrialization and economic growth, its environmental costs are becoming increasingly apparent. Another point to consider is that India also has to cater to a vastly increasing power demand from both domestic and industrial sectors. Without proper long-term investments in renewable energy, a coal phase-out plan shortly is seemingly improbable. Looking at the employment figures, a phase-out of coal is expected to lay off more than 70,000 mine workers in India. (The Wire,2023) Thus, a coal phase-out not only imposes a certain degree of economic consequence but also impacts the social lives of millions of workers employed in the coal and allied sectors.

5.3. Social Impacts of Phasing Out of Coal

With a looming coal phase-out, the most significantly affected are the mine workers, who face a livelihood crisis. These workers are often unskilled laborers who don't have the necessary skills or education to be employed in other sectors (Marais et al., 2022). Their loss of livelihood is also exacerbated by the fact that many of these workers belong to the indigenous communities belonging to the land where these mines are located. After the closure of mines, they are often left unemployed because there is no longer a means of employment left in the region where they live.

Coal mining impacts the mining region significantly. The cycle of exploitation starts at the point of contention, where coal is found. Coal assets in India are mostly located in regions with a history of low Human Development Index (HDI) (Sharma & Loginova, 2024) combined with numerous social and political conflicts. India's top-performing coal-producing states rank among the lowest on socioeconomic factors. The millions of informal workers in this sector are among the most vulnerable, while the coal-rich states gain revenue from their labor.

A coal phase-out will also have far-reaching effects on the coal value chain, affecting both formal and informal workers, service providers, and downstream industrial sectors like steel-making and railways (Sharma et al., 2021). This underscores the complexity and interconnectedness of India's coal ecosystem, highlighting the need for careful planning and consideration of social and economic implications in any transition away from coal.

Coal mining also exerts profound effects on biodiversity across various spatial scales, including site, landscape, regional, and global levels (Sonter et al., 2018). These impacts stem from both direct activities, such as mineral extraction, and indirect processes involving industries supporting mining operations and external stakeholders accessing biodiversity-rich areas resulting from mining activities. The shift from traditional mining to large-scale mechanized mining has also increased the pressure in regions that have an abundance of coal. These regions are spread across the biodiversity hotspots in the states of Chhattisgarh, Odisha, and Jharkhand (Roy & Schaffartzik, 2021), where conflicts between the indigenous population and the state have ensued for a long time.

India's commitments to a coal phase-out are seemingly hollow in the face of continued conflicts ensuing in parts of Chhattisgarh and Goa, where the state wants to open up protected land for mining coal. The auction of 40 coal blocks, part of which is inside the Hasdeo forest in Chhattisgarh, has sparked massive protests led by the tribal population living in this region. Further, these blocks have been opened for private players to enter the coal mining industry (Peterson, 2020). Mining in this area by private players will not only destroy the natural resources but also displace thousands of tribals whose livelihoods solely depend on these resources.

While coal mining leads to environmental degradation and the marginalization of the people dependent on this environment, it is also necessary for a nation's development. Though there is no alternative for mining operations, options as to the location and technology of processing can minimize the damage to the environment (Goswami, 2015). There is an urgent need to improve the assessment methods better to understand the environmental and social costs of mining activities. This will ensure that these costs are addressed without necessitating any social and environmental conflicts.

5.4. Environmental Impacts of Transitioning Away From Oil Based Energy

India's energy transition is a lot more complex than an initial phase-down of coal followed by its phase-out and requires structural and policy reforms along with climate finance (Haldar et al., 2023). Significant institutional costs are not taken into consideration, especially in the pursuit of minerals, which are becoming increasingly important for effecting this energy transition. India has made significant strides in green energy initiatives, particularly in the realm of solar and wind energy. However, these renewable energies are mostly concentrated in the country's western and southern regions (Sharma & Loginova, 2024).

There is a huge demand to replace internal combustion engines with electric vehicles, which is equivalent to displacing oil demand with electricity. This shift in demand necessitates the mining of critical minerals such as cobalt and lithium, which are key elements of electric vehicles. (Nevshehir, 2023). The Geological Survey of India announced its discovery of 5.9 MT of lithium in the Salal-Haimana area of Jammu and Kashmir's Reasi district in 2022 (Basrur, 2023). This development in the Kashmir region has brought more complications to the already conflict-ridden zone. The extraction of this mineral could critically damage the local ecology due to deforestation accompanied by land and water contamination with mining byproducts. On one hand, this discovery could help India with its Net Zero commitments, but on the other hand, the location of this discovery brings in its own set of problems. The mineral has been discovered in a region near the India-Pakistan border, which is heavily militarized due to the presence of militancy in the region. The mining of lithium presents here, thus, poses significant challenges not only at the ecological level but also at the geopolitical level (Ellison, 2023).

India has also released a list of critical mineral blocks that have been opened up for mining by private players. (PIB,2023) While a majority of these are found near existing mines, the mining of these critical minerals will result in further environmental damage in the regions surrounding these mines. The social conflicts that will arise as a result of the mining will be similar to those explained earlier in the chapter. However, these costs of the energy transition are not limited to mining activities. The expansion of solar and wind farms to increase India's renewable energy capacity is accompanied by land grabs, which largely impact agrarian populations. Thus, in a situation where land as a resource is taken away from the people, monetary compensation of any form cannot rehabilitate the displaced.

An energy transition to clean energy is dependent on critical minerals like lithium, cobalt, and rare earth metals, which form a crucial part of energy storage systems. A shift away from coal and other fossil fuel-based systems requires heavy investment in the mining of these critical minerals. There are also many challenges to the mining of these critical minerals, as they are more often found in remote areas. (Zheng, 2023)

5.5. Social Impact of Building New Renewable Energy Projects

5.5.1. Competing Land Uses and Contested Land Designations: Phasing out coal and oil production and building new renewable energy projects, such as solar farms, must compete with possible alternative uses for land, especially food production, environmental preservation, and human settlement, including increasing urbanization. The abandonment of productive agricultural land seems to be a generally accepted principle in this transition. The terms "zero land", "barren land", "unused land" or the official term "wasteland" imply that such land has no value. And they can be a suitable choice for renewable energy projects. However, this is fiercely contested by groups claiming ownership or use rights to such land, as in the case of the Charanka Solar Park in Gujarat or by farmers in Assam opposing a solar plant. (Worringham,2021)

5.6. Environmental Impact of Building New Renewable Energy Projects

5.6.1. Conservation and Ecosystem Value & Conflict with Wildlife Preservation: Environmental advocates point out that supposed "wasteland" areas can be fragile and harbor unique ecosystems. These areas include deserts, rock and boulder fields, grasslands, and savannahs, which they refer to as "open natural ecosystems". Their ecological value is often underestimated, as is their ability to feed hundreds of millions of people and provide about half the fodder for India's 500 million livestock. The fact that renewable energy plants can conflict with nature conservation, even in sparsely populated areas, was underlined by a recent Supreme Court ruling. The court has demanded that transmission lines for solar energy in Rajasthan must be laid underground, as the small remaining population of the iconic Indian Great Bustard could be further threatened by overhead lines; proponents have appealed against this decision. (Worringham, 2021)

5.7. Inclusion of Displaced Workers Through Upskilling and Reskilling

According to the Central Electricity Authority (CEA March 2024), India's total installed electricity capacity is more than 441.19 GW, of which 243.21 GW is coal-based. However, as the world is moving towards a low-carbon, sustainable economy and phasing out coal, the Indian coal industry is facing a major transition. However, the Global Energy Monitor has reported According to the expected closure dates, almost 990,200 jobs will be lost in almost 1,000 coal mines by 2050. In India, Coal India Limited (CIL) will have to cut 73,800 jobs by then. (Prasad, 2023)

According to the International Energy Agency (IEA), the transition to clean energy will lead to the creation of 14 million jobs by 2030. In addition, investments in energy-efficient appliances, electric vehicles, fuel cell vehicles, retrofitting buildings, and energy-efficient construction will require an additional 16 million workers. However, it is also important to note that these employment opportunities are located in different regions, require different skills, and may belong to different sectors than the jobs that will be lost due to the decline or loss of fossil fuel-related jobs. (Layke,2021)

When we talk about the ongoing transition in the transportation sector, in the form of greening the fleet, we are seeing a switch from diesel engines to electric vehicles to reduce emissions. A summary report prepared by CUTS International highlights that the ongoing shift in the global automotive industry towards alternative energy options, particularly electric vehicles (EVs), is significantly impacting India, the world's third-largest automobile manufacturing market. This transition, motivated by the rising cost of oil imports, concerns about air pollution, and climate change commitments, poses complicated challenges for India's large automotive industry workforce, estimated at nearly 32 million where these are either employed directly or indirectly. (CUTS,2023)

Further, the summary document also highlighted the role of trade unions. Trade unions have an important role to play in advocating for workers' rights and job security during this transition. This involves issues such as the need for modern training facilities, comprehensive tripartite consultation between the government, trade unions, and employees, and implementing effective social security measures. Based on Germany's experience, collective agreements, regional dialogs, and partnerships between government and stakeholders can be essential strategies. However, challenges remain in India, including the lack of a safety net, exclusionary social security regulations, and legislative changes undermining worker protection. Other reasons, such as the weakening of the "National Productivity Council" in India over the past seven or eight years, are also cited as reasons, as this council used to be a platform for discussing productivity issues in the country and the role of trade unions in this context. Also, cooperation among trade unions around the world is essential for setting common standards and ensuring a just transition, while ratification of international labor standards and cooperation with national governments are essential for protecting workers and strengthening trade unions. (CUTS,2023)

To meet this challenge at the company and/or agency level, companies must provide or facilitate training and development programs for existing employees in the energy sector. This means creating pathways to improve skills to adapt to new clean energy technologies and practices. (VBeyond,2024)

6. CASE STUDY

The Cobalt mines of the Democratic Republic of Congo (DRC) are used as a case study here. The thematic analysis of the Book "Cobalt Red: How the Blood of the Congo Powers Our Lives" by Siddhartha Kara was done to understand the implications of Mining critical minerals (here cobalt) on communities for replacing oil-based fuels and switching to electric vehicles (EV)

6.1. Introduction

Siddharth Kara's book "Cobalt Red" is a harrowing exposé of the human rights abuses and environmental destruction associated with cobalt mining in the Democratic Republic of Congo (DRC). Based on extensive research and interviews with cobalt miners, Kara sheds light on the harsh conditions and exploitation to which these people are subjected. This thematic analysis aims to highlight the key findings from the book and provide a deeper understanding of the complexity of cobalt mining in the DRC.

6.2. Insights

6.2.1 Dangerous and Inhumane Working Conditions

One of the most harrowing insights from "Cobalt Red" is the harsh working conditions suffered by cobalt miners in the Democratic Republic of Congo. Kara vividly describes the grueling experiences of the miners who toil under inhumane conditions. These miners often work in militia-controlled areas where violence and exploitation are the order of the day. They are exposed to toxic chemicals such as cobalt dust, which leads to severe respiratory problems and other health issues. In addition, miners are often exposed to physical hazards such as cave-ins and landslides in the unstable, hand-dug mines. Extreme temperatures and long working hours without proper protective equipment exacerbate the risks and lead to numerous injuries and deaths.

6.2.2 Environmental Destruction and Pollution

Another insight from the book was the environmental destruction caused by cobalt mining in the Democratic Republic of Congo. Kara meticulously documents the destruction of natural habitats and the resulting loss of biodiversity. Mining has led to the deforestation of vast areas, destroying local ecosystems. In addition, the pollution of water sources through the leaching of heavy metals and chemicals from mining waste has had a devastating impact on local communities. Groundwater resources have been depleted, exacerbating water scarcity in the region and leaving communities with contaminated water sources that pose a serious health risk.

6.2.3. Entrenched Social Inequality and Exploitation

In "Cobalt Red," the author sheds light on the deeply ingrained social inequalities that contribute to the exploitation of cobalt miners. Kara describes how the lack of access to necessities such as education and healthcare perpetuates a cycle of poverty for miners. Many miners, including children, are forced to work in hazardous conditions due to economic desperation, earning minimal wages. Moreover, the absence of labor regulations and enforcement of workers' rights further exacerbate their vulnerability, limiting their opportunities for social mobility and economic advancement.

6.2.4 Economic Disparity and Market Domination by Multinational Companies

The book also addresses the economic inequality and market dominance of a few major corporations in the cobalt industry. Kara illustrates how multinational companies profit significantly from cobalt mined in the DRC, while local communities receive little to no economic benefit. These corporations and a small group of elites concentrate on the profits from cobalt mining, leading to widespread economic inequality and underdevelopment among the local population.

6.2.5 Conclusion

Siddharth Kara's "Cobalt Red" presents a clear picture of the harsh realities of cobalt mining in the Democratic Republic of the Congo. The book highlights the dangerous working conditions, environmental degradation, deep-rooted social inequality, and economic disparity associated with cobalt mining. The exploitation of miners, including children, and the concentration of profits with multinational corporations and elites perpetuate poverty and hinder the development of local communities.

7. EXPERTS' CONSULTATION

Consultations with experts in the fields of energy and environment were conducted to gather professional insights and perspectives on the topic. These consultations helped to validate the findings and provide a comprehensive view of the issues involved.

7.1. Shivani Ilangovan, Former Project Associate, Waatavaran, Mumbai

Shivani Ilangovan is a former project associate at Waatavaran (Mumbai). She worked on a biodiversity mapping project in urban parks to document the biodiverse pockets and all their unique features in Mumbai. She holds an M.Sc in Ecology and Environment Sciences degree from Pondicherry University, Puducherry, and a B.Sc in Biotechnology also from the University of Mumbai. Water, Environment, Climate change, Gender, Religion, and caste are her core interests.

Shivani quoted and discussed a lot of research papers to validate her points on the costs and concerns of the energy transition during the consultation.

India has committed to net zero emissions by 2070, which paves the way toward an energy transition from fossil fuels to renewable energy. Shivani started with the need to focus on the multiple intersections of the 'Environmental' and 'Social' components of ESG. While these intersections leave people dependent on coal-based industries for their livelihoods vulnerable, the vulnerabilities faced by women and marginalized communities formally or informally dependent on coal-based industries for their livelihoods are exacerbated multifold. Hence, it is more important than ever to focus on the JUST energy transition now while facing the enormous target of net zero emissions by 2070.

Shivani stated that the transition away from coal-based industries would leave the states that lead fossil fuel production in a vulnerable situation, specifically Chhattisgarh, Jharkhand, Madhya Pradesh, Odisha, and West Bengal, which would face increased socioeconomic complications. The energy transition will impact the fiscal capacity of the states, as the higher the state's dependency on coal-based industries, the more economically vulnerable and energy insecure it will become because of the transition.

The International Labour Organization defines just transition as "fair and inclusive as possible to everyone concerned, creating decent work opportunities, and leaving no one behind." The majority of the laborers or informal workers in the coal-based industry are migrants and displaced people hailing from Dalit and Adivasi communities since this sector has a high demand for a workforce. Oftentimes, the Dalit and Adivasi communities working and living in areas of coal-based industries are not recognized as stakeholders in the conversation and decision-making regarding energy transition in terms of employment due to the systemic oppression in place they have been put through throughout history. The formal employees of coal-based industries will have to be reskilled to be employable and are offered alternate employment, while the informal and contractual workers are left without any safeguard for their employment. Shivani emphasized the need for a socially inclusive dialogue on the just energy transition in India.

Multiple corporations are now focusing on the employment impacts of the energy transition through CSR interventions and stakeholder engagement. The failure to implement just procedures for land acquisition and dispossession of local communities for renewable energy projects leaves them resentful towards renewable energy projects. The interventions to ensure the participation and empowerment of local communities end up reproducing caste and class-based iniquities as the dominant households in the area utilize these opportunities.

Shivani stated that a just energy transition process needs to visualize the often invisibilized labor of Dalit and Adivasi communities and women in the coal sector. It is also very important to consider that gender, caste, and class-based iniquities are reproduced over generations in the coal sector. A just transition policy is needed to create alternate opportunities for people engaged as laborers in the coal sector for generations. Multiple barriers are faced by women in the coal industry, starting with the entry barrier in the Mines Act of 1952, which led women to become informal laborers and coal scavengers, along with being engaged in unpaid domestic and care work at the household level. Recognition and representation of women are needed in the just energy transition away from coal to ensure gender-inclusive development and opportunities.

The formal work opportunity in the coal sector is only given to landowners as compensation for land acquisition. Dalits who were landless or had inferior land quality did not have the opportunity to become formal workers, while the dominant caste landowners had the opportunity to become formal workers. This leads to Dalits becoming daily wage earners by washing, scavenging, or transporting coal. This kind of gap in work opportunities based on caste and land ownership is seen among direct beneficiaries. It is also reproduced through generations owing to the neoliberal nature of our economy.

The gender, caste, and class-based iniquities entrenched in our society are also reflected in the political economy of coal-based industries with the transition. While the energy transition might reproduce gender, caste, and class-based iniquities, it also allows us to break away from these systems of oppression through a just transition by creating equal opportunities for everyone. A just transition needs to ensure Dalit and Adivasi daily wage earners are not rehabilitated to become daily wage earners in a different sector to transform generational iniquities into equal job opportunities. Shivani emphasizes economic diversification or alternative livelihood generation as the way forward to correct historical injustices against Dalits, Adivasis, and women and leave no one behind in the journey of just energy transition.

7.2. Taslima Rahi, Research Associate, Morningstar-Sustainalytics, Mumbai

Taslima Rahi is a Research Associate at Morningstar-Sustainalytics (Mumbai), where she researches climate-related data for assessing the low-carbon transition by evaluating companies' progress on their stated net-zero commitments. She holds a Master's degree in Environment, Climate Change, and Sustainability Studies from Tata Institute of Social Sciences, Mumbai.

Rahi emphasized the importance of addressing the social and human aspects of India's transition from fossil fuels to renewable energy. India has set ambitious targets for the deployment of renewable energy, such as a target of 500 GW by 2035 and a commitment to achieve net zero emissions by 2070. However, Rahi emphasized that the transition must focus on equity for those affected by the shift away from coal-based industries.

Rahi pointed out the disproportionate impact of moving away from coal on communities that rely on coal mines for their livelihoods. About 90% of India's coal-based energy comes from two state-owned companies (PSUs): Coal India and Nevyeli Lignite. About 50 lakh people are directly dependent on coal mining in India; therefore, the human aspect of the transition cannot be overlooked. Many of these workers lack alternative skills and face socio-economic challenges, including inadequate social security. In some regions, such as Jharkhand, the implementation of tribal laws and governance is also poor.

Furthermore, Rahi criticized the top-down approach of the policy, which prioritizes the technological and economic aspects of the transition while neglecting the needs of the affected communities. She argued that a just transition requires proactive measures, such as the provision of training, upskilling, and alternative employment opportunities for displaced workers. In her work, Rahi evaluates companies on their just transition efforts. She assessed whether companies are providing training and upskilling opportunities, providing alternative employment for workers affected by the transition, and responding to the needs of communities affected by their operations. However, she pointed out that companies face no consequences if they do not adhere to these aspects of transition, making it a voluntary effort rather than a requirement.

The International Labor Organization (ILO) has guidelines for the qualification of workers in this transition phase. However, they are not being followed or implemented due to a lack of pressure from workers who do not form a strong social base. Rahi emphasizes the need for political will to drive upskilling at the company level through funding and incentives, especially given the available company-specific data on workers and the health and environmental safety concerns associated with coal mining. It also criticized the insufficient flow of climate finance from developed countries to support just transition initiatives in developing countries such as India.

The G20 has acknowledged that finance is needed to support the transition, with some of this funding going towards upskilling workers. However, Rahi pointed out that despite several pledges, commitments, and high-level meetings, developed countries are not providing sufficient funding and that countries are mostly dependent on financing their green transition. When developed countries do provide finance, it is mostly in the form of loans, which increases the country's debt burden and leaves workers behind. And when financing takes the form of loans, technological and economic feasibility takes precedence over social justice. This shows that the international community needs to do more to ensure a just transition in developing countries like India, she said.

Rahi emphasized the link between the principles of just transition and the Sustainable Development Goals (SDGs). A just transition can help drive climate action while making progress on all the Sustainable Development Goals, especially those on affordable and clean energy, decent work and economic growth, reducing inequalities, and responsible production and consumption.

She warned of the possible consequences of urban migration driven by the closure of coal mines, which could exacerbate urban poverty and the emergence of slums without adequate upskilling and integration measures. The transition to renewable energy offers the opportunity to create new jobs and promote sustainable development, but it must be done in a way that respects the rights, dignity, and livelihoods of affected workers and communities. She says: "Transition is inevitable, justice is not."

Rahi suggested a comprehensive approach that includes government intervention, corporate responsibility, and regulatory pressure to address these challenges. She advocated for upskilling initiatives at the corporate level, supported by government incentives and funding, and emphasized the importance of political will to drive the transition. She believes that social dialog, social protection, rights at work, and employment are essential building blocks for sustainable development and must be at the heart of policies for strong, sustainable, and inclusive growth and development.

7.3. Debashree Hazarika, PhD Scholar at IITB-Monash Academy

Debashree Hazarika is a PhD scholar at IITB-Monash Academy and is a master's graduate from IIT Guwahati in Development Studies. Her area of interest is predominantly public policy, with a specific focus on addressing social conflict, public health, and advancing gender equality.

Hazarika highlighted the vital connection between gender dynamics and the shift towards sustainable energy in Northeast India. She focused on the northeast region, particularly Meghalaya, where women played a crucial role in traditional matriarchal societies, often being the primary breadwinners, especially in industries such as coal mining.

She drew upon the theory of intersectionality, which emphasises the interconnected nature of social categorisations such as gender, race, and economic class. It was evident that the energy transition in Northeast India had to consider differential impacts on various social groups, including women. The shift towards renewable energy sources is a crucial step in addressing climate change and reducing greenhouse gas emissions, particularly in Meghalaya, where the traditional energy sector has been dominated by coal mining. However, this transition also brought about social and environmental costs that must be carefully considered, particularly in terms of gender dynamics.

As the energy landscape has evolved, Hazarika has highlighted the challenges faced by these women. The decline in coal-related jobs left them financially vulnerable, worsening their economic situation and pushing them further to marginalisation.

The lack of necessary skills and limited opportunities for retraining exacerbates these difficulties.

Hazarika also emphasised the necessity of gender-sensitive policies in the realm of sustainable energy transition. She advocated the inclusion of gender-specific data and tailoring skill-development programs to meet the unique needs of women. Additionally, she stressed the importance of investing in education, awareness, and empowerment programs aimed at women, who often play key roles in household decision-making.

She also discussed the gendered impact of energy transitions. For instance, the gender wage gap, which persists in many industries including renewable energy, could exacerbate women's financial vulnerability during the transition. Additionally, the unequal distribution of unpaid care work between men and women, as highlighted by feminist economists, could further limit women's participation in the renewable energy sector.

To address these challenges, she suggested that policymakers adopt a gender-responsive approach to energy transition that considers the intersectional nature of social categorizations and unique experiences of women in Meghalaya. This approach could include measures such as targeted skill development programs for women, incentives for renewable energy companies to hire and promote women, and policies to address the gender wage gap in the renewable energy sector.

Hazarika's analysis highlights the critical role of gender-inclusive strategies in achieving a fair and sustainable energy transition and the importance of empowering women, addressing their specific challenges, and leveraging their potential as catalysts for change in their journey towards a clean energy future.

7.4. Kishlay Ranjan, Research Associate, Morningstar-Sustainalytics, Mumbai

Kishlay Ranjan is a Research Associate at Morningstar-Sustainalytics (Mumbai), and holds a Master's degree from TISS, Mumbai, in Water Policy and Governance. In the Social (Human Capital) division of ESG at Morningstar, Kishlay's role involves conducting indicator research and assigning ratings to global companies based on ESG parameters. His areas of interest revolve around Water, Climate Change, Energy, Policy, and the ESG.

Kishlay Ranjan, an associate in the ESG domain, addressed the costs of shifting from fossil fuel-based energy sources to renewable energy sources in India. He pointed out that unemployment, particularly among coal workers, would be a major concern, as India committed to achieving net zero emissions by 2070. There is also a fear that the government might adopt a top-down approach to meet this net zero-emission goal.

He pointed out that this transition is expected to be challenging for India, primarily because of the high unemployment rate and the necessity of upskilling workers' skills to fit into the renewable energy sector to facilitate a smoother transition. The lack of financial resources, technological progress, and demand for climate justice further complicate the transition. India is committed to transitioning to renewable energy sources while maintaining high growth rates, which is difficult, given its low per capita income and heavy dependence on coal for power generation.

Ranjan pointed out that this transition would have significant implications for workers, including the necessity for new skills and education. The slow progress of the government in addressing this issue poses a major challenge. He highlighted the importance of a fair transition that prioritized the needs of workers and communities dependent on coal mining. He then deliberated on the obstacles faced in the development of infrastructure, specifically the production of renewable energy sources. India's reliance on China for manufacturing solar modules and wind farms has resulted in increased costs for constructing renewable energy sources. He stated that India should enhance its infrastructure to enable independent production of renewable sources.

Ranjan also highlighted the need for demand-side interventions to reduce energy consumption, particularly in the context of Western lifestyles, which are promoted in India. Limiting waste generation, promoting sustainable consumption, and making sustainable choices in day-to-day life are crucial for reducing energy consumption. Furthermore, Ranjan pointed out that the renewable sector could look green, but this was not always the case. He provided an example of electric vehicles, where the car's manufacturing process was carbon-intensive and the input of lithium, which came from mining in South America, had a significant environmental impact.

Additionally, he also pointed toward the need for policies that address all the factors contributing to pollutants, not just carbon. Ranjan's insights highlight the complexities and challenges of transitioning to renewable energy sources in India. The transition would require significant investment, infrastructure development, and a just transition that prioritizes the needs of workers and communities dependent on coal mining. The challenges of infrastructure development, the need for demand-side interventions, and the need for policies that address all the factors contributing to pollutants, not just carbon, were particularly noteworthy.

8. DISCUSSION

The shift from fossil fuels-based economy to a renewable energy-based economy is essential for limiting greenhouse gas emissions, addressing climate change, and achieving sustainable development goals. However, this transition presents a range of challenges and implications across social, economic, and environmental dimensions. This "discussion" section consolidates findings from an extensive literature review, a case study on cobalt mining in the DRC, and expert consultations to outline the complexities and obstacles associated with this global shift towards clean energy.

8.1. Insights From Literature Review

The literature review highlighted key insights concerning the transition from coal mining in India and land use conflicts that arose from the construction of new renewable projects. India's industrialization and energy sector have relied heavily on coal, as coal-based thermal power plants generate a significant portion of the country's electricity. Despite commitments to decrease carbon emissions, India continues to invest in and expand its coal-based power infrastructure, indicating difficulties in transitioning to low-carbon alternatives such as renewable energy. This reliance presents a major challenge in achieving sustainable energy objectives and indicates the need for a nuanced path forward necessitating well-balanced strategies.

Socially, the phasing out of coal mining disproportionately affects marginalized communities, particularly mine workers, who often lack alternative skills or education for employment in other sectors. Many impacted workers come from indigenous communities residing in areas with low Human Development Index (HDI) scores, exacerbating existing socioeconomic inequalities. The closure of coal mines not only results in immediate job losses but also disrupts local economies and cultural identities linked to mining activities. It raises the importance of inclusive policies that assist affected communities in transitioning to sustainable livelihood options and social safeguards.

Moreover, the environmental impacts associated with coal mining and clean energy production are substantial, resulting in the loss of biodiversity and degradation of ecosystems in key coal-rich regions such as Chhattisgarh, Odisha, and Jharkhand. These regions are critical areas of high biodiversity that are currently experiencing conflicts between indigenous communities and government authorities over land use and resource exploitation. Achieving a balance between economic development and environmental conservation is of utmost importance, necessitating the enhancement of assessment methods to mitigate negative effects on biodiversity and minimize environmental conflicts.

When it comes to the challenges of transitioning to renewable energy sources like solar and wind power, there are intricate trade-offs involved, including conflicts related to land use and environmental considerations. The establishment of renewable energy projects often competes with agricultural land and conservation priorities, pointing towards the need for sustainable land-use planning and active engagement with stakeholders to effectively navigate these conflicts.

Lastly, the shift away from coal presents opportunities for job creation in the renewable energy sectors, but it requires substantial investments in the upskilling and reskilling of the affected workers. Policies that support workforce development and social security measures are vital to ensure a fair transition for workers and communities that rely on the coal industry. Collaboration between the government, industry, and civil society stakeholders is essential for implementing comprehensive strategies that effectively address the economic, social, and environmental aspects of India's energy transition.

8.2. Insights From Case Study

A case study on cobalt mining in the Democratic Republic of Congo (DRC), based on Siddharth Kara's book "Cobalt Red: How the Blood of the Congo Powers Our Lives," reveals distressing insights into the industry. The study documents the hazardous conditions endured by miners, including exposure to toxic chemicals and physical dangers like cave-ins. Their living conditions are exacerbated further as most of the mining areas are militia-controlled. Environmental degradation, such as extensive deforestation and water pollution from mining waste, severely impacts local ecosystems. Socially, the study exposes entrenched inequalities where miners, including children, face exploitation due to economic deprivation, lack of education, and inadequate healthcare. Economically, multinational corporations profit significantly from cobalt extraction, widening the economic gap between them and local communities that receive minimal benefits. These findings highlights the urgent need for ethical mining practices and equitable distribution of benefits to mitigate the humanitarian and environmental crises associated with cobalt mining in the DRC.

8.3. Insights From Experts' Consultation

The discussions with experts from various backgrounds yielded comprehensive insights into the opportunities and challenges associated with India's shift from fossil fuels to renewable energy. The key takeaways are as follows:

● Shivani Ilangovan emphasized the crucial need for an inclusive dialogue during the energy transition process. She stressed that marginalized communities, specifically Dalits and Adivasis, who have traditionally relied on coal-based industries for their livelihoods, should not be left behind. Shivani pointed towards the significance of acknowledging and addressing inequalities based on gender, caste, and class that are perpetuated by the energy sector transition.

- Taslima Rahi focused on the socio-economic impacts of energy transition on workers in coal-dependent communities. She highlighted the importance of proactive measures such as providing training for new skills, creating alternative employment opportunities, and implementing social protections to mitigate the adverse effects on affected communities. Rahi criticized the current top-down approach and advocated for stronger regulatory frameworks to ensure that companies adhere to the principles of a fair transition.

- Debashree Hazarika drew attention to the gender dynamics in India's energy transition, specifically in Northeast India. She emphasized the disproportionate impact on women, who often experience heightened economic vulnerability and social marginalization as traditional coal-related jobs decline. Hazarika called for gender-responsive policies that include targeted skill development and empowerment initiatives to support women's active participation in the renewable energy sector.

- Kishlay Ranjan addressed the wider implications of the transition, addressing fears of unemployment among coal workers and the obstacles to achieving net zero emissions by 2070. He emphasized the need to promote infrastructure and autonomous production capacities for renewable energy sources to reduce dependence on imports. In addition, Ranjan placed great emphasis on demand-side measures and a comprehensive policy that includes all environmental pollutants and goes beyond carbon emissions alone.

9. CONCLUSION

The global transition from fossil fuels to renewable energy sources is a crucial and complex endeavor with profound social, economic, and environmental implications. India's heavy dependence on coal highlights the socio-economic challenges associated with phasing out coal, especially the disproportionate impact on vulnerable communities and the environment. Environmental degradation and land use conflicts highlight the need for strategies that balance economic development with environmental sustainability. The case study on cobalt mining in the Democratic Republic of Congo also highlights serious human rights violations and environmental damage associated with the extraction of critical minerals to switch to electric vehicles. The findings from the expert consultations emphasize the importance of inclusive dialog and proactive measures to support affected communities through training, job security, and a sound regulatory framework. Governments, trade unions, and employers should collaborate to design and implement policies that prioritize fairness, equity, and sustainability to facilitate a smoother transition. Investments in renewable energy infrastructure, alongside skill development programs and social safety nets, are crucial to supporting affected workers and communities. Furthermore, meaningful engagement with stakeholders, particularly marginalized groups, is essential to ensure their voices are heard and their concerns addressed in policy formulation and implementation.

By adopting a just and inclusive approach to the energy transition, we can create a future that is not only environmentally sustainable but also socially and economically equitable. It is through collective action and shared commitment that we can navigate the challenges of this transition and build a more resilient and inclusive society for all.

REFERENCES

All india installed capacity (in mw) of power stations. (2024, March 31). Central Electricity Authority - CEA. https://cea.nic.in/wp-content/uploads/installed/2024/03/IC_Mar_2024_allocation_wise.pdf

Anisie, Y. A., Bianco, E., Blanco, H., Boshell, F., Casals Seck, X., Feng, J., Guadarrama, C., Hawila, D., Kang, S., López-Peña, A., Nagpal, D., Parajuli, B., Pragada, G., Prakash, G., Rana, F., Renner, M., Seck, G. S., Taibi, E., & Vaid, A. (2022). *WORLD ENERGY TRANSITIONS OUTLOOK 2022*.IRENA. https://www.irena.org/-/media/Files/IRENA/Agency/Publication/2022/Mar/IRENA_World_Energy_Transitions_Outlook_2022.pdf?rev=6ff451981b0948c6894546661c6658a1

Basrur, A. (2023, November 23). *Implications of lithium reserves in Jammu and Kashmir*. ORF. https://www.orfonline.org/expert-speak/implications-of-lithium-reserves-in-jammu-and-kashmir

Casals, X. G., Parajuli, B., & Ferroukhi, R. (2020). *Measuring the Socio-economics of Transition: Focus on Jobs*. IRENA. https://www.irena.org/-/media/Files/IRENA/Agency/Publication/2020/Feb/IRENA_Transition_jobs_2020.pdf

Coal India Could Layoff More Than 70,000 Workers by 2050: Report. (2023, October 10). The wire. https://www.google.com/url?q=https://thewire.in/energy/coal-india-could-layoff-70000-workers-2050-just transition&sa=D&source=docs&ust=1718860754262411&usg=AOvVaw3_V9DHK4crT7UsM8S5HDfT

Ellison, T. (2023, March 30). *INDIA'S LITHIUM RESOURCES IN KASHMIR HIGHLIGHT CONFLICT RISKS AROUND CRITICAL MINERALS*. center for Climate and Security. https://councilonstrategicrisks.org/wp-content/uploads/2023/03/48-KashmirLithium.pdf

EVolution:Aligning the Just Energy Transition in the Electric Mobility Ecosystem with the G20 Framework. (n.d.). ccier. https://cuts-ccier.org/pdf/summary-of-podcasts-evolution.pdf

Goswami, S. (2017, April 24). *Impact of Coal Mining on Environment: A Study of Raniganj and Jharia Coal Field in India*. The International Academic Forum (IAFOR). https://iafor.org/journal/iafor-journal-of-arts-and-humanities/volume-3-issue-1/article-1/

Haldar, S., Peddibhotla, A., & Bazaz, A. (2023, March 9). *Analysing intersections of justice with energy transitions in India: A systematic literature review*. Lund University. https://portal.research.lu.se/en/publications/analysing-intersections-of-justice-with-energy-transitions-in-ind

Hanna, R., Heptonstall, P., & Gross, R. (2024, January 11). *Job creation in a low carbon transition to renewables and energy efficiency: A review of international evidence*. SpringerLink. https://link.springer.com/article/10.1007/s11625-023-01440-y

How the clean energy transition affects workers and communities. (2020, August 11). Environmental Defense Fund. https://www.edf.org/how-clean-energy-transition-affects-workers-and-communities

India to burn 38% more coal every year with new plans for thermal power. (2023, September 19). Business Standard. https://www.google.com/url?q=https://www.business-standard.com/industry/news/india-to-burn-38-more-coal-every-year-with-new-plans-for-thermal-power-123091900478_1.html%255B4&sa=D&source=docs&ust=1718864827070774&usg=AOvVaw2tFkJht3xiRJLe6ZcVmpTk

Keith, D., & Krol, A. (2023, July 24). *Electric vehicles*. MIT Climate Portal. https://climate.mit.edu/explainers/electric-vehicles

Layke, J., Jaeger, J., Pastor, K., Levin, K., & Searchinger, T. (2021, May 21). *5 things to know about the IEA's roadmap to net zero by 2050*. World Resources Institute. https://www.wri.org/insights/5-things-know-about-ieas-roadmap-net-zero-2050

Marais, L., Burton, J., Campbell, M., & Nel, E. (2021). Chapter 3 mine closure in the coal industry: Global and national perspectives. Coal and Energy in South Africa, 34-43. https://doi.org/10.1515/9781474487078-009

Nevshehir, N. (2021, February 19). *These are the biggest hurdles on the path to clean energy*. World Economic Forum. https://www.weforum.org/agenda/2021/02/heres-why-geopolitics-could-hamper-the-energy-transition/

Petersen, H. E. (2020, August 8). *India plans to fell ancient forest to create 40 new coalfields*. The Guardian. https://www.theguardian.com/world/2020/aug/08/india-prime-minister-narendra-modi-plans-to-fell-ancient-forest-to-create-40-new-coal-fields

Poudel, S. S. (2021, November 11). *India commits to net-zero emissions by 2070*. The Diplomat – Asia-Pacific Current Affairs Magazine. https://thediplomat.com/2021/11/india-commits-to-net-zero-emissions-by-2070/

Powering the future: Workplace skill development and recruitment in the clean energy transition. (2024, January25). VBeyond.https://vbeyond.com/powering-the-future-workplace-skill-development-and-recruitment-in-the-clean-energy-transition/#:~:text=Reskilling%20and%20upskilling%3A%20Agencies%20must,and%20methodologies%20in%20green%20energy

Prasad, S. (2023, October 11). *By 2050 coal India limited may have to lay off 73,800 jobs: Global energy monitor.* DTE. https://www.downtoearth.org.in/news/india/by-2050-coal-india-limited-may-have-to-lay-off-73-800-jobs-global-energy-monitor-92237

Roy, B., & Schaffartzik, A. (2021, February). *Talk renewables, walk coal: The paradox of India's energy transition.* Ecological Economics. https://www.sciencedirect.com/science/article/pii/S0921800920303232

Safarzynska, K. (2021). *A macro-evolutionary approach to energy policy.* ScienceDirect., https://www.sciencedirect.com/science/article/abs/pii/B9780128147122000142?via%3Dihub10.1016/B978-0-12-814712-2.00014-2

Sharma, V., Greig, C., & Lant, P. (2021, August). *What is stopping India's rapid decarbonisation? Examining social factors, speed, and institutions in Odisha.* ScienceDirect. https://www.sciencedirect.com/science/article/abs/pii/S2214629621002103

Sharma, V., & Loginova, J. (2023, September). *The Social Aspects of India's Energy Transition.* Google. https://www.google.com/url?q=https://www.researchgate.net/publication/373665379_The_Social_Aspects_of_India%2527s_Energy_Transition&sa=D&source=docs&ust=1718863811157703&usg=AOvVaw0t_pcMcFIVfaohunQinFp0

Sonter, L. J., & Ali, S. H. (2018, December 5). *Mining and biodiversity: key issues and research needs in conservation science.* The Royal Society. https://royalsocietypublishing.org/doi/10.1098/rspb.2018.1926

Thirty minerals listed as critical minerals for India. (2023, December 11). Press Information Bureau. https://pib.gov.in/PressReleseDetail.aspx?PRID=1984942

Varadhan, S. (2024, February 1). *India to increase coal-fired capacity in 2024 by the most in at least 6 years.* reuters.com. https://www.reuters.com/business/energy/india-increase-coal-fired-capacity-2024-by-most-least-6-years-2024-02-01/

World Energy Investment 2023. (2023, May). IEA. https://iea.blob.core.windows.net/assets/8834d3af-af60-4df0-9643-72e2684f7221/WorldEnergyInvestment2023.pdf

Worringham, C. (2021, September). *Renewable Energy and Land Use in India by Mid-Century Careful Planning Today Can Maximise the Benefits and Minimise the Costs of India's History-Making Energy Transition.* IEEFA | Institute for Energy Economics and Financial Analysis. https://ieefa.org/wp-content/uploads/2021/09/Renewable-Energy-and-Land-Use-in-India-by-Mid-Century_September-2021.pdf?ftag=MSF0951a18

Zabin, C. (2020, June). *Putting California on the high road*. UC Berkeley Labor Center. https://laborcenter.berkeley.edu/wp-content/uploads/2020/09/Putting-California-on-the-High-Road.pdf

Zheng, M. (2023, March 31). *The Environmental Impacts of Lithium and Cobalt Mining*. Earth.org.https://www.bing.com/search?pglt=41&q=zheng+%2C+lithium+and+cobalt+mining&cvid=a1c39363c1824aa0a2496203f39a3f52&gs_lcrp=EgZjaHJvbWUyBggAEEUYOTIGCAEQABhAMgYIAhAAGEAyBggDEAAYQDIGCAQQABhAMgYIBRAAGEDSAQg3NDY4ajBqMagCALACAA&FORM=ANNTA1&PC=HCTS

Compilation of References

Abad, D., Cutillas-Gomariz, M. F., Sánchez-Ballesta, J. P., & Yagüe, J. (2018). Real earnings management and information asymmetry in the equity market. *European Accounting Review*, 27(2), 209–235. 10.1080/09638180.2016.1261720

Abazi-Alili, H. R. Ç. (2016). Encouragement factors of social entrepreneurial activities in Europe. *International Journal of Foresight and Innovation Policy*, 11(4), 225. 10.1504/IJFIP.2016.084529

Abbasi, T., Premalatha, M., & Abbasi, S. A. (2011). The return to renewables: Will it help in global warming control? *Renewable & Sustainable Energy Reviews*, 15(1), 891–894. 10.1016/j.rser.2010.09.048

Abbott, L. J., Parker, S., & Peters, G. F. (2004). Audit Committee Characteristics and Restatements. *Auditing*, 23(1), 69–87. 10.2308/aud.2004.23.1.69

Abdelhalim, K., & Eldin, A. (2019). Can CSR help achieve sustainable development? Applying a new assessment model to CSR cases from Egypt. *The International Journal of Sociology and Social Policy*, 39(9–10), 773–795. 10.1108/IJSSP-06-2019-0120

Abdul Rahman, R., & Alsayegh, M. F. (2021). Determinants of corporate environment, social and governance (ESG) reporting among Asian firms. *Journal of Risk and Financial Management*, 14(4), 167. 10.3390/jrfm14040167

Abdullah, A., Yamak, S., Korzhenitskaya, A., Rahimi, R., & McClellan, J. (2024). Sustainable development: The role of sustainability committees in achieving ESG targets. *Business Strategy and the Environment*, 33(3), 2250–2268. 10.1002/bse.3596

Aboody, D., Hughes, J., & Liu, J. (2005). Earnings quality, insider trading, and cost of capital. *Journal of Accounting Research*, 43(5), 651–673. 10.1111/j.1475-679X.2005.00185.x

Abu Afifa, M. M., & Saadeh, M. (2023). Does information asymmetry mediate the relationship between voluntary disclosure and cost of capital? Evidence from a developing economy. *Journal of Financial Reporting and Accounting, ahead-of-print*(ahead-of-print).

Accenture. (2023). *360° Value Report*. Retrieved from https://www.accenture.com/content/dam/accenture/final/corporate/corporate-initiatives/sustainability/document/360-Value-Report-2023.pdf

Accenture. (2023). *Responsible Business: The Future of ESG*. Retrieved from https://www .accenture.com/us-en/insights/consulting/future-esg-responsible-business

Accenture. (2023). *Uniting technology and sustainability*. Retrieved from https://www.accenture .com/in-en/insights/technology/uniting-technology-sustainability

Adams, R. B., & Ferreira, D. (2009). Women in the boardroom and their impact on governance and performance. *Journal of Financial Economics*, 94(2), 291–309. 10.1016/j.jfineco.2008.10.007

Ademi, B., & Klungseth, N. J. (2022). Does it pay to deliver superior ESG performance? Evidence from US S&P 500 companies. *Journal of Global Responsibility*, 13(4), 421–449. Advance online publication. 10.1108/JGR-01-2022-0006

Adeneye, Y. B., Fasihi, S., Kammoun, I., & Albitar, K. (2024). Does earnings management constrain ESG performance? The role of corporate governance. *International Journal of Disclosure and Governance*, 21(1), 69–92. 10.1057/s41310-023-00181-9

Afridi, S. H. S., Rehman, A., Mubashir, M., & Zeeshan, M. (2020). Risk Adjusted Performance, Market Timing and Selectivity of Mutual Funds: A Comparative Analysis of Islamic and Conventional Mutual Funds of Pakistan. *Journal of Management Research*, 6(2), 1–22.

Ahmed, S., & Siddiqui, D. A. (2020). Factors affecting fund flows in islamic and conventional mutual funds of Pakistan. *Available atSSRN* 3681179. 10.2139/ssrn.3681179

Ahsan, M. J. (2024). Unlocking sustainable success: Exploring the impact of transformational leadership, organizational culture, and CSR performance on financial performance in the Italian manufacturing sector. *Social Responsibility Journal*, 20(4), 783–803. 10.1108/SRJ-06-2023-0332

Akadırı, S. S., Alola, A. A., & Usman, O. (2021). Energy mix outlook and the EKC hypothesis in BRICS countries: A perspective of economic freedom vs. economic growth. *Environmental Science and Pollution Research International*, 28(7), 8922–8926. 10.1007/s11356-020-11964-w33410045

Akerlof, G. A. (1970). The Market for" Lemons": Quality Uncertainty and the Market Mechanism, 84Q. *Journal of Economics*, 488, 489–490.

Alam, M. J., Begum, I. A., Buysse, J., Rahman, S., & Van Huylenbroeck, G. (2011). Dynamic modeling of causal relationship between energy consumption, CO2 emissions and economic growth in India. *Renewable & Sustainable Energy Reviews*, 15(6), 3243–3251. 10.1016/j.rser.2011.04.029

Alam, M. M., & Murad, M. W. (2020). The impacts of economic growth, trade openness and technological progress on renewable energy use in organization for economic co-operation and development countries. *Renewable Energy*, 145, 382–390. 10.1016/j.renene.2019.06.054

Alatawi, I. A., Ntim, C. G., Zras, A., & Elmagrhi, M. H. (2023). CSR, financial and non-financial performance in the tourism sector: A systematic literature review and future research agenda. *International Review of Financial Analysis*, 89, 102734. 10.1016/j.irfa.2023.102734

Compilation of References

Albitar, K., Hussainey, K., Kolade, N., & Gerged, A. M. (2020). ESG disclosure and firm performance before and after IR: The moderating role of governance mechanisms. *International Journal of Accounting and Information Management*, 28(3), 429–444. 10.1108/IJAIM-09-2019-0108

Al-Hadrami, A., Rafiki, A., & Sarea, A. (2020). The impact of an audit committee's independence and competence on investment decision: A study in Bahrain. *Asian Journal of Accounting Research*, 5(2), 299–313. 10.1108/AJAR-02-2020-0008

Alibakhshi, R., & Sadeghi Moghadam, M. R. (2016). A new algorithm for mutual funds evaluation based on multiple attribute decision making techniques. *Kybernetes*, 45(8), 1194–1212. 10.1108/K-10-2015-0256

Ali, H. Y., Danish, R. Q., & Asrar-ul-Haq, M. (2019). How corporate social responsibility boosts firm financial performance: The mediating role of corporate image and customer satisfaction. *Corporate Social Responsibility and Environmental Management*, 27(1), 166–177. 10.1002/csr.1781

Ali, W., Danni, Y., Latif, B., Kouser, R., & Baqader, S. (2021). Corporate Social Responsibility and Customer Loyalty in Food Chains—Mediating Role of Customer Satisfaction and Corporate Reputation. *Sustainability (Basel)*, 13(16), 8681. 10.3390/su13168681

Ali, W., Frynas, J. G., & Mahmood, Z. (2017). Determinants of Corporate Social Responsibility (CSR) Disclosure in Developed and Developing Countries: A Literature Review. *Corporate Social Responsibility and Environmental Management*, 24(4), 273–294. 10.1002/csr.1410

Alkhammash, R. (2023). Bibliometric, network, and thematic mapping analyses of metaphor and discourse in COVID-19 publications from 2020 to 2022. *Frontiers in Psychology*, 13, 1062943. 10.3389/fpsyg.2022.106294336726506

All india installed capacity (in mw) of power stations. (2024, March 31). Central Electricity Authority - CEA. https://cea.nic.in/wp-content/uploads/installed/2024/03/IC_Mar_2024_allocation_wise.pdf

Allen, F., Qian, J., & Qian, M. (2005). Law, finance, and economic growth in China. *Journal of Financial Economics*, 77(1), 57–116. 10.1016/j.jfineco.2004.06.010

Almubarak, W. I., Chebbi, K., & Ammer, M. A. (2023). Unveiling the Connection among ESG, Earnings Management, and Financial Distress: Insights from an Emerging Market. *Sustainability (Basel)*, 15(16), 16. 10.3390/su151612348

Alqudah, H., Amran, N. A., Hassan, H., Lutfi, A., Alessa, N., alrawad, M., & Almaiah, M. A. (2023). Examining the critical factors of internal audit effectiveness from internal auditors' perspective: Moderating role of extrinsic rewards. *Heliyon*, 9(10), e20497. 10.1016/j.heliyon.2023.e2049737842607

Alsaadi, A., Ebrahim, M. S., & Jaafar, A. (2017). Corporate social responsibility, Shariah-compliance, and earnings quality. *Journal of Financial Services Research*, 51(2), 169–194. 10.1007/s10693-016-0263-0

Al-Shaer, H., & Zaman, M. (2018). Credibility of sustainability reports: The contribution of audit committees. *Business Strategy and the Environment*, 27(7), 973–986. 10.1002/bse.2046

Alshehhi, A., Nobanee, H., & Khare, N. (2018). The impact of sustainability practices on corporate financial performance: Literature trends and future research potential. *Sustainability (Basel)*, 10(2), 494. 10.3390/su10020494

ALTAN, İ. M. (2022). Thematic investment strategies: Cointegration relationship between robotic investment index and Bist100. *International Journal of Mechanical Engineering*.

Amaral, M. R., Willerding, I. V. A., & Lapolli, É. M. (2023). ESG and sustainability: The impact of the pillar social. *Concilium*, 23(13), 186–199. 10.53660/CLM-1643-23J43

Amel-Zadeh, A., & Serafeim, G. (2018). Why and how investors use ESG information: Evidence from a global survey. *Financial Analysts Journal*, 74(3), 87–103. 10.2469/faj.v74.n3.2

Amihud, Y., & Mendelson, H. (1986). Asset pricing and the bid-ask spread. *Journal of Financial Economics*, 17(2), 223–249. 10.1016/0304-405X(86)90065-6

Amin, M. H., Ali, H., & Mohamed, E. K. (2024). Corporate social responsibility disclosure on Twitter: Signalling or greenwashing? Evidence from the UK. *International Journal of Finance & Economics*, 29(2), 1745–1761. 10.1002/ijfe.2762

Ammann, M., Oesch, D., & Schmid, M. M. (2011). Corporate governance and firm value: International evidence. *Journal of Empirical Finance*, 18(1), 36–55. 10.1016/j.jempfin.2010.10.003

Amran, A., Lee, S. P., & Devi, S. S. (2015). The influence of governance structure and strategic corporate social responsibility toward sustainability reporting quality. *Business Strategy and the Environment*, 23(4), 249–264. 10.1002/bse.1767

An, X., Cui, Y., & Qi, E. (2010). *Study on eco-efficiency evaluation of manufacturing system based on Circular economy*. https://doi.org/https://doi.org/10.1109/icieem.2010.5646545

Anderson, R. C., & Fraser, D. R. (2000). Corporate control, bank risk taking, and the health of the banking industry. *Journal of Banking & Finance*, 24(8), 1383–1398. 10.1016/S0378-4266(99)00088-6

Ang, A., & Bekaert, G. (2002). International asset allocation with regime shifts. *Review of Financial Studies*, 15(4), 1137–1187. 10.1093/rfs/15.4.1137

Anginer, D., Cerutti, E., & Martínez Pería, M. S. (2017). Foreign bank subsidiaries' default risk during the global crisis: What factors help insulate affiliates from their parents? *Journal of Financial Intermediation*, 29, 19–31. 10.1016/j.jfi.2016.05.004

Anginer, D., Demirguc-Kunt, A., Huizinga, H., & Ma, K. (2018). Corporate governance of banks and financial stability. *Journal of Financial Economics*, 130(2), 327–346. 10.1016/j.jfineco.2018.06.011

Compilation of References

Anisie, Y. A., Bianco, E., Blanco, H., Boshell, F., Casals Seck, X., Feng, J., Guadarrama, C., Hawila, D., Kang, S., López-Peña, A., Nagpal, D., Parajuli, B., Pragada, G., Prakash, G., Rana, F., Renner, M., Seck, G. S., Taibi, E., & Vaid, A. (2022). *WORLD ENERGY TRANSITIONS OUTLOOK 2022*. IRENA. https://www.irena.org/-/media/Files/IRENA/Agency/Publication/2022/Mar/IRENA_World_Energy_Transitions_Outlook_2022.pdf?rev=6ff451981b0948c6894546661c6658a1

Antoncic, M., Bekaert, G., Rothenberg, R. V., & Noguer, M. (2020, August 1). *Sustainable Investment - Exploring the Linkage between Alpha, ESG, and SDG's*. Papers.*ssrn*.com. https://ssrn.com/abstract=362345910.2139/ssrn.3623459

Apergis, N., & Danuletiu, D. C. (2014). Renewable energy and economic growth: Evidence from the sign of panel long-run causality. *International Journal of Energy Economics and Policy*, 4(4), 578–587.

Apergis, N., & Payne, J. E. (2010). Renewable energy consumption and economic growth: Evidence from a panel of OECD countries. *Energy Policy*, 38(1), 656–660. 10.1016/j.enpol.2009.09.002

Appuhami, R., & Tashakor, S. (2017). The Impact of Audit Committee Characteristics on CSR Disclosure: An Analysis of Australian Firms. *Australian Accounting Review*, 27(4), 400–420. 10.1111/auar.12170

Aragon, G. O., Li, L., & Qian, J. Q. J. (2019). The use of credit default swaps by bond mutual funds: Liquidity provision and counterparty risk. *Journal of Financial Economics*, 131(1), 168–185. 10.1016/j.jfineco.2018.07.014

Arantes, R. F. M., Zanon, L. G., Calache, L. D. D. R., Bertassini, A. C., & Carpinetti, L. C. R. (2022). A fuzzy multicriteria group decision approach for circular business models prioritization. *Production, 32*. https://doi.org/10.1590/0103-6513.20220019

Aria, M., & Cuccurullo, C. (2017). bibliometrix: An R-tool for comprehensive science mapping analysis. *Journal of Informetrics*, 11(4), 959–975. 10.1016/j.joi.2017.08.007

Armstrong, C. S., Core, J. E., Taylor, D. J., & Verrecchia, R. E. (2011). When does information asymmetry affect the cost of capital? *Journal of Accounting Research*, 49(1), 1–40. 10.1111/j.1475-679X.2010.00391.x

Arnold, M., Bassen, A., & Frank, R. (2018). Timing effects of corporate social responsibility disclosure: An experimental study with investment professionals. *Journal of Sustainable Finance & Investment*, 8(1), 45–71. 10.1080/20430795.2017.1368229

Asante-Appiah, B., & Lambert, T. A. (2023). The role of the external auditor in managing environmental, social, and governance (ESG) reputation risk. *Review of Accounting Studies*, 28(4), 2589–2641. 10.1007/s11142-022-09706-z

Ascioglu, A., Hegde, S. P., Krishnan, G. V., & McDermott, J. B. (2012). Earnings management and market liquidity. *Review of Quantitative Finance and Accounting*, 38(2), 257–274. 10.1007/s11156-010-0225-9

Ashforth, B. E., & Reingen, P. H. (2014). Functions of dysfunction: Managing the dynamics of an organizational duality in a natural food cooperative. *Administrative Science Quarterly*, 59(3), 474–516. 10.1177/0001839214537811

Ashraf, D. (2013). Performance evaluation of Islamic mutual funds relative to conventional funds: Empirical evidence from Saudi Arabia. *International Journal of Islamic and Middle Eastern Finance and Management*, 6(2), 105–121. 10.1108/17538391311329815

Asif, M. A. (2018). The Role of Social Entrepreneurship in Pakistan and its Impact on Economy. *International Journal of Business. Economics and Management*, 5(5), 117–127.

Asif, M., Searcy, C., & Castka, P. (2023). ESG and Industry 5.0: The role of technologies in enhancing ESG disclosure. *Technological Forecasting and Social Change*, 195, 122806. 10.1016/j.techfore.2023.122806

Aslam, F., Ferreira, P., & Mohti, W. (2023). Investigating efficiency of frontier stock markets using multifractal detrended fluctuation analysis. *International Journal of Emerging Markets*, 18(7), 1650–1676. 10.1108/IJOEM-11-2020-1348

Atkinson, K. R., & Rosler, A. L. (2017). The relationship between corporate social responsibility, brand reputation and consumer trust. *Environmental Science & Policy*, 61, 11–21.

Atstaja, D., Uvarova, I., Kamilla Kambala, D., Alberte, V., Stokmane, K., Gegere-Zetterstroma, A., Kraze, S., & Zapletnuka, G. (2020). Investments to Develop Business Models and Projects in the Circular Economy. *IOP Conference Series. Earth and Environmental Science*, 578(1), 012029. Advance online publication. 10.1088/1755-1315/578/1/012029

Atz, U., Van Holt, T., Liu, Z. Z., & Bruno, C. C. (2023). Does sustainability generate better financial performance? Review, meta-analysis, and propositions. *Journal of Sustainable Finance & Investment*, 13(1), 1–24. 10.1080/20430795.2022.2106934

Aureli, S., Del Baldo, M., Lombardi, R., & Nappo, F. (2020). Nonfinancial reporting regulation and challenges in sustainability disclosure and corporate governance practices. *Business Strategy and the Environment*, 29(6), 2392–2403. 10.1002/bse.2509

Ausloos, M., Bartolacci, F., Castellano, N. G., & Cerqueti, R. (2018). Exploring how innovation strategies at time of crisis influence performance: A cluster analysis perspective. *Technology Analysis and Strategic Management*, 30(4), 484–497. 10.1080/09537325.2017.1337889

Aydoğmuş, M., Gülay, G., & Ergun, K. (2022). Impact of ESG performance on firm value and profitability. *Borsa Istanbul Review*, 22, S119–S127. 10.1016/j.bir.2022.11.006

Azmi, W., Hassan, M. K., Houston, R., & Karim, M. S. (2020). ESG activities and banking performance: International evidence from emerging economies. *Journal of International Financial Markets, Institutions and Money*, 70, 101277. 10.1016/j.intfin.2020.101277

Bae, G.-K., Lee, S.-M., & Luan, B.-K. (2023). The impact of ESG on brand trust and word of mouth in food and beverage companies: Focusing on Jeju Island tourists. *Sustainability (Basel)*, 15(3), 2348. Advance online publication. 10.3390/su15032348

Compilation of References

Bae, J. W., Bali, T. G., Sharifkhani, A., & Zhao, X. (2022). Labor Market Networks, Fundamentals, and Stock Returns. *Georgetown McDonough School of Business Research, Paper No. 3951333*. 10.2139/ssrn.3951333

Bae, K. H., Bailey, W., & Mao, C. X. (2006). Stock market liberalization and the information environment. *Journal of International Money and Finance*, 25(3), 404–428. 10.1016/j.jimonfin.2006.01.004

Baldi, F., & Lambertides, N. (2024). Exploring the role of ESG for the performance and risks of infrastructure investing: Evidence from the international funds' market. *Managerial Finance*, 50(1), 92–117. 10.1108/MF-01-2023-0024

Baldi, F., & Pandimiglio, A. (2022). The role of ESG scoring and greenwashing risk in explaining the yields of green bonds: A conceptual framework and an econometric analysis. *Global Finance Journal*, 52, 100711. 10.1016/j.gfj.2022.100711

Balmer, J. M. T., Powell, S. M., & Greyser, S. A. (2011). Explicating Ethical Corporate Marketing. Insights from the BP Deepwater Horizon Catastrophe: The Ethical Brand that Exploded and then Imploded. *Journal of Business Ethics*, 102(1), 1–14. 10.1007/s10551-011-0902-1

Bandeira, G. L., Duarte, Gardi, L. H., Sodario, M., & Simioni, C. G. (2023). *Developing an ESG Strategy and Roadmap: An Integrated Perspective in an O&G Company*. 10.4043/32600-MS

Baraibar-Diez, E., & Odriozola, D., M. (2019). CSR committees and their effect on ESG performance in UK, France, Germany, and Spain. *Sustainability*, 11(18), 5077. 10.3390/su11185077

Barney, J. B. (1991). Firm resources and sustained competitive advantage. *Journal of Management*, 17(1), 99–120. 10.1177/014920639101700108

Bartkutė, R., Streimikiene, D., & Kačerauskas, T. (2023). Between Fast and Sustainable Fashion: The Attitude of Young Lithuanian Designers to the Circular Economy. *Sustainability (Basel)*, 15(13), 9986. Advance online publication. 10.3390/su15139986

Bartleet, M., & Gounder, R. (2010). Energy consumption and economic growth in New Zealand: Results of trivariate and multivariate models. *Energy Policy*, 38(7), 3508–3517. 10.1016/j.enpol.2010.02.025

Bartolacci, F., Caputo, A., & Soverchia, M. (2020). Sustainability and financial performance of small and medium sized enterprises: A bibliometric and systematic literature review. *Business Strategy and the Environment*, 29(3), 1297–1309. 10.1002/bse.2434

Basrur, A. (2023, November 23). *Implications of lithium reserves in Jammu and Kashmir*. ORF. https://www.orfonline.org/expert-speak/implications-of-lithium-reserves-in-jammu-and-kashmir

Baz, K., Cheng, J., Xu, D., Abbas, K., Ali, I., Ali, H., & Fang, C. (2021). Asymmetric impact of fossil fuel and renewable energy consumption on economic growth: A nonlinear technique. *Energy*, 226, 120357. 10.1016/j.energy.2021.120357

Bear, S., Rahman, N., & Post, C. (2010). The impact of board diversity and gender composition on corporate social responsibility and firm reputation. *Journal of Business Ethics*, 97(2), 207–221. 10.1007/s10551-010-0505-2

Beasley, M. S., Carcello, J. V., Hermanson, D. R., & Neal, T. L. (2009). The Audit Committee Oversight Process*. *Contemporary Accounting Research*, 26(1), 65–122. 10.1506/car.26.1.3

Beattie, V. (2005). Moving the financial accounting research front forward: The UK contribution. *The British Accounting Review*, 37(1), 85–114. 10.1016/j.bar.2004.09.004

Bebchuk, L. A. (2005). The case for increasing shareholder power. *Harvard Law Review*, 118(3), 833–914. https://ssrn.com/abstract=387940

Bebchuk, L. A., Cohen, A., & Ferrell, A. (2009). What matters in corporate governance? *Review of Financial Studies*, 22(2), 783–827. 10.1093/rfs/hhn099

Behl, A., Kumari, P. S. R., Makhija, H., & Sharma, D. (2021). Exploring the relationship of ESG score and firm value using cross-lagged panel analyses: Case of the Indian energy sector. *Annals of Operations Research*, 313(1), 231–256. 10.1007/s10479-021-04189-8

Bekaert, G., Rothenberg, R., & Noguer, M. (2023). Sustainable investment – Exploring the linkage between alpha, ESG, and SDGs. *Sustainable Development (Bradford)*, 31(5), 3831–3842. 10.1002/sd.2628

Bekun, F. V., Emir, F., & Sarkodie, S. A. (2019). Another look at the relationship between energy consumption, carbon dioxide emissions, and economic growth in South Africa. *The Science of the Total Environment*, 655, 759–765. 10.1016/j.scitotenv.2018.11.27130476856

Bellardini, L., Murro, P., & Previtali, D. (2024). Measuring the risk appetite of bank-controlling shareholders: The Risk-Weighted Ownership index. *Global Finance Journal*, 60, 100935. 10.1016/j.gfj.2024.100935

Bento, P. F. (2018). How Social Entrepreneurship Promotes Sustainable Development: With Some Examples from Developed and Developing Countries. *Studies on entrepreneurship, structural change and industrial dynamics*, 283–297.

Berg, F., Kölbel, J. F., & Rigobon, R. (2022). Aggregate Confusion: The Divergence of ESG Ratings. *Review of Finance*, 26(6), 1315–1344. 10.1093/rof/rfac033

Berman, S. L., Wicks, A. C., Kotha, S., & Jones, T. M. (1999). Does stakeholder orientation matter? The relationship between stakeholder management models and firm financial performance. *Academy of Management Journal*, 42(5), 488–506. 10.2307/256972

Bernardi, R. A., & Threadgill, V. H. (2010). Women Directors and Corporate Social Responsibility. EJBO, Vol. 15, No. 2, p. 15-21. https://urn.fi/URN:NBN:fi:jyu-201201301096

Bernardi, C., & Stark, A. W. (2018). Environmental, social and governance disclosure, integrated reporting, and the accuracy of analyst forecasts. *The Effects of Environmental. The British Accounting Review*, 50(1), 16–31. 10.1016/j.bar.2016.10.001

Compilation of References

Berrone, P., Rousseau, H. E., Ricart, J. E., Brito, E., & Giuliodori, A. (2023). How Can Research Contribute to the Implementation of Sustainable Development goals? an Interpretive Review of SDG Literature in Management. *International Journal of Management Reviews*, 25(2), 318–339. 10.1111/ijmr.12331

Bharath, S. T., Sunder, J., & Sunder, S. V. (2008). Accounting quality and debt contracting. *The Accounting Review*, 83(1), 1–28. 10.2308/accr.2008.83.1.1

Bhasin, M. L. (2016). Unethical accounting practices in connivance with top management: A case study of satyam. *International Journal of Management Sciences and Business Research*, 5(9), 5–19.

Bhatia, A., & Makkar, B. (2020). CSR disclosure in developing and developed countries: A comparative study. *Journal of Global Responsibility*, 11(1), 1–26. 10.1108/JGR-04-2019-0043

Bhattacharya, B., Khadka, I., & Mani, D. (2022). Shaking up (and keeping intact) the old boys' network: The impact of the mandatory gender quota on the board of directors in India. *Journal of Business Ethics*, 177(4), 763–778. 10.1007/s10551-022-05099-w

Bhattacharya, N., Desai, H., & Venkataraman, K. (2013). Does earnings quality affect information asymmetry? Evidence from trading costs. *Contemporary Accounting Research*, 30(2), 482–516. 10.1111/j.1911-3846.2012.01161.x

Bianchi, N., Carretta, A., Farina, V., & Fiordelisi, F. (2021). Does espoused risk culture pay? Evidence from European banks. *Journal of Banking & Finance*, 122, 105767. 10.1016/j.jbankfin.2020.105767

Biju, A. V. N., Kodiyatt, S. J., Krishna, P. P. N., & Sreelekshmi, G. (2023). ESG sentiments and divergent ESG scores: Suggesting a framework for ESG rating. *SN Business & Economics*, 3(12), 209. 10.1007/s43546-023-00592-4

Bildirici, M. E., & Bakirtas, T. (2014). The relationship among oil, natural gas and coal consumption and economic growth in BRICTS (Brazil, Russian, India, China, Turkey and South Africa) countries. *Energy*, 65, 134–144. 10.1016/j.energy.2013.12.006

BinMahfouz, S., & Hassan, M. K.BinMahfouz. (2012). A comparative study between the investment characteristics of Islamic and conventional equity mutual funds in Saudi Arabia. *Journal of Investing*, 21(4), 128–143. 10.3905/joi.2012.21.4.128

Biswas, S. (2021). Female directors and risk-taking behavior of Indian firms. *Managerial Finance*, 47(7), 1016–1037. 10.1108/MF-05-2020-0274

Bizjak, J., Lemmon, M., & Whitby, R. (2009). Option backdating and board interlocks. *Review of Financial Studies*, 22(11), 4821–4847. 10.1093/rfs/hhn120

BlackRock. (2023). Investment Stewardship Annual Report. Retrieved from https://www.blackrock.com/corporate/literature/publication/annual-stewardship-report-2023-summary.pdf

Blair, M. M. (2001). Corporate Governance. In Smelser, N. J., & Baltes, P. B. (Eds.), *International Encyclopedia of the Social & Behavioral Sciences* (pp. 2797–2803). Pergamon., 10.1016/B0-08-043076-7/04292-3

Blanding, M. (2011). *The coke machine: The dirty truth behind the world's favorite soft drink.* Penguin.

Bloomberg Intelligence. (2022). ESG assets may hit $53 trillion by 2025, a third of global AUM. Retrieved from https://www.bloomberg.com/professional/blog/esg-assets-may-hit-53-trillion-by-2025-a-third-of-global-aum/

Bocken, N., & Konietzko, J. (2022). Experimentation capability for a circular economy: A practical guide. *The Journal of Business Strategy*, 44(6), 406–414. https://doi.org/https://doi.org/10.1108/jbs-02-2022-0039. 10.1108/JBS-02-2022-0039

Bonacorsi, L., Cerasi, V., Galfrascoli, P., & Manera, M. (2024). ESG Factors and Firms' Credit Risk. *Journal of Climate Finance*, 6, 100032. 10.1016/j.jclimf.2024.100032

Bonilla-Priego, M. J., Font, X., & del Rosario Pacheco-Olivares, M. (2014). Corporate sustainability reporting index and baseline data for the cruise industry. *Tourism Management*, 44, 149–160. 10.1016/j.tourman.2014.03.004

Boston Consulting Group. (2023). Building the Supply Chain of the Future. Retrieved from https://www.bcg.com/publications/2023/building-the-supply-chain-of-the-future

Botosan, C. A. (1997). Disclosure level and the cost of equity capital. *The Accounting Review*, •••, 323–349.

Boubaker, S., Cellier, A., Manita, R., & Saeed, A. (2020). Does corporate social responsibility reduce financial distress risk? *Economic Modelling*, 91, 835–851. 10.1016/j.econmod.2020.05.012

Boufounou, P., Moustairas, I., Toudas, K., & Malesios, C. (2023). ESGs and customer choice: Some empirical evidence. *Circular Economy and Sustainability*, 3(4), 1841–1874. Advance online publication. 10.1007/s43615-023-00251-836685983

Branco, M., & Lima Rodrigues, L. (2006). Corporate Social Responsibility and Resource-Based Perspectives. *Journal of Business Ethics*, 69(2), 111–132. 10.1007/s10551-006-9071-z

Bran, F., Ioan, I., Radulescu, C. V., & Ardeleanu, M. P. (2011). Sustainable development at corporate level. *Rivista di Studi sulla Sostenibilità*, 1(1), 101–131. 10.3280/RISS2011-001012

Bravo, F., & Reguera-Alvarado, N. (2019). Sustainable development disclosure: Environmental, social, and governance reporting and gender diversity in the audit committee. *Business Strategy and the Environment*, 28(2), 418–429. 10.1002/bse.2258

Breitung, J. 2000. The local power of some unit root tests for panel data. Advances in Econometrics, Volume 15: Nonstationary Panels, Panel Cointegration, and Dynamic Panels, ed. B. H. Baltagi, 161–178. Amsterdam: JAY Press. 10.1016/S0731-9053(00)15006-6

Compilation of References

Brennan, M. J., & Subrahmanyam, A. (1996). Market microstructure and asset pricing: On the compensation for illiquidity in stock returns. *Journal of Financial Economics*, 41(3), 441–464. 10.1016/0304-405X(95)00870-K

Broadstock, D. C., Matousek, R., Meyer, M., & Tzeremes, N. G. (2020). Does corporate social responsibility impact firms' innovation capacity? The indirect link between environmental & social governance implementation and innovation performance. *Journal of Business Research*, 119, 99–110. 10.1016/j.jbusres.2019.07.014

Brooks, C., & Oikonomou, I. (2018). The effects of environmental, social and governance disclosures and performance on firm value: A review of the literature in accounting and finance. *The Effects of Environmental. The British Accounting Review*, 50(1), 1–15. 10.1016/j.bar.2017.11.005

Brown, T. J., & Dacin, P. A. (1997). The Company and the Product: Corporate Associations and Consumer Product Responses. *Journal of Marketing*, 61(1), 68–84. 10.1177/002224299706100106

Bruce, C., & Laroiya, A. (2007). The production of eco-labels. *Environmental and Resource Economics*, 36(3), 275–293. 10.1007/s10640-006-9028-9

Bryndin, E. (2023). Transition of Countries to Currency and Trade Sustainable International Cooperation on the BRICS Platform. *Japan and the World Economy*, 2(1), 1–6. 10.56397/JWE.2023.03.01

Buallay, A. (2020). Sustainability reporting and firm's performance: Comparative study between manufacturing and banking sectors. *International Journal of Productivity and Performance Management*, 69(3), 431–445. 10.1108/IJPPM-10-2018-0371

Buallay, A., Hamdan, R., Barone, E., & Hamdan, A. (2022). Increasing female participation on boards: Effects on sustainability reporting. *International Journal of Finance & Economics*, 27(1), 111–124. 10.1002/ijfe.2141

Buhr, N. (2001). Corporate silence: Environmental disclosure and the North American free trade agreement. *Critical Perspectives on Accounting*, 12(4), 405–421. 10.1006/cpac.2000.0434

Burgstahler, D. C., & Dichev, I. D. (1997). Earnings, adaptation and equity value. *The Accounting Review*, ●●●, 187–215.

Busch, T., Bauer, R., & Orlitzky, M. (2016). Sustainable development and financial markets: Old paths and new avenues. *Business & Society*, 55(3), 303–329. 10.1177/0007650315570701

Bushman, R. M., & Smith, A. J. (2001). Financial accounting information and corporate governance. *Journal of Accounting and Economics*, 32(1), 237–333. 10.1016/S0165-4101(01)00027-1

Caiado, R. G. G., Scavarda, L. F., Gavião, L. O., Ivson, P., Nascimento, D. L. de M., & Garza-Reyes, J. A. (2021). A fuzzy rule-based industry 4.0 maturity model for operations and supply chain management. *International Journal of Production Economics*, 231, 107883. Advance online publication. 10.1016/j.ijpe.2020.107883

Cambrea, D. R., Paolone, F., & Cucari, N. (2023). Advisory or monitoring role in ESG scenario: Which women directors are more influential in the Italian context? *Business Strategy and the Environment*, 32(7), 4299–4314. 10.1002/bse.3366

Camilleri, M. A. (2015). Environmental, social and governance disclosures in Europe. *Sustainability Accounting. Management and Policy Journal*, 6(2), 224–242.

Camilleri, M. A. (2017). Corporate sustainability and responsibility: Creating value for business, society and the environment. *Asian Journal of Sustainability and Social Responsibility*, 2(1), 59–74. 10.1186/s41180-017-0016-5

Cao, Q., Zhu, T., & Yu, W. (2024). ESG investment and bank efficiency: Evidence from China. *Energy Economics*, 133, 107516. 10.1016/j.eneco.2024.107516

Capotă, L.-D., Giuzio, M., Kapadia, S., & Salakhova, D. (2022). *Are ethical and green investment funds more resilient?* Carhart, M. M. (1997). On Persistence in Mutual Fund Performance. *The Journal of Finance*, 52(1), 57–82. https://doi.org/https://doi.org/10.1111/j.1540-6261.1997.tb03808.x

Carroll, A. B. (1991). The pyramid of corporate social responsibility: Toward the moral management of organizational stakeholders. *Business Horizons*, 34(4), 39–48. 10.1016/0007-6813(91)90005-G

Carroll, A. B. (1999). Corporate Social Responsibility: Evolution of a Definitional Construct. *Business & Society*, 38(3), 268–295. 10.1177/000765039903800303

Carter, D. A., Simkins, B. J., & Simpson, W. G. (2003). Corporate governance, board diversity, and firm value. *Financial Review*, 38(1), 33–53. 10.1111/1540-6288.00034

Casals, X. G., Parajuli, B., & Ferroukhi, R. (2020). *Measuring the Socio-economics of Transition: Focus on Jobs*. IRENA. https://www.irena.org/-/media/Files/IRENA/Agency/Publication/2020/Feb/IRENA_Transition_jobs_2020.pdf

Casey, R. J., & Grenier, J. H. (2015). Understanding and Contributing to the Enigma of Corporate Social Responsibility (CSR) Assurance in the United States. *Auditing*, 34(1), 97–130. 10.2308/ajpt-50736

Çek, K., & Eyupoglu, S. (2020). Does environmental, social and governance performance influence economic performance? *Journal of Business Economics and Management*, 21(4), 1165–1184. 10.3846/jbem.2020.12725

Cerciello, M., Busato, F., & Taddeo, S. (2023). The effect of sustainable business practices on profitability. Accounting for strategic disclosure. *Corporate Social Responsibility and Environmental Management*, 30(2), 802–819. 10.1002/csr.2389

Chaney, P. K., & Lewis, C. M. (1995). Earnings management and firm valuation under asymmetric information. *Journal of Corporate Finance*, 1(3-4), 319–345. 10.1016/0929-1199(94)00008-I

Chang, D.-Y. (1996). Applications of the extent analysis method on fuzzy AHP. In *European Journal of Operational Research* (Vol. 95). 10.1016/0377-2217(95)00300-2

Chang, C. C. (2010). A multivariate causality test of carbon dioxide emissions, energy consumption and economic growth in China. *Applied Energy*, 87(11), 3533–3537. 10.1016/j.apenergy.2010.05.004

Chang, S. C., Chung, T. Y., & Lin, W. C. (2010). Underwriter reputation, earnings management and the long-run performance of initial public offerings. *Accounting and Finance*, 50(1), 53–78. 10.1111/j.1467-629X.2009.00329.x

Chatterjee, C., & Nag, T. (2023). Do women on boards enhance firm performance? Evidence from top Indian companies. *International Journal of Disclosure and Governance*, 20(2), 155–167. 10.1057/s41310-022-00153-5

Chatterji, A. K., Durand, R., Levine, D. I., & Touboul, S. (2016). Do ratings of firms converge? Implications for managers, investors and strategy researchers. *Strategic Management Journal*, 37(8), 1597–1614. 10.1002/smj.2407

Chen, G., & Wang, M. (2023). Stock market liberalization and earnings management: Evidence from the China–Hong Kong stock connects. *Finance Research Letters*, 58, 104417. 10.1016/j.frl.2023.104417

Cheng, B. S. (1999). Causality between energy consumption and economic growth in India: An application of cointegration and error-correction modeling. *Indian Economic Review*, ●●●, 39–49.

Cheng, B. S., & Lai, T. W. (1997). An investigation of co-integration and causality between energy consumption and economic activity in Taiwan. *Energy Economics*, 19(4), 435–444. 10.1016/S0140-9883(97)01023-2

Cheng, B., Ioannou, I., & Serafeim, G. (2014). Corporate social responsibility and access to finance. *Strategic Management Journal*, 35(1), 1–23. 10.1002/smj.2131

Chen, H., Chen, J. Z., Lobo, G. J., & Wang, Y. (2011). Effects of audit quality on earnings management and cost of equity capital: Evidence from China. *Contemporary Accounting Research*, 28(3), 892–925. 10.1111/j.1911-3846.2011.01088.x

Chen, L., & Bouvain, P. (2009). Is corporate responsibility converging? A comparison of corporate responsibility reporting in the USA, UK, Australia, and Germany. *Journal of Business Ethics*, 87(1), 299–317. 10.1007/s10551-008-9794-0

Chen, P., Chu, Z., & Zhao, M. (2024). The Road to corporate sustainability: The importance of artificial intelligence. *Technology in Society*, 76, 102440. 10.1016/j.techsoc.2023.102440

Cherubini, U., Mulinacci, S., Gobbi, F., & Romagnoli, S. (2011). *Dynamic copula methods in finance*. John Wiley & Sons. 10.1002/9781118467404

Cheruvalath, R. (2017). NEED FOR A SHIFT FROM A PHILANTHROPIC TO A HUMANISTIC APPROACH TO CORPORATE SOCIAL RESPONSIBILITY. *Annals of Public and Cooperative Economics*, 88(1), 121–136. 10.1111/apce.12146

Chiew, D., Qiu, J., Treepongkaruna, S., Yang, J., & Shi, C. (2021). Performance of Portfolios Based on the Expected Utility-Entropy Fund Rating Approach. *Entropy (Basel, Switzerland)*, 23(4), 481. 10.3390/e2304048133919622

Chih, H. L., Shen, C. H., & Kang, F. C. (2008). Corporate social responsibility, investor protection, and earnings management: Some international evidence. *Journal of Business Ethics*, 79(1-2), 179–198. 10.1007/s10551-007-9383-7

Chin, W. W. (1998). The partial least squares approach to structural equation modeling. *Modern methods for business research, 295*(2), 295-336.

Cho, C. H., Freedman, M., & Patten, D. M. (2012). Corporate disclosure of environmental capital expenditures: A test of alternative theories. *Accounting, Auditing & Accountability Journal*, 25(3), 486–507. 10.1108/09513571211209617

Cho, E., & Chun, S. (2016). Corporate social responsibility, real activities earnings management, and corporate governance: Evidence from Korea. *Asia-Pacific Journal of Accounting & Economics*, 23(4), 400–431. 10.1080/16081625.2015.1047005

Choi, B. B., Lee, D., & Park, Y. (2013). Corporate Social Responsibility, Corporate Governance and Earnings Quality: Evidence from K orea. *Corporate Governance*, 21(5), 447–467. 10.1111/corg.12033

Choi, D., Gam, Y. K., Kang, M. J., & Shin, H. (2024). The effect of ESG-motivated turnover on firm financial risk. *The British Accounting Review*, 101373, 101373. Advance online publication. 10.1016/j.bar.2024.101373

Choi, Y. K., Han, S. H., & Kwon, Y. (2019). CSR activities and internal capital markets: Evidence from Korean business groups. *Pacific-Basin Finance Journal*, 55, 283–298. 10.1016/j.pacfin.2019.04.008

Cho, S. Y., Lee, C., & Pfeiffer, R. J.Jr. (2013). Corporate social responsibility performance and information asymmetry. *Journal of Accounting and Public Policy*, 32(1), 71–83. 10.1016/j.jaccpubpol.2012.10.005

Chouaibi, Y., & Zouari, G. (2022). The mediating role of real earnings management in the relationship between CSR practices and cost of equity: Evidence from European ESG data. *EuroMed Journal of Business, ahead-of-print*(ahead-of-print).

Chouaibi, S., & Affes, H. (2021). The effect of social and ethical practices on environmental disclosure: Evidence from an international ESG data. *Corporate Governance (Bradford)*, 21(7), 1293–1317. 10.1108/CG-03-2020-0087

Cho, Y. N., & Baskin, E. (2018). It's a match when green meets healthy in sustainability labeling. *Journal of Business Research*, 86, 119–129. 10.1016/j.jbusres.2018.01.050

Christensen, D. M., Hail, L., & Leuz, C. (2019). Economic analysis of widespread adoption of CSR and sustainability reporting standards. *SSRN*, 57(4), 931–972. 10.2139/ssrn.3315673

Christensen, H. B., Serafeim, G., & Sikochi, A. (2022). Why is corporate virtue in the eye of the beholder? The case of ESG ratings. *The Accounting Review*, 97(1), 147–175. 10.2308/TAR-2019-0506

Christoffersen, P., & Langlois, H. (2013). The joint dynamics of equity market factors. *Journal of Financial and Quantitative Analysis*, 48(5), 1371–1404. 10.1017/S0022109013000598

Chu, N., Dao, B., Pham, N., Nguyen, H., & Tran, H. (2022). Predicting Mutual Funds' Performance using Deep Learning and Ensemble Techniques. *ArXiv Preprint ArXiv:2209.09649.*

Citterio, A., & King, T. (2023). The role of Environmental, Social, and Governance (ESG) in predicting bank financial distress. *Finance Research Letters*, 51, 103411. 10.1016/j.frl.2022.103411

Clark, G. L., Feiner, A., & Viehs, M. (2015). From the stockholder to the stakeholder: How sustainability can drive financial outperformance. *University of Oxford and Arabesque Partners.* 10.2139/ssrn.2508281

Clément, A., Robinot, É., & Trespeuch, L. (2023). The use of ESG scores in academic literature: a systematic literature review. *Journal of Enterprising Communities*. https://doi.org/10.1108/JEC-10-2022-0147/FULL/XML

Clementino, E., & Perkins, R. (2021). How Do Companies Respond to Environmental, Social and Governance (ESG) ratings? Evidence from Italy. *Journal of Business Ethics*, 171(2), 379–397. 10.1007/s10551-020-04441-4

Coal India Could Layoff More Than 70,000 Workers by 2050: Report. (2023, October 10). The wire. https://www.google.com/url?q=https://thewire.in/energy/coal-india-could-layoff-70000-workers-2050-just transition&sa=D&source=docs&ust=1718860754262411&usg=AOv-Vaw3_V9DHK4crT7UsM8S5HDfT

Coelho, R., Jayantilal, S., & Ferreira, J. J. (2023). The impact of social responsibility on corporate financial performance: A systematic literature review. *Corporate Social Responsibility and Environmental Management*, 30(4), 1535–1560. 10.1002/csr.2446

Cohen, J. (1998). *Statistical power analysis for the behavioural sciences, xxi.* L Erlbaum Associates.

Cohen, J., Holder-Webb, L., Nath, L., & Wood, D. (2011). Retail investors' perceptions of the decision-usefulness of economic performance, governance, and corporate social responsibility disclosures. *Behavioral Research in Accounting*, 23(1), 109–129. 10.2308/bria.2011.23.1.109

Coleman, L., & Coleman, L. (2016). The Mutual Fund Industry: Structure and Conduct. *Applied Investment Theory: How Markets and Investors Behave, and Why*, 121–129.

Coleman, J. S. (1988). Social Capital in the Creation of Human Capital. *American Journal of Sociology*, 94, S95–S120. 10.1086/228943

Coles, J. L., Loewenstein, U., & Suay, J. (1995). On equilibrium pricing under parameter uncertainty. *Journal of Financial and Quantitative Analysis*, 30(3), 347–364. 10.2307/2331345

Collier, P., & Gregory, A. (1999). Audit committee activity and agency costs. *Journal of Accounting and Public Policy*, 18(4–5), 311–332. 10.1016/S0278-4254(99)00015-0

Consolandi, C., Phadke, H., Hawley, J., & Eccles, R. G. (2020). Material ESG outcomes and SDG externalities: Evaluating the health care sector's contribution to the SDGs. *Organization & Environment*, 33(4), 511–533. 10.1177/1086026619899795

Cooper, E. W., & Uzun, H. (2022). Busy outside directors and ESG performance. *Journal of Sustainable Finance & Investment*, 1–20. Advance online publication. 10.1080/20430795.2022.2122687

Core, J. E. (2001). A review of the empirical disclosure literature [discussion]. *Journal of Accounting and Economics*, 31(1-3), 441–456. 10.1016/S0165-4101(01)00036-2

Cormier, D., Houle, S., & Ledoux, M. J. (2013). The incidence of earnings management on information asymmetry in an uncertain environment: Some Canadian evidence. *Journal of International Accounting, Auditing & Taxation*, 22(1), 26–38. 10.1016/j.intaccaudtax.2013.02.002

Cormier, D., Ledoux, M. J., & Magnan, M. (2011). The informational contribution of social and environmental disclosures for investors. *Management Decision*, 49(8), 1276–1304. 10.1108/00251741111163124

Cornett, M. M., McNutt, J. J., & Tehranian, H. (2009). Corporate governance and earnings management at large US bank holding companies. *Journal of Corporate Finance*, 15(4), 412–430. 10.1016/j.jcorpfin.2009.04.003

Cox, P., & Wicks, P. G. (2011). Institutional interest in corporate responsibility: Portfolio evidence and ethical explanation. *Journal of Business Ethics*, 103(1), 143–165. 10.1007/s10551-011-0859-0

Crapa, G., Latino, M. E., & Roma, P. (2024). The performance of green communication across social media: Evidence from large-scale retail industry in Italy. *Corporate Social Responsibility and Environmental Management*, 31(1), 493–513. 10.1002/csr.2581

Creyer, E. H., & Ross, W. T. (2017). The influence of firm behavior on purchase intention: Do consumers really care about business ethics? *Journal of Consumer Marketing*, 34(2), 82–96. 10.1108/07363769710185999

Crilly, D., Hansen, M., & Zollo, M. (2016). The grammar of decoupling: Stakeholder heterogeneity and firm decoupling of sustainability practices. *Academy of Management Journal*, 59, 705–729. 10.5465/amj.2015.0171

Crilly, D., Zollo, M., & Hansen, M. T. (2012). Faking it or muddling through? Understanding decoupling in response to stakeholder pressures. *Academy of Management Journal*, 55(6), 1429–1448. 10.5465/amj.2010.0697

Crisóstomo, V. L., De Azevedo Prudêncio, P., & Forte, H. C. (2017). An analysis of the adherence to GRI for disclosing information on social action and sustainability concerns. *Advances in Environmental Accounting and Management*, 6, 69–103. 10.1108/S1479-359820160000006002

Compilation of References

Cruz Villares, L. (2022). *Environmental Management and Data for the SDGs*. IoT Applications Computing., 10.5772/intechopen.97685

Cuadrado-Ballesteros, B., Garcia-Sanchez, I. M., & Martinez Ferrero, J. (2016). How are corporate disclosures related to the cost of capital? The fundamental role of information asymmetry. *Management Decision*, 54(7), 1669–1701. 10.1108/MD-10-2015-0454

Cucari, N., Esposito De Falco, S., & Orlando, B. (2018). Diversity of board of directors and environmental social governance: Evidence from Italian listed companies. *Corporate Social Responsibility and Environmental Management*, 25(3), 250–266. 10.1002/csr.1452

Cuervo-Cazurra, A. (2006). Who cares about corruption? *Journal of International Business Studies*, 37(6), 807–822. 10.1057/palgrave.jibs.8400223

Cui, J., Jo, H., & Na, H. (2018). Does corporate social responsibility affect information asymmetry? *Journal of Business Ethics*, 148(3), 549–572. 10.1007/s10551-015-3003-8

Curcio, D., Gianfrancesco, I., Onorato, G., & Vioto, D. (2024). Do ESG scores affect financial systemic risk? Evidence from European banks and insurers. *Research in International Business and Finance*, 69, 102251. 10.1016/j.ribaf.2024.102251

Curtis, Q., Fisch, J., & Robertson, A. Z. (2021). Do ESG mutual funds deliver on their promises? *Michigan Law Review*, 120(120.3), 393. 10.36644/mlr.120.3.ESG

Dai, Y., Kong, D., & Wang, L. (2013). Information asymmetry, mutual funds and earnings management: Evidence from China. *China Journal of Accounting Research*, 6(3), 187–209. 10.1016/j.cjar.2013.03.001

Damiongraham. (2023, August 29). *The Catalyst for Change: The Role of Social Entrepreneurship in Economic Development*. Retrieved from Economic Impact Catalyst: https://economicimpactcatalyst.com/social-entrepreneurship/

Danisman, G. O., & Tarazi, A. (2024). ESG activity and bank lending during financial crises. *Journal of Financial Stability*, 70, 101206. 10.1016/j.jfs.2023.101206

Daňo, F., Drábik, P., & Hanuláková, E. (2020). Circular Business Models in Textiles and Apparel Sector in Slovakia. *Central European Business Review, 9*(1), 1–19. https://doi.org/https://doi.org/10.18267/j.cebr.226

Davino, C., & D'Alesio, N. (2023). Sustainable development goals: classifying European countries through self-organizing maps. *Proceedings E Report (Online)*, 95–100. 10.36253/979-12-215-0106-3.17

Davis, E. P. (2002). Institutional investors, corporate governance and the performance of the corporate sector. *Economic Systems*, 26(3), 203–229. 10.1016/S0939-3625(02)00044-4

de Freitas Netto, S. V., Sobral, M. F. F., Ribeiro, A. R. B., & Soares, G. R. D. L. (2020). Concepts and forms of greenwashing: A systematic review. *Environmental Sciences Europe*, 32(1), 1. Advance online publication. 10.1186/s12302-020-0300-3

De la Torre, O., Galeana, E., & Aguilasocho, D. (2016). The use of the sustainable investment against the broad market one. A first test in the Mexican stock market. *European Research on Management and Business Economics*, 22(3), 117–123. 10.1016/j.iedee.2015.08.002

Dechow, P. M., Sloan, R. G., & Sweeney, A. P. (1995). Detecting earnings management. *The Accounting Review*, ●●●, 193–225.

Deegan, C. (2000). *Financial Accounting Theory*. McGraw-Hill Education Australia.

Deegan, C. (2002). Introduction: The legitimising effect of social and environmental disclosures–a theoretical foundation. *Accounting, Auditing & Accountability Journal*, 15(3), 282–311. 10.1108/09513570210435852

Degeorge, F., Patel, J., & Zeckhauser, R. (1999). Earnings management to exceed thresholds. *The Journal of Business*, 72(1), 1–33. 10.1086/209601

Del Gesso, C., & Lodhi, R. N. (2024). Theories underlying environmental, social and governance (ESG) disclosure: A systematic review of accounting studies. *Journal of Accounting Literature*. Advance online publication. 10.1108/JAL-08-2023-0143

Delgado-Ceballos, J., Ortiz-De-Mandojana, N., Antolín-López, R., & Montiel, I. (2023). Connecting the Sustainable Development Goals to firm-level sustainability and ESG factors: The need for double materiality. *Business Research Quarterly*, 26(1), 2–10. 10.1177/23409444221140919

Delmas, M. A., & Burbano, V. C. (2011). The drivers of greenwashing. *California Management Review*, 54(1), 64–87. 10.1525/cmr.2011.54.1.64

Delmas, M., & Toffel, M. W. (2004). Stakeholders and environmental management practices: An institutional framework. *Business Strategy and the Environment*, 13(4), 209–222. 10.1002/bse.409

Deloitte. (2022). *The Evolution of ESG: A Focus on Mainstreaming*. Retrieved from https://www2.deloitte.com/global/en/pages/about-deloitte/articles/esg-evolution-mainstreaming.html

Deloitte. (2023). *ESG preparedness survey report*. Retrieved from https://www2.deloitte.com/content/dam/Deloitte/in/Documents/about-deloitte/in-Deloitte-India-ESG-Preparedness-Survey-Report_noexp.pdf

Deloitte. (2023). *ESG, Sustainability & Climate*. Retrieved from https://www2.deloitte.com/ba/en/pages/risk/articles/ESG-sustainability-and-climate.html

Demitriades, E., & Zilakaki, E. (2019). The effect of corporate social responsibility on customer loyalty in mobile telephone companies. *International Journal of Economics and Business Administration*, VII(4), 433–450. Advance online publication. 10.35808/ijeba/356

Deng, X., Kang, J., & Low, B. S. (2013). Corporate social responsibility and stakeholder value maximization: Evidence from mergers. *Journal of Financial Economics*, 110(1), 87–109. 10.1016/j.jfineco.2013.04.014

Dergiades, T., Martinopoulos, G., & Tsoulfidis, L. (2013). Energy consumption and economic growth: Parametric and non-parametric causality testing for the case of Greece. *Energy Economics*, 36, 686–697. 10.1016/j.eneco.2012.11.017

Devroye, L. (1986). *Non-Uniform Random Variate Generation*. Springer-Verlag, New York European Sustainable Investment Forum. (2018). *European SRI Study 2018*. Brussels. 10.1007/978-1-4613-8643-8

Dhaliwal, D. S., Li, O. Z., Tsang, A., & Yang, Y. G. (2011). Voluntary nonfinancial disclosure and the cost of equity capital: The initiation of corporate social responsibility reporting. *The Accounting Review*, 86(1), 59–100. 10.2308/accr.00000005

Dhaliwal, D. S., Radhakrishnan, S., Tsang, A., & Yang, Y. G. (2012). Nonfinancial disclosure and analyst forecast accuracy: International evidence on corporate social responsibility disclosure. *The Accounting Review*, 87(3), 723–759. 10.2308/accr-10218

Dharmapala, D., & Khanna, V. (2018). The impact of mandated corporate social responsibility: Evidence from India's Companies Act of 2013. *International Review of Law and Economics*, 56, 92–104. 10.1016/j.irle.2018.09.001

Diamond, D. W. (1985). Optimal release of information by firms. *The Journal of Finance*, 40(4), 1071–1094. 10.1111/j.1540-6261.1985.tb02364.x

Diamond, D. W., & Verrecchia, R. E. (1991). Disclosure, liquidity, and the cost of capital. *The Journal of Finance*, 46(4), 1325–1359. 10.1111/j.1540-6261.1991.tb04620.x

Díaz-López, C., Martín-Blanco, C., De la Torre Bayo, J. J., Rubio-Rivera, B., & Zamorano, M. (2021). Analyzing the Scientific Evolution of the Sustainable Development Goals. *Applied Sciences (Basel, Switzerland)*, 11(18), 8286. 10.3390/app11188286

Diaz-Sarachaga, J. M. (2021). Shortcomings in reporting contributions towards the sustainable development goals. *Corporate Social Responsibility and Environmental Management*, 28(4), 1299–1312. Advance online publication. 10.1002/csr.2129

Dimson, E., Karakaş, O., & Li, X. (2023). Coordinated engagements. *European Corporate Governance Institute–Finance Working Paper, 721*. 10.2139/ssrn.3209072

Dimson, E., Karakaş, O., & Li, X. (2015). Active ownership. *Review of Financial Studies*, 28(12), 3225–3268. 10.1093/rfs/hhv044

Dixon, R., Mousa, G. A., & Woodhead, A. D. (2004). The necessary characteristics of environmental auditors: A review of the contribution of the financial auditing profession. *Accounting Forum*, 28(2), 119–138. 10.1016/j.accfor.2004.01.001

Docekalova, M. P., & Kocmanova, A. (2015). Evaluation of the Effectiveness of Manufacturing Companies by Financial and Non-financial Indicators. *20th International Scientific Conference 'Economics and Management 2015 (ICEM-2015)', 213*, 491–496. 10.1016/j.sbspro.2015.11.439

Donaldson, T., & Preston, L. E. (1995). The stakeholder theory of the corporation: Concepts, evidence, and implications. *Academy of Management Review*, 20(1), 65–91. 10.2307/258887

Dwekat, A., Meqbel, R., Seguí-Mas, E., & Tormo-Carbó, G. (2022). The role of the audit committee in enhancing the credibility of CSR disclosure: Evidence from STOXX Europe 600 members. *Business Ethics, the Environment & Responsibility*, 31(3), 718–740. 10.1111/beer.12439

Dye, R. A. (1988). Earnings management in an overlapping generations model. *Journal of Accounting Research*, 26(2), 195–235. 10.2307/2491102

Dziuba, R., Jabłońska, M., Ławińska, K., & Wysokińska, Z. (2022). Overview of EU and Global Conditions for the Transformation of the TCLF Industry on the Way to a Circular and Digital Economy (Case Studies from Poland). *Comparative Economic Research*, 25(1), 75–94. 10.18778/1508-2008.25.05

Easley, D., & O'hara, M. (2004). Information and the cost of capital. *The Journal of Finance*, 59(4), 1553–1583. 10.1111/j.1540-6261.2004.00672.x

Eccles, R. G., Ioannou, I., & Serafeim, G. (2014). The impact of corporate sustainability on organizational processes and performance. *Management Science*, 60(11), 2835–2857. 10.1287/mnsc.2014.1984

Eccles, R. G., & Klimenko, S. (2019). The Investor Revolution. *Harvard Business Review*, 97(3), 106–116.

Eccles, R. G., & Klimenko, S. (2019). The investor revolution. *Harvard Business Review*, 97(3), 106–116. https://hbr.org/2019/05/the-investor-revolution

Eccles, R. G., & Krzus, M. P. (2010). Integrated Reporting for a Sustainable Strategy. *Financial Executive*, 26(2), 28–32.

Eccles, R. G., & Stroehle, J. C. (2018). Exploring social origins in the construction of ESG measures. *Available atSSRN* 3212685. 10.2139/ssrn.3212685

Efthymiou, L., Kulshrestha, A., & Kulshrestha, S. (2023). A Study on Sustainability and ESG in the Service Sector in India: Benefits, Challenges, and Future Implications. *Administrative Sciences*, 13(7), 7. 10.3390/admsci13070165

Egri, C. P., & Ralston, D. A. (2008). Corporate responsibility: A review of international management research from 1998 to 2007. *Journal of International Management*, 14(4), 319–339. 10.1016/j.intman.2007.09.003

Ehrenhard, M. L., & Fiorito, T. L. (2018). Corporate values of the 25 largest European banks: Exploring the ambiguous link with corporate scandals. *Journal of Public Affairs*, 18(1), e1700. Advance online publication. 10.1002/pa.1700

El Ghoul, S., Guedhami, O., Kim, H., & Park, K. (2018). Corporate environmental responsibility and the cost of capital: International evidence. *Journal of Business Ethics*, 149(2), 335–361. 10.1007/s10551-015-3005-6

Compilation of References

El Ghoul, S., Guedhami, O., Kwok, C. C., & Mishra, D. R. (2011). Does corporate social responsibility affect the cost of capital? *Journal of Banking & Finance*, 35(9), 2388–2406. 10.1016/j.jbankfin.2011.02.007

El Ghoul, S., Guedhami, O., & Pittman, J. (2016). Cross-country evidence on the importance of Big Four auditors to equity pricing: The mediating role of legal institutions. *Accounting, Organizations and Society*, 54, 60–81. 10.1016/j.aos.2016.03.002

El Khoury, R., Nasrallah, N., & Alareeni, B. (2021). ESG and financial performance of banks in the MENAT region: Concavity–convexity patterns. *Journal of Sustainable Finance & Investment*, ●●●, 1–25. 10.1080/20430795.2021.1929807

Elbadry, A., Gounopoulos, D., & Skinner, F. (2015). Governance quality and information asymmetry. *Financial Markets, Institutions and Instruments*, 24(2-3), 127–157. 10.1111/fmii.12026

Eliwa, Y., Haslam, J., & Abraham, S. (2016). The association between earnings quality and the cost of equity capital: Evidence from the UK. *International Review of Financial Analysis*, 48, 125–139. 10.1016/j.irfa.2016.09.012

Elkington, J. (1994). Towards the sustainable corporation: Win-win-win business strategies for sustainable development. *California Management Review*, 36(2), 90–100. 10.2307/41165746

Elkington, J. (1997). *Cannibals with Forks: The Triple Bottom Line of 21st Century Business*. New Society Publishers.

Ellison, T. (2023, March 30). *INDIA'S LITHIUM RESOURCES IN KASHMIR HIGHLIGHT CONFLICT RISKS AROUND CRITICAL MINERALS*. center for Climate and Security. https://councilonstrategicrisks.org/wp-content/uploads/2023/03/48-KashmirLithium.pdf

Eng, L. L., & Mak, Y. T. (2003). Corporate governance and voluntary disclosure. *Journal of Accounting and Public Policy*, 22(4), 325–345. 10.1016/S0278-4254(03)00037-1

Erhardt, N. L., Werbel, J. D., & Shrader, C. B. (2003). Board of director diversity and firm financial performance. *Corporate Governance*, 11(2), 102–111. 10.1111/1467-8683.00011

Erhemjamts, O., Huang, K., & Tehranian, H. (2024). Climate risk, ESG performance, and ESG sentiment in US commercial banks. *Global Finance Journal*, 59, 100924. 10.1016/j.gfj.2023.100924

Ernst & Young (EY). (2023). *ESG Reporting and Disclosure: Building Trust and Transparency*. Retrieved from https://www.ey.com/en_us/sustainability/creating-long-term-value/esg-reporting-disclosure

Escrig-Olmedo, E., Fernández-Izquierdo, M. Á., Ferrero-Ferrero, I., Rivera-Lirio, J. M., & Muñoz-Torres, M. J. (2019). Rating the raters: Evaluating how ESG rating agencies integrate sustainability principles. *Sustainability (Basel)*, 11(3), 915. 10.3390/su11030915

European Commission. (2020). *Taxonomy: Final report of the technical expert group on sustainable finance*. Retrieved from https://ec.europa.eu/info/sites/info/files/business_economy_euro/banking_and_finance/documents/200309-sustainable-finance-teg-final-report-taxonomy_en.pdf

European Commission. (2023). *Regulation of the European Parliament and of the Council on the Transparency and Integrity of Environmental, Social and Governance (ESG) rating activities.* Retrieved from https://eur-lex.europa.eu/resource.html?uri=cellar:50922493-1ce4-11ee-806b -01aa75ed71a1.0001.02/DOC_1&format=PDF

EVolution:Aligning the Just Energy Transition in the Electric Mobility Ecosystem with the G20 Framework. (n.d.). ccier. https://cuts-ccier.org/pdf/summary-of-podcasts-evolution.pdf

EY Global Insights Team. (2022, July 14). Five priorities to build trust in ESG. EY. https://www .ey.com/en_gl/insights/public-policy/five-priorities-to-build-trust-in-esg

Fang, J. X., & Hong, J. Q. (2007). Listed firms' information disclosure quality and securities analysts' earnings forecasts. *Securities Market Herald*, 3, 25–30.

Fan, Y., Li, S., & Yang, W. (2024). Research on the impact of the percentage of female directors on corporate ESG score. *Finance Research Letters*, 105376, 105376. Advance online publication. 10.1016/j.frl.2024.105376

Fatemi, A., Glaum, M., & Kaiser, S. (2018). ESG performance and firm value: The moderating role of disclosure. *Global Finance Journal*, 38, 45–64. 10.1016/j.gfj.2017.03.001

Fatimah, Y. A., Kannan, D., Govindan, K., & Hasibuan, Z. A. (2023). Circular economy e-business model portfolio development for e-business applications: Impacts on ESG and sustainability performance. *Journal of Cleaner Production*, 415, 137528. 10.1016/j.jclepro.2023.137528

Fatma, M., & Khan, I. (2023). Impact of CSR on Customer Citizenship Behavior: Mediating the Role of Customer Engagement. *Sustainability (Basel)*, 15(7), 5802. 10.3390/su15075802

Feng, Y., & Zhao, T. (2022). Exploring the Nonlinear Relationship between Renewable Energy Consumption and Economic Growth in the Context of Global Climate Change. *International Journal of Environmental Research and Public Health*, 19(23), 15647. 10.3390/ijerph19231564736497722

Ferrero-Ferrero, I. I., Fernández-Izquierdo, M., & Muñoz-Torres, M. (2016). The effect of environmental, social and governance consistency on economic results. *Sustainability (Basel)*, 8(10), 1005. 10.3390/su8101005

Ferrero-Ferrero, I., Muñoz-Torres, M. J., Rivera-Lirio, J. M., Escrig-Olmedo, E., & Fernández-Izquierdo, M. Á. (2023). SDG reporting: An analysis of corporate sustainability leaders. *Marketing Intelligence & Planning*, 41(4), 457–472. 10.1108/MIP-07-2022-0332

Ferriani, F., & Natoli, F. (2021). ESG risks in times of Covid-19. *Applied Economics Letters*, 28(18), 1537–1541. 10.1080/13504851.2020.1830932

Ferris, S. P., Javakhadze, D., & Rajkovic, T. (2017). The international effect of managerial social capital on the cost of equity. *Journal of Banking & Finance*, 74, 69–84. 10.1016/j.jbank-fin.2016.10.001

Filipiak, B. Z., & Kiestrzyn, M. (2021). Potential ESG Risks in Entities of the Healthcare System. In Adapting and Mitigating Environmental, Social, and Governance Risk in Business (pp. 74-102). IGI Global. 10.4018/978-1-7998-6788-3.ch005

Flammer, C., & Luo, J. (2017). Corporate social responsibility as a conflict between shareholders. *Journal of Management*, 43(6), 1851–1875. 10.1007/s10551-010-0496-z

Flammer, C., & Luo, J. (2017). Corporate social responsibility as an employee governance tool: Evidence from a quasi-experiment. *Strategic Management Journal*, 38(2), 163–183. 10.1002/smj.2492

Fong, K. Y. L., Parwada, J. T., & Yang, J. W. (2018). Algorithmic Trading and Mutual Fund Performance. *Available atSSRN* 3111598.

Font, X., & Harris, C. (2004). Rethinking standards from green to sustainable. *Annals of Tourism Research*, 31(4), 986–1007. 10.1016/j.annals.2004.04.001

Fooladi, I. J., & Hebb, G. (2022). Drivers of differences in performance of ESG-focused funds relative to their underlying benchmarks. *Global Finance Journal*, 56, 100745. 10.1016/j.gfj.2022.100745

Forgione, A. F., & Migliardo, C. (2020). CSR engagement and market structure: Evidence from listed banks. *Finance Research Letters*, 35, 101592. 10.1016/j.frl.2020.101592

Fornell, C., & Larcker, D. F. (1981). Evaluating structural equation models with unobservable variables and measurement error. *JMR, Journal of Marketing Research*, 18(1), 39–50. 10.1177/002224378101800104

Fowler, S. J., & Hope, C. (2007). A critical review of sustainable business indices and their impact. *Journal of Business Ethics*, 76(3), 243–252. 10.1007/s10551-007-9590-2

Francis, J., LaFond, R., Olsson, P. M., & Schipper, K. (2004). Costs of equity and earnings attributes. *The Accounting Review*, 79(4), 967–1010. 10.2308/accr.2004.79.4.967

Freeman, R. & Mcvea, John. (2001). A Stakeholder Approach to Strategic Management. *SSRN Electronic Journal*. DOI: 10.2139/ssrn.263511

Freeman, R. E. (1984). *Strategic Management: A Stakeholder Approach*. Pitman Publishing.

Freeman, R. E. (1999). Divergent stakeholder theory. *Academy of Management Review*, 24(2), 233–236.

Friede, G. (2019). Why don't we see more action? A meta-synthesis of the investor impediments to integrate environmental, social, and governance factors. *Business Strategy and the Environment*, 28(6), 1260–1282. Advance online publication. 10.1002/bse.2346

Friede, G., Busch, T., & Bassen, A. (2015). ESG and financial performance: Aggregated evidence from more than 2000 empirical studies. *Journal of Sustainable Finance & Investment*, 5(4), 210–233. 10.1080/20430795.2015.1118917

Friedman, M. (1953). *Essays in Positive Economics*. University Of Chicago Press.

Fuadah, L. L., Mukhtarudin, M., Andriana, I., & Arisman, A.Luk Luk Fuadah. (2023). Environmental, Social and Governance (ESG). *Integrated Journal of Business and Economics*, 7(2), 459–459. 10.33019/ijbe.v7i2.706

Gaio, C., Gonçalves, T., & Sousa, M. V. (2022). Does corporate social responsibility mitigate earnings management? *Management Decision*, 60(11), 2972–2989. 10.1108/MD-05-2021-0719

Galeazzo, A., Miandar, T., & Carraro, M. (2023). SDGs in corporate responsibility reporting: A longitudinal investigation of institutional determinants and financial performance. *The Journal of Management and Governance*. Advance online publication. 10.1007/s10997-023-09671-y

Galletta, S., Goodell, J. W., Mazzù, S., & Paltrinieri, A. (2023). Bank reputation and operational risk: The impact of ESG. *Finance Research Letters*, 51, 103494. 10.1016/j.frl.2022.103494

Gangi, F., Meles, A., D'Angelo, E., & Daniele, L. M. (2019). Sustainable development and corporate governance in the financial system: Are environmentally friendly banks less risky? *Corporate Social Responsibility and Environmental Management*, 26(3), 529–547. 10.1002/csr.1699

Gao, H., Shen, Z., Li, Y., Mao, X., & Shi, Y. (2020). Institutional Investors, Real Earnings Management and Cost of Equity: Evidence from Listed High-tech Firms in China. *Emerging Markets Finance & Trade*, 56(14), 3490–3506. 10.1080/1540496X.2019.1650348

Gao, W., Li, M., & Zou, C. (2023). Analysis of the Impact of ESG on Corporate Financial Performance under the Epidemic Based on Static and Dynamic Panel Data. *Wireless Communications and Mobile Computing*, 2023, 1–1. 10.1155/2023/9816809

Garcia, A. S., & Orsato, R. J. (2020). Testing the institutional difference hypothesis: A study about environmental, social, governance, and financial performance. *Business Strategy and the Environment*, 29(8), 3261–3272. 10.1002/bse.2570

Garcia, R., & Tsafack, G. (2011). Dependence structure and extreme comovements in international equity and bond markets. *Journal of Banking & Finance*, 35(8), 1954–1970. 10.1016/j.jbankfin.2011.01.003

Gardas, B. B., Mangla, S. K., Raut, R. D., Narkhede, B., & Luthra, S. (2019). Green talent management to unlock sustainability in the oil and gas sector. *Journal of Cleaner Production*, 229, 850–862. 10.1016/j.jclepro.2019.05.018

Gargouri, R. M., Shabou, R., & Francoeur, C. (2010). The relationship between corporate social performance and earnings management. *Canadian Journal of Administrative Sciences/Revue Canadienne Des Sciences De l'Administration, 27*(4), 320-334.

Gatti, L., Pizzetti, M., & Seele, P. (2021). Green lies and their effect on intention to invest. *Journal of Business Research*, 127, 228–240. 10.1016/j.jbusres.2021.01.028

Compilation of References

Gatti, L., Seele, P., & Rademacher, L. (2019). Grey zone in–greenwash out. A review of green-washing research and implications for the voluntary-mandatory transition of CSR. *International Journal of Corporate Social Responsibility*, 4(1), 1. Advance online publication. 10.1186/s40991-019-0044-9

Gavana, G., Gottardo, P., & Moisello, A. (2017). Earnings management and CSR disclosure. Family vs. non-family firms. *Sustainability (Basel)*, 9(12), 2327. 10.3390/su9122327

Gbolarumi, F. T., Wong, K. Y., & Olohunde, S. T. (2021). Sustainability Assessment in The Textile and Apparel Industry: A Review of Recent Studies. *IOP Conference Series. Materials Science and Engineering*, 1051(1), 012099. 10.1088/1757-899X/1051/1/012099

Geetha, S., & Biju, A. V. N. (2024). Is green FinTech reshaping the finance sphere? Unravelling through a systematic literature review. *Environmental Science and Pollution Research International*, 31(2), 1790–1810. 10.1007/s11356-023-31382-y38057679

Geissdoerfer, M., Pieroni, M. P. P., Pigosso, D. C. A., & Soufani, K. (2020). Circular business models: A review. In *Journal of Cleaner Production* (Vol. 277). Elsevier Ltd., 10.1016/j.jclepro.2020.123741

Geissdoerfer, M., Savaget, P., Bocken, N. M., & Hultink, E. J. (2017). The Circular Economy – A new sustainability paradigm? *Journal of Cleaner Production*, 143, 757–768. 10.1016/j.jclepro.2016.12.048

Geisser, S. (1974). A predictive approach to the random effect model. *Biometrika*, 61(1), 101–107. 10.1093/biomet/61.1.101

GEM. (2017). *GEM 2016/2017 Global Report*. London: GEM. Retrieved from https://www.gemconsortium.org/report/gem-2016-2017-global-report

Ghafran, C., & O'Sullivan, N. (2013). The Governance Role of Audit Committees: Reviewing a Decade of Evidence. *International Journal of Management Reviews*, 15(4), 381–407. 10.1111/j.1468-2370.2012.00347.x

Ghasemi Doudkanlou, M., Chandro, P., & Banihashemi, S. (2023). The Effect of Exit Time and Entropy on Asset Performance Evaluation. *Entropy (Basel, Switzerland)*, 25(9), 1252. 10.3390/e2509125237761551

Gibson, R., Krueger, P., & Schmidt, P. S. (2021). ESG rating disagreement and stock returns. *Financial Analysts Journal*, 77(4), 104–127. 10.1080/0015198X.2021.1963186

Giese, G., Lee, L. E., Melas, D., Nagy, Z., & Nishikawa, L. (2019). Foundations of ESG investing: How ESG affects equity valuation, risk, and performance. *Journal of Portfolio Management*, 45(5), 69–83. 10.3905/jpm.2019.45.5.069

Gillan, S. L., Koch, A., & Starks, L. T. (2021). Firms and social responsibility: A review of ESG and CSR research in corporate finance. *Journal of Corporate Finance*, 66, 101889. 10.1016/j.jcorpfin.2021.101889

Ginesti, G., Campa, D., Spano', R., Allini, A., & Maffei, M. (2023). The role of CSR committee characteristics on R&D investments. *International Business Review*, 32(5), 102147. 10.1016/j.ibusrev.2023.102147

Global Reporting Initiative (GRI). (2020). *GRI standards: Consolidated set of GRI standards 2020*. Retrieved from https://www.globalreporting.org/standards/gri-standards-download-center/consolidated-set-of-gri-standards-2020/

Global Sustainable Investment Alliance (GSIA). (2022). *Global Sustainable Investment Review*. Retrieved from https://www.gsi-alliance.org/wp-content/uploads/2023/12/GSIA-Report-2022.pdf

Glushakova, O. V., & Chernikova, O. P. (2023). Institutionalization of ESG-principles at the international level and in the Russian Federation, their impact on ferrous metallurgy enterprises. Part 1. *Izvestiâ Vysših Učebnyh Zavedenij. Černaâ Metallurgiâ, 66*(2), 253–264. 10.17073/0368-0797-2023-2-253-264

Gokkaya, S., Liu, X., Pool, V. K., Xie, F., & Zhang, J. (2023). Is there investment value in the soft-dollar arrangement? Evidence from mutual funds. *Review of Financial Studies*, 36(8), 3122–3162. 10.1093/rfs/hhad010

Gonçalves, T. C., Barros, V., & Avelar, J. V. (2023). Environmental, social and governance scores in Europe: What drives financial performance for larger firms? *Economics and Business Letters*, 12(2), 121–131. 10.17811/ebl.12.2.2023.121-131

Gonçalves, T., Pimentel, D., & Gaio, C. (2021). Risk and performance of European green and conventional funds. *Sustainability (Basel)*, 13(8), 4226. 10.3390/su13084226

Goodell, J. W., Li, M., Liu, D., & Wang, Y. (2024). Aligning empirical evidence on ESG with ancient conservative traditions. *International Review of Financial Analysis*, 94, 103284. 10.1016/j.irfa.2024.103284

Gordeev, V. A., Knyazev, A. G., & Shemyakin, A. E. (2012). Selection of copula model for inter-market dependence. *Model Assisted Statistics and Applications : An International Journal*, 7(4), 315–325. 10.3233/MAS-2012-0243

Górka, J., & Kuziak, K. (2022). Volatility modeling and dependence structure of ESG and conventional investments. *Risks*, 10(1), 20. 10.3390/risks10010020

Goswami, S. (2017, April 24). *Impact of Coal Mining on Environment: A Study of Raniganj and Jharia Coal Field in India*. The International Academic Forum (IAFOR). https://iafor.org/journal/iafor-journal-of-arts-and-humanities/volume-3-issue-1/article-1/

Goswami, M., & Krishnan, B. (2022). eHED2SDG: A Framework Towards Sustainable Professionalism and Attaining SDG Through Online Holistic Education in Indian Higher Education. *ECS Transactions*, 107(1), 15337–15347. 10.1149/10701.15337ecst

Govindan, K., Khodaverdi, R., & Jafarian, A. (2013). A fuzzy multi criteria approach for measuring sustainability performance of a supplier based on triple bottom line approach. *Journal of Cleaner Production*, 47, 345–354. 10.1016/j.jclepro.2012.04.014

Compilation of References

Govindan, K., Kilic, M., Uyar, A., & Karaman, A. S. (2021). Drivers and value-relevance of CSR performance in the logistics sector: A cross-country firm-level investigation. *International Journal of Production Economics*, 231, 107835. 10.1016/j.ijpe.2020.107835

Gozgor, G., Lau, C. K. M., & Lu, Z. (2018). Energy consumption and economic growth: New evidence from the OECD countries. *Energy*, 153, 27–34. 10.1016/j.energy.2018.03.158

Gras-Gil, E., Manzano, M. P., & Fernández, J. H. (2016). Investigating the relationship between corporate social responsibility and earnings management: Evidence from Spain. *Business Research Quarterly*, 19(4), 289–299. 10.1016/j.brq.2016.02.002

Gray, P., Koh, P. S., & Tong, Y. H. (2009). Accruals quality, information risk and cost of capital: Evidence from Australia. *Journal of Business Finance & Accounting*, 36(1-2), 51–72. 10.1111/j.1468-5957.2008.02118.x

Gray, R., Kouhy, R., & Lavers, S. (1995). Corporate social and environmental reporting: A review of the literature and a longitudinal study of UK disclosure. *Accounting, Auditing & Accountability Journal*, 8(2), 47–77. 10.1108/09513579510146996

Greiner, M., & Sun, J. (2021). How corporate social responsibility can incentivize top managers: A commitment to sustainability as an agency intervention. *Corporate Social Responsibility and Environmental Management*, 28(4), 1360–1375. 10.1002/csr.2148

Grewal, D., Gauri, D. K., Roggeveen, A. L., & Sethuraman, R. (2021). Strategizing retailing in the new technology era. *Journal of Retailing*, 97(1), 6–12. 10.1016/j.jretai.2021.02.004

Grissom, A. R. (2018). Workplace diversity and inclusion. *Reference and User Services Quarterly*, 57(4), 242–247. https://www.jstor.org/stable/90022643. 10.5860/rusq.57.4.6700

Grossman, S. J., & Hart, O. D. (1980). Disclosure laws and takeover bids. *The Journal of Finance*, 35(2), 323–334. 10.1111/j.1540-6261.1980.tb02161.x

Guerard, J. B. (1997). Is there a cost to being socially responsible in investing? *Journal of Forecasting*, 16(7), 475–490. 10.1002/(SICI)1099-131X(199712)16:7<475::AID-FOR668>3.0.CO;2-X

Gupta, H., & Chaudhary, R. (2023). An Analysis of Volatility and Risk-Adjusted Returns of ESG Indices in Developed and Emerging Economies. *Risks*, 11(10), 182. 10.3390/risks11100182

Guthrie, J., & Parker, L. D. (1990). Corporate social disclosure practice: a comparative international analysis. *Advances in public interest accounting, 3*, 159-175.

Gu, W., Pan, H., Hu, Z., & Liu, Z. (2022). The Triple Bottom Line of Sustainable Entrepreneurship and Economic Policy Uncertainty: An Empirical Evidence from 22 Countries. *International Journal of Environmental Research and Public Health*, 19(13), 7758. 10.3390/ijerph1913775835805416

Gwalani, H., & Mazumdar, S. (2022). ESG Reporting – Genesis And Significance. *The Management Accountant Journal*, 57(3), 53. 10.33516/maj.v57i3.53-57p

Habib, A. M. (2023). Do business strategies and environmental, social, and governance (ESG) performance mitigate the likelihood of financial distress? A multiple mediation model. *Heliyon*, 9(7), e17847. 10.1016/j.heliyon.2023.e1784737483754

Hahn, T., Pinkse, J., Preuss, L., & Figge, F. (2015). Tensions in corporate sustainability: Towards an integrative framework. *Journal of Business Ethics*, 127(2), 297–316. 10.1007/s10551-014-2047-5

Hair, F.Jr, J., Sarstedt, M., Hopkins, L., & G. Kuppelwieser, V. (. (2014). Partial least squares structural equation modeling (PLS-SEM) An emerging tool in business research. *European Business Review*, 26(2), 106–121. 10.1108/EBR-10-2013-0128

Hair, J. F.Jr, Matthews, L. M., Matthews, R. L., & Sarstedt, M. (2017). PLS-SEM or CB-SEM: Updated guidelines on which method to use. *International Journal of Multivariate Data Analysis*, 1(2), 107–123. 10.1504/IJMDA.2017.087624

Haldar, S., Peddibhotla, A., & Bazaz, A. (2023, March 9). *Analysing intersections of justice with energy transitions in India: A systematic literature review.* Lund University. https://portal .research.lu.se/en/publications/analysing-intersections-of-justice-with-energy-transitions-in-ind

Halme, M., Rintamäki, J., Knudsen, J. S., Lankoski, L., & Kuisma, M. (2020). When Is There a Sustainability Case for CSR? Pathways to Environmental and Social Performance Improvements. *Business & Society*, 59(6), 1181–1227. 10.1177/0007650318755648

Halttunen, L., & Inkilä, J. (2014). Corporate responsibility reporting on the consumer perspective: Case: Coca-Cola Company.

Hamed, R. S., Al-Shattarat, B. K., Al-Shattarat, W. K., & Hussainey, K. (2022). The impact of introducing new regulations on the quality of CSR reporting: Evidence from the UK. *Journal of International Accounting, Auditing & Taxation*, 46, 100444. 10.1016/j.intaccaudtax.2021.100444

Hamrouni, A., Bouattour, M., Ben Farhat Toumi, N., & Boussaada, R. (2021). Corporate social responsibility disclosure and information asymmetry: Does boardroom attributes matter? *Journal of Applied Accounting Research*, 23(5), 897–920. 10.1108/JAAR-03-2021-0056

Hanna, R., Heptonstall, P., & Gross, R. (2024, January 11). *Job creation in a low carbon transition to renewables and energy efficiency: A review of international evidence.* SpringerLink. https://link.springer.com/article/10.1007/s11625-023-01440-y

Hardjono, T. W., & van Marrewijk, M. (2001). The Social Dimensions of Business Excellence. *Corporate Environmental Strategy*, 8(3), 223–233. 10.1016/S1066-7938(01)00125-7

Harnos, R. (2022). ESG (Environmental Social Governance) beim Vertrieb von Finanzprodukten. *Zeitschrift Für Das Gesamte Bank- Und Börsenwesen*, 70(12), 882. 10.47782/oeba202212088201

Härri, A., & Levänen, J. (2024). "It should be much faster fashion"— Textile industry stakeholders' perceptions of a just circular transition in Tamil Nadu, India. *Discover Sustainability*, 5(1), 39. Advance online publication. 10.1007/s43621-024-00211-8

Compilation of References

Harris, R. D. F., & Tzavalis, E. (1999). Inference for unit roots in dynamic panels where the time dimension is fixed. *Journal of Econometrics*, 91(2), 201–226. 10.1016/S0304-4076(98)00076-1

Hart, S. L., & Milstein, M. B. (2003). Creating Sustainable Value. *The Academy of Management Perspectives*, 17(2), 56–67. 10.5465/ame.2003.10025194

Hartzmark, S. M., & Sussman, A. B. (2019). Do investors value sustainability? A natural experiment examining ranking and fund flows. *The Journal of Finance*, 74(6), 2789–2837. 10.1111/jofi.12841

Harvard Business Review. (2024). *Two Factors that Determine When ESG Creates Shareholder Value*. Retrieved from https://hbr.org/2024/02/two-factors-that-determine-when-esg-creates -shareholder-value

Hauff, J. C., & Nilsson, J. (2022). Is ESG mutual fund quality in the eye of the beholder? An experimental study of investor responses to ESG fund strategies. *Business Strategy and the Environment*. Advance online publication. 10.1002/bse.3181

Haw, I., Hu, B., Hwang, L. S., & Wu, W. (2004). Ultimate ownership, income management, and legal and extra-legal institutions. *Journal of Accounting Research*, 42(2), 423–462. 10.1111/j.1475-679X.2004.00144.x

Hawkins, G. (2011). Packaging water: Plastic bottles as market and public devices. *Economy and Society*, 40(4), 534–552. 10.1080/03085147.2011.602295

Hawley, J. P., & Williams, A. T. (2000). *The rise of fiduciary capitalism: How institutional investors can make corporate America more democratic*. University of Pennsylvania Press.

Hawn, O., Chatterji, A. K., & Mitchell, L. (2018). Do investors actually value sustainability? New evidence from investor reactions to the Dow Jones sustainability index (DJSI). *Strategic Management Journal*, 39(4), 949–976. 10.1002/smj.2752

Haws, J. W. (2022). Cherry red greenwashing: The rhetoric behind corporate recycling narratives (Doctoral dissertation, Brigham Young University). ProQuest Dissertations Publishing.

Heal, G. M. (2008). *When principles pay: corporate social responsibility and the bottom line*. Columbia University Press. 10.7312/heal14400

Healy, P. M., & Palepu, K. G. (2001). Information asymmetry, corporate disclosure, and the capital markets: A review of the empirical disclosure literature. *Journal of Accounting and Economics*, 31(1-3), 405–440. 10.1016/S0165-4101(01)00018-0

Healy, P. M., & Wahlen, J. M. (1999). A review of the earnings management literature and its implications for standard setting. *Accounting Horizons*, 13(4), 365–383. 10.2308/acch.1999.13.4.365

Helms, B. (2023). *5 Ways to Better support social entrepreneurs*. Forbes.

Hengst, I. A., Jarzabkowski, P., Hoegl, M., & Muethel, M. (2020). Toward a process theory of making sustainability strategies legitimate in action. *Academy of Management Journal*, 63(1), 246–271. 10.5465/amj.2016.0960

He, W. P., Lepone, A., & Leung, H. (2013). Information asymmetry and the cost of equity capital. *International Review of Economics & Finance*, 27, 611–620. 10.1016/j.iref.2013.03.001

Hillman, A. J., Cannella, A. A., & Paetzold, R. L. (2000). The resource dependency role of corporate directors: Strategic adaptation of board composition in response to environmental change. *Journal of Management Studies*, 37(2), 235–256. 10.1111/1467-6486.00179

HKEX. 2020. Performance of ESG Equity Indices Versus Traditional Equity Indices. Available online: https://www.hkex.com.hk/-/media/HKEX-Market/News/Research-Reports/HKEx -Research-Papers/2020/CCEO_ESGEqIdx_202011_e.pdf

Hoang, H. V., Ha, S. T., Tran, M. L., & Nguyen, T. T. T. (2022). Is auditor tolerant of earnings management in socially responsible firms? Evidence from China. *Asian Review of Accounting*, 30(5), 669–690. 10.1108/ARA-01-2022-0001

Hofert, M., Kojadinovic, I., Maechler, M., & Yan, J. (2014). Copula: Multivariate dependence with copulas. R package version 0.999-9, URL http://CRAN. R-project. org/package= copula, C225.

Hofert, M., & Mächler, M. (2011). Nested Archimedean copulas meet R: The nacopula package. *Journal of Statistical Software*, 39(9), 1–20. 10.18637/jss.v039.i09

Holcomb, J. L., Upchurch, R. S., & Okumus, F. (2007). Corporate social responsibility: What are top hotel companies reporting? *International Journal of Contemporary Hospitality Management*, 19(6), 461–475. 10.1108/09596110710775129

Holtström, J., Bjellerup, C., & Eriksson, J. (2019). Business model development for sustainable apparel consumption: The case of Houdini Sportswear. *Journal of Strategy and Management*, 12(4), 481–504. 10.1108/JSMA-01-2019-0015

Holzendorff, G. D. (2013). Living on the Coke side of thirst: The Coca-Cola Company and responsibility for water shortage in India. *Journal of European Management & Public Affairs Studies*, 1(1), 1–4. 10.15771/2199-1618_2013_1_1_6

Hong, H., & Kacperczyk, M. (2009). The price of sin: The effects of social norms on markets. *Journal of Financial Economics*, 93(1), 15–36. 10.1016/j.jfineco.2008.09.001

Hopkins, M. J. D. (2002). Sustainability in the Internal Operations of Companies. *Corporate Environmental Strategy*, 9(4), 398–408. 10.1016/S1066-7938(02)00121-5

Hopkins, M., & Cowe, R. (2003). *Corporate social responsibility: is there a business case.* ACCA UK.

Hora, S. T., Bungau, C., Negru, P. A., & Radu, A.-F. (2023). Implementing Circular Economy Elements in the Textile Industry: A Bibliometric Analysis. *Sustainability (Basel)*, 15(20), 15130. 10.3390/su152015130

Compilation of References

Hosseinniakani, M., Overland, C., & Samani, N. (2024). Do key audit matters matter? Correspondence between auditor and management disclosures and the role of audit committees. *Journal of International Accounting, Auditing & Taxation*, 55, 100617. 10.1016/j.intaccaudtax.2024.100617

Hou, F., Ng, J., Rusticus, T., & Xu, X. (2019). Foreign capital and earnings management: International evidence from equity market openings. University of Hawai'i. http://hdl.handle.net/10125/59269

How the clean energy transition affects workers and communities. (2020, August 11). Environmental Defense Fund. https://www.edf.org/how-clean-energy-transition-affects-workers-and-communities

Hoyas, S. (2022). *ASDG — An AI-based framework for automatic classification of impact on the SDGs.* 10.1145/3560107.3560128

Huang, Q., Li, Y., Lin, M., & McBrayer, G. A. (2022). Natural disasters, risk salience, and corporate ESG disclosure. *Journal of Corporate Finance*, 72, 102152. 10.1016/j.jcorpfin.2021.102152

Hughes, J. S., Liu, J., & Liu, J. (2007). Information asymmetry, diversification, and cost of capital. *The Accounting Review*, 82(3), 705–729. 10.2308/accr.2007.82.3.705

Hummel, K., & Schlick, C. (2016). The relationship between sustainability performance and sustainability disclosure–Reconciling voluntary disclosure theory and legitimacy theory. *Journal of Accounting and Public Policy*, 35(5), 455–476. 10.1016/j.jaccpubpol.2016.06.001

Hung, M., Shi, J., & Wang, Y. (2015). Mandatory CSR disclosure and information asymmetry: Evidence from a quasi-natural experiment in China. In *The Asian Finance Conference 2013.*

Hung, N. T. (2021). Green bonds and asset classes: New evidence from time-varying copula and transfer entropy models. *Global Business Review*, 097215092110340. Advance online publication. 10.1177/09721509211034095

Hunton, J. E., Libby, R., & Mazza, C. L. (2006). Financial reporting transparency and earnings management (retracted). *The Accounting Review*, 81(1), 135–157. 10.2308/accr.2006.81.1.135

Hutchins, M. J., & Sutherland, J. W. (2008). An exploration of measures of social sustainability and their application to supply chain decisions. *Journal of Cleaner Production*, 16(15), 1688–1698. 10.1016/j.jclepro.2008.06.001

Ielasi, F., & Rossolini, M. (2019a). A New Approach to Sustainable and Responsible Investment: The Sustainability-Themed Mutual Funds. *Socially Responsible Investments: The Crossroads Between Institutional and Retail Investors*, 125–148.

Ielasi, F., & Rossolini, M. (2019b). Responsible or thematic? The true nature of sustainability-themed mutual funds. *Sustainability (Basel)*, 11(12), 3304. 10.3390/su11123304

Ielasi, F., Rossolini, M., & Limberti, S. (2018). Sustainability-themed mutual funds: An empirical examination of risk and performance. *The Journal of Risk Finance*, 19(3), 247–261. 10.1108/JRF-12-2016-0159

Ihsani, A. N., Nidar, S. R., & Kurniawan, M. (2023). Does ESG Performance Affect Financial Performance? Evidence from Indonesia. *Wiga : Jurnal Penelitian Ilmu Ekonomi*, 13(1), 46–61. 10.30741/wiga.v13i1.968

Ilieva, M. V. (2022). Chapter 7. The Interconnection Among Social, Environmental, and Economic Aspects of the 17 SDGs. *Nomos Verlagsgesellschaft MbH & Co. KG EBooks*, 127–150. 10.5771/9783748933090-127

ILO. (2021). *ILO global estimates on international migrant workers: Results and methodology.* International Labour Organization. Retrieved from https://www.ilo.org/international-labour -standards

Im, K. S., Pesaran, M. H., & Shin, Y. (2003). Testing for unit roots in heterogeneous panels. *Journal of Econometrics*, 115(1), 53–74. 10.1016/S0304-4076(03)00092-7

India to burn 38% more coal every year with new plans for thermal power. (2023, September 19). Business Standard. https://www.google.com/url?q=https://www.business-standard.com/ industry/news/india-to-burn-38-more-coal-every-year-with-new-plans-for-thermal-power -123091900478_1.html%255B4&sa=D&source=docs&ust=1718864827070774&usg= AOvVaw2tFkJht3xiRJLe6ZcVmpTk

Indrayani, L., & Triwiswara, M. (2020). Implementation green industry standard at textile industry and textile product. *IOP Conference Series. Earth and Environmental Science*, 456(1), 012049. Advance online publication. 10.1088/1755-1315/456/1/012049

Inglesi-Lotz, R. (2016). The impact of renewable energy consumption to economic growth: A panel data application. *Energy Economics*, 53, 58–63. 10.1016/j.eneco.2015.01.003

Inoue, Y., & Lee, S. (2011). Effects of different dimensions of corporate social responsibility on corporate financial performance in tourism-related industries. *Tourism Management*, 32(4), 790–804. 10.1016/j.tourman.2010.06.019

Ioannou, I., & Serafeim, G. (2012). What drives corporate social performance? The role of nation-level institutions. *Journal of International Business Studies*, 43(9), 834–864. 10.1057/jibs.2012.26

Iqbal, M. (2022). *Pakistan sees growing culture of innovation amid tech startup boom.* Atlantic Council.

Işık, C., & Ongan, S. Islam, H., Pinzon, S., & Jabeen, G. (2024). Navigating sustainability: Unveiling the interconnected dynamics of ESG factors and SDGs in BRICS-11. *Sustainable Development*. Advance online publication. 10.1002/sd.2977

Islam, M. M., Perry, P., & Gill, S. (2021). Mapping environmentally sustainable practices in textiles, apparel and fashion industries: A systematic literature review. *Journal of Fashion Marketing and Management*, 25(2), 331–353. 10.1108/JFMM-07-2020-0130

ISO. (2021). *ISO 26000: Guidance on social responsibility.* Retrieved from https://www.iso.org/ standard/42546.html

Compilation of References

Jack, L. Treynor. (1961). Market Value, Time, and Risk. SSRN.

Jain, K., & Tripathi, P. S. (2023). Mapping the environmental, social and governance literature: A bibliometric and content analysis. *Journal of Strategy and Management*. 10.1108/JSMA-05-2022-0092

Jain, M., Sharma, G. D., & Srivastava, M. (2019). Can sustainable investment yield better financial returns: A comparative study of ESG indices and MSCI indices. *Risks*, 7(1), 15. 10.3390/risks7010015

Jamali, D. (2008). A Stakeholder Approach to Corporate Social Responsibility: A Fresh Perspective into Theory and Practice. *Journal of Business Ethics*, 82(1), 213–231. 10.1007/s10551-007-9572-4

Jamali, D. R., Ahmad, I., Aboelmaged, M., & Usman, M. (2024). Corporate social responsibility in the United Arab Emirates and globally: A cross-national comparison. *Journal of Cleaner Production*, 434, 140105. 10.1016/j.jclepro.2023.140105

Jamali, D., & Karam, C. (2018). Corporate Social Responsibility in Developing Countries as an Emerging Field of Study. *International Journal of Management Reviews*, 20(1), 32–61. 10.1111/ijmr.12112

Jamali, D., & Mirshak, R. (2006). Corporate Social Responsibility (CSR): Theory and Practice in a Developing Country Context. *Journal of Business Ethics*, 72(3), 243–262. 10.1007/s10551-006-9168-4

James, A. S. J., & Kent, A. (2019). Clothing Sustainability and Upcycling in Ghana. *Fashion Practice*, 11(3), 375–396. 10.1080/17569370.2019.1661601

Jana, S. K. (2022). Sustainable energy development in emerging economies: A study on BRICS. In *Environmental Sustainability, Growth Trajectory and Gender: Contemporary Issues of Developing Economies* (pp. 23-35). Emerald Publishing Limited. 10.1108/978-1-80262-153-220221002

Janjuha-Jivraj, S., & Pasha, N. (2021). *Futureproof Your Career: How to Lead and Succeed in a Changing World*. Bloomsbury Publishing.

Jehan. (2022). *10 sustainability startups in Pakistan*. Katalystlabs.

Jemel-Fornetty, H., Louche, C., & Bourghelle, D. (2011). Changing the dominant convention: The role of emerging initiatives in mainstreaming ESG. *Critical Studies on Corporate Responsibility. Governance and Sustainability*, 2, 85–117. 10.1108/S2043-9059(2011)0000002011/FULL/XML

Jenkins, H., & Yakovleva, N. (2006). Corporate social responsibility in the mining industry: Exploring trends in social and environmental disclosure. *Journal of Cleaner Production*, 14(3-4), 271–284. 10.1016/j.jclepro.2004.10.004

Jensen, J. C., & Berg, N. (2012). Determinants of traditional sustainability reporting versus integrated reporting. An institutionalist approach. *Business Strategy and the Environment*, 21(5), 299–316. 10.1002/bse.740

Jensen, M. C. (1968). The performance of mutual funds in the period 1945-1964. *The Journal of Finance*, 23(2), 389–416.

Jensen, M. C., & Meckling, W. H. (1976). Theory of the firm: Managerial behavior, agency costs and ownership structure. *Journal of Financial Economics*, 3(4), 305–360. 10.1016/0304-405X(76)90026-X

Jha, A. K., & Verma, N. K. (2023). Social media sustainability communication: An analysis of firm behaviour and stakeholder responses. *Information Systems Frontiers*, 25(3), 723–742. 10.1007/s10796-022-10257-6

Jiao, J., Tong, L., & Yan, A. (2021). Catering incentive and corporate social responsibility. [Preprint]. *SSRN*. http://dx.doi.org/10.2139/ssrn.3536960

Jin, I. (2022). ESG-screening and factor-risk-adjusted performance: The concentration level of screening does matter. *Journal of Sustainable Finance & Investment*, 12(4), 1125–1145. 10.1080/20430795.2020.1837501

Joe, H. (1997). *Multivariate Models and Multivariate Dependence Concepts*. Chapman and Hall.

Jo, H., & Harjoto, M. A. (2011). Corporate governance and firm value: The impact of corporate social responsibility. *Journal of Business Ethics*, 103(3), 351–383. 10.1007/s10551-011-0869-y

Jo, H., Kim, H., & Park, K. (2015). Corporate Environmental Responsibility and Firm Performance in the Financial Services Sector. *Journal of Business Ethics*, 131(2), 257–284. 10.1007/s10551-014-2276-7

Jo, H., & Kim, Y. (2007). Disclosure frequency and earnings management. *Journal of Financial Economics*, 84(2), 561–590. 10.1016/j.jfineco.2006.03.007

Johnson, S., Boone, P., Breach, A., & Friedman, E. (2000). Corporate governance in the Asian financial crisis. *Journal of Financial Economics*, 58(1), 141–186. 10.1016/S0304-405X(00)00069-6

Joh, S. W. (2003). Corporate governance and firm profitability: Evidence from Korea before the economic crisis. *Journal of Financial Economics*, 68(2), 287–322. 10.1016/S0304-405X(03)00068-0

Jondeau, E. (2016). Asymmetry in tail dependence in equity portfolios. *Computational Statistics & Data Analysis*, 100, 351–368. 10.1016/j.csda.2015.02.014

Jones, E. (2019). Rethinking greenwashing: Corporate discourse, unethical practice, and the unmet potential of ethical consumerism. *Sociological Perspectives*, 62(5), 728–754. 10.1177/0731121419849095

Jones, P., Comfort, D., & Hillier, D. (2006). Reporting and reflecting on corporate social responsibility in the hospitality industry: A case study of pub operators in the UK. *International Journal of Contemporary Hospitality Management*, 18(4), 329–340. 10.1108/09596110610665339

Compilation of References

Jones, P., Comfort, D., & Hillier, D. (2017). Corporate social responsibility in the boardroom: Balancing shareholder and stakeholder interests. *Business Strategy and the Environment*, 26(3), 297–312.

Jones, T. M. (1995). Instrumental stakeholder theory: A synthesis of ethics and economics. *Academy of Management Review*, 20(2), 404–437. 10.2307/258852

Jørgensen, M. S., & Remmen, A. (2018). A Methodological Approach to Development of Circular Economy Options in Businesses. *Procedia CIRP*, 69, 816–821. 10.1016/j.procir.2017.12.002

Kabir, S. M., & Rabbi, F. (2017). Corporate sustainability reporting on environmental issue: An assessment of CSR framework for Lever Brothers Bangladesh. *Malaysian Construction Research Journal, Special Issue 1*(1). https://researchonline.nd.edu.au/bus_article/90

Kao C. Spurious regression and residual-based tests for cointegration in paneldata. J Econom 1999;90:1e44. .10.1016/S0304-4076(98)00023-2

Kao, T.-Y., Chen, J. C. H., Wu, J.-T. B., & Yang, M.-H. (2016). Poverty Reduction through Empowerment for Sustainable Development: A Proactive Strategy of Corporate Social Responsibility. *Corporate Social Responsibility and Environmental Management*, 23(3), 140–149. 10.1002/csr.1365

Katamba, D. (n.d.). *STRENGTHENING HEALTH CARE SYSTEMS: PRIVATE FOR-PROFIT COMPANIES' CORPORATE SOCIAL RESPONSIBILITY ENGAGEMENTS - Document - Gale Academic OneFile*. Retrieved June 22, 2024, from https://go.gale.com/ps/i.do?id=GALE%7CA513854428&sid=googleScholar&v=2.1&it=r&linkaccess=abs&issn=23304103&p=AONE&sw=w&userGroupName=anon%7E29efc51f&aty=open-web-entry

Katmon, N., Mohamad, Z. Z., Norwani, N. M., & Farooque, O. A. (2019). Comprehensive Board Diversity and Quality of Corporate Social Responsibility Disclosure: Evidence from an Emerging Market. *Journal of Business Ethics*, 157(2), 447–481. 10.1007/s10551-017-3672-6

Kaur, N., & Singh, V. (2021). Empirically examining the impact of corporate social responsibility on financial performance: Evidence from Indian steel industry. *Asian Journal of Accounting Research*, 6(2), 134–151. 10.1108/AJAR-07-2020-0061

Kazemi, H., & Rahmani, F. (2013). Relationship between information asymmetry and cost of capital. *Management Science Letters*, 3(1), 321–328. 10.5267/j.msl.2012.10.026

Keinath, A. K., & Walo, J. C. (2004). Audit Committee Responsibilities: Focusing on Oversight, Open Communication, and Best Practices. *The CPA Journal*, ●●●, 22–28.

Keith, D., & Krol, A. (2023, July 24). *Electric vehicles*. MIT Climate Portal. https://climate.mit.edu/explainers/electric-vehicles

Kennedy, S., Grewatsch, S., Liboni, L., & Cezarino, L. O. (2021). *A systems approach to business sustainability education*. Proceedings., 10.5465/AMBPP.2021.227

Keshavarz Ghorabaee, M., Amiri, M., Zavadskas, E. K., Turskis, Z., & Antucheviciene, J. (2017). A new multi-criteria model based on interval type-2 fuzzy sets and EDAS method for supplier evaluation and order allocation with environmental considerations. *Computers & Industrial Engineering*, 112, 156–174. 10.1016/j.cie.2017.08.017

Khadke, S., Gupta, P., Rachakunta, S., Mahata, C., Dawn, S., Sharma, M., Verma, D., Pradhan, A., Krishna, A. M. S., Ramakrishna, S., Chakrabortty, S., Saianand, G., Sonar, P., Biring, S., Dash, J. K., & Dalapati, G. K. (2021). Efficient Plastic Recycling and Remolding Circular Economy Using the Technology of Trust–Blockchain. *Sustainability (Basel)*, 13(16), 16. 10.3390/su13169142

Khan, A., Muttakin, M. B., & Siddiqui, J. (2013). Corporate Governance and Corporate Social Responsibility Disclosures: Evidence from an Emerging Economy. *Journal of Business Ethics*, 114(2), 207–223. 10.1007/s10551-012-1336-0

Khanchel, I., & Lassoued, N. (2022). ESG Disclosure and the Cost of Capital: Is There a Ratcheting Effect over Time? *Sustainability (Basel)*, 14(15), 9237. 10.3390/su14159237

Khan, I., & Fatma, M. (2023). CSR Influence on Brand Image and Consumer Word of Mouth: Mediating Role of Brand Trust. *Sustainability (Basel)*, 15(4), 3409. 10.3390/su15043409

Khan, I., Hou, F., Zakari, A., & Tawiah, V. K. (2021). The dynamic links among energy transitions, energy consumption, and sustainable economic growth: A novel framework for IEA countries. *Energy*, 222, 119935. 10.1016/j.energy.2021.119935

Khan, M., Serafeim, G., & Yoon, A. (2016). Corporate sustainability: First evidence on materiality. *The Accounting Review*, 91(6), 1697–1724. 10.2308/accr-51383

Khanna, T., & Palepu, K. (2000). Is group affiliation profitable in emerging markets? *The Journal of Finance*, 55(2), 867–891. 10.1111/0022-1082.00229

Khan, O., Daddi, T., & Iraldo, F. (2020). Microfoundations of dynamic capabilities: Insights from circular economy business cases. *Business Strategy and the Environment*, 29(3), 1479–1493. 10.1002/bse.2447

Khuong, M. N., Truong an, N. K., & Thanh Hang, T. T. (2021). Stakeholders and Corporate Social Responsibility (CSR) programme as key sustainable development strategies to promote corporate reputation—Evidence from vietnam. *Cogent Business & Management*, 8(1), 1917333. 10.1080/23311975.2021.1917333

Khurram, M. U., Abbassi, W., Chen, Y., & Chen, L. (2024). Outward foreign investment performance, digital transformation, and ESG performance: Evidence from China. *Global Finance Journal*, 60, 100963. 10.1016/j.gfj.2024.100963

Khutorova, N. A., Gazizova, A. V., & Gazizov, D. N. (2023). ESG approaches in strategic management of economic systems at the federal and regional levels. *Nacional nye Interesy: Prioritety I Bezopasnost , 19*(5), 866–882. https://doi.org/10.24891/ni.19.5.866

Compilation of References

Kihn, E. A., Zhizhin, M., Siquig, R., & Redmon, R. (2004). The Environmental Scenario Generator (ESG): A distributed environmental data archive analysis tool. *Data Science Journal*, 3, 10–28. 10.2481/dsj.3.10

Kilanioti, I., & Papadopoulos, G. A. (2023). A knowledge graph-based deep learning framework for efficient content similarity search of Sustainable Development Goals data. *Data Intelligence (Online)*, 1–19. 10.1162/dint_a_00206

Kim, C.-S. (2019). Can socially responsible investments be compatible with financial performance? A meta-analysis. *Asia-Pacific Journal of Financial Studies*, 48(1), 30–64. 10.1111/ajfs.12244

Kim, D.-G., Grieco, E., Bombelli, A., Hickman, J. E., & Sanz-Cobena, A. (2021). Challenges and opportunities for enhancing food security and greenhouse gas mitigation in smallholder farming in sub-Saharan Africa: A review. *Food Security*, 13(2), 457–476. 10.1007/s12571-021-01149-9

Kim, D., Park, J., & Wiersema, M. (2023). ESG Performance and Firm Value: The Moderating Role of Industry Competition and Demand Growth. *Strategic Management Journal*, 44(2), 402–423.

Kim, E.-H., & Lyon, T. (2011). When does institutional investor activism increase shareholder value? The Carbon Disclosure Project. *The B.E. Journal of Economic Analysis & Policy*, 11(1), 50–50. 10.2202/1935-1682.2676

Kim, J. B., & Sohn, B. C. (2013). Real earnings management and cost of capital. *Journal of Accounting and Public Policy*, 32(6), 518–543. 10.1016/j.jaccpubpol.2013.08.002

Kim, Y., Park, M. S., & Wier, B. (2012). Is earnings quality associated with corporate social responsibility? *The Accounting Review*, 87(3), 761–796. 10.2308/accr-10209

Kirk, M. P., & Vincent, J. D. (2014). Professional investor relations within the firm. *The Accounting Review*, 89(4), 1421–1452. 10.2308/accr-50724

Kodiyatt, S. J., Nair, B. A. V., Jacob, M. S., & Reddy, K. (2024). Does green bond issuance enhance market return of equity shares in the Indian stock market?*. *Asia-Pacific Journal of Financial Studies*, 02(3), 1–20. 10.1111/ajfs.12459

Koh, H.-K., Burnasheva, R., & Suh, Y. (2022). Perceived ESG (Environmental, Social, Governance) and consumers' responses: The mediating role of brand credibility, brand image, and perceived quality. *Sustainability (Basel)*, 14(8), 4515. Advance online publication. 10.3390/su14084515

Kojadinovic, I., & Yan, J. (2010). Modeling Multivariate distributions with continuous margins using the copula RPackage. *Journal of Statistical Software*, 34(9). Advance online publication. 10.18637/jss.v034.i09

Kolk, A., & Pinkse, J. (2010). The integration of corporate governance in corporate social responsibility disclosures. *Corporate Social Responsibility and Environmental Management*, 17(1), 15–26. 10.1002/csr.196

Konrad, A. M., Kramer, V., & Erkut, S. (2008). The impact of three or more women on corporate boards. *Organizational Dynamics*, 37(2), 145–164. 10.1016/j.orgdyn.2008.02.005

Koroleva, E., Baggieri, M., & Nalwanga, S. (2020). Company performance: Are environmental, social, and governance factors important. *International Journal of Technology*, 11(8), 1468–1477. 10.14716/ijtech.v11i8.4527

Kothari, S. P., Leone, A. J., & Wasley, C. E. (2005). Performance matched discretionary accrual measures. *Journal of Accounting and Economics*, 39(1), 163–197. 10.1016/j.jacceco.2004.11.002

Kotsantonis, S., Pinney, C., & Serafeim, G. (2016). ESG integration in investment management: Myths and realities. *The Bank of America Journal of Applied Corporate Finance*, 28(2), 10–16. http://highmeadowsinstitute.org/wp-content/uploads/2014/05/JACF-ESG-Integration-Myths-and-Realities.pdf. 10.1111/jacf.12169

KPMG. (2020). *KPMG International Survey of Sustainability Reporting 2020*. KPMG International Cooperative.

KPMG. (2021). *Climate change and corporate value*. https://assets.kpmg.com/content/dam/kpmg/xx/pdf/2021/03/climate-change-and-corporate-value.pdf

KPMG. (2023). *Transparency Report 2023*. Retrieved from https://assets.kpmg.com/content/dam/kpmg/ie/pdf/2024/05/ie-transparency-report-2023.pdf

Kraft, J., & Kraft, A. (1978). On the relationship between energy and GNP. *The Journal of Energy and Development*, 401-403.

Krasodomska, J., Simnett, R., & Street, D. L. (2021). Extended external reporting assurance: Current practices and challenges. *Journal of International Financial Management & Accounting*, 32(1), 104–142. 10.1111/jifm.12127

Kräussl, R., Oladiran, T., & Stefanova, D. (2024). A review on ESG investing: Investors' expectations, beliefs and perceptions. *Journal of Economic Surveys*, 38(2), 476–502. 10.1111/joes.12599

Kumar, V., & Srivastava, A. (2016). Performance Evaluation of Private Sector Mutual Funds. *International Journal of Trend in Research of Development*, 3(1), 201–210.

Kwok, K. (2022). *The 6 Ps of empowering youth social entrepreneurs*. World Economic Forum.

La Porta, R., Lopez-de-Silanes, F., Shleifer, A., & Vishny, R. (2000). Investor protection and corporate governance. *Journal of Financial Economics*, 58(1), 3–27. 10.1016/S0304-405X(00)00065-9

Lai, A., Melloni, G., & Stacchezzini, R. (2016). Corporate Sustainable Development: Is 'Integrated Reporting' a Legitimation Strategy? *Business Strategy and the Environment*, 25(3), 165–177. 10.1002/bse.1863

Lai, S., & Li, H. (2008). The performance evaluation for fund of funds by comparing asset allocation of mean–variance model or genetic algorithms to that of fund managers. *Applied Financial Economics*, 18(6), 485–501. 10.1080/09603100600970099

Lal Bhasin, M. (2013). Corporate Accounting Fraud: A Case Study of Satyam Computers Limited. *Open Journal of Accounting*, 02(02), 26–38. 10.4236/ojacct.2013.22006

Compilation of References

Laluc, C. (2020). *Social Entrepreneurs Have Improved 622 Million Lives: Schwab Foundation Report*. Davos: WEF. Retrieved from https://www.weforum.org/press/2020/01/social-entrepreneurs -have-improved-622-million-lives-schwab-foundation-report/

Lambert, R. A., Leuz, C., & Verrecchia, R. E. (2011). Information asymmetry, information precision, and the cost of capital. *Review of Finance*, 16(1), 1–29. 10.1093/rof/rfr014

Lambert, R., Leuz, C., & Verrecchia, R. E. (2007). Accounting information, disclosure, and the cost of capital. *Journal of Accounting Research*, 45(2), 385–420. 10.1111/j.1475-679X.2007.00238.x

Lamm, E., Tosti-Kharas, J., & King, C. E. (2015). Empowering Employee Sustainability: Perceived Organizational Support Toward the Environment. *Journal of Business Ethics*, 128(1), 207–220. 10.1007/s10551-014-2093-z

Lamy, E. (2019). How to Make Social Entrepreneurship Sustainable? A Diagnosis and a Few Elements of a Response. *Journal of Business Ethics*, 155(3), 645–662. 10.1007/s10551-017-3485-7

Landrum, N. E., & Ohsowski, B. (2018). Identifying Worldviews on Corporate Sustainability: A Content Analysis of Corporate Sustainability Reports. *Business Strategy and the Environment*, 27(1), 128–151. 10.1002/bse.1989

Lanthorn, K. R. (2013). It's all about the green: The economically driven greenwashing practices of Coca-Cola. *Augsburg Honors Review, 6*(1), 13. https://idun.augsburg.edu/honors_review/ vol6/iss1/13

Lapointe, V. (2015). Financial Performance of Socially Responsible Investment: Does the Visibility of Firms in the Portfolio Matter? *Available at SSRN* 2386015.

Lapsley, J., & Eggertsson, M. (2022). Managing ESG in a Global Enterprise. *International Journal of Business Research*, 22(2), 14–24. 10.18374/IJBR-22-2.2

Lassala, C., Apetrei, A., & Sapena, J. (2017). Sustainability matter and financial performance of companies. *Sustainability (Basel)*, 9(9), 1498. 10.3390/su9091498

Laufer, W. S. (2003). Social accountability and corporate greenwashing. *Journal of Business Ethics*, 43(3), 253–261. 10.1023/A:1022962719299

Laux, C., & Leuz, C. (2009). The crisis of fair-value accounting: Making sense of the recent debate. *Accounting, Organizations and Society*, 34(6-7), 826–834. 10.1016/j.aos.2009.04.003

Lawal, E., May, G., & Stahl, B. (2017). The Significance of Corporate Social Disclosure for High-Tech Manufacturing Companies: Focus on Employee and Community Aspects of Sustainable Development. *Corporate Social Responsibility and Environmental Management*, 24(4), 295–311. 10.1002/csr.1397

Layke, J., Jaeger, J., Pastor, K., Levin, K., & Searchinger, T. (2021, May 21). *5 things to know about the IEA's roadmap to net zero by 2050*. World Resources Institute. https://www.wri.org/ insights/5-things-know-about-ieas-roadmap-net-zero-2050

Le Blanc, D. (2015). Towards Integration at Last? The Sustainable Development Goals as a Network of Targets. *Sustainable Development (Bradford)*, 23(3), 176–187. 10.1002/sd.1582

Leal Filho, W., Azeiteiro, U., Alves, F., Pace, P., Mifsud, M., Brandli, L., Caeiro, S. S., & Disterheft, A. (2018). Reinvigorating the sustainable development research agenda: The role of the sustainable development goals (SDG). *International Journal of Sustainable Development and World Ecology*, 25(2), 131–142. 10.1080/13504509.2017.1342103

Le, B., & Moore, P. H. (2021). The impact of audit quality on earnings management and cost of equity capital: Evidence from a developing market. *Journal of Financial Reporting and Accounting*, 21(3), 695–728. 10.1108/JFRA-09-2021-0284

Lee, C.-C., Lu, M., Wang, C.-W., & Cheng, C.-Y. (2024). ESG engagement, country-level political risk and bank liquidity creation. *Pacific-Basin Finance Journal*, 83, 102260. 10.1016/j.pacfin.2024.102260

Lee, D. S., Fahey, D. W., Skowron, A., Allen, M. R., Burkhardt, U., Chen, Q., Doherty, S. J., Freeman, S., Forster, P. M., Fuglestvedt, J., Gettelman, A., De León, R. R., Lim, L. L., Lund, M. T., Millar, R. J., Owen, B., Penner, J. E., Pitari, G., Prather, M. J., & Wilcox, L. J. (2021). The contribution of global aviation to anthropogenic climate forcing for 2000 to 2018. *Atmospheric Environment*, 244, 117834. 10.1016/j.atmosenv.2020.11783432895604

Lee, J. E., & Yang, Y. S. (2022). The Impact of Corporate Social Responsibility Performance Feedback on Corporate Social Responsibility Performance. *Frontiers in Psychology*, 13, 893193. Advance online publication. 10.3389/fpsyg.2022.89319335664210

Lee, J., Koh, K., & Shim, E. D. (2024). Managerial incentives for ESG in the financial services industry: Direct and indirect association between ESG and executive compensation. *Managerial Finance*, 50(1), 10–27. 10.1108/MF-03-2023-0149

Lee, M. T., Raschke, R. L., & Krishen, A. S. (2022). Signaling green! Firm ESG signals in an interconnected environment that promote brand valuation. *Journal of Business Research*, 138, 1–11. 10.1016/j.jbusres.2021.08.061

Lee, W. H., Han, M.-Y., & Kim, S. (2023). ESG, Style Investing, and Integration. *Asian Review of Financial Research*, 36(3), 105–145. 10.37197/ARFR.2023.36.3.4

Lefort, F., & González, R. (2008). Hacia un mejor gobierno corporativo en Chile. *Revista Abante*, 11(1), 17–37.

Leitão, N. C., Balsalobre-Lorente, D., & Cantos-Cantos, J. M. (2021). The impact of renewable energy and economic complexity on carbon emissions in BRICS countries under the EKC scheme. *Energies*, 14(16), 4908. 10.3390/en14164908

Leland, H. E. (1992). Insider trading: Should it be prohibited? *Journal of Political Economy*, 100(4), 859–887. 10.1086/261843

Leuz, C., & Verrecchia, R. (2000). The economic consequences of increased disclosure. *Journal of Accounting Research*, 38, 91–124. 10.2307/2672910

Leuz, C., & Verrecchia, R. E. (1999). The economic consequences of increased disclosure. *Available atSSRN* 171975.

Levy, S. E., & Park, S. Y. (2011). An Analysis of CSR Activities in the Lodging Industry. *Journal of Hospitality and Tourism Management*, 18(1), 147–154. 10.1375/jhtm.18.1.147

Lima, F. R.Junior, Osiro, L., & Carpinetti, L. C. R. (2014). A comparison between Fuzzy AHP and Fuzzy TOPSIS methods to supplier selection. *Applied Soft Computing*, 21, 194–209. 10.1016/j. asoc.2014.03.014

Ling, A., Li, J., & Zhang, Y. (2023). Can firms with higher ESG ratings bear higher bank systemic tail risk spillover?—Evidence from Chinese A-share market. *Pacific-Basin Finance Journal*, 80, 102097. 10.1016/j.pacfin.2023.102097

Lin, J. W., Li, J. F., & Yang, J. S. (2006). The effect of audit committee performance on earnings quality. *Managerial Auditing Journal*, 21(9), 921–933. 10.1108/02686900610705019

Liu, D., & Jin, S. (2023). How Does Corporate ESG Performance Affect Financial Irregularities? *Sustainability (Basel)*, 15(13), 9999. Advance online publication. 10.3390/su15139999

Liu, G., Qian, H., Shi, Y., Yuan, D., & Zhou, M. (2024). How do firms react to capital market liberalization? Evidence from ESG reporting greenwashing. *Corporate Social Responsibility and Environmental Management*, csr.2808. Advance online publication. 10.1002/csr.2808

Liu, H., Wu, K., & Zhou, Q. (2022). Whether and How ESG Impacts on Corporate Financial Performance in the Yangtze River Delta of China. *Sustainability (Basel)*, 14(24), 16584. Advance online publication. 10.3390/su142416584

Liu, K., Wang, J., Liu, L., & Huang, Y. (2023). Mixed-ownership reform of SOEs and ESG performance: Evidence from China. *Economic Analysis and Policy*, 80, 1618–1641. 10.1016/j. eap.2023.10.016

Liu, Z., & Li, X. (2024). The impact of bank fintech on ESG greenwashing. *Finance Research Letters*, 62, 105199. 10.1016/j.frl.2024.105199

Loewen, B. (2022). Coal, green growth and crises: Exploring three European Union policy responses to regional energy transitions. *Energy Research & Social Science*, 93, 102849. 10.1016/j. erss.2022.102849

Lombardo, D., & Pagano, M. (2002). Law and equity markets: A simple model. *Corporate governance regimes: Convergence and diversity*, 343-362.

Long, H., Feng, G.-F., Gong, Q., & Chang, C.-P. (2023). ESG performance and green innovation: An investigation based on quantile regression. *Business Strategy and the Environment*, 32(7), 5102–5118. 10.1002/bse.3410

LSEG (2024). https://www.lseg.com/content/dam/marketing/en_us/documents/methodology/ refinitiv-esg-scores-methodology.pdf

Lubbe, S., Parker, G., & Hoard, A. (1995). The profit impact of IT investment. *Journal of Information Technology*, 10(1), 44–51. 10.1177/026839629501000106

Lu, C. W., & Chueh, T. S. (2015). Corporate social responsibility and information asymmetry. *Journal of Applied Finance & Banking*, 5(3), 105–122.

Luo, X., & Bhattacharya, C. (2006). Corporate Social Responsibility, Customer Satisfaction, and Market Value. *Journal of Marketing*, 70(4), 1–18. 10.1509/jmkg.70.4.001

Lu, Z., Liang, Y., Hu, Y., & Liu, Y. (2024). Is managerial myopia detrimental to corporate ESG performance? *International Review of Economics & Finance*, 92, 998–1015. Advance online publication. 10.1016/j.iref.2024.02.061

Lyon, T. P., & Maxwell, J. W. (2011). Greenwash: Corporate environmental disclosure under threat of audit. *Journal of Economics & Management Strategy*, 20(1), 3–41. 10.1111/j.1530-9134.2010.00282.x

Lyon, T. P., & Montgomery, A. W. (2013). Tweetjacked: The impact of social media on corporate greenwash. *Journal of Business Ethics*, 118(4), 747–757. 10.1007/s10551-013-1958-x

Machado, M. A. D., de Almeida, S. O., Bollick, L. C., & Bragagnolo, G. (2019). Second-hand fashion market: Consumer role in circular economy. *Journal of Fashion Marketing and Management*, 23(3), 382–395. 10.1108/JFMM-07-2018-0099

MacLean, T. L., & Behnam, M. (2010). The dangers of decoupling: The relationship between compliance programs, legitimacy perceptions, and institutionalized misconduct. *Academy of Management Journal*, 53(6), 1499–1520. 10.5465/amj.2010.57319198

Macpherson, M., Gasperini, A., & Bosco, M. (2021). Implications for artificial intelligence and ESG data. 10.2139/ssrn.3863599

Mahoney, L. S., Thorne, L., Cecil, L., & LaGore, W. (2013). A research note on standalone corporate social responsibility reports: Signaling or greenwashing? *Critical Perspectives on Accounting*, 24(4–5), 350–359. 10.1016/j.cpa.2012.09.008

Maidin, A. J. (2022). Governance of SDGs. *Routledge EBooks*, 222–231. 10.4324/9781003230724-19

Majid, K. A., & Russell, C. A. (2015). Giving green a second thought: Modeling the value retention of green products in the secondary market. *Journal of Business Research*, 68(5), 994–1002. 10.1016/j.jbusres.2014.10.001

Maletič, M., Maletič, D., & Gomišček, B. (2016). The impact of sustainability exploration and sustainability exploitation practices on the organisational performance: A cross-country comparison. *Journal of Cleaner Production*, 138, 158–169. 10.1016/j.jclepro.2016.02.132

Mamun, A., Torst, N., & Sabantina, L. (2023). Advancing towards a Circular Economy in the Textile Industry. *Engineering Proceedings*, 56(1), 18. Advance online publication. 10.3390/ASEC2023-15244

Managi, S., Okimoto, T., & Matsuda, A. (2012). Do socially responsible investment indexes outperform conventional indexes? *Applied Financial Economics*, 22(18), 1511–1527. 10.1080/09603107.2012.665593

Manchiraju, H., & Rajgopal, S. (2017). Does Corporate Social Responsibility (CSR) Create Shareholder Value? Evidence from the Indian Companies Act 2013. *Journal of Accounting Research*, 55(5), 1257–1300. 10.1111/1475-679X.12174

Mangena, M., & Pike, R. (2005). The effect of audit committee shareholding, financial expertise and size on interim financial disclosures. *Accounting and Business Research*, 35(4), 327–349. 10.1080/00014788.2005.9729998

Mansor, F., Bhatti, M. I., Rahman, S., & Do, H. Q. (2020). The investment performance of ethical equity funds in Malaysia. *Journal of Risk and Financial Management*, 13(9), 219. 10.3390/jrfm13090219

Mansouri, S., & Momtaz, P. P. (2022). Financing sustainable entrepreneurship: ESG measurement, valuation, and performance. *Journal of Business Venturing*, 37(6), 106258. 10.1016/j.jbusvent.2022.106258

Maqbool, S., & Zameer, M. N. (2018). Corporate social responsibility and financial performance: An empirical analysis of Indian banks. *Future Business Journal*, 4(1), 84–93. 10.1016/j.fbj.2017.12.002

Maquieira, C. P., Arias, J. T., & Espinosa-Méndez, C. (2024). The impact of ESG on the default risk of family firms: International evidence. *Research in International Business and Finance*, 67, 102136. 10.1016/j.ribaf.2023.102136

Marais, L., Burton, J., Campbell, M., & Nel, E. (2021). Chapter 3 mine closure in the coal industry: Global and national perspectives. Coal and Energy in South Africa, 34-43. https://doi.org/10.1515/9781474487078-009

Marano, V., Sauerwald, S., & Van Essen, M. (2022). The influence of culture on the relationship between women directors and corporate social performance. *Journal of International Business Studies*, 53(7), 1315–1342. 10.1057/s41267-022-00503-z

Marcel, T., Zenglian, Z., Yanick, O. A., & Paulin, B. (2024). Entrepreneurship and High-Quality Development of Enterprises—Empirical Research Based on Chinese-Listed Companies. *Journal of the Knowledge Economy*, 1–27. 10.1007/s13132-024-01922-z

Marcus, J., Kurucz, E. C., & Colbert, B. A. (2010). Conceptions of the Business-Society-Nature Interface: Implications for Management Scholarship. *Business & Society*, 49(3), 402–438. 10.1177/0007650310368827

Markopoulos, E., & Maria Barbara Ramonda. (2022). An ESG-SDGs alignment and execution model based on the Ocean Strategies transition in emerging markets. *AHFE International*. 10.54941/ahfe1001511

Markopoulos, E., Zhao, K., Samkova, M., & Vanharanta, H. (2023). *ESG and UN SDGs Driven Strategy Generation Process for Green and Pink Oceans.* Openaccess.cms-Conferences.org; AHFE Open Acces. 10.54941/ahfe1003878

Marquis, C., & Qian, C. (2014). Corporate social responsibility reporting in China: Symbol or substance? *Organization Science*, 25(1), 127–148. 10.1287/orsc.2013.0837

Marquis, C., Toffel, M. W., & Zhou, Y. (2016). Scrutiny, norms, and selective disclosure: A global study of greenwashing. *Organization Science*, 27(2), 483–504. 10.1287/orsc.2015.1039

Martínez-Ferrero, J., Banerjee, S., & García-Sánchez, I. M. (2016). Corporate social responsibility as a strategic shield against costs of earnings management practices. *Journal of Business Ethics*, 133(2), 305–324. 10.1007/s10551-014-2399-x

Martínez-Ferrero, J., Gallego-Álvarez, I., & García-Sánchez, I. M. (2015). A bidirectional analysis of earnings management and corporate social responsibility: The moderating effect of stakeholder and investor protection. *Australian Accounting Review*, 25(4), 359–371. 10.1111/auar.12075

Marzuki, A., & Atta, A. A. B. (2020). *Mutual Fund Families in Saudi Arabia, Malaysia, Indonesia And Pakistan: How Persist Their Performance Are?*

Massa, M., & Yadav, V. (n.d.). *Do Mutual Funds Play a Sentiment-based Strategy?*

Masud, M. H., Anees, F., & Ahmed, H. (2017). Impact of corporate diversification on earnings management. *Journal of Indian Business Research*, 9(2), 82–106. 10.1108/JIBR-06-2015-0070

Mateus, , I. BMateus, , CTodorovic, , N. (2019). Review of new trends in the literature on factor models and mutual fund performance. *International Review of Financial Analysis, 63*, 344–354.

Matten, D., & Moon, J. (2008). "Implicit" and "explicit" CSR: A conceptual framework for a comparative understanding of corporate social responsibility. *Academy of Management Review*, 33(2), 404–424. 10.5465/amr.2008.31193458

Mazumdar, S. C., & Sengupta, P. (2005). Disclosure and the loan spread on private debt. *Financial Analysts Journal*, 61(3), 83–95. 10.2469/faj.v61.n3.2731

Mazzacurati, J. (2021). *ESG ratings: Status and key issues ahead.*

McInnis, J. (2010). Earnings smoothness, average returns, and implied cost of equity capital. *The Accounting Review*, 85(1), 315–341. 10.2308/accr.2010.85.1.315

McKinsey & Company. (2020). *The ESG Premium: New Perspectives on Value and Performance.* Retrieved from https://www.mckinsey.com/~/media/mckinsey/business%20functions/sustainability/our%20insights/the%20esg%20premium%20new%20perspectives%20on%20value%20and%20performance/the-esg-premium-new-perspectives-on-value-and-performance.pdf

McKinsey & Company. (2022). *The Business Case for ESG.* Retrieved from https://www.mckinsey.com/business-functions/sustainability/our-insights/the-business-case-for-esg

Compilation of References

McKinsey & Company. (2023). *Diversity and Inclusion*. Retrieved from https://www.mckinsey.com/featured-insights/diversity-and-inclusion

Mcneil, A. J., Frey, R., & Embrechts, P. (2015). *Quantitative Risk Management: Concepts, Techniques and Tools*. Princeton University Press.

McWilliams, A., Siegel, D. S., & Wright, P. M. (2006). Corporate social responsibility: Strategic implications. *Journal of Management Studies*, 43(1), 1–18. 10.1111/j.1467-6486.2006.00580.x

Mensi, W., Hammoudeh, S., Al-Jarrah, I. M. W., Sensoy, A., & Kang, S. H. (2017). Dynamic risk spillovers between gold, oil prices and conventional, sustainability and Islamic equity aggregates and sectors with portfolio implications. *Energy Economics*, 67, 454–475. 10.1016/j.eneco.2017.08.031

Menz, K. M. (2010). Corporate social responsibility: Is it rewarded by the corporate bond market? A critical note. *Journal of Business Ethics*, 96(1), 117–134. 10.1007/s10551-010-0452-y

Merton, R. C. (1987). A simple model of capital market equilibrium with incomplete information. *The Journal of Finance*, 42(3), 483–510. 10.1111/j.1540-6261.1987.tb04565.x

Methling, F., & von Nitzsch, R. (2019). Naïve diversification in thematic investing: Heuristics for the core satellite investor. *Journal of Asset Management*, 20(7), 568–580. 10.1057/s41260-019-00136-2

Michaels, A., & Grüning, M. (2017). Relationship of corporate social responsibility disclosure on information asymmetry and the cost of capital. *Journal of Management Control*, 28(3), 251–274. 10.1007/s00187-017-0251-z

Michelon, G., Pilonato, S., & Ricceri, F. (2015). CSR reporting practices and the quality of disclosure: An empirical analysis. *Critical Perspectives on Accounting*, 33, 59–78. 10.1016/j.cpa.2014.10.003

Ministry of Statistics and Programme Implementation. (2023). *Energy Statistics India*. Government of India.

Minutolo, M. C., Kristjanpoller, W. D., & Stakeley, J. (2019). Exploring environmental, social, and governance disclosure effects on the S&P 500 financial performance. *Business Strategy and the Environment*, 28(6), 1083–1095. 10.1002/bse.2303

Miozzo, M., & Dewick, P. (2002). Building competitive advantage: Innovation and corporate governance in European construction. *Research Policy*, 31(6), 989–1008. 10.1016/S0048-7333(01)00173-1

Miralles-Quiros, M. del M., Miralles-Quiros, J. L., & Arraiano, I. G. (2017). Sustainable development, sustainability leadership and firm valuation: Differences across Europe. *Business Strategy and the Environment*, 26(7), 1014–1028. 10.1002/bse.1964

Miralles-Quirós, M. M., Miralles-Quirós, J. L., & Redondo-Hernández, J. (2019). The impact of environmental, social, and governance performance on stock prices: Evidence from the banking industry. *Corporate Social Responsibility and Environmental Management*, 26(6), 1446–1456. 10.1002/csr.1759

Mirovic, V., Kalas, B., Djokic, I., Milicevic, N., Djokic, N., & Djakovic, M. (2023). Green loans in bank portfolio: Financial and marketing implications. *Sustainability (Basel)*, 15(7), 5914. 10.3390/su15075914

Mishra, M., Sudarsan, D., Santos, Mishra, S. K., Abu, Goswami, S., Kalumba, A. M., Biswal, R., Silva, Antonio, C., & Baral, K. (2023). *A bibliometric analysis of SDGs: a review of progress, challenges, and opportunities.* 10.1007/s10668-023-03225-w

Mishra, L. (2021). Corporate social responsibility and sustainable development goals: A study of Indian companies. *Journal of Public Affairs*, 21(1), e2147. 10.1002/pa.2147

Mitchell, R. K., Agle, B. R., & Wood, D. J. (1997). Toward a theory of stakeholder identification and salience: Defining the principle of who and what really counts. *Academy of Management Review*, 22(4), 853–886. 10.2307/259247

Mitton, T. (2002). A cross-firm analysis of the impact of corporate governance on the East Asian financial crisis. *Journal of Financial Economics*, 64(2), 215–241. 10.1016/S0304-405X(02)00076-4

Modak, N. M., Kazemi, N., & Cárdenas-Barrón, L. E. (2019). Investigating structure of a two-echelon closed-loop supply chain using social work donation as a Corporate Social Responsibility practice. *International Journal of Production Economics*, 207, 19–33. 10.1016/j.ijpe.2018.10.009

Money, K., & Schepers, H. (2007). Are CSR and corporate governance converging?: A view from boardroom directors and company secretaries in FTSE100 companies in the UK. *Journal of General Management*, 33(2), 1–11. 10.1177/030630700703300201

Montecchia, A., Giordano, F., & Grieco, C. (2016). Communicating CSR: Integrated approach or Selfie? Evidence from the Milan Stock Exchange. *Journal of Cleaner Production*, 136, 42–52. 10.1016/j.jclepro.2016.01.099

Moorhouse, D., & Moorhouse, D. (2017). Sustainable Design: Circular Economy in Fashion and Textiles. *Design Journal, 20*(sup1), S1948–S1959. https://doi.org/10.1080/14606925.2017.1352713

Morgan Stanley. (2023). *Sustainable Funds Show Continued Outperformance and Positive Flows in 2023 Despite a Slower Second Half.* Institute of Sustainable Investing.

MSCI (2024) https://www.msci.com/documents/1296102/34424357/MSCI+ESG+Ratings+Methodology+-+Process.pdf/820e4152-4804-fe33-0a67-8ee4c6a8fd7d?t=1666300410683

Muttakin, M. B., Khan, A., & Subramaniam, N. (2015). Firm characteristics, board diversity and corporate social responsibility: Evidence from Bangladesh. *Pacific Accounting Review*, 27(3), 353–372. 10.1108/PAR-01-2013-0007

Compilation of References

Naeem, N., Cankaya, S., & Bildik, R. (2022). Does ESG performance affect the financial performance of environmentally sensitive industries? A comparison between emerging and developed markets. *Borsa Istanbul Review*, 22, S128–S140. 10.1016/j.bir.2022.11.014

Naimy, V., El Khoury, R., & Iskandar, S. (2021). ESG Versus Corporate Financial Performance: Evidence from East Asian Firms in the Industrials Sector. *Estudios de Economía Aplicada*, 39(3). Advance online publication. 10.25115/eea.v39i3.4457

Nain, M. Z., Ahmad, W., & Kamaiah, B. (2017). Economic growth, energy consumption and CO2 emissions in India: A disaggregated causal analysis. *International Journal of Sustainable Energy*, 36(8), 807–824. 10.1080/14786451.2015.1109512

Naqvi, N. (2019). Manias, panics and crashes in emerging markets: An empirical investigation of the post-2008 crisis period. *New Political Economy*, 24(6), 759–779. 10.1080/13563467.2018.1526263

Naqvi, S. K., Shahzad, F., Rehman, I. U., Qureshi, F., & Laique, U. (2021). Corporate social responsibility performance and information asymmetry: The moderating role of analyst coverage. *Corporate Social Responsibility and Environmental Management*, 28(6), 1549–1563. 10.1002/csr.2114

Narang, M. (2018). Performance Evaluation of Selected Equity Mutual Funds. *Performance Evaluation*.

Nascimento, J., & Powell, W. (2010). Dynamic programming models and algorithms for the mutual fund cash balance problem. *Management Science*, 56(5), 801–815. 10.1287/mnsc.1100.1143

Natter, M., Rohleder, M., Schulte, D., & Wilkens, M. (2017). Bond mutual funds and complex investments. *Journal of Asset Management*, 18(6), 433–456. 10.1057/s41260-017-0046-7

Nayak, R., Panwar, T., & Van Thang Nguyen, L. (2019). Sustainability in fashion and textiles: A survey from developing country. In *Sustainable Technologies for Fashion and Textiles* (pp. 3–30). Elsevier., 10.1016/B978-0-08-102867-4.00001-3

Nayal, K., Raut, R. D., Yadav, V. S., Priyadarshinee, P., & Narkhede, B. E. (2022). The impact of sustainable development strategy on sustainable supply chain firm performance in the digital transformation era. *Business Strategy and the Environment*, 31(3), 845–859. 10.1002/bse.2921

Nekhili, M., & Gatfaoui, H. (2013). Are Demographic Attributes and Firm Characteristics Drivers of Gender Diversity? Investigating Women's Positions on French Boards of Directors. *Journal of Business Ethics*, 118(2), 227–249. 10.1007/s10551-012-1576-z

Neumann, T. (2021). The impact of entrepreneurship on economic, social and environmental welfare and its determinants: A systematic review. *Management Review*, 71, 553–584.

Nevshehir, N. (2021, February 19). *These are the biggest hurdles on the path to clean energy.* World Economic Forum. https://www.weforum.org/agenda/2021/02/heres-why-geopolitics-could-hamper-the-energy-transition/

Ng, A. C., & Rezaee, Z. (2015). Business sustainability performance and cost of equity capital. *Journal of Corporate Finance*, 34, 128–149. 10.1016/j.jcorpfin.2015.08.003

Nguyen, T. T. H., Yang, Z., Nguyen, N., Johnson, L. W., & Cao, T. K. (2019). Greenwash and green purchase intention: The mediating role of green skepticism. *Sustainability (Basel)*, 11(9), 2653. 10.3390/su11092653

Nicolescu, L., & Tudorache, F. G. (2018). Romania, Slovakia and Hungary: evolution of mutual funds in recent years. *Proceedings of the International Conference on Business Excellence, 12*(1), 695–710.

Nicolo, G., Zampone, G., Sannino, G., & Tiron-Tudor, A. (2023). Worldwide evidence of corporate governance influence on ESG disclosure in the utilities sector. *Utilities Policy*, 82, 101549. 10.1016/j.jup.2023.101549

Niels Bosma, T. S. (2016). *Global Entrepreneurship Monitor 2015 to 2016: Special Report on Social Entrepreneurship*. Global Entrepreneurship Research Association.

Nielsen, S., & Huse, M. (2010). The contribution of women on boards of directors: Going beyond the surface. *Corporate Governance*, 18(2), 136–148. 10.1111/j.1467-8683.2010.00784.x

Noe, T. H., & Rebello, M. J. (1996). Asymmetric information, managerial opportunism, financing, and payout policies. *The Journal of Finance*, 51(2), 637–660. 10.1111/j.1540-6261.1996.tb02697.x

Nofsinger, J., & Varma, A. (2014). Socially responsible funds and market crises. *Journal of Banking & Finance*, 48, 180–193. 10.1016/j.jbankfin.2013.12.016

Nor, A. I. (2024). Entrepreneurship Development as a Tool for Employment Creation, Income Generation, and Poverty Reduction for the Youth and Women. *Journal of the Knowledge Economy*, ●●●, 1–24. 10.1007/s13132-024-01747-w

Norris, L. (2013). Aesthetics and ethics: Upgrading textile production in northern Kerala. *Geoforum*, 50, 221–231. 10.1016/j.geoforum.2013.09.006

Nygaard, S., Kokholm, A. R., & Huulgaard, R. D. (2022). Incorporating the sustainable development goals in small- to medium-sized enterprises. *Journal of Urban Economics*, 8(1), juac022. Advance online publication. 10.1093/jue/juac022

Nyilasy, G., Gangadharbatla, H., & Paladino, A. (2014). Perceived greenwashing: The interactive effects of green advertising and corporate environmental performance on consumer reactions. *Journal of Business Ethics*, 125(4), 693–707. 10.1007/s10551-013-1944-3

OECD. (2015). *G20/OECD principles of corporate governance*. OECD Publishing., 10.1787/9789264236882-

Orazalin, N., Kuzey, C., Uyar, A., & Karaman, A. S. (2024). Does CSR contribute to the financial sector's financial stability? The moderating role of a sustainability committee. *Journal of Applied Accounting Research*, 25(1), 105–125. 10.1108/JAAR-12-2022-0329

Orazalin, N., & Mahmood, M. (2021). Toward sustainable development: Board characteristics, country governance quality, and environmental performance. *Business Strategy and the Environment*, 30(8), 3569–3588. 10.1002/bse.2820

Orlitzky, M., Schmidt, F. L., & Rynes, S. L. (2003). Corporate social and financial performance: A meta-analysis. *Organization Studies*, 24(3), 403–441. 10.1177/0170840603024003910

Ortas, E., Gallego-Alvarez, I., & Álvarez Etxeberria, I. (2014). Financial factors influencing the quality of corporate social responsibility and environmental management disclosure: A quantile regression approach. *Corporate Social Responsibility and Environmental Management*, 22(6), 362–380. 10.1002/csr.1351

Ostermann, C. M., Nascimento, L. da S., Steinbruch, F. K., & Callegaro-de-Menezes, D. (2021). Drivers to implement the circular economy in born-sustainable business models: A case study in the fashion industry. *Revista de Gestao*, 28(3), 223–240. 10.1108/REGE-03-2020-0017

Owusu, P. A., & Asumadu-Sarkodie, S. (2016). A review of renewable energy sources, sustainability issues and climate change mitigation. *Cogent Engineering*, 3(1), 1167990. 10.1080/23311916.2016.1167990

Pancholi, D. (2022). Hedge Funds: Resolving Myths about ESG Integration. *Journal of Alternative Investments*, 25(2), 8–13. 10.3905/jai.2022.1.172

Panda, P. K. (2016). A Review on Evolution of Mutual Funds Market in India: Current Status and Problems. *Indian Journal of Economics & Business*, 15(1), 153–172.

Parguel, B., Benoit-Moreau, F., & Larceneux, F. (2011). How sustainability ratings might deter 'greenwashing': A closer look at ethical corporate communication. *Journal of Business Ethics*, 102(1), 15–28. 10.1007/s10551-011-0901-2

Park, S. R., & Jang, J. Y. (2021). The Impact of ESG Management on Investment Decision: Institutional Investors' Perceptions of Country-Specific ESG Criteria. *International Journal of Financial Studies*, 9(3), 3. 10.3390/ijfs9030048

Parmar, B. L., Freeman, R. E., Harrison, J. S., Wicks, A. C., Purnell, L., & de Colle, S. (2010). Stakeholder Theory: The State of the Art. *The Academy of Management Annals*, 4(1), 403–445. 10.5465/19416520.2010.495581

Pascual, U., Balvanera, P., Díaz, S., Pataki, G., Roth, E., Stenseke, M., Watson, R. T., Başak Dessane, E., Islar, M., Kelemen, E., Maris, V., Quaas, M., Subramanian, S. M., Wittmer, H., Adlan, A., Ahn, S. E., Al-Hafedh, Y. S., Amankwah, E., Asah, S. T., & Yagi, N. (2017). Valuing nature's contributions to people: The IPBES approach. *Current Opinion in Environmental Sustainability*, 26, 7–16. 10.1016/j.cosust.2016.12.006

Pater, L. R., & Cristea, S. L. (2016). Systemic Definitions of Sustainability, Durability and Longevity. *13th International Symposium in Management: Management During and After the Economic Crisis, 221*, 362–371. 10.1016/j.sbspro.2016.05.126

Patro, A., & Kanagaraj, A. (2016). Is Earnings Management a Technique to Reduce Cost of Capital? Exploratory Study on Indian Companies. *Journal of Modern Accounting and Auditing*, 12(5), 243–249.

Patton, A. J. (2012). A review of copula models for economic time series. *Journal of Multivariate Analysis*, 110, 4–18. 10.1016/j.jmva.2012.02.021

Paul, S., & Bhattacharya, R. N. (2004). Causality between energy consumption and economic growth in India: A note on conflicting results. *Energy Economics*, 26(6), 977–983. 10.1016/j.eneco.2004.07.002

Pejovic, B., Backovic, T., & Karadzic, V. (2023). Analysis of the Relationship Between Energy Consumption and Economic Growth in Transition Countries. *Eastern European Economics*, ●●●, 1–21. 10.1080/00128775.2023.2216690

Pesaran MH. General diagnostic tests for cross section dependence in panels. Iza 2004;1e42.

Pesaran MH. J Appl Econom 2007;21:1e21. https://doi.org/.10.1002/jae

Petersen, H. E. (2020, August 8). *India plans to fell ancient forest to create 40 new coalfields*. The Guardian. https://www.theguardian.com/world/2020/aug/08/india-prime-minister-narendra-modi-plans-to-fell-ancient-forest-to-create-40-new-coal-fields

Petersen, H., & Vredenburg, H. (2009). Corporate governance, social responsibility and capital markets: exploring the institutional investor mental model. *Corporate Governance: The international journal of business in society, 9*(5), 610-622.

Petersen, A., Herbert, S., & Daniels, N. (2022). The likely adoption of the IFRS Foundation's proposed sustainability reporting standards. *The Business and Management Review*, 13(2). Advance online publication. 10.24052/BMR/V13NU02/ART-03

Peters, M., Godfrey, C., Mcinerney, P., Munn, Z., Trico, A., & Khalil, H. (2020). *Scoping Reviews.*, 10.46658/JBIMES-20-12

Pfajfar, G., Shoham, A., Małecka, A., & Zalaznik, M. (2022). Value of corporate social responsibility for multiple stakeholders and social impact – Relationship marketing perspective. *Journal of Business Research*, 143, 46–61. 10.1016/j.jbusres.2022.01.051

Pham Vo Ninh, B., Do Thanh, T., & Vo Hong, D. (2018). Financial distress and bankruptcy prediction: An appropriate model for listed firms in Vietnam. *Economic Systems*, 42(4), 616–624. 10.1016/j.ecosys.2018.05.002

Phillips PCB, Sul D. Dynamic panel estimation and homogeneity testing under cross section dependence. Econom J 2003;6:217e59. .10.1111/1368-423X.00108

Phillips, R. (2003). *Stakeholder Theory and Organizational Ethics*. Berrett-Koehler Publishers.

Pincus, S. M., & Huang, W.-M. (1992). Approximate entropy: Statistical properties and applications. *Communications in Statistics. Theory and Methods*, 21(11), 3061–3077. 10.1080/03610929208830963

Pisani, N., Kourula, A., Kolk, A., & Meijer, R. (2017). How global is international CSR research? Insights and recommendations from a systematic review. *Journal of World Business*, 52(5), 591–614. 10.1016/j.jwb.2017.05.003

Plastun, A., Bouri, E., Gupta, R., & Ji, Q. (2022). Price effects after one-day abnormal returns in developed and emerging markets: ESG versus traditional indices. *The North American Journal of Economics and Finance*, 59, 101572. 10.1016/j.najef.2021.101572

Plumlee, M., Brown, D., & Marshall, S. (2008). The impact of voluntary environmental disclosure quality on firm value. *Available atSSRN* 1140221.

Pokrovskaia, N. N., Mordovets, V. A., & Nataly Yu. Kuchieva. (2023). Regulation of ESG-Ecosystem: Context and Content Evolution: Energy Sector Study. *Springer Proceedings in Business and Economics*, 159–179. 10.1007/978-3-031-30498-9_15

Pollock, D., Peters, M. D. J., Khalil, H., McInerney, P., Alexander, L., Tricco, A. C., Evans, C., de Moraes, É. B., Godfrey, C. M., Pieper, D., Saran, A., Stern, C., & Munn, Z. (2023). Recommendations for the extraction, analysis, and presentation of results in scoping reviews. *JBI Evidence Synthesis*, 21(3), 520–532. 10.11124/JBIES-22-0012336081365

Porter, M. E., & Kramer, M. R. (2006, December 1). Strategy and Society: The Link Between Competitive Advantage and Corporate Social Responsibility. *Harvard Business Review*. https://hbr.org/2006/12/strategy-and-society-the-link-between-competitive-advantage-and-corporate-social-responsibility

Porter, M. E., & Kramer, M. R. (2006). Strategy and society: The link between competitive advantage and corporate social responsibility. *Harvard Business Review*, 84(12).17183795

Porter, M. E., & Kramer, M. R. (2011). Creating shared value. *Harvard Business Review*, 89(1/2), 62–77. https://hbr.org/2011/01/the-big-idea-creating-shared-value

Post, C., Rahman, N., & McQuillen, C. (2015). From Board Composition to Corporate Environmental Performance Through Sustainability-Themed Alliances. *Journal of Business Ethics*, 130(2), 423–435. 10.1007/s10551-014-2231-7

Poudel, S. S. (2021, November 11). *India commits to net-zero emissions by 2070*. The Diplomat – Asia-Pacific Current Affairs Magazine. https://thediplomat.com/2021/11/india-commits-to-net-zero-emissions-by-2070/

Powering the future: Workplace skill development and recruitment in the clean energy transition. (2024,January25). VBeyond.https://vbeyond.com/powering-the-future-workplace-skill-development-and-recruitment-in-the-clean-energy-transition/#:~:text=Reskilling%20and%20upskilling%3A%20Agencies%20must,and%20methodologies%20in%20green%20energy

Prajapati, K. N. S. H. M. F. (2008). *Performance Evaluation of Public & Private Mutual Fund Schemes in India.*

Prakash, A., & Potoski, M. (2006). *The voluntary environmentalists: Green clubs, ISO 14001, and voluntary environmental regulations.* Cambridge University Press. 10.1017/CBO9780511617683

Prasad, S. (2023, October 11). *By 2050 coal India limited may have to lay off 73,800 jobs: Global energy monitor.* DTE. https://www.downtoearth.org.in/news/india/by-2050-coal-india-limited-may-have-to-lay-off-73-800-jobs-global-energy-monitor-92237

Prashar, A. (2021). Moderating effects on sustainability reporting and firm performance relationships: A meta-analytical review. *International Journal of Productivity and Performance Management*, 72(4), 1154–1181. 10.1108/IJPPM-04-2021-0183

PricewaterhouseCoopers (PwC). (2023). *ESG: What does it mean?* Retrieved from https://www.pwc.com/us/en/services/audit-assurance/library/esg-introduction.html

Prior, D., Surroca, J., & Tribó, J. A. (2008). Are socially responsible managers really ethical? Exploring the relationship between earnings management and corporate social responsibility. *Corporate Governance*, 16(3), 160–177. 10.1111/j.1467-8683.2008.00678.x

Proimos, A. (2005). Strengthening corporate governance regulations. *Journal of Investment Compliance*, 6(4), 75–84. 10.1108/15285810510681900

Pucker, K. P. (2021). Overselling sustainability reporting. *Harvard Business Review*, 99(3), 90–99. https://hbr.org/2021/05/overselling-sustainability-reporting

Pureza, A. P., & Lee, K.-H. (2020). Corporate social responsibility leadership for sustainable development: An institutional logics perspective in Brazil. *Corporate Social Responsibility and Environmental Management*, 27(3), 1410–1424. 10.1002/csr.1894

Purvis, B., Mao, Y., & Robinson, D. (2019). Three pillars of sustainability: In search of conceptual origins. *Sustainability Science*, 14(3), 681–695. 10.1007/s11625-018-0627-5

Putnam, R. D. (1993). The Prosperous Community: Social Capital and Public Life. *The American Prospect*, 35–42.

Putra, H. B. D., Trisnawati, R., & Sasongko, N. (2016). Cost of Equity Capital and Real Earnings Management on Listed Companies in LQ-45 and Jakarta Islamic Index.

PwC Global. (2022, December 6). The CEO's ESG dilemma. PwC. https://www.pwc.com/gx/en/issues/esg/ceo-esg-dilemma.html

PwC. (2024). *ESG reporting and preparation of a Sustainability Report.* Retrieved from https://www.pwc.com/sk/en/environmental-social-and-corporate-governance-esg/esg-reporting.html

Qamar, U. A. (2020). Social entrepreneurship in Pakistan: Challenges and prospects. *Journal of Management Research*, 7(2), 1–41.

Qian, W., Parker, L., & Zhu, J. (2024). Corporate environmental reporting in the China context: The interplay of stakeholder salience, socialist ideology and state power. *The British Accounting Review*, 56(1), 101198. 10.1016/j.bar.2023.101198

Quirici, M. C. (2023). The European Blue Economy Framework and Blue Bonds as New Instruments of Blue Finance. In *ESG Integration and SRI Strategies in the EU: Challenges and Opportunities for Sustainable Development* (pp. 175–194). Springer. 10.1007/978-3-031-36457-0_9

Radu, O.-M., Dragomir, V. D., & Feleagă, L. (2023). The Link between Corporate ESG Performance and the UN Sustainable Development Goals. *Proceedings of the ...International Conference on Business Excellence, 17*(1), 776–790. 10.2478/picbe-2023-0072

Raghunandan, A., & Rajgopal, S. (2022). Do ESG funds make stakeholder-friendly investments? *Review of Accounting Studies*, 27(3), 822–863. 10.1007/s11142-022-09693-1

Rahaman, M. T., Pranta, A. D., Repon, M. R., Ahmed, M. S., & Islam, T. (2024). Green production and consumption of textiles and apparel: Importance, fabrication, challenges and future prospects. In *Journal of Open Innovation: Technology, Market, and Complexity* (Vol. 10, Issue 2). Elsevier B.V. https://doi.org/10.1016/j.joitmc.2024.100280

Rahim, H. L.–1. (2015). Social Entrepreneurship: A Different Perspective. *International Academic Research Journal of Business and Technology*, 1(1), 9–15.

Raimo, N., Vitolla, F., Marrone, A., & Rubino, M. (2020). Do audit committee attributes influence integrated reporting quality? An agency theory viewpoint. *Business Strategy and the Environment*, 30(1), 522–534. 10.1002/bse.2635

Raj, A., Biswas, I., & Srivastava, S. K. (2018). Designing supply contracts for the sustainable supply chain using game theory. *Journal of Cleaner Production*, 185, 275–284. 10.1016/j.jclepro.2018.03.046

Rajesh, R. (2020). Exploring the sustainability performances of firms using environmental, social, and governance scores. *Journal of Cleaner Production*, 247, 119600. 10.1016/j.jclepro.2019.119600

Rajesh, R., & Rajendran, C. (2020). Relating Environmental, Social, and Governance scores and sustainability performances of firms: An empirical analysis. *Business Strategy and the Environment*, 29(3), 1247–1267. 10.1002/bse.2429

Rajwani, S., & Kumar, D. (2019). Measuring dependence between the USA and the Asian economies: A time-varying copula approach. *Global Business Review*, 20(4), 962–980. 10.1177/0972150919845240

Rametse, N. a. (2012). Investigating Social Entrepreneurship in Developing Countries. *SSRN*. 10.2139/ssrn.2176557

Rands, M. R., Adams, W. M., Bennun, L., Butchart, S. H., Clements, A., Coomes, D., Entwistle, A., Hodge, I., Kapos, V., Scharlemann, J. P. W., Sutherland, W. J., & Vira, B. (2010). Biodiversity conservation: Challenges beyond 2010. *Science*, 329(5997), 1298–1303. 10.1126/science.118913820829476

Raut, R. D., Luthra, S., Narkhede, B. E., Mangla, S. K., Gardas, B. B., & Priyadarshinee, P. (2019). Examining the performance oriented indicators for implementing green management practices in the Indian agro sector. *Journal of Cleaner Production*, 215, 926–943. 10.1016/j.jclepro.2019.01.139

Renneboog, L., Ter Horst, J., & Zhang, C. (2008). The price of ethics and stakeholder governance: The performance of socially responsible mutual funds. *Journal of Corporate Finance*, 14(3), 302–322. 10.1016/j.jcorpfin.2008.03.009

Renneboog, L., Ter Horst, J., & Zhang, C. (2011). Is ethical money financially smart? Nonfinancial attributes and money flows of socially responsible investment funds. *Journal of Financial Intermediation*, 20(4), 562–588. 10.1016/j.jfi.2010.12.003

Rényi, A. (1961). On measures of entropy and information. *Proceedings of the Fourth Berkeley Symposium on Mathematical Statistics and Probability,* Volume 1*: Contributions to the Theory of Statistics, 4*, 547–562.

Reverte, C. (2012). The impact of better corporate social responsibility disclosure on the cost of equity capital. *Corporate Social Responsibility and Environmental Management*, 19(5), 253–272. 10.1002/csr.273

Reynold, J., & Santos, A. (1999). Cronbach's alpha: A tool for assessing the reliability of scales. *Journal of Extension*, 37(7), 36–35.

Rezaee, Z., & Tuo, L. (2019). Are the Quantity and Quality of Sustainability Disclosures Associated with the Innate and Discretionary Earnings Quality? *Journal of Business Ethics*, 155(3), 763–786. 10.1007/s10551-017-3546-y

Richardson, A. J., & Welker, M. (2001). Social disclosure, financial disclosure and the cost of equity capital. *Accounting, Organizations and Society*, 26(7-8), 597–616. 10.1016/S0361-3682(01)00025-3

Richardson, V. J. (2000). Information asymmetry and earnings management: Some evidence. *Review of Quantitative Finance and Accounting*, 15(4), 325–347. 10.1023/A:1012098407706

Rigdon, E. E. (1998). The equal correlation baseline model for comparative fit assessment in structural equation modeling. *Structural Equation Modeling*, 5(1), 63–77. 10.1080/10705519809540089

Rizqi, M. A., & Munari, M. (2023). Effect ESG on Financial Performance. *Owner*, 7(3), 2537–2546. 10.33395/owner.v7i3.1600

Rodrigo, F. (2024). Impact on the performance of ESG indices: A comparative study in Brazil and international markets. *Applied Economics*, •••, 1–12. 10.1080/00036846.2024.2342069

Compilation of References

Rogers, E. M. (2003). *Diffusion of Innovations*. Free Press.

Rosenberg, J. V., & Schuermann, T. (2006). A general approach to integrated risk management with skewed, fat-tailed risks. *Journal of Financial Economics*, 79(3), 569–614. 10.1016/j.jfineco.2005.03.001

Roy, B., & Schaffartzik, A. (2021, February). *Talk renewables, walk coal: The paradox of India's energy transition*. Ecological Economics. https://www.sciencedirect.com/science/article/pii/S0921800920303232

Ruan, H. (2018). *Essays on Mutual Funds*.

Ruhana, F., Suwartiningsih, S., Mulyandari, E., Handoyo, S., & Afrilia, U. A. (2024). Innovative Strategies for Achieving Sustainable Development Goals Amidst Escalating Global Environmental and Social Challenges. *The International Journal of Science in Society*, 6(1), 662–677. 10.54783/ijsoc.v6i1.1054

Rymar, I. E. (2016). Information asymmetry and its impact on cost of equity capital: Volkswagen case.

Saad, W., & Taleb, A. (2018). The causal relationship between renewable energy consumption and economic growth: Evidence from Europe. *Clean Technologies and Environmental Policy*, 20(1), 127–136. 10.1007/s10098-017-1463-5

Saaty, R. W. (1987). *The Analytic Hierarchy Process-What it is And How it is Used* (Vol. 9, Issue 5).

Saaty, T. L. (2004). *Decision Making-The Analytic Hierarchy and Network Processes (AHP/ANP)* (Vol. 13, Issue 1).

Sachin, N., & Rajesh, R. (2022). An empirical study of supply chain sustainability with financial performances of Indian firms. *Environment, Development and Sustainability*, 24(5), 6577–6601. 10.1007/s10668-021-01717-134393619

Sachs, J. D.-T.-D. (2019). *SDG Index and Dashboards Report 2019*. Bertelsmann Stiftung and Sustainable Development Solutions Network (SDSN).

Sadaa, A. M., Ganesan, Y., Yet, C. E., Alkhazaleh, Q., Alnoor, A., & aldegis, A. M. (2023). Corporate governance as antecedents and financial distress as a consequence of credit risk. Evidence from Iraqi banks. *Journal of Open Innovation*, 9(2), 100051. 10.1016/j.joitmc.2023.100051

Sadorsky, P. (2014). Modeling volatility and conditional correlations between socially responsible investments, gold and oil. *Economic Modelling*, 38, 609–618. 10.1016/j.econmod.2014.02.013

Saeidi, S. P., Sofian, S., Saeidi, P., Saeidi, S. P., & Saaeidi, S. A. (2015). How does corporate social responsibility contribute to firm financial performance? The mediating role of competitive advantage, reputation, and customer satisfaction. *Journal of Business Research*, 116(2), 13–23. 10.1016/j.jbusres.2014.06.024

Safarzynska, K. (2021). *A macro-evolutionary approach to energy policy*. ScienceDirect., https://www.sciencedirect.com/science/article/abs/pii/B9780128147122000142?via%3Dihub10.1016/B978-0-12-814712-2.00014-2

Saha, P., Akhter, S., & Hassan, A. (2021). Framing Corporate Social Responsibility to Achieve Sustainability in Urban Industrialization: Case of Bangladesh Ready-Made Garments (RMG). *Sustainability (Basel)*, 13(13), 6988. Advance online publication. 10.3390/su13136988

Sahin, G. (2022). Investigation into the Effects of Energy Transition in Terms. *Handbook of Energy Transitions*, 343.

Saini, M., Aggarwal, V., Dhingra, B., Kumar, P., & Yadav, M. (2023). ESG and financial variables: A systematic review. *International Journal of Law and Management*, 65(6), 663–682. 10.1108/IJLMA-02-2023-0033

Sajeev, A., Kaur, H., & Kaur, S. (2015). Cereal and fuel price interactions: Econometric evidence from India. *Journal of Business Thought*, ●●●, 14–43.

Sajeev, A., & Kaur, S. (2020). Environmental sustainability, trade and economic growth in India: Implications for public policy. *International Trade. Politics and Development*, 4(2), 141–160. 10.1108/ITPD-09-2020-0079

Salmon, M., & Schleicher, C. (2006). Pricing multivariate currency options with copulas. In *Copulas: From Theory to Application in Finance*. Risk Books, London.

Sandberg, J., & Sjöström, E. (2021). *Motivations for investment in sustainable consumption and production. Sustainable Consumption and Production* (Vol. I). Challenges and Development., 10.1007/978-3-030-56371-4_7/COVER

Santis, P., Albuquerque, A., & Lizarelli, F. (2016). Do sustainable companies have a better financial performance? A study on Brazilian public companies. *Journal of Cleaner Production*, 133, 735–745. 10.1016/j.jclepro.2016.05.180

Sardana, D., Gupta, N., Kumar, V., & Terziovski, M. (2020). CSR 'sustainability' practices and firm performance in an emerging economy. *Journal of Cleaner Production*, 258, 120766. 10.1016/j.jclepro.2020.120766

Sarhan, A. A., & Al-Najjar, B. (2023). The influence of corporate governance and shareholding structure on corporate social responsibility: The key role of executive compensation. *International Journal of Finance & Economics*, 28(4), 4532–4556. 10.1002/ijfe.2663

Sarkar, S., Nair, S., & Datta, A. (2023). *Role of Environmental, Social, and Governance in achieving the UN Sustainable Development Goals: A special focus on India*. https://doi.org/10.1002/ep.14204

Sarwat, S., Godil, D. I., Ali, L., Ahmad, B., Dinca, G., & Khan, S. A. R. (2022). The role of natural resources, renewable energy, and globalization in testing EKC Theory in BRICS countries: Method of Moments Quantile. *Environmental Science and Pollution Research International*, 29(16), 1–13. 10.1007/s11356-021-17557-534811617

Sattar, M., Biswas, P. K., & Roberts, H. (2023). Private firm performance: Do women directors matter? *Meditari Accountancy Research*, 31(3), 602–634. 10.1108/MEDAR-03-2021-1233

Schäfer, H. (2004). Ethical Investment of German Non-Profit Organzations-Conceptual Outline and Empirical Results. *Business Ethics (Oxford, England)*, 13(4), 269–287. 10.1111/j.1467-8608.2004.00370.x

Schaltegger, S., & Figge, F. (2000). Environmental shareholder value: Economic success with corporate environmental management. *Eco-Management and Auditing*, 7(1), 29–42. 10.1002/(SICI)1099-0925(200003)7:1<29::AID-EMA119>3.0.CO;2-1

Schipper, K. (1989). Earnings management. *Accounting Horizons*, 3(4), 91.

Schoenmaker, D., & Schramade, W. (2018). *Principles of sustainable finance.* Oxford University Press., https://www.researchgate.net/profile/Dirk-Schoenmaker/publication/330359025 _Principles_of_Sustainable_Finance/links/5c3c3d1992851c22a3736593/Principles-of -Sustainable-Finance.pdf

Scholtens, B., & Kang, F. C. (2013). Corporate social responsibility and earnings management: Evidence from Asian economies. *Corporate Social Responsibility and Environmental Management*, 20(2), 95–112. 10.1002/csr.1286

Schonherr, N., Findler, F., & Martinuzzi, A. (2017). Exploring the interface of CSR and the Sustainable Development Goals. *Transnational Corporations*, 24(3), 33–47. 10.18356/cfb5b8b6-en

Schwab Foundation for Social Entrepreneurship. (2020). *Two Decades of Impact.* Geneva: World Economic Forum.

SECP. (2023). *Draft Guidelines on ESG Disclosures for Listed Companies.* Securities and Exchange Commission of Pakistan.

Seele, P., & Gatti, L. (2017). Greenwashing revisited: In search of a typology and accusation-based definition incorporating legitimacy strategies. *Business Strategy and the Environment*, 26(2), 239–252. 10.1002/bse.1912

Sehgal, S., & Babbar, S. (2017). Evaluating alternative performance benchmarks for Indian mutual fund industry. *Journal of Advances in Management Research*, 14(2), 222–250. 10.1108/JAMR-04-2016-0028

Sehgal, S., & Jain, S. (2012). Short-term prior return patterns in stocks and sector returns: Evidence for BRICKS markets. *Investment Management and Financial Innovations*, 9(1), 93–114.

Sehgal, S., & Jhanwar, M. (2007). Short-term persistence in mutual funds performance: evidence from India. *10th Capital Markets Conference,* Indian Institute of Capital Markets. 10.2139/ssrn.962829

Sekar, A., & Krishnan, R. (2022). ESG - Marching Towards Sustainable Development Goals. *The Management Accountant Journal*, 57(3), 17. 10.33516/maj.v57i3.17-21p

Senbet, L. W., & Seward, J. K. (1995). Financial distress, bankruptcy and reorganization. In *Handbooks in Operations Research and Management Science* (Vol. 9, pp. 921–961). Elsevier., 10.1016/S0927-0507(05)80072-6

Serra, D., & De Oliveira, T. (2023). Environmental, Social and Governance (ESG). *Revista Direito E Sexualidade*, 49–71. 10.9771/rds.v4i1.52207

Shahzad, M., Qu, Y., Javed, S. A., Zafar, A. U., & Rehman, S. U. (2020). Relation of environment sustainability to CSR and green innovation: A case of Pakistani manufacturing industry. *Journal of Cleaner Production*, 253, 119938. 10.1016/j.jclepro.2019.119938

Shannon, C. E. (1948). A mathematical theory of communication. *The Bell System Technical Journal*, 27(3), 379–423. 10.1002/j.1538-7305.1948.tb01338.x

Sharma, V., & Loginova, J. (2023, September). *The Social Aspects of India's Energy Transition.* Google. https://www.google.com/url?q=https://www.researchgate.net/publication/373665379 _The_Social_Aspects_of_India%2527s_Energy_Transition&sa=D&source=docs&ust= 1718863811157703&usg=AOvVaw0t_pcMcFIVfaohunQinFp0

Sharma, V., Greig, C., & Lant, P. (2021, August). *What is stopping India's rapid decarbonisation? Examining social factors, speed, and institutions in Odisha.* ScienceDirect. https://www .sciencedirect.com/science/article/abs/pii/S2214629621002103

Sharma, E. (2019). A review of corporate social responsibility in developed and developing nations. *Corporate Social Responsibility and Environmental Management*, 26(4), 712–720. 10.1002/csr.1739

Sharpe, W. F. (1964). 1964 Sharpe - Capital Asset Prices. *The Journal of Finance*, 19(3).

Shayan, N. F., Mohabbati-Kalejahi, N., Alavi, S., & Zahed, M. A. (2022). Sustainable Development Goals (SDGs) as a Framework for Corporate Social Responsibility (CSR). *Sustainability (Basel)*, 14(3), 1222. Advance online publication. 10.3390/su14031222

Sheptytska, L., & Liudmyla, K. O. (2024). Social entrepreneurship in scientific and social discourses of Ukraine (the beginning of the 21st century. *East European HistoricalBulletin*, (30), 191–199.

Siew, R. Y., Balatbat, M. C., & Carmichael, D. G. (2016). The impact of ESG disclosures and institutional ownership on market information asymmetry. *Asia-Pacific Journal of Accounting & Economics*, 23(4), 432–448. 10.1080/16081625.2016.1170100

Simao, M. S., Dagnese, L. L., Ribeiro, E., Aurelio, M., Green, V., & Tomaz, K. D. (2022). Multisectoral Sustainable Development Impacts Survey From the Application of the SDGs-IAE Framework: A Case Study. *2022 IEEE Sustainable Power and Energy Conference (ISPEC)*. 10.1109/iSPEC54162.2022.10032985

Singhania, M., & Saini, N. (2023). Institutional framework of ESG disclosures: Comparative analysis of developed and developing countries. *Journal of Sustainable Finance & Investment*, 13(1), 516–559. 10.1080/20430795.2021.1964810

Compilation of References

Singh, H. V., Bocca, R., Gomez, P., Dahlke, S., & Bazilian, M. (2019). The energy transitions index: An analytic framework for understanding the evolving global energy system. *Energy Strategy Reviews*, 26, 100382. 10.1016/j.esr.2019.100382

Sklar, M. (1959). Fonctions de répartition à n dimensions et leurs marges. In Annales de l'ISUP (Vol. 8, No. 3, pp. 229-231).

Smith, R. (2003). *Audit Committtees Combined Code Guidance.* https://www.ecgi.global/sites/default/files/codes/documents/ac_report.pdf

Society for Human Resource Management (SHRM). (2023). *THE INTERSECTION OF ESG AND HR*. Retrieved from https://www.shrm.org/content/dam/en/shrm/executive-network/en-insights-forums/March%202023%20Insights%20Forum.pdf

Sodano, V., & Hingley, M. (2018). Corporate social responsibility reporting: The case of the agri-food sector. *Economia Agro-Alimentare*, 20(1), 93–120. 10.3280/ECAG2018-001006

Sokolova, N. A., & Teymurov, E. S. (2022). Correlation of Sustainable Development Goals and ESG principles. [MSAL]. *Courier of Kutafin Moscow State Law University*, 12(12), 171–183. 10.17803/2311-5998.2021.88.12.171-183

Soni, T. K. (2023). Demystifying the relationship between ESG and SDG performance: Study of emerging economies. *Investment Management and Financial Innovations*, 20(3), 1–12. 10.21511/imfi.20(3).2023.01

Sonter, L. J., & Ali, S. H. (2018, December 5). *Mining and biodiversity: key issues and research needs in conservation science.* The Royal Society. https://royalsocietypublishing.org/doi/10.1098/rspb.2018.1926

Soobaroyen, T., & Mahadeo, J. D. (2016). Community disclosures in a developing country: Insights from a neo-pluralist perspective. *Accounting, Auditing & Accountability Journal*, 29(3), 452–482. Advance online publication. 10.1108/AAAJ-08-2014-1810

Sougné, D., & Ajina, A. (2014). Examining the Effect of Earnings Management on Bid-Ask Spread and Market Liquidity. *European Journal of Business and Management*, 9(28).

Soussou, K., & Omri, A. (2022). Mutual Funds' Performance Sensitivity to Funds' Attributes. Case Study: Saudi Mutual Funds. *Financial Markets. Institutions and Risks*, 6(4), 32–50. 10.21272/fmir.6(4).32-50.2022

Srivastava, A., & Anand, A. (2023). ESG performance and firm value: The moderating role of ownership concentration. *Corporate Ownership and Control.*, 20(3), 169–179. 10.22495/cocv20i3art11

Staicu, D., & Pop, O. (2018). Mapping the interactions between the stakeholders of the circular economy ecosystem applied to the textile and apparel sector in Romania. *Management and Marketing*, 13(4), 1190–1209. 10.2478/mmcks-2018-0031

Statman, M., & Glushkov, D. (2016). Classifying and measuring the performance of socially responsible mutual funds. *Journal of Portfolio Management*, 42(2), 140–151. 10.3905/jpm.2016.42.2.140

Stavins, R., Reinhardt, F., & Vietor, R. (2008). Corporate Social Responsibility Through an Economic Lens. *Review of Environmental Economics and Policy*, 2(2), 219–239. 10.1093/reep/ren008

Steen, M., Moussawi, J. T., & Gjolberg, O. (2020). Is there a relationship between Morningstar's ESG ratings and mutual fund performance? *Journal of Sustainable Finance & Investment*, 10(4), 349–370. 10.1080/20430795.2019.1700065

Stern, D. I. (1993). Energy and economic growth in the USA: A multivariate approach. *Energy Economics*, 15(2), 137–150. 10.1016/0140-9883(93)90033-N

Stern, D. I. (2000). A multivariate cointegration analysis of the role of energy in the US macroeconomy. *Energy Economics*, 22(2), 267–283. 10.1016/S0140-9883(99)00028-6

Stern, N. H. (2007). *The economics of climate change: the Stern review*. Cambridge University press. 10.1017/CBO9780511817434

Stone, M. (1974). Cross-validation and multinomial prediction. *Biometrika*, 61(3), 509–515. 10.1093/biomet/61.3.509

Strobl, G. (2013). Earnings manipulation and the cost of capital. *Journal of Accounting Research*, 51(2), 449–473. 10.1111/1475-679X.12008

Suchman, M. C. (1995). Managing legitimacy: Strategic and institutional approaches. *Academy of Management Review*, 20(3), 571–610. 10.2307/258788

Suharti, T., Aminda, R. S., Bimo, W. A., Nurhayati, I., & Dewi, S. M. (2022). Performance of Conventional and Sharia Mutual Funds Using Sharpe, Treynor and Jensens Methods. *Proceedings of The International Halal Science and Technology Conference*, 15(1), 48–58. 10.31098/ihsatec.v15i1.594

Sullivan, D. M. (2007). Stimulating social entrepreneurship: Can support from cities make a difference? *The Academy of Management Perspectives*, 21(1), 77–78. 10.5465/amp.2007.24286169

Sustainalytics (2024). https://www.sustainalytics.com/material-esg-issues-resource-center

Suto, M., & Takehara, H. (2017). CSR and cost of capital: Evidence from Japan. *Social Responsibility Journal*, 13(4), 798–816. 10.1108/SRJ-10-2016-0170

Syed Samar Hasnain, S. B. (2017). *Green Banking Guidelines*. State Bank of Pakistan.

Szabo, S., & Webster, J. (2021). Perceived greenwashing: The effects of green marketing on environmental and product perceptions. *Journal of Business Ethics*, 171(4), 719–739. 10.1007/s10551-020-04461-0

Szetey, K., Moallemi, E. A., & Bryan, B. A. (2023). Knowledge Co-Production Reveals Nuanced Societal Dynamics and Sectoral Connections in Mapping Sustainable Human–Natural Systems. *Earth's Future*, 11(9), e2022EF003326. Advance online publication. 10.1029/2022EF003326

Compilation of References

Talan, G., & Sharma, G. (2019). Doing well by doing good: A systematic review and research agenda for sustainable investment. *Sustainability (Basel)*, 11(2), 353. 10.3390/su11020353

Tariq, S., Yunis, M. S., Shoaib, S., Abdullah, F., & Khan, S. W. (2022). Perceived corporate social responsibility and pro-environmental behaviour: Insights from business schools of Peshawar, Pakistan. In *Frontiers in Psychology* (Vol. 13). Frontiers Media S.A., 10.3389/fpsyg.2022.948059

Tateishi, E. (2017). Craving gains and claiming "green" by cutting greens? An exploratory analysis of greenfield housing developments in Iskandar Malaysia. *Journal of Urban Affairs*, 40(3), 370–393. 10.1080/07352166.2017.1355667

Teichmann, F. M. J., Wittmann, C., & Sergi, B. S. S. (2023). What are the consequences of corporate greenwashing? A look into the consequences of greenwashing in consumer and financial markets. *Journal of Information. Communication and Ethics in Society*, 21(3), 290–301. 10.1108/JICES-10-2022-0090

Teng, X., Ge, Y., Wu, K. S., Chang, B. G., Kuo, L., & Zhang, X. (2022). Too little or too much? Exploring the inverted U-shaped nexus between voluntary environmental, social and governance and corporate financial performance. *Frontiers in Environmental Science*, 10, 969721. Advance online publication. 10.3389/fenvs.2022.969721

Teoh, S. H., Welch, I., & Wong, T. J. (1998). Earnings management and the long-run market performance of initial public offerings. *The Journal of Finance*, 53(6), 1935–1974. 10.1111/0022-1082.00079

Terrachoice Environmental Marketing Inc. (2007). *The 'Six Sins of Greenwashing': A study of environmental claims in North American consumer markets*. Global Ecolabelling Network.

The Forum for Sustainable and Responsible Investment. (2018). *Report on US Sustainable. Responsible and Impact Investing Trends.*

The World Bank. (2024, April 20). *The World Bank*. Retrieved from Understanding Poverty: https://www.worldbank.org/en/topic/poverty/overview

Thirty minerals listed as critical minerals for India. (2023, December 11). Press Information Bureau. https://pib.gov.in/PressReleseDetail.aspx?PRID=1984942

Thomas, A. S., Jayachandran, A., & Biju, A. V. N. (2024). Strategic mapping of the environmental social governance landscape in finance – A bibliometric exploration through concepts and themes. *Corporate Social Responsibility and Environmental Management*, •••, 1–26. 10.1002/csr.2805

Tian, Z., Shen, Y., & Chen, Z. (2024). How does bank branch expansion affect ESG: Evidence from Chinese commercial banks. *Economic Analysis and Policy*, 82, 502–514. 10.1016/j.eap.2024.03.025

Tiba, S., & Omri, A. (2017). Literature survey on the relationships between energy, environment and economic growth. *Renewable & Sustainable Energy Reviews*, 69, 1129–1146. 10.1016/j.rser.2016.09.113

Todaro, D. L., & Torelli, R. (2024). From greenwashing to ESG-washing: A focus on the circular economy field. *Corporate Social Responsibility and Environmental Management*, csr.2786. Advance online publication. 10.1002/csr.2786

Torelli, R., Balluchi, F., & Lazzini, A. (2020). Greenwashing and environmental communication: Effects on stakeholders' perceptions. *Business Strategy and the Environment*, 29(2), 407–421. 10.1002/bse.2373

Tran, N. T. (2022). Impact of corporate social responsibility on customer loyalty: Evidence from the Vietnamese jewellery industry. *Cogent Business & Management*, 9(1), 2025675. Advance online publication. 10.1080/23311975.2022.2025675

Transparency International. (2020). *Corruption perceptions index 2020*. Retrieved from https://www.transparency.org/en/cpi/2020/index/nzl

Trendafilova, S., Babiak, K., & Heinze, K. (2013). Corporate social responsibility and environmental sustainability: Why professional sport is greening the playing field. *Sport Management Review*, 16(3), 298–313. 10.1016/j.smr.2012.12.006

Tricco, A. C., Lillie, E., Zarin, W., O'Brien, K. K., Colquhoun, H., Levac, D., Moher, D., Peters, M. D. J., Horsley, T., Weeks, L., Hempel, S., Akl, E. A., Chang, C., McGowan, J., Stewart, L., Hartling, L., Aldcroft, A., Wilson, M. G., Garritty, C., & Straus, S. E. (2018). PRISMA Extension for Scoping Reviews (PRISMA-ScR): Checklist and Explanation. *Annals of Internal Medicine*, 169(7), 467–473. 10.7326/M18-085030178033

Tricco, A. C., Lillie, E., Zarin, W., O'Brien, K., Colquhoun, H., Kastner, M., Levac, D., Ng, C., Sharpe, J. P., Wilson, K., Kenny, M., Warren, R., Wilson, C., Stelfox, H. T., & Straus, S. E. (2016). A scoping review on the conduct and reporting of scoping reviews. *BMC Medical Research Methodology*, 16(1), 15. 10.1186/s12874-016-0116-426857112

Tripathi, V., & Bhandari, V. (2015). Socially responsible stocks: A boon for investors in India. *Journal of Advances in Management Research*, 12(2), 209–225. 10.1108/JAMR-03-2014-0021

Tripopsakul, S., & Puriwat, W. (2022). Understanding the impact of ESG on brand trust and customer engagement. *Journal of Human, Earth, and Future*, 3(4), 430–440. 10.28991/HEF-2022-03-04-03

Trueman, B., & Titman, S. (1988). An explanation for accounting income smoothing. *Journal of Accounting Research*, 26, 127–139. 10.2307/2491184

Tsai, T.-J., Yang, C.-B., & Peng, Y.-H. (2011). Genetic algorithms for the investment of the mutual fund with global trend indicator. *Expert Systems with Applications*, 38(3), 1697–1701. 10.1016/j.eswa.2010.07.094

Tse, , TEsposito, , MGoh, , D. (2024). The impact of artificial intelligence on environmental, social and governance investing: the case of Nexus FrontierTech. *International Journal of Teaching and Case Studies*, 14(3), 256-275. https://doi.org/10.1504/IJTCS.2024.137516

Compilation of References

Tugcu, C. T., Ozturk, I., & Aslan, A. (2012). Renewable and non-renewable energy consumption and economic growth relationship revisited: Evidence from G7 countries. *Energy Economics*, 34(6), 1942–1950. 10.1016/j.eneco.2012.08.021

Tykvová, T., & Borell, M. (2012). Do private equity owners increase risk of financial distress and bankruptcy? *Journal of Corporate Finance*, 18(1), 138–150. 10.1016/j.jcorpfin.2011.11.004

Uduji, J. I., Okolo-Obasi, E. N., & Asongu, S. A. (2019). Corporate social responsibility and the role of rural women in sustainable agricultural development in sub-Saharan Africa: Evidence from the Niger Delta in Nigeria. *Sustainable Development (Bradford)*, 27(4), 692–703. 10.1002/sd.1933

Uduji, J. I., Okolo-Obasi, E. N., & Asongu, S. A. (2021). Sustainable peacebuilding and development in Nigeria's post-amnesty programme: The role of corporate social responsibility in oil host communities. *Journal of Public Affairs*, 21(2), e2200. 10.1002/pa.2200

Ukko, J., Nasiri, M., Saunila, M., & Rantala, T. (2019). Sustainability strategy as a moderator in the relationship between digital business strategy and financial performance. *Journal of Cleaner Production*, 236, 117626. 10.1016/j.jclepro.2019.117626

UN. (2011). *Guiding principles on business and human rights: Implementing the United Nations "Protect, Respect and Remedy" framework.* United Nations Human Rights Office of the High Commissioner. Retrieved from https://www.ohchr.org/documents/publications/guidingprinciples businesshr_en.pdf

UNDP. (2024, April 15). *Multi Dimensional Poverty Index2023.* Retrieved from UNDP. Paksitan: https://hdr.undp.org/sites/default/files/Country-Profiles/MPI/PAK.pdf#:~:text=The%20intensity %20of%20deprivations%20in%20Pakistan%2C%20which,the%20intensity%20of%20the%20 deprivations%2C%20is%200.198

Unilever (2023). *The Unilever Compass for Sustainable Growth.* Retrieved from https://www .unilever.com/files/8f9a3825-2101-411f-9a31-7e6f176393a4/the-unilever-compass.pdf

United Nations Environment Programme. International Resource Panel, United Nations Environment Programme. Sustainable Consumption, & Production Branch. (2011). *Decoupling natural resource use and environmental impacts from economic growth.* UNEP/Earthprint. Retrieved from https://www.unep.org/resources/report/decoupling-natural-resource-use-and-environmental -impacts-economic-growth

United Nations Framework Convention on Climate Change. Secretariat. (1992). *United Nations framework convention on climate change.* UNFCCC.

US SIF Foundation. (2022). Highlights: 2022 Report on US Sustainable Investing Trends from US SIF Foundation. US SIF Trends 2022 Highlights. https://trends2022highlights.com/

Usman, M., Zhang, J., Wang, F., Sun, J., & Makki, M. A. M. (2018). Gender diversity in compensation committees and CEO pay: Evidence from China. *Management Decision*, 56(5), 1065–1087. 10.1108/MD-09-2017-0815

Uyar, A., Kilic, M., Koseoglu, M. A., Kuzey, C., & Karaman, A. S. (2020). The link among board characteristics, corporate social responsibility performance, and financial performance: Evidence from the hospitality and tourism industry. *Tourism Management Perspectives*, 35, 100714. 10.1016/j.tmp.2020.100714

van Asselt, H. (2023). The SDGs and fossil fuel subsidy reform. *International Environmental Agreement: Politics, Law and Economics*, 23(2), 191–197. 10.1007/s10784-023-09601-1

Vanaja, V., & Karrupasamy, R. (2016). Performance Evaluation of select Public Sector and Private Sector Mutual Funds in India. *Asian Journal of Research in Social Sciences and Humanities*, 6(7), 1532–1547. 10.5958/2249-7315.2016.00527.X

Varadhan, S. (2024, February 1). *India to increase coal-fired capacity in 2024 by the most in at least 6 years*. reuters.com. https://www.reuters.com/business/energy/india-increase-coal-fired -capacity-2024-by-most-least-6-years-2024-02-01/

Velte, P. (2017). Does ESG performance have an impact on financial performance? Evidence from Germany. *Journal of Global Responsibility*, 8(2), 169–178. 10.1108/JGR-11-2016-0029

Verheyden, T., Eccles, R. G., & Feiner, A. (2016). ESG for all? The impact of ESG screening on return, risk, and diversification. *The Bank of America Journal of Applied Corporate Finance*, 28(2), 47–55. 10.1111/jacf.12174

Verrecchia, R. E. (1983). Discretionary disclosure. *Journal of Accounting and Economics*, 5, 179–194. 10.1016/0165-4101(83)90011-3

Verrecchia, R. E. (2001). Essays on disclosure. *Journal of Accounting and Economics*, 32(1-3), 97–180. 10.1016/S0165-4101(01)00025-8

Vidal-García, J., & Vidal, M. (2024). The Relation between Mutual Fund Performance and Investment Style Changes. *Available atSSRN* 4021259.

Vidyarthi, H. (2013). Energy consumption, carbon emissions and economic growth in India. *World Journal of Science. Technology and Sustainable Development*, 10(4), 278–287. 10.1108/WJSTSD-07-2013-0024

Visalli, F., Patrizio, A., Lanza, A., Papaleo, P., Nautiyal, A., Pupo, M., Scilinguo, U., Oro, E., & Ruffolo, M. (2023). ESG data collection with adaptive AI. In *Proceedings of the 25th International Conference on Enterprise Information Systems - Volume 1: ICEIS* (pp. 468-475). SciTePress. https://doi.org/10.5220/0011844500003467

Vormedal, I., & Ruud, A. (2009). Sustainability reporting in Norway: An assessment of performance in the context of legal demands and socio-political drivers. *Business Strategy and the Environment*, 18(4), 207–222. 10.1002/bse.560

Walker, K., & Wan, F. (2012). The harm of symbolic actions and green-washing: Corporate actions and communications on environmental performance and their financial implications. *Journal of Business Ethics*, 109(2), 227–242. 10.1007/s10551-011-1122-4

Walsh, H., & Dowding, T. J. (2012). Sustainability and The Coca-Cola Company: The global water crisis and Coca-Cola's business case for water stewardship. *International Journal of Business Insights & Transformation, 4.*

Wang, S., & D'Souza, J. (2006). Earnings management: The effect of accounting flexibility on R&D investment choices. *Johnson School Research Paper Series*, (33-06).

Wang, J. (1993). A model of intertemporal asset prices under asymmetric information. *The Review of Economic Studies*, 60(2), 249–282. 10.2307/2298057

Wang, K., Chen, X., & Wang, C. (2023). The impact of sustainable development planning in resource-based cities on corporate ESG–Evidence from China. *Energy Economics*, 127, 107087. 10.1016/j.eneco.2023.107087

Wang, K., Huang, S., & Chen, Y.-H. (2008). Mutual fund performance evaluation system using fast adaptive neural network classifier. *2008 Fourth International Conference on Natural Computation, 2*, 479–483. 10.1109/ICNC.2008.756

Wang, K., Li, T., San, Z., & Gao, H. (2023). How does corporate ESG performance affect stock liquidity? Evidence from China. *Pacific-Basin Finance Journal*, 80, 102087. 10.1016/j.pacfin.2023.102087

Wang, Q., Dong, Z., Li, R., & Wang, L. (2022). Renewable energy and economic growth: New insight from country risks. *Energy*, 238, 122018. 10.1016/j.energy.2021.122018

Wang, S., & Chang, Y. (2024). A study on the impact of ESG rating on green technology innovation in enterprises: An empirical study based on informal environmental governance. Journal of Environmental Management, 358. *Journal of Environmental Management*, 358, 120878. Advance online publication. 10.1016/j.jenvman.2024.120878

Wang, Z., Ran, Y., Chen, Y., Yu, H., & Zhang, G. (2020). Failure mode and effects analysis using extended matter-element model and AHP. *Computers & Industrial Engineering*, 140, 106233. Advance online publication. 10.1016/j.cie.2019.106233

Wang, Z., & Sarkis, J. (2017). Corporate social responsibility governance, outcomes, and financial performance. *Journal of Cleaner Production*, 162, 1607–1616. 10.1016/j.jclepro.2017.06.142

Ward, H. (2006). *Corporate Social Responsibility at a Crossroads: Futures for CSR in the UK to 2015.* IIED.

Warfield, T. D., Wild, J. J., & Wild, K. L. (1995). Managerial ownership, accounting choices, and informativeness of earnings. *Journal of Accounting and Economics*, 20(1), 61–91. 10.1016/0165-4101(94)00393-J

Weiss, T. G., & Wilkinson, R. (2023). *International Organization and Global Governance.* Taylor & Francis. 10.4324/9781003266365

Welker, M. (1995). Disclosure policy, information asymmetry, and liquidity in equity markets. *Contemporary Accounting Research*, 11(2), 801–827. 10.1111/j.1911-3846.1995.tb00467.x

Wheeler, D., Fabig, H., & Boele, R. (2002). Paradoxes and dilemmas for stakeholder responsive firms in the extractive sector: *Lessons from the case of Shell and the Ogoni.Journal of Business Ethics*, 39(3), 297–318. 10.1023/A:1016542207069

Widyawati, L. (2019). A systematic literature review of socially responsible investment and environmental social governance metrics. *Business Strategy and the Environment*, 29(2), 619–637. 10.1002/bse.2393

Williams, Z. (2022). The Materiality Challenge of ESG Ratings. *Economics and Culture*, 19(2), 97–108. 10.2478/jec-2022-0019

Wiseman, J. (1982). An evaluation of environmental disclosures made in corporate annual reports. *Accounting, Organizations and Society*, 7(1), 53–63. 10.1016/0361-3682(82)90025-3

Wiyadi, A Veno, N & Sasongko. (2015). Information Asymmetry And Earnings Management: Good Corporate Governance As Moderating Variable. South East Asia Journal of Contemporary Business. *Economics and Law*, 7, 54–61.

Wong, K. K. K. (2013). Partial least squares structural equation modeling (PLS-SEM) techniques using SmartPLS. *Marketing Bulletin*, 24(1), 1–32.

Wong, W. C., Batten, J. A., Ahmad, A. H., Mohamed-Arshad, S. B., Nordin, S., & Adzis, A. A. (2021). Does ESG certification add firm value? *Finance Research Letters*, 39, 101593. 10.1016/j.frl.2020.101593

World Economic Forum. (2022). *ESG Governance: Integrating Sustainability into Corporate Strategy*. Retrieved from https://www.weforum.org/agenda/2022/06/why-sustainability-is-crucial-for-corporate-strategy/

World Energy Investment 2023. (2023, May).IEA. https://iea.blob.core.windows.net/assets/8834d3af-af60-4df0-9643-72e2684f7221/WorldEnergyInvestment2023.pdf

Worringham, C. (2021, September). *Renewable Energy and Land Use in India by Mid-Century Careful Planning Today Can Maximise the Benefits and Minimise the Costs of India's History-Making Energy Transition*. IEEFA | Institute for Energy Economics and Financial Analysis. https://ieefa.org/wp-content/uploads/2021/09/Renewable-Energy-and-Land-Use-in-India-by-Mid-Century_September-2021.pdf?ftag=MSF0951a18

Wu, J., Lodorfos, G., Dean, A., & Gioulmpaxiotis, G. (2015). The market performance of socially responsible investment during periods of the economic cycle - Illustrated using the case of FTSE. *MDE. Managerial and Decision Economics*, 38(2), 238–251. 10.1002/mde.2772

Wu, M.-W., Shen, C.-H., Hsu, H.-H., & Chiu, P.-H. (2023). Why did a bank with good governance perform worse during the financial crisis? The views of shareholder and stakeholder orientations. *Pacific-Basin Finance Journal*, 82, 102127. 10.1016/j.pacfin.2023.102127

Wu, Y., Zhang, K., & Xie, J. (2020). Bad greenwashing, good greenwashing: Corporate social responsibility and information transparency. *Management Science*, 66(7), 3095–3112. 10.1287/mnsc.2019.3340

Compilation of References

Xia, L. J., & LU, X. N. (2005). On the Relationship between Earnings Management and Information Disclosure Quality of Listed Firms [J]. *Geological Technoeconomic Management, 5*.

Xiao, K. (2023). How does Environment, Social and Governance Affect the Financial Performance of Enterprises? *SHS Web of Conferences, 163*, 04015. 10.1051/shsconf/202316304015

Xia, Q., Liu, Y., & Wei, F. (2023). How can ESG funds improve their performance? Based on the DEA-Malmquist productivity index and fsQCA method. *Journal of University of Science and Technology of China, 53*(8), 0803. Advance online publication. 10.52396/JUSTC-2023-0017

Xie, J., Nozawa, W., Yagi, M., Fujii, H., & Managi, S. (2019). Do environmental, social, and governance activities improve corporate financial performance? *Business Strategy and the Environment, 28*(2), 286–300. 10.1002/bse.2224

Xu, S., Liu, D., & Huang, J. (2015). Corporate social responsibility, the cost of equity capital and ownership structure: An analysis of Chinese listed firms. *Australian Journal of Management, 40*(2), 245–276. 10.1177/0312896213517894

Xu, Z., Peng, J., Qiu, S., Liu, Y., Dong, J., & Zhang, H. (2022). Responses of spatial relationships between ecosystem services and the Sustainable Development Goals to urbanization. *The Science of the Total Environment, 850*, 157868. 10.1016/j.scitotenv.2022.15786835944627

Yadav, P., & Prashar, A. (2022). Board gender diversity: Implications for environment, social, and governance (ESG) performance of Indian firms. *International Journal of Productivity and Performance Management, 72*(9), 2654–2673. 10.1108/IJPPM-12-2021-0689

Yadav, P., Singh, J., Srivastava, D. K., & Mishra, V. (2021). Environmental pollution and sustainability. In Singh, P., Verma, P., Perrotti, D., & Srivastava, K. K. (Eds.), *Environmental Sustainability and Economy* (pp. 111–120). Elsevier., 10.1016/B978-0-12-822188-4.00015-4

Yang, Z., Nguyen, T. T. H., Nguyen, H. N., Nguyen, T. T. N., & Cao, T. T. (2020). Greenwashing behaviours: Causes, taxonomy and consequences based on a systematic literature review. *Journal of Business Economics and Management, 21*(5), 1486–1507. 10.3846/jbem.2020.13225

Yang, Z., & Zhao, Y. (2014). Energy consumption, carbon emissions, and economic growth in India: Evidence from directed acyclic graphs. *Economic Modelling, 38*, 533–540. 10.1016/j.econmod.2014.01.030

Yan, J. (2007). Enjoy the joy of copulas: With a package copula. *Journal of Statistical Software, 21*(4). Advance online publication. 10.18637/jss.v021.i04

Yi, I., & Yi, I. (2023). The Sustainable Development Goals. *Edward Elgar Publishing EBooks*, 310–320. 10.4337/9781803920924.00054

Ying, M., Tikuye, G. A., & Shan, H. (2021). Impacts of Firm Performance on Corporate Social Responsibility Practices: The Mediation Role of Corporate Governance in Ethiopia Corporate Business. *Sustainability (Basel), 13*(17), 9717. 10.3390/su13179717

Yousaf, M., Ziaullah, M., & Tariq, M. G. (2023). The Performance of Pakistani Equity Mutual Funds During Bull and Bear Market. *Global Social Sciences Review*, VIII(II), 592–615. 10.31703/gssr.2023(VIII-II).53

Yu, G. (2010). Accounting standards and international portfolio holdings: Analysis of cross-border holdings following mandatory adoption of IFRS. *Unpublished Paper, Harvard University*.

Yu, E. P. Y., Van Luu, B., & Chen, C. H. (2020). Greenwashing in environmental, social and governance disclosures. *Research in International Business and Finance*, 52, 101192. 10.1016/j.ribaf.2020.101192

Yu, J. (2024). Stabilizing leverage, financial technology innovation, and commercial bank risks: Evidence from China. *Economic Modelling*, 131, 106599. 10.1016/j.econmod.2023.106599

Yu, J.-R., Chiou, W.-J. P., Lee, W.-Y., & Yu, K.-C. (2017). Does entropy model with return forecasting enhance portfolio performance? *Computers & Industrial Engineering*, 114, 175–182. 10.1016/j.cie.2017.10.007

Zabin, C. (2020, June). *Putting California on the high road*. UC Berkeley Labor Center. https://laborcenter.berkeley.edu/wp-content/uploads/2020/09/Putting-California-on-the-High-Road.pdf

Zahoor, N., Lew, Y. K., Arslan, A., Christofi, M., & Tarba, S. Y. (2023). International corporate social responsibility and post-entry performance of developing market INVs: The moderating role of corporate governance mechanisms. *Journal of International Management*, 29(4), 101036. 10.1016/j.intman.2023.101036

Zeeshan, M., Han, J., Rehman, A., Saleem, K., Shah, R. U., Ishaque, A., Farooq, N., & Hussain, A. (2020). Conventional mutual funds out perform Islamic mutual funds in the context of Pakistan. A myth or reality. *International Journal of Economics and Financial Issues*, 10(4), 151–157. 10.32479/ijefi.10090

Zhang, C., & Zhang, D. (2023). Executive incentives, team stability and corporate innovation performance. *Finance Research Letters*, 58, 104690. 10.1016/j.frl.2023.104690

Zhang, D. (2022). Environmental regulation and firm product quality improvement: How does the greenwashing response. *International Review of Financial Analysis*, 80, 1–8. 10.1016/j.irfa.2022.102058

Zhang, D., & Liu, L. (2022). Does ESG Performance Enhance Financial Flexibility? Evidence from China. *Sustainability (Basel)*, 14(18), 11324. Advance online publication. 10.3390/su141811324

Zhang, D., Wang, C., & Dong, Y. (2022). How Does Firm ESG Performance Impact Financial Constraints? An Experimental Exploration of the COVID-19 Pandemic. *European Journal of Development Research*, 35(1), 219–239. Advance online publication. 10.1057/s41287-021-00499-635002102

Zhang, Y., Mirza, S. S., Safdar, R., Huang, C., & Zhang, C. (2023). Business strategy and sustainability of Chinese SMEs: Determining the moderating role of environmental uncertainty. *Ekonomska Istrazivanja*, 36(3), 2218468. 10.1080/1331677X.2023.2218468

Compilation of References

Zheng, M. (2023, March 31). *The Environmental Impacts of Lithium and Cobalt Mining*. Earth. org.https://www.bing.com/search?pglt=41&q=zheng+%2C+lithium+and+cobalt+mining&cvid =a1c39363c1824aa0a2496203f39a3f52&gs_lcrp=EgZjaHJvbWUyBggAEEUYOTIGCAEQ ABhAMgYIAhAAGEAyBggDEAAYQDIGCAQQABhAMgYIBRAAGEDSAQg3NDY4ajBq MagCALACAA&FORM=ANNTA1&PC=HCTS

Zhixin, Z., & Xin, R. (2011). Causal relationships between energy consumption and economic growth. *Energy Procedia*, 5, 2065–2071. 10.1016/j.egypro.2011.03.356

Zhou, D., Saeed, U. F., & Agyemang, A. O. (2024). Assessing the Role of Sustainability Disclosure on Firms' Financial Performance: Evidence from the Energy Sector of Belt and Road Initiative Countries. *Sustainability (Basel)*, 16(2), 2. Advance online publication. 10.3390/su16020930

About the Contributors

Biju Ajithakumari Vijayappan Nair is an Associate Professor at the Dept. of Commerce, School of Business Management & Legal studies, University of Kerala. His research interests include corporate credit, personal finance, Market Microstructure, Nudging and Social Finance, Crypto Market, ML in Finance, Green Washing, Green Bonds, Sustainability Reporting, ESG and Surveillance capitalism. He is a research supervisor in the Faculty of Commerce and Faculty of Management at the University of Kerala. He is the author of five textbooks for the M Com programme at the University of Kerala and several papers in popular journals having a high impact factor. He received the best paper award from the IIM Nagpur conference in 2022. He has collaborated with the Research Sans frontier (RSF) in Dubai. He is acting as the visiting faculty of the University of Wollongong, UAE. He collaborates with Khalifa University, Abu Dhabi, and James Cook University, Australia. He serves as the editorial board member of springer, Wiley, Inderscience and IGI Global journals such as the SN Business and Economics, International Journal of Applied Management Science, International Journal of E-business Research (IJEBR) and International Journal of Business Analytics (IJBAN). His papers appeared in the Employees Responsibilities and Rights Journal, Business strategy and development, S N business and economics, Asia pacific journal of finance studies and Digital Finance and the International Journal of Human Capital and Information Technology Professional (IJHCIT)by IGI Global.

Glenn Muschert is a professor of sociology in the Department of Public Health and Epidemiology at Khalifa University of Science and Technology (ÌÇãÚÉ ÌáÍÝÉ) in Abu Dhabi, UAE. He has served as a research advisor to the Abu Dhabi Department of Community Development and has been appointed as the Len Jessup Professor of Leadership and Organizational Change at Woxsen University in Hyderabad, India. Previously he served appointments on the Law and Society faculty at Purdue University (USA) and the Sociology, Social Justice Studies, and Comparative Media Studies faculties at Miami University (USA). His research focuses on the metaverse, digital inequalities, sustainable development, and the ethical resolution of social problems. Dr. Muschert earned a Ph.D. (2002) in sociology from the University of Colorado (USA), and a BS (1992) in International Studies from Drexel University (USA). He has been a visiting scholar at various universities worldwide, including Seoul City University (South Korea), Erzincan University (Turkey), and Atatürk University (Turkey). He is proficient in various qualitative and quantitative methodologies of social research inquiry and frequently serves as a reviewer and editorial board member for dozens of academic journals. With over 25 years of experience as a university instructor, the UAE Ministry of Education has certified him as an External Reviewer for the Council on Academic Accreditation. Dr. Muschert is a member of international professional associations such as the Academy of International Business (AIB) and the Society for the Study of Social Problems (SSSP), where he is a lifetime member and has served since 2010 as SSSP Secretary. He has written or edited over a dozen academic volumes/special issues of journals, dozens of academic research articles, and dozens of chapters in academic volumes. Major books include Theorizing Digital Divides (Routledge), The Digital Divide: The Internet and Social Inequality in International Perspective (Routledge), and multiple volumes of Agenda for Social Justice (Policy Press).

About the Contributors

Ambili Jayachandran is a keen and passionate academic researcher with interests in topics of Sustainability, ESG, International Business, Macroeconomics and Econometric analysis. She is currently working as a Research Associate under the ICSSR-funded project titled "Effect of Investor Sentimentality on Sustainability and ESG Ratings on Performance of Indian Companies". Awarded Ph.D in Commerce under the University of Kerala in April 2022 for the presentation of the research thesis titled "Implications of Asian Monetary Unit in Indian Business Environment: A Feasibility Study". She has publications in the areas of Exchange rate dynamics, International Business and Indian Banking

***

Ayyoob A is a distinguished Senior Research Scholar in Commerce, currently pursuing his Ph.D. at the Department of Commerce and Management Studies (DCMS), School of Business Studies, University of Calicut, Kerala. His research delves into the intricate realms of Corporate Governance, Corporate Sustainability, Strategic CSR, ESG, DEIB, and SDGs, marking him as a pivotal figure in his field. Among his impressive scholarly contributions is a notable paper on Diversity, Equity, and Inclusion (DE&I) published by Routledge, alongside several other papers focused on sustainability, which are under review in prestigious journals indexed in Scopus and ABDC. Mr. Ayyoob A's dedication to advancing sustainability is evident through his consistent delivery of valuable insights, profoundly influencing both theoretical frameworks and practical applications within his domain. His commitment is further demonstrated by his active participation in the academic community, having attended and presented over 15 papers at various international conferences organized by esteemed institutions. Beyond his research endeavors, Mr. Ayyoob A extends his expertise through consultancy services to researchers and students, both domestically and internationally. His consultancy work is complemented by his role as an educator, where he handles lectures and workshops focusing on research methodology and data analysis. His ability to demystify complex concepts and impart practical knowledge has made him a sought-after mentor and speaker. In his academic journey, Mr. Ayyoob A has not only contributed significantly to the body of knowledge in his field but also demonstrated a profound commitment to fostering a deeper understanding of sustainability and corporate responsibility. His multifaceted contributions, from groundbreaking research to impactful teaching and consultancy, underscore his role as a key influencer in the realms of commerce and management studies. Through his unwavering dedication and scholarly excellence, Mr. Ayyoob A continues to inspire and shape the future of corporate sustainability and governance.

Aparna A.S is a Senior Research Fellow at the Department of Commerce, University of Kerala. Her area of interest includes Behavioural economics, Nudges and choice architecture, Retirement planning, ESG, Cryptocurrencies, etc.

Haseena Akbar is a Post Doctoral Fellow (RUSA 2.0 Project) at the Centre for Budget Studies, Cochin University of Science and Technology, Kerala, India.Her Research interest includes Labour Migration, Sustainable development and macroeconomics.

El Houssan Attak, holds a PhD in Business Administration from Aix-Marseille University and a Master's degree in Research from the University Paris-Panthéon-Assas. He is a professor at the National School of Business and Management at Cadi Ayyad University in Marrakesh. Dr. Attak has published papers in Scopus-indexed journals and contributed chapters to Scopus-indexed books.

Muhammad bin Ashfaq is affiliated with the MBBS department of Rawal Institute of Health Sciences . With a keen interest in social sciences and its correlation with his own field of work, he has co authored more than 4 research papers pertaining to emotional resilience, extremism and social entrepreneurship .

Showkat Ahmad Busru has received his PhD Degree from Pondicherry Central University in the area of Finance and has completed his Post-graduate degree in Accounting and Finance from Central University of Rajasthan. In addition, he has also completed Post Graduate Diploma in Computer Application from Pondicherry Central University. He got awarded UGC NET in Commerce conducted by UGC. On his credit are several research publications in reputed journals and has also attended numerous National as well as International Conferences conducted by prestigious Institutions of the Country

Sreelekshmi G. is a doctoral student at the Department of Commerce, School of Business Management and Legal Studies, University of Kerala. Keenly interested in sustainable finance, after completing her B.Com. and M.Com. with first position in both the programmes from the University of Kerala, she is pursuing research on the topic of green bonds under the guidance of Dr. Biju A. V. under the UGC JRF scheme.

Taji Hanaa earned a Doctorate in Management Sciences from the National School of Business and Management in Agadir in 2022, with a dissertation on creating ethical indices for the Casablanca Stock Exchange; Taji completed a Master's degree in Economic and Social Administration, specializing in Governance and Organizational Management, at Université d'Évry Val d'Essonne, Paris, in 2015. In 2013, Taji obtained a diploma from the National School of Business and Management Agadir, specializing in Financial and Accounting Management. Taji's research interests include Corporate Social Responsibility (CSR) and financial performance, ESG (Environmental, Social, and Governance) and Islamic rating, and the development of ESG Islamic indices.

Smiju Sudevan, is currently working as an Assistant Professor in Information Systems at Cochin University of Science and Technology. He has seventeen years of professional experience in teaching Information Systems at the university level in both national and international colleges like BITS-Pilani and MCBS, Oman. Dr Smiju holds a MTech in software engineering and a PhD in software project management from Cochin University of Science and Technology, India. The main research areas of his interest are Software engineering and Software project management with emphasis on Stakeholder management along with agile methodologies. He has completed his PostDoc from IIT, Hyderabad while working as the project manager for Suzuki V2X Project. He is a member of PMI, Scrum Allianze ,ACM and IEEE. Dr Smiju Sudevan has delivered numerous workshops and seminars on project management nationally and internationally and has also published numerous papers in reputed journals.

Sanobar Imam is a master's graduate in Water Policy and Governance from Tata Institute of Social Sciences, Mumbai, and is currently working as a research associate at CUTS International, Jaipur, in climate finance, climate change, environment, ecology, energy, and water verticals. She has co-authored a report titled "Decarbonization of Freight Sector in India". She has also co-authored a briefing paper on public-private synergy in climate financing, addressing the climate finance gap to achieve climate mitigation and adaptation targets. She also wrote an opinion piece titled, "The Demand for Green Transportation Looming the Future of Miners in Congo". She is currently a part of the global campaign titled "Innovative Finance for Climate and the Planet (IFCP)," where she is advocating for establishing a 'Fund of Funds' to leverage various non-governmental financial sources for addressing climate and biodiversity challenges, given their interconnection and common governance in many countries. She loves playing Badminton, watching Cricket, and writing.

Jose John is a research scholar from the School of Management Studies, Cochin University of Science and Technology. His area of interest lies in the domains of Corporate Social Responsibility, Corporate Social Work, Agile Methodologies and Stakeholder Engagement. He has a master's degree in Social Work and is a JRF holder.

Joseph M. K. is an experienced social work educator and a development Practitioner. He retired as the Head of the social work department at Rajagiri College of Social Sciences, Kerala, India. His doctoral thesis was on the village milk cooperatives in Kerala. He has many research projects, including UGC, IMPRESS, MGNCRE, and DSIR, funded projects to his credit and has published several journal articles and edited volumes. He is the recipient of the COADY international fellowship (Canada) and was a visiting scholar at Western Michigan University, USA. His teaching and research interests are in community development, social entrepreneurship, and developing partnerships for Civil society organisations and rural producer organisations.

About the Contributors

Mohammed K embarked on a rewarding journey with Bank of New York Mellon (BNY Mellon), contributing my efforts for two impactful years. I proudly served as a General Manager at Fiveberg India Ltd., soaking in the challenges and triumphs of the entrepreneurial landscape for a thrilling 1.5 years and my journey has led me to Aifer Institute, where I am dedicated to coaching NTA JRF aspirants, sharing knowledge and inspiring the next generation of thinkers. My passion as a researcher has taken me deep into the realm of Environmental, Social, and Governance (ESG) disclosures of Indian companies.I believe in the power of knowledge and the impact it can make.

Harpreet Kaur is an Associate Professor, Department of Economics, Sri Guru Gobind Singh College of Commerce, University of Delhi, India. She has two decades of teaching experience and has taught papers on 'Statistical Methods for Economics', Mathematical Methods for Economics', 'Introductory Econometrics', 'Macro Economics' and 'Managerial Economics'. She completed her Master's in Economics from Delhi School of Economics and has done her M.Phil from the Department of Business Economics, University of Delhi and earned her Ph.D. from Faculty of Management Studies, University of Delhi. Her dissertation was on "Food Security in South Asia: Implications for Public Policy". Her research interests include open economy macroeconomics, managerial economics, development economics and public policy.

Santhosh Kumar P K is the Director and Associate Professor of Economics at the Centre for Budget Studies, Cochin University of Science and Technology (CUSAT). He specializes in finance and macroeconomic modeling, bringing a wealth of expertise to these areas. Dr. Santhosh has an extensive publication record, with numerous articles featured in highly regarded international and national journals. His research encompasses a wide range of economic topics, contributing significantly to the field through his rigorous analytical work and insightful findings. His academic and professional endeavors have earned him a distinguished reputation in the economics community.

Vimal George Kurian is an Assistant Professor at the Department of Commerce, CMS College Kottayam (Autonomous). He obtained his PhD in finance from the University of Madras. He is had made contirbutions in the field of behavioural finance through his publications. His publications primarily focused on market and investor sentiments. He is interested in areas like sustainability, and stock predictions using machine learning.

Moni M is a PhD research scholar at the Department of Commerce, University of Kerala, with a current research focus on asset pricing models. His profound interest lies in the fields of asset pricing models, econophysics, cryptocurrencies, ESG, sustainability, and financial market dynamics. He has also published works in domains such as finance and cryptocurrencies. He has received several best paper awards from international conferences.

Silpa Krishnan MP is a PhD research scholar in the finance domain at the University of Kerala, with her current research focus on Fintech and the digital economy. She holds MPhil degree from the Department of Commerce, University of Kerala. Her profound interest lies in the fields of AI, Fintech, the digital economy, and financial econometrics. She has received best paper awards from international conference.

Adwait Madkaikar has a master's in Sociology from Tata Institute of Social Sciences and a bachelor's in Engineering Physics from IIT Bombay. He is presently working as a Researcher in the Political Domain. His areas of interest are Policy and Legislative Research, Urban Studies, Environment and Climate Change Mitigation.

Ria Mammen is working as an Assistant Professor at the Department of Commerce, St. Thomas College, Pathanamthitta, India with nine years of experience. She obtained hes PhD in commerce from the University of Kerala. She specializes in accounting, retailing and e-commerce and had published papers in the area of finance in various peer-reviewed journals. Also she had made presentations at various international conferences. In addition her area of interest included sustainability, and stock market dynamics.

Vineetha Mathew is a passionate researcher in management, specializing in personal finance, gender studies, and wellbeing. With publications in Scopus and ABDC indexed journals, her research interests lie in unravelling the dynamics of human psychology, behaviour and its influence on decision-making, driving impactful insights in her field.

Fahad P has received his PhD Degree from Pondicherry Central University in the area of Finance and has completed his Post-graduate degree in Business Finance from Pondicherry Central University.

Mubarak Rahman P completed PhD from Pondicherry University on the topic of Innovation management in SMEs. Currently, I am working as an assistant professor in the management department at LEAD college Management Palakkad. I have more than 3 years of teaching experience.

Barbara Pisker is an Associate Professor of University of Osijek Faculty of Tourism and Rural Development. She specialises in Digital Sociology, Corporate Social Responsibility, Business Communication and Consumer Behaviour.

Hareesh Ramanathan is a teaching and research professional with sound experience in academic leadership, administration, international relations and institution building. Has got immense experience in making wonderful workplaces and a true practitioner of camaraderie. Two times recipient of European Union ERASMUS + fellowship for international teaching. An IBM certified data analyst who has made impact by analytical consultancies and publications. An acclaimed trainer and teacher in the field of analytics and research methods who had conducted many talks and workshops in India and abroad to benefit the research fraternity. A social as well as a sports enthusiast and hence passionately associating with many LSGs, NGOs, GOs and Sports clubs.

Faryal Razzaq is the managing Director for Center for Ethical Leadership at KSBL. She is a social entrepreneur and a seminal mentor for startups, and trainer for soft skills. Her area of expertise are emotional intelligence at workplace, ethics, Extremism, instructional design, learning styles. She has a keen interest in uplifting social problems, women empowerment, emotional well being, countering terrorism and extremism and developing ethical leaders

Aparna Sajeev is an Assistant Professor at the Department of Commerce and Management Studies, School of Business Studies, University of Calicut. She pursued her doctoral degree in macro-policy management at the Faculty of Management Studies, University of Delhi. Her key research areas include sustainable Development and Climate Change, Sustainable Finance, Psychometric Analysis, and Impact Assessment. She has three years of Education industry experience as a Senior Research Manager - Impact Assessment and continues her work in education sector engagements as a consultant. She collaborated with the Berkeley Evaluation and Assessment Research Center. With over a decade of research experience, she is presently a research supervisor at the Department of Commerce, University of Calicut. She received a 2 million Won -Selected Research Paper award from Kyunghee University, Seoul (2020).

About the Contributors

Aghila Sasidharan is an Assistant Professor specializing in Financial Management at the Indian Institute of Forest Management, Bhopal. She brings a rich academic background with four years of prior experience at Jindal Global Business School of O.P Jindal Global University. She also serves as a Visiting Faculty at Nalanda University, Rajgir, Bihar, where she continues to share her expertise and foster academic growth. She is passionate about teaching and mentorship. She engages with her students through innovative teaching methodologies, encouraging critical thinking and practical application of financial theories. Beyond academia, she actively participates in various professional forums and conferences, presenting her research and contributing to policy discussions. Her involvement in these platforms highlights her dedication to bridging the gap between academic research and real-world financial practices She earned her Ph.D. from the prestigious Indian Institute of Technology (IIT) Madras. Her doctoral research focused on Corporate Governance and Corporate Finance, reflecting her deep commitment to understanding the complexities and dynamics of financial management in corporate settings. Her research interests span a broad spectrum of critical and contemporary topics, including Environmental, Social, and Governance (ESG) issues, Sustainable Finance, Corporate Governance, and Corporate Finance. Aghila contributes significantly to the academic discourse in these areas through her rigorous scholarly endeavours. She has a strong publication record, with her research work appearing in top-tier ABDC and Scopus-indexed journals, underscoring the quality and impact of her contributions to the field. Her studies often delve into the intersection of finance and sustainability, providing valuable insights and fostering a deeper understanding of responsible financial practices.

Vitaliy Serzhanov currently serves as the Dean of the Faculty of Economics at Uzhhorod National University, Ukraine. He specializes in investment policy, economic growth, and corruption prevention. His research focuses on enhancing national economic systems through innovation and effective state regulation.

Nisha Sheen is a proactive and dedicated independent researcher committed with 20 + years of experience in multidisciplinary research with related expertise in Aging. Passionate towards research, teaching, and community services with publications in Social Sciences journals, a confident presenter at conferences, and a seasoned educator. I possess commendable communication, planning, supervision, and teamwork skills to promote quality education and research. I now serve as the School of Interdisciplinary Studies and Pathways faculty at ST Lawrence College, Ontario, Canada.

Shreyanshu Singh is an Assistant Professor of Management at BBD University, Lucknow, India. He has completed his doctorate in Applied Economics from the University of Lucknow, where he held a position as both JRF & SRF. His area of specialization is Marketing, Business Statistics and Operations Research. He has qualified UGC-NET seven times and UGC-JRF thrice in Management and Commerce. He holds a Master's degree in Electronics, Business Administration and Commerce. He also holds a Post Graduate Diploma in International Business Operations. He has numerous publications in ABDC, Scopus, UGC, and peer-reviewed refereed journals. As the editor, He contributed to the academic community with the publications of two books focusing on digital transformation. He has reviewed many papers for Web of Science-indexed and peer-reviewed refereed journals. He has more than nine years of research and teaching experience in different institutes and universities. He also had more than two years of Industry Experience in the FMCG sector. He has presented 31 research papers at various national and international conferences and seminars. He is associated with Indira Gandhi National Open University (IGNOU) as an Academic Counselor. He is an Editorial Board Member at the international peer-reviewed e-journal Multidisciplinary Cosmopolitan Journal of Research (MUCOJOR) and Edwin Group of Journals. He is a registered Ph.D. Co-Guide at JJT University, Rajasthan. He is an active life member of the Indian Commerce Association (ICA) and Indian Accounting Association (IAA).

Asha SP is a research scholar currently pursuing her PhD in Commerce at SN College, Kollam, research center, University of Kerala, India. Her research focuses on the necessity of forensic accounting. Her publications have been primarily focused on finance and forensic accounting. She had attended and presented papers on forensic accounting at various international conferences. In addition, she has a keen interest in research on sustainability, and blue economy.

Kiran Thampi is currently HOD of the Department of Social Work, Rajagiri and also the Assistant Director of the Office of International Relations (Kalamassery campus). He has done his PhD and government-funded research in the organizational practices of Non-Government organizations. Research and publication interests include Social Audit, Participatory Rural Appraisal, Mental Health of professionals and youth, and international social work. He was appointed as an Adjunct faculty member in the School of Health and Human Services, Nazareth College, USA, for the summer of 2015. He has published articles in Scopus Indexed journals and is the peer reviewer of International Social Work, Social Work Education, Journal of Emergency Management etc. He also serves as the Editorial Review Board Member of the International Journal of Gerontology and Geriatric Medicine.

Ann Susan Thomas is a PhD research scholar at the Department of Commerce, University of Kerala, with her current research focus on ESG Investments and Momentum strategies in Asian Emerging Markets. She holds an MPhil degree from the same institution. She pursued her academic journey at Mar Ivanios College, Thiruvananthapuram, completing both her undergraduate and postgraduate degrees. Her profound interest lies in the fields of ESG, sustainability and financial market dynamics. She also has publications in domains like AI in finance and cryptocurrencies.

Dany Thomas is an academician passionate about research, with experience as an assistant professor for five years. He had completed hid Ph.D. in commerce from the University of Kerala, Thiruvananthapuram, India. His research concentrated on stock market movements and the factors affecting it during the pre-post GST era. During his academic journey he had developed a keen interest in the dynamics of the financial market, sustainability, algorithmic trading, and machine learning. He is currently working as a field investigator for the ICSSR funded project titled "Effect of Investor Sentimentality on Sustainability and ESG Ratings on Performance of Indian Companies." He has publications in financial market, digital payments, and forensic accounting.

Sreeraj V completed his postgraduation in commerce from University of Kerala, specializing in finance and accounting. He is currently working as a field investigator for the Indian Council of Social Science Research (ICSSR) on the project titled "Effect of Investors' Sentiments on Sustainability and ESG Ratings on the Performance of Indian Companies." His research primarily focuses on econometrics and econophysics, with a special emphasis on sustainability and standard finance. He has also published works in domains such as finance and cryptocurrencies. He has received several best paper awards from international conferences.

Rinki Verma is a proficient academician in the field of management and has extensive research experience. She carries a wide experience of 15 years in academics and corporate. She shouldered responsibilities from IQAC and NAAC in her current and prior serving institutions. She is presently associated with an ICSSR-funded project as a Project Director. Currently, she is an Associate Professor at Babu Banarasi Das University, Lucknow. She holds a doctorate from an institute of national importance, MNNIT, Allahabad. She has qualified UGC NET in Management. She has many national and international research papers in her credit, which are published in ABDC, Scopus, UGC CARE, and reputed peer-reviewed journals. She made significant contributions to the academic field as the editor, publishing two books centered on the theme of digital transformation. She is passionate, purposeful, high-spirited and has a never-ending approach to learning. She has supervised many students for their PhD and Masters dissertations.

Index

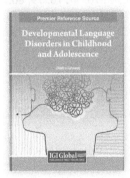

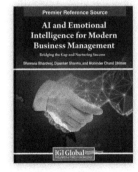

  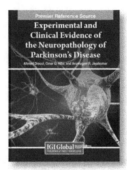 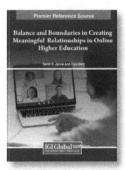